Financial Econometrics

Financial Econometrics is a contribution to modern financial econometrics, overviewing both theory and application. It covers, in detail, three important topics in the field that have recently drawn the attention of the academic community and practitioners, with low-frequency data (trend determination, bubble detection, and factor-augmented regressions) and examines various topics in high-frequency financial econometrics with continuous time models and discretized data. Also included are the estimation of stochastic volatility models, posterior-based hypothesis testing, and posterior-based model selection. Exploring topics at the forefront of research in the field of financial econometrics, this book offers an accessible introduction to the research and provides the groundwork for the development of new econometric techniques.

Shuping Shi is a professor at Macquarie University. She received the Discovery Early Career Researcher Award from the Australian Research Council (2019–2021) and the 2022 Young Economist Award from the Economic Society of Australia. She is an econometrician with a research agenda that is both theoretically grounded and policy-relevant, and has published in the *Journal of Econometrics*, *Management Science*, *International Economic Review*, *Econometric Theory*, *Journal of Financial Econometrics*, and *Journal of Banking and Finance*, and more.

Xiaohu Wang is an associate professor at the School of Economics, Fudan University. His research is on financial econometrics and empirical asset pricing. His works appear in the *Journal of Econometrics*, *Econometrics Journal*, *Journal of International Money and Finance*, *Econometric Reviews*, *Advances in Econometrics*, *Quantitative Finance*, *and Economics Letters.*

Tao Zeng is an associate professor at the School of Economics and Academy of Financial Research, Zhejiang University. His research areas include Bayesian econometrics, empirical asset pricing, and machine learning. His works appear in the *Journal of Econometrics*, *Journal of Financial Econometrics*, *Advances in Econometrics*, and more.

Themes in Modern Econometrics

Series Editor

PETER C. B. PHILLIPS, *Yale University, University of Auckland, and Singapore Management University*

Themes in Modern Econometrics provides an organized sequence of advanced textbooks in econometrics aimed directly at the student population and is the first series in the discipline to have this as its express aim. Written at a level accessible to those who have completed an introductory course in econometrics, each book addresses topics and themes that students and researchers encounter daily. All areas of econometrics are covered within the series. Particular emphasis is given to theory fundamentals and practical implementation in breaking research areas that are relevant to empirical applications. Each book stands alone as an authoritative survey in its own right. The distinct emphasis throughout is on pedagogic excellence and accessibility.

Books in the Series

Econometric Analysis of Stochastic Dominance (2019) YOON-JAE WHANG
Structural Vector Autoregressive Analysis (2017) LUTZ KILIAN *and* HELMUT LÜTKEPOHL
Almost All About Unit Roots (2015) IN CHOI
Granularity Theory with Applications to Finance and Insurance (2014) PATRICK GAGLIARDINI *and* CHRISTIAN GOURIÉROUX
Econometric Modeling with Time Series (2012) VANCE MARTIN, STAN HURN, *and* DAVID HARRIS
Economic Modeling and Inference (2007) JEAN-PIERRE FLORENSE, VELAYOUDOM MARIMOUTOU, *and* ANNE PEGUIN-FEISSOLLE
Translated by JOSEF PERKTOLD *and* MARINE CARRASCO
Introduction to the Mathematical and Statistical Foundations of Econometrics (2004) HERMAN J. BIERENS
Applied Time Series Econometrics (2004) HELMUT LÜTKEPOHL *and* MARKUS KRÄTZIG
Semiparametric Regression for the Applied Econometrician (2003) ADONIS YATCHEW
The Econometric Analysis of Seasonal Time Series (2001) ERIC GHYSELS *and* DENISE R. OSBORN
Econometrics of Qualitative Dependent Variables (2000) CHRISTIAN GOURIEROUX
Translated by PAUL B. KLASSEN
Nonparametric Econometrics (1999) ADRIAN PAGAN *and* AMAN ULLAH
Generalized Method of Moments Estimation (1999) *Edited by* LÁSZLÓ MÁTYÁS
Unit Roots, Cointegration, and Structural Change (1999) G.S. MADDALA *and* IN-MOO KIM
Time Series and Dynamic Models (1997) CHRISTIAN GOURIEROUX *and* ALAIN MONFORT *Translated and edited by* GIAMPIERO GALLO
Statistics and Econometric Models: Volumes 1 and 2 (1995) CHRISTIAN GOURIEROUX *and* ALAIN MONFORT *Translated by* QUANG VUONG

FINANCIAL ECONOMETRICS

Theory and Applications

Edited by

SHUPING SHI
Macquarie University

XIAOHU WANG
Fudan University

TAO ZENG
Zhejiang University

CAMBRIDGE
UNIVERSITY PRESS

CAMBRIDGE
UNIVERSITY PRESS

Shaftesbury Road, Cambridge CB2 8EA, United Kingdom

One Liberty Plaza, 20th Floor, New York, NY 10006, USA

477 Williamstown Road, Port Melbourne, VIC 3207, Australia

314–321, 3rd Floor, Plot 3, Splendor Forum, Jasola District Centre, New Delhi – 110025, India

103 Penang Road, #05-06/07, Visioncrest Commercial, Singapore 238467

Cambridge University Press is part of Cambridge University Press & Assessment, a department of the University of Cambridge.

We share the University's mission to contribute to society through the pursuit of education, learning and research at the highest international levels of excellence.

www.cambridge.org
Information on this title: www.cambridge.org/9781108843294

DOI: 10.1017/9781108910095

When citing this work, please include a reference to the DOI 10.1017/9781108910095

First published 2025

A catalogue record for this publication is available from the British Library.

A Cataloging-in-Publication data record for this book is available from the Library of Congress

ISBN 978-1-108-84329-4 Hardback

Contents

Contributors

YE CHEN
Capital University of Economics and Business

YONG LI
Renmin University of China

CHENG LIU
Wuhan University

XIAOBIN LIU
Sun Yat-sen University

YIU LIM LUI
Dongbei University of Finance and Economics

PETER C. B. PHILLIPS
Yale University, University of Auckland, and Singapore Management University

SHUPING SHI
Macquarie University

XIAOHU WANG
Fudan University

WEILIN XIAO
Zhejiang University

TAO ZENG
Zhejiang University

XILI ZHANG
Zhejiang University

YONGHUI ZHANG
Renmin University of China

Foreword

A defining characteristic of econometrics in the first two decades of the twenty-first century is the growth and importance of financial econometrics. The subject was born in the 1980s as a field of time series econometrics concerned with modelling volatility, a prominent feature of financial assets that is amenable to estimation and inference conditional on past history. As such it is interdisciplinary, bringing together finance and econometrics in productive ways that guide theory, reveal empirical regularities, and enhance industry practice. During the 1990s with the development of global internet connectivity and the emergence of high-frequency, high-dimensional market observations, the possibility of utilizing vast amounts of financial data became apparent. Important linkages were forged with earlier research on continuous time econometrics and ongoing probabilistic research in the stochastic process modelling of quadratic variation and higher-order quantities such as quarticity. Amidst these technical developments and a thundering avalanche of data driving the discipline, the shape of modern financial econometrics began to emerge and led with surprising rapidity to a discipline and profession supported by its own society and journals.

Concomitant with these developments and motivated by the opportunity that a young university has to invest in human capital, the School of Economics at Singapore Management University took the bold step of building an econometrics unit within its expanding economics faculty to face the challenges of this emergent discipline. In this mission SMU was supported by successive deans, provosts, and presidents, making several key appointments that proved capable of the task. One of these appointments was Jun Yu, a young associate professor recruited in 2004 from the University of Auckland. In 2008 a PhD program was established based on the North American model of advanced coursework complemented by a substantial dissertation. At the same time, the Sim Kee Boon Institute for Financial Economics was founded with a Centre of Financial Econometrics for which Jun served as the deputy director, later assuming the role of full director of the Institute itself for a three-year term. In the following years, the faculty grew steadily with increasing breadth and depth in econometrics; and the PhD program blossomed, producing at the time of writing over 75 PhD graduates, some 32 of whom are in econometrics with a goodly fraction in financial econometrics.

Jun Yu has been a central figure in all of these developments. In supervision, he has chaired or co-chaired the dissertations of around one half of the PhD students; in research he has written over 80 published articles in finance and econometrics, many in leading journals and many with his students, former students, and colleagues; as an instructor and workshop leader he is deeply valued by all his students; and in teaching, research, supervision, and administration he has played a major role in helping guide the PhD program to become a leading cradle of econometrics training in the entire Asia-Pacific region. Within a period of some 15 years this is a major accomplishment.

The present volume is a contribution to modern financial econometrics written in honour of Professor Jun Yu on the occasion of his 50th birthday by his colleagues and former students. The book is an extended overview of econometric theory and empirical applications intended for advanced students and researchers in financial econometrics. The volume has eleven chapters separated into three parts according to content. Part I deals with major issues concerned primarily with low-frequency phenomena that are prominent in long historical financial data. The chapters in Part II address various topics in high-frequency financial econometrics with continuous time models and discretized data. Part III is concerned with the estimation of stochastic volatility models, hypothesis testing, and model selection based on Bayesian posterior analysis. All topics covered in the volume are at the forefront of research in the field of financial econometrics. The individual chapters are written with a level of exposition designed to enhance readability, making it particularly suitable for a graduate advanced course or a supplementary text or reference work.

Since the turn of the millenium, financial econometrics has embarked on a striking individual journey with methodologies drawn and developed from multiple disciplines that include stochastic process probability, high-dimensional statistical analysis, and advanced time series econometrics. This eclectic approach has opened many doors to understanding the complexities of the modern world of financial, commodity, and real estate markets. The editors and contributors join me in hoping that this volume will assist graduate students and researchers of financial econometrics in their own scholarly journeys within this exciting field. As such it belongs to the tradition of graduate training in econometrics that is now well established at Singapore Management University.

Peter C. B. Phillips
Sterling Professor Emeritus, Yale University
Distinguished Professor, University of Auckland
Distinguished Term Professor, Singapore Management University

Acknowledgments

Shi acknowledges the support from the Research Excellence Support Scheme of Macquarie Business School. Wang expresses gratitude for financial support from the Shanghai Pujiang Program (No. 22PJC022). Zeng acknowledges the financial support of the National Natural Science Foundation of China (No. 72073121).

We are also grateful to the School of Economics, the School of Digital Finance at the Polytechnic Institute, and the Academy of Financial Research (AFR) at Zhejiang University for hosting the "2019 Advanced Symposium on Financial Time Series." The insightful discussions and academic exchanges that took place during this symposium have been invaluable in the planning and development of this book volume.

Part I

Trend Determination, Asset Price Bubbles, and Factor-Augmented Regressions

1 Asymptotics of Polynomial Time Trend Estimation and Hypothesis Testing under Rank Deficiency

PETER C. B. PHILLIPS *Yale University, University of Auckland, and Singapore Management University*

1.1 Introduction

Under very general conditions Grenander and Rosenblatt (1954) proved a major theorem which showed that in regression with polynomial and trigonometric polynomial trend regressors and stationary errors simple application of ordinary least squares (OLS) is asymptotically equivalent to generalized least squares (GLS) and thereby efficient. This important property provided an asymptotic justification for the use of OLS in trend regression and made trend elimination by polynomial time trend regression a popular procedure in empirical research. A key condition underlying this Grenander–Rosenblatt (GR) theorem is that the regression errors are stationary and have positive spectral density at the origin, which ensures that the long-run variance of the errors is necessarily positive. A similar finding to the GR theorem holds in the case of trend regression with integrated regressors, so the result is not confined to deterministic regressors but includes pure cointegrated regression models in which the regressors are strictly exogenous (Phillips and Park, 1988). While these asymptotic properties, including the conditions for the limiting equivalence of OLS-GLS, are well established, there remain some interesting unexplored aspects of trend regression.

This chapter studies two such issues that can arise in estimation and inference with polynomial time trend regression: (i) problems in the limit theory that arise from a moving average (MA) error with a unit root that produces a zero error spectrum at the origin and leads to failure in standard invariance principle arguments and failure in the GR theorem; and (ii) problems of rank deficiency

This chapter provides an extended solution to a graduate take-home examination at Singapore Management University in April 2022. The examination problem provided a challenge similar to that of a research project, working from a familiar foundation towards arenas that are unfamiliar and that require some technical novelty and notational innovation to resolve. Such challenges are part of normal research and play an important role in graduate student apprenticeship training in econometrics. Research support is acknowledged from NSF Grant No. SES 18-50860, a Kelly Fellowship at the University of Auckland, and a Lee Kong Chian Fellowship at Singapore Management University.

and singularity that arise in trend regression when testing multiple hypotheses using Wald statistics. Both of these might be considered graduate student problems. They are not dealt with in graduate textbooks of econometrics but, as shown here, they are the type of problem that can easily arise in research when dealing with new models and nonstationary data. We focus on the simplest case of deterministic trend regression. But related issues do occur in cases of stochastic regressors (Phillips, 1987, 1995; Park and Phillips, 1988, 1989) as well as explosive model cases (Phillips and Magdalinos, 2013) and nonparametric kernel regression problems (Phillips et al., 2017) where unexpected singularities can occur in the asymptotic theory. A general treatment of rank deficiency and singularities in econometric testing is available in Magdalinos and Phillips (2018). In spite of the simplicity of the present deterministic trend model, considerable technical complexities arise in the general case, which require some innovations and notational aids to resolve adequately and to secure definitive results. These techniques should have wider applicability beyond the trend regression models of the present study.

This chapter is largely pedagogical in nature and is written specifically for this advanced textbook series. The development proceeds from a common model of deterministic trend regression where standard asymptotics hold to one where the limit theory and convergence rates of the usual OLS estimator and associated test statistics differ from the standard theory. To aid exposition a progression of examples are given that assist in building up the notation and techniques required to resolve the general case under study. It should therefore be accessible to graduate students and some undergraduates with advanced training in econometrics.

The trend regression model is given in the next section with key conditions that enable the asymptotic development given in Section 1.3 for estimation and in Section 1.4 for inference. Section 1.5 provides some final discussion. A brief appendix on Wiener stochastic integration is included for completeness to facilitate development of the limit theory.

1.2 Deterministic Trend Regression

We study limit theory in the simple linear trend regression model

$$y_t = x_t'\beta + u_t, \quad t = 0, 1, \ldots, n \tag{1.1}$$

where the deterministic trend regressor $x_t = (1, t, t^2, \ldots, t^m)'$ and the errors u_t are generated by the linear process $u_t = C(L)\varepsilon_t = \sum_{j=0}^{\infty} c_j \varepsilon_{t-j}$ with coefficients c_j satisfying the summability condition $\sum_{j=0}^{\infty} j|c_j| < \infty$ and innovations $\varepsilon_t \sim iid\left(0, \sigma^2\right)$.

Using the Phillips–Solo device (Phillips and Solo, 1992) gives the valid Beveridge–Nelson decomposition

$$u_t = C(L)\varepsilon_t = \sum_{j=0}^{\infty} c_j \varepsilon_{t-j} = C(1)\varepsilon_t - (1-L)\tilde{C}(L)\varepsilon_t = C(1)\varepsilon_t + \tilde{\varepsilon}_{t-1} - \tilde{\varepsilon}_t, \tag{1.2}$$

where $\tilde{\varepsilon}_t = \tilde{C}(L)\varepsilon_t$ and $\tilde{C}(L) = \sum_{j=0}^{\infty} \tilde{c}_j L^j$ with $\tilde{c}_j = \sum_{s=j+1}^{\infty} c_s$. The series representation $\tilde{\varepsilon}_t = \sum_{j=0}^{\infty} \tilde{c}_j \varepsilon_{t-j}$ converges almost surely in view of the summability condition $\sum_{j=0}^{\infty} j|c_j| < \infty$. The long-run behavior of u_t is primarily determined by the long-run moving average coefficient $C(1)$, which directly affects the value of the spectral density at the origin and is therefore instrumental in the long-run properties of the time series u_t.

The $(m+1)\times 1$ parameter vector $\beta = (\beta_0, \beta_1, \ldots, \beta_m)'$ in (1.1) is estimated by ordinary least squares (OLS) regression using $\hat{\beta} = (X'X)^{-1} X'y$ where $X' = [x_1, \ldots, x_n]$ and $y' = [y_1, \ldots, y_n]$. The remainder of the chapter considers the asymptotic theory of $\hat{\beta}$ and Wald tests based on $\hat{\beta}$ under different conditions that determine the long-run behavior of the equation error u_t. We look at two cases. The first is the standard model where $C(1) \neq 0$; the second is the degenerate unit root moving average case where $C(1) = 0$.

When $C(1) = 0$ it is clear from the decomposition (1.2) that the regression error u_t has the MA unit root form $u_t = -(1-L)\tilde{\varepsilon}_t$. Models with MA unit roots or near unit roots can arise in empirical work with time series data when there is overdifferencing or where multicointegration is present (Kheifets and Phillips, 2023; Phillips and Kheifets, 2024). The GR asymptotic equivalence theorem fails in such cases because the spectral density of u_t is $f_u(\lambda) = \frac{\sigma^2}{2\pi}|C(e^{i\lambda})|^2 = \frac{\sigma^2}{2\pi}|1 - e^{i\lambda}|^2|\tilde{C}(e^{i\lambda})|^2$ and so at the origin $f_u(0) = 0$. As will be shown, the asymptotic theory for $\hat{\beta}$ changes considerably. Convergence rates of the components of $\hat{\beta}$ differ from when $C(1) \neq 0$ and conventional invariance principle asymptotics fail, causing difficulties with inference. A simple procedure for dealing with this failure is developed.

In both $C(1) \neq 0$ and $C(1) = 0$ cases, Wald tests of general hypotheses concerning β suffer from rank deficiency and singularity asymptotically that arise from the differing signal strengths in the nonstationary components of the regressor x_t and consequent differing convergence rates in the components of $\hat{\beta}$. These differences affect the Wald statistic limit theory and hypothesis testing. Related problems of rank deficiency in cointegrated regression and VARs were studied in Phillips (1995). Readers are referred to Magdalinos and Phillips (2018) for the first general treatment of matrix normalization problems in inference.

1.3 Limit Theory

1.3.1 The Standard Case: $C(1) \neq 0$

The $(m+1) \times 1$ parameter vector β in (1.1) is estimated by ordinary least squares regression using $\hat{\beta} = \left(X'X\right)^{-1} X'y$ where $X' = [x_1, \ldots, x_n]$ and $y' = [y_1, \ldots, y_n]$. The limit behavior of $\hat{\beta}$ follows by standard manipulations.

Let $D_n = \text{diag}\{1, n, n^2, \ldots, n^m\}$. For $r \in [0,1]$, $D_n^{-1} x_{\lfloor nr \rfloor} \rightarrow X(r) = (1, r, r^2, \ldots, r^m)'$ as $n \rightarrow \infty$. It follows by Riemann integration that

$$n^{-1} D_n^{-1} X'XD_n^{-1} = n^{-1} \sum_{t=1}^{n} D_n^{-1} x_t x_t' D_n^{-1} \rightarrow \int_0^1 X(r)X(r)'dr$$
$$=: M, \quad \text{as } n \rightarrow \infty. \tag{1.3}$$

Under the given conditions, normalized partial sums of u_t satisfy the functional central limit law $n^{-1/2} \sum_{t=1}^{\lfloor nr \rfloor} u_t \rightsquigarrow B_u(r)$ where B_u is Brownian motion with variance given by the long-run variance $\omega^2 = \sigma^2 C(1)^2$ of u_t. Setting $u' = [u_1, \ldots, u_n]$ we find using Wiener integral limit theory (see Lemma 1.6.1 in the Appendix) that

$$\frac{1}{\sqrt{n}} D_n^{-1} X'u = \sum_{t=1}^{n} D_n^{-1} x_t \frac{u_t}{\sqrt{n}} \rightsquigarrow \int_0^1 X(r)dB_u(r). \tag{1.4}$$

It follows directly from (1.3) and (1.4) that

$$\sqrt{n} D_n(\hat{\beta} - \beta) = \left(\frac{1}{n} D_n^{-1} X'XD_n^{-1}\right)^{-1} \frac{1}{\sqrt{n}} D_n^{-1} X'u$$
$$\rightsquigarrow \left(\int_0^1 X(r)X(r)'dr\right)^{-1} \left(\int_0^1 X(r)dB_u(r)\right) = \mathcal{N}\left(0, \omega^2 M^{-1}\right), \tag{1.5}$$

since $\int_0^1 X(r)dB_u(r) =_d \mathcal{N}\left(0, \omega^2 M\right)$.

1.3.2 The Degenerate Case: $C(1) = 0$

Using partial summation as in the proof of Lemma 1.6.1 we obtain

$$D_n^{-1} X'u = D_n^{-1} \sum_{t=1}^{n} x_t \Delta \tilde{\varepsilon}_t = D_n^{-1}(x_n \tilde{\varepsilon}_n - x_0 \tilde{\varepsilon}_0) - D_n^{-1} \sum_{t=1}^{n} \Delta x_t \tilde{\varepsilon}_{t-1}$$
$$\rightsquigarrow X(1)\tilde{\varepsilon}_\infty - e_1 \tilde{\varepsilon}_0, \tag{1.6}$$

where $D_n^{-1} x_n \rightarrow X(1)$ and $\tilde{\varepsilon}_n \rightsquigarrow \tilde{\varepsilon}_\infty =_d \tilde{\varepsilon}_t$ as $n \rightarrow \infty$, $e_1 = (1, 0, \ldots, 0)'$ and $D_n^{-1} x_0 = e_1$. Note also that $\Delta x_t \approx (0, 1, 2t, \ldots, mt^{m-1})'$ for large t and then

$\sqrt{n}D_n^{-1}\Delta x_{t=\lfloor nr \rfloor} \sim_a (0, \frac{1}{n^{1/2}}, \frac{2\lfloor nr \rfloor}{n^{3/2}}, \ldots, \frac{m\lfloor nr \rfloor^{m-1}}{n^{m-1/2}})' = O(\frac{1}{\sqrt{n}}) \to 0$ as $n \to \infty$ for all $r \in [0, 1]$. It follows that

$$D_n^{-1}\sum_{t=1}^{n}\Delta x_t \tilde{\varepsilon}_{t-1} = \sum_{t=1}^{n}\sqrt{n}D_n^{-1}\Delta x_t \frac{\tilde{\varepsilon}_{t-1}}{\sqrt{n}} \to_p 0, \tag{1.7}$$

confirming (1.6). We deduce that

$$nD_n(\hat{\beta} - \beta) = \left(\frac{1}{n}D_n^{-1}X'XD_n^{-1}\right)^{-1} D_n^{-1}X'u \rightsquigarrow M^{-1}\left(X(1)\tilde{\varepsilon}_\infty - e_1\tilde{\varepsilon}_0\right), \tag{1.8}$$

so that $\hat{\beta}$ is consistent with convergence rate nD_n but no invariance principle applies, leading to difficulties with robust inference about β. However, observe that the convergence rate of $\hat{\beta}$ in (1.8) is nD_n, which is $O(\sqrt{n})$ faster than the convergence rate $\sqrt{n}D_n$ for the same estimator in the case where $C(1) \neq 0$. Thus, degeneracy in the long-run behavior of the equation error leads to an acceleration in convergence. But it does not lead to an invariance principle at least for this OLS estimator because its limit distribution depends on the distribution of $\tilde{\varepsilon}_t$, thereby causing the difficulties for inference.

If $\tilde{\varepsilon}_0 = 0$ then

$$nD_n(\hat{\beta} - \beta) \rightsquigarrow \left(\int_0^1 X(r)X(r)'dr\right)^{-1} X(1)\tilde{\varepsilon}_\infty = M^{-1}X(1)\tilde{\varepsilon}_\infty, \tag{1.9}$$

which has mean zero and variance $\mathbb{V}ar(\tilde{\varepsilon}_\infty)M^{-1}X(1)X(1)'M^{-1}$, which is singular of rank unity when $m > 0$. When $m = 0$ and $x_t = 1$, we have $X(r) = 1$ and the limit variance is simply $\mathbb{V}ar(\tilde{\varepsilon}_\infty)$. But when $m > 1$ there is a (nonrandom) direction where the convergence rate is faster than nD_n because of the singularity in (1.9). In particular, if $G_\perp$ is an $(m+1) \times m$ orthogonal complement of the vector $g = M^{-1}X(1)$ then it follows from (1.9) that $nG_\perp' D_n(\hat{\beta} - \beta) = o_p(1)$. This degenerate feature of the limit theory indicates that there may be another procedure that can accelerate convergence, which we now consider.

1.3.3 Use of Temporal Aggregation

Temporal aggregation of the model (1.1) leads to the equation

$$Y_t = X_t'\beta + U_t, \quad t = 1, \ldots, n, \tag{1.10}$$

where $Y_t = \sum_{s=1}^{t} y_s$, $X_t = \sum_{s=1}^{t} x_s = \sum_{s=1}^{t}(1, s, s^2, \ldots, s^m)'$ and when $C(1) = 0$ we have $U_t = \sum_{s=1}^{t} \Delta\tilde{\varepsilon}_s = \tilde{\varepsilon}_t - \tilde{\varepsilon}_0$, so that

$$Y_t = X_t'\beta + \tilde{\varepsilon}_t - \tilde{\varepsilon}_0, \quad t = 1, \ldots, n. \tag{1.11}$$

The parameter vector β in (1.10) is again estimated by OLS regression giving $\tilde{\beta} = \left(\tilde{X}'\tilde{X}\right)^{-1}\tilde{X}'\tilde{Y}$ where $\tilde{X}' = [X_1, \ldots, X_n]$ and $\tilde{Y}' = [Y_1, \ldots, Y_n]$. Similarly, we define $\tilde{U}' = [U_1, \ldots, U_n] = [\tilde{\varepsilon}_1 - \tilde{\varepsilon}_0, \ldots, \tilde{\varepsilon}_n - \tilde{\varepsilon}_0]$.

To find the limit behavior of $\tilde{\beta}$ we use $F_n = nD_n$ and note that $F_n^{-1}X_{\lfloor nr \rfloor} = \frac{1}{n}\sum_{s=1}^{\lfloor nr \rfloor} D_n^{-1}x_s \to \tilde{X}(r) := \int_0^r X(s)ds = \int_0^r (1, s, s^2, \ldots, s^m)' ds = \left(r, \frac{r^2}{2}, \ldots, \frac{r^{m+1}}{m+1}\right)'$. It follows by Riemann integration that

$$\frac{1}{n}\sum_{t=1}^{\lfloor nr \rfloor} F_n^{-1}X_t = \frac{1}{n}\sum_{t=1}^{\lfloor nr \rfloor}\frac{1}{n}\sum_{s=1}^{t} D_n^{-1}x_s \to \int_0^r \tilde{X}(p)dp, \tag{1.12}$$

and

$$\frac{1}{n}F_n^{-1}\tilde{X}'\tilde{X}F_n^{-1} = n^{-1}\sum_{t=1}^{n} F_n^{-1}X_tX_t'F_n^{-1} \to \int_0^1 \tilde{X}(r)\tilde{X}(r)'\,dr =: \tilde{M}, \tag{1.13}$$

as $n \to \infty$. Next observe that

$$\begin{aligned}\frac{1}{n}F_n^{-1}\tilde{X}'\tilde{U} &= \frac{1}{n}\sum_{t=1}^{n} F_n^{-1}X_t\tilde{\varepsilon}_t - \frac{1}{n}\sum_{t=1}^{n} F_n^{-1}X_t\tilde{\varepsilon}_0 \\ &= \frac{1}{\sqrt{n}}\sum_{t=1}^{n} F_n^{-1}X_t\frac{\tilde{\varepsilon}_t}{\sqrt{n}} - \frac{1}{n}\sum_{t=1}^{n} F_n^{-1}X_t\tilde{\varepsilon}_0 \\ &= O_p\left(\frac{1}{\sqrt{n}}\right) - \left(\frac{1}{n}\sum_{t=1}^{n} F_n^{-1}X_t\right)\tilde{\varepsilon}_0 \rightsquigarrow -\int_0^1 \tilde{X}(p)dp\;\tilde{\varepsilon}_0.\end{aligned} \tag{1.14}$$

To confirm (1.14) first note that under the stated summability conditions $\tilde{\varepsilon}_t = \tilde{C}(L)\varepsilon_t$ is zero mean stationary with long-run variance $\tilde{\omega}^2 = \sigma^2\tilde{C}(1)^2$ and so partial sums of $\tilde{\varepsilon}_t$ satisfy the functional law $n^{-1/2}\sum_{s=1}^{\lfloor nr \rfloor}\tilde{\varepsilon}_s \rightsquigarrow B_{\tilde{\varepsilon}}(r)$ where $B_{\tilde{\varepsilon}}$ is Brownian motion with variance $\tilde{\omega}^2 > 0$ provided $\tilde{C}(1) \neq 0$. It follows by using the summation by parts argument in Lemma 1.6.1 that $\sum_{t=1}^{n} F_n^{-1}X_t\frac{\tilde{\varepsilon}_t}{\sqrt{n}} \rightsquigarrow \int_0^1 \tilde{X}(r)dB_{\tilde{\varepsilon}}(r)$ so that $\frac{1}{\sqrt{n}}\sum_{t=1}^{n} F_n^{-1}X_t\frac{\tilde{\varepsilon}_t}{\sqrt{n}} = O_p\left(\frac{1}{\sqrt{n}}\right)$, which leads to (1.14). If $\tilde{C}(1) = 0$, then a further level of complexity arises that can be treated by similar methods but which we do not address in the present chapter. We deduce from (1.13) and (1.14) that

$$\begin{aligned}F_n(\tilde{\beta} - \beta) &= \left(\frac{1}{n}F_n^{-1}\tilde{X}'\tilde{X}F_n^{-1}\right)^{-1}\left(\frac{1}{n}F_n^{-1}\tilde{X}'\tilde{U}\right) \\ &\rightsquigarrow -\tilde{M}^{-1}\int_0^1 \tilde{X}(p)dp\;\tilde{\varepsilon}_0,\end{aligned} \tag{1.15}$$

so that $\tilde{\beta}$ is consistent with rate of convergence $F_n = nD_n$ but no invariance principle applies, leading to continuing difficulties with robust inference about β.

Remark 1.3.1 *We deduce that temporal aggregation of the data and estimation of* (1.10) *raises the convergence rate of OLS regression from the rate* $\sqrt{n}D_n$ *for* $\hat{\beta}$ *by* $O(\sqrt{n})$ *to the rate* $F_n = nD_n$ *for* $\tilde{\beta}$. *This rise in the convergence rate is explained by the rise in the signal strength associated with the signal matrix* $\tilde{X}'\tilde{X}$ *in the regression formula* $(\frac{1}{n}F_n^{-1}\tilde{X}'\tilde{X}F_n^{-1})^{-1}(\frac{1}{n}F_n^{-1}\tilde{X}'\tilde{U})$ *in* (1.15). *Temporal aggregation is a simple mechanism for taking into account the MA unit root and zero long-run variance of* u_t *in the general model* (1.1) *when* $C(1) = 0$, *leading to* (1.10). *This procedure may therefore be regarded as an important partial step toward implementing GLS. It is not a full implementation of GLS because the residual* $\tilde{\varepsilon}_t$ *in* (1.10) *is generally autocorrelated with spectrum* $f_{\tilde{\varepsilon}}(\lambda) = \sigma^2|\tilde{C}(e^{i\lambda})|^2$ *that is not necessarily flat. Thus, taking account of the MA unit root and the zero long-run variance of* u_t *leads to accelerated convergence and asymptotic normality. So the conventional OLS trend regression estimator* $\hat{\beta}$ *is asymptotically infinitely deficient by a* $\sqrt{n}$ *factor, relative to the partial use of GLS that leads to* $\tilde{\beta}$, *manifesting the failure of the GR asymptotic equivalence theorem.*

The rise in convergence rate that results from the use of OLS regression in the temporally aggregated model does not resolve difficulties concerning inference because the limit theory (1.15) involves the distribution of $\tilde{\varepsilon}_0$. This difficulty in the limit theory is addressed by an adjustment to the estimation technique, as explained in the next section.

1.3.4 The Effect of Intercept Adjustment

We propose to estimate the parameter vector β in (1.10) by OLS regression with a fitted intercept in the regression. The model may therefore be written in the form

$$Y_t = X_t'\beta + \tilde{\varepsilon}_t - \tilde{\varepsilon}_0 = \mu + X_t'\beta + \tilde{\varepsilon}_t,\ t = 1, \ldots, n \tag{1.16}$$

with (random) intercept $\mu = \tilde{\varepsilon}_0$. The presence of the intercept in the OLS regression leads to all variables in the model being demeaned. We use the daggered affix variable $A_t^\dagger$ to signify that the variable A_t is demeaned, so that $A_t^\dagger := A_t - \frac{1}{n}\sum_{s=1}^n A_s$. For the matrix of observations $A = [A_1, \ldots, A_n]'$ of A_t we correspondingly denote the observation matrix of demeaned variables $A_t^\dagger$ by $A^\dagger$.

With this notation in hand, the algebra and asymptotics in the aggregated model with a fitted intercept are determined with the following modifications of those given above. In particular, setting $X_t^\dagger := X_t - \frac{1}{n}\sum_{s=1}^n X_s$ and by taking limits as $n \to \infty$ and Riemann integration we have

$$\begin{aligned} F_n^{-1} X_{\lfloor nr \rfloor}^\dagger &= \frac{1}{n}\sum_{s=1}^{\lfloor nr \rfloor} D_n^{-1} x_s - \frac{1}{n}\sum_{t=1}^{n}\frac{1}{n}\sum_{s=1}^{t} D_n^{-1} x_s \\ &\to \tilde{X}(r) - \int_0^1 \tilde{X}(p)dp = \int_0^r X(s)ds \\ &\quad - \int_0^1 \int_0^p X(s)dsdp =: X^\dagger(r). \end{aligned} \tag{1.17}$$

The limit function $X^\dagger(r)$ is the demeaned form of $\tilde{X}(r) = \int_0^r X(s)ds$ in the function space $C[0,1]$ and this function correspondingly satisfies $\int_0^1 X^\dagger(r)dr = 0$. We now obtain as $n \to \infty$

$$\frac{1}{n}F_n^{-1}\tilde{X}^{\dagger\prime}\tilde{X}^\dagger F_n^{-1} = n^{-1}\sum_{t=1}^{n} F_n^{-1}X_t^\dagger X_t^{\dagger\prime}F_n^{-1} \to \int_0^1 X^\dagger(r)X^\dagger(r)'dr =: M^\dagger. \tag{1.18}$$

Next observe that $\sum_{t=1}^n X_t^\dagger \tilde{\varepsilon}_0 = \tilde{\varepsilon}_0 \sum_{t=1}^n X_t^\dagger = 0$ by virtue of the definition of the demeaned variable $X_t^\dagger$, thereby eliminating the effect of $\tilde{\varepsilon}_0$. It follows that

$$\begin{aligned} \frac{1}{\sqrt{n}}F_n^{-1}\tilde{X}^{\dagger\prime}\tilde{U}^\dagger &= \frac{1}{\sqrt{n}}\sum_{t=1}^{n} F_n^{-1}X_t^\dagger\tilde{\varepsilon}_t - \frac{1}{\sqrt{n}}\sum_{t=1}^{n} F_n^{-1}X_t^\dagger\tilde{\varepsilon}_0 \\ &= \sum_{t=1}^{n} F_n^{-1}X_t^\dagger\frac{\tilde{\varepsilon}_t}{\sqrt{n}} \rightsquigarrow \int_0^1 X^\dagger(r)dB_{\tilde{\varepsilon}}(r), \end{aligned} \tag{1.19}$$

where $B_{\tilde{\varepsilon}}$ is Brownian motion with variance $\tilde{\omega}^2 = \sigma^2\tilde{C}(1)$ in view of the functional law $n^{-1/2}\sum_{s=1}^{\lfloor nr \rfloor}\tilde{\varepsilon}_s \rightsquigarrow B_{\tilde{\varepsilon}}(r)$ indicated above, which holds provided $\tilde{C}(1) \neq 0$. The limit theory in (1.19) involves Wiener integration with respect to the process $B_{\tilde{\varepsilon}}$ and is validated, as in Lemma 1.6.1, by the bounded variation property of the demeaned trend function $X^\dagger(r)$ and the weak convergence of the standardized partial sum process $n^{-1/2}\sum_{s=1}^{\lfloor nr \rfloor}\tilde{\varepsilon}_s$.

Combining the limits in (1.18) and (1.19), we obtain the asymptotic behavior of the OLS estimator $\hat{\beta}^\dagger = \left(\tilde{X}^{\dagger\prime}\tilde{X}^\dagger\right)^{-1}\left(\tilde{X}^{\dagger\prime}\tilde{Y}^\dagger\right)$ after centering and scaling, namely,

$$\sqrt{n}F_n(\hat{\beta}^\dagger - \beta) = \left(\frac{1}{n}F_n^{-1}\tilde{X}^{\dagger\prime}\tilde{X}^\dagger F_n^{-1}\right)^{-1}\left(\frac{1}{n}F_n^{-1}\tilde{X}^{\dagger\prime}\tilde{U}\right)$$

$$\rightsquigarrow \left(\int_0^1 X^\dagger(r)X^\dagger(r)'dr\right)^{-1}\int_0^1 X^\dagger(r)dB_{\tilde{\varepsilon}}(r)$$
$$=_d \mathcal{N}\left(0,\tilde{\omega}^2 M^{\dagger-1}\right). \tag{1.20}$$

As is apparent from (1.20), the OLS estimator $\hat{\beta}^\dagger$ obtained from the temporally aggregated model (1.16) with a fitted intercept in the regression satisfies an invariance principle and is asymptotically normal with a simple covariance matrix structure involving the inverse limiting signal matrix $M^{\dagger-1}$ and the scalar factor $\tilde{\omega}^2$, which is the long-run variance of the equation errors $\tilde{\varepsilon}_t$ in (1.16). It is further apparent that under the given conditions the spectral density $f_{\tilde{\varepsilon}}(\lambda) = \frac{\sigma^2}{2\pi}|\tilde{C}(e^{i\lambda})|^2 \in (0,\infty)$ of $\tilde{\varepsilon}_t$ satisfies the conditions in the GR theorem for the asymptotic equivalence of OLS and GLS. Hence, asymptotic efficiency in the regression (1.16) can be achieved by the use of OLS without any knowledge of the spectral density $f_{\tilde{\varepsilon}}(\lambda)$.

Consistent estimation of $\tilde{\omega}^2$ may be conducted by standard HAC methods applied to the residuals of the regression, namely,

$$\hat{U}_t^\dagger = Y_t - \hat{\mu}^\dagger - X_t'\hat{\beta}^\dagger = Y_t^\dagger - X_t^{\dagger\prime}\hat{\beta}^\dagger, \tag{1.21}$$

where the intercept estimate is $\hat{\mu}^\dagger = \frac{1}{n}\sum_{t=1}^n Y_t - \frac{1}{n}\sum_{t=1}^n X_t'\hat{\beta}^\dagger$. The nonparametric estimate has the usual form $\hat{\tilde{\omega}}^2 = \sum_{\ell=-L}^{L} k\left(\frac{\ell}{L}\right)\hat{\gamma}_{\hat{U}^\dagger}(\ell)$, where $\gamma_{\hat{U}^\dagger}(\ell) = \frac{1}{n}\sum_{1\le t,t+\ell\le n}\hat{U}_t^\dagger\hat{U}_{t+\ell}^\dagger$ and $k(\cdot)$ is a symmetric lag kernel such as the Bartlett or Parzen kernel. Since $\hat{\beta}^\dagger \to_p \beta$ it follows that $\hat{U}_t^\dagger = \tilde{\varepsilon}_t + o_p(1)$ and $\gamma_{\hat{U}^\dagger}(\ell) \to_p \gamma_{\tilde{\varepsilon}}(\ell) = \mathbb{E}(\tilde{\varepsilon}_t\tilde{\varepsilon}_{t+\ell})$ for all finite ℓ as $n \to \infty$. Then the kernel long-run variance estimator $\hat{\tilde{\omega}}^2 \to_p \tilde{\omega}^2$ under standard conditions on the kernel $k(\cdot)$ and the lag truncation parameter $L = L_n \to \infty$ as $n \to \infty$, which are henceforth assumed to hold.

With the limit theory (1.20) and consistent estimation of $\tilde{\omega}^2$ it might appear that inference about the regression coefficients β can be conducted using standard t-tests and Wald tests. However, the asymptotic distribution in (1.20) involves matrix normalization by F_n to account for the differing magnitudes in the trend regressors X_t. This matrix normalization and multiple hypotheses about the coefficients together lead to some additional complexities in the limit theory for Wald tests. A general treatment of hypothesis testing in regression under matrix normalization is developed in Magdalinos and Phillips (2018). The present discussion will focus on the potential deficiencies and their impact on the asymptotic theory induced by the presence of the deterministic trend polynomials X_t and multiple convergence rates in the regression (1.16).

Unlike Wald tests of general hypotheses, inference procedures for individual coefficients β_i follow directly from (1.20). For instance, to test null hypotheses such as $\mathcal{H}_0: \beta_i = \beta_i^0$, standard t-tests can be employed using the limit theory

$$t_{\beta_i} = \frac{\hat{\beta}_i^{\dagger} - \beta_i^0}{\hat{\omega}^2 \left[\left(\tilde{X}^{\dagger\prime} \tilde{X}^{\dagger} \right)^{-1} \right]_{ii}} \rightsquigarrow \mathcal{N}(0,1), \text{ as } n \to \infty, \tag{1.22}$$

where $[A]_{ii}$ denotes the ith diagonal element of the matrix A. Tests of multiple hypotheses involving several of the coefficients β_i need to respect the different rates of convergence of the elements $\hat{\beta}_i$ that are evident in (1.20). Coefficient estimates with lower convergence rates then dominate the limit theory, which has some interesting features that are explored in Section 1.4.

1.3.5 Temporal Aggregation in the Standard Case Where $C(1) \neq 0$

We next consider the effect of estimating the parameter vector β in the temporally aggregated model (1.10) by OLS regression with a fitted intercept in the regression but in the case where $C(1) \neq 0$ and there is no degeneracy induced by an MA unit root. The model may therefore be written in the form

$$Y_t = X_t'\beta + U_t = \mu + X_t'\beta + U_t, \; t = 1, \ldots, n \tag{1.23}$$

with $\mu = 0$ and $U_t = \sum_{s=1}^t u_s$. The OLS estimator $\hat{\beta}^{\dagger} = (\tilde{X}^{\dagger\prime}\tilde{X}^{\dagger})^{-1}(\tilde{X}^{\dagger\prime}\tilde{Y}^{\dagger})$ has the same form as before but now the estimation error is $\hat{\beta}^{\dagger} - \beta = (\tilde{X}^{\dagger\prime}\tilde{X}^{\dagger})^{-1}(\tilde{X}^{\dagger\prime}\tilde{U})$ and in place of (1.19) the sample covariance factor has the following limit:

$$\frac{1}{n^{3/2}} F_n^{-1} \tilde{X}^{\dagger\prime} \tilde{U} = \frac{1}{n} \sum_{t=1}^{n} F_n^{-1} X_t^{\dagger} \frac{U_t}{\sqrt{n}} \rightsquigarrow \int_0^1 X^{\dagger}(r) B_u(r) dr. \tag{1.24}$$

Upon centering and scaling, the limit distribution follows by standard methods giving

$$\begin{aligned} \frac{1}{\sqrt{n}} F_n (\hat{\beta}^{\dagger} - \beta) &= \left(\frac{1}{n} F_n^{-1} \tilde{X}^{\dagger\prime} \tilde{X}^{\dagger} F_n^{-1} \right)^{-1} \left(\frac{1}{n^{3/2}} F_n^{-1} \tilde{X}^{\dagger\prime} \tilde{U} \right) \\ &\rightsquigarrow M^{\dagger -1} \int_0^1 X^{\dagger}(r) B_u(r) dr \\ &=_d \mathcal{N}\left(0, \omega^2 M^{\dagger -1} \int_0^1 \int_0^1 X^{\dagger}(r) r \wedge s X^{\dagger}(s)' dr ds M^{\dagger -1} \right). \end{aligned} \tag{1.25}$$

The rate of convergence of $\hat{\beta}^{\dagger}$ is $\frac{1}{\sqrt{n}} F_n$ and is therefore slower by $O(n)$ than the MA unit root case where the error is $u_t = \tilde{\varepsilon}_{t-1} - \tilde{\varepsilon}_t$. Also, the variance matrix in the limit distribution (1.25) has a sandwich form, which arises from the fact that the temporally aggregated model (1.23) is a polynomial regression with a highly autocorrelated $I(1)$ error process U_t. The regressor in (1.23) is, for large t, $X_t = \sum_{s=1}^t x_s \sim_a (t, t^2, \ldots, t^{m+1})'$, whose component of lowest degree is the linear trend t which has the sample signal $\sum_{t=1}^n t^2 = O(n^3)$. This signal of $O(n^3)$ exceeds that of the $I(1)$ error U_t, which is $\sum_{t=1}^{n} U_t^2 = O_p(n^2)$), by order $O_p(n)$. It follows that the OLS estimator $\hat{\beta}^{\dagger}$ is consistent with the lowest convergence rate $O(\sqrt{n})$ for the coefficient β_0.

The fitted intercept $\hat{\mu}^{\dagger}$, on the other hand, is inconsistent. To show this, note that $\hat{\mu}^{\dagger} = \frac{1}{n}\sum_{t=1}^{n} Y_t - \frac{1}{n}\sum_{t=1}^{n} X_t'\hat{\beta}^{\dagger}$ and

$$\begin{aligned}\frac{1}{\sqrt{n}}\hat{\mu}^{\dagger} &= \frac{1}{n}\sum_{t=1}^{n}\frac{U_t}{\sqrt{n}} - \frac{1}{n}\sum_{t=1}^{n} X_t'F_n^{-1}\frac{1}{\sqrt{n}}F_n\left(\hat{\beta}^{\dagger} - \beta\right) \\ &\rightsquigarrow \int_0^1 B_u(r)dr - \int_0^1 X(r)'dr\left(\int_0^1 X^{\dagger}(r)X^{\dagger}(r)'dr\right)^{-1} \\ &\quad\times \int_0^1 X^{\dagger}(r)B_u(r)dr, \end{aligned} \tag{1.26}$$

so that $\hat{\mu}^{\dagger} = O_p(\sqrt{n})$ diverges as $n \to \infty$. The divergence of the fitted intercept is a consequence of the fact that the temporally aggregated model error U_t is an $I(1)$ time series whose signal exceeds that of the constant regressor associated with the intercept. The fitted equation therefore manifests a partially spurious regression property in which the intercept is not consistently estimated but the time polynomial regression coefficients are consistent because their signal is stronger, as discussed earlier.

1.4 Wald Statistic Inference

Before commencing a general treatment we illustrate the issues involved with some examples. These help in developing a notation that is suited for a complete discussion of the general case. In these examples and the subsequent treatment we continue to work with the temporally aggregated model in which $C(1) = 0$ and the model has a fitted intercept, as in (1.16). The analysis for the case where $C(1) \neq 0$ is entirely analogous, allowing for the different convergence rates of the estimated coefficients and different estimate of the residual long-run error variance.[1]

[1] In practical situations it is typically unknown, at least without testing, whether $C(1) = 0$ or $C(1) \neq 0$. Then an additional issue arises in the construction of the Wald test statistic, because the statistic depends on a consistent estimate of the variance matrix of the coefficient estimates, which in turn depends on whether $C(1) = 0$ or $C(1) \neq 0$. Readers are referred to Phillips and Kheifets (2024) for a systematic analysis of this issue in the case of a possibly multicointegrated system. That model involves stochastic trends but the ideas underlying the construction of the Wald statistic may be applied in the present context. A full analysis of that case is not presented here to avoid unnecessary lengthening of the chapter.

1.4.1 Example 1

We start with the case of a simple null hypothesis about all the coefficients of the form $\mathcal{H}_0 \colon \beta_0 = \beta_1 = \beta_2 = \cdots = \beta_m$. This hypothesis can be written as $\mathcal{H}_0 \colon H\beta = h$ using the $m \times (m+1)$ matrix $H = [\iota_m, -I_m]$ and vector $h = 0$ with the m-vector $\iota_m = (1, 1, \ldots, 1)'$ and order m identity matrix I_m. The Wald statistic for testing $\mathcal{H}_0$ is then

$$\begin{aligned} W_n &= (H\hat{\beta}^{\dagger} - h)' \left[H \left(\tilde{X}^{\dagger\prime} \tilde{X}^{\dagger} \right)^{-1} H' \right]^{-1} (H\hat{\beta}^{\dagger} - h) / \hat{\tilde{\omega}}^2 \\ &= \hat{\beta}^{\dagger\prime} H' \left[H \left(\tilde{X}^{\dagger\prime} \tilde{X}^{\dagger} \right)^{-1} H' \right]^{-1} H\hat{\beta}^{\dagger} / \hat{\tilde{\omega}}^2. \end{aligned} \tag{1.27}$$

The analysis that follows proceeds with the case studied in Section 1.3.4 where $C(1) = 0$ and an intercept is included in the regression as in (1.16). Using the normalization matrix $F_n = nD_n = \text{diag}(n, n^2, \ldots, n^{m+1})$, and setting $G_n = \text{diag}(n^2, \ldots, n^{m+1})$, we have $G_n^{-1} = O(n^{-2})$ and observe that $HF_n^{-1} = [\iota_m, -I_m]F_n^{-1} = [n^{-1}\iota_m, -G_n^{-1}] = \frac{1}{n}[\iota_m, -nG_n^{-1}]$. Then

$$\begin{aligned} n^{3/2} HF_n^{-1} F_n(\hat{\beta}^{\dagger} - \beta) &= \left[\iota_m, -nG_n^{-1} \right] \sqrt{n} F_n(\hat{\beta}^{\dagger} - \beta) \\ &\sim_a \left[\iota_m, -nG_n^{-1} \right] \left(\int_0^1 X^{\dagger}(r) X^{\dagger}(r)' dr \right)^{-1} \int_0^1 X^{\dagger}(r) dB_{\tilde{\varepsilon}}(dr) \\ &\sim_a \mathcal{N} \left(0, \tilde{\omega}^2 \left[\iota_m, -nG_n^{-1} \right] M^{\dagger -1} \left[\iota_m, -nG_n^{-1} \right]' \right) \\ &\rightsquigarrow \mathcal{N} \left(0, \tilde{\omega}^2 \left[\iota_m, 0_{m \times m} \right] M^{\dagger -1} \left[\iota_m, 0_{m \times m} \right]' \right), \end{aligned} \tag{1.28}$$

as $n \to \infty$ because $nG_n^{-1} = O(n^{-1})$ and so $\left[\iota_m, -nG_n^{-1} \right] \to [\iota_m, 0_{m \times m}]$. Observe that the limit distribution given in (1.28) is singular because the transform matrix $[\iota_m, 0_{m \times m}]$ has rank $1 < m$. This rank deficiency affects the limit distribution of the Wald statistic and the degrees of freedom of the resulting chi-squared statistic. In particular, we have

$$\begin{aligned} & \hat{\beta}^{\dagger\prime} H' \left[H \left(\tilde{X}^{\dagger\prime} \tilde{X}^{\dagger} \right)^{-1} H' \right]^{-1} H\hat{\beta}^{\dagger} / \hat{\tilde{\omega}}^2 \\ &= \hat{\beta}^{\dagger\prime} H' \left[\frac{1}{n} HF_n^{-1} \left(\frac{1}{n} F_n^{-1} \tilde{X}^{\dagger\prime} \tilde{X}^{\dagger} F_n^{-1} \right)^{-1} F_n^{-1} H' \right]^{-1} H\hat{\beta}^{\dagger} / \hat{\tilde{\omega}}^2 \\ &= \frac{1}{n} \hat{\beta}^{\dagger\prime} \sqrt{n} F_n F_n^{-1} H' \left[\frac{1}{n} HF_n^{-1} \left(\frac{1}{n} F_n^{-1} \tilde{X}^{\dagger\prime} \tilde{X}^{\dagger} F_n^{-1} \right)^{-1} F_n^{-1} H' \right]^{-1} \\ &\quad \times HF_n^{-1} \sqrt{n} F_n \hat{\beta}^{\dagger} / \hat{\tilde{\omega}}^2 \end{aligned}$$

$$
\begin{aligned}
&\sim_a \hat{\beta}^{\dagger\prime}\sqrt{n}F_nF_n^{-1}H'\left[\left[\frac{1}{n}\iota_m,-G_n^{-1}\right]M^{\dagger-1}\left[\frac{1}{n}\iota_m,-G_n^{-1}\right]'\right]^{-1} \\
&\quad\times HF_n^{-1}\sqrt{n}F_n\hat{\beta}^{\dagger}/\tilde{\omega}^2 \\
&\sim_a \int_0^1 dB_{\tilde{\varepsilon}}(r)X^{\dagger\prime}(r)M^{\dagger-1}\left[\frac{1}{n}\iota_m,-G_n^{-1}\right]' \\
&\quad\times\left[\left[\frac{1}{n}\iota_m,-G_n^{-1}\right]M^{\dagger-1}\left[\frac{1}{n}\iota_m,-G_n^{-1}\right]'\right]^{-1} \\
&\quad\times\left[\frac{1}{n}\iota_m,-G_n^{-1}\right]M^{\dagger-1}\int_0^1 X^{\dagger}(r)dB_{\tilde{\varepsilon}}(r)/\tilde{\omega}^2 \\
&\sim_a \int_0^1 dB_{\tilde{\varepsilon}}(r)X^{\dagger}(r)'M^{\dagger-1}\left[\iota_m,-nG_n^{-1}\right]' \\
&\quad\times\left[\left[\iota_m,-nG_n^{-1}\right]M^{\dagger-1}\left[\iota_m,-nG_n^{-1}\right]'\right]^{-1} \\
&\quad\times\left[\iota_m,-nG_n^{-1}\right]M^{\dagger-1}\int_0^1 X^{\dagger}(r)dB_{\tilde{\varepsilon}}(r)/\tilde{\omega}^2 \\
&= \int_0^1 dW_{\tilde{\varepsilon}}(r)X^{\dagger}(r)'M^{\dagger-1/2}P_{\mathcal{A}_n}M^{\dagger-1/2}\int_0^1 X^{\dagger}(r)dW_{\tilde{\varepsilon}}(r) \\
&= \mathcal{Z}'P_{\mathcal{A}_n}\mathcal{Z} \rightsquigarrow \mathcal{Z}'P_{\mathcal{A}}\mathcal{Z} =_d \chi_1^2. \qquad (1.29)
\end{aligned}
$$

Here $W_\varepsilon := (1/\tilde{\omega})B_\varepsilon$ is standard Brownian motion and $\mathcal{Z}'P_{\mathcal{A}_n}\mathcal{Z}$ is a quadratic form in the Gaussian vector $\mathcal{Z} := \left(\int_0^1 X^{\dagger}(r)X^{\dagger}(r)'dr\right)^{-1/2}\int_0^1 X^{\dagger}(r)dW_{\tilde{\varepsilon}}(r) =_d \mathcal{N}(0, I_m)$. The projection matrix $P_{\mathcal{A}_n} = \mathcal{A}_n\left(\mathcal{A}_n'\mathcal{A}_n\right)^{-1}\mathcal{A}_n'$ is deterministic of rank $m = \operatorname{rank}\left(\left[\iota_m, -nG_n^{-1}\right]\right)$ for finite n. $P_{\mathcal{A}_n}$ projects onto the m-dimensional range space of the matrix $\mathcal{A}_n$ where

$$
\begin{aligned}
\mathcal{A}_n' &= \left[\iota_m,-nG_n^{-1}\right]M^{\dagger-1/2} = \left[\iota_m, O\left(\frac{1}{n}\right)\right]M^{\dagger-1/2} \\
&\to \left[\iota_m, 0_{m\times m}\right]M^{\dagger-1/2} =: \mathcal{A}'. \qquad (1.30)
\end{aligned}
$$

The $(m+1)\times(m+1)$ dimensional limiting projection matrix $P_{\mathcal{A}} = \mathcal{A}\left(\mathcal{A}'\mathcal{A}\right)^{+}\mathcal{A}'$ has rank unity, where $\left(\mathcal{A}'\mathcal{A}\right)^{+}$ is the Moore–Penrose inverse[2] of $\mathcal{A}'\mathcal{A}$. The projector $P_{\mathcal{A}}$ can be simplified as follows. Let a' be the first row of the symmetric matrix $M^{\dagger-1/2} = \left(\int_0^1 X^{\dagger}(r)X^{\dagger}(r)'dr\right)^{-1/2}$. Then

$$
\mathcal{A}' = \left[\iota_m, 0\right]M^{\dagger-1/2} = \iota_m a', \qquad (1.31)
$$

[2] For an $n\times k$ matrix X of rank $k < n$ the Moore–Penrose inverse of XX' is $(XX')^{+} = X(X'X)^{-2}X'$ and the Moore–Penrose inverse of X is $X^{+} = X'(XX')^{+}$.

and

$$P_{\mathcal{A}} = a\iota_m'(\iota_m a' a \iota_m')^{+}\iota_m a' = a(a'a)^{-1}a'\iota_m'(\iota_m\iota_m')^{+}\iota_m$$
$$= P_a\iota_m'(\iota_m\iota_m')^{+}\iota_m = P_a, \tag{1.32}$$

since the Moore–Penrose inverse $(\iota_m\iota_m')^{+} = \iota_m(\iota_m'\iota_m)^{-2}\iota_m$ and thus

$$\iota_m'(\iota_m\iota_m')^{+}\iota_m = \iota_m'\iota_m(\iota_m'\iota_m)^{-2}\iota_m'\iota_m = 1.$$

It follows that $\mathcal{Z}'P_{\mathcal{A}}\mathcal{Z} = \mathcal{Z}'P_a\mathcal{Z} =_d \chi_1^2$, giving (1.29).

This example illustrates a key asymptotic deficiency in the Wald test in which a test of m different hypotheses leads to a statistic whose limit distribution is chi-square with only a single degree of freedom. The dimension reduction that occurs in this limit theory of the Wald statistic is associated with the concentration of the range space of the projector $P_{\mathcal{A}_n}$ to the lower dimensional range space of the projector $P_{\mathcal{A}} = P_a$. The dimension reduction occurs in the limit distribution of the Wald statistic as the sample size $n \to \infty$ and thereby affects inference but it does not occur in the limit distribution of the estimated coefficient vector $\hat{\beta}^{\dagger}$ itself, as is clear from (1.20). More specifically, it is the matrix metric $H\left(\tilde{X}^{\dagger\prime}\tilde{X}^{\dagger}\right)^{-1}H'$, which is used to measure distance from the null hypothesis in the Wald statistic (1.27), that collapses in dimension as $n \to \infty$. This collapse in dimension at infinity is the result of the differing signal strengths in the signal matrix $\tilde{X}^{\dagger\prime}\tilde{X}^{\dagger}$ that determine the convergence rates of the elements of the estimated coefficient vector $\hat{\beta}$. It is captured by the replacement of this metric, upon appropriate matrix normalization, by the projector $P_{\mathcal{A}_n}$ which collapses to $P_{\mathcal{A}} = P_a$ as $n \to \infty$.

In the present case the null hypothesis is $\mathcal{H}_0: \beta_0 = \beta_1 = \ldots, \beta_m$ and involves m restrictions on $m+1$ coefficients. But the limit distribution of the Wald test is simply χ_1^2 rather than the usual χ_m^2 where the number of degrees of freedom equals the number of restrictions. The reason for the reduced degrees of freedom in the limit distribution is that the estimates of the individual coefficients $\{\beta_1, \ldots, \beta_m\}$ of the trend terms all have faster rates of convergence given the stronger signal associated with their regressors. This difference means that the variances of the differentials in the regression coefficients are all dominated by the variance of $\hat{\beta}_0$. For instance, in the regression (1.16) for the temporally aggregated equation, the difference in the first two coefficients $\hat{\beta}_0 - \hat{\beta}_1$ satisfies

$$n^{3/2}(\hat{\beta}_0 - \hat{\beta}_1) = n^{3/2}(\hat{\beta}_0\beta_1) - n^{3/2}(\hat{\beta}_1 - \beta_1) = n^{3/2}(\hat{\beta}_0 - \beta_1) + O_p\left(\frac{1}{n}\right), \tag{1.33}$$

since $n^{5/2}(\hat{\beta}_1 - \hat{\beta}_1) = O_p(1)$. Recall that the regressor $X_t = \sum_{s=1}^{t} x_s = \sum_{s=1}^{t}(1, s, s^2, \ldots, s^m)'$ in (1.16). So the components of X_t corresponding to the coefficients β_0 and β_1 are $X_{1t} = t$ and $X_{2t} = \sum_{s=1}^{t} s = t(t+1)/2$. The convergence rate of $\hat{\beta}_0$ is then $n^{3/2}$, corresponding to the order of magnitude of the signal $\sum_{t=1}^{n} X_{1t}^2 = O(n^3)$ and the convergence rate of $\hat{\beta}_1$ is $n^{5/2}$ corresponding to the signal order $\sum_{t=1}^{n} X_{2t}^2 = O(n^5)$. Hence, the limit distribution in the Wald test is determined as if the coefficients of the higher-order trend terms were known. In effect, the greater rates of convergence of the higher-order coefficient estimates in the trend regression imply that their variances do not contribute to the limit distribution of the Wald statistic and only the variance of $\hat{\beta}_0$ figures in the limit theory. But $\hat{\beta}_0$ has only a single dimension and this is what leads to the χ_1^2 limit distribution in (1.29).

Remarks

(i) The reduction in dimension that occurs in the limit theory of the Wald statistic W_n in (1.29) from the rank m of H to unity matches the reduction in dimension of the limit theory of the transformed estimator (1.28) following matrix normalization. Importantly, in the derivation of this limit theory there is no reduction in dimension for finite n. The collapse in dimension occurs in the limit when $n \to \infty$. Notably, the singular covariance matrix $\tilde{\omega}^2 [\iota_m, 0_{m\times m}] \left(\int_0^1 X^\dagger(r) X^\dagger(r)' dr\right)^{-1} [\iota_m, 0_{m\times m}]'$ of the limit distribution in (1.28) of the normalized, transformed, and centered estimator $n^{3/2} H F_n^{-1} F_n(\hat{\beta}^\dagger - \beta)$ is consistently estimated by the matrix $\hat{\tilde{\omega}}^2 \left[\iota_m, -nG_n^{-1}\right] \left(\frac{1}{n} F_n^{-1} \tilde{X}^{\dagger\prime} \tilde{X}^\dagger F_n^{-1}\right)^{-1} \left[\iota_m, -nG_n^{-1}\right]'$. This means that, although a generalized inverse is involved in our analysis of the limit distribution theory of the Wald statistic, it is not necessary to consider limits of generalized inverses as $n \to \infty$ in determining the limit theory of the Wald statistic as in the analyses of Stewart (1969), Puri et al. (1984), and Andrews (1987). The situation in this example where consistent estimation of the limiting covariance matrix is available is instead similar to the case studied in Vuong (1987).

(ii) As is apparent in the derivation leading to (1.29), the details of the dimensional reduction rely on the form of the null hypothesis $\mathcal{H}_0$ and in particular the form of the matrix H. The asymptotic theory can be complex and the final limit distribution of the Wald test is contingent on the interaction between the normalization matrix F_n and the hypothesis matrix H. This is the essence of the difficulties involved in matrix normalization.

1.4.2 Example 2

The next example gives a different scenario in the limit theory which displays no asymptotic deficiency but more complex matrix normalization. The null hypothesis is $\mathcal{H}_0 : H\beta = h$ with $h = 0$ and

$$H = H_{2\times m+1} = \begin{bmatrix} 1 & -2 & 0 & 0 & 0 & \cdots & 0 \\ 0 & 0 & 1 & 1 & 0 & \cdots & 0 \end{bmatrix} =: \left[H_1, H_2, 0_{2\times(m-3)}\right], \tag{1.34}$$

with

$$H_1 = \begin{bmatrix} 1 & -2 \\ 0 & 0 \end{bmatrix}, \; H_2 = \begin{bmatrix} 0 & 0 \\ 1 & 1 \end{bmatrix}, \tag{1.35}$$

so that the null hypothesis is simply $\mathcal{H}_0\colon \beta_0 = 2\beta_1$ and $\beta_2 + \beta_3 = 0$.

We now partition the normalization matrix as $F_n = nD_n = \operatorname{diag}(n, n^2, \ldots, n^{m+1}) = \operatorname{blockdiag}[F_{1n}, F_{2n}, F_{3n}]$, where $F_{1n} = \operatorname{diag}(n, n^2)$, $F_{2n} = \operatorname{diag}(n^3, n^4)$, and $F_{3n} = \operatorname{diag}(n^5, \ldots, n^{m+1})$, so that $F_{3n}^{-1} = O(n^{-5})$. Next observe that

$$\begin{aligned} HF_n^{-1} &= \left[H_1, H_2, 0_{2\times(m-3)}\right] F_n^{-1} = \left[H_1 F_{1n}^{-1}, H_2 F_{2n}^{-1}, 0_{2\times(m-3)}\right] \\ &= \begin{bmatrix} \frac{1}{n} & -\frac{2}{n^2} & 0 & 0 & 0 & \cdots & 0 \\ 0 & 0 & \frac{1}{n^3} & \frac{1}{n^4} & 0 & \cdots & 0 \end{bmatrix} \\ &= \begin{bmatrix} \frac{1}{n} & 0 \\ 0 & \frac{1}{n^3} \end{bmatrix} \begin{bmatrix} 1 & -\frac{2}{n} & 0 & 0 & 0 & \cdots & 0 \\ 0 & 0 & 1 & \frac{1}{n} & 0 & \cdots & 0 \end{bmatrix} =: Q_n \times R_n, \end{aligned} \tag{1.36}$$

with $Q_n = \operatorname{diag}(n^{-1}, n^{-3})$ and $R_n = \begin{bmatrix} 1 & -\frac{2}{n} & 0 & 0 & 0 & \cdots & 0 \\ 0 & 0 & 1 & \frac{1}{n} & 0 & \cdots & 0 \end{bmatrix}$ has dimension $2 \times (m+1)$ and rank 2. Then

$$\begin{aligned} &\sqrt{n} Q_n^{-1} H F_n^{-1} F_n(\hat{\beta}^\dagger - \beta) = R_n \sqrt{n} F_n(\hat{\beta}^\dagger - \beta) \\ &\sim_a R_n M^{\dagger -1} \int_0^1 X^\dagger(r) dB_{\tilde{\varepsilon}}(dr) \\ &=_d \mathcal{N}\left(0,\ \tilde{\omega}^2 R_n M^{\dagger -1} R_n'\right) \rightsquigarrow \mathcal{N}\left(0,\ \tilde{\omega}^2 R M^{\dagger -1} R'\right), \end{aligned} \tag{1.37}$$

where $R_n \to R = \begin{bmatrix} 1 & 0 & 0 & 0 & 0 & \cdots & 0 \\ 0 & 0 & 1 & 0 & 0 & \cdots & 0 \end{bmatrix}$. Observe that the limit distribution of $\hat{\beta}^\dagger - \beta$ given in (1.37) is of full rank 2 but requires a more complex matrix normalization involving the normalization matrix Q_n than does that of the earlier result given in (1.28). With this limit theory for the estimator in hand we can obtain the limit distribution of the Wald statistic for testing $\mathcal{H}_0\colon H\beta = h = 0$ as follows.

$$\begin{aligned} W_n &= \hat{\beta}^{\dagger\prime} H' \left[H \left(\tilde{X}^{\dagger\prime} \tilde{X}^\dagger \right)^{-1} H' \right]^{-1} H\hat{\beta}^\dagger / \hat{\tilde{\omega}}^2 \\ &= \hat{\beta}^{\dagger\prime} H' \left[\frac{1}{n} H F_n^{-1} \left(\frac{1}{n} F_n^{-1} \tilde{X}^{\dagger\prime} \tilde{X}^\dagger F_n^{-1} \right)^{-1} F_n^{-1} H' \right]^{-1} H\hat{\beta}^\dagger / \hat{\tilde{\omega}}^2 \end{aligned}$$

$$= \frac{1}{n}\hat{\beta}^{\dagger\prime}\sqrt{n}F_nR_n'Q_n'\left[\frac{1}{n}Q_nR_n\left(\frac{1}{n}F_n^{-1}\tilde{X}^{\dagger\prime}\tilde{X}^{\dagger}F_n^{-1}\right)^{-1}R_n'Q_n'\right]^{-1}$$

$$\times Q_nR_n\sqrt{n}F_n\hat{\beta}^{\dagger}/\hat{\bar{\omega}}^2$$

$$= \hat{\beta}^{\dagger\prime}\sqrt{n}F_nR_n'\left[R_n\left(\frac{1}{n}F_n^{-1}\tilde{X}^{\dagger\prime}\tilde{X}^{\dagger}F_n^{-1}\right)^{-1}R_n'\right]^{-1}$$

$$R_n\sqrt{n}F_n\hat{\beta}^{\dagger}/\hat{\bar{\omega}}^2 \rightsquigarrow \chi_2^2, \tag{1.38}$$

in view of (1.37) and the fact that rank$(R) = 2$. Hence, in this case the distribution has the usual limiting chi-squared distribution with degrees of freedom that match the number of (independent) restrictions involved in the null hypothesis $\mathcal{H}_0\colon H\beta = h$ with the restriction matrix H given in (1.34).

1.4.3 Example 3

We now combine the features of Examples 1 and 2 in a third more complex case involving the null hypothesis $\mathcal{H}_0\colon H\beta = h$ with $h = 0$ and the $m \times (m+1)$ restriction matrix

$$H = \begin{bmatrix} 1 & -1 & 0 & 0 & 0 & \cdots & 0 \\ 2 & 0 & 1 & 0 & 0 & \cdots & 0 \\ 0 & 3 & 0 & -2 & 0 & \cdots & 0 \\ 0 & 0 & 1 & -1 & 0 & \cdots & 0 \\ 0 & 0 & 1 & 0 & -1 & \cdots & 0 \\ \vdots & \vdots & \vdots & \vdots & \vdots & \ddots & \vdots \\ 0 & 0 & 1 & 0 & 0 & \cdots & -1 \end{bmatrix}, \tag{1.39}$$

giving $q = m$ restrictions on β. So the null hypothesis is $\mathcal{H}_0\colon \beta_0 - \beta_1 = 0,\ 2\beta_0 + \beta_2 = 0,\ 3\beta_1 + 2\beta_3 = 0\ \beta_3 = \beta_4 = \cdots = \beta_m$ or equivalently $\bar{\mathcal{H}}_0\colon \beta_0 - \beta_1 = 0,\ \beta_0 + \frac{1}{2}\beta_2 = 0,\ \beta_1 + \frac{2}{3}\beta_3 = 0,\ \beta_3 = \beta_4 = \cdots = \beta_m$. For this equivalent null hypothesis $\bar{\mathcal{H}}_0\colon\ \bar{H}\beta = 0$ we have the normalized $m \times (m+1)$ restriction matrix

$$\bar{H} = \begin{bmatrix} 1 & -1 & 0 & 0 & \cdots & 0 \\ 1 & 0 & \frac{1}{2} & 0 & \cdots & 0 \\ 0 & 1 & 0 & -\frac{2}{3} & \cdots & 0 \\ 0_{m-3} & 0_{m-3} & \iota_{m-3} & & -I_{m-3} & \end{bmatrix}$$

$$= \left[\begin{array}{cccccc} \iota_2 & -1 & 0 & 0 & \cdots & 0 \\ & 0 & \frac{1}{2} & 0 & \cdots & 0 \\ \hline 0 & 1 & 0 & -\frac{2}{3} & \cdots & 0 \\ 0_{m-3} & 0_{m-3} & \iota_{m-3} & & -I_{m-3} & \end{array}\right]. \tag{1.40}$$

Setting $G_n = \text{diag}(n^4, n^5, \cdots, n^{m+1})$ we now have

$$
\begin{aligned}
\bar{H}F_n^{-1} &= \left[\begin{array}{c|ccccc} \frac{1}{n}\iota_2 & \begin{matrix} -\frac{1}{n^2} \\ 0 \end{matrix} & \begin{matrix} 0 \\ \frac{1}{2n^3} \end{matrix} & \begin{matrix} 0 \\ 0 \end{matrix} & \begin{matrix} \cdots \\ \cdots \end{matrix} & \begin{matrix} 0 \\ 0 \end{matrix} \\ \hline \begin{matrix} 0 \\ 0_{m-3} \end{matrix} & \begin{matrix} \frac{1}{n^2} \\ 0_{m-3} \end{matrix} & \begin{matrix} 0 \\ \frac{1}{n^3}\iota_{m-3} \end{matrix} & \begin{matrix} -\frac{2}{3n^4} \\ \end{matrix} & \begin{matrix} \cdots \\ -G_n^{-1} \end{matrix} & \begin{matrix} 0 \\ \end{matrix} \end{array}\right] \\
&= \begin{bmatrix} \frac{1}{n}I_2 & 0 & 0 & 0\cdots & 0 \\ 0 & \frac{1}{n^2} & 0 & 0\cdots & 0 \\ 0 & 0 & & \frac{1}{n^3}I_{m-3} & \end{bmatrix} \\
&\quad \times \left[\begin{array}{c|ccccc} \iota_2 & \begin{matrix} -\frac{1}{n} \\ 0 \end{matrix} & \begin{matrix} 0 \\ \frac{1}{2n^2} \end{matrix} & \begin{matrix} 0 \\ 0 \end{matrix} & \begin{matrix} \cdots \\ \cdots \end{matrix} & \begin{matrix} 0 \\ 0 \end{matrix} \\ \hline \begin{matrix} 0 \\ 0_{m-3} \end{matrix} & \begin{matrix} 1 \\ 0_{m-3} \end{matrix} & \begin{matrix} 0 \\ \iota_{m-3} \end{matrix} & \begin{matrix} -\frac{2}{3n^2} \\ \end{matrix} & \begin{matrix} \cdots \\ -n^3G_n^{-1} \end{matrix} & \begin{matrix} 0 \\ \end{matrix} \end{array}\right] \\
&=: Q_n \times R_n, \qquad (1.41)
\end{aligned}
$$

where Q_n is an $m \times m$ normalization matrix and R_n is an $m \times m + 1$ matrix of rank m for finite n which captures the implied normalized form of the restriction matrix. Similar to (1.37) in Example 2 we can now obtain the limit theory for the appropriately normalized estimated error in the restrictions $\bar{H}(\hat{\beta}^{\dagger} - \beta)$, namely,

$$
\begin{aligned}
&\sqrt{n}Q_n^{-1}\bar{H}F_n^{-1}F_n(\hat{\beta}^{\dagger} - \beta) = R_n\sqrt{n}F_n(\hat{\beta}^{\dagger} - \beta) \\
&\sim_a R_nM^{\dagger-1}\int_0^1 X^{\dagger}(r)dB_{\bar{\varepsilon}}(dr) \rightsquigarrow \mathcal{N}\left(0, \bar{\omega}^2RM^{\dagger-1}R'\right), \qquad (1.42)
\end{aligned}
$$

since

$$
R_n \to R = \left[\begin{array}{c|ccccc} \iota_2 & \begin{matrix} 0 \\ 0 \end{matrix} & \begin{matrix} 0 \\ 0 \end{matrix} & \begin{matrix} \cdots \\ \cdots \end{matrix} & \begin{matrix} 0 \\ 0 \end{matrix} \\ \hline \begin{matrix} 0 \\ 0_{m-3} \end{matrix} & \begin{matrix} 1 \\ 0_{m-3} \end{matrix} & \begin{matrix} 0 \\ \iota_{m-3} \end{matrix} & \begin{matrix} \cdots \\ \end{matrix} & \begin{matrix} 0 \\ 0_{m-3\times m-2} \end{matrix} \end{array}\right]_{m\times(m+1)}. \qquad (1.43)
$$

Observe that the limit matrix R has rank $3 < m$ and, correspondingly, the limit distribution in (1.42) is singular with deficient rank 3. As in Example 1, this singularity affects the limit distribution of the Wald statistic and the degrees of freedom of the resulting chi-squared statistic. The derivation follows the same lines but is more complex than that leading to (1.29) in Example 1 because there are now two sources of degeneracy, not one, and these are of different dimension. The Wald statistic has the following form (replacing H with $\bar{H}$):

$$
\begin{aligned}
&\hat{\beta}^{\dagger\prime}\bar{H}'\left[\bar{H}\left(\tilde{X}^{\dagger\prime}\tilde{X}^{\dagger}\right)^{-1}\bar{H}'\right]^{-1}\bar{H}\hat{\beta}^{\dagger}/\hat{\tilde{\omega}}^{2}\\
&=\hat{\beta}^{\dagger\prime}\bar{H}'\left[\frac{1}{n}\bar{H}F_n^{-1}\left(\frac{1}{n}F_n^{-1}\tilde{X}^{\dagger\prime}\tilde{X}^{\dagger}F_n^{-1}\right)^{-1}F_n^{-1}\bar{H}'\right]^{-1}\bar{H}\hat{\beta}^{\dagger}/\hat{\tilde{\omega}}^{2}\\
&=\frac{1}{n}\hat{\beta}^{\dagger\prime}\sqrt{n}F_nF_n^{-1}\bar{H}'Q_n^{-1}\left[\frac{1}{n}Q_n^{-1}\bar{H}F_n^{-1}\left(\frac{1}{n}F_n^{-1}\tilde{X}^{\dagger\prime}\tilde{X}^{\dagger}F_n^{-1}\right)^{-1}\right.\\
&\quad\left.\times F_n^{-1}\bar{H}'Q_n^{-1}\right]^{-1}Q_n^{-1}\bar{H}F_n^{-1}\sqrt{n}F_n\hat{\beta}^{\dagger}/\hat{\tilde{\omega}}^{2}\\
&\sim_a\hat{\beta}^{\dagger\prime}\sqrt{n}F_nR_n'\left[R_nM^{\dagger-1}R_n'\right]^{-1}R_n\sqrt{n}F_n\hat{\beta}^{\dagger}/\tilde{\omega}^{2}\\
&\sim_a\int_0^1 dB_{\tilde{\varepsilon}}(r)X^{\dagger}(r)'M^{\dagger-1}R_n'\left[R_nM^{\dagger-1}R_n'\right]^{-1}R_nM^{\dagger-1}\\
&\quad\times\int_0^1 X^{\dagger}(r)dB_{\tilde{\varepsilon}}(r)/\tilde{\omega}^{2}\\
&=\int_0^1 dW_{\tilde{\varepsilon}}(r)X^{\dagger}(r)'M^{\dagger-1/2}P_{\mathcal{A}_n}M^{\dagger-1/2}\times\int_0^1 X^{\dagger}(r)dW_{\tilde{\varepsilon}}(r)\\
&=\mathcal{Z}'P_{\mathcal{A}_n}\mathcal{Z}\rightsquigarrow\mathcal{Z}'P_{\mathcal{A}}\mathcal{Z}=_d\chi_3^2.
\end{aligned}
\tag{1.44}
$$

As in (1.29) $W_{\tilde{\varepsilon}} := (1/\tilde{\omega})B_{\tilde{\varepsilon}}$ is standard Brownian motion and $\mathcal{Z}'P_{\mathcal{A}_n}\mathcal{Z}$ is a quadratic form in the Gaussian vector $\mathcal{Z} := M^{\dagger-1/2}\int_0^1 X^{\dagger}(r)dW_{\tilde{\varepsilon}}(r) =_d \mathcal{N}(0, I_m)$. The projection matrix $P_{\mathcal{A}_n} = \mathcal{A}_n\left(\mathcal{A}_n'\mathcal{A}_n\right)^{-1}\mathcal{A}_n'$ is deterministic of rank $m = \text{rank}(\mathcal{A}_n) = \text{rank}(R_n)$ for all finite n. $P_{\mathcal{A}_n}$ projects onto the m-dimensional range space of the $(m+1)\times m$ matrix $\mathcal{A}_n$, where in (1.44) we have

$$
\mathcal{A}_n' = R_nM^{\dagger-1/2} \to RM^{\dagger-1/2} =: \mathcal{A}',
\tag{1.45}
$$

for which the limiting rank is $\text{rank}(\mathcal{A}) = 3$, the same as the matrix R. The $(m+1)$-dimensional limiting projection matrix $P_{\mathcal{A}} = \mathcal{A}\left(\mathcal{A}'\mathcal{A}\right)^{+}\mathcal{A}'$ therefore has rank 3. An explicit form of the projector $P_{\mathcal{A}}$ can be expressed as follows. Let a_1', a_2' and a_3' be the first, second and third rows of the symmetric matrix positive definite matrix $M^{\dagger-1/2} = \left(\int_0^1 X^{\dagger}(r)X^{\dagger}(r)'dr\right)^{-1/2}$. Then the $(m+1)\times m$ matrix $\mathcal{A}$ has the explicit form

$$
\mathcal{A} = M^{\dagger-1/2}R' = \begin{bmatrix} a_1\iota_2' & a_2 & a_3\iota_{m-3}' \end{bmatrix},
\tag{1.46}
$$

in which there are only three linearly independent columns, which we collect in the $(m+1)\times 3$ matrix $A = [a_1, a_2, a_3]$. It follows directly that the projector $P_{\mathcal{A}}$ projects onto the range space of A and is therefore equivalent to the projector

P_A by virtue of uniqueness. We deduce that the limit distribution of the Wald statistic is $\mathcal{Z}'P_{\mathcal{A}}\mathcal{Z} = \mathcal{Z}'P_A\mathcal{Z} =_d \chi_3^2$, as given in (1.44).

1.4.4 The General Case

From these examples, we now proceed to a general treatment of the limit theory for Wald tests in trend polynomial regression. The analysis continues to use the time-aggregated regression model (1.16), again with $C(1) = 0$. We start by formulating a generalized version of (1.40) for the normalized restriction matrix $\bar{H}$ in which: (i) the rows of $\bar{H}$ are assembled so that the corresponding hypotheses are ordered according to the time polynomial power of the respective coefficients; and (ii) the first nonzero coefficient in each row, corresponding to the lowest power of the associated time polynomial, is set to unity, as in (1.40). With this ordering and normalization and recognizing that hypotheses can involve different elements of the coefficient vector β that relate to time polynomials of different degrees, we partition the $q \times (m+1)$ restriction matrix $\bar{H}$ of the null hypothesis to accord with these elements in rising polynomial degree form as follows:

$$\bar{H} = \begin{bmatrix} h_{1,1} & h_{1,2} & h_{1,3} & \cdots & h_{1,m+1} \\ 0 & h_{2,2} & h_{2,3} & \cdots & h_{2,m+1} \\ 0 & 0 & h_{3,3} & \cdots & h_{3,m+1} \\ \vdots & \vdots & \vdots & \ddots & \vdots \\ 0 & 0 & 0 & \cdots & h_{p,m+1} \end{bmatrix}_S$$
$$=: \left[\bar{H}^{(1)}, \bar{H}^{(2)}, \bar{H}^{3}, \cdots, \bar{H}^{(m+1)} \right]. \tag{1.47}$$

In this representation there are p block rows indicated and $m+1$ columns. Each block diagonal entry of $\bar{H}$ is a vector of the form $h_{i,i} = c_i \iota_{q_i}$ in which $\iota_{q_i} = (1, 1, \ldots, 1)'$ has dimension q_i and $c_i = \mathbb{j}_{S_i}$ is the selector function of the block row i, which indicates whether that block row enters the matrix or not. In particular, block row i occurs in the matrix if the entry is $c_i = \mathbb{j}_{S_i} = 1$, which signifies that there are restrictions involving the coefficient β_{i-1} of t^{i-1}, namely, the lowest trend degree coefficient in block row i. On the other hand, if the entry $c_i = \mathbb{j}_{S_i} = 0$, then row i is removed from the matrix altogether as the selector $\mathbb{j}_{S_i} = 0$ signifies that there is no restriction involving β_{i-1} – so the ith-block row is removed entirely in the specification $\bar{H}_S$. The affix S on $\bar{H}_S$ in the upper block triangular matrix (1.47) means that selection may have taken place in the matrix and then $r = \sum_{i=1}^{p} \mathbb{1}\{c_i \neq 0\}$ is the actual number of block rows in the matrix $\bar{H}_S$. This arrangement implies that the q restrictions that comprise the rows of $\bar{H}$ are partitioned into r groups whose numbers sum to $q = \sum_{i=1}^{p} q_i \mathbb{1}\{c_i \neq 0\}$ in total. Upon selection of its relevant rows the restriction matrix $\bar{H} = \bar{H}_S$ is then of dimension $q \times (m+1)$ with full rank q.

In the first example above where $\bar{H} = \bar{H}_S = [\iota_m, -I_m]$ there is only one block row in the restriction matrix $\bar{H}$ and so $r = 1$, $q_1 = q = m$, $c_1 = 1$, and $c_j = 0$ for all $j > 1$. In the second example presented earlier

$$\bar{H} = \bar{H}_S = \begin{bmatrix} 1 & -2 & 0 & 0 & 0 & \cdots & 0 \\ 0 & 0 & 1 & 1 & 0 & \cdots & 0 \end{bmatrix},$$

and there are only two rows in the restriction matrix, so that $r = q = 2$, $q_1 = q_3 = 1$, $c_1 = c_3 = 1$, and $c_j = 0$ for all $j \notin \{1, 3\}$. In the third example presented earlier where

$$\bar{H} = \left[\begin{array}{cccccc} \iota_2 & \begin{matrix} -1 \\ 0 \end{matrix} & \begin{matrix} 0 \\ \frac{1}{2} \end{matrix} & \begin{matrix} 0 \\ 0 \end{matrix} & \begin{matrix} \cdots \\ \cdots \end{matrix} & \begin{matrix} 0 \\ 0 \end{matrix} \\ \hline 0 & 1 & 0 & -\frac{2}{3} & \cdots & 0 \\ 0_{m-3} & 0_{m-3} & \iota_{m-3} & & -I_{m-3} & \end{array}\right], \tag{1.48}$$

there are three blocks of restrictions so that $r = 3, q_1 = 2, q_2 = 1, q_3 = m - 3$, $q = m$, and $c_1 = c_2 = c_3 = 1$.

In the general case with restriction matrix (1.47) the normalization matrix is $F_n = \mathrm{diag}(n, n^2, \ldots, n^{m+1})$ and we write the effect of normalization by F_n^{-1} on the $q \times (m+1)$ restriction matrix $\bar{H}$ in the following partitioned matrix form which uses the selection matrix notation

$$\begin{aligned}
\bar{H}F_n^{-1} &= \left[\bar{H}^{(1)}, \bar{H}^{(2)}, \bar{H}^{3}, \cdots, \bar{H}^{(m+1)}\right] F_n^{-1} \\
&= \left[\frac{1}{n}\bar{H}^{(1)}, \frac{1}{n^2}\bar{H}^{(2)}, \frac{1}{n^3}\bar{H}^{(3)}, \cdots, \frac{1}{n^{m+1}}\bar{H}^{(m+1)}\right] \\
&= \begin{bmatrix} \frac{1}{n}h_{1,1} & \frac{1}{n^2}h_{1,2} & \frac{1}{n^3}h_{1,3} & \cdots & \frac{1}{n^{m+1}}h_{1,m+1} \\ 0 & \frac{1}{n^2}h_{2,2} & \frac{1}{n^3}h_{2,3} & \cdots & \frac{1}{n^{m+1}}h_{2,m+1} \\ 0 & 0 & \frac{1}{n^3}h_{3,3} & \cdots & \frac{1}{n^{m+1}}h_{3,m+1} \\ \vdots & \vdots & \vdots & \ddots & \vdots \\ 0 & 0 & 0 & \cdots & \frac{1}{n^{m+1}}h_{p,m+1} \end{bmatrix}_S \\
&= \begin{bmatrix} \frac{c_1}{n}I_{q_1} & 0 & 0 & \cdots & 0 \\ 0 & \frac{c_2}{n^2}I_{q_2} & 0 & \cdots & 0 \\ 0 & 0 & \frac{c_3}{n^3}I_{q_3} & \cdots & 0 \\ \vdots & \vdots & \vdots & \ddots & \vdots \\ 0 & 0 & 0 & \cdots & \frac{c_p}{n^p}I_{q_p} \end{bmatrix}_S
\end{aligned}$$

$$\times \begin{bmatrix} c_1 \iota_{q_1} & \frac{1}{n} h_{1,2} & \frac{1}{n^2} h_{1,3} & \cdots & \frac{1}{n^{r-1}} h_{1,p} & \cdots & \frac{1}{n^m} h_{1,m+1} \\ 0 & c_2 \iota_{q_2} & \frac{1}{n} h_{2,3} & \cdots & \frac{1}{n^{r-2}} h_{2,p} & \cdots & \frac{1}{n^{m-1}} h_{2,m+1} \\ 0 & 0 & c_3 \iota_{q_3} & \cdots & \frac{1}{n^{r-3}} h_{3,p} & \cdots & \frac{1}{n^{m-2}} h_{3,m+1} \\ \vdots & \vdots & \vdots & \ddots & \vdots & \vdots & \vdots \\ 0 & 0 & 0 & \cdots & c_p \iota_{q_p} & \cdots & \frac{1}{n^{m-r+1}} h_{p,m+1} \end{bmatrix}_S$$

$$=: Q_{n,S^+} \times R_{n,S}. \tag{1.49}$$

In the matrix Q_{n,S^+} the affix S^+ signifies selection and retention of rows *and* columns according to the rule that $c_i = 1$ and the removal of those rows *and* columns for which $c_i = 0$. Thus, Q_{n,S^+} is a diagonal $q \times q$ matrix that is conformable with the $q \times (m+1)$ matrix $R_{n,S}$ defined by (1.49).

With this framework in the general case we can now obtain the limit theory as $n \to \infty$ for the appropriately normalized estimated error in the restrictions $\bar{H}(\hat{\beta}^\dagger - \beta)$, namely,

$$\begin{aligned} \sqrt{n} Q_{n,S^+}^{-1} \bar{H} F_n^{-1} F_n(\hat{\beta}^\dagger - \beta) &= R_{n,S} \sqrt{n} F_n(\hat{\beta}^\dagger - \beta) \\ &\sim_a R_{n,S} \left(\int_0^1 X^\dagger(r) X^\dagger(r)' dr \right)^{-1} \int_0^1 X^\dagger(r) dB_{\tilde{\varepsilon}}(dr) \\ &\rightsquigarrow \mathcal{N}\left(0,\ \tilde{\omega}^2 R_S M^{\dagger -1} R_S'\right), \end{aligned} \tag{1.50}$$

with

$$R_{n,S} \to R_S := \begin{bmatrix} c_1 \iota_{q_1} & 0 & 0 & 0 & 0 & \cdots & 0 \\ 0 & c_2 \iota_{q_2} & 0 & \cdots & 0 & \cdots & 0 \\ 0 & 0 & c_3 \iota_{q_3} & \cdots & 0 & \cdots & 0 \\ \vdots & \vdots & \vdots & \ddots & \vdots & \vdots & \vdots \\ 0 & 0 & 0 & \cdots & c_p \iota_{q_p} & \cdots & 0 \end{bmatrix}_S, \tag{1.51}$$

where R_S is a $q \times (m+1)$ matrix of rank $r = \sum_{i=1}^p \mathbb{1}\{c_i \neq 0\} \leq q = \sum_{i=1}^p q_i \mathbb{1}\{c_i \neq 0\}$. When $r < q$, the limit distribution given in (1.50) is singular of rank r.

As in Examples 1 and 3, rank deficiency in the limit transformation matrix R_S in (1.51) and singularity of the limiting normal distribution in (1.50) affects the limit distribution of the Wald statistic and the degrees of freedom of the resulting chi-squared statistic. Following the earlier approach we have developed above, the limit distribution of the Wald statistic $W_n = \hat{\beta}^{\dagger\prime} \bar{H}' \left[\bar{H} \left(\tilde{X}^{\dagger\prime} \tilde{X}^\dagger \right)^{-1} \bar{H}' \right]^{-1} \bar{H} \hat{\beta}^\dagger / \hat{\tilde{\omega}}^2$ for testing the null hypothesis $\mathcal{H}_0:\ \bar{H}\beta = 0$ is

$$
\begin{aligned}
W_n &= \hat{\beta}^{\dagger\prime}\bar{H}'\left[\frac{1}{n}\bar{H}F_n^{-1}\left(\frac{1}{n}F_n^{-1}\tilde{X}^{\dagger\prime}\tilde{X}^{\dagger}F_n^{-1}\right)^{-1}F_n^{-1}\bar{H}'\right]^{-1}\bar{H}\hat{\beta}^{\dagger}/\hat{\tilde{\omega}}^2 \\
&= \frac{1}{n}\hat{\beta}^{\dagger\prime}\sqrt{n}F_nF_n^{-1}\bar{H}'Q_{n,S}^{-1}\left[\frac{1}{n}Q_{n,S}^{-1}\bar{H}F_n^{-1}\left(\frac{1}{n}F_n^{-1}\tilde{X}^{\dagger\prime}\tilde{X}^{\dagger}F_n^{-1}\right)^{-1}\right. \\
&\qquad \left.\times F_n^{-1}\bar{H}'Q_{n,S}^{-1}\right]^{-1}Q_{n,S}^{-1}\bar{H}F_n^{-1}\sqrt{n}F_n\hat{\beta}^{\dagger}/\hat{\tilde{\omega}}^2 \\
&\sim_a \hat{\beta}^{\dagger\prime}\sqrt{n}F_nR_{n,S}'\left[R_{n,S}M^{\dagger-1}R_{n,S}'\right]^{-1}R_{n,S}\sqrt{n}F_n\hat{\beta}^{\dagger}/\tilde{\omega}^2 \\
&\sim_a \int_0^1 dB_{\tilde{\varepsilon}}(r)X^{\dagger}(r)'M^{\dagger-1}R_{n,S}'\left[R_{n,S}M^{\dagger-1}R_{n,S}'\right]^{-1}R_{n,S}M^{\dagger-1} \\
&\qquad \times \int_0^1 X^{\dagger}(r)dB_{\tilde{\varepsilon}}(r)/\tilde{\omega}^2 \\
&= \int_0^1 dW_{\tilde{\varepsilon}}(r)X^{\dagger}(r)'M^{\dagger-1/2}P_{\mathcal{A}_{n,S}}M^{\dagger-1/2}\int_0^1 X^{\dagger}(r)dW_{\tilde{\varepsilon}}(r) \\
&= \mathcal{Z}'P_{\mathcal{A}_{n,S}}\mathcal{Z} \rightsquigarrow \mathcal{Z}'P_{\mathcal{A}_S}\mathcal{Z} =_d \chi_r^2. \qquad (1.52)
\end{aligned}
$$

Justification of (1.52) follows as before, albeit with the additional notational complications of this general case. $\mathcal{Z} = M^{\dagger-1/2}\int_0^1 X^{\dagger}(r)dW_{\tilde{\varepsilon}}(r) =_d \mathcal{N}(0, I_m)$ and $\mathcal{Z}'P_{\mathcal{A}_{n,S}}\mathcal{Z}$ is a Gaussian quadratic form. The projection matrix $P_{\mathcal{A}_{n,S}} = \mathcal{A}_{n,S}\left(\mathcal{A}_{n,S}'\mathcal{A}_{n,S}\right)^{-1}\mathcal{A}_{n,S}'$ has rank $q = \text{rank}(\mathcal{A}_{n,S}) = \text{rank}(R_{n,S})$ for all finite n and is deterministic. This matrix projects onto the q-dimensional range space of the $(m+1)\times m$ matrix $\mathcal{A}_{n,S}$, where in (1.52) we have

$$
\mathcal{A}_{n,S}' = R_{n,S}M^{\dagger-1/2} \to R_SM^{\dagger-1/2} =: \mathcal{A}_S', \qquad (1.53)
$$

for which the limiting rank is $\text{rank}(\mathcal{A}_S) = r$, the same as the rank of the matrix R_S. The $(m+1)$-dimensional limiting projection matrix $P_{\mathcal{A}_S} = \mathcal{A}_S\left(\mathcal{A}_S'\mathcal{A}_S\right)^{+}\mathcal{A}_S'$ therefore has rank r. As in the examples discussed above, an explicit form of the projector $P_{\mathcal{A}}$ can be found as follows. Use the expression for the limit matrix R_s given in (1.51), and let $\{a_i'\}_{i=1}^{m+1}$ be the rows of the positive definite matrix $M^{\dagger-1/2} = (\int_0^1 X^{\dagger}(r)X^{\dagger}(r)'dr)^{-1/2}$. Then the $(m+1)\times q$ matrix $\mathcal{A}_S$ can be written as

$$
\mathcal{A}_S = M^{\dagger-1/2}R_S' = \begin{bmatrix} c_1a_1\iota_{q_1}', & c_2a_2\iota_{q_2}', & \cdots, & c_pa_p\iota_{q_p}' \end{bmatrix}_S \qquad (1.54)
$$

in which the selection operator S removes those columns for which $c_j = 0$ so that $\mathcal{A}_S$ has the stated dimension $(m+1)\times q$ with $q = \sum_{i=1}^{p} q_i\mathbb{1}\{c_i \neq 0\}$. What remains in the matrix $\mathcal{A}_S$ are r linearly independent columns which we assemble in the $(m+1)\times r$ matrix $A_S = \left[c_1a_1, c_2a_2, \cdots, c_pa_p\right]_S$, which is easily seen to have full rank r because the matrix $(\int_0^1 X^{\dagger}(r)X^{\dagger}(r)'dr)^{-1/2}$ is nonsingular.

It follows directly that the projector $P_{\mathcal{A}_S}$ projects onto the range space of the matrix A_S and is therefore equivalent to the projector P_{A_S} by uniqueness. The limit distribution of the Wald statistic W_n is then $\mathcal{Z}'P_{\mathcal{A}_S}\mathcal{Z} = \mathcal{Z}'P_{A_S}\mathcal{Z} =_d \chi_r^2$, as stated in (1.52).

1.5 Conclusion

As is apparent from the analysis in the last section, testing multiple hypotheses in models with trend regressors involves complexities that can affect the degrees of freedom of the limiting χ^2 distribution. Whereas the least squares coefficients themselves, upon suitable centering and matrix normalization, have a standard limiting nonsingular normal distribution, Wald statistics based on them can suffer from degeneracies that are induced by the nature of the hypotheses being tested. These arise through the algebraic interaction of the normalizing matrix and the matrix form of the hypotheses being tested. The heuristic explanation is that lower rates of convergence in estimated coefficients inevitably dominate the limit theory, so that hypotheses involving linear combinations of coefficients estimated at different rates end up in the asymptotic theory being dominated by the variation of the coefficients estimated at the lowest rates, a feature that can induce degeneracy in multiple hypothesis testing when several hypotheses are of this type. As we have seen, this degeneracy leads to some algebraic complexity in a general analysis. But the heuristics remain accurate even in such cases and should enable a straightforward computation of the nondegenerate component in the Wald statistic limit theory and the appropriate degrees of freedom in the limiting χ^2 distribution.

While these features of trend regression induce potential degeneracies in the limit theory of Wald statistics for multiple hypotheses, the finite sample distributions typically do not suffer from the same reductions in degrees of freedom, as the analyses above make clear. The higher-order terms that disappear in limit theory may have a considerable influence in finite samples. These effects and the adequacy of the asymptotic theory may be investigated by simulation experiments and formal asymptotic expansions to reveal their importance in practice. Such an investigation is left for future research.

1.6 Appendix

Lemma 1.6.1 *In the deterministic m-vector sequence* $a_{tn} = a\left(\frac{t}{n}\right)$*, the function* $a(\cdot)$ *is assumed to be of bounded variation and partial sums of* u_t *are assumed to satisfy the functional law* $\frac{1}{\sqrt{n}}\sum_{t=1}^{\lfloor nr \rfloor} u_t \rightsquigarrow B_u(r)$ *where* B_u *is Brownian motion with variance* $\omega^2 = \mathbb{V}^{LR}(u_t) = 2\pi f_u(0) > 0$*. Then* $\frac{1}{\sqrt{n}}\sum_{t=1}^{n} a_{tn}u_t \rightsquigarrow \int_0^1 a(r)dB_u(r) = \mathcal{N}\left(0, \omega^2 \int_0^1 a(r)a(r)'dr\right)$.

Proof The proof is by partial summation. Note that $\Delta(f_t g_t) = (\Delta f_t)g_t + f_{t-1}\Delta g_t$. Summing the left side of this equality gives $\sum_{t=1}^n \Delta(f_t g_t) = f_n g_n - f_0 g_0$ and summing the right side gives $\sum_{t=1}^n (\Delta f_t)g_t + \sum_{t=1}^n f_{t-1}\Delta g_t$, which leads to the following partial summation formula

$$\sum_{t=1}^{n}(\Delta f_t)g_t = f_n g_n - f_0 g_0 - \sum_{t=1}^{n} f_{t-1}\Delta g_t. \tag{1.55}$$

Define the partial sum process $S_t = \sum_{j=1}^t u_j$ with $S_0 = 0$. Applying partial summation as in (1.55) we have $\sum_{t=1}^n a(\frac{t}{n})u_t = \sum_{t=1}^n a(\frac{t}{n})\Delta S_t = a(1)S_n - \sum_{t=1}^n S_{t-1}\left(a(\frac{t}{n}) - a(\frac{t-1}{n})\right)$. Then upon standardization by $\sqrt{n}$ the following weak convergence holds as $n \to \infty$:

$$\begin{aligned}\sum_{t=1}^{n} a\left(\frac{t}{n}\right)\frac{u_t}{\sqrt{n}} &= a(1)\frac{S_n}{\sqrt{n}} - \sum_{t=1}^{n}\frac{S_{t-1}}{\sqrt{n}}\Delta a\left(\frac{t}{n}\right)\\ &\rightsquigarrow a(1)B_u(1) - \int_0^1 B_u(r)da(r),\end{aligned} \tag{1.56}$$

because $\frac{1}{\sqrt{n}}\sum_{t=1}^{\lfloor nr \rfloor} u_t \rightsquigarrow B_u(r)$ and $\sum_{t=1}^n \frac{S_{t-1}}{\sqrt{n}}\Delta a\left(\frac{t}{n}\right) \rightsquigarrow \int_0^1 B_u(r)da(r)$ by virtue of Riemann–Stieltjes integration which may be employed because the limit process $B_u(\cdot)$ is continuous almost surely and $a(\cdot)$ is of bounded variation by assumption. We may then define the Wiener stochastic integral $\int_0^1 a(r)dB_u(r)$ with respect to Brownian motion by virtue of the integration by parts formula

$$\begin{aligned}\int_0^1 a(r)dB_u(r) &= [a(r)B(r)]_0^1 - \int_0^1 B_u(r)da(r)\\ &= a(1)B_u(1) - \int_0^1 B_u(r)da(r).\end{aligned} \tag{1.57}$$

The functional $\int_0^1 a(r)dB_u(r)$ is Gaussian with zero mean and variance matrix $\omega^2\int_0^1 a(r)a(r)'dr$ since Brownian motion has independent increments and $\mathbb{E}\left(dB_u(s)dB_u(r)\right) = \omega^2 dr\mathbb{1}\{r = s\}$. The special case considered in the paper involves time polynomials of the form $a(\frac{t}{n}) = (\frac{t}{n})^k$ for integer $k \geq 0$ and then $\int_0^1 r^p dB_u(r) = \mathcal{N}\left(0, \omega^2\int_0^1 r^{2p}dr\right) = \mathcal{N}\left(0, \frac{\omega^2}{2p+1}\right)$. ■

Remark

(iii) More general versions of Lemma 1.6.1 hold and are proved in the same manner allowing for stochastic integration of bounded variation functions, including stochastic functions, and for functional laws to continuous stochastic processes other than Brownian motion. For instance, suppose the time series u_t is such that $\frac{1}{d_n}\sum_{t=1}^{\lfloor nr \rfloor} u_t \rightsquigarrow Y(r)$ where d_n is an increasing numerical sequence with $d_n \to \infty$ and $Y(r)$ is a limiting stochastic process with continuous sample paths almost surely. Then

$$\sum_{t=1}^{n} a\left(\frac{t}{n}\right)\frac{u_t}{d_n} = a(1)\frac{S_n}{d_n} - \sum_{t=1}^{n}\frac{S_{t-1}}{d_n}\Delta a\left(\frac{t}{n}\right)$$
$$\rightsquigarrow a(1)Y(1) - \int_0^1 Y(r)da(r) =: \int_0^1 a(r)dY(r). \tag{1.58}$$

With an appropriate choice of the normalization sequence d_n, (1.58) includes the case where $Y(r) = B_H(r)$ is fractional Brownian motion with Hurst parameter H. Further, if $P_t = \sum_{s=1}^{t} S_s$ then it follows by continuous mapping that a suitably normalized version of P_t satisfies the weak convergence $\frac{1}{nd_n}P_{\lfloor nr \rfloor} = \frac{1}{n}\sum_{s=1}^{t}\frac{S_s}{d_n} \rightsquigarrow \int_0^r Y(q)dq =: \bar{Y}(r)$, which is of bounded variation because $Y(q)$ is continuous. We therefore have

$$\frac{1}{nd_n}\sum_{t=1}^{n} P_t\frac{u_t}{d_n} = \frac{P(1)}{nd_n}\frac{S_n}{d_n} - \sum_{t=1}^{n}\frac{S_{t-1}}{d_n}\frac{1}{nd_n}\Delta P_t$$
$$\rightsquigarrow \int_0^1 Y(q)dqY(1) - \int_0^1 Y(r)d\bar{Y}(r)$$
$$= \bar{Y}(1)Y(1) - \int_0^1 Y(r)^2dr =: \int_0^1 \bar{Y}(r)dY(r), \tag{1.59}$$

by Riemann–Stieltjes integration, thereby defining the Wiener stochastic integral $\int_0^1 \bar{Y}(r)dY(r)$ with respect to $Y(r)$.

Bibliography

Andrews, D. W. (1987). Asymptotic results for generalized Wald tests. *Econometric Theory 3*(3), 348–358.

Grenander, U. and M. Rosenblatt (1954). Regression analysis of time series with stationary residuals. *Proceedings of the National Academy of Sciences of the United States of America 40*(9), 812.

Kheifets, I. and P. C. B. Phillips (2023). Fully modified least squares cointegrating parameter estimation in multicointegrated systems. *Journal of Econometrics*, 232(2), 300–319.

Magdalinos, T. and P. C. B. Phillips (2018). Wald testing with matrix normalization. Working Paper, *University of Southampton.*

Park, J. Y. and P. C. B. Phillips (1988). Statistical inference in regressions with integrated processes: Part 1. *Econometric Theory 4*(3), 468–497.

Park, J. Y. and P. C. B. Phillips (1989). Statistical inference in regressions with integrated processes: Part 2. *Econometric Theory 5*(1), 95–131.

Phillips, P. C. B. (1987, 12). Multiple regression with integrated time series. *Contemporary Mathematics 80*, 79–106.

Phillips, P. C. B. (1995). Fully modified least squares and vector autoregression. *Econometrica 63*, 1023–1078.

Phillips, P. C. B. and I. L. Kheifets (2024). High-dimensional IV cointegration estimation and inference. *Journal of Econometrics*, 238(2), 105622.

Phillips, P. C. B., D. Li, and J. Gao (2017). Estimating smooth structural change in cointegration models. *Journal of Econometrics 196*(1), 180–195.

Phillips, P. C. B. and T. Magdalinos (2013). Inconsistent var regression with common explosive roots. *Econometric Theory 29*(4), 808–837.

Phillips, P. C. B. and J. Y. Park (1988). Asymptotic equivalence of ordinary least squares and generalized least squares in regressions with integrated regressors. *Journal of the American Statistical Association 83*(401), 111–115.

Phillips, P. C. B. and V. Solo (1992). Asymptotics for linear processes. *The Annals of Statistics 20*(2), 971–1001.

Puri, M. L., C. T. Russell, and T. Mathew (1984). Convergence of generalized inverses with applications to asymptotic hypothesis testing. *Sankhyā: The Indian Journal of Statistics, Series A 46*(2), 277–286.

Stewart, G. W. (1969). On the continuity of the generalized inverse. *SIAM Journal on Applied Mathematics 17*(1), 33–45.

Vuong, Q. H. (1987). Generalized inverses and asymptotic properties of Wald tests. *Economics Letters 24*(4), 343–347.

2 Econometric Analysis of Asset Price Bubbles

SHUPING SHI *Macquarie University*
Peter C. B. Phillips *Yale University, University of Auckland, and Singapore Management University*

2.1 Introduction

The history of financial bubbles demonstrates the potential of these financial phenomena to inflict harm on real economic activity. During the expansion phase of a financial bubble a typical consequence is resource misallocation as funds are directed toward asset speculation rather than productive enterprises (Caballero and Krishnamurthy, 2006; Hirano et al., 2015). This process of diversion raises the risk to lending institutions of foreclosure in the event of a bubble collapse and the risk of economic downturn or even general economic crisis in its aftermath (Case et al., 2000). The demise of the hedge fund Long Term Capital Management in 1998 during the Russian financial crisis, the dot-com bubble collapse over 2001–2002, and the subsequent 2008 subprime mortgage crisis with the bankruptcy of Lehman Brothers and the advent of the great recession provide three recent examples. In recognition of the major economic implications of financial bubbles, policymakers have emphasized the urgency of research designed to deepen understanding of financial bubble phenomena and to develop measures to address them in order to avoid further crises or to ameliorate their consequences and to maintain economic and financial stability. Correspondingly, there has been a significant surge of academic interest in financial bubbles among economists and in the development of econometric tools to facilitate bubble identification, particularly in real time so that policy measures may be implemented to avert the more serious economic and financial consequences of collapse. There is now a wide literature, and for recent econometric research in the field readers are directed to Phillips and Yu (2011); Phillips et al. (2011); Homm and Breitung (2012); Phillips et al. (2015a,b,c); Lee and Phillips (2016); Harvey et al. (2013, 2016, 2020); Pavlidis et al. (2016, 2017); Hu and Oxley (2017); Phillips and Shi

Shi acknowledges support from the Australian Research Council Discovery Projects funding scheme (project No.: DP190102049). Phillips acknowledges support from the Kelly Fund at the University of Auckland and the NSF under Grant No. SES 18-50860. Shuping Shi email: shuping.shi@mq.edu.au. Peter C. B. Phillips email: peter.phillips@yale.edu.

(2018, 2020); Shi and Phillips (2023); Chen et al. (2023) and Wang and Yu (2023), among others.

There is a general agreement among economists seeking to model asset prices that in the presence of bubbles asset prices are driven by two separate components, one involving economic fundamentals that relate to the activity and another, the bubble component, carrying the impact of speculative interest. Both these components are theoretical constructs and need precise formulation for empirical research, typically related to particular applications. Various definitions appear in the literature. For example, the definitions presented in Shi (2017) and Shi and Phillips (2023) for housing markets are derived from underlying accounting identities involving returns. These are often expressed in logarithmic form, with the fundamental component being a function of payoffs received from the particular asset (e.g., dividends in the case of equities or rents in the case of housing) and the real interest rates. On the other hand, the definitions used in Phillips et al. (2011, 2015b) are based on the present value identity assuming a constant discount factor and expressed in either levels or logarithmic form and the fundamental component is related only to the payoffs of the asset. The relationships among the various definitions in use in empirical research are not always apparent. This chapter provides a framework that embodies many of these definitions and reveals their connections.

A major challenge for bubble identification is the unobservability of the bubble component in asset prices. This component has complex dynamics, exhibiting explosive behavior during the expansion phase followed by decline or collapse in the bubble downturn. The most common solution to the problem of the unobservable bubble component is to monitor its impact through the analysis of realized asset prices or prices adjusted for some observed returns. During the expansionary phase, explosive unit root tests may be applied to simple proxies of the bubble component such as real asset prices or log price-payoff ratios. This approach is successful because in the presence of an expansionary bubble its explosive dynamic typically dominates the time series behavior of asset prices. Nonetheless, the presence of market fundamentals, which are commonly believed to be at most I(1), can compromise the performance of explosive root tests on these simple proxies for the bubble component (Shi and Phillips, 2023). An alternative solution is to estimate the fundamentals separately and remove them from the proxies before applying explosive root tests. While the first approach is easy to implement and has enjoyed widespread use in the literature, the second approach has been investigated only recently (Shi, 2017; Shi et al., 2020; Shi and Phillips, 2023) and has not attracted as much attention, especially in equity markets. The empirical application of the present work applies both approaches to the S&P 500 stock market and reveals the importance of controlling for market fundamentals in identifying bubbles in equity markets.

This chapter focuses on the econometric technique of bubble detection that utilizes the recursive evolving explosive root test of Phillips et al. (2015b,c,

PSY hereafter). The PSY procedure utilizes historical information and, by applying the detector to the data as it evolves through the observed sample, the procedure serves as a real-time monitoring device as well as a general purpose detector. The approach also accounts for the periodically collapsing feature of bubbles and provides consistent estimates for bubble origination and termination dates even when there are multiple bubble episodes within the same sample period. This procedure has been shown to outperform several alternative methods (Phillips et al., 2011; Homm and Breitung, 2012) and has been applied to many different markets, including equity, real estate, and commodity markets. See Wöckl (2019) and Shi and Phillips (2023) for recent surveys of the field.

Although all statistical tests have a nonzero probability of drawing false-positive conclusions, a complex multiplicity issue arises when a particular test is implemented many times on the same data set, as it is in recursive investigations of episodic financial bubbles and their initiation and termination dates. In such applications the probability of making at least one false-positive conclusion rises rapidly toward 100 percent as the number of tests increases. In the context of real-time bubble monitoring, the PSY procedure is implemented each period as new information arrives. So the multiplicity issue cannot be ignored in empirical testing for financial bubbles. We illustrate the problem by Monte Carlo simulations. To address the issue we propose the use of a multiple-testing algorithm for the computation of suitable critical values for the PSY test. With the use of multiple-testing critical values, the performance of the real-time bubble monitoring procedure is shown to be satisfactory in terms of its family-wise error rates under the null hypothesis of no bubbles and to be successful in its detection rates and estimation accuracy of bubble origination and termination dates under the alternative of bubbles being present in the data.

The rest of the chapter is organized as follows. Section 2.2 discusses bubble definitions. Section 2.3 outlines bubble identification strategies. The PSY explosive root test and its asymptotic properties are introduced in Section 2.4. Section 2.5 overviews the multiplicity issue that arises in recursive testing, introduces the multiple-testing algorithm for critical value computation, and explores the finite sample performance of the associated bubble monitoring procedure. The empirical application to the S&P 500 is reported in Section 2.6. Section 2.7 concludes the chapter. An Appendix is included to explain the IVX estimation procedure used in the chapter.

2.2 Bubble Definitions

A standard theory-based approach to the definition of a rational bubble starts from the accounting identity of asset returns (R_{t+1}) over the period of $[t, t+1]$ as

$$1 + R_{t+1} = \frac{P_{t+1} + D_{t+1}}{P_t}, \tag{2.1}$$

where P_t is the price of a financial asset and D_t is the payoff received from the asset, such as rental income for houses and dividend income for stocks. Taking conditional expectations at period t and re-organization of Equation (2.1) leads to the standard no arbitrage condition

$$P_t = \rho_t \mathbb{E}_t \left(P_{t+1} + D_{t+1}\right) \text{ with } \rho_t = \frac{1}{1 + \mathbb{E}_t \left(R_{t+1}\right)}, \tag{2.2}$$

where the quantity $\rho_t \in (0, 1)$ is typically referred to as the (time-varying) discount factor.

2.2.1 *Log Linear Approximation*

Let $p_t = \log (P_t)$, $d_t = \log (D_t)$, and $r_t = \log(1 + R_t)$. The return identity (2.1) can be rewritten using notations p_t, d_t, and r_t as

$$r_{t+1} = \log(P_{t+1} + D_{t+1}) - \log P_t = p_{t+1} - p_t + \log(1 + e^{d_{t+1} - p_{t+1}}). \tag{2.3}$$

Applying a Taylor series expansion of $\log(1 + e^{d_{t+1} - p_{t+1}})$ at the sample mean of p_t and d_t ($\bar{p}$ and $\bar{r}$) as in Campbell and Shiller (1988), we obtain the (approximate) relation

$$r_{t+1} = \kappa + \delta p_{t+1} + (1 - \delta) d_{t+1} - p_t, \tag{2.4}$$

where

$$\delta = \frac{1}{1 + \exp(\bar{d} - \bar{p})} \quad \text{and} \quad \kappa = -\delta \log \delta - (1 - \delta) \log(1 - \delta).$$

By recursive substitution of (2.4) and taking conditional expectations with respect to information available at period t, we can write the difference $p_t - d_t$ in the form of a sum of a fundamental component f_t and a bubble component b_t as

$$p_t - d_t = f_t + b_t, \tag{2.5}$$

where the two components are written as

$$f_t = \frac{\kappa}{1 - \delta} + \sum_{k=0}^{\infty} \delta^k \mathbb{E}_t(\Delta d_{t+1+k} - r_{t+1+k}), \tag{2.6}$$

$$b_t = \lim_{i \to \infty} \delta^i \mathbb{E}_t(p_{t+i}). \tag{2.7}$$

Equations (2.6) and (2.7) provide convenient definitions for the market fundamental component and the rational bubble component of the log price dividend ratio in (2.5).

Fundamentals f_t are determined in terms of a discounted present value involving dividend growth and returns. The bubble component involves the eventual discounted present expectation of the asset price. In the absence of a bubble, the transversality condition holds and $b_t = \lim_{i\to\infty} \delta^i \mathbb{E}_t(p_{t+i}) = 0$, so that eventual discounted expected value is zero. In the presence of speculative sentiment, the transversality condition does not apply and the bubble component b_t satisfies the submartingale property

$$\mathbb{E}_t\left(b_{t+1}\right) = \lim_{i\to\infty} \mathbb{E}_t\left(\delta^i p_{t+1+i}\right) = \frac{1}{\delta} \lim_{i\to\infty} \mathbb{E}_t\left(\delta^{i+1} p_{t+1+i}\right) = \frac{1}{\delta} b_t. \tag{2.8}$$

Since $1/\delta > 1$, Equation (2.8) reveals that the speculative bubble component b_t is expected to be larger in the next period than it is today, that is, $\mathbb{E}_t\left(b_{t+1}\right) > b_t$. In other words, the variable b_t follows an explosive process. Many of the latest econometric techniques for bubble identification are based on this unique explosive feature of bubbles. See, for example, Diba and Grossman (1988); Phillips et al. (2011, 2015b); and Pavlidis et al. (2016).

The log linear approximation of $\log(1 + e^{d_{t+1} - p_{t+1}})$ typically relies on the presumption that the sample mean $\bar{p} - \bar{d}$ converges to the population mean of $p_t - d_t$. In the case that p_t and d_t are integrated and with a cointegration vector $[1, -1]$, the approximation is valid. In the presence of bubbles, $p_t - d_t$ is itself explosive and the log linear approximation is only valid under certain conditions. Explosive behavior in the time series $p_t - d_t$ leads to an explosive sample mean $\bar{p} - \bar{d}$ so that $\delta = \frac{1}{1+\exp(\bar{d}-\bar{p})} \to 1$, thereby potentially compromising the validity of the representation (2.6). Interestingly, Lee and Phillips (2016) show that both the log linear approximation and the present value identity (2.5) remain valid as long as the duration of the bubble is asymptotically negligible.

2.2.2 *Constant Discount Factor*

It is often convenient to take the special case of a constant discount factor, namely, $\rho_t = \rho \in (0, 1)$. By recursive substitution, Equation (2.2) then becomes

$$P_t = \sum_{i=0}^{\infty} \rho^i \mathbb{E}_t\left(D_{t+i}\right) + \lim_{i\to\infty} \mathbb{E}_t\left(\rho^i P_{t+i}\right). \tag{2.9}$$

In this event, fundamentals and bubbles are sometimes defined as the two components

$$F_t = \sum_{i=0}^{\infty} \rho^i \mathbb{E}_t\left(D_{t+i}\right) \text{ and } B_t = \lim_{i\to\infty} \mathbb{E}_t\left(\rho^i P_{t+i}\right). \tag{2.10}$$

Since the discount rate $\rho \in (0,1)$, B_t continues to satisfy a submartingale property where

$$\mathbb{E}_t\left(B_{t+1}\right) = \frac{1}{\rho}B_t. \tag{2.11}$$

Further, under a constant discount factor we have $\mathbb{E}_t(r_{t+1+k}) = -\log\rho$ by virtue of the definition of ρ_t and r_{t+1}. We can then write Equation (2.6) in simpler form as

$$f_t = \frac{\kappa + \log\rho}{1-\delta} + \sum_{k=0}^{\infty}\delta^k\mathbb{E}_t(\Delta d_{t+1+k}), \tag{2.12}$$

which is another commonly used definition of fundamentals. In the absence of bubbles and when the growth rate of dividends Δd_{t+1+k} is stationary, then $p_t - d_t = f_t$ is I(0). For instance, if Δd_t is stationary autoregressive, satisfying $\Delta d_t = \alpha\Delta d_{t-1} + \zeta_t$ with $|\alpha| < 1$ and $\zeta_t \sim iid(0,\sigma_\zeta^2)$, then

$$f_t = \frac{\kappa + \log\rho}{1-\delta} + \frac{\alpha}{1-\alpha\delta}\sum_{s=0}^{\infty}\alpha^s\zeta_{t-s} \tag{2.13}$$

is a stationary linear autoregressive process. So p_t and d_t are cointegrated. But in the presence of a bubble process b_t, the dynamics of $p_t - d_t$ are dominated by b_t and hence become explosive. Evidence of explosive dynamics in the log price-to-rent ratio can therefore serve as a signal for the presence of a speculative bubble component in the generating mechanism.

2.2.3 Time-Varying Discount Factor

The log gross return r_{t+1} is assumed to equal the return of a baseline asset g_{t+1} plus a risk premium φ_{t+1} (Campbell and Shiller, 1988; Shi, 2017), so that

$$r_{t+1} = g_{t+1} + \varphi_{t+1}.$$

The baseline return can be three-month treasury bill rates in the case of equities or real mortgage interest rates in the case of housing. It is further assumed that the time-varying risk premium fluctuates around a long-term risk premium level φ (Shi, 2017; Shi et al., 2020), so that

$$\varphi_{t+1} = \varphi + \varepsilon_{t+1},$$

where ε_{t+1} is a zero mean disturbance. The expected log return of the asset is the sum of the expected return of the baseline asset and the expected long-run risk premium, that is,

$$\mathbb{E}_t\left(r_{t+1}\right) = \varphi + \mathbb{E}_t\left(g_{t+1}\right).$$

By definition, the logarithmic discount factor is $\log \rho_t = -\mathbb{E}_t(r_{t+1})$, and under this assumed model structure, the fundamental component in (2.6) then becomes

$$f_t = \frac{\kappa - \varphi}{1-\delta} + \sum_{k=0}^{\infty} \delta^k \mathbb{E}_t(\Delta d_{t+1+k} - g_{t+1+k}), \tag{2.14}$$

which serves as the basis for the fundamental-bubble decomposition used in Section 2.3.2.

2.2.4 Collapsing Bubbles

Historical evidence indicates that bubbles are typically transitory with alternate stages of expansion and collapse in asset prices. Various models have been proposed to capture such dynamics. Examples are the early probabilistic bubble generating mechanisms of Blanchard and Watson (1982) and Evans (1991) and a recent behavioral model of Phillips (2016). In Blanchard and Watson (1982) bubbles are generated according to the model

$$B_{t+1} = \begin{cases} (\pi\rho)^{-1} B_t + \varepsilon_{t+1} & \text{with probability } \pi \\ \varepsilon_{t+1} & \text{with probability } 1-\pi \end{cases}, \tag{2.15}$$

where ε_{t+1} is an error term. In this model the probability of a bubble in each time period is set *a priori* to π and the probability of a bubble collapse is $1-\pi$. The expansion rate of the bubble is the autoregressive parameter $(\pi\rho)^{-1}$ during the bubble expansion phase. The conditional expectation of B_{t+1} is given by

$$\mathbb{E}_t(B_{t+1}) = \mathbb{E}_t\left\{\pi\left[(\pi\rho)^{-1} B_t + \varepsilon_{t+1}\right] + (1-\pi)\,\varepsilon_{t+1}\right\} = \rho^{-1}B_t.$$

So, the bubble generating process satisfies the submartingale property $\mathbb{E}_t(B_{t+1}) > B_t$.

Unlike Blanchard and Watson (1982), Evans (1991) considers a bubble model with three stages. At the initial stage, the bubble expands at a rate of ρ^{-1}. After exceeding the threshold b, the expansion accelerates with a rate of $(\pi\rho)^{-1}$ and during this period faces a probability of collapse. The collapse mechanism is governed by a Bernoulli process θ_t, which takes the value one with probability π and zero otherwise. More specifically,

$$B_{t+1} = \begin{cases} \rho^{-1} B_t \varepsilon_{B,t+1} & \text{if } B_t < b \\ \left[\upsilon + (\pi\rho)^{-1}\theta_{t+1}(B_t - \rho\upsilon)\right]\varepsilon_{B,t+1} & \text{if } B_t \geq b \end{cases}. \tag{2.16}$$

The error term in this model is multiplicative, rather than additive, and takes the form of $\varepsilon_{B,t+1} = \exp\left(v_{t+1} - w^2/2\right)$ with $v_{t+1} \overset{i.i.d}{\sim} \mathcal{N}\left(0, w^2\right)$, which ensures that

$$\mathbb{E}_t(B_{t+1}) = \rho^{-1}B_t.$$

The approach taken in Phillips (2016) constructs a behavioral model of asset markets that produces episodes of exuberance, collapse, and recovery. These episodes emerge because of subjective investor-based rational expectations about the impact of fundamentals on the market price. Investors are assumed to have heterogeneous sentiments about the market, allowing them to be exuberant or cautious or strict followers of fundamentals. This is achieved via boundary conditions that describe their respective views of the expected market impact of the same economic fundamentals. Equilibrium solution paths take multiple forms, depending on the dominating market sentiment. This rational expectations model of asset pricing produces market bubbles when exuberant sentiment dominates and then gives way to cautionary and negative sentiment.

2.3 Bubble Identification

As indicated earlier, a significant challenge to empirical bubble identification is the unobservability of the bubble component in the decomposition of asset prices into bubble and fundamental components. The problem is in some respects analogous to another common time series identification problem, the separation of trend and cycle components in nonstationary data. Various econometric approaches have been proposed to address this challenge of unobservable components and the main ideas are reviewed in what follows.

2.3.1 Strategy I: Use Simple Proxies

Consider the fundamental and bubble definitions given in Equations (2.9)–(2.10). In the absence of bubbles, the transversality condition $\lim_{i\to\infty} \mathbb{E}_t \left(\rho^i P_{t+i}\right) = 0$ is assumed to hold and the asset price in (2.9) is at most I(1), as the dividend process D_t is generally believed to be integrated of order one. On the other hand, in the presence of speculation, P_t is dominated by the bubble component and accordingly follows an explosive process during the expansionary phase of the bubble. Similarly, from (2.5)–(2.7), $p_t - d_t$ is at most I(1) in the absence of speculative behavior but becomes explosive when speculation overtakes the market. An immediate solution to the unobservable bubble component problem is to apply explosive root tests to P_t or $p_t - d_t$ for bubble identification directly in the observable price or price/dividend ratio data. The approach seeks to detect the explosive dynamics in P_t or $p_t - d_t$ that are induced by the underlying bubble component.

The accuracy of this approach to bubble identification can be compromised when the fundamental component (which is taken as residual noise in this approach) is highly persistent. Since the fundamental process F_t is a weighted linear function of the dividend process D_{t+i}, which is itself generally believed to be $I(1)$, F_t can be expected to manifest persistence. The fundamental component

f_t of $p_t - d_t$ given in (2.13) is related to the growth rate of dividends Δd_{t+1+k}, which may be taken as stationary. In other words, under the constant discount factor assumption, f_t in (2.13) is less persistent than F_t. Therefore, we focus on $p_t - d_t$ for subsequent discussions on bubble identification. Nevertheless, when the discount factor is allowed to be time-varying, the fundamental of $p_t - d_t$ in (2.14) is also related to returns of a baseline asset, which may well not be stationary. In fact, most time series of real interest rates are either highly persistent or fractionally integrated, and may be considered nonstationary (Rose, 1988; Mishkin, 1995; Rapach and Weber, 2004; Sun and Phillips, 2004; Phillips, 2005).

2.3.2 Strategy II: Decomposition

To control the impact of market fundamentals on tests designed to detect explosive root behavior in time series such as $p_t - d_t$, Shi (2017) proposed to remove the residual noise element by decomposing the observed series $p_t - d_t$ into fundamental and nonfundamental components. The explosive root tests could then be conducted directly on the empirically estimated nonfundamental component.

Two different approaches have been suggested for performing this decomposition. Campbell and Shiller (1988) introduced a structural decomposition method based on (2.14). The decomposition involves three steps: (i) forecasting the future stream $\Delta d_{t+1+k} - g_{t+1+k}$ using a VAR model; (ii) calibrating parameters κ, φ, and δ; and (iii) combining the results from the first two steps in Equation (2.14) to obtain an estimate of f_t. This approach requires asset prices and dividends or rents data to be available in their actual dollar values.

The second approach is a reduced form method proposed recently in Shi and Phillips (2023). Working with the reduced form involves fewer steps than the structural approach, which has the added advantage of reducing the potential impact of estimation or calibration errors on the final outcome. Additionally, the price and dividend or rent series can be measured in either index form or dollar values, which significantly improves the feasibility of this approach in practice. The following discussion gives an overview of the method.

The reduced form econometric model of the key variables is assumed to have the following general form:

$$y_t = \alpha + \beta X_t + \varepsilon_t, \tag{2.17}$$

$$X_t = d_X + \rho_X X_{t-1} + u_{Xt}, \tag{2.18}$$

where y_t is the first difference of $p_t - d_t$ and the regressor X_t includes payoffs of the asset, d_t, returns of a baseline asset, g_t, and other relevant observable fundamentals. The regressor X_t is $k \times 1$ and its components are assumed to have varying unknown degrees of persistence, including I(1), near I(1), or forms of mild stationarity. A convenient way of formulating this is to assume that the autoregressive coefficient matrix in (2.18) allows for such possibilities via a general specification of the form

$$\rho_X = I_k + \frac{C_X}{T^\alpha}, \tag{2.19}$$

where I_k is a $k \times k$ identity matrix, $C_X = \text{diag}(c_{X1}, \ldots, c_{Xk})$ with $c_{Xi} \leq 0$, and $\alpha \in (0, 1]$. The errors ε_t in the regression equation (2.17) are assumed to be generated by the following mechanism:

$$\varepsilon_t = \sum_{i=1}^{q} \phi_i \varepsilon_{t-i} + \sigma_t \eta_t, \tag{2.20}$$

$$\sigma_t^2 = c_0 + \sum_{l=1}^{m} \omega_l \varepsilon_{t-l}^2 + \sum_{j=1}^{n} \gamma_j \sigma_{t-j}^2, \tag{2.21}$$

where $\eta_t \overset{i.i.d}{\sim} (0, 1)$, allowing for both weak dependence and conditional heteroskedasticity. The simple case of no serial correlation and homoskedasticity is included when $\phi_i = \omega_l = \gamma_j = 0$ for all (i, l, j).

The system (2.17)–(2.18) is similar to typical predictive regression formulations. But the present goal is to estimate the fundamental component rather than to forecast $p_t - d_t$. It is therefore important in the formulation not to include variables that are contaminated by speculative behavior in the regression. For example, consumer sentiment, which measures how optimistic or pessimistic consumers feel about the market, could be one of the driving forces behind speculative market behavior. Further, the time-varying risk premium (i.e., $\varphi_{t+1} = r_{t+1} - g_{t+1}$) is a linear function of asset returns r_{t+1} which may itself embody consequences of a bubble component. So, neither consumer sentiment nor time-varying risk premia are considered for inclusion in the regression. On the other hand, the real interest rate, which reflects borrowing costs, is believed to be a key fundamental driving factor for asset prices, in addition to expected future payoffs. For housing markets, prices may be related to other variables that affect housing demand (e.g., population, immigration, employment, personal income) and housing supply (Shi, 2017). Even though most of these variables manifest varying degrees of persistence, the specification (2.18)–(2.19) for X_t suitably accommodates them all.

When regressors are highly persistent, it is well known that least squares estimation leads to bias and nonstandard limit theory, invalidating inference by conventional t and Wald tests. Endogeneity is a further complication, typically arising from joint determination of y_t and X_t, omitted variables, or errors in variables. Various methods have been proposed to address these problems but most of these are practical only in the case of a scalar X_t, which is unrealistic in most applications. One method that addresses all of these complications is the IVX instrumental variable estimation method, proposed in Phillips and

Magdalinos (2009). This method has many advantages, a particularly important one in many applications being its use of endogenous instruments, which avoids the need to find external instruments that satisfy suitable orthogonality and relevance conditions. Kostakis et al. (2015) extended this method to account for potential heteroskedasticity, and a further extension to deal more successfully with serially correlated errors than the original IVX method was given by Yang et al. (2020).

The basic idea of the IVX method is to construct instrumental variables from X_t that are less persistent than X_t when X_t is highly persistent. For completeness, details of the IVX estimation method and the internal instrument construction process are provided in the appendix. The following discussion shows how the method is implemented in the present context.

Let $\widehat{\alpha}$ and $\widehat{\beta}$ be the IVX estimates of α and β in (2.17) and the corresponding fitted regression equation be

$$\widehat{y}_t = \widehat{\alpha} + \widehat{\beta} X_{t-1},$$

so that $\widehat{y}_t$ is the regression estimate of y_t, the first difference of $p_t - d_t$. Using this regression equation, the estimated market fundamental component, $\hat{f}_t$, and estimated nonfundamental component, $\hat{e}_t$, are obtained as follows:

$$\hat{f}_t = \hat{f}_1 + \sum_{i=2}^{t} \hat{y}_t \text{ and } \hat{e}_t = p_t - d_t - \hat{f}_t \tag{2.22}$$

so that $\hat{f}_t$ is a partial sum of the regression fitted values $\widehat{y}_t$ taken from the initialization $\hat{f}_1 = p_1 - d_1$, thereby providing an estimate of the fundamental component of $p_t - d_t$. The residual component $\hat{e}_t = p_t - d_t - \hat{f}_t$ therefore contains estimation errors as well as components that cannot be explained by the fundamentals. The residuals $\hat{e}_t$ can be expected to mirror explosive behavior in the bubble component of $p_t - d_t$ when bubbles are present in the data. Having removed the fundamental component $\hat{f}_t$ from $p_t - d_t$, the residual term $\hat{e}_t$ should be less contaminated by noise from fundamentals and serve as a better proxy for the bubble component.

2.4 The PSY Explosive Root Test

The overarching goal of bubble identification procedures is to detect the presence of speculative behavior in each period using only historical data. The PSY explosive root test is applied to historical data x_t, where x_t constitutes different time series data depending on the particular bubble identification strategy. For the two strategies considered in the previous section we have

$$x_t = \begin{cases} p_t - d_t & \text{Strategy I} \\ \hat{e}_t & \text{Strategy II} \end{cases} .$$

The null hypothesis is that there is no bubble present in period t and the alternative hypothesis is that observation t carries a speculative bubble component. Since x_t is at most I(1) in the absence of bubbles, the null hypothesis can be translated into a unit root model given by the equation

$$\mathcal{H}_0: x_t = c_T + x_{t-1} + u_t, \tag{2.23}$$

where the intercept satisfies $c_T = c_0 T^{-\gamma}$ for some constant c_0, with power coefficient $\gamma > 1/2$, and T being the total number of observations. The setting $\gamma > 1/2$ ensures that the drift induced by the intercept c_T is asymptotically negligible as $T \to \infty$.[1] See Phillips et al. (2014) for more discussion.

Under the alternative, x_t is driven by a bubble mechanism and follows a mildly explosive process (Phillips and Magdalinos, 2007) such that

$$\mathcal{H}_A: x_t = \delta_T x_{t-1} + u_t \text{ with } \delta_T = 1 + cT^{-\alpha}, \tag{2.24}$$

where $c > 0$ and $\alpha \in (0, 1)$. Detecting the presence of a bubble component in the generating mechanism at period t is therefore equivalent to distinguishing a martingale process (2.23) (possibly with negligible drift) from a mildly explosive process (2.24) at a specific data point.

2.4.1 The PWY Data Generating Process

Blanchard and Watson (1982) and Evans (1991) used stochastic mechanisms for bubble generation in which bubbles are turned on and off according to a certain probabilistic rule (i.e., Equations (2.15) and (2.16)). Alternative methods, like the reduced form methods considered earlier, involve direct empirical specifications with deterministic break dates that can be estimated econometrically. Several methods of this type have been considered in the literature and employed for the econometric analysis of bubble origination and termination dates (Phillips and Yu, 2009; Phillips et al., 2011; Phillips et al., 2015b,c; Phillips and Shi, 2018).

The data generating process proposed by Phillips et al. (2011) is for x_t and takes the form

$$x_t = \begin{cases} x_{t-1} + \varepsilon_t & t \in [1, t_e) \cup [t_c + 1, T] \\ \delta_T x_{t-1} + \varepsilon_t & t \in [t_e, t_c - 1] \\ X^*_{T_c} & t = t_c \end{cases}, \tag{2.25}$$

[1] Suppose the T equidistant observations span over N years in total. The distance between two observations is Δ, taking values $\Delta = \{1/256, 1/52, 1/12\}$, respectively, for daily, weekly, and monthly observations. We have $T = N/\Delta$ and $c_T = c_0 N^{-\gamma} \Delta^{\gamma}$. In finite samples, the magnitude of the drift depends on the sampling frequency Δ. Suppose the time period N is fixed. The higher the sampling frequency (or equivalently the smaller the value of Δ), the smaller the drift value c_T.

where $\varepsilon_t \overset{i.i.d}{\sim} (0, \sigma^2)$, t_e is the bubble origination date, t_c is the date of bubble collapse, and δ_T is specified as in (2.24). The variable x_t follows a unit root process in the normal market regimes $t \in [1, t_e) \cup [t_c + 1, T]$ and is mildly explosive with autoregressive coefficient δ_T in the bubble expansion regime $t \in [t_e, t_c - 1]$. The rate of bubble expansion is controlled by the magnitude of the power parameter α and that of the localizing coefficient $c > 0$.[2] When the bubble episode collapses it does so in a single period and adjusts to the level around that of the bubble origination level with a small perturbation, namely, $X_{t_c}^* = X_{t_e} + O_p(1)$.

This data generating process can be generalized to allow for multiple bubbles as in Phillips et al. (2015b,c) and to include a small drift in the normal regime or allow for various rates of bubble collapse as in Phillips and Shi (2018). Figure 2.1 displays a typical realization of the data generating process (2.25). The parameter settings are $x_0 = 100$, $c = 1$, $\sigma = 6.79$, $\alpha = 0.6$, $t_e = \lfloor 0.4T \rfloor$, $t_c = \lfloor 0.6T \rfloor$, and $T = 120$, as in Phillips et al. (2015b), where the floor function $\lfloor . \rfloor$ delivers the integer part of the argument. As is apparent from the trajectory shown, when the bubble process begins there is little indication of any change in its character or the generating mechanism. But this quickly changes as the bubble takes hold and the explosive behavior becomes manifest. The abrupt collapse at the termination of the bubble is the consequence of the single period transition to the region of the process at the point of bubble origination.

2.4.2 The PSY Recursive Evolving Algorithm

Policy makers, regulators, financial institutions, and individual investors are all intensely interested in learning whether market conditions have changed from normal to abnormal behavior. From an econometric perspective, this interest translates into learning from the data whether observations of x_s are generated by a martingale process under normal efficient market conditions as in (2.23) or whether speculative behavior has overtaken the market with a mildly explosive dynamic as in (2.24). The recursive algorithms suggested in Phillips et al. (2011, 2015b,c) deliver test procedures that provide a mechanism for answering this important question of whether a subtle change has occurred in the generating process that may ultimately lead to significant changes in market behavior that carry attendant risks of market readjustment or collapse.

The PSY procedure employs an evolving recursion to compute the test statistic. The recursion starts by generating a sequence of augmented Dickey–Fuller (ADF) statistics from subsamples of the data. Let t_1 and t_2 be the starting and ending dates of a subsample such that $t_2 > t_1 \geq 1$ giving a window size

[2] Smaller α and larger c lead to greater values of the autoregressive coefficient $\delta_T > 1$ and hence stronger explosive behavior.

$t_w = t_2 - t_1 + 1 \geq t_{\min}$, where $t_{\min}$ is the minimum window size required to run the regression. The fitted ADF regression equation is

$$\Delta x_t = \hat{\beta}_0 + \hat{\beta}_1 x_{t-1} + \sum_{j=1}^{K} \hat{\psi}_j \Delta x_{t-i} + \hat{\varepsilon}_t, \tag{2.26}$$

where t runs from t_1 to t_2, K is the lag order, and $\hat{\varepsilon}_t$ is the residual. The regression is fitted by ordinary least squares. The t-statistic for the significance of $\hat{\beta}_1$ is referred to as the ADF statistic and is denoted ADF_{t_1,t_2}. This statistic is computed in an evolving fashion over the data from varying points of initialization.

The goal in this evolving recursion is to determine whether the data generating process has a bubble component. As attention moves through the sample observations, suppose the current observation of interest is s. In this evolving recursion, the end dates of all the subsamples are fixed on the observation of interest (in this case $t_2 = s$), whereas the starting date varies from the first observation to $s - t_{\min} + 1$. Consider, for example, the sample path displayed in Figure 2.1 and suppose $s = 60$. The recursive algorithm together with its attendant calculations are illustrated in Figure 2.2. The PSY test statistic,

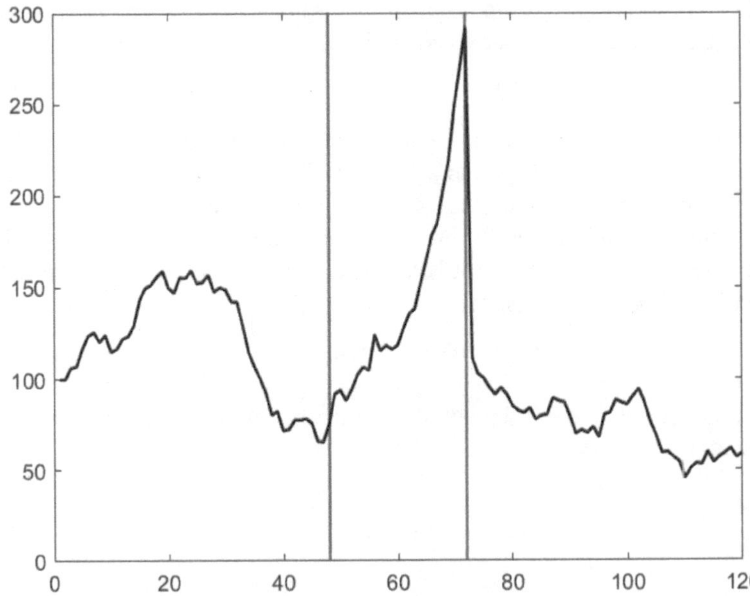

Figure 2.1 A typical realization of the data generating process (2.25) proposed in Phillips et al. (2011). The two vertical lines indicate the locations of the bubble origination and bubble termination dates.

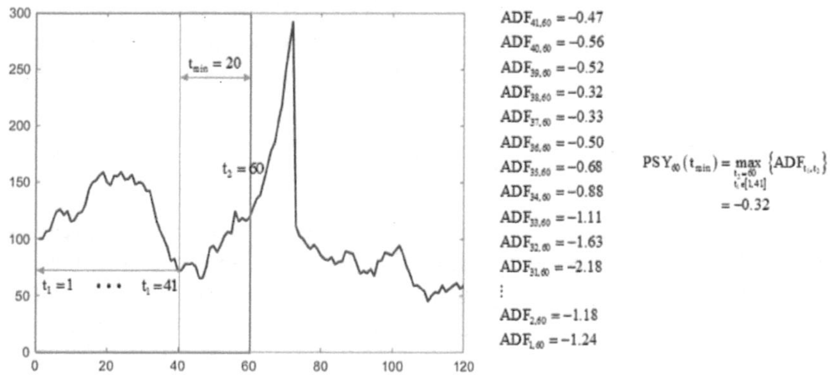

Figure 2.2 The recursive evolving algorithm: $t_2 = s$ and $t_1 \in [1, s - t_{\min} + 1]$.

denoted by $PSY_s(t_{\min})$, is computed as the extremum of the individual ADF statistics ADF_{t_1,t_2}, namely,

$$PSY_s(t_{\min}) = \max_{\substack{t_2=s,\\ t_1\in[1,s-t_{\min}+1]}} \left\{ADF_{t_1,t_2}\right\}.$$

Let $cv_s(\beta_T)$ be the $100\beta_T\%$ critical value of the $PSY_s(t_{\min})$ statistic.[3] The null hypothesis is rejected and observation s is taken as driven by a speculative bubble if the critical value is exceeded; that is, if

$$PSY_s(t_{\min}) > cv_s(\beta_T).$$

Otherwise, we conclude that the null is not rejected and there is no bubble component in the data at period s. The feasible range for s runs from $t_{\min}$ to T, the lower point of the range $t_{\min}$ being determined by the requirement of a minimum window size for the ADF regressions. The first chronological observation at which the PSY statistic exceeds the critical value is taken as the estimated bubble origination date, so that

$$\hat{t}_e = \inf_{s\in[t_{\min},T]} \left\{PSY_s(t_{\min}) > cv_s(\beta_T)\right\}.$$

In similar fashion, the termination date of the bubble is estimated by the first chronological observation after $\hat{t}_e$ that falls below its corresponding critical value, that is,

$$\hat{t}_c = \inf_{s\in[\hat{t}_e,T]} \left\{PSY_s(t_{\min}) < cv_s(\beta_T)\right\}.$$

[3] Critical values of the PSY statistic are computed numerically by simulation, evolve according to the position of the time period s, and depend on the setting of the minimum window size $t_{\min}$. For ease of notation they are written here as $cv_s(\beta_T)$, although $cv_s(\beta_T, t_{\min})$ would be more precise.

The nuisance parameter $t_{\min}$ is usually set according to the rule recommended in Phillips et al. (2015b) on the basis of extensive simulations, namely, $t_{\min} = \lfloor 0.01T + 1.8\sqrt{T} \rfloor$.

2.4.3 Asymptotic Theory

The properties of the evolving recursion are analyzed in Phillips et al. (2015b,c) under both the null and alternative hypotheses using asymptotic theory as the sample size $T \to \infty$ and finite sample simulations. This section reviews the limit properties of the PSY procedure and the dating estimators that emerge from it. We use the notation $\Rightarrow$ to signify weak convergence, $:=$ to represent definitional equivalence, $\sim_a$ to indicate distributional equivalence, $\to^p$ to represent convergence in probability, and τ to denote fractional observations (i.e., $\tau_1 = t_1/T$, $\tau_2 = t_2/T$, $\tau_w = t_w/T$, $\tau_{\min} = t_{\min}/T$, $\tau = s/T$, $\tau_e = t_e/T$, and $\tau_c = t_c/T$).

The error term u_t in $\mathcal{H}_0$ may be weakly dependent and is assumed to satisfy the following linear process conditions to facilitate the development of the asymptotics (Phillips and Solo, 1992).

Assumption 2.4.1 *Let $u_t = \psi(L)\varepsilon_t = \sum_{j=0}^{\infty} \psi_j \varepsilon_{t-j}$, where L is the lag operator, the summability condition $\sum_{j=0}^{\infty} j\left|\psi_j\right| < \infty$ holds, and $\{\varepsilon_t\}$ is an i.i.d. sequence with zero mean, variance σ^2, and $\mathbb{E}\left|\varepsilon_t\right|^{4+\delta} < \infty$ for some $\delta > 0$.*

Under the null hypothesis of (2.23) and Assumption 2.4.1, Phillips et al. (2015b) show that

$$ADF_{t_1,t_2} \Rightarrow$$
$$\frac{\frac{1}{2}\tau_w\left[W(\tau_2)^2 - W(\tau_1)^2 - \tau_w\right] - \int_{\tau_1}^{\tau_2} W(r)\,dr\left[W(\tau_2) - W(\tau_1)\right]}{\tau_w^{1/2}\left\{\tau_w \int_{\tau_1}^{\tau_2} W(r)^2\,dr - \left[\int_{\tau_1}^{\tau_2} W(r)\,dr\right]^2\right\}^{1/2}} := \Upsilon_{\tau_1,\tau_2},$$

where $W(.)$ is a standard Wiener process. By virtue of continuous mapping arguments, the PSY statistic is found to have the following pivotal asymptotic distribution (Phillips et al., 2015b):

$$PSY_s(t_{\min}) \Rightarrow$$
$$\sup_{\substack{\tau_2=\tau,\\ \tau_1\in[0,\tau_2-\tau_{\min}]}} \left\{\frac{\frac{1}{2}\tau_w\left[W(\tau_2)^2 - W(\tau_1)^2 - \tau_w\right] - \int_{\tau_1}^{\tau_2} W(r)\,dr\left[W(\tau_2) - W(\tau_1)\right]}{\tau_w^{1/2}\left\{\tau_w \int_{\tau_1}^{\tau_2} W(r)^2\,dr - \left[\int_{\tau_1}^{\tau_2} W(r)\,dr\right]^2\right\}^{1/2}}\right\}$$
$$:= \Upsilon_{\tau}(\tau_{\min}).$$

The asymptotic $100\beta_T\%$ critical value of $PSY_s(t_{\min})$ is taken as the 100 $(1-\beta_T)$th percentile of the distribution $\Upsilon_\tau(\tau_{\min})$.

Next, we review limiting properties of the PSY statistic under the data generating process (2.25), which has a single bubble episode. For ease of notation, we refer to the two normal periods (i.e., $[1, t_e)$ and $[t_c+1, T]$) as N_0 and N_1 and the bubble period $[t_e, t_c-1]$ as B. The asymptotic properties of ADF_{t_1,t_2} depend on the location of the subsample. There are four possible scenarios:

(1) $t_1 \in N_0$ and $t_2 \in N_0$,

(2) $t_1 \in N_0$ and $t_2 \in B$,

(3) $t_1 \in N_0$ and $t_2 \in C$,

(4) $t_1 \in N_0$ and $t_2 \in N_1$.

Except for the first episode N_0, all the other cases involve structural breaks. For case (2) the subsample begins in the normal regime N_0 with a structural break introducing the bubble component to the data generating mechanism and the bubble regime B ends just before the collapse period (3). In regime B the regression is dominated by bubble dynamics with a mildly explosive autoregression. In this regime, rather than converging to a random variable as in case (1), the ADF statistic diverges to positive infinity at rate $O_p\left(T^{1-\alpha/2}\right)$. For cases (3) and (4), the sample period includes both expansion and collapse stages of the bubble. The initial strong reverting autoregressive pattern within the subsample causes the ADF statistic to diverge to negative infinity at rate $O_p\left(T^{(1-\alpha)/2}\right)$, which signals the collapse regime C. More specifically, Phillips et al. (2015c) show that under the DPG (2.25),

$$ADF_{t_1,t_2} \sim_a \begin{cases} \Upsilon_{\tau_1,\tau_2} & t_1 \in N_0 \text{ and } t_2 \in N_0 \\ T^{1-\alpha/2}\frac{\tau_w^{3/2}}{\sqrt{2(\tau_e-\tau_1)}} \to +\infty & t_1 \in N_0 \text{ and } t_2 \in B \\ -T^{(1-\alpha)/2}\sqrt{\frac{1}{2}c\tau_w} \to -\infty & t_1 \in N_0 \text{ and } t_2 \in C \\ -T^{(1-\alpha)/2}\sqrt{\frac{1}{2}c\tau_w} \to -\infty & t_1 \in N_0 \text{ and } t_2 \in N_1 \end{cases}. \tag{2.27}$$

By continuous mapping arguments the asymptotic behavior of the PSY statistic in the various locations is given by

$$PSY_s(t_{\min}) \sim_a \begin{cases} \Upsilon_\tau(\tau_{\min}) & s \in N_0 \\ T^{1-\alpha/2}\sup_{\tau_1\in[0,\tau-\tau_{\min}]}\left\{\frac{(\tau-\tau_1)^{3/2}}{\sqrt{2(\tau_e-\tau_1)}}\right\} \to +\infty & s \in B \\ -T^{(1-\alpha)/2}\left(\frac{c\tau}{2}\right)^{1/2} \to -\infty & s \in C \\ -T^{(1-\alpha)/2}\left(\frac{c\tau}{2}\right)^{1/2} \to -\infty & s \in N_1 \end{cases}.$$

The PSY statistic is asymptotically equivalent to a random variable (i.e., $O_p(1)$) when the observation of interest s falls in the normal regime N_0. It diverges to positive infinity at rate $O_p(T^{1-\alpha/2})$ when s is in the bubble regime and diverges to negative infinity when s falls in regimes C and N_1.

Consistency of the bubble origination and termination date estimators, namely, $\hat{t}_e/T \to^p \tau_e$ and $\hat{t}_c/T \to^p \tau_c$, follows under the following simple condition on the respective expansion rate of the critical value $cv_\tau(\beta_T)$ and the power coefficient α that controls the mildly explosive rate in the bubble regime:

$$\frac{1}{cv_\tau\left(\beta_T\right)} + \frac{cv_\tau\left(\beta_T\right)}{T^{1-\alpha/2}} \to 0.$$

We assume that $\beta_T \to 0$ and hence $cv_\tau\left(\beta_T\right) \to \infty$ as $T \to \infty$, to eliminate Type I errors asymptotically, and the second condition requires the rate of divergence to be slower than $O_p\left(T^{1-\alpha/2}\right)$.

Readers are referred to Phillips et al. (2015b,c,a) for proofs of these asymptotic results, generalizations that include multiple bubble episodes, and further discussion, including extensive simulation findings of the properties of these procedures in finite samples. Phillips and Shi (2018) provide further asymptotic results under DGPs with various rates of bubble collapse, and Chen et al. (2023) give an extension in which the DGP includes multiple assets in which the dynamics are driven by common factors and the asymptotic performance of the PSY procedure in detecting a common factor bubble is analyzed.

2.5 The Multiplicity Issue

In all hypothesis testing the prospect of making a false decision is always present with nonzero probabilities of a false positive (a Type I error controlled by size) and a false negative (a Type II error of failing to reject the null, determined by test power). The basic principle underlying Neyman–Pearson testing is to cap size (i.e., control size to some preassigned level β, say) and use a test that maximizes power against the alternative of interest. The multiplicity issue is concerned with the failure to cap size at the required level when performing multiple hypothesis tests. This problem is universal when repeated testing occurs, as in recursive test procedures. In the context of bubble identification, it refers to the situation where a speculative bubble is falsely identified in repeated testing of the same null hypothesis. For each hypothesis test, suppose the probability of making a Type I error is β_T which is often set to be 5 percent and referred to as the "nominal size." Dependence of the size on the sample size T is often convenient for asymptotic theory to ensure test consistency, as seen earlier. The multiplicity issue arises when the test is implemented many times, as it is when the test is employed recursively over subsets of the sample observations. The presence of Type I error distortion among a large number of such tests is almost guaranteed unless corrective measures are taken.

Suppose a real-time analysis is conducted on a sample containing T observations with the PSY procedure. The PSY statistic is computed for each observation running from t_{min} to T and inferences of bubble existence are drawn for each of the $T - t_{min} + 1$ individual observations. The probability of making a false positive conclusion for each test may be set to 5 percent. But collectively the probability of making at least one false positive conclusion among the $T - t_{min} + 1$ tests (commonly known as the family-wise error rate, FWER) is close to 100 percent if the number of tests is large. Such "false discovery" can grossly distort inference and potentially mislead investors and policymakers. It is therefore important to address the issue.

2.5.1 *Multiple Testing Algorithm*

The goal in dealing with multiplicity is to quantify the degree of Type I error accumulation that arises when many hypothesis tests are performed and with this information control size by suitable adjustment. Suppose the window width used in multiple testing for the presence of a bubble is T_w. The focus in controlling multiplicity is then on samples that are of the effective size T_w. We propose the following procedure for simulating finite sample critical values to employ in multiple testing. The approach is in the same spirit as bootstrapping methods that have been developed to address data mining and multiplicity in recursive testing (White, 2000; Shi et al., 2020; Shi and Phillips, 2023). Let $T^* = t_{min} + T_w - 1$.

- Step 1: generate a sample path with T^* observations from the model

$$x_t^{(m)} = x_{t-1} + \varepsilon_t.$$

- Step 2: compute the PSY statistic sequence $\left\{PSY_s^{(m)}(t_{\min})\right\}_{s=t_{\min}}^{T^*}$ from the simulated data series.
- Step 3: compute

$$MPSY^{(m)} = \max_{s\in[t_{\min},T^*]} \left\{PSY_s^{(m)}(t_{\min})\right\}.$$

- Step 4: repeat Steps 1–3 M^* times.
- Step 5: take the 95th percentile of $\left\{MPSY^{(m)}\right\}_{m=1}^{M^*}$ as the critical value of the PSY test, denoted by cv^* (0.05).

There are two differences between the standard procedure for simulating finite sample critical values and the algorithm just proposed. First, in Step 1, instead of generating T observations as in the standard procedure, T^* observations are generated so that the resulting PSY statistic sequence from the

Table 2.1 *The family-wise error rates of the PSY procedure*

FWER / Sample Size	Quarterly $T = 40$	Monthly $T = 120$	Weekly $T = 520$
PSY (standard)	0.55	0.78	0.93
PSY (multiple)	0.04	0.06	0.05

simulated data is of the correct dimension T_w. Second, in Step 5 the 95th percentile is taken from the distribution of $MPSY^{(m)}$ instead of $PSY_s^{(m)}$ for each $s \in [t_{\min}, T]$ as in the standard procedure. This step ensures that the false rejection probability for the observation with the largest PSY statistic within the control window is 5 percent.

2.5.2 Simulations

We compare the family-wise error rate of the PSY test with the standard and the multiple testing procedures, labeled respectively as "PSY (standard)" and "PSY (multiple)," for computing critical values. The minimum window size of the PSY procedure is set according the rule of Phillips et al. (2015b) and the lag order K of the ADF model is set to one. The data are generated under the null hypothesis (2.23) over a 10-year period with sampling frequencies of quarterly, monthly, and weekly (i.e., $T = \{40, 120, 520\}$). For each parameter constellation, the simulation is repeated $M = 2{,}000$ times.

Let $I_s^{(m)}$ be the bubble indicator for observation s from the mth simulated data series, taking value one when $PSY_s^{(m)}$ is above the critical value and zero otherwise. The family-wise error rate is defined as

$$FWER = \frac{1}{M}\sum_{m=1}^{M} 1\left(\sum_{s=t_{\min}}^{T} I_s^{(m)} > 0\right),$$

where 1 (.) is an indication function taking value one when the condition is satisfied and zero otherwise.

Table 2.1 shows the family-wise error rates of the "PSY (standard)" and "PSY (multiple)" tests. For the PSY (multiple), the FWER is controlled within the whole sample period ($T_w = T$). Evidently, with the use of standard critical values, the FWER is lowest when $T = 40$ but still badly distorted at 55 percent, and then rises rapidly to 93 percent when T increases to 520. In sharp contrast, the FWER of the multiple testing procedure is stable around 5 percent under all settings.

It is important to recognize that there is a trade-off between the use of FWER and Type II errors. Fewer Type I errors typically result in more Type II errors, meaning that there is greater chance of failure to identify small bubbles or to detect a bubble at its later stage of development. To examine the performance

Table 2.2 *The successful detection rates and the biases of the estimated bubble origination and collapsing dates. Numbers in the parentheses are standard deviations.*

$T = 120$	SDR	$\frac{1}{M}\sum_{m=1}^{M}(\hat{t}_e^{(m)} - t_e)$	$\frac{1}{M}\sum_{m=1}^{M}(\hat{t}_c^{(m)} - t_c)$
PSY (standard)	0.84	7.56 (4.99)	0.79 (1.72)
PSY (multiple)	0.75	12.20 (5.33)	0.77 (1.71)

of the PSY procedure under the alternative, we consider the bubble-generating process (2.25). Parameters are set as in Figure 2.1. It is standard in the literature to report the power of a test, which is the probability of rejecting the null hypothesis when it is false. This is equivalent to the FWER in multiple testing, but the computation is made under the alternative. However, the power statistic does not reveal the estimation accuracy of bubble locations and does not preclude Type I errors. An important example of the latter is the inconsistency that arises when the test falsely rejects the null for observation $t \in [1, t_e - 1]$ but fails to detect bubbles in $[t_e, t_c - 1]$. Although this is an undesirable scenario, it would still be counted toward test power. We therefore use two alternative measures to measure success under the alternative: (i) the successful detection rate (SDR); and (ii) the averaged delays in the estimated bubble origination and collapse dates.

The SDR measures the probability of the estimated bubble origination date falling between the true start and collapse dates, given by

$$SDR = \frac{1}{M}\sum_{m=1}^{M} 1\left(t_e \leq \hat{t}_e^{(m)} \leq t_c\right).$$

Averaged delay in dating the bubble is computed by the following two measures, one for origination and one for collapse

$$\frac{1}{M}\sum_{m=1}^{M}(\hat{t}_e^{(m)} - t_e) \text{ and } \frac{1}{M}\sum_{m=1}^{M}(\hat{t}_c^{(m)} - t_c).$$

Evidently, the control of Type I errors comes at a cost. From Table 2.2, the successful detection rate of PSY (multiple) is lower (75% versus 84%) and the bias in the estimated bubble origination date is larger (12.20 months versus 7.56 months), although there is a slight improvement in the identification accuracy of the bubble termination date. In practice, one could take an intermediate position between the two procedures, depending on the purpose and subject to individual preferences. That is, instead of controlling the Type I error over the entire 10-year period, it may be more realistic and useful to manage it over a smaller window, for example, one year, two years, or five years. As

Table 2.3 *The finite sample performance of the PSY test with the multiple testing procedure for critical values. The control window T_w is set to be one year, two years, and five years. The sample size $T = 120$. Numbers in the parentheses are standard deviations.*

$T = 120$	Null		Alternative		
	FWER	# of Rejections	SDR	$\frac{1}{M}\sum_{m=1}^{M}(\hat{t}_e^{(m)} - t_e)$	$\frac{1}{M}\sum_{m=1}^{M}(\hat{t}_c^{(m)} - t_c)$
T_w: 1 years	0.44	1.67 (3.26)	0.84	8.76 (5.21)	0.85 (1.32)
T_w: 2 years	0.22	0.57 (1.53)	0.80	10.44 (5.37)	0.78 (1.71)
T_w: 5 years	0.10	0.22 (0.84)	0.77	11.53 (5.33)	0.84 (1.36)

such, one would expect a smaller delay should there be a bubble within the window. This approach to testing and estimation is analogous to using a loss function that takes size and power into account, rather than strictly following the principle of capping size.

The performance of the multiple testing procedure under alternative settings of T_w is investigated in Table 2.3. The data generating process is the same as before. In addition to FWER, we report the average numbers of rejections (ANR) under the null, that is,

$$ANR = \frac{1}{M}\sum_{m=1}^{M}\sum_{s=t_{\min}}^{T} I_s^{(m)},$$

which complements the FWER rate as a measure for Type I errors. The performance of the test under the alternative is again evaluated by SDR and by the average delays in identifying bubble start and collapse dates.

Although the FWER remains sizeable (44%) when the control window is one year, by comparison with the 78 percent of the standard procedure (Table 2.1), it is already a dramatic improvement. The average number of false rejections within each sample path is 1.67, with a standard deviation of 3.26. On the other hand, we observe a slight deterioration in the bubble identification accuracy. The average delay in identifying the bubble origination date is slightly longer (8.76 observations), while the SDR is the same as that of the standard procedure (84%). As the control window T_w increases from one year to five years, the family-wise error rate declines from 44 percent to 10 percent, and the average number of false rejections decreases from 1.67 to 0.22. Meanwhile, the successful detection rate reduces to 77 percent, and the delay in identifying bubble origination increases to 11.53 months. We do not observe obvious changes in the estimation accuracy of the bubble termination date.

In practice, the choice of the control window T_w is subjective. The selection of a larger control window results in more conservative testing with a lower possibility of making false-positive conclusions. In contrast, a small control window enables a higher probability of detecting the presence of a bubble as well as earlier detection.

2.6 Empirical Application: S&P 500 Stock Market

As an illustration, we conduct a pseudo real-time analysis monitoring for a bubble in the S&P 500 stock market at the monthly frequency, starting from January 1990 and terminating in June 2020. The sample period covers the dot-com expansion in the late 1990s and the 2007–2009 subprime mortgage crisis period. Figure 2.3 displays the logarithmic price-dividend ratios of the S&P 500 composite index. The price and dividend series are obtained from Robert Shiller's website.[4] The data series experienced a decade-long expansion at the beginning of the sample period and peaked in March 2000. The expansion is followed by a market downturn that leads to a reversion to the market's 1997 level in 2003. The data exhibit a V-shape dynamic around the subprime mortgage crisis period.

We apply the two bubble identification strategies detailed in Section 2.3 to the market. The first strategy is to apply the PSY explosive root test to the log price-dividend ratios. The second is to estimate the fundamental component of the log price-dividend ratios and apply the PSY test to the nonfundamental/residual component. The decomposition is based on Equations

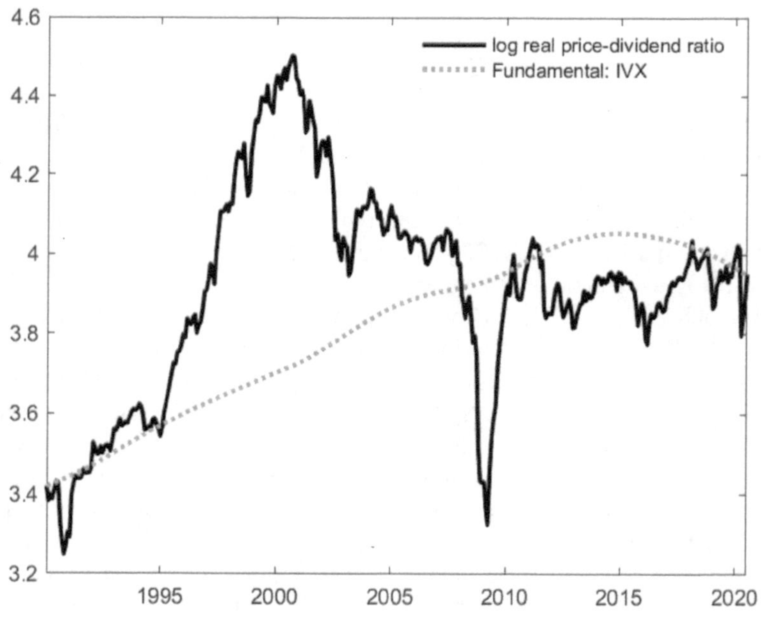

Figure 2.3 The log price-dividend ratios of the S&P 500 composite index and the estimated residual component from January 1990 to June 2020.

[4] See www.econ.yale.edu/~shiller/data.htm.

(2.17)–(2.18), where y_t is the first difference of $p_t - d_t$ and X_t includes real dividends and three-month treasury bill rates. The real dividend series is from Robert Shiller's website and three-month treasury bill rates are from the FRED database.[5] The regression model is estimated using IVX detailed in the appendix. The estimated fundamental component is plotted along with the log price-dividend ratios in Figure 2.3. We observe a general upward trend in the data series. The residual component is computed as the difference between the log price-dividend ratios and the estimated fundamentals and captures fluctuations around the trend.

For the PSY procedure, the minimum window contains 38 observations, which is set according to the rule of $t_{\min} = 0.01T + 1.8\sqrt{T}$. Monitoring starts from February 1993 onwards. Critical values are obtained from the standard procedure in the first row of Figure 2.4 and the multiple testing procedure in the second and third rows, with the control window being two years and five years respectively (i.e., $T_w = \{24, 60\}$). The black lines are the x_t series, and the green shaded areas are periods when the PSY statistic exceeds its critical value. The bubble signal is switched on for two sample periods: the late 1990s and 2008–2009. While the first episode is associated with upward expansion of the market, the second episode overlaps with a market plunge. When using the PSY (standard) test on the residuals, this test also identifies a market downturn between 2002 and 2003. Although the PSY test was initially designed for identifying explosive bubbles, Phillips and Shi (2019) show that this procedure can also detect crises. For analysis and further detail on crisis identification readers may refer to Phillips and Shi (2019).

Some further comments are worth mentioning regarding the dot-com bubble episode. First, the identified origination (respectively, termination) date is earlier (later) when the multiplicity issue is not accounted for or when the control window T_w is smaller. This result is consistent with the simulation findings in Section 2.5, where both the family-wise error rate and the successful detection rate are higher with PSY (standard) or when PSY (multiple) is used with a smaller control window. Second, the identified bubble period is shorter when we control for the impact of market fundamentals using the approach of Shi and Phillips (2023). It suggests that the expansion was first driven by fundamentals followed by speculative sentiment and investment in 1997–1998, in a similar way to the behavioral model of Phillips (2016). Third, the multiple testing procedure indicates that the bubble signal switched off almost two years before the market reached its peak. This finding is coherent with results in Laurent and Shi (2020) and has potent implications for investors who aim to withdraw investments in anticipation of a market collapse.

[5] See https://fred.stlouisfed.org/.

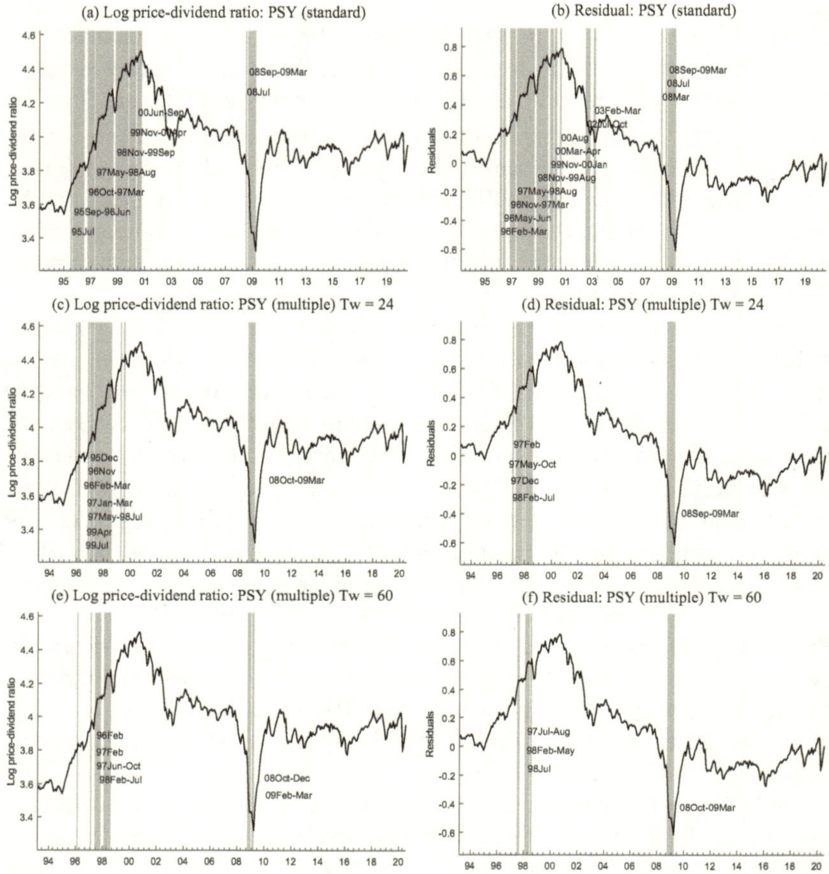

Figure 2.4 The PSY explosive root tests. The black lines are the log price-dividend ratios in the first column and the estimated nonfundamental components in the second column. The shaded areas are periods when the PSY statistic is larger than its critical value.

2.7 Conclusion

In the presence of a financial bubble asset, prices may be written as the sum of two components, one determined by economic fundamentals and the other following an explosive dynamic that constitutes a bubble. The common strategy for bubble identification in empirical work is to apply explosive autoregressive root tests to proxies for the unobserved bubble. In practice proxies are typically constructed by using asset prices themselves or by standardizing prices in some way (e.g., by taking ratios) using observed fundamentals that are considered relevant to the asset. This paper outlines an alternative approach that provides a theoretical framework for the construction of a bubble series that is simple to use and general enough to apply in the case of many different assets.

The two most commonly used proxies for bubbles are real prices and log price–payoff ratios. During a speculative bubble, both asset prices and log price–payoff ratios are explosive because the dynamics of the bubble component dominate the observed data. Market fundamentals are typically near integrated time series, so these proxies of the bubble component are therefore contaminated by highly persistent series, a feature that inevitably influences the sensitivity and performance of explosive root tests.

A new strategy in the literature is to estimate the fundamental component itself and remove it from the proxy variable before applying explosive root tests. The additional step in this strategy helps to reduce the persistent noise element in the proxy and enable more accurate bubble identification. This approach has led to new bubble test results in several housing markets but has yet to be applied to equities. The present chapter overviews the fundamental-bubble decomposition approach proposed by Shi and Phillips (2023) and provides an empirical application of the bubble identification strategy to the S&P 500 stock market.

Explosive autoregressive root tests play a crucial role in bubble identification. This chapter reviews the popular PSY real-time explosive root test strategy. The PSY approach aims to detect explosive dynamics, accounting for their nonlinearity and using this characteristic to provide a consistent real-time dating strategy. The procedure employs a recursive evolving algorithm that has been shown to outperform other methods. Nevertheless, recursive testing of the type employed by PSY inevitably faces multiplicity problems with size control. These issues are discussed and illustrated by simulations.

To address multiplicity the chapter provides a multiple-testing algorithm to generate critical values for the PSY test that are designed to control family-wise size. Simulation results show that the standard PSY procedure can have extremely high family-wise error rates, whereas the new procedure PSY (multiple) has good size control and satisfactory performance overall in detection rates under bubble alternatives. An empirical application to the S&P 500 stock market reveals the importance of controlling for market fundamentals and addressing the multiplicity issue in testing for bubble behavior in equity markets. In particular, controlling for the impact of market fundamentals leads to a shorter dot-com bubble period in the 1990s and suggests that the expansive phase was first driven by fundamentals that then led to speculative behavior. Attention to the consequences of multiple testing produced a further material change in existing findings on the dot-com bubble by switching off the bubble signal in the data sometime before the market peak.

2.8 Appendix: IVX Estimation

The IVX method was proposed by Phillips and Magdalinos (2009), extended to allow for heteroskedastic errors in Kostakis et al. (2015) and subsequently with Cochrane–Orcutt-type parametric adjustments for serial correlation in Yang et al. (2020). In what follows we outline the IVX-AR method of Yang et al. (2020).

Define the transformed dependent and explanatory variables as $y_{\phi,t} = y_t - \sum_{j=1}^{q} \phi_j y_{t-j}$ and $X_{\phi,t} = X_t - \sum_{j=1}^{q} \phi_j X_{t-j}$, where $\phi = (\phi_1, \ldots, \phi_q)$ and $\{\phi_i\}$ are the coefficients in (2.20). Rewrite the regression equation (2.17) as

$$y_{\phi,t} = \alpha_\phi + \beta X_{\phi,t-1} + \eta_t,$$

where $\alpha_\phi = \alpha \left(1 - \sum_{j=1}^{q} \phi_j\right)$. The IVX estimation method uses instrumental variables $z_{\phi,t}$ constructed from the predictors $X_{\phi,t}$ as follows:

$$z_{\phi,t} = \sum_{j=1}^{t} \rho_z^{t-j} \Delta X_{\phi,j} \text{ with } \rho_z = I_k + \frac{C_z}{T^\beta} \text{ for some } C_z \text{ and } \beta \in (0,1),$$

where $t = 2, \ldots, T$, $z_{\phi,1} = 0$, k is the dimension of X_t, and I_k is the $k \times k$ identity matrix. When the X_t are unit root or near unit root processes, the instrumental variables $z_{\phi,t}$ are less persistent than X_t because the autoregressive coefficient matrix ρ_z generates mildly integrated time series from $\Delta X_{\phi,t}$. The IVX parameters are set to $C_z = -I_k$ and $\beta = 0.95$, following the recommendation of Kostakis et al. (2015).

Let $\underline{Y}_\phi = \left(\underline{y}_{\phi,1}, \ldots, \underline{y}_{\phi,T}\right)'_{T\times 1}$, $\underline{X}_\phi = \left(\underline{x}_{\phi,1}, \ldots, \underline{x}_{\phi,T}\right)'_{T\times k}$, and $Z_\phi = \left(z_{\phi,1}, \ldots, z_{\phi,T}\right)'_{T\times k}$, where $\underline{y}_{\phi,t} = y_{\phi,t} - \frac{1}{T}\sum_{t=1}^{T} y_{\phi,t}$ and $\underline{X}_{\phi,t} = X_{\phi,t} - \frac{1}{T}\sum_{t=1}^{T} X_{\phi,t}$ denote the demeaned series of $y_{\phi,t}$ and $X_{\phi,t}$. The IVX-AR estimation method is implemented as follows.

Step 1: Compute the IVX estimator with a given $\phi \in \left[\underline{\phi}, \overline{\phi}\right]$,

$$\hat{\beta}^{(\phi)} = \underline{Y}'_\phi Z_\phi \left(\underline{X}'_\phi Z_\phi\right)^{-1},$$

and obtain the residuals $\hat{\eta}_{\phi,t} = \underline{y}_{\phi,t} - \hat{\beta}^{(\phi)} \underline{X}_{\phi,t}$.

Step 2: Find the optimal moving average coefficients ϕ^* by minimizing the sum of squared residuals

$$\phi^* = \operatorname{argmin}_\phi \left(\sum_{t=1}^{T} \hat{\eta}_{\phi,t}^2\right).$$

Step 3: Compute the IVX-AR estimator $\hat{\beta}_{IVX}$ with ϕ^* as

$$\hat{\beta}_{IVX} = \underline{Y}'_{\phi^*} Z_{\phi^*} \left(\underline{X}'_{\phi^*} Z_{\phi^*} \right)^{-1},$$

and the corresponding fitted intercept $\hat{\alpha}_{IVX} = \bar{y} - \hat{\beta}_{IVX} \bar{X}$ with $\bar{y}$ and $\bar{X}$ being the sample means of y_t and X_t.

The asymptotic and finite sample properties of the IVX-AR method are explored in Yang et al. (2020). This method has all the advantages of the usual IVX method, including endogenous instrumentation and valid asymptotic inference, for use in the reduced form regression (2.17) for the determination of fundamentals via predictive regression. These advantages are coupled with anticipated improvements in the method's finite sample properties over standard IVX arising from the AR transform of the system in the presence of serially correlated errors, which help to capture in the equation's fitted values the essential characteristics of innovations in fundamentally driven prices. Construction of the fundamentals time series then proceeds as in (2.22) with the residuals capturing the bubble component. Simulations show that this method works well in practice for testing the presence of bubbles in asset prices.

Bibliography

Blanchard, O. J. and M. W. Watson (1982). Bubbles, rational expectations and financial markets. NBER Working Paper No. 0945. DOI: https://doi.org/10.3386/w0945

Caballero, R. J. and A. Krishnamurthy (2006). Bubbles and capital flow volatility: Causes and risk management. *Journal of Monetary Economics 53*(1), 35–53.

Campbell, J. Y. and R. J. Shiller (1988). Stock prices, earnings, and expected dividends. *The Journal of Finance 43*(3), 661–676.

Case, K. E., E. L. Glaeser, and J. A. Parker (2000). Real estate and the macroeconomy. *Brookings Papers on Economic Activity 2000*(2), 119–162.

Chen, Y., P. C. B. Phillips, and S. Shi (2023). Common bubble detection in large dimensional financial systems. *Journal of Financial Econometrics 21*(4), 989–1063.

Diba, B. T. and H. I. Grossman (1988). Explosive rational bubbles in stock prices? *The American Economic Review 78*(3), 520–530.

Evans, G. W. (1991). Pitfalls in testing for explosive bubbles in asset prices. *The American Economic Review 81*(4), 922–930.

Harvey, D. I., S. J. Leybourne, and R. Sollis (2013). Recursive right-tailed unit root tests for an explosive asset price bubble. *Journal of Financial Econometrics 13*(1), 166–187.

Harvey, D. I., S. J. Leybourne, R. Sollis, and A. R. Taylor (2016). Tests for explosive financial bubbles in the presence of non-stationary volatility. *Journal of Empirical Finance 38B*, 548–574.

Harvey, D. I., S. J. Leybourne, and Y. Zu (2020). Sign-based unit root tests for explosive financial bubbles in the presence of deterministically time-varying volatility. *Econometric Theory 36*(1), 122–169.

Hirano, T., M. Inaba, and N. Yanagawa (2015). Asset bubbles and bailouts. *Journal of Monetary Economics 76, Supplement*, S71–S89.

Homm, U. and J. Breitung (2012). Testing for speculative bubbles in stock markets: A comparison of alternative methods. *Journal of Financial Econometrics 10*(1), 198–231.

Hu, Y. and L. Oxley (2017). Exuberance, bubbles or froth? Some historical results using long run house price data for Amsterdam, Norway and Paris. Technical Report 16/08, Working Paper, University of Waikato.

Kostakis, A., T. Magdalinos, and M. P. Stamatogiannis (2015). Robust econometric inference for stock return predictability. *The Review of Financial Studies 28*(5), 1506–1553.

Laurent, S. and S. Shi (2020). Volatility estimation and jump detection for drift–diffusion processes. *Journal of Econometrics 217*(2), 259–290.

Lee, J. H. and P. C. B. Phillips (2016). Asset pricing with financial bubble risk. *Journal of Empirical Finance 38B*, 590–622.

Mishkin, F. S. (1995). Nonstationarity of regressors and tests on real-interest-rate behavior. *Journal of Business & Economic Statistics 13*(1), 47–51.

Pavlidis, E. G., I. Paya, and D. A. Peel (2017). Testing for speculative bubbles using spot and forward prices. *International Economic Review 58*(4), 1191–1226.

Pavlidis, E. G., A. Yusupova, I. Paya, D. A. Peel, E. Martínez-García, A. Mack, and V. Grossman (2016). Episodes of exuberance in housing markets: In search of the smoking gun. *The Journal of Real Estate Finance and Economics 53*(4), 419–449.

Phillips, P. C. B. (2005). Econometric analysis of Fisher's equation. *American Journal of Economics and Sociology 64*(1), 125–168.

Phillips, P. C. B. (2016). Modeling speculative bubbles with diverse investor expectations. *Research in Economics 70*(3), 375–387.

Phillips, P. C. B. and T. Magdalinos (2007). Limit theory for moderate deviations from a unit root. *Journal of Econometrics 136*(1), 115–130.

Phillips, P. C. B. and T. Magdalinos (2009). Unit root and cointegrating limit theory when initialization is in the infinite past. *Econometric Theory 25*(06), 1682–1715.

Phillips, P. C. B. and S. Shi (2018). Financial bubble implosion and reverse regression. *Econometric Theory 34*(4), 705–753.

Phillips, P. C. B. and S. Shi (2019). Detecting financial collapse and ballooning sovereign risk. *Oxford Bulletin of Economics and Statistics 81*(6), 1336–1361.

Phillips, P. C. B. and S. Shi (2020). Real time monitoring of asset markets: Bubbles and crises. In *Handbook of Statistics*, Volume 42, pp. 61–80. Elsevier.

Phillips, P. C. B., S. Shi, and J. Yu (2014). Specification sensitivity in right-tailed unit root testing for explosive behaviour. *Oxford Bulletin of Economics and Statistics 76*(3), 315–333.

Phillips, P. C. B., S. Shi, and J. Yu (2015a). Supplement to two papers on multiple bubbles. *International Economic Review 56*(4), 99 pages.

Phillips, P. C. B., S. Shi, and J. Yu (2015b). Testing for multiple bubbles: Historical episodes of exuberance and collapse in the S&P 500. *International Economic Review 56*(4), 1043–1078.

Phillips, P. C. B., S. Shi, and J. Yu (2015c). Testing for multiple bubbles: Limit theory of real-time detectors. *International Economic Review 56*(4), 1079–1134.

Phillips, P. C. B. and V. Solo (1992). Asymptotics for linear processes. *The Annals of Statistics 20*(2), 971–1001.

Phillips, P. C. B., Y. Wu, and J. Yu (2011). Explosive behavior in the 1990s Nasdaq: When did exuberance escalate asset values? *International Economic Review 52*(1), 201–226.

Phillips, P. C. B. and J. Yu (2009). Limit theory for dating the origination and collapse of mildly explosive periods in time series data. Working Paper, Singapore Management University.

Phillips, P. C. B. and J. Yu (2011). Dating the timeline of financial bubbles during the subprime crisis. *Quantitative Economics 2*(3), 455–491.

Rapach, D. E. and C. E. Weber (2004). Are real interest rates really nonstationary? New evidence from tests with good size and power. *Journal of Macroeconomics 26*(3), 409–430.

Rose, A. K. (1988). Is the real interest rate stable? *The Journal of Finance 43*(5), 1095–1112.

Shi, S. (2017). Speculative bubbles or market fundamentals? An investigation of US regional housing markets. *Economic Modelling 66*, 101–111.

Shi, S., S. Hurn, and P. C. B. Phillips (2020). Causal change detection in possibly integrated systems: Revisiting the money–income relationship. *Journal of Financial Econometrics 18*(1), 158–180.

Shi, S. and P. C. B. Phillips (2023). Diagnosing housing fever with an econometric thermometer. *Journal of Economic Surveys 37*(1), 159–186.

Shi, S., A. Rahman, and B. Z. Wang (2020). Australian housing market booms: Fundamentals or speculation? *Economic Record 96*(315), 381–401.

Sun, Y. and P. C. B. Phillips (2004). Understanding the Fisher equation. *Journal of Applied Econometrics 19*(7), 869–886.

Wang, X. and J. Yu (2023). Bubble testing under polynomial trends. *The Econometrics Journal 26*(1), 25–44.

White, H. (2000). A reality check for data snooping. *Econometrica 68*(5), 1097–1126.

Wöckl, I. (2019). Bubble detection in financial markets: A survey of theoretical bubble models and empirical bubble detection tests. Available at SSRN 3460430.

Yang, B., W. Long, L. Peng, and Z. Cai (2020). Testing the predictability of US housing price index returns based on an IVX-AR model. *Journal of the American Statistical Association 115*(532), 1598–1619.

3 Factor-Augmented Regressions and Their Applications to Financial Markets: A Selective Review

YONGHUI ZHANG *Renmin University of China*

3.1 Introduction

Due to rapid technological advances in data collection and the accumulation of massive amounts of information, economists now have the luxury of working in a data-rich environment. Common factor models, as an efficient way to summarize and extract information from large data sets, have received much attention in this revolutionary era of data science and have been widely used in empirical studies. Partial previous applications of factor models in economics and finance include the arbitrage pricing theory (APT) of Ross (1976), the disaggregate business cycle model in Gregory and Head (1999) and Forni and Reichlin (1998), monitoring and forecasting with diffusion indices in Bai and Ng (2006) and Stock et al. (1998); Stock and Watson (2002a,b), the demand system in Gorman (1981), and the identification of common factors for exchange rate in Greenaway-McGrevy et al. (2018), and other works. See Bai and Ng (2008), Bai and Wang (2016), Xu et al. (2016), Swanson and Xiong (2018), Karabiyik et al. (2019), and Fan et al. (2021) for selective reviews on factor models from different perspectives.

This chapter provides a selective review of factor-augmented regression (FAR) models and their applications in finance. In the framework of FAR, the factors are usually estimated from a large set of observed data and then, as "generated regressors" that enter into other models such as linear predictive models, quantile regression models, or panel regression models, and so on. Since the seminal paper of Stock and Watson (2002b), FAR models have been broadly used for many purposes. Once the factor components have been extracted, they can be used to date the recession (Stock and Watson, 2016), compare forecasts (Boivin and Ng, 2005), measure uncertainty (Jurado et al., 2015), and evaluate monetary policy (Bernanke and Boivin, 2003).

Useful comments from an anonymous referee led to a considerably improved version of the paper. Zhang gratefully acknowledges the financial support from National Natural Science Foundation of China (Project No.71973141). All errors are the authors' sole responsibilities. Yonghui Zhang, School of Economics, Renmin University of China. *E-mail address*: yonghui.zhang@hotmail.com.

In the literature on factor models, different methods, such as a principal component analysis (PCA) based on an eigen-analysis of the sample covariance matrix of the data, a maximum likelihood estimation (MLE), or some low-rank regularization methods that use the low-rank structure of factor models, have been proposed to estimate factor models. Among all the estimation methods, PCA is the most popular in empirical applications. As a simple way of transforming the information content in a large number of series into a smaller number of manageable series, PCA can provide consistent estimates for some rotation of common factors under certain assumptions. This chapter focuses on the method of PCA.

The rest of the chapter is organized as follows. We provide an introduction to the factor model and its PCA estimators in Section 3.2. Section 3.3 reviews the FAR with time series data, which mainly includes the diffusion index model and the issue of model selection. Section 3.4 focuses on the nonlinear FAR models covering factor-augmented quantile regression models, factor-augmented nonlinear models, and FARs with structural breaks and threshold effects. Section 3.5 surveys a FAR with a panel data set. Two applications of FARs to financial markets are mentioned in Section 3.6. Section 3.7 presents concluding remarks.

3.2 Factor Models and Principal Component Analysis

In this section, we first introduce the large-dimensional factor models in Bai (2003) and then review the main theories of PCA estimators.

A typical factor model has the following representation:

$$X_{it} = \lambda_i' F_t + e_{it}, \tag{3.1}$$

$i = 1, \ldots, N$, $t = 1, \ldots, T$, where X_{it} is the observed data for the ith cross-section unit or variable at time t, F_t is a vector $(r \times 1)$ of common latent factors, λ_i is a vector $(r \times 1)$ of factor loadings, and e_{it} is the idiosyncratic error. Both F_t's and λ_i's are not observable. We are usually interested in the estimation of common factors $F = (F_1, \ldots, F_T)'$, factor loadings $\Lambda = (\lambda_1, \ldots, \lambda_N)'$, and the common components $C_{it} \equiv \lambda_i' F_t$ when both N and T tend to infinity simultaneously.

In this chapter, we focus on stationary factor models where both $\{F_t\}_{t=1}^T$ and $\{e_{it}\}_{t=1}^T$ are stationary. For an excellent review of nonstationary factor models, see Chapter 6 of Bai and Ng (2008). In the literature, there are two general approaches to estimate the factor model (3.1). One is the PCA method, and the other is low-rank regularization. In this review, we restrict our interest to the PCA estimators, which is much simpler and more popular than other methods in applications. For the low-rank regularization of factor models, see section 3.2 of Fan et al. (2020).

Let $X_i = (X_{i1},\ldots,X_{iT})'$, $X = (X_1,\ldots,X_N)$, $e_i = (e_{i1},\ldots,e_{iT})'$, and $e = (e_1,\ldots,e_N)$. Then, the model (3.1) can be written in T-vector form $X_i = F\lambda_i + e_i$ or matrix form

$$X = F\Lambda' + e.$$

Note that $F\Lambda' = FHH^{-1}\Lambda'$ for any invertible $r \times r$ matrix H, F and Λ are not separately identifiable. Bai and Ng (2002) impose the following identification restrictions:

$$F'F/T = I_r \text{ and } \Lambda'\Lambda \text{ being diagonal.}$$

The r^2 restrictions given by the normalization of F and the diagonalization of $\Lambda'\Lambda$ fix the r^2 free parameters in matrix H. However, the column signs of F and Λ are still not fixed. Alternatively, one can use the normalization of factor loadings $\Lambda'\Lambda/N = I_r$ and the diagonalization that $F'F$ is diagonal. For other identification restrictions, see Bai and Ng (2013). For any $k(k \leq \min[T,N])$, the PCA estimator with k factors is given by

$$\left(\hat{F}^k, \hat{\Lambda}^k\right) = \arg\min_{F^k,\Lambda^k} S(k) \text{ with}$$

$$\begin{aligned} S(k) &= \frac{1}{NT}\sum_{i=1}^{N}\sum_{t=1}^{T}\left(X_{it} - \lambda_i^{k\prime}F_t^k\right)^2 \\ &= \frac{1}{NT}\mathtt{tr}\left[\left(X - F\Lambda'\right)\left(X - F\Lambda'\right)'\right], \end{aligned}$$

subject to

$$\text{(PC1) } F^{k\prime}F^k/T = I_k \text{ and } \Lambda^{k\prime}\Lambda^k \text{being diagonal; or}$$

$$\text{(PC2) } \Lambda^{k\prime}\Lambda^k/N = I_k \text{ and } F^{k\prime}F^k \text{ being diagonal.}$$

Under restriction (PC1), we can cancel Λ^k by using $\Lambda^{k\prime} = \left(F^{k\prime}F^k\right)^{-1}F^{k\prime}X = F^{k\prime}X/T$ and obtain

$$\begin{aligned} \hat{F}^k &= \arg\min_{F^k}\mathtt{tr}\left(X'M_{F^k}X\right) = \arg\max_{F^k}\mathtt{tr}\left(X'P_{F^k}X\right) \\ &= \arg\max_{F^k}\mathtt{tr}\left(F^{k\prime}XX'F^k\right), \end{aligned}$$

where $M_{F^k} = I_T - F^k\left(F^{k\prime}F^k\right)^{-1}F^{k\prime} = I_T - F^kF^{k\prime}/T$ and $P_{F^k} = F^k\left(F^{k\prime}F^k\right)^{-1}F^{k\prime} = F^kF^{k\prime}/T$. The estimated factor matrix $\hat{F}^k$ is given by $\sqrt{T}$ times the eigenvectors that correspond to the k largest eigenvalues of the $T \times T$ matrix XX', and the factor loadings are estimated by $\hat{\Lambda}^{k\prime} = \hat{F}^{k\prime}X/T$ by using restriction (PC1). Now, the restriction $\Lambda^{k\prime}\Lambda^k$ being diagonal is satisfied automatically. Alternatively, one can use restriction (PC2) and concentrate out F^k to obtain another set of estimators $\left(\tilde{F}^k, \tilde{\Lambda}^k\right)$: $\tilde{\Lambda}^k$ is $\sqrt{N}$ times the eigenvectors that correspond to the k largest eigenvalues of the $N \times N$ matrix $X'X$, and $\tilde{F}^{k\prime} = X\tilde{\Lambda}^k/N$. Let $\tilde{V}_k$ be the $k \times k$ diagonal matrix that consists of the first k largest eigenvalues of the matrix $X'X/(TN)$ (or $XX'/(TN)$)[1], arranged in decreasing order. It can be shown easily that

$$\frac{\hat{\Lambda}^{k\prime}\hat{\Lambda}^k}{N} = \frac{\tilde{F}^{k\prime}\tilde{F}^k}{T} = \tilde{V}_k, \tilde{F}^k = \hat{F}^k\left(\tilde{V}_k\right)^{1/2}, \text{ and } \hat{\Lambda}^{k\prime} = \tilde{\Lambda}^k\left(\tilde{V}_k\right)^{1/2}.$$

For the determination of the number of factors k, Bai and Ng (2002) propose estimating it by minimizing the following information criteria:

$$\hat{k}_{IC} = \arg\min_{0 \le k \le k_{\max}} IC(k) \text{ with } IC(k) = \log S(k) + kg(N, T),$$

or

$$\hat{k}_{PC} = \arg\min_{0 \le k \le k_{\max}} PC(k) \text{ with } PC(k) = S(k) + \bar{\sigma}^2 kg(N, T),$$

where $k_{\max} \ge r$ is a prespecified large number, $S(k) = \frac{1}{NT}\sum_{i=1}^{N}\sum_{t=1}^{T}\left(X_{it} - \hat{\lambda}_i^{k\prime}\hat{F}_t^k\right)^2$, $\bar{\sigma}^2$ is used as the proper scaling penalty term in $PC(k)$, and $g(N,T)$ is a penalty function that satisfies (i) $g(N,T) \to 0$ and (ii) $\delta_{NT} \cdot g(N,T) \to \infty$ as $(N,T) \to \infty$, where $\delta_{NT} \equiv \min[\sqrt{N}, \sqrt{T}]$. The typical function $g(N,T)$ includes $g_1 = \frac{N+T}{NT}\ln\left(\frac{NT}{N+T}\right)$, $g_2 = \frac{N+T}{NT}\ln\left(\delta_{NT}^2\right)$, and $g_3 = \frac{\ln \delta_{NT}^2}{\delta_{NT}^2}$. For $PC(k)$, $\bar{\sigma}^2$ can be estimated by $S(k_{\max}) = \frac{1}{NT}\sum_{i=1}^{N}\sum_{t=1}^{T}(X_{it} - \hat{\lambda}_i^{k_{\max}\prime}\hat{F}_t^{k_{\max}})^2$. Under standard conditions on factor models, Bai and Ng (2002) show that

$$\Pr\left(\hat{k}_{IC} = r\right) \to 1 \text{ and } \Pr\left(\hat{k}_{PC} = r\right) \to 1$$

as $(N,T) \to \infty$. As shown by Bai and Ng (2002), all criteria (IC, PC) with g_1, g_2, and g_3 perform very well in simulation when both N and T are large. When either N or T is small and errors are uncorrelated across i and t, the ICs with g_1 and g_2 have better finite sample performance. In this chapter, we assume a known r because the large sample theories of the estimated factors and factor loadings are not affected when the number of factors is estimated using information criteria. There are some other criteria on the determination of the number of factors; for example, see Onatski (2009) for a testing approach based on large random matrix theory, Ahn and Horenstein (2013) for the eigenvalue ratio (ER) and the growth ratio (GR) estimator based on the calculation of eigenvalues, Alessi et al. (2010) for the modified information criterion of Bai and Ng (2002) with an additional tuning multiplicative constant in the penalty, and Li et al. (2017) for the information criteria for the factor model with a diverging number of factors.

[1] Note that $X'X$ and XX' have the same nonzero eigenvalues.

Since the review focuses on the FARs, we are interested in the large sample properties of the factors estimated by PCA. Therefore, we only state the limiting theories for the estimated factors in Bai (2003). For the limiting distributions of the estimated factor loadings and common components, see Theorems 2–3 in Bai (2003). Let F_t^0 and λ_i^0 denote the true factors and factor loadings, respectively. Under the standard conditions on factor models, Bai (2003) shows that

(i) If $\sqrt{N}/T \to 0$, then for each t,

$$\sqrt{N}\left(\hat{F}_t - H'F_t^0\right) = V_{NT}^{-1}\left(\frac{\hat{F}'F^0}{T}\right)\frac{1}{\sqrt{N}}\sum_{i=1}^{N}\lambda_i^0 e_{it} + O_p\left(\frac{\sqrt{N}}{T}\right) \quad (3.2)$$

$$\xrightarrow{d} N\left(0, V^{-1}Q\Gamma_t Q'V^{-1}\right), \quad (3.3)$$

where $H = V_{NT}^{-1}\left(\hat{F}'F^0/T\right)\left(\Lambda'\Lambda/N\right)$ is an asymptotically invertible $r \times r$ matrix, V_{NT} is a diagonal matrix that consists of the first r eigenvalues of $(NT)^{-1}XX'$ in decreasing order, $V = \mathtt{diag}(v_1, \ldots, v_r)$ and $Q = \text{plim}_{T\to\infty} \hat{F}'F^0/T = V^{1/2}\Upsilon\Sigma_\Lambda^{-1/2}$, $v_1 > \cdots > v_r$ are the eigenvalues of $\Sigma_\Lambda^{1/2}\Sigma_F\Sigma_\Lambda^{1/2}$, and Υ is the corresponding eigenvector matrix such that $\Upsilon'\Upsilon = I_r$ with $\Sigma_\Lambda = \text{plim}_{N\to\infty} \Lambda^{0\prime}\Lambda^0/N$ and $\Sigma_F = \text{plim}_{T\to\infty} F^{0\prime}F^0/T$, and $\Gamma_t = \lim_{N\to\infty} N^{-1}\sum_{i=1}^{N}\sum_{j=1}^{N}\lambda_i^0\lambda_j^{0\prime}E\left(e_{it}e_{jt}\right)$.

(ii) If $\liminf \sqrt{N}/T \geq \tau > 0$, then

$$T\left(\hat{F}_t - H'F_t^0\right) = O_p(1). \quad (3.4)$$

From the preceding results, we conclude that the convergence rate for each estimated factor is $\min[N^{1/2}, T]$, and the asymptotic normality generally holds when $\sqrt{N}/T \to 0$. The rate $\min[N^{1/2}, T]$ reflects the fact that the factor loadings are estimated. If the λ_i^0's are all known, then the convergence rate for the cross-sectional least square estimator for F_t^0 should be $\sqrt{N}$.

To make inference about the estimated factors when $\sqrt{N}/T \to 0$, a consistent estimator for the asymptotic variance $\mathtt{Avar}(\hat{F}_t) = V^{-1}Q\Gamma_t Q'V^{-1}$ is needed. Bai (2003) proposes the following estimator

$$\widehat{\mathtt{Avar}}(\hat{F}_t) = V_{NT}^{-1}\hat{\Gamma}_t V_{NT}^{-1}, \quad (3.5)$$

where the $r \times r$ covariance matrix $\hat{\Gamma}_t$ can be estimated by

$$\text{(a) } \hat{\Gamma}_t = \frac{1}{N}\sum_{i=1}^{N}\hat{e}_{it}^2\hat{\lambda}_i\hat{\lambda}_i'; \text{ (b) } \hat{\Gamma}_t = \hat{\sigma}_e^2\frac{1}{N}\sum_{i=1}^{N}\hat{\lambda}_i\hat{\lambda}_i'; \text{ or}$$

$$\text{(c) } \hat{\Gamma} = \frac{1}{n}\sum_{i=1}^{n}\sum_{j=1}^{n}\hat{\lambda}_i\hat{\lambda}_j'\frac{1}{T}\sum_{t=1}^{T}\hat{e}_{it}\hat{e}_{jt},$$

where $\frac{n}{\min[N,T]} \to 0$ in (c) and $\hat{e}_{it} = X_{it} - \hat{\lambda}_i'\hat{F}_t$. The estimator in (a) works when e_{it} are uncorrelated with e_{jt} for $i \neq j$, and (b) works when e_{it} are uncorrelated with e_{jt} for $i \neq j$ and $E\left(e_{it}^2\right) = \sigma_e^2$ for all i's and t's. As argued by Bai (2003), when a small degree of cross-section correlation in the error terms exists, sometimes restricting them to be 0 could be desirable because the sampling variability from estimating them could generate nontrivial efficiency loss. The estimator in (c) is termed the cross-section and heteroskedastic autocorrelation consistent (CS-HAC) estimator by Bai (2003) and is appropriate for cross-sectional dependent errors with an additional covariance stationarity assumption that $E\left(e_{it}e_{jt}\right) = \sigma_{ij}$ for all t's. As for the choice of n in (c), one simple rule is to use $n = \min\left\{\lfloor N^{1/2}\rfloor, \lfloor T^{1/2}\rfloor\right\}$ as suggested by Bai (2003), where $\lfloor a\rfloor$ denotes the largest integer less than a.

Since we focus on the cases where the estimated factors are used as regressors in the next stage, the following rough uniform consistency result for the estimated factors $\hat{F}_t$ is given by

$$\max_{1\leq t\leq T}\left\|\hat{F}_t - H'F_t^0\right\| = O_p\left(T^{-1/2}\right) + O_p\left((T/N)^{1/2}\right).$$

Bai and Ng (2008) provide a sharper bound. If there exists $\ell \geq 4$ such that $E\left\|F_t^0\right\|^{\ell} \leq M$ and $E\left\|N^{-1/2}\sum_{i=1}^N \lambda_i^0 e_{it}\right\|^{\ell} \leq M$ for all t, then

$$\max_{1\leq t\leq T}\left\|\hat{F}_t - H'F_t^0\right\| = O_p\left(T^{-1+1/\ell}\right) + O_p\left(T^{1/\ell}/N^{1/2}\right).$$

When $\ell = 4$, $\max_{1\leq t\leq T}\left\|\hat{F}_t - H'F_t^0\right\| = O_p\left(T^{-3/4}\right) + O_p\left(T^{1/4}/N^{1/2}\right) \to 0$ given that $T/N^2 \to 0$. In addition, the following results are relevant for the FAR:

(i) $T^{-1}\sum_{t=1}^T\left\|\hat{F}_t - H'F_t^0\right\|^2 = O_p\left(\delta_{NT}^{-2}\right)$;

(ii) Assume that ξ_t is uncorrelated with e_{it} for all i and t and $E\left|\xi_t\right|^2 \leq M$ for all t; then, $T^{-1}\sum_{t=1}^T\left(\hat{F}_t - H'F_t^0\right)\xi_t = O_p\left(\delta_{NT}^{-2}\right)$.

3.3 FARs with Time Series Data

In this section, we mainly review the forecast model using the FARs in Stock and Watson (2002a,b) and Bai and Ng (2006).

3.3.1 Diffusion Index Forecasting Model

When a FAR model is applied to time series data, it is typically for the aim of forecasting some target variables in a data-rich environment. Consider the following h-step ahead forecasting model for y_t with $h \geq 1$:

$$y_{t+h} = \alpha'F_t + \beta'W_t + \varepsilon_{t+h},\ t = 1,\ldots,T, \tag{3.6}$$

where F_t is an $r \times 1$ vector of unobservable factors, and W_t is a vector of a small number of observables, which typically includes the intercept and the lags of y_t or seasonal dummies, and ε_{t+h} is the error term. Clearly, given $E(\varepsilon_{t+h}|\Omega_T) = 0$, where $\Omega_T = [F_T, W_T, F_{T-1}, W_{T-1}, \cdots]$, the optimal predictor for y_{T+h} at the Tth period is

$$y_{T+h|T} \equiv E(y_{T+h}|\Omega_T) = \alpha' F_t + \beta' W_t. \tag{3.7}$$

However, based on the observed data set $\{W_t, y_t\}_{t=1}^{T}$, it is impossible to obtain the conventional mean-squared optimal prediction of $y_{T+h|T}$ because F_t are unobservable.

In a data-rich environment, suppose that there is a large number of series $\underline{X}_t = (X_{1t}, \ldots, X_{Nt})'$ at the tth period that has a factor structure as follows:

$$X_{it} = \lambda_i' F_t + e_{it}. \tag{3.8}$$

Clearly, X_{it} is correlated with the latent factors F_t and is a noisy predictor for y_{t+h}. However, one cannot directly regress y_{t+h} on $\underline{X}_t$ and W_t to construct the forecast due to the large dimension of $\underline{X}_t$ (N) without imposing some special structure. Instead, one can extract the factors from the observables X_{it}'s through PCA and then provide a feasible forecast by using the PC estimates for the latent factors.

When the target variable y_{t+h} is a scalar, the framework in (3.6) and (3.8) is the famous *diffusion index* (DI) forecasting model proposed by Stock and Watson (2002b). The DI can reduce the dimension of the predictors from N to a much smaller number r, namely, the dimension of F_t. That is, it can exploit the information underlying a large data set in a parsimonious way. Due to its advantage in modeling large data sets, the DI framework has been widely used by government agencies in different countries and many academic researchers.

Now, we turn to the construction of the DI forecast. Consider the PCA estimator $\hat{F}_t$ in the model (3.8) based on data $\{X_{it}, i = 1, \ldots, N, t = 1, \ldots, T\}$, which is a consistent estimator of $H' F_t$ for some invertible rotation matrix H according to (3.2)–(3.4) in Section 3.2. Then, regress y_{t+h} on $\hat{F}_t$ and W_t to obtain $\hat{\delta} \equiv \left(\hat{\alpha}', \hat{\beta}'\right)'$ by using the usual least square method, namely,

$$\hat{\delta} = \left(\sum_{t=1}^{T-h} \hat{z}_t \hat{z}_t'\right)^{-1} \sum_{t=1}^{T-h} \hat{z}_t y_{t+h},$$

where $\hat{z}_t \equiv \left(\hat{F}_t', W_t'\right)'$. Let $\delta \equiv (\alpha' H^{-1}, \beta')'$ and $z_t \equiv \left(F_t', W_t'\right)'$. Rewriting

$$\begin{aligned} y_{t+h} &= \alpha' F_t + \beta' W_t + \varepsilon_{t+h} \\ &= \alpha' H^{-1} \hat{F}_t + \beta' W_t + \varepsilon_{t+h} + \alpha' H^{-1} \left(H F_t - \hat{F}_t\right) \\ &= \delta' \hat{z}_t + \varepsilon_{t+h} + \alpha' H^{-1} \left(H F_t - \hat{F}_t\right) \end{aligned}$$

leads to the following decomposition:

$$\sqrt{T}\left(\hat{\delta}-\delta\right)=\left(\frac{1}{T}\sum_{t=1}^{T-h}\hat{z}_t\hat{z}_t'\right)^{-1}\frac{1}{\sqrt{T}}\sum_{t=1}^{T-h}\hat{z}_t\varepsilon_{t+h}$$
$$+\left(\frac{1}{T}\sum_{t=1}^{T-h}\hat{z}_t\hat{z}_t'\right)^{-1}\frac{1}{\sqrt{T}}\sum_{t=1}^{T-h}\hat{z}_t\left(HF_t-\hat{F}_t\right)'H^{-1}\alpha,$$

where the first term is $O_p(1)$ and becomes the leading term when $\sqrt{T}/N\to 0$, and the second term is $O_p\left(T^{1/2}/N+T^{-1/2}\right)$ according to lemma A.1 (iii) in Bai and Ng (2006). Under some regular conditions, Bai and Ng (2006) show that when $\sqrt{T}/N\to 0$, $\hat{\delta}$ is $\sqrt{T}$-consistent as the estimator of δ and is asymptotically normally distributed. Specifically, when $\sqrt{T}/N\to 0$, Bai and Ng (2006) establish that

$$\sqrt{T}\left(\hat{\delta}-\delta\right)\xrightarrow{d}N\left(0,\Sigma_\delta\right), \tag{3.9}$$

where $\Sigma_\delta\equiv\Phi_0^{-1}\Sigma_{zz}^{-1}\Sigma_{zz,\varepsilon}\Sigma_{zz}^{-1}\Phi_0^{-1}$ with $\Phi_0\equiv\mathtt{diag}\left(V^{-1}Q\Sigma_\Lambda,I\right)$, $\Sigma_{zz}\equiv\operatorname{plim}_{T\to\infty}T^{-1}\sum_{t=1}^{T}z_tz_t'$ and $\Sigma_{zz,\varepsilon}\equiv\operatorname{plim}_{T\to\infty}T^{-1}\sum_{t=1}^{T}z_tz_t'\varepsilon_{t+h}^2$. Let $\hat{\varepsilon}_{t+h}\equiv y_{t+h}-\hat{y}_{t+h|t}$. A heteroskedasticity consistent (HC) estimator for Σ_δ is given by

$$\hat{\Sigma}_\delta=\left(\frac{1}{T_h}\sum_{t=1}^{T-h}\hat{z}_t\hat{z}_t'\right)^{-1}\left(\frac{1}{T_h}\sum_{t=1}^{T-h}\hat{z}_t\hat{z}_t'\hat{\varepsilon}_{t+h}^2\right)\left(\frac{1}{T_h}\sum_{t=1}^{T-h}\hat{z}_t\hat{z}_t'\right)^{-1}, \tag{3.10}$$

where $T_h=T-h$.

Given the consistency of $\hat{\delta}$, a feasible prediction for y_{T+h} is given by

$$\hat{y}_{T+h|T}=\hat{\alpha}'\hat{F}_T+\hat{\beta}'W_T=\hat{z}_T'\hat{\delta}. \tag{3.11}$$

To make inference about the feasible predictor, write

$$\hat{y}_{T+h|T}-y_{T+h|T}=\hat{z}_T'\hat{\delta}-z_T'\delta=\alpha'H^{-1}\left(\hat{F}_t-HF_t\right)+\hat{z}_T'\left(\hat{\delta}-\delta\right), \tag{3.12}$$

which has two components due to the estimation of F_t and δ. Recall that as $\sqrt{N}/T\to 0$, $\sqrt{N}\left(\hat{F}_T-H'F_T\right)\xrightarrow{d}N\left(0,\mathtt{Avar}\left(\hat{F}_T\right)\right)$, where $\mathtt{Avar}\left(\hat{F}_T\right)\equiv V^{-1}Q\Gamma_tQ'V^{-1}$. This result combined with (3.9) gives the following:

$$\frac{\hat{y}_{T+h|T}-y_{T+h|T}}{\sqrt{Var\left(\hat{y}_{T+h|T}\right)}}\xrightarrow{d}N(0,1),$$

where

$$Var\left(\hat{y}_{T+h|T}\right)=\frac{1}{T}\hat{z}_T'\mathtt{Avar}\left(\hat{\delta}\right)\hat{z}_T+\frac{1}{N}\hat{\alpha}'\mathtt{Avar}\left(\hat{F}_T\right)\hat{\alpha}.$$

The forecast error is given by

$$\hat{\varepsilon}_{T+h|T} \equiv \hat{y}_{T+h|T} - y_{T+h} = \left(\hat{y}_{T+h|T} - y_{T+h|T}\right) + \varepsilon_{T+h}$$

and its variance is given by $Var\left(\hat{\varepsilon}_{T+h|T}\right) = Var\left(\hat{y}_{T+h|T}\right) + Var\left(\varepsilon_{T+h}\right)$. If one imposes a further assumption that ε_t is normal with variance σ_ε^2, then the forecasting error also becomes approximately normal:

$$\hat{\varepsilon}_{T+h|T} \overset{a}{\sim} N\left(0, \sigma_\varepsilon^2 + Var\left(\hat{y}_{T+h|T}\right)\right),$$

so that the confidence intervals (CIs) can be constructed for the forecasts.

Given the consistent estimators for $\mathtt{Avar}(\hat{\delta})$ in (3.10) and $\mathtt{Avar}(\hat{F}_T)$ in (3.5), the prediction intervals can be straightforwardly constructed. For example, the 95% CI for the forecasting variable y_{T+h} can be given by

$$\left[\hat{y}_{T+h|T} - 1.96\sqrt{\hat{\sigma}_\varepsilon^2 + \widehat{Var}\left(\hat{y}_{T+h|T}\right)}, \hat{y}_{T+h|T} + 1.96\sqrt{\hat{\sigma}_\varepsilon^2 + \widehat{Var}\left(\hat{y}_{T+h|T}\right)}\right]$$

where $\widehat{Var}\left(\hat{y}_{T+h|T}\right) = \frac{1}{T}\hat{z}_T' \widehat{\mathtt{Avar}}\left(\hat{\delta}\right)\hat{z}_T + \frac{1}{N}\hat{\alpha}'\widehat{\mathtt{Avar}}\left(\hat{F}_T\right)\hat{\alpha}$ and $\hat{\sigma}_\varepsilon^2 = T^{-1}\sum_{t=h+1}^{T}\hat{\varepsilon}_t^2$ with $\hat{\varepsilon}_{t+h} = y_{t+h} - \hat{z}_t'\hat{\delta}$. For the bootstrap prediction intervals for factor models, see Gonçalves et al. (2017). The bootstrap can relax the assumption of the Gaussianity of the innovations and construct valid prediction intervals under more general conditions. Moreover, even under the Gaussianity assumption, the bootstrap procedure leads to more accurate intervals when N is relatively small.

The estimated factors $\hat{F}_t$ can be combined with an m-vector of W_t to form a factor-augmented vector autoregression (FAVAR) model, which was originally proposed by Bernanke et al. (2005) to measure monetary policy. A FAVAR model assumes that a large number of economic variables are driven by a small vector autoregression (VAR), which includes both latent and observed variables. To be specific, in a FAVAR, both the unobserved factors F_t and the observed factors W_t affect a large number of observed variables X_{it},

$$X_{it} = \lambda_i' F_t + \gamma_i' W_t + e_{it},$$

and the random vector $G_t \equiv \left(F_t', W_t'\right)'$ follows a VAR of finite order,

$$\Phi(L)G_t = u_t.$$

where $\{u_t\}$ are i.i.d. $(0, \sigma_u^2)$. For the preceding model, two ways have been proposed to analyze the system by Bernanke et al. (2005). The first one is a two-step method: Step 1. Form estimates of the space spanned by both F_t and W_t with PCA, where various identification approaches can be used to obtain the estimates $\hat{F}_t$; Step 2. The estimated factors are treated as observed in conducting a VAR analysis of $\hat{G}_t = \left(\hat{F}_t', W_t'\right)'$. Due to the problem of "generated regressors," the two-step estimator has a different inferential theory from the standard large factor models; see Bai et al. (2016). The second method considers the joint estimation of the latent factors and impulse responses with a one-step likelihood approach that uses Gibbs sampling. These two methods can complement one another, with the first one being computationally simple and the second providing possibly better finite sample inference but at a heavier computational cost. See Bernanke et al. (2005), Stock and Watson (2012), and Bai and Wang (2016) for more discussion.

3.3.2 *Model Selection of the Diffusion Index Forecasting Model*

In the DI forecasting model, the predictor constructed in (3.11) relies on the fact that both the target variable y_{t+h} and the large set of variables X_{it}, $i = 1, \ldots, N$, have the same set of factors. In practice, some factors extracted from the observable X_{it}'s may provide useless information for predicting the target variable. In the literature, different approaches to select the significant predictors exist (the estimated factors and observable predictors), such as model selection criteria, a generalized cross-validation, a shrinkage estimation with sparsity assumptions, and model averaging techniques.

In the following section, we review three commonly used model selection criteria in DI forecasting models.

Groen and Kapetanios (2013) model selection criteria. Let $\hat{F} = \left(\hat{F}_1, \ldots, \hat{F}_T\right)'$ be the $T \times r$ matrix of the estimated factors by applying PCA to model (3.8), where the number of factors r can be determined by the criteria in Bai and Ng (2002). Let

$$\hat{\mathcal{F}} = \left\{\left\{\hat{F}_t^{(1)}\right\}_{t=1}^T, \left\{\hat{F}_t^{(2)}\right\}_{t=1}^T, \ldots, \left\{\hat{F}_t^{(s)}\right\}_{t=1}^T\right\}$$

denote the set of estimated factor variables, where $\hat{F}_t^{(l)}$ indicates the lth candidate vector of the estimated factors at time t and includes the d_l elements of $\hat{F}_t$,; the number of all candidate sets is s. Let $\hat{F}^{(l)} = \left(\hat{F}_1^{(l)}, \ldots, \hat{F}_T^{(l)}\right)'$ be the $T \times d_l$ matrix of the estimated factors for the lth candidate set. Clearly, $s \leq 2^r$ because there are 2^r distinct forecasting models when there are r estimated factors. When r is not too large, all 2^r subsets can be considered; but when the number of combinations is too large, a much smaller subset of them can be considered. Furthermore, let

$$\mathcal{F} = \left\{\left\{F_t^{(1)}\right\}_{t=1}^\infty, \left\{F_t^{(2)}\right\}_{t=1}^\infty, \ldots, \left\{F_t^{(s)}\right\}_{t=1}^\infty\right\},$$

where $F_t^{(l)} \equiv \text{plim}_{N,T\to\infty} \hat{F}_t^{(l)}$ is the probability limit of $\hat{F}_t^{(l)}$ for $l = 1, \ldots, s$. To select the correct specification of factors in the predictive regression, Groen and Kapetanios (2013) propose the following information criteria (IC):

$$IC_l = \frac{T}{2} \ln\left(\hat{\sigma}_\varepsilon^2\right) + d_l \tilde{C}_{N,T},$$

where $\hat{\sigma}_\varepsilon^2 \equiv T^{-1}\sum_{t=h+1}^{T}\hat{\varepsilon}_t^2$, with $\hat{\varepsilon}_t$'s being the ordinary least squares (OLS) residuals from the linear regression

$$y_{t+h} = \hat{z}_t^{(l)\prime}\delta^{(l)} + \varepsilon_{t+h}$$

with $\hat{z}_t^{(l)} \equiv \left(\hat{F}_t^{(l)\prime}, W_t'\right)'$, d_l is the number of factors included in $\hat{F}_t^{(l)}$, and $\tilde{C}_{N,T}$ denotes a penalty term that satisfies $\tilde{C}_{NT} = o(T)$ and $\lim_{N,T\to\infty} T^{-1}\min(N,T)\,\tilde{C}_{N,T} = \infty$. Let F_t^0 be the true factors in the target predictor variable y_{t+h}. Under the standard assumptions in Bai and Ng (2006), Groen and Kapetanios (2013) establish the following factor selection consistency result:

(i) If there exists a matrix A such that $F_t^0 = AF_t^{(l)}$ for $\forall t$, but no such matrix exists for $F_t^{(j)}$ when $l \neq j$, then

$$\lim_{N,T\to\infty} \Pr\left(IC_l < IC_j\right) = 1; \tag{3.13}$$

(ii) If there exist matrices $A^{(l)}$ and $A^{(m)}$ such that $F_t^0 = A^{(l)}F_t^{(l)}$ and $F_t^0 = A^{(m)}F_t^{(m)}$ for $\forall t$ and $d_l < d_m$, then (3.13) holds.

The model selection consistency results include two parts: (i) any set of estimated factors whose probability limits span the true factors will be chosen over any set of estimated factors that do not span the true factors, given the penalty term being $o(T)$; and (ii) if two sets of estimated factors both span the set of true factors, then the one with the smaller dimension will be chosen.

Note that the conditions on $\tilde{C}_{N,T}$ allow for all popular ICs such as the Bayesian IC (BIC) and the HQIC. To gain a better finite sample performance, Groen and Kapetanios (2013) propose the following modified BIC and HQIC:

$$BICM = \frac{T}{2}\ln\left(\hat{\sigma}_\varepsilon^2\right) + d\ln(T)\left(1+\frac{T}{N}\right) \text{ and}$$

$$HQICM = \frac{T}{2}\ln\left(\hat{\sigma}_\varepsilon^2\right) + 2d\ln(\ln T)\left(1+\frac{T}{N}\right).$$

When other variables W_t such as the lags of the target variable in the forecasting regression also need selection, Groen and Kapetanios (2013) provide the modified criteria to select the estimated factors and other predictors jointly:

$$BICM = \frac{T}{2}\ln\left(\hat{\sigma}_\varepsilon^2\right) + k\ln T + d\ln(T)\left(1+\frac{T}{N}\right) \text{ and}$$

$$HQICM = \frac{T}{2}\ln\left(\hat{\sigma}_\varepsilon^2\right) + 2k\ln(\ln T) + 2d\ln(\ln T)\left(1+\frac{T}{N}\right),$$

where k is the number of variables in the subset of W_t used in the forecasting regression.

Ando and Tsay (2014) PMSE criterion. Let $u_{1+h},\ldots,u_{T+h}$ be replicates of the target variables $y_{1+h},\ldots,y_{T+h}$, given the true values of factors $F_1,\ldots,F_T$.

To assess the predictive ability of the estimated model, the predictive mean squared error (PMSE) is considered:

$$\eta \equiv \frac{1}{T}\int\left[\sum_{t=1}^{T}\left(u_{t+h}-\hat{z}_t'\hat{\delta}\right)^2\right]dG(\mathbf{u}), \tag{3.14}$$

where $dG(\mathbf{u})$ is the Lebesgue measure with respect to the probability density $g(\mathbf{u})$ of the joint distribution of $\mathbf{u} = (u_{1+h}, \ldots, u_{T+h})'$. The PMSE is positive unless $u_{t+h} = \hat{z}_t'\hat{\delta}$ almost surely holds. The best statistical model is chosen by minimizing the PMSE. However, the PMSE depends on (a) the unobserved replicates $u_{1+h}, \ldots, u_{T+h}$, (b) the observed data (through the estimate $\hat{\delta}$), and (c) the use of proxies $\hat{z}_1, \ldots, \hat{z}_T$ because the true factors in z_t are unobservable. A natural estimator for η in (3.14) is given by

$$\hat{\eta} = \frac{1}{T}\sum_{t=1}^{T}\left(y_{t+h}-\hat{z}_t'\hat{\delta}\right)^2,$$

which replaces the unknown distribution $G(\mathbf{u})$ with an empirical distribution with a mass of $1/T$ on each observation. However, $\hat{\eta}$ is biased due to the estimation error. The bias is given by

$$b = \int\left\{\frac{1}{T}\int\left[\sum_{t=1}^{T}\left(u_{t+h}-\hat{z}_t'\hat{\delta}\right)^2\right]dG(\mathbf{u}) - \frac{1}{T}\sum_{t=1}^{T}\left(y_{t+h}-\hat{z}_t'\hat{\delta}\right)^2\right\}dG(\mathbf{y}).$$

Assuming that $\hat{b}$ estimates b consistently by using some procedure, the following bias-corrected PMSE is considered:

$$PMSE = \hat{\eta} - \hat{b}. \tag{3.15}$$

See Remark 4 in Ando and Tsay (2014) for a detailed discussion of b and its consistent estimator $\hat{b}$. Ando and Tsay (2014) choose the best diffusion-index model that minimizes this PMSE score in (3.15). Based on the bias-corrected PMSE, the criterion is a natural extension of the traditional Akaike information criterion (AIC), but it relaxes the restrictive distributional assumptions for the likelihood.

Djogbenou (2021) selection procedures for FAR models. The first procedure is a generalization of leave-d-out cross-validation (CV), which can select the smallest basis for the space spanned by the true factors. Given the b random draws of d indexes S in $\{1, \ldots, T\}$ called validation samples, for each draw $S = \{s(1), \ldots, s(d)\}$, define

$$\mathbf{y}_S = \begin{pmatrix} y_{s(1)} \\ y_{s(2)} \\ \vdots \\ y_{s(d)} \end{pmatrix} \text{ and } \hat{\mathbf{Z}}_S(m) = \begin{pmatrix} \hat{F}_{s(1)}(m) & W_{s(1)} \\ \hat{F}_{s(2)}(m) & W_{s(2)} \\ \vdots & \vdots \\ \hat{F}_{s(d)}(m) & W_{s(d)} \end{pmatrix},$$

where $\hat{F}_t(m)$ is a subset from the $r \times 1$ estimated factors $\hat{F}_t$ by using PCA, and m is any of the 2^r subsets of indices in $\{1, \ldots, r\}$ denoted $\mathcal{M}$ including the empty set. The corresponding construction sample is indexed by $S^c = \{1, \ldots, T\} \backslash S$ with $\mathbf{y}_{S^c}$ being the complement of $\mathbf{y}_S$ in $\mathbf{y}$, and $\hat{\mathbf{Z}}_{S^c}$ being the complement of $\hat{\mathbf{Z}}_S$ in $\hat{\mathbf{Z}} = (\hat{z}_1, \ldots, \hat{z}_T)'$. Denote $\hat{\mathbf{y}}_S(m) = \hat{\mathbf{Z}}_S(m)\hat{\delta}_S(m)$, $\hat{\delta}_S(m) = \left(\hat{\mathbf{Z}}'_{S^c}\hat{\mathbf{Z}}_{S^c}\right)^{-1}\hat{\mathbf{Z}}'_{S^c}\mathbf{y}_{S^c}$. The Monte Carlo leave-$d$-out CV estimated model is obtained by minimizing

$$CV_d(m) = \frac{1}{d \cdot b}\sum_{S \in \mathcal{R}} \left\| \mathbf{y}_S - \hat{\mathbf{y}}_S(m) \right\|^2,$$

where $\mathcal{R}$ represents a collection of b subsets of size d randomly drawn from $\{1, \ldots, T\}$. When $d = 1$, $S = \{t\}$, and $\mathcal{R} = \{\{1\}, \ldots, \{T\}\}$, $CV_1(m)$ is the usual leave-one-out CV objective function. The consistency of the leave-d-out CV for the diffusion index model is established in Djogbenou (2021). In addition, Djogbenou (2021) shows that the usual CV fails to give consistent model selections.

The second procedure proposed by Djogbenou (2021) is a generalization of the bootstrap approximation of the squared error of prediction of Shao (1996). Djogbenou (2021) proves the validity of the described bootstrap scheme under some conditions. The algorithm for bootstrapping the squared error of prediction is as follows:

Step 1. Obtain the estimates $\hat{F}$ and $\hat{\Lambda}$ for F and Λ from X with the PCA method.
Step 2. For each model m:

1. Compute $\hat{\delta}(m)$ by regressing $\mathbf{y}$ on $\hat{\mathbf{Z}}(m) = \left(\hat{F}(m), W\right)$.
2. Generate B bootstrap samples $X^*_{it} = \hat{F}'_t\hat{\lambda}_i + e^*_{it}$, $\mathbf{y}^*(m) = \hat{\mathbf{Z}}(m)\hat{\delta}(m) + \varepsilon^*$, where $\{e^*_{it}\}$ and $\{\varepsilon^*_t\}$ are the bootstrap errors based on $\{\hat{e}_{it}\}$ and $\{\hat{\varepsilon}_t\}$, respectively, with $\hat{\varepsilon}_t$ being the residual when all the estimated factors are used.
3. $\{e^*_{it}\}$ are obtained by multiplying $\{\hat{e}_{it}\}$ i.i.d. external draws η_{it} with $E\eta_{it} = 0$ and $Var(\eta_{it}) = 1$ for $i = 1, \ldots, N$, and $t = 1, \ldots T$.
4. $\{\varepsilon^*_t\}_{t=1,\ldots,T}$ are the i.i.d. draws of $\left\{\frac{\sqrt{T/\kappa}}{\sqrt{1-(r+q)/T}}\left(\hat{\varepsilon}_t - T^{-1}\sum_{t=1}^{T}\hat{\varepsilon}_t\right)\right\}$, with $\kappa \to \infty$ and $\frac{\kappa}{\min[N,T]} \to 0$, and q is the dimension of W_t.
5. For each bootstrap sample, extract $\hat{F}^*$ from X^* and estimate $\hat{\delta}^*_\kappa(m)$ based on $\hat{\mathbf{Z}}^*(m) = \left(\hat{F}^*(m), W\right)$ and $y^*(m)$.

Step 3. Obtain $\hat{m}$ as the model that minimizes the average of $\hat{\Gamma}^j_\kappa(m) = T^{-1}\left\|\mathbf{y} - \hat{\mathbf{Z}}^{*j}(m)\hat{\delta}^{*j}_\kappa(m)\right\|^2$ over the B samples indexed by j, as given by $\hat{\Gamma}_\kappa(m) = B^{-1}\sum_{j=1}^{B}\hat{\Gamma}^j_\kappa(m)$.

Other Recent Developments For a slightly different forecasting model, where both latent factors and idiosyncratic components from a large set of predictors may enter the predictive regression, Fosten (2017) proposes some model selection criteria that considers the uncertainty in estimating both components. The criteria can jointly select the estimated factors and idiosyncratic components consistently. For other approaches to determine the forecasting model with FAR, see Bai and Ng (2009) for the boosting approach to diffusion index, Cheng and Hansen (2015) for the forecast combination with FAR based on frequentist model averaging criteria, Kelly and Pruitt (2015) for the three-pass filter regression approach, and Carrasco and Rossi (2016) for the regularization methods for in-sample inference and forecasting in misspecified factor models.

3.4 Nonlinear FARs

The FAR framework is also useful in nonlinear or semiparametric regressions. Recent developments for FAR in nonlinear models include a factor-augmented functional-coefficient predictive regression, factor-augmented quantile prediction regression, factor-augmented forecasting model with structural changes or threshold effects, and so on. In this section, we give a selective review on nonlinear FAR models.

3.4.1 Factor-Augmented Functional-Coefficient Predictive Regression Models

Li et al. (2020) introduce a new class of functional-coefficient predictive regression models, where the regressors consist of lagged target variables and latent factor regressors, and the coefficients vary with certain index variables. Specifically, they consider the following one-step ahead predictive regression model:

$$\begin{aligned} y_{t+1} &= \sum_{l=1}^{q_n} \alpha_{1l}(u_t) z_{tl} + \sum_{j=1}^{d_0} \alpha_{2j}(u_t) y_{t+1-j} + \varepsilon_{t+1} \\ &= Z_t' \alpha_1(u_t) + Y_t' \alpha_2(u_t) + \varepsilon_{t+1}, \end{aligned} \tag{3.16}$$

with $t = 1, \ldots, T$, where y_{t+1} is the dependent variable, $Z_t = (z_{t1}, \ldots, z_{tq_T})$ is a $q_T \times 1$ vector of exogenous covariates with $q_T \to \infty$ as $T \to \infty$, $Y_t = (y_t, \ldots, y_{t-d_0+1})'$ includes fixed d_0 lags of the response, u_t is a univariate index variable, $\alpha_1(\cdot) = [\alpha_{11}(\cdot), \ldots, \alpha_{1q_T}(\cdot)]'$ and $\alpha_2(\cdot) = [\alpha_{21}(\cdot), \ldots, \alpha_{2d_0}(\cdot)]'$ are two vectors of coefficient functions, and ε_{t+1} is the error. When $u_t \equiv t/T$ is the time regressor, the model (3.16) becomes the time-varying coefficient (TVC) model. In the preceding predictive model, Z_t are determined by some latent factors outside of the models, and Y_t are determined within the model.

When the dimension of regressors is extremely high or moderately large, some commonly used approaches such as a shrinkage estimation or screening method are used to remove the insignificant regressors or reduce the model dimension. However, as Fan and Lv (2008) point out, when irrelevant regressors are highly correlated with some relevant ones, both methods tend to select these irrelevant regressors into the model with higher priority than some other relevant regressors, which then causes high false positive rates and low true positive rates. In time series models, the problem may be more severe since regressors often contain the lags of the dependent variable and cause strong correlations among the regressors.

To address this problem, Li et al. (2020) develop an alternative dimension-reduction technique for the high-dimensional functional-coefficient predictive regression model by imposing a factor structure on Z_t:

$$Z_t = \mathbb{B}_T F_t + V_t, \tag{3.17}$$

where $\mathbb{B}_T$ is a $q_T \times r$ matrix of factor loadings, F_t is a $r \times 1$ vector of latent common factors that is stationary and weakly dependent, and V_t is a q_n-dimensional vector of idiosyncratic errors. The number of factors r is usually unknown and may increase slowly as the sample size increases; see Li et al. (2017). Using the structure model in (3.17), Li et al. (2020) consider the following functional-coefficient predictive model by using the factor regressors:

$$y_{t+1} = F_t'\beta_1(u_t) + Y_t'\beta_2(u_t) + \varepsilon_{t+1}, \tag{3.18}$$

where $\beta_1(\cdot) = (\beta_{11}(\cdot), \ldots, \beta_{1r}(\cdot))' = \mathbb{B}_T'\alpha_1(\cdot)$, $\beta_2(\cdot) = \alpha_2(\cdot)$, and $\varepsilon_{t+1} = V_t'\alpha_1(u_t) + \varepsilon_{t+1}$. The model in (3.17) and (3.18) is called the *factor-augmented functional-coefficient model (FA-FCM)*. Noting that the factor regressors are unobservable in (3.18), Li et al. (2020) propose to replace them by their PC estimators with data Z_t's. Specifically, they introduce a two-stage estimation procedure.

Step 1. Estimate the factor regressors by using PCA. Let $\hat{\mathbb{F}}_T \equiv \left(\hat{F}_1, \ldots, \hat{F}_T\right)'$ be the PC estimators, which are an $T \times r$ matrix that consists of the r eigenvectors (multiplied by $\sqrt{n}$) associated with the r largest eigenvalues of $\mathbb{Z}_T\mathbb{Z}_T'/(Tq_T)$ (ranked in descending order), where $\mathbb{Z}_T = (Z_1, \ldots, Z_T)'$.

Step 2. Estimate the rotated coefficient functions by the local linear (LL) smoothing method. Let $X_t = \left[(HF_t)', Y_t'\right]'$ and $\beta_H(\cdot) = \left[\beta_1'(\cdot)H, \beta_2'(\cdot)\right]'$. Write the model (3.18) as follows:

$$y_{t+1} = X_t'\beta_H(u_t) + \varepsilon_{t+1}.$$

Assuming that the coefficient functions $\beta_H(u_t)$ have continuous second-order derivatives, one can estimate the preceding model with the LL smoothing method by using the estimated factors in Step 1. Let $\hat{X}_t = \left[\hat{F}_t', \hat{Y}_t'\right]'$, $\mathbb{Y}_T = (y_2, \ldots, y_T)'$,

$$\hat{\mathbb{X}}_T(u) = \begin{pmatrix} \hat{X}_1' & \hat{X}_1'(u_1 - u) \\ \vdots & \vdots \\ \hat{X}_n' & \hat{X}_n'(u_1 - u) \end{pmatrix}, \text{ and}$$

$$\mathbb{W}_T(u) = \mathtt{diag}\{K_b(u_1, u), \ldots, K_b(u_T, u)\},$$

where $K_b(u_i, u) \equiv K((u_i - u)/b)$, $K(\cdot)$ is a kernel function, and b is the bandwidth. The local linear estimate of $\beta_H(u)$ is given by

$$\hat{\beta}_H(u) = \left[I_{r+d_0}, 0_{(r+d_0)\times(r+d_0)}\right]\left[\hat{\mathbb{X}}_T'(u)\,\mathbb{W}_T(u)\hat{\mathbb{X}}_T(u)\right]^{-1} \times \hat{\mathbb{X}}_T'(u)\,\mathbb{W}_T(u)\mathbb{Y}_T, \tag{3.19}$$

where $u \in \mathcal{U}$ with $\mathcal{U}$ is the support of the index variable u_t.

Given the feasible LL estimate in (3.19), the one-step ahead prediction of y_{T+1} is given by

$$\hat{y}_{T+1|T} = \hat{\beta}_{H,T-1}(u_T)'\,\hat{X}_T, \tag{3.20}$$

where $\hat{\beta}_{H,T-1}$ is the LL estimate as in (3.19) that uses the sample (y_{t+1}, u_t, Z_t), $t = 1, \ldots, T$. Clearly, $\hat{y}_{T+1|T}$ in (3.20) is an estimate for

$$y_{T+1|T} = F_T'\beta_1(u_T) + Y_T'\beta_T(u_t) = X_T'\beta_H(u_T).$$

For a given $0 < \alpha < 1$, the $(1-\alpha)$ CI of $y_{T+1|T}$ can be defined by

$$\left[\hat{y}_{T+1|T} - c_{\alpha/2}\sqrt{\widehat{Var}(\hat{y}_{T+1|T})}, \hat{y}_{T+1|T} + c_{\alpha/2}\sqrt{\widehat{Var}(\hat{y}_{T+1|T})}\right],$$

where $c_{\alpha/2}$ is the upper $\alpha/2$-percentile of $\left(\hat{y}_{T+1|T} - y_{T+1|T}\right)/\sqrt{\widehat{Var}(\hat{y}_{T+1|T})}$, and $\widehat{Var}(\hat{y}_{T+1|T})$ is the estimate of the variance of $\hat{y}_{T+1|T}$. To construct the feasible CI, these quantities have to be estimated by using the asymptotic result (e.g., theorem 3 in Li et al. (2020)). However, due to the slow convergence rate caused by the nonparametric nature, such CI construction based on asymptotic theory usually does not perform well in finite samples. Li et al. (2020) propose the use of a wild bootstrap procedure to estimate $c_{\alpha/2}$ and $\widehat{Var}(\hat{y}_{T+1|T})$, and we then proceed to construct the prediction interval.

Under some regularity conditions on factor models, Li et al. (2020) establish the asymptotic properties of the proposed methods:

(i) $\sup_{u\in\mathcal{U}}\left\|\hat{\beta}_H(u) - \tilde{\beta}_H(u)\right\| = o_p\left((Tb)^{-1/2}\right)$, where $\tilde{\beta}_H(u)$ is the infeasible estimator that uses the true factors.

(ii) $\sqrt{Tb}D_T\left(\hat{\beta}_H(u) - \beta_H(u) - \frac{1}{2}\mu_2\beta_H^{(2)}(u)\,b^2\right) \xrightarrow{d} N\left(0_{r+d_0}, \Xi(u)\right)$, where $\mu_2 = \int u^2 K(u)\,du$.

(iii) Let $\Delta(u_T, X_T) \equiv \left[\hat{\beta}_{H,T-1}(u_T) - \beta_H(u_T)\right]' X_T$. For a fixed r,

$$\hat{y}_{T+1|T} - y_{T+1|T} = \Delta(u_T, X_T) - \varepsilon_{T+1} + o_p\left(1/(Tb)^{1/2}\right),$$

and conditional on $u_T = u^*$ and $X_T = X^*$,

$$\sqrt{Tb}\left[\Delta\left(u^*, X^*\right) - \frac{1}{2}\mu_2 b^2 X^{*\prime}\beta_H^{(2)}\left(u^*\right)\right] \xrightarrow{d} N\left(0, \Sigma^*\right);$$

where D_T, $\Xi(u)$, and Σ^* are well-defined matrices in Li et al. (2020). The result in (i) shows that the LL estimator and the nonlinear forecast that uses the estimated factor regressors are asymptotically equivalent to those that use the true latent factor regressors. Result (ii) gives the pointwise asymptotic distribution of the LL estimator of the functional coefficient, and result (iii) presents the limiting distribution of the feasible predictor. In practice, to implement the estimation and forecasting method, Li et al. (2020) use the forward selection criterion as a screening tool and adopt the BIC as the stopping rule to estimate d_0 and r.

3.4.2 Factor-Augmented Quantile Regressions

Since the seminal work by Koenker and Bassett Jr (1978), quantile regressions (QRs) have been widely used in empirical studies such as labor economics, macroeconomics, and risk management in finance, and their theoretical properties have been extensively investigated in the econometric and statistical literature. In a data-rich environment, the factor structure, as an efficient tool that summarizes the information in a large set of predictors or regressors, is incorporated into a QR. For example, Ando and Tsay (2011) study the estimation of factor-augmented conditional QR models and propose an information criterion based on the bias-corrected expected log-likelihood to select the estimated factors and observable predictors; Ohno and Ando (2018) adopt a factor-augmented quantile predictive regression system to predict the stock returns with the shrinkage method to select the useful predictors. Other recent developments include the model averaging approach to forecasting with factor-augmented quantile autoregressions in Phella (2020) and the quantile-based asset pricing model in Ando et al. (2019) and Belloni et al. (2023). In the literature of factor-augmented QR models, another strand of works treat the factors as unknown parameters to be estimated; see Ando and Bai (2020), Chen et al. (2021), and Ma et al. (2021). In this subsection, we focus on the developments of the factor-augmented approach to QRs.

Ando and Tsay (2011) consider the τth conditional quantile of y_t given X_t and W_t:

$$q_\tau(y_t|z_t;\gamma) = \alpha(\tau)' F_t + \beta(\tau)' W_t \equiv \gamma(\tau)' z_t, \tag{3.21}$$

where $\gamma(\tau) = (\alpha(\tau)', \beta(\tau)')'$ is a vector of the coefficients that depend on the quantile τ, and $z_t = (F_t', W_t')'$. If $\tau = 0.5$, then the model in (3.21) reduces to the conditional median regression, which is more robust to outliers than the usual conditional mean regression. In addition, the set of latent factors F_t also enters a panel data set

$$\underline{X}_t = \Lambda F_t + \varepsilon_t, t = 1, \ldots, T,$$

where $\underline{X}_t = (X_{1t}, \ldots, X_{Nt})'$ is an N-dimensional observable random vector.

The estimation procedure consists of two stages. In the first stage, common factors are estimated from the panel data set $\{X_t\}$ with PCA. In the second stage, the estimated factors are used in the standard quantile regression. Putting the estimated factors into the model yields

$$q_\tau(y_t|\hat{z}_t;\gamma) = \alpha(\tau)' \hat{F}_t + \beta(\tau)' W_t \equiv \gamma(\tau)' \hat{z}_t,$$

where $\hat{z}_t = (\hat{F}_t', W_t')'$, and $\hat{F}_t$ is the r-dimensional PC estimator for common factors F_t. The unknown parameters $\gamma(\tau)$ are estimated by maximizing the log-likelihood function:

$$l_\tau\left(\mathbf{y}_T; \gamma(\tau), \hat{Z}\right) = \frac{1}{T}\log\left[\tau(1-\tau)\exp\left\{-\sum_{t=1}^{T}\rho_\tau\left(y_t - \gamma(\tau)'\hat{z}_t\right)\right\}\right],$$

with $\rho_\tau(u) = u(\tau - \mathbf{1}(u < 0))$, $\mathbf{y}_T = (y_1, \ldots, y_T)'$, and $\hat{Z} = (\hat{z}_1, \ldots, \hat{z}_T)'$. The estimate $\hat{\gamma}(\tau)$ is obtained as a solution of $\partial l_\tau(\gamma)/\partial\gamma = 0$, which is a linear optimization problem. Koenker and Bassett Jr (1978) show that the solution is

$$\hat{\gamma}(\tau) = \hat{Z}^{-1}(h_\tau)\, y(h_\tau),$$

where h_τ is a p-element index subset from the set $\{1, 2, \ldots, T\}$, $\hat{Z}(h_\tau)$ refers to indexed rows in $\hat{Z}$, and $y(h_\tau)$ refers to the elements in y selected by h_τ. The asymptotic normality of $\hat{\gamma}(\tau)$ is established by Bai and Ng (2008). Under some mild conditions and $T^{5/8}/N \to 0$,

$$\sqrt{T}\left[\hat{\gamma}(\tau) - \gamma(\tau)\right] \xrightarrow{d} N(0, \Omega_\tau),$$

where Ω_τ is the positive asymptotic variance matrix; see lemma A.2 in Ando and Tsay (2011) for the detailed expression of Ω_τ.

By replacing the unknown parameter $\gamma(\tau)$ with $\hat{\gamma}(\tau)$, we obtain the estimated quantile regression model with factor-augmented predictors:

$$q_\tau\left(y_t|\hat{z}_t; \hat{\gamma}(\tau)\right) = \hat{\gamma}(\tau)' \hat{z}_t, t = 1, 2, \ldots, T.$$

The asymptotic properties of $q_\tau\left(y_t|\hat{z}_t;\hat{\gamma}(\tau)\right)$ can be analyzed similar to the term in (3.12). After estimating the model, the goodness of fit can be assessed from a predictive point of view. Let $\mathbf{u}_T = (u_1,\ldots,u_T)'$ be replicates of the dependent variable $\mathbf{y}_T$ drawn from $g(u)$, which is the target probability that generates the data. The goodness of fit for $q_\tau\left(y_t|\hat{z}_t;\hat{\gamma}\right)$ can be given by the *expected log-likelihood*

$$\eta_\tau\left(G,\hat{\gamma},\hat{Z}\right) = \int l_\tau\left(\mathbf{u}_T;\hat{\gamma}(\tau),\hat{Z}\right) dG(\mathbf{u}_T), \tag{3.22}$$

where $dG(\mathbf{u})$ is the Lebesgue measure with respect to the true probability density $g(u)$. The best candidate model should maximize the expected log-likelihood function in (3.22). In this sense, the optimal number of factors is defined as the value of r that maximizes the expected log-likelihood function.

Note that the true distribution $G(\mathbf{u})$ is unknown, which can be replaced by the empirical distribution $\hat{G}(\cdot)$. Thus, a natural estimator of the expected log-likelihood is the sample-based log-likelihood:

$$\begin{aligned}\eta_\tau\left(\hat{G},\hat{\gamma},\hat{Z}\right) &= \int l_\tau\left(\mathbf{y}_T;\hat{\gamma}(\tau),\hat{Z}\right) d\hat{G}(\mathbf{y}_T)\\ &= \log\left[\tau(1-\tau)\right] - \frac{1}{T}\sum_{t=1}^{T}\rho_\tau\left(y_t - \gamma(\tau)'\hat{z}_t\right).\end{aligned} \tag{3.23}$$

However, the estimate in (3.23) is positively biased because the same data are used in both the estimation of unknown parameters and the evaluation of the expected log-likelihood. The bias term is given by

$$b_\tau(G) = \int\left[\eta_\tau\left(\hat{G},\hat{\gamma},\hat{Z}\right) - \eta_\tau\left(G,\hat{\gamma},\hat{Z}\right)\right] dG(Y_T).$$

A consistent estimator $\hat{b}_\tau(G)$ is given by theorem 3.1 of Ando and Tsay (2011). Then, based on the bias-corrected estimator for the expected log-likelihood, a model selection criterion for evaluating the estimate is given by

$$IC = -2l_\tau\left(\mathbf{y}_T;\hat{\gamma}(\tau),\hat{Z}\right) + 2T\hat{b}_\tau(G). \tag{3.24}$$

Let $B_{NT} = \min\left[N, T^{3/2}\right]$. Ando and Tsay (2011) show that the IC in (3.24) is a consistent estimator of the expected log-likelihood with order $O_p\left(B_{NT}^{-1}\right)$ and then can asymptotically select the optimal number of factors that maximizes the expected log-likelihood.

Recently, Ohno and Ando (2018) have used the factor-augmented quantile predictive regression system to predict stock returns, where a shrinkage method is adopted to select the useful estimated factors and observed predictors. To be specific, they consider the following quantile predictive model:

$$q_\tau\left(y_{t+h}|z_t;\gamma\right) = \alpha(\tau)'F_t + \beta(\tau)'W_t \equiv \gamma(\tau)'z_t,$$

$$X_{it} = \lambda_i' F_t + \varepsilon_{it}, t = 1, \ldots, T, i = 1, \ldots, N.$$

A two-stage estimation procedure is considered. In the first stage, the factors are estimated with PCA from the observables X_{it}'s. In the second stage, the shrinkage method is combined with the usual quantile regression to select the predictors. The unknown parameters $\gamma(\tau)$ are estimated by using a shrinkage method, which is obtained by minimizing

$$\frac{1}{T}\sum_{t=1}^{T-h} \rho_\tau \left(y_{t+h} - \gamma(\tau)' \hat{z}_t\right) + p_\delta(\gamma(\tau)),$$

where $\rho_\tau(\cdot)$ is the check function, and $p_\delta(\cdot)$ is a penalty function of the coefficients indexed by a regularization parameter δ that controls the trade-off between the loss function and the penalty. They propose the use of a smoothly clipped absolute deviation (SCAD) penalty in Fan and Li (2001) $p_\delta(\gamma) = \sum_{k=1}^{p} p_{\kappa,\delta}(\gamma_k)$, where

$$p_{\delta,\kappa}(\gamma_k) = \begin{cases} \kappa\,|\gamma_k|, & \text{if } |\gamma_k| \le \kappa \\ \frac{\kappa\delta|\gamma_k| - 0.5(\gamma_k^2 + \kappa^2)}{\delta - 1}, & \text{if } \kappa < |\gamma_k| \le \kappa\delta \\ 0.5\kappa^2(\delta + 1), & \text{if } \kappa\delta < |\gamma_k| \end{cases}$$

for $\kappa > 0$ and $\delta > 2$. For the algorithm for QR with the SCAD penalty, see Wu and Liu (2009). Ohno and Ando (2018) establish the variable selection consistency and asymptotic normality of the estimator under some mild conditions. The regularization parameter is selected by using the prediction error because the aim is to predict the behavior of the stock market. The FAR quantile predictive model is applied to analyze the Tokyo Stock Exchange, and they show that macroeconomic variables play an important role in predicting the characteristics of the stock market of Japan even after controlling the various asset-pricing factors.

3.4.3 Time-Varying DI Forecasting Model

The standard DI forecasting model assumes *time-invariant* factor loadings and coefficients in the predictive regression model. However, considerable empirical evidence of parameter instability and time-varying effects has been found in the literature of macroeconomics and finance. Ignoring such instabilities in the diffusion model may lead to inconsistent estimators of the factors (Bates et al., 2013) or an inconsistent estimation of the coefficients (Clements and Hendry, 1996). Although the rolling window (RW) method is usually used to address the unstable parameters in empirical applications, the choice of windows is arbitrary or just based on past experience. As Rossi and Inoue (2012) and Inoue et al. (2017) point out, the forecasting performance of the RW scheme is sensitive to the choice of the window size since it balances the estimation efficiency and the misspecification bias.

To accommodate the time-varying factor loadings and time-varying regression coefficients, Wei and Zhang (2020) propose a general time-varying DI forecasting model. Given N observable predictors $\underline{X}_t = (X_{1t}, \cdots, X_{Nt})'$ and a target variable y_t, they consider forecasting $y_{T+\ell}$ for some integer $\ell > 0$ given the information set up according to the Tth period. Assume that X_{it} has a static factor representation with time-varying factor loadings as Su and Wang (2017):

$$X_{it} = \lambda_{it}' F_t + e_{it},\ i = 1, \ldots, N, t = 1, \ldots, T, \tag{3.25}$$

where F_t is an $r \times 1$ vector of the latent factors, $\lambda_{it} \equiv \lambda_i(t/T)$ are the time-varying factor loadings, with $\lambda_i(\cdot) : [0, 1] \to \mathbb{R}^r$ being a vector of unknown piecewise smooth functions, and e_{it} being the idiosyncratic error. Meanwhile, the target variable to be predicted is also driven by the same set of common factors and some other observables:

$$y_{t+\ell} = \alpha_t' F_t + \beta_t' W_t + \varepsilon_{t+\ell}, \tag{3.26}$$

where W_t is a $p \times 1$ vector of the observed variables including the constant, the lags of y_t or time trends, $\alpha_t \equiv \alpha(t/T)$ and $\beta_t \equiv \beta(t/T)$ are the TVCs for predictors F_t and W_t, respectively, with $\alpha(\cdot)$ and $\beta(\cdot)$ being unknown smooth functions on [0, 1], and $\varepsilon_{t+\ell}$ is the error term. The models (3.25) and (3.26) are termed the time-varying diffusion index (TVDI) forecasting models. If F_t is observable and the conditional mean of $\varepsilon_{t+\ell}$ is zero given the past information, then the (mean-squared) optimal prediction of $y_{T+\ell}$ is given by

$$y_{T+\ell|T} = E(Y_{T+\ell}|F_T, W_T, F_{T-1}, W_{T-1}, \cdots) = \alpha'(1)F_T + \beta'(1)W_T.$$

Here, factors F_T and TVCs $\alpha(1)$ and $\beta(1)$ are all unknown. To address this issue, it is tempting to follow the road map of Bai and Ng (2006) to estimate F_t's first from the large number of observed predictors and then use them as generated regressors to estimate $\alpha(1)$ and $\beta(1)$ nonparametrically in (3.26). The two-step procedure to construct the time-varying DI forecast is as follows:

Step 1. Apply the local principal component analysis (LPCA) in Su and Wang (2017) to estimate the locally weighted factors from a large number of predictors. Let $K_h(\cdot) \equiv h^{-1}K(\cdot/h)$ and $K_{h,tr} \equiv K_h(\tau_t - \tau_r)$, where $\tau_s \equiv s/T$ for $1 \leq s \leq T$, and $h \to 0$ is the bandwidth as $(N, T) \to \infty$. At the Tth period, estimate $\{\lambda_{iT}\}_{r=1}^{T}$ and $\{F_t\}_{t=1}^{T}$ by minimizing the following kernel-weighted least squares objective function:

$$\min_{\{\lambda_{iT}\}_{i=1}^{N}, \{F_t\}_{t=1}^{T}} \frac{1}{NT} \sum_{i=1}^{N} \sum_{t=1}^{T} \left(X_{it} - \lambda_{iT}' F_t\right)^2 K_{h,tT}$$

$$\Leftrightarrow \min_{\Lambda_T, F^{(T)}} \sum_{i=1}^{N} \sum_{t=1}^{T} (X_{it}^{(T)} - \lambda_{iT}' F_t^{(T)})^2$$
$$= \text{tr}[(X^{(T)} - F^{(T)}\Lambda_T')(X^{(T)} - F^{(T)}\Lambda_T')'], \tag{3.27}$$

where $X_{it}^{(T)} \equiv X_{it}K_{h,tT}^{1/2}$, $X_i^{(T)} \equiv (X_{i1}^{(T)}, \cdots, X_{iN}^{(T)})'$, $X^{(T)} \equiv (X_1^{(T)}, \cdots, X_N^{(T)})$, $F_t^{(T)} \equiv F_t K_{h,tT}^{1/2}$, $F^{(T)} \equiv (F_1^{(T)}, \cdots, F_T^{(T)})'$, and $\Lambda_T \equiv (\lambda_{1T}, \cdots, \lambda_{NT})'$. To identify $F^{(T)}$ and Λ_T in (3.27), the usual restrictions for PCA are used: $F^{(T)\prime}F^{(T)}/T = I_r$ and $\Lambda_T'\Lambda_T$ is a diagonal matrix, where I_r is the $r \times r$ identity matrix. After concentrating out Λ_T, we can estimate $F^{(T)}$ by

$$\hat{F}^{(T)} = \arg\max_{F^{(T)}} \text{tr}\left[F^{(T)\prime}X^{(T)}X^{(T)\prime}F^{(T)}\right] \tag{3.28}$$

subject to $F^{(T)\prime}F^{(T)}/T = I_r$. The estimator $\hat{F}^{(T)} = (\hat{F}_1^{(T)}, \cdots, \hat{F}_T^{(T)})'$ is $\sqrt{T}$ times the eigenvectors that correspond to the r largest eigenvalues of the matrix $X^{(T)}X^{(T)\prime}$, arranged in descending order, and $\hat{\Lambda}_T = X^{(T)\prime}\hat{F}^{(T)}(\hat{F}^{(T)\prime}\hat{F}^{(T)})^{-1} = X^{(T)\prime}\hat{F}^{(T)}/T$. To mitigate the boundary bias problem since T is at the right boundary, a boundary-corrected kernel function should be used.

Step 2. Augment the forecasting regression with the estimated factors in (3.28) to estimate the TVCs with the kernel method. Because t is near T, transform (3.26) as follows:

$$\begin{aligned} y_{t+\ell} &= \alpha'(\tau_t)[H^{(T)\prime}]^{-1} \times K_{h,tT}^{-1/2} H^{(T)\prime} F_t^{(T)} + \beta'(\tau_t)W_t + \varepsilon_{t+\ell} \\ &\equiv \gamma^{(T)}(\tau_t)'D_t^{(T)} + \beta'(\tau_t)W_t + \varepsilon_{t+\ell} \\ &= \gamma^{(T)}(\tau_t)'\hat{D}_t^{(T)} + \beta'(\tau_t)W_t + \varepsilon_{t+\ell}^* \\ &= \delta^{(T)\prime}(\tau_t)\hat{G}_t^{(T)} + \varepsilon_{t+\ell}^* \end{aligned}$$

where $\gamma^{(T)}(\tau_t)' \equiv \alpha'(\tau_t)[H^{(T)\prime}]^{-1}$, $D_t^{(T)} \equiv K_{h,tT}^{-1/2} H^{(T)\prime} F_t^{(T)}$, $\hat{D}_t^{(T)} \equiv K_{h,tT}^{-1/2}\hat{F}_t^{(T)}$, $\delta^{(T)}(\tau_t) = \left(\gamma^{(T)}(\tau_t)', \beta(\tau_t)'\right)'$ and $\hat{G}_t^{(T)} = \left(\hat{D}_t^{(T)}, W_t\right)$. In the third equation, the unobservable composite regressors $D_t^{(T)}$ are replaced by their consistent estimators $\hat{D}_t^{(T)} \equiv K_{h,tT}^{-1/2}\hat{F}_t^{(T)}$, which come from the local PCA in Step 1. Note that $\delta^{(T)}(\tau_t)$ are the TVCs. A feasible forecast is proposed by combining the estimated factors and the nonparametric estimators of the coefficients. The proposed feasible forecast for $Y_{T+\ell}$ follows as

$$\hat{y}_{T+\ell|T} = \hat{\delta}^{(T)\prime}(1)\hat{G}_T^{(T)},$$

where $\hat{\delta}^{(T)\prime}(1) = \left(\sum_{t=1}^{T-\ell} \hat{G}_t^{(T)} \hat{G}_t^{(T)\prime} K_{h^*,Tt}\right)^{-1} \sum_{t=1}^{T-\ell} \hat{G}_t^{(T)} y_{t+\ell} K_{h^*,Tt}$ is the local constant estimator of $\delta^{(T)}(1)$, with h^* being the bandwidth parameter.

For the model in (3.25) and (3.26) without W_t, Corradi and Swanson (2014) are concerned with testing the following hypotheses:

$$\mathbb{H}_0 : \Lambda_t = (\lambda_{1t}, \ldots, \lambda_{Nt}) = \Lambda_0 \text{ and } \alpha_t = \alpha_0 \text{ for all } t,$$

versus

$$\mathbb{H}_1 : \Lambda_t = \begin{cases} \Lambda_{0,1} & \text{for } t/T \leq \tau_\lambda^{(1)} \\ \Lambda_{0,2} & \text{for } \tau_\lambda^{(1)} + 1 \leq t/T \leq \tau_\lambda^{(2)} \\ \vdots & \\ \Lambda_{0,q_\lambda+1} & \text{for } \tau_\lambda^{(q_\lambda)} + 1 \leq t/T \leq 1 \end{cases} \quad \text{and/or}$$

$$\alpha_t = \begin{cases} \alpha_{0,1} & \text{for } t/T \leq \tau_\alpha^{(1)} \\ \alpha_{0,2} & \text{for } \tau_\alpha^{(1)} + 1 \leq t/T \leq \tau_\alpha^{(2)} \\ \vdots & \\ \alpha_{0,q_\alpha+1} & \text{for } \tau_\alpha^{(q_\alpha)} + 1 \leq t/T \leq 1 \end{cases}$$

where the factor loadings Λ_t and slopes α_t are time-invariant under the null hypothesis and may have shifted under the alternative hypothesis. To construct the test, they proceed in three steps. First, the IC of Bai and Ng (2002) is used to determine the number of breaks by using the full sample. Second, the factors are estimated by again using the full sample. The PC estimator is denoted as $\hat{G}_T$. Third, an estimator of the sample covariance between $y_{t+\ell}$ and the estimated factors is constructed by using both the full sample and rolling windows of observations. The difference between the full sample and the rolling estimators of the covariance between $y_{t+\ell}$ and the estimated factors is the key ingredient of their statistic. For $\ell = 1$, the testing statistic is constructed as follows:

$$Z_{P,R} = \sqrt{P}\left[\frac{1}{T}\sum_{t=2}^{T} \hat{G}_{t-1} y_t - \frac{1}{P}\sum_{t=R+1}^{T}\left(\frac{1}{R}\sum_{j=t-1+R}^{t} \hat{G}_{j-1} y_t\right)\right],$$

where R is the window for the rolling estimator, and $P = T - R$. The statistic is more in the spirit of a Hausman-type test than tests for structural stability. Indeed, they compare two estimators that converge to the same probability limit under the null hypothesis but to different probability limits under the alternative hypotheses. Furthermore, under the null hypothesis, the full sample estimator is more efficient. Under some conditions, such as $\sqrt{T}/N \to 0$ and $P/R \to \pi > 0$, then under $\mathbb{H}_0$,

$$Z_{P,R} \xrightarrow{d} N(0, \Omega_0)$$

for some positive matrix Ω_0, and

$$\lim_{P\to\infty} \Pr\left(P^{-1/2}\left\|Z_{P,R}\right\| \geq \varepsilon\right) = 1.$$

To implement the test, they propose using the quadratic form $Z'_{P,R}\hat{\Omega}_T^{-1}Z_{P,R}$, where $\hat{\Omega}_T$ is a consistent estimator for Ω_0. Clearly, $Z'_{P,R}\hat{\Omega}_T^{-1}Z_{P,R} \to_d \chi_r^2$ under $\mathbb{H}_0$ and $\Pr\left(P^{-1}Z'_{P,R}\hat{\Omega}_T^{-1}Z_{P,R} \geq \varepsilon\right) \to 1$ under $\mathbb{H}_1$ for any $\varepsilon > 0$.

3.4.4 FAR Models with Structural Breaks or Threshold Effects

Massacci (2019) considers an unstable diffusion index model as follows:

$$\underline{X}_t = 1\,(t/T \leq \pi_x)\,\Lambda_1 F_t + 1\,(t/T > \pi_x)\,\Lambda_2 F_t + e_t, \tag{3.29}$$

$$\begin{aligned} y_{t+h} &= 1\left(t/T \leq \pi_y\right)\left(\gamma_1' F_t + \beta_1' W_t\right) \\ &\quad + 1\left(t/T > \pi_y\right)\left(\gamma_2' F_t + \beta_2' W_t\right) + \varepsilon_{t+h}, \end{aligned} \tag{3.30}$$

where $t = 1, \ldots, T$, $\underline{X}_t = (X_{1t}, \cdots, X_{Nt})'$, F_t is a $k \times 1$ vector of factors, $\Lambda_l = \left(\Lambda'_{l1}, \cdots \Lambda'_{lN}\right)'$ is a $N \times k$ matrix of factor loadings, $l = 1, 2$, γ_1 and γ_2 are $k \times 1$ vectors of the coefficients for factor F_t, β_1, β_2 are $p \times 1$ vectors of the coefficients for W_t in the predictive model, and $h \geq 0$. Obviously, there are structural changes in the factor model of X_{it} and the predictive regression model of y_{t+h}.

For the breakpoint factor model in (3.29), for a given number R of factors, the joint objective function to be minimized is

$$S\left(\Lambda^R, F^R, \pi_x\right) = \frac{1}{NT}\sum_{t=1}^{T}\left\{\left\|\underline{X}_t - 1_{1t}\,(\pi_x)\,\Lambda_1^R F_t^R - 1_{2t}\,(\pi_x)\,\Lambda_2^R F_t^R\right\|^2\right\},$$

where $1_{1t}\,(\pi_x) = 1\,(t/T \leq \pi_x)$, $1_{2t}(\pi_x) = 1(t/T > \pi_x)$. $\Lambda^R = \left(\Lambda_1^R, \Lambda_2^R\right)$, and $F^R = \left(F_1^R, \ldots, F_T^R\right)$. For the preceding optimization problem, for a given π_x, the PCA method is used to estimate the factors and factor loadings, and π_x is estimated with the concentrated least squares method. See Massacci (2017) for the estimation of threshold factor models. Once the factors and breakpoints are estimated, we can estimate the model (3.30) by minimizing the following feasible objective function:

$$\begin{aligned} L\left(\theta, \pi_y\right) = T^{-1}\sum_{t=1}^{T-h}\Big[y_{t+h} &- 1_{1t}\left(\pi_y\right)\left(\gamma_1'\hat{F}_t + \beta_1' W_t\right) \\ &- 1_{2t}\left(\pi_y\right)\left(\gamma_2'\hat{F}_t + \beta_2' W_t\right)\Big]^2, \end{aligned}$$

where $\theta = \left(\gamma_1', \gamma_2', \beta_1', \beta_2'\right)'$. As the usual threshold model, we can obtain the estimators $\hat{\theta}$ and $\hat{\pi}_y$ for the unknown coefficients and breakpoint, respectively.

The consistency of the estimator $\hat{\pi}_y$ of π and the limiting distribution for the estimated coefficients are established under some mild conditions. A test for structural change in (3.30) is also provided by Massacci (2019).

Other recent developments include Wang et al. (2015), where a structural break in the coefficient of W_t is studied, and Yan and Cheng (2022) for factor-augmented forecasting regressions with a threshold effect in the coefficient of F_t in (3.30), where the threshold effect is caused by some common random variables.

3.5 FAR with Panel Data

In this section, we review the development of factor augmented panel regression models.

A prototypical panel data regression model with a factor error structure is given by

$$y_{it} = \beta' X_{it} + u_{it}, \tag{3.31}$$

$$u_{it} = \lambda_i^{u\prime} F_t^u + \varepsilon_{it}, \tag{3.32}$$

with $i = 1, \ldots, N$, $t = 1, \ldots, T$, where X_{it} is a $p \times 1$ vector of the explanatory variables, F_t^u is an r-vector of the latent common factors in the composite error u_{it}, λ_i^u is a $r \times 1$ vector of factor loadings, and ε_{it} is the idiosyncratic error. The regressor X_{it} is allowed to be correlated with common component $\lambda_i^{u\prime} F_t^u$. This correlation causes the endogeneity bias issue when the least squares (LS) or least-squares dummy variables (LSDV) methods are adopted to estimate the unknown parameters β.

In the literature, several methods have been proposed to estimate unknown parameters in the panel data models with multifactor structural errors. For example, Ahn et al. (2013) estimate the model based on moment restrictions on the error terms, and Bai (2009) considers the joint estimation of the β, factor space $\{F_1^u, \ldots, F_T^u\}$, and factor loadings $\{\lambda_1^u, \ldots, \lambda_N^u\}$ by using the iterated PCA method. Alternatively, one may augment the panel regression directly with the estimated factors or their proxies from the observable data X_{it}'s or (y_{it}, X_{it})'s. For example, Pesaran (2006) proposes the common correlated effects (CCE) estimators that use the cross-sectional averages of $\left(y_{it}, X_{it}'\right)'$ as the proxies of the unobservable factors. However, the consistency of CCE relies on the rank condition, which is usually difficult to verify in practice. In contrast, Kapetanios and Pesaran (2007) and Greenaway-McGrevy et al. (2012) estimate the latent factors from the observables by using the PCA method, which avoids the rank condition in CCE. For a comprehensive comparison between the CCE and PC approaches, see Westerlund and Urbain (2015) and Reese and Westerlund (2018). For some empirical applications of factor-augmented panel regressions, see Giannone et al. (2010) for the study of the international saving-investment relationship with the global factor being extracted from the observables and

Kapetanios and Pesaran (2007) for modeling asset returns. Now, write the model (3.31)–(3.32) in vector form:

$$y_i = X_i\beta + F^u\lambda_i^u + \varepsilon_i \tag{3.33}$$

where $y_i = (y_{i1}, \ldots, y_{iT})'$, $X_i = (X_{i1}, \ldots, X_{iT})'$, $F^u = \left(F_1^u, \ldots, F_T^u\right)'$, and $\varepsilon_i = (\varepsilon_{i1}, \ldots, \varepsilon_{iT})'$. The correlation between X_{it} and the common component $\lambda_i^{u\prime}F_t^u$ is modeled through a latent factor structure in X_{it}, namely,

$$X_{it} = F_t^{X\prime}\lambda_i^X + V_{it}, \tag{3.34}$$

where F_t^X is a vector of the latent factors underlying X_{it}, λ_i^X is the corresponding vector of factor loadings, and $F_t^{X\prime}\lambda_i^X$ can be correlated with $F_t^{u\prime}\lambda_i^u$. In matrix form, (3.34) can be written as $X_i = F^X\lambda_i^X + V_i$, where $F^X = \left(F_1^X, \ldots, F_T^X\right)'$, and $V_i = (V_{i1}, \ldots, V_{iT})'$. Let $F^y = \left(F_1^y, \ldots, F_T^y\right)'$ denote the common factors in y_i and λ_i^y denote the associated factor loadings. Define F to be the $T \times m$ matrix that consists of a subset of the columns of F^X and F^y such that $T^{-1}F'F$ is nonsingular, and

$$F^X = FA^X \text{ and } F^y = FA^y$$

for some selection matrices A^X and A^y. That is, F contains all unique columns in F^X and F^y. When X_i and y_i share the same factor, it is included only once as a column in F. Then,

$$F^u\lambda_i^u = F^y\lambda_i^y - F^X\lambda_i^X\beta = F\left(A^y\lambda_i^y - A^X\lambda_i^X\beta\right) \equiv F\left(\lambda_{y,i} - \lambda_{X,i}\beta\right) \equiv F\lambda_{u,i}.$$

Replacing F^u with the full set of factors F, we can write the model (3.33) as

$$y_i = X_i\beta + F\lambda_{u,i} + \varepsilon_i,$$

with $\lambda_{u,i}$ satisfying $F\lambda_{u,i} = F^u\lambda_i^u$. Then, an infeasible ordinary factor-augmented estimator is given by

$$\hat{b}_{I,FAE} = \left(\sum_{i=1}^N X_i'M_F X_i\right)^{-1} \sum_{i=1}^N X_i'M_F y_i,$$

where $M_F = I_T - F\left(F'F\right)^{-1}F'$. When F is replaced with a PC estimate $\hat{F}$ from the observables $\{(y_{it}, X_{it}), i = 1, \ldots, N, t = 1, \ldots, T\}$, a feasible estimator is given by

$$\begin{aligned}\hat{b}_{FAE} &= \left(\sum_{i=1}^N X_i'M_{\hat{F}} X_i\right)^{-1} \sum_{i=1}^N X_i'M_{\hat{F}} y_i \\ &= \beta + \left(\sum_{i=1}^N X_i'M_{\hat{F}} X_i\right)^{-1} \sum_{i=1}^N X_i'M_{\hat{F}}\varepsilon_i + \left(\sum_{i=1}^N X_i'M_{\hat{F}} X_i\right)^{-1} \sum_{i=1}^N X_i'M_{\hat{F}} F\lambda_{u,i},\end{aligned}$$

where $M_{\hat{F}} = I_T - \hat{F}\left(\hat{F}'\hat{F}\right)^{-1}\hat{F}'$. The properties of $\hat{b}_{FAE}$ depend heavily on the last term. In particular, consistency requires that $(NT)^{-1}\sum_{i=1}^{N}\sum_{i=1}^{N}X_i'M_{\hat{F}}X_i(\varepsilon_i + F\lambda_{u,i}) \rightarrow_p 0$, while to make $\hat{b}_{FAE}$ have an unbiased limiting distribution, we require $(NT)^{-1/2}\sum_{i=1}^{N}\sum_{i=1}^{N}X_i'M_{\hat{F}}X_i(\varepsilon_i+F\lambda_{u,i})$ to be centered at zero. The consistency of $\hat{b}_{FAE}$ is established for the general estimated factors that are not limited to the PC estimator. Given that $T^{-1}\left\|\hat{F} - FH\right\|^2 = o_p(1)$ for some nonsingular matrix H, as $(N, T) \rightarrow \infty$,

$$\hat{b}_{FAE} \xrightarrow{p} \beta.$$

This result shows that the consistency of a standard FAE requires only the consistency of the associated factor estimator, given the PC estimator $\hat{F}$ in the sense that

$$T^{-1}\left\|\hat{F} - FH\right\|^2 = O_p(\delta_{NT}^{-2}),$$

with $\delta_{NT} = \min[\sqrt{N}, \sqrt{T}]$ and for some asymptotic nonsingular H. Denote the $\hat{b}_{FAE}$ by using PCs as $\hat{b}_{PCA}$. With the above convergence rate for the PC estimators, when $T/N \rightarrow 0$, $N/T^3 \rightarrow 0$, then

$$\sqrt{NT}\left(\hat{b}_{PCA} - \hat{b}_{I,FAE}\right) = o_p(1).$$

The preceding result suggests that if N is large compared to T and if T is not too small, then the asymptotic distribution of the PCA is equivalent to that of its infeasible counterpart. Under the requirement on (N, T),

$$\sqrt{NT}\left(\hat{b}_{PCA} - \hat{b}_{I,FAE}\right) \rightarrow_d N(0, \Xi),$$

where $\Xi = \Sigma_V^{-1}\Omega_0\Sigma_V^{-1}$ with $\Omega_0 = \text{plim}_{N,T\rightarrow\infty}\frac{1}{NT}\sum_{i=1}^{N}X_i'M_F\varepsilon_i\varepsilon_i'M_FX_i$ and $\Sigma_V = \text{plim}_{N,T\rightarrow\infty}\frac{1}{NT}\sum_{i=1}^{N}X_i'M_FX_i$. However, if $T > N$, then the asymptotic distribution of $\sqrt{NT}\left(\hat{b}_{PCA} - \beta\right)$ is biased. If $N/T \rightarrow \in (0, \infty)$, then the asymptotic distribution of $\hat{b}_{PCA}$ is biased. A bias correction as proposed in Bai (2009) should be used to carry out a valid statistical inference.

Finally, we mention the factor-augmented panel regression model where the factors may have mixed factor strength. Despite the generated regressor problem caused by the use of estimated rather than known factors, the PC estimators of β are still $\sqrt{NT}$-consistent and asymptotically normal. This requires strong factors. However, in practice, some factors are only weakly influential; see Chudik et al. (2011) and Chudik and Pesaran (2015b) for some motivating examples. Bai and Ng (2008) and Boivin and Ng (2006) find that PC factors can be severely impaired when the factors are not strong. Chudik et al. (2011) investigate the implications of weak, semi-weak, and semi-strong factors on the

CCE estimator and find that the CCE estimator performs better and has fewer size distortions than the iterated PC approach of Bai (2009). The findings are because the presence of weak or semi-strong factors leads to inconsistent PC estimates of the (rotated) factors but does not affect the CCE estimator since its aim is to address the endogeneity that arises from error cross-section dependence. In addition, Onatski (2012) studies the case when some of the included factors are semi-strong within the context of a PC estimation of a pure common factor model and finds that the presence of such factors causes the PC estimator to be inconsistent.

Recently, Reese and Westerlund (2018) offer an analysis of the effect of weak, semi-weak, and semi-strong factors on two of the most popular estimators for FARs, namely, PC and CCE. As a comparison, we present the main findings for two popular estimators that may facilitate the choice of estimators in applications. They set factor loadings that go to zero at the rate of N^{-a} to capture the different weaknesses of the factor, where $a \in [0, 1]$ and N are related to T via $T = N^k$. Under the standard assumption of homogeneous slopes, the main findings are summarized as follows.

(i) To ensure $\sqrt{NT}$-consistency and to alimit normal distributions, both estimators require strong or semi-strong factors ($a < 1/2$). The requirement on k generally differs between the estimators. However, both sets shrink toward 1 as the factors become weaker ($a \to 0$).

(ii) Unless $k < 1$, both estimators are asymptotically biased.

(iii) Both estimators can be consistent when the factors are semi-weak ($a < 1$), but only PC allows for a consistent estimation in the weak factor case ($a = 1$) with additional requirements on k. CCE has binding restrictions on k only for semi-weak factors. By contrast, PC restricts k from below for semi-strong factors and requires that $k > 3$ when the factors are weak, which is restrictive.

3.6 Two Applications of FAR in Finance

FAR has been widely used in finance. In this section, we present two typical applications of FAR to financial markets: Ludvigson and Ng (2009) use the FAR to study the bond risk premia, and Qiu et al. (2022) use a factor-augmented HAR model to forecast the realized volatility (RV).

3.6.1 Ludvigson and Ng's (2009) Factor Models for Bond Risk Premia

Ludvigson and Ng (2009) use the methodology of a dynamic factor analysis for large data sets to study the possible linkages between forecastable variation in excess bond returns and macroeconomic fundamentals. They consider the following model for excess bond returns:

$$rx_{t+1}^{(n)} = \beta' Z_t + \gamma' \underline{X}_t + \varepsilon_{t+1},$$

where $rx_{t+1}^{(n)}$ is the continuously compounded (log) excess return on an n-year discount bond in period $t+1$, Z_t is a set of K predetermined conditioning variables at time t and may include the individual forward rates, the single forward factor, or other predictors based on a few macroeconomic series, $\underline{X}_t = (X_{1t}, \ldots, X_{Nt})'$ is a $N \times 1$ vector of macroeconomic fundamentals, and N is large and possibly larger than the number of time periods (T). To handle the large dimension of the regressors, they assume that X_{it} has a factor structure:

$$X_{it} = \lambda_i' f_t + e_{it},$$

where f_t is an $r \times 1$ vector of latent common factors, λ_i is the corresponding $r \times 1$ vector of factor loadings, and e_{it} is a vector of idiosyncratic errors. One prominent feature for the factor structure of X_{it} is $r << N$, so that substantial dimension reduction can be achieved by considering the regression

$$rx_{t+1}^{(n)} = \alpha' F_t + \beta' Z_t + \varepsilon_t,$$

where $F_t \subset f_t$ because the factors that are pervasive for the panel of data X_{it} need not be important for predicting $rx_{t+1}^{(n)}$.

The common factors f_t are estimated by $\hat{f}_t$ with PCA. To determine the composition of $\hat{F}_t$, form different subsets of $\hat{f}_t$ and/or functions of $\hat{f}_t$ (such as $\hat{f}_{1t}^2$), run regression of $rx_{t+1}^{(n)}$ on $\hat{F}_t$ and Z_t, and evaluate the corresponding Bayesian information criterion (BIC) and $\bar{R}^2$. Following Stock and Watson (2002b), minimizing the BIC yields the preferred set of factors $\hat{F}_t$.

The preceding method is used to study the predictability of excess returns on US government bonds. The empirical results show that there is a strong predictable variation in excess bond returns that is associated with macroeconomic activity. The predictive power of the estimated factors is not only statistically significant but also economically important, with factors explaining between 21 percent and 26 percent of one-year-ahead excess bond returns. The selected factors also exhibit stable and strongly statistically significant out-of-sample forecasting power for future returns. In addition, risk premia are found to be substantially higher in recessions when the macroeconomic factors are added to the information already contained in current bond market data.

3.6.2 Qiu et al.'s (2022) Panel HAR Model to Forecast Volatility

Qiu et al. (2022) propose a heterogeneous autoregressive panel (HARP) model with error cross-sectional dependence to control for possibly unobserved common effects in volatility across a class of assets. Let y_{it} be the RV of the ith individual asset at time t. Consider the h-period direct forecasting panel data model for y_{it}:

$$y_{i,t+h} = \alpha_i' d_t + \sum_{l \in \mathcal{L}} \phi_i^{(l)} \bar{y}_{it}^{(l)} + \beta_i' X_{it} + u_{i,t+h}, \tag{3.35}$$

with $i = 1, \ldots, N$, $t = 1, \ldots, T$, where $\bar{y}_{it}^{(l)} = l^{-1} \sum_{s=0}^{l} y_{i,t-l}$, d_t is a vector of the observed common effects that may include the constant, the deterministic trends or seasonal dummies, X_{it} is a $k \times 1$ vector of regressors specific to cross-sectional unit i at time t, and α_i and β_i are parameter vectors specific for the h-period forecasting model. Note that the HAR component $\bar{y}_{it}^{(l)}$ is the average of previous l periods of y_{it}, and $\phi_i^{(l)}$ is the corresponding coefficient. $\mathcal{L}$ is the set of lag index vectors of l. Furthermore, assume that the error term, u_{it}, comprises m unobserved common factors:

$$u_{it} = \lambda_i' F_t + \varepsilon_{it}, \tag{3.36}$$

where F_t is the $m \times 1$ vector of the unobserved common factors, λ_i is the $m \times 1$ vector of the factor loadings, and ε_{it} are the idiosyncratic errors. With the factor structure error, the RV of individual stocks is correlated beyond what can be explained by the observed determinants. Finally, F_t can be modeled by a VAR or by a more general relationship:

$$F_{t+h} = \Phi F_t + \zeta_{t+h}. \tag{3.37}$$

Given the model setup in (3.35)–(3.37), they are interested in forecasting y_{T+h} at the Tth period. Plugging (3.36) into (3.35) leads to

$$y_{i,t+h} = \alpha_i' d_t + \sum_{l \in \mathcal{L}} \phi_i^{(l)} \bar{y}_{it}^{(l)} + \beta_i' X_{it} + \lambda_i' F_{t+h} + \varepsilon_{i,t+h}$$

and the optimal forecast for $y_{i,T+h}$ is given by

$$y_{i,T+h|T} = \alpha_i' d_T + \sum_{l \in \mathcal{L}} \phi_i^{(l)} \bar{y}_{iT}^{(l)} + \beta_i' X_{iT} + \lambda_i' F_{T+h|T}.$$

Clearly, an estimator for $y_{i,T+h|T}$ can be constructed as

$$\hat{y}_{i,T+h|T} = \hat{\alpha}_i' d_T + \sum_{l \in \mathcal{L}} \hat{\phi}_i^{(l)} \bar{y}_{iT}^{(l)} + \hat{\beta}_i' X_{iT} + \hat{\lambda}_i' \hat{F}_{T+h|T},$$

where each estimated quantity is obtained as follows:

(i) Obtain $\hat{\alpha}_i$, $\hat{\phi}_i^{(l)}$'s, and $\hat{\beta}_i$ based on the dynamic CCE in Chudik and Pesaran (2015a).

(ii) Given the CCE estimators, define

$$\hat{u}_{it} = y_{it} - \hat{\alpha}_i' d_{t-h} + \sum_{l \in \mathcal{L}} \hat{\phi}_i^{(l)} \bar{y}_{i,t-h}^{(l)} + \hat{\beta}_i' X_{i,t-h}, t = h+1, \ldots T,$$

which has an approximate factor structure. By applying the PCA method to $\{\hat{u}_{it}\}$ to obtain the estimators, $\hat{\lambda}_i$ for $i = 1, \ldots, N$, and $\hat{F}_t$ for $t = h+1, \ldots, T$.

(iii) Based on $\left\{\hat{F}_t\right\}_{t=h+1}^{T}$, obtain the usual least-squares estimate $\hat{\Phi}$ for Φ and the estimate for $F_{T+h|T}$:

$$\hat{F}_{T+h|T} = \hat{\Phi} \hat{F}_T.$$

They use the model in (3.35)–(3.37), to study the linkage among the realized volatilities of component stocks and find that the linkage is important to forecast the relevant index volatility. Empirical studies show that the RV models that exploit the linkage effects lead to significantly better out-of-sample forecast performance, for example, an up to 32 percent increase in the pseudo R^2.

3.7 Concluding Remarks

In this chapter, we give a selective review of FARs and their applications to financial markets. For the estimation of factor models, we focus on the PCA method. We emphasize that many important topics are not covered in the chapter since too many breakthrough methodologies and applications have been developed for factor models in the literature. For example, the factor structure is used in the multiple testing, model selection, and robust estimation of high-dimensional models to control the correlation among regressors or errors. More importantly, many learning theories and methods on the low-rank structure of high-dimensional models have refreshed the modern understanding of econometric modeling in the last ten years. The low-rank structure is one of the key features of factor models. It provides a new perspective and opportunities to study factor models and leads to many new discoveries and understanding. For a more comprehensive account on this topic, see chapters 9–11 of Fan et al. (2020).

Bibliography

Ahn, S. C. and A. R. Horenstein (2013). Eigenvalue ratio test for the number of factors. *Econometrica 81*(3), 1203–1227.

Ahn, S. C., Y. H. Lee, and P. Schmidt (2013). Panel data models with multiple time-varying individual effects. *Journal of Econometrics 174*(1), 1–14.

Alessi, L., M. Barigozzi, and M. Capasso (2010). Improved penalization for determining the number of factors in approximate factor models. *Statistics & Probability Letters 80*(23–24), 1806–1813.

Ando, T. and J. Bai (2020). Quantile co-movement in financial markets: A panel quantile model with unobserved heterogeneity. *Journal of the American Statistical Association 115*(529), 266–279.

Ando, T., J. Bai, M. Nishimura, and J. Yu (2019). A quantile-based asset pricing model. Working paper.

Ando, T. and R. S. Tsay (2011). Quantile regression models with factor-augmented predictors and information criterion. *The Econometrics Journal 14*(1), 1–24.

Ando, T. and R. S. Tsay (2014). A predictive approach for selection of diffusion index models. *Econometric Reviews 33*(1–4), 68–99.

Bai, J. (2003). Inferential theory for factor models of large dimensions. *Econometrica 71*(1), 135–171.

Bai, J. (2009). Panel data models with interactive fixed effects. *Econometrica 77*(4), 1229–1279.

Bai, J., K. Li, and L. Lu (2016). Estimation and inference of FAVAR models. *Journal of Business & Economic Statistics 34*(4), 620–641.

Bai, J. and S. Ng (2002). Determining the number of factors in approximate factor models. *Econometrica 70*(1), 191–221.

Bai, J. and S. Ng (2006). Confidence intervals for diffusion index forecasts and inference for factor-augmented regressions. *Econometrica 74*(4), 1133–1150.

Bai, J. and S. Ng (2008). *Large dimensional factor analysis*. Now Publishers Inc.

Bai, J. and S. Ng (2009). Boosting diffusion indices. *Journal of Applied Econometrics 24*(4), 607–629.

Bai, J. and S. Ng (2013). Principal components estimation and identification of static factors. *Journal of Econometrics 176*(1), 18–29.

Bai, J. and P. Wang (2016). Econometric analysis of large factor models. *Annual Review of Economics 8*, 53–80.

Bates, B. J., M. Plagborg-Møller, J. H. Stock, and M. W. Watson (2013). Consistent factor estimation in dynamic factor models with structural instability. *Journal of Econometrics 177*(2), 289–304.

Belloni, A., M. Chen, O. H. Madrid Padilla, and Z. Wang (2023). High-dimensional latent panel quantile regression with an application to asset pricing. *The Annals of Statistics 51*(1), 96–121.

Bernanke, B., J. Boivin, and P. Eliasz (2005). Measuring the effects of monetary policy: A factor-augmented vector autoregressive (FAVAR) approach. *The Quarterly Journal of Economics 120*(1), 387–422.

Bernanke, B. S. and J. Boivin (2003). Monetary policy in a data-rich environment. *Journal of Monetary Economics 50*(3), 525–546.

Boivin, J. and S. Ng (2005). Understanding and comparing factor-based forecasts. *International Journal of Central Banking 1*(3), 117–152.

Boivin, J. and S. Ng (2006). Are more data always better for factor analysis. *Journal of Econometrics 132*, 169–194.

Carrasco, M. and B. Rossi (2016). In-sample inference and forecasting in misspecified factor models. *Journal of Business & Economic Statistics 34*(3), 313–338.

Chen, L., J. J. Dolado, and J. Gonzalo (2021). Quantile factor models. *Econometrica 89*(2), 875–910.

Cheng, X. and B. E. Hansen (2015). Forecasting with factor-augmented regression: A frequentist model averaging approach. *Journal of Econometrics 186*(2), 280–293.

Chudik, A. and M. H. Pesaran (2015a). Common correlated effects estimation of heterogeneous dynamic panel data models with weakly exogenous regressors. *Journal of Econometrics 188*(2), 393–420.

Chudik, A. and M. H. Pesaran (2015b). Large panel data models with cross-sectional dependence: A survey. Technical report, Oxford University Press.

Chudik, A., M. H. Pesaran, and E. Tosetti (2011). Weak and strong cross-section dependence and estimation of large panels. *The Econometrics Journal 1*(14), C45–C90.

Clements, M. P. and D. F. Hendry (1996). Intercept corrections and structural change. *Journal of Applied Econometrics 11*(5), 475–494.

Corradi, V. and N. R. Swanson (2014). Testing for structural stability of factor augmented forecasting models. *Journal of Econometrics 182*(1), 100–118.

Djogbenou, A. A. (2021). Model selection in factor-augmented regressions with estimated factors. *Econometric Reviews 40*(5), 470–503.

Fan, J., K. Li, and Y. Liao (2021). Recent developments in factor models and applications in econometric learning. *Annual Review of Financial Economics 13*, 401–430.

Fan, J. and R. Li (2001). Variable selection via nonconcave penalized likelihood and its oracle properties. *Journal of the American Statistical Association 96*(456), 1348–1360.

Fan, J., R. Li, C.-H. Zhang, and H. Zou (2020). *Statistical foundations of data science*. Chapman and Hall/CRC.

Fan, J. and J. Lv (2008). Sure independence screening for ultrahigh dimensional feature space. *Journal of the Royal Statistical Society: Series B (Statistical Methodology) 70*(5), 849–911.

Forni, M. and L. Reichlin (1998). Let's get real: A factor analytical approach to disaggregated business cycle dynamics. *The Review of Economic Studies 65*(3), 453–473.

Fosten, J. (2017). Model selection with estimated factors and idiosyncratic components. *Journal of Applied Econometrics 32*(6), 1087–1106.

Giannone, D., M. Lenza, and L. Reichlin (2010). Business cycles in the euro area. In A. Alesina and F. Giavazzi (Eds.), *Europe and the Euro*, pp. 141–167. Cambridge, MA: National Bureau of Economic Research: University of Chicago Press.

Gonçalves, S., B. Perron, and A. Djogbenou (2017). Bootstrap prediction intervals for factor models. *Journal of Business & Economic Statistics 35*(1), 53–69.

Gorman, W. M. (1981). *Some Engel curves*. Cambridge University Press.

Greenaway-McGrevy, R., C. Han, and D. Sul (2012). Asymptotic distribution of factor augmented estimators for panel regression. *Journal of Econometrics 169*(1), 48–53.

Greenaway-McGrevy, R., N. C. Mark, D. Sul, and J.-L. Wu (2018). Identifying exchange rate common factors. *International Economic Review 59*(4), 2193–2218.

Gregory, A. W. and A. C. Head (1999). Common and country-specific fluctuations in productivity, investment, and the current account. *Journal of Monetary Economics 44*(3), 423–451.

Groen, J. J. and G. Kapetanios (2013). Model selection criteria for factor-augmented regressions. *Oxford Bulletin of Economics and Statistics 75*(1), 37–63.

Inoue, A., L. Jin, and B. Rossi (2017). Rolling window selection for out-of-sample forecasting with time-varying parameters. *Journal of Econometrics 196*(1), 55–67.

Jurado, K., S. C. Ludvigson, and S. Ng (2015). Measuring uncertainty. *American Economic Review 105*(3), 1177–1216.

Kapetanios, G. and M. H. Pesaran (2007). Alternative approaches to estimation and inference in large multifactor panels: Small sample results with an application to modelling of asset returns. In G. Phillips and E. Tzavalis (Eds.), *The Refinement of Econometric Estimation and Test Procedures: Finite Sample and Asymptotic Analysis*, pp. 239 – 281. Cambridge: Cambridge University Press.

Karabiyik, H., F. C. Palm, and J.-P. Urbain (2019). Econometric analysis of panel data models with multifactor error structures. *Annual Review of Economics 11*, 495–522.

Kelly, B. and S. Pruitt (2015). The three-pass regression filter: A new approach to forecasting using many predictors. *Journal of Econometrics 186*(2), 294–316.

Koenker, R. and G. Bassett Jr (1978). Regression quantiles. *Econometrica 46*(1), 33–50.

Li, D., J. Tosasukul, and W. Zhang (2020). Nonlinear factor-augmented predictive regression models with functional coefficients. *Journal of Time Series Analysis 41*(3), 367–386.

Li, H., Q. Li, and Y. Shi (2017). Determining the number of factors when the number of factors can increase with sample size. *Journal of Econometrics 197*(1), 76–86.

Ludvigson, S. C., and S. Ng (2009). Macro factors in bond risk premia. *The Review of Financial Studies 22*(12), 5027–5067.

Ma, S., O. Linton, and J. Gao (2021). Estimation and inference in semiparametric quantile factor models. *Journal of Econometrics 222*(1), 295–323.

Massacci, D. (2017). Least squares estimation of large dimensional threshold factor models. *Journal of Econometrics 197*(1), 101–129.

Massacci, D. (2019). Unstable diffusion indexes: With an application to bond risk premia. *Oxford Bulletin of Economics and Statistics 81*(6), 1376–1400.

Ohno, S. and T. Ando (2018). Stock return predictability: A factor-augmented predictive regression system with shrinkage method. *Econometric Reviews 37*(1), 29–60.

Onatski, A. (2009). A formal statistical test for the number of factors in the approximate factor models. *Econometrica 77*(5), 1447–1480.

Onatski, A. (2012). Asymptotics of the principal components estimator of large factor models with weakly influential factors. *Journal of Econometrics 168*(2), 244–258.

Pesaran, M. H. (2006). Estimation and inference in large heterogeneous panels with a multifactor error structure. *Econometrica 74*(4), 967–1012.

Phella, A. (2020). Forecasting with factor-augmented quantile autoregressions: A model averaging approach. *arXiv preprint arXiv:2010.12263*.

Qiu, Y., T. Xie, J. Yu, and Q. Zhou (2022). Forecasting equity index volatility by measuring the linkage among component stocks. *Journal of Financial Econometrics 20*(1), 160–186.

Reese, S. and J. Westerlund (2018). Estimation of factor-augmented panel regressions with weakly influential factors. *Econometric Reviews 37*(5), 401–465.

Ross, S. A. (1976). The arbitrage theory of capital asset pricing. *Journal of Economic Theory 13*(3), 341–360.

Rossi, B. and A. Inoue (2012). Out-of-sample forecast tests robust to the choice of window size. *Journal of Business & Economic Statistics 30*(3), 432–453.

Shao, J. (1996). Bootstrap model selection. *Journal of the American Statistical Association 91*(434), 655–665.

Stock, J. H. and M. W. Watson (1998). Diffusion indexes. Technical report, National Bureau of Economic Research, Inc.

Stock, J. H. and M. W. Watson (2002a). Forecasting using principal components from a large number of predictors. *Journal of the American Statistical Association 97*(460), 1167–1179.

Stock, J. H. and M. W. Watson (2002b). Macroeconomic forecasting using diffusion indexes. *Journal of Business & Economic Statistics 20*(2), 147–162.

Stock, J. H. and M. W. Watson (2012). Dynamic factor models. In M. P. Clements and D. F. Hendry (Eds.), *The Oxford Handbook of Economic Forecasting*. New York: Oxford University Press.

Stock, J. H. and M. W. Watson (2016). Dynamic factor models, factor-augmented vector autoregressions, and structural vector autoregressions in macroeconomics. In *Handbook of Macroeconomics*, Volume 2, pp. 415–525. Elsevier.

Su, L. and X. Wang (2017). On time-varying factor models: Estimation and testing. *Journal of Econometrics 198*(1), 84–101.

Swanson, N. R. and W. Xiong (2018). Big data analytics in economics: What have we learned so far, and where should we go from here? *Canadian Journal of Economics/Revue canadienne d'économique 51*(3), 695–746.

Wang, S., G. Cui, and K. Li (2015). Factor-augmented regression models with structural change. *Economics Letters 130*, 124–127.

Wei, J. and Y. Zhang (2020). A time-varying diffusion index forecasting model. *Economics Letters 193*, 109337.

Westerlund, J. and J.-P. Urbain (2015). Cross-sectional averages versus principal components. *Journal of Econometrics 185*(2), 372–377.

Wu, Y. and Y. Liu (2009). Variable selection in quantile regression. *Statistica Sinica 19*(2), 801–817.

Xu, Q.-H., Z.-W. Cai, and Y. Fang (2016). Panel data models with cross-sectional dependence: A selective review. *Applied Mathematics: A Journal of Chinese Universities 31*(2), 127–147.

Yan, Y. and T. Cheng (2022). Factor-augmented forecasting regressions with threshold effects. *The Econometrics Journal 25*(1), 134–154.

Part II

Continuous-Time Models and High-Frequency Financial Econometrics

4 Finite Sample Theory in Continuous-Time Models

XIAOHU WANG *School of Economics, Fudan University*

4.1 Introduction

Let $X(t)$ denote a stochastic process with t taking values continuously over the period of $[0, T]$, where T is the time span of the process. Stochastic differential equations (SDEs) driven by Brownian motion provide a convenient way to model the evolution of $X(t)$ over infinitesimal time intervals. The use of SDEs to model variables in economics and finance has many advantages. For example, SDEs can capture interactions among variables during the unit observation period and make a clear distinction between the treatment of stock variables and the treatment of flow variables. A detailed discussion can be found in Bergstrom (1966). Because of these advantages, continuous-time models are widely applied in many core areas of economics and finance, including neoclassical growth theory, capital accumulation, game theory, the asset pricing of financial derivatives, volatility modeling, and term structure theory. Certain examples are summarized in Bergstrom (1990), Merton (1992), Sundaresan (2000), and Piazzesi (2010).

This chapter focuses primarily on scalar, time-homogeneous SDEs that take the form of

$$dX(t) = a(X(t); \theta)\, dt + \sigma(X(t); \theta)\, dW(t), \tag{4.1}$$

where $dX(t)$ denotes the change of $X(t)$ over an infinitesimal instant, $a(\cdot; \theta)$ and $\sigma(\cdot; \theta)$ are the drift and the diffusion functions, θ is a vector of unknown parameters, and $W(t)$ denotes standard Brownian motion. The initial value of $X(t)$ at time $t = 0$ is denoted as $X(0) = O_p(1)$. The model in (4.1) indicates that $dX(t)$ follows a conditional normal distribution with mean $a(X(t); \theta)\, dt$ and variance $\{\sigma(X(t); \theta)\}^2\, dt$. The term $dW(t)$ represents shocks to the system, whose effect on $dX(t)$ is scaled by the variance term $\sigma(X(t); \theta)$.

Although modeled in continuous time, observations of the process are typically available at discrete time points, for example, at $n = T/\Delta$ equally spaced points $\{t\Delta\}_{t=1}^{n}$, where Δ is the sampling interval. If an observation measures the value of $X(t)$ at a particular time point, it is referred to as stock data. In contrast, if an observation represents the value of $X(t)$ over a time interval, it is referred to as flow data. In addition, many ultrahigh-frequency stock data in finance are available at random and unequally spaced points (see, e.g., Aït-Sahalia et al. (2010)). The interface between models formulated in continuous time and data collected at discrete points is fundamental to the econometric treatment of continuous systems and leads to issues that are quite different from those typically encountered in a discrete time-series analysis. In this chapter, we only discuss the estimation issues for equally spaced stock data.

Under regular conditions, the maximum likelihood (ML) estimators of the parameters in the diffusion process (4.1) are consistent, asymptotically normal, and asymptotically efficient. Due to these optimal asymptotic properties, the ML approach is suitable for estimating the model whenever it is available (e.g., Lo (1988)). The likelihood function is the product of the transition densities. When the transition density is available in closed form, the ML estimation is easy to implement. However, except for some exceptional cases, the transition densities of discrete-time observations are unavailable in closed-form. Accordingly, various approximate ML methods have been proposed. A partial list includes methods based on approximate discrete-time models such as the Euler, trapezoidal, and Norman approximations proposed in Bergstrom (1966), Florens-Zmirou (1989), and Nowman (1997), respectively, along with the Hermit approximation method developed in Aït-Sahalia (1999, 2002, 2008), Aït-Sahalia and Kimmel (2007), and Li (2013), and the infill simulation method attributable to Pedersen (1995), Santa-Clara (1997), and Durham and Gallant (2002).

In addition to those approximate ML methods, a variety of moment-based estimation approaches have been developed, such as the generalized method of moments by Chan et al. (1992) and Hansen and Scheinkman (1995), the efficient method of moments by Gallant and Tauchen (1996), the empirical characteristic function method by Singleton (2001) and Knight and Yu (2002), and the Bayesian Markov Chain Monte Carlo methods by Eraker (2001) and Elerian et al. (2001).

The preceding methods have achieved significant success in estimating the SDEs consistently and efficiently in asymptotics. However, in virtually every one of these methods, the estimation of certain critical parameters suffers from severe finite-sample bias. Moreover, that bias does not disappear even when the sample size increases unboundedly under the asymptotic scheme of $\Delta \to 0$ with a fixed T. Thus, the availability of high-frequency data provides no help in reducing the magnitude of the bias.

Take the Ornstein–Uhlenbeck (OU) process as an example:

$$dX(t) = \kappa\left(\mu - X(t)\right) dt + \sigma dW(t), \tag{4.2}$$

where κ, μ, and σ are three constants. For this simple process, the exact transition density of the discrete-time observations $\{X_{t\Delta}\}$ is available in closed form.

Many studies in the literature point out that the ML estimator of κ, denoted by $\widehat{\kappa}_{ML}$, has substantial finite-sample bias; see, for example, Ball and Torous (1996), Chapman and Pearson (2000), Phillips and Yu (2005, 2009), and Yu and Phillips (2001). In addition, Tang and Chen (2009) and Yu (2012) provide explicit expressions to approximate the bias. Their formulae reveal that the leading term of the bias is a function of T and not Δ, implying that the bias disappears only when T, the number of observation years, goes to infinity. However, in most empirical applications, data are available only for a small value of T. It is not realistic to expect time-series data in the real world to last for many years without any structural breaks.

Wang et al. (2011) argue that the quasi-ML estimator of κ based on the Euler approximation of the OU process outperforms $\widehat{\kappa}_{ML}$ and other estimators based on higher-order approximations in terms of finite-sample bias. The bias of the quasi-ML estimator consists of two parts, namely, the estimation bias and the discretization bias. Wang et al. (2011) prove that the two types of bias have opposite directions. Therefore, the estimation bias is offset by the discretization bias, making the total bias of the quasi-ML estimator smaller than that of the exact ML estimator. However, the bias of the Euler quasi-ML estimator remains large.

In finance, SDEs are often applied to model the dynamics of asset prices, exchange rates, volatility, and short-term interest rates. Thus, the prices of financial derivatives, such as bonds and options, are developed as functions of SDEs' parameters. These functions are often nonlinear and can be sensitive to certain parameters in SDEs. Well-known examples include Black and Scholes (1973), Merton (1973), and Hull and White (1987) for stock options, and Vasicek (1977), Cox et al. (1985), Chan et al. (1992), Heston (1993), and Duffie et al. (2000) for interest-rate–contingent claims. As a result, the finite-sample bias of the estimated parameters in SDEs will propagate to and generate bias in the price calculations of financial derivatives.

Phillips and Yu (2005) comprehensively study the finite-sample bias problem in pricing rate–contingent claims. Both univariate models and multivariate models are considered. Phillips and Yu (2009) extend their study to the bias issue of price calculations of stock options for models with and without stochastic volatility. These articles propose two alternative methods to reduce the finite-sample pricing bias: the jackknife method and the indirect-inference method. They further point out that due to the nonlinearity of pricing formulae, applying the bias-correction methods directly to the contingent claims works better in reducing pricing bias than the method of obtaining the bias-reduction estimates of the SDE parameters first and then plugging the estimates into the pricing formulae of contingent claims. Simulations and empirical studies by Phillips and Yu (2005, 2009) show that the two methods can achieve considerable bias reduction compared with the ML estimation in pricing financial derivatives.

The purpose of this chapter is to provide a systematic introduction to the finite-sample bias problem in estimating SDEs' parameters and pricing financial derivatives. In Section 4.2, the applications of SDEs to modeling short-term interest rates are briefly introduced. Furthermore, the OU process provides an example to show the connections between the prices of interest-rate–contingent claims and the SDE parameters. Section 4.3 gives the bias formulae of the ML and quasi-ML estimators of the parameters in SDEs and discusses how the parameter bias translates into contingent claim pricing. The two bias-correction techniques are studied in detail in Section 4.4. Simulation examples are provided in Sections 4.3 and 4.4 to show the gravity of the bias problem and the performance of the bias-correction methods. Section 4.5 concludes the chapter.

4.2 Applications in Term Structure Modeling

As application examples in finance, this section introduces the use of diffusion processes in the term structure literature. In Subsection 4.2.1, we briefly summarize the scalar diffusions applied in modeling the short-term risk-free interest rates. For the case in which the dynamics of the short-term rate follow the OU process defined in (4.2), the contingent claims based on interest rates have closed-form pricing formulae. Subsection 4.2.2 displays these pricing formulae to show the roles of SDE parameters in pricing contingent claims.

4.2.1 Modeling Short-Term Interest Rates

The short-term risk-free interest rate can be defined with the help of zero-coupon bonds. A bond that makes a terminal payoff without the risk of default and without paying any intermediate coupons is called a zero-coupon bond. Let us normalize the terminal payoff as \$1 and use $P(t,s)$ to denote the price of the bond that is issued at time t with maturity date s. Holding the bond until its maturity generates a risk-free per-period return as

$$\gamma_t^{(s)} = -\frac{\log P(t,s)}{s-t}. \tag{4.3}$$

$\gamma_t^{(s)}$ is often referred to as yield to maturity. The short-term risk-free interest rate is defined as the limit of $\gamma_t^{(s)}$ when $s \to t$:

$$r(t) = \lim_{s\to t} \gamma_t^{(s)} = \lim_{s\to t} -\frac{\log P(t,s)}{s-t}.$$

The short-term rate is a fundamental factor in the valuation of nearly all of the derivatives in the financial markets. In addition, interest-rate variability is a major source of risk for banks and other financial institutions. Unsurprisingly, therefore, problems related to short-term interest rates attract enormous attention in the economics and finance literature. One important branch of inquiry

Table 4.1 *Alternative model specifications for short-term interest rates. In this table, $r := r(t)$ denotes the interest rate at time t, $W := W(t)$ is the standard Brownian motion, and $\{\alpha_i\}_{i=1}^4$ and $\{\beta_i\}_{i=1}^4$ are unknown parameters. Moreover, GBM, BS (1980), CIR VR (1980), and Aït (1996) refer to geometric Brownian motion, Brennan and Schwartz (1980), Cox et al. (1980), and Aït-Sahalia (1996), respectively.*

Merton (1973)	$dr = \alpha_1 dt + \beta_1 dW$
Vasicek (1977)	$dr = (\alpha_1 + \alpha_2 r)\, dt + \beta_1 dW$
CIR (1985)	$dr = (\alpha_1 + \alpha_2 r)\, dt + \beta_2 r^{1/2} dW$
Dothan (1978)	$dr = \beta_2 r dW$
GBM	$dr = \alpha_2 r dt + \beta_2 r dW$
BS (1980)	$dr = (\alpha_1 + \alpha_2 r)\, dt + \beta_2 r dW$
CIR VR (1980)	$dr = \beta_2 r^{3/2} dW$
CKLS (1992)	$dr = (\alpha_1 + \alpha_2 r)\, dt + \beta_3 r^{\beta_4} dW$
Tauchen (1995)	$dr = \left(\alpha_1 + \alpha_2 r + \alpha_3 r^2 + \alpha_4 / r\right) dt + \beta_3 r^{\beta_4} dW$
Aït (1996)	$dr = \left(\alpha_1 + \alpha_2 r + \alpha_3 r^2 + \alpha_4 / r\right) dt + \left(\beta_1 + \beta_2 r + \beta_3 r^{\beta_4}\right) dW$

on this topic is concerned with how best to model the short-term rate dynamics. Over the past 50 years, many single-factor and multifactor interest-rate models specified by various SDEs have been proposed. Table 4.1 displays some prominent single-factor models that have achieved remarkable success in modeling and forecasting short-term rates.

Multifactor models assume that the short-term rate depends on a state vector $Z(t)$, namely, $r(t) = f(Z(t))$, where $f(\cdot)$ is a real-valued function. Various multivariate diffusion processes have been applied to model the dynamics of $Z(t)$. Examples of multifactor models can be found in Duffie and Kan (1996), Gouriéroux and Sufana (2006), and their references.

Another group of models for short-term interest rates is that of continuous-time models with stochastic volatility. Many empirical studies show that the short-term rate exhibits properties such as fat tails and persistent volatility patterns. Stochastic volatility models can better fit these properties. An incomplete list of references includes Hull and White (1987), Andersen and Lund (1997), Gallant and Tauchen (1998), Eraker (2001), Durham (2003), and Trolle and Schwartz (2009).

4.2.2 Pricing Formulae of Contingent Claims

The univariate OU process defined in (4.2) is identical to the Vasicek model in Table 6.1, with the relationship between the parameters being $\alpha_1 = \kappa\mu$, $\alpha_2 = -\kappa$, and $\beta_1 = \sigma$. Assuming that the short-term rate follows an OU process, Vasicek (1977) derives an explicit pricing formula for the zero-coupon bond. Jamshidian (1989) obtains the pricing formula for European options, with bonds as the underlying assets. To display these pricing formulae, we assume in this subsection that the short-term rate follows the OU process defined in (4.2) and specify it here again by letting $r(t) := X(t)$ for convenience:

$$dr(t) = \kappa(\mu - r(t))\,dt + \sigma\,dW(t). \tag{4.4}$$

By holding a zero-coupon bond to its maturity date s, a risk-free return is possible. However, the bond is tradable at random prices at any time before its maturity. Holding a bond from time t to period $t+h < s$ generates a holding-period return defined as

$$hpr_t^{t+h} = \frac{\log P(t+h,s) - \log P(t,s)}{h},$$

which is a random variable due to the uncertainty of the price $P(t+h,s)$. Hence, zero-coupon bonds are risky assets.

The bond price $P(t,s)$ depends on t and the short-term rate $r(t)$. Hence, by using Ito's lemma, the bond price has the dynamics

$$\begin{aligned} dP(t,s) &= P_t dt + P_r dr + \frac{1}{2}P_{rr}(dr)^2 \\ &= \left(P_t + \kappa(\mu - r(t))P_r + \frac{1}{2}\sigma^2 P_{rr}\right)dt + \sigma P_r dW(t), \end{aligned}$$

where P_t denotes the first-order derivative of the bond price with respect to t, and P_r and P_{rr} are the first- and second-order derivatives, respectively, with respect to the short-term rate $r(t)$. It is further obtained that

$$\begin{aligned} \frac{dP(t,s)}{P(t,s)} &= \frac{\left(P_t + \kappa(\mu - r(t))P_r + \frac{1}{2}\sigma^2 P_{rr}\right)}{P(t,s)}dt + \frac{\sigma P_r}{P(t,s)}dW(t) \\ &= \mu_p dt + \sigma_p dW(t). \end{aligned}$$

where μ_p represents the conditional expected return of the bond, and σ_p^2 is the conditional variance. Define the market price of risk as the expected excess return per unit risk, that is, $\lambda := \left(\mu_p - r\right)/\sigma_p$. This definition yields the equation of

$$\mu_p - r = \lambda\sigma_p,$$

which shows that the expected excess return of the bond equals the market price of risk multiplying the standard deviation associated with the bond. Substituting for the representations of μ_p and σ_p gives a partial differential equation (PDE) of the bond price P:

$$P_t + \kappa\left(\mu - \frac{\lambda\sigma}{\kappa} - r(t)\right)P_r + \frac{1}{2}\sigma^2 P_{rr} - rP = 0. \tag{4.5}$$

The solution of the PDE with the boundary condition of $P(s,s) = 1$ gives the bond pricing formula derived in Vasicek (1977). We report this formula in Theorem 4.2.1.

Theorem 4.2.1 *Assume the short-term rate $r(t)$ follows the OU process given in (4.4). At time period t, the price of the zero-coupon bond with the terminal payoff* \$1 *and the maturity date s follows the formula of*

$$P(t,s) = A(t,s)\, e^{-B(t,s)r(t)}, \tag{4.6}$$

where

$$A(t,s) = \exp\left\{\left(\mu - \frac{\lambda\sigma}{\kappa} - \frac{\sigma^2}{2\kappa^2}\right)[B(t,s) - s + t] - \frac{\sigma^2}{4\kappa}[B(t,s)]^2\right\}, \tag{4.7}$$

and

$$B(t,s) = \frac{1}{\kappa}\left(1 - e^{-\kappa(s-t)}\right). \tag{4.8}$$

The pricing formula in (4.6) makes the yield-to-maturity defined in (4.3) an affine function of the short-term rate:

$$\gamma_t^{(s)} = -\frac{\log P(t,s)}{s-t} = -\frac{\log A(t,s)}{s-t} + \frac{B(t,s)}{s-t} r(t).$$

Hence, the Vasicek model is a special case of the affine term structure models.

Another way to price bonds is with the help of a risk-neutral probability measure. Imagine that there is a probability measure, denoted by Q^*, under which the short-term rate has the following dynamics

$$dr(t) = \kappa\left(\mu^* - r(t)\right) dt + \sigma\, dW^*(t),$$

where $\mu^* = \mu - (\lambda\sigma)/\kappa$, and $W^*(t)$ is a standard Brownian motion under Q^*. The application of Ito's lemma gives the dynamics of the bond price under Q^* as

$$dP(t,s) = \left(P_t + \kappa\left(\mu^* - r(t)\right) P_r + \frac{1}{2}\sigma^2 P_{rr}\right) dt + \sigma P_r dW^*(t).$$

From Equation (4.5), it is obtained that the expected excess return of the bond under the measure Q^* is zero, namely,

$$\frac{\left(P_t + \kappa(\mu^* - r(t)) P_r + \frac{1}{2}\sigma^2 P_{rr}\right)}{P(t,s)} - r = 0.$$

In other words, under the probability measure Q^*, investors are risk-neutral in the sense that they do not require excess returns for any risk they bear.

This property gives the reason for Q^* being named as a risk-neutral probability measure. Furthermore, due to the risk-neutral attitude, the bond price can be calculated as the expected values of its further payoff discounted at the short-term rate, namely,

$$P(t,s) = E_t^* \left[\exp\left(-\int_t^{t+s} r(\tau)\, d\tau \right) \right],$$

where E_t^* denotes the expectation under the measure Q^* and the information available at time t. Providing a thorough discussion of the risk-neutral pricing theory and the connections between physical probability measures and the associated risk-neutral measures is beyond the scope of this chapter. Interested readers can find classic textbooks for more details, for example, Shreve (2004).

We end this subsection by introducing the pricing formulae of bond options developed in Jamshidian (1989). A European option is a contract that gives the holders a right to buy or sell a bond at a particular time (expiration date) for a predetermined price. This predetermined price is called the strike price of the option. Consider a zero-coupon bond with a fixed maturity date s and a terminal payoff (also called principal value) L. The current price of this bond is determined by

$$P(t,s) = L \times A(t,s)\, e^{-B(t,s)r(t)}, \tag{4.9}$$

where $A(t,s)$ and $B(t,s)$ are given in (4.7) and (4.8), respectively. Jamshidian (1989) derived explicit pricing formulae for options written on this bond, which are reported in Theorem 4.2.2.

Theorem 4.2.2 *Consider a zero-coupon bond that gives a terminal payoff L at the maturity date s.*
(a) A European call option written on this bond with strike price K and expiration date τ $(t < \tau < s)$ has the pricing formula of

$$C_{OP}(t,\tau,s,K) = LP(t,s)\,\Phi(h) - KP(t,\tau)\,\Phi\left(h - \delta_P\right); \tag{4.10}$$

(b) The price of a corresponding put option takes the form of

$$P_{OP}(t,\tau,s,K) = KP(t,\tau)\,\Phi\left(\delta_P - h\right) - LP(t,s)\,\Phi(-h),$$

where $P(t,s)$ is given in (4.9), $\Phi(\cdot)$ denotes the standard normal cumulative function,

$$\delta_P = \frac{\sigma}{\kappa}\left(1 - e^{-\kappa(s-\tau)}\right)\sqrt{\frac{1 - e^{-2\kappa(\tau - t)}}{2\kappa}},$$

and

$$h = \delta_p^{-1} \log\left(\frac{P(t,s)L}{P(t,\tau)K}\right) + \frac{\delta_p}{2}.$$

4.3 Estimation and Finite-Sample Bias

4.3.1 Vasicek Model with an Unknown Mean

Although modeled by a continuous-time diffusion process, the short-term rate $r(t)$ can only be observed at discrete time points. Assume that observations of $r(t)$ are available at equally spaced discrete time points from time zero to time T with the sampling interval Δ. This means that the observations are collected at time points $\{t\Delta\}_{t=0}^{n}$ from $t = 0$ to $t = n$, with $n := T/\Delta$ being the total number of observations. The short-term rate $r(t)$ is often taken as the normalized annual rate. Thus, in the term structure literature, if $r(t)$ is observed at daily (weekly or monthly) frequency over 10 years, it is often set as $\Delta = 1/252$ $(1/52$ or $1/12)$, and $T = 10$ represents the number of observing years. T is referred to as the time span of the data. In the rest of this chapter, we use $\{r_{t\Delta}\}$ to represent the observations of $r(t)$, and we write the term simply as $\{r_t\}$ when there is no confusion.

To estimate the continuous-time diffusion processes, the ML estimators are asymptotically optimal under regular conditions; accordingly, they are often adopted when available. The simple Vasicek process in (4.4) has an equivalent discretization (see, e.g., Phillips (1972)):

$$r_t = e^{-\kappa\Delta} r_{t-1} + \mu\left(1 - e^{-\kappa\Delta}\right) + \varepsilon_t, \tag{4.11}$$

where the errors

$$\varepsilon_t = \sigma \int_{(t-1)\Delta}^{t\Delta} e^{-\kappa(t\Delta - s)} dW(s),$$

for $t = 1, 2, \ldots, n$, are a sequence of independent and identically distributed (i.i.d.) variables with the normal distribution $N\left(0, \sigma^2\left(1 - e^{-2\kappa\Delta}\right)/(2\kappa)\right)$. The transition density of the observations is readily obtained as

$$r_t | r_{t-1} \sim N\left(e^{-\kappa\Delta} r_{t-1} + \mu\left(1 - e^{-\kappa\Delta}\right), \sigma^2\left(1 - e^{-2\kappa\Delta}\right)/(2\kappa)\right).$$

Therefore, the log likelihood function

$$\mathcal{L}(\theta) = \sum_{t=1}^{n} \ln f(r_t | r_{t-1})$$

has a simple, explicit expression, where $f(r_t | r_{t-1})$ denotes the conditional density function of r_t given r_{t-1}. Tang and Chen (2009) provide explicit formulae of the ML estimators as

$$\widehat{\kappa}_n^{ML} = -\frac{1}{\Delta}\ln\left(\widehat{\varphi}_1\right) \quad \text{with } \widehat{\varphi}_1 = \frac{\sum_{t=1}^{n} r_t r_{t-1} - n^{-1}\sum_{t=1}^{n} r_t \sum_{t=1}^{n} r_{t-1}}{\sum_{t=1}^{n} r_{t-1}^2 - n^{-1}\left(\sum_{t=1}^{n} r_{t-1}\right)^2}, \tag{4.12}$$

$$\widehat{\mu}_n^{ML} = \widehat{\varphi}_2 \quad \text{with } \widehat{\varphi}_2 = \frac{n^{-1}\sum_{t=1}^{n}\left(r_t - \widehat{\varphi}_1 r_{t-1}\right)}{1-\widehat{\varphi}_1},$$

and

$$\widehat{\sigma}_n^{ML} = \sqrt{\frac{2\widehat{\kappa}\widehat{\varphi}_3}{1-\widehat{\varphi}_1^2}} \quad \text{with } \widehat{\varphi}_3 = n^{-1}\sum_{t=1}^{n}\left[r_t - \widehat{\varphi}_1 r_{t-1} - \widehat{\varphi}_2\left(1-\widehat{\varphi}_1\right)\right]^2.$$

When $\kappa > 0$, the Vasicek process in (4.4) is stationary. Under stationarity, Tang and Chen (2009) prove the asymptotic normality of the ML estimators when $T \to \infty$ with a fixed Δ. In addition, they derive the bias formula for each ML estimator. Their results show that the biases of $\widehat{\mu}_n^{ML}$ and $\widehat{\sigma}_n^{ML}$ are negligible when the sample size n is reasonably large. However, the estimator $\widehat{\kappa}_n^{ML}$ suffers from substantial finite-sample bias even when $n \to \infty$, as long as the time span T is small. Theorem 4.3.1 reports the bias formula of $\widehat{\kappa}_n^{ML}$ developed in Tang and Chen (2009).

Theorem 4.3.1 *The ML estimator $\widehat{\kappa}_n^{ML}$ given in (4.12) has the bias formula of*

$$Bias\left(\widehat{\kappa}_n^{ML}\right) = E\left(\widehat{\kappa}_n^{ML}\right) - \kappa = \frac{1}{T}\left(\frac{5}{2} + e^{\kappa\Delta} + \frac{1}{2}e^{2\kappa\Delta}\right) + O\left(n^{-2}\right). \tag{4.13}$$

To examine the performance of the bias formula in (4.13), Figure 4.1 compares the values calculated from the bias formula with the simulated finite-sample bias. The range of κ is $(0, 3]$, which covers the reasonable values found in empirical studies of short-term interest rates. We simulate data from the Vasicek process in (4.4), with $T = 4$, $\Delta = 1/52$, and $\Delta = 1/252$, respectively, corresponding to four years of weekly data and daily data. For each simulated sample path, κ is estimated by the ML method. We replicate this experiment 1,000 times to obtain the simulated bias of $\widehat{\kappa}_n^{ML}$, which can provide an excellent approximation of the actual bias. The solid black line in Figure 4.1 draws the simulated bias of $\widehat{\kappa}_n^{ML}$. The dotted blue line reports the values calculated from the leading term of the bias formula in (4.13).

Several features appear in Figure 4.1. First, the actual bias of $\widehat{\kappa}_n^{ML}$ is a nonlinear function of κ, and the curvature is large when κ is small. Second, instead of going to zero, the bias increases sharply as $\kappa \to 0$. Thus, the bias percentage

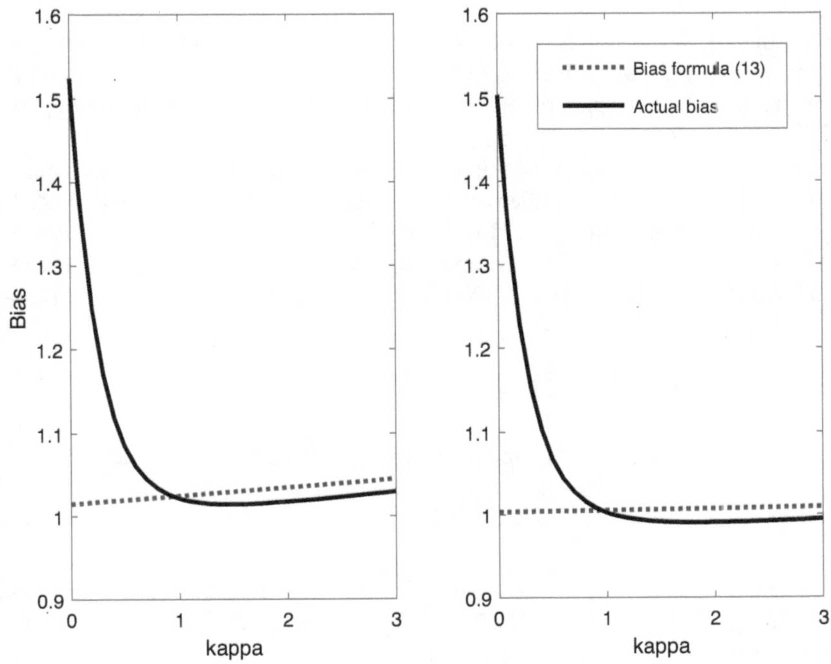

Figure 4.1 Bias of $\widehat{\kappa}_n^{ML}$ as a function of κ. From left to right, the two panels correspond to weekly data ($\Delta = 1/52$) and daily data ($\Delta = 1/252$), respectively.

is very high when κ is low. Third, the bias magnitude has almost no change when the sampling frequency changes from weekly to daily, showing that the availability of high-frequency data cannot reduce the bias. Fourth, the bias formula in (4.13) provides a very good approximation of the actual bias when κ is large. However, when κ is small, the bias formula (4.13) fails to capture the curvature of the actual bias; thus, it does not perform well in approximating the actual bias.

To better understand the bias property of $\widehat{\kappa}_n^{ML}$ and the bias formula in (4.13), we expand $(\widehat{\varphi}_1)$ about the point $\varphi_1 = \exp\{-\kappa\Delta\}$:

$$\begin{aligned}\widehat{\kappa}_n^{ML} &= -\frac{1}{\Delta}\ln(\widehat{\varphi}_1) \\ &= -\frac{1}{\Delta}\left\{\ln(\varphi_1) + \frac{1}{\varphi_1}(\widehat{\varphi}_1 - \varphi_1) - \frac{1}{2\varphi_1^2}(\widehat{\varphi}_1 - \varphi_1)^2 + \cdots\right\}.\end{aligned}$$

The preceding Taylor expansion leads to the formula

$$E\left(\widehat{\kappa}_n^{ML}\right) = \kappa - \frac{1}{\Delta}\left\{\frac{1}{\varphi_1}E(\widehat{\varphi}_1 - \varphi_1) - \frac{1}{2\varphi_1^2}E(\widehat{\varphi}_1 - \varphi_1)^2 + \cdots\right\}. \tag{4.14}$$

Note that $\varphi_1 = \exp\{-\kappa\Delta\}$ is the autoregressive (AR) root of the discretization in (4.11), and $\widehat{\varphi}_1$, as defined in (4.12), is the ML estimation. Formula (4.14) reveals that the moments of $\widehat{\varphi}_1 - \varphi_1$ of every order contribute to the bias of $\widehat{\kappa}_n^{ML}$.

The finite sample properties of $\widehat{\varphi}_1$ have been well studied in the literature. Alternative bias formulae under various model settings have been developed. A partial list includes Hurvicz (1950), Kendall (1954), Marriott and Pope (1954), White (1961), Shenton and Johnson (1965), Yamamoto and Kunitomo (1984), and Vinod and Shenton (1996). The bias formula derived in Marriott and Pope (1954) is

$$E(\widehat{\varphi}_1 - \varphi_1) = -\frac{3\varphi_1 + 1}{n} + o\left(\frac{1}{n}\right).$$

Bartlett (1946) develops an approximation of the finite-sample variance:

$$Var(\widehat{\varphi}_1) = \frac{1 - \varphi_1^2}{n} + o\left(\frac{1}{n}\right).$$

The bias formula of $\widehat{\kappa}_n^{ML}$ given in (4.13) is obtained by substituting the bias formula of Marriott and Pope (1954) and the variance formula of Bartlett (1946) into the Taylor expansion (4.14) and ignoring all the higher-order moments of $\widehat{\varphi}_1 - \varphi_1$. Involving only the first two moments of $\widehat{\varphi}_1$ omits the bias of $\widehat{\kappa}_n^{ML}$ contributed by the higher-order moments of $\widehat{\varphi}_1$, such as the skewness and the kurtosis. Yu (2012) argues that including higher-order moments of $\widehat{\varphi}_1$ can lead to a bias formula of $\widehat{\kappa}_n^{ML}$ that captures the nonlinearity of the actual bias when the values of κ are small. He proves this argument for a Vasicek model with $\mu = 0$, which we will introduce in the following subsection.

4.3.2 Vasicek Model with $\mu = 0$

The Vasicek process with $\mu = 0$ has the expression

$$dr(t) = -\kappa r(t)\,dt + \sigma\,dW(t), \tag{4.15}$$

whose exact discretization is a first-order AR model without intercept:

$$r_t = \varphi r_{t-1} + \varepsilon_t,$$

where $\varphi = e^{-\kappa\Delta}$ and

$$\varepsilon_t \overset{i.i.d}{\sim} N\left(0, \sigma^2\left(1 - e^{-2\kappa\Delta}\right)/(2\kappa)\right).$$

The ML estimator of κ, in this case, takes the form of

$$\widehat{\kappa} = -\frac{1}{\Delta}\ln(\widehat{\varphi}) \quad \text{with } \widehat{\varphi} = \left(\sum_{t=1}^{n} r_t r_{t-1}\right) / \sum_{t=1}^{n} r_{t-1}^2. \tag{4.16}$$

The Taylor expansion reveals the following relationship between the bias of $\widehat{\kappa}$ and the moments of $\widehat{\varphi}$:

$$E(\widehat{\kappa}) = \kappa - \frac{1}{\Delta}\left\{\frac{1}{\varphi}E(\widehat{\varphi}-\varphi) - \frac{1}{2\varphi^2}E(\widehat{\varphi}-\varphi)^2 + \cdots\right\}.$$

Yu (2012), at the beginning of the paper, provides a bias formula of $\widehat{\kappa}$ by only calculating the first two moments of $\widehat{\varphi}-\varphi$:

$$E(\widehat{\kappa}) - \kappa = \frac{2}{T}\left(1+\frac{1}{n}\right) + \frac{1}{2T}\left(e^{2\kappa\Delta}-1\right) + o\left(\frac{1}{T}\right). \tag{4.17}$$

The paper then argues that if $\kappa \to 0$, it has $e^{2\kappa\Delta} - 1 \to 0$, which makes the constant term $\frac{2}{T}\left(1+\frac{1}{n}\right)$ the only one dominating in the bias approximation. Hence, the nonlinearity of the actual bias of $\widehat{\kappa}$ as $\kappa \to 0$ is not captured by the bias approximation in (4.17).

To better capture the nonlinearity of the actual bias when κ is small, Yu (2012) develops another bias approximation that involves the information from the higher-order moments of $\widehat{\varphi}-\varphi$. This bias approximation is presented in Theorem 4.3.2.

Theorem 4.3.2 *The estimator $\widehat{\kappa}$ given in (4.16) has the bias formula of*

$$\begin{aligned} E(\widehat{\kappa}) - \kappa = {} & \frac{2}{T}\left(1+\frac{1}{n}\right) + \frac{1}{2T}\left(e^{2\kappa\Delta}-1\right) \\ & - \frac{2\left(1-e^{-2n\kappa\Delta}\right)}{Tn\left(1-e^{-2\kappa\Delta}\right)}\left\{1+\frac{2}{n}-\frac{1-e^{-2n\kappa\Delta}}{n^2\left(1-e^{-2\kappa\Delta}\right)}\right\} + o\left(\frac{1}{T}\right). \end{aligned} \tag{4.18}$$

Compared with (4.17), the bias formula given in Theorem 4.3.2 has the additional term

$$-\frac{2\left(1-e^{-2n\kappa\Delta}\right)}{Tn\left(1-e^{-2\kappa\Delta}\right)}\left\{1+\frac{2}{n}-\frac{1-e^{-2n\kappa\Delta}}{n^2\left(1-e^{-2\kappa\Delta}\right)}\right\}.$$

When $\kappa \to 0$, it has

$$\frac{1-e^{-2n\kappa\Delta}}{n\left(1-e^{-2\kappa\Delta}\right)} \to 1,$$

and

$$-\frac{2\left(1-e^{-2n\kappa\Delta}\right)}{Tn\left(1-e^{-2\kappa\Delta}\right)}\left\{1+\frac{2}{n}-\frac{1-e^{-2n\kappa\Delta}}{n^2\left(1-e^{-2\kappa\Delta}\right)}\right\} \to -\frac{2}{T}\left(1+\frac{1}{n}\right).$$

Therefore, when $\kappa \to 0$, the additional term has the same order as the leading term in the bias formula and cannot be ignored in the bias approximation. More importantly, the limit of the additional term will cancel out the leading term in the bias formula when $\kappa \to 0$. As a result, it is the middle term in the bias formula (4.18), namely, $\frac{1}{2T}\left(e^{2\kappa\Delta} - 1\right)$, which plays a dominating role as $\kappa \to 0$. This middle term can well capture the nonlinearity of the actual bias for small values of κ.

In addition, Yu (2012) proves that when $\Delta \to 0$ with a fixed time-span T, it has $n = T/\Delta \to \infty$, and

$$E\left(\widehat{\kappa}\right) - \kappa \approx \frac{2}{T} + \frac{1 - e^{2\kappa T}}{T^2\kappa},$$

which clearly shows that the bias does not disappear when high-frequency observations are available.

Figure 4.2 compares the performance of formulae (4.17) and (4.18) in approximating the actual bias of $\widehat{\kappa}$. The dotted blue line and the dashed red line report the bias values calculated from formulae (4.17) and (4.18), respectively. The solid black line gives the actual bias from simulations that are replicated

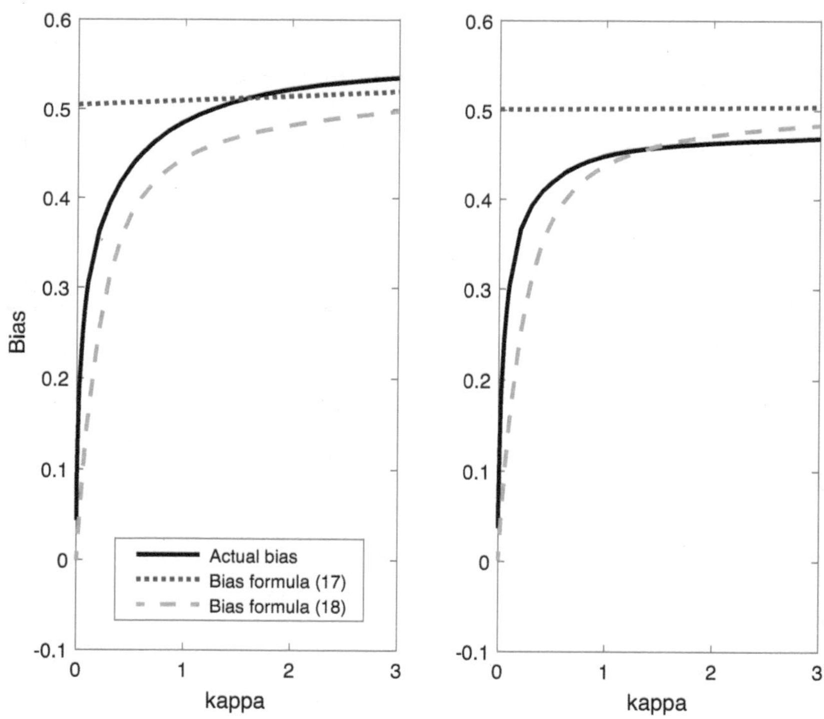

Figure 4.2 Bias of $\widehat{\kappa}$ as a function of κ. From left to right, the two panels correspond to weekly data ($\Delta = 1/52$) and daily data ($\Delta = 1/252$), respectively.

1,000 times. The data are simulated based on the Vasicek process in (4.15) with $T = 4$, $\Delta = 1/52$, and $\Delta = 1/252$, respectively. For each simulated sample path, κ is estimated by the estimator $\widehat{\kappa}$ defined in (4.16).

Two critical features can be seen in Figure 4.2. First, the bias approximation from Formula (4.17), which uses only the information from the first two moments of $\widehat{\varphi} - \varphi$, can well approximate the actual bias when κ is large. In contrast, the bias approximation from Formula (4.18), which involves the information from higher-order moments of $\widehat{\varphi} - \varphi$, accurately approximates the actual bias for all concerned values of κ and perfectly captures the nonlinearity of the bias when $\kappa \to 0$. Second, the actual bias of $\widehat{\kappa}$ goes to zero as $\kappa \to 0$. This feature sharply differs from the case where the intercept of the Vasicek process is unknown, as shown in Figure 4.1.

4.3.3 Bias of Quasi-ML Estimators

Wang et al. (2011) point out that although the exact ML approach is optimal asymptotically, the associated estimators may not perform the best in terms of the finite-sample properties. They derive the bias formulae of the quasi-ML estimators of κ that are obtained based on various approximate discretizations of the OU process. It is shown that the estimator based on the first-order Euler discretization has a smaller finite-sample bias than the estimators based on high-order approximations, which in turn perform better than the exact ML estimator. The reason for this finding is that the bias can be decomposed into two parts, the estimation bias and the discretization bias, which have opposite signs. A lower-order approximation generates a more significant discretization bias that helps reduce the magnitude of the total bias.

For the OU process with an unknown mean, as described in (4.4), integrating both sides of the equation over the interval from $(t-1)\Delta$ to $t\Delta$ leads to the equation

$$r_t - r_{t-1} = -\kappa \int_{(t-1)\Delta}^{t\Delta} r(s)\, ds + \kappa\mu\Delta + \varepsilon_t,$$

where $\varepsilon_t = \sigma\left(W_{t\Delta} - W_{(t-1)\Delta}\right)$ is an i.i.d. sequence of random variables with the normal distribution $N\left(0, \sigma^2\Delta\right)$. The Euler approximation is defined as

$$\int_{(t-1)\Delta}^{t\Delta} r(s)\, ds \approx r_{t-1} \cdot \Delta,$$

which leads to the following approximate discretization of the OU process:

$$r_t \approx (1 - \kappa\Delta)\, r_{t-1} + \kappa\mu\Delta + \varepsilon_t. \tag{4.19}$$

For convenience, Equation (4.19) is referred to as Euler discretization hereafter.

The Euler discretization in (4.19) presents an AR(1) regression with normally distributed errors. The ML estimator of the AR root, $\widehat{\varphi}_1$, is given by (4.12). From the relationship between κ and the AR root in the regression of (4.19), the quasi-ML estimator of κ based on the Euler discretization has the form of

$$\widehat{\kappa}_{Euler} = \frac{1}{\Delta}\left(1 - \widehat{\varphi}_1\right). \tag{4.20}$$

The Taylor expansion of $\varphi_1 = \exp\{-\kappa\Delta\}$ shows that

$$\varphi_1 = \sum_{i=0}^{\infty} \frac{(-\kappa\Delta)^i}{i!} = 1 - \kappa\Delta + H,$$

where $H = \sum_{i=2}^{\infty} \frac{(-\kappa\Delta)^i}{i!} = O\left(\Delta^2\right)$ as $\Delta \to 0$. Therefore,

$$\kappa = \Delta^{-1}\left(1 - \varphi_1\right) + \Delta^{-1}H$$

and

$$\widehat{\kappa}_{Euler} - \kappa = -\frac{1}{\Delta}\left(\widehat{\varphi}_1 - \varphi_1\right) - \frac{H}{\Delta}.$$

The bias of the Euler estimator $\widehat{\kappa}_{Euler}$ is then expressed as

$$\text{Bias}\left(\widehat{\kappa}_{Euler}\right) = E\left(\widehat{\kappa}_{Euler} - \kappa\right) = -\frac{1}{\Delta}E\left(\widehat{\varphi}_1 - \varphi_1\right) - \frac{H}{\Delta}.$$

It becomes clear that the bias of $\widehat{\kappa}_{Euler}$ has two components. The first component is $-\frac{1}{\Delta}E\left(\widehat{\varphi}_1 - \varphi_1\right)$. This component is called the estimation bias, which comes from estimating the AR root in the regression of (4.19). The second component is $-H/\Delta$, which is attributable to the truncation of the Taylor expansion of $\varphi_1 = \exp\{-\kappa\Delta\}$. This component is named the discretization bias. It has been well demonstrated in the discrete-time AR regression literature that the estimator $\widehat{\varphi}_1$ has a downward bias. Hence, the estimation bias of $\widehat{\kappa}_{Euler}$ is positive. In contrast, the representation of H suggests that the discretization bias $-H/\Delta$ should be negative when $\kappa\Delta$ is reasonably small. Therefore, the two bias components have opposite signs and partially cancel each other out. As a result, the magnitude of the total bias of $\widehat{\kappa}_{Euler}$ is reduced. Theorem 4.3.3 gives the explicit form of the bias formula of $\widehat{\kappa}_{Euler}$ developed in Wang et al. (2011).

Theorem 4.3.3 *Assume the short-term rate $r(t)$ follows the OU process in (4.4) with $\kappa > 0$. The estimator $\widehat{\kappa}_{Euler}$ has the bias of*

$$Bias\left(\widehat{\kappa}_{Euler}\right) = \frac{1 + 3\exp\{-\kappa\Delta\}}{T} - \frac{H}{\Delta} + o\left(\frac{1}{T}\right), \tag{4.21}$$

where $\left(1 + 3\exp\{-\kappa\Delta\}\right)/T > 0$ is the estimation bias, and $-\frac{H}{\Delta} < 0$ is the discretization bias.

Remark 4.3.4 *Wang et al. (2011) prove that as long as* $T < 8\left(1+O(\Delta)\right)/\left(\kappa^2\Delta\right)$*, the first term of the bias formula (4.21) dominates the second term in magnitude. In other words, the estimation bias of* $\widehat{\kappa}_{Euler}$ *has a greater magnitude than the discretization bias. Therefore, the total bias of* $\widehat{\kappa}_{Euler}$ *takes the same sign as the estimation bias, which is positive. However, because the discretization bias is negative, the total bias of* $\widehat{\kappa}_{Euler}$ *takes a smaller value than the estimation bias. Notably,* $8/\left(\kappa^2\Delta\right)$ *accounts for very large values in empirically relevant cases.*

To compare the Euler estimator $\widehat{\kappa}_{Euler}$ with that of the exact ML estimator $\widehat{\kappa}_n^{ML}$, we have

$$\begin{aligned}
&\text{Bias}\left(\widehat{\kappa}_n^{ML}\right) - \text{Bias}\left(\widehat{\kappa}_{Euler}\right)\\
&= \frac{5+2e^{\kappa\Delta}+e^{2\kappa\Delta}}{2T} - \frac{1+3e^{-\kappa\Delta}}{T} + \frac{H}{\Delta} + o\left(\frac{1}{T}\right)\\
&= \frac{3+2e^{\kappa\Delta}+e^{2\kappa\Delta}-6e^{-\kappa\Delta}}{2T} + \frac{H}{\Delta} + o\left(\frac{1}{T}\right)\\
&= \frac{3+2\left(1+\kappa\Delta\right)+\left(1+2\kappa\Delta\right)-6\left(1-\kappa\Delta\right)+O\left(\Delta^2\right)}{2T} + \frac{H}{\Delta} + o\left(\frac{1}{T}\right)\\
&= \frac{10\kappa\Delta+O\left(\Delta^2\right)}{2T} + \frac{H}{\Delta} + o\left(\frac{1}{T}\right) > 0.
\end{aligned}$$

Hence, the quasi-ML estimator $\widehat{\kappa}_{Euler}$ has a smaller finite-sample bias than the exact ML estimator when $\kappa > 0$ and Δ is small.

Moreover, from the equation in (4.20), the variance of $\widehat{\kappa}_{Euler}$ has the representation of

$$Var\left(\widehat{\kappa}_{Euler}\right) = \frac{1}{\Delta^2} Var\left(\widehat{\varphi}_1\right).$$

In contrast, the delta method suggests that the exact ML estimator $\widehat{\kappa}_n^{ML}$ has the variance of

$$Var\left(\widehat{\kappa}_n^{ML}\right) = \frac{1}{\Delta^2}\frac{1}{\varphi_1^2}\left(Var\left(\widehat{\varphi}_1\right) + O\left(n^{-3/2}\right)\right),$$

when $n \to \infty$ with a fixed Δ. When $\kappa > 0$, which makes $\varphi_1 = \exp\{-\kappa\Delta\} < 1$, we have

$$Var\left(\widehat{\kappa}_{Euler}\right) < Var\left(\widehat{\kappa}_n^{ML}\right).$$

Therefore, the Euler estimator $\widehat{\kappa}_{Euler}$ can perform better than the exact ML estimator in terms of finite-sample variance.

In addition to Euler discretization, Wang et al. (2011) examine the finite-sample performance of alternative quasi-ML estimators from a variety of approximation methods, including the trapezoidal approximation, the Milstein approximation, and the Norman approximation. Their results show that when a higher-order approximation method is adopted, the discretization bias of the estimator decreases, but the estimation bias increases. Because the discretization bias plays a role in offsetting the estimation bias, a higher-order approximation leads to an estimator with a more significant total bias. Therefore, the total bias of the Euler estimator is smaller than that of the estimator based on any higher-order approximation.

Wang et al. (2011) further extend their results to include the OU process with a known mean, general univariate diffusion processes (such as the CIR process), and multivariate OU processes.

Figures 4.3–4.4 provide simulation results to compare the finite-sample performance of κ's alternative estimators. For simplicity, we simulate data from the OU process with a known mean of $\mu = 0$:

$$dr(t) = -\kappa r(t)\, dt + \sigma\, dW(t)\,.$$

For each simulation, we let $T = 4$ and $\Delta = 1/52$, which corresponds to four years of weekly observations. We replicate the simulation 1,000 times to

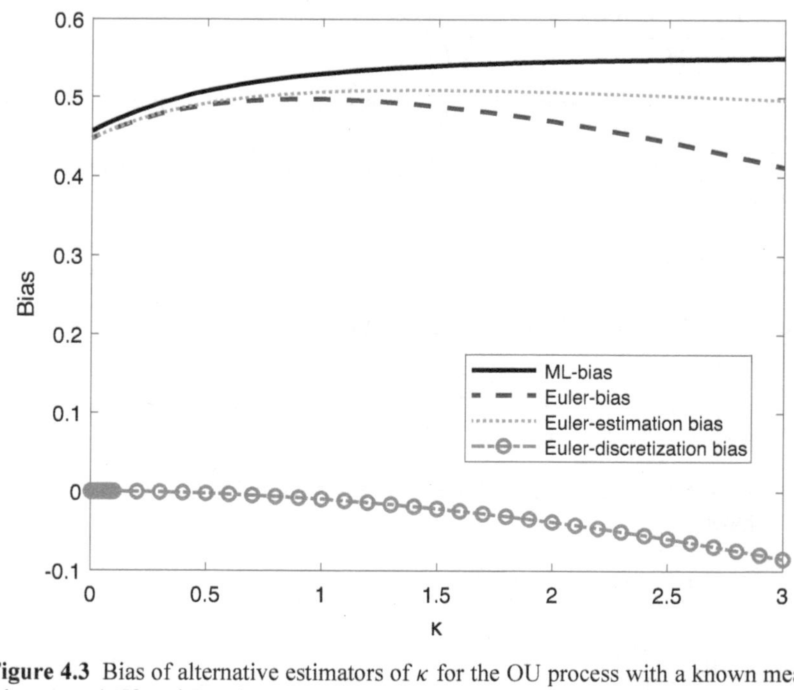

Figure 4.3 Bias of alternative estimators of κ for the OU process with a known mean when $\Delta = 1/52$ and $T = 4$.

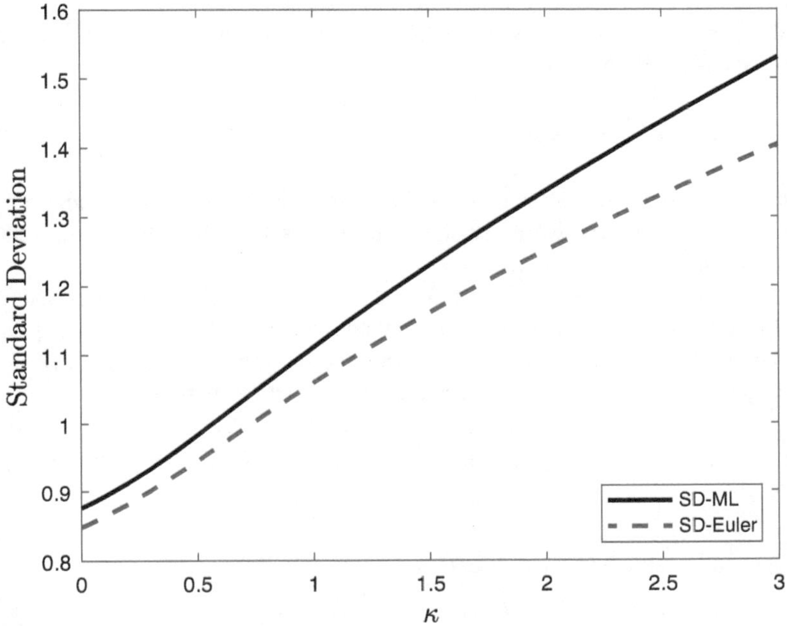

Figure 4.4 Standard deviations of alternative estimators of κ for the OU process with a known mean when $\Delta = 1/52$ and $T = 4$.

calculate the bias and the variance of the Euler estimator and the exact ML estimator of κ. Figure 4.3 reports the bias values. Figure 4.4 displays the simulated variance.

Figures 4.3–4.4 clearly show that the Euler estimator performs better than the exact ML estimator in terms of both finite-sample bias and variance. Figure 4.3 also plots the estimation bias and the discretization bias of the Euler estimator, showing that these two types of bias have opposite signs. Therefore, the estimation bias is offset partially by the discretization bias, reducing the magnitude of the total bias of the Euler estimator.

4.3.4 Bias for General Diffusion Processes

Estimation of general diffusion processes also encounters the issue of finite sample bias. Consider the following general diffusion process with a linear drift:

$$dr(t) = \kappa(\mu - r(t))\,dt + \sigma q(r(t);\psi)\,dW(t), \tag{4.22}$$

where ψ is the vector of unknown parameters, and $q(r(t);\psi)$ is a function of $r(t)$ and ψ. The diffusion process in (4.22) includes most of the models listed in Table 6.1 as special cases. The exact discretization of this general diffusion process takes the form of

$$r_t = e^{-\kappa\Delta} r_{t-1} + \mu\left(1 - e^{-\kappa\Delta}\right) + \int_{(t-1)\Delta}^{t\Delta} e^{\kappa(s-t\Delta)} \sigma q\left(r(s);\psi\right) dW(s).$$

The preceding discretization gives an AR(1) regression with heteroskedasticity. The estimation of the AR root suffers from finite-sample bias, which translates into the estimation of κ in the end.

Due to the complexity of the function $q(r(t);\psi)$, the transitional density of the general diffusion process is not analytically available. Thus, quasi-ML methods based on various approximation methods are often adopted. For example, Nowman (1997) proposes the approximation method as

$$\begin{aligned}\int_{(t-1)\Delta}^{t\Delta} e^{\kappa(s-t\Delta)} \sigma q\left(r(s);\psi\right) dW(s) &\approx q\left(r_{t-1};\psi\right) \int_{(t-1)\Delta}^{t\Delta} e^{\kappa(s-t\Delta)} \sigma\, dW(s) \\ &:= q\left(r_{t-1};\psi\right) \varepsilon_t,\end{aligned}$$

which leads to the Nowman discretization

$$r_t \approx e^{-\kappa\Delta} r_{t-1} + \mu\left(1 - e^{-\kappa\Delta}\right) + q\left(r_{t-1};\psi\right)\varepsilon_t, \tag{4.23}$$

where $\{\varepsilon_t\}$ is an i.i.d. sequence with $N\left(0, \sigma^2\left(1 - e^{-2\kappa\Delta}\right)/(2\kappa)\right)$ distribution. Then, the approximate transition density function, the log-likelihood function, and the associated quasi-ML estimators of parameters can be obtained. The Nowman discretization can provide an excellent approximation of the exact discretization when the sampling interval Δ is reasonably small.

Take the famous CIR process as an example, where $r(t)$ follows the general diffusion process (4.22) with $q(r(t);\psi) = \sqrt{r(t)}$:

$$dr(t) = \kappa\left(\mu - r(t)\right) dt + \sigma\sqrt{r(t)}\, dW(t). \tag{4.24}$$

The Nowman method gives the following approximate discretization:

$$r_t \approx e^{-\kappa\Delta} r_{t-1} + \mu\left(1 - e^{-\kappa\Delta}\right) + \sqrt{r_{t-1}}\varepsilon_t.$$

Tang and Chen (2009) develop the corresponding quasi-ML estimator of κ as

$$\widehat{\kappa}_{CIR-Nowman} = -\frac{1}{\Delta}\ln\left(\widehat{\beta}_1\right),$$

where $\widehat{\beta}_1$ is the quasi-ML estimator of the AR root in the Nowman discretization that takes the form of

$$\widehat{\beta}_1 = \frac{n^{-2}\sum_{t=1}^{n} r_t \sum_{t=1}^{n} r_{t-1}^{-1} - n^{-1}\sum_{t=1}^{n} r_t r_{t-1}^{-1}}{n^{-2}\sum_{t=1}^{n} r_{t-1}\sum_{t=1}^{n} r_{t-1}^{-1} - 1}.$$

$\widehat{\beta}_1$ is a biased estimator, whose bias translates into $\widehat{\kappa}_{CIR-Nowman}$. Tang and Chen (2009) provide an explicit bias formulae for $\widehat{\kappa}_{CIR-Nowman}$, which we report in Theorem 4.3.5.

Theorem 4.3.5 *For a stationary CIR process as given in (4.24) with $2\kappa\mu/\sigma^2 > 2$, the quasi-ML estimator $\widehat{\kappa}_{CIR-Nowman}$ has the bias as*

(a) when $n \to \infty$ with a fixed Δ,

$$Bias\left(\widehat{\kappa}_{CIR-Nowman}\right) = \frac{1}{T}B_3\left(\theta;\Delta\right) + O\left(n^{-2}\right);$$

(b) when $n \to \infty$ with $T \to \infty$ and $\Delta \to 0$, and for some $c > 2$, $T\Delta^{1/c} \to \infty$,

$$Bias\left(\widehat{\kappa}_{CIR-Nowman}\right) = \frac{4}{T} + o\left(T^{-1}\right),$$

where $B_3\left(\theta;\Delta\right)$ takes a complicated form that can be found in Tang and Chen (2009), which is omitted here for space limit.

Wang et al. (2011) propose using the Euler approximation to estimate the CIR model and compare the finite-sample performance of the Euler estimator with that of the estimator from the Nowman approximation. Unlike the OU process, the quasi-ML estimator of the diffusion parameter σ^2 of the CIR process has a substantial finite-sample bias. Detailed analysis and the bias formula can be found in Tang and Chen (2009).

4.3.5 Bias in Pricing Contingent Claims

As studied in Subsection 4.2.2, the pricing formulae of contingent claims, such as bonds and bond options, are nonlinear functions of the parameters in the diffusion process. Therefore, the bias in estimating SDEs' parameters translates into the price calculation of contingent claims. In addition, the estimation variance of the SDEs' parameters may significantly contribute to the bias in pricing contingent claims, because of the nonlinearity of the pricing formulae. In other words, even if all the parameter estimations have no bias, the estimation of the contingent claims prices can still suffer from a severe bias problem.

To investigate the bias issue in pricing contingent claims, let us assume the short-term rate $r(t)$ follows the OU process defined in (4.4), and all the parameters are known except for κ. Use $P(\kappa)$, a function of κ, to denote the price of contingent claims, which is either the price of a zero-coupon bond as given in (4.6) or the price of a bond option as listed in (4.10). Let $\widehat{\kappa}_n^{ML}$ be the ML estimator of κ defined in (4.12). By virtue of the invariance principle, replacing κ in $P(\kappa)$ by $\widehat{\kappa}_n^{ML}$ generates the ML estimate of $P(\kappa)$, denoted by

$$\widehat{P}_n^{ML} = P\left(\widehat{\kappa}_n^{ML}\right).$$

The Taylor expansion about point κ leads to the following equation:

$$\widehat{P}_n^{ML} = P(\kappa) + \frac{\partial P(\kappa)}{\partial \kappa}\left(\widehat{\kappa}_n^{ML} - \kappa\right) + \frac{\partial^2 P(\kappa)}{\partial \kappa^2}\left(\widehat{\kappa}_n^{ML} - \kappa\right)^2 + \cdots.$$

Taking expectations on both sides of the preceding equation, we have

$$E\left(\widehat{P}_n^{ML}\right) - P(\kappa) = \frac{\partial P(\kappa)}{\partial \kappa} E\left(\widehat{\kappa}_n^{ML} - \kappa\right) + \frac{\partial^2 P(\kappa)}{\partial \kappa^2} E\left(\widehat{\kappa}_n^{ML} - \kappa\right)^2 + \cdots. \tag{4.25}$$

Equation (4.25) reveals two important facts of the bias of $\widehat{P}_n^{ML}$. First, the bias of $\widehat{\kappa}_n^{ML}$ translates into $\widehat{P}_n^{ML}$, amplified or reduced by the multiplier $\partial P(\kappa)/\partial \kappa$. Second, the mean-squared-error (MSE) of $\widehat{\kappa}_n^{ML}$ contributes to the bias of $\widehat{P}_n^{ML}$. Its influence on the bias is scaled by $\partial^2 P(\kappa)/\partial \kappa^2$. When the price formula $P(\kappa)$ has strong nonlinearity, which makes the magnitude of $\partial^2 P(\kappa)/\partial \kappa^2$ significant, the finite-sample bias of $\widehat{P}_n^{ML}$ can be very substantial even if $\widehat{P}_n^{ML}$ has no bias.

In a more realistic situation where all the parameters $\theta = (\kappa, \mu, \sigma)$ in the OU process are unknown, the finite-sample bias and variance of the estimation of each parameter contribute to the bias of the contingent-claim price $P(\theta)$. Define

$$\widehat{P}_n^{ML} := P\left(\widehat{\theta}_n^{ML}\right) = P\left(\widehat{\kappa}_n^{ML}, \widehat{\mu}_n^{ML}, \widehat{\sigma}_n^{ML}\right).$$

First, expanding $P\left(\widehat{\theta}_n^{ML}\right)$ about the true value of the parameter vector θ, then taking the expectations, we can have

$$E\left(\widehat{P}_n^{ML}\right) \approx P(\theta) + \begin{bmatrix} \frac{\partial P(\theta)}{\partial \kappa} & \frac{\partial P(\theta)}{\partial \mu} & \frac{\partial P(\theta)}{\partial \sigma} \end{bmatrix} \begin{bmatrix} E\left(\widehat{\kappa}_n^{ML}\right) - \kappa \\ E\left(\widehat{\mu}_n^{ML}\right) - \mu \\ E\left(\widehat{\sigma}_n^{ML}\right) - \sigma \end{bmatrix}$$
$$+ E\left\{ \left(\widehat{\theta}_n^{ML} - \theta\right) \begin{bmatrix} \frac{\partial^2 P(\theta)}{\partial \kappa^2} & \frac{\partial^2 P(\theta)}{\partial \kappa \partial \mu} & \frac{\partial^2 P(\theta)}{\partial \kappa \partial \sigma} \\ \frac{\partial^2 P(\theta)}{\partial \mu \partial \kappa} & \frac{\partial^2 P(\theta)}{\partial \mu^2} & \frac{\partial^2 P(\theta)}{\partial \mu \partial \sigma} \\ \frac{\partial^2 P(\theta)}{\partial \sigma \partial \kappa} & \frac{\partial^2 P(\theta)}{\partial \sigma \partial \mu} & \frac{\partial^2 P(\theta)}{\partial \sigma^2} \end{bmatrix} \left(\widehat{\theta}_n^{ML} - \theta\right)' \right\},$$

where $\widehat{\theta}_n^{ML} - \theta$ is a 1×3 row vector and $(\cdot)'$ denotes the vector transpose. In this case, besides the bias and variance, the covariance of the estimators $\left(\widehat{\kappa}_n^{ML}, \widehat{\mu}_n^{ML}, \widehat{\sigma}_n^{ML}\right)$ also contributes to the bias of $\widehat{P}_n^{ML}$.

We provide some simulation results in Table 4.2 to further illustrate the bias problem in pricing contingent claims. The simulation settings are similar to those in Phillips and Yu (2005, 2009), where the bias problem has been systematically studied and more simulation results can be found.

Table 4.2 *Bias in pricing contingent claims. The left panel reports the simulation results for the Vasicek model, where* $\widehat{BP}_n^{ML}$ *is the estimate of the price of a three-year discount bond and* $\widehat{OP}_n^{ML}$ *represents the estimate of the price of a two-year call option written on the discount bond. The right panel gives the simulation results for the Black–Scholes model, where* $\widehat{OP}_n^{ML}$ *denotes the estimate of the price of a one-week call option written on a stock.*

	Vasicek model			Black–Scholes	
	$\widehat{\kappa}_n^{ML}$	$\widehat{BP}_n^{ML}$	$\widehat{OP}_n^{ML}$	$\widehat{\sigma}_n^{2,ML}$	$\widehat{OP}_n^{ML}$
True	0.02	83.12	5.5098	0.45	5.44
Mean	0.063	82.37	5.0944	0.4478	6.25
Bias (in %)	215.09	−0.909	−7.54	−0.4791	14.96

The left panel of Table 4.2 reports the simulation results for the Vasicek model. The data are simulated from the OU process with $\kappa = 0.02$, $\mu = 0.12$, and $\sigma = 0.01$. Let κ be the only unknown parameter and $\widehat{\kappa}$ the ML estimator defined in (4.16). Use BP to denote the price of a three-year discount bond with the terminal payoff $L = \$100$, and OP as the price of a two-year call option written on the discount bond. Set the annual interest rate to be 6 percent, and the strike price of the option as $K = 105 \times \exp\{-3 \times 0.06\}$. The true values of BP and OP are calculated by using the pricing formulae given in (4.9) and (4.10), respectively. We assume the market price of risk to be $\lambda = 0$ for simplicity. Replacing κ in the pricing formulae by $\widehat{\kappa}$ yields the ML estimates of the bond price and the option price, denoted by $\widehat{BP}_n^{ML}$ and $\widehat{OP}_n^{ML}$, respectively. For each sample path, we simulate 5,000 data with $T = 30$ and $\Delta = 1/250$, corresponding to 30 years of daily observations. We replicate the simulation 5,000 times to calculate the bias of $\widehat{\kappa}$, $\widehat{BP}_n^{ML}$ and $\widehat{OP}_n^{ML}$.

Two features are apparent in the left panel of Table 4.2. First, the ML estimator $\widehat{\kappa}$ is severely upward biased. The bias percentage is 215.09 percent. Second, $\widehat{BP}_n^{ML}$ and $\widehat{OP}_n^{ML}$ have negative bias. Although economically significant, the bias percentage of the bond price is −0.909 percent only. In contrast, the bias percentage of the option price is much more substantial, reaching −7.54 percent.

The right panel of Table 4.2 reports simulation results for the Black–Scholes option pricing model, in which we can see that the parameter of the underlying diffusion process has almost no estimation bias, whereas the estimation of the option price has substantial bias. In the Black–Scholes model, the stock price $S(t)$ is assumed to be a process of geometric Brownian motion (GBM):

$$dS(t) = \alpha S(t)\, dt + \sigma S(t)\, dB(t), \tag{4.26}$$

where α and σ are two constants. Consider a European call option written on this stock with a strike price K and a maturity τ. The Black–Scholes option pricing formula takes the form of

$$OP = S(t)\,\Phi(d_1) - Ke^{-r\tau}\,\Phi(d_2), \tag{4.27}$$

where $d_1 = \left[\ln(S(t)/K) + \left(r + 0.5\sigma^2\right)\tau\right] / \left(\sigma\sqrt{\tau}\right)$, $d_2 = d_1 - \sigma\sqrt{\tau}$, $\Phi(\cdot)$ denotes the cumulative function of the standard normal distribution, and r is the averaged annual interest rate from time t to $t+\tau$. In this example, the only unknown parameter in the option price is σ^2. Lo (1988) advocates the following ML estimator of σ^2 with discrete-time price observations $\{S_t\}_{t=0}^{n}$:

$$\widehat{\sigma}_n^{2,ML} = \frac{1}{n}\sum_{t=0}^{n-1}\left(\ln\frac{S_{t+1}}{S_t} - n^{-1}\sum_{t=0}^{n-1}\ln\frac{S_{t+1}}{S_t}\right)^2. \tag{4.28}$$

Putting $\widehat{\sigma}_n^{2,ML}$ into the pricing formula yields the ML estimate of the option price $\widehat{OP}_n^{ML} = OP\left(\widehat{\sigma}_n^{2,ML}\right)$.

We simulate data from the GBM defined in (4.26) with $\alpha = 0$, $\sigma^2 = 0.45$, $\Delta = 1/250$, and $n = T/\Delta = 250$, corresponding to one year of daily observations. Assume that the initial price of the stock is $S(0) = 100$. Consider a deep out-of-money call option with $K = 1.4S(0)\,e^{r\tau}$, $r = 6\%$, and $\tau = 5/250$ (the option expires in one week). For each simulated sample path, calculate the ML estimates of $\widehat{\sigma}_n^{2,ML}$ and $\widehat{OP}_n^{ML}$. We replicate the experiment 5,000 times to obtain the bias of the ML estimates, and report them in the right panel of Table 4.2.

The simulation results show that the ML estimator of the parameter in the diffusion price, $\widehat{\sigma}_n^{2,ML}$, has almost no bias. In contrast, the estimate of the option price, $\widehat{OP}_n^{ML}$, is severely upward biased, with the bias percentage of 14.96 percent. The bias in pricing option is attributable to the nonlinearity of the price formula with respect to σ^2. In the same spirit of Equation (4.25), it is easy to get

$$\begin{aligned} &E\left(\widehat{OP}_n^{ML}\right) - OP\left(\sigma^2\right) \\ &= \frac{\partial OP\left(\sigma^2\right)}{\partial\sigma^2}E\left(\widehat{\sigma}_n^{2,ML} - \sigma^2\right) + \frac{\partial^2 OP\left(\sigma^2\right)}{\partial\left(\sigma^2\right)^2}E\left(\widehat{\sigma}_n^{2,ML} - \sigma^2\right)^2 + \cdots. \end{aligned}$$

When $\widehat{\sigma}_n^{2,ML}$ has almost no bias, the contribution of the first term in the preceding equation to the option pricing bias becomes negligible. However, $\widehat{\sigma}_n^{2,ML}$ can have significant variance, and hence significant MSE. Phillips and Yu (2009) point out that the price of the deep-out-money call option is a strongly nonlinear function of σ^2. That means $\frac{\partial^2 OP(\sigma^2)}{\partial(\sigma^2)^2}$ has a large magnitude. Therefore, the MSE of $\widehat{\sigma}_n^{2,ML}$ is amplified by the multiplier $\frac{\partial^2 OP(\sigma^2)}{\partial(\sigma^2)^2}$, making $\widehat{OP}_n^{ML}$ have substantial finite-sample bias.

4.4 Bias-Correction Methods

To reduce the estimation bias of κ in the OU process defined in (4.4), it is possible to simply apply the explicit bias formulae, such as those in (4.13), (4.18), and (4.21), to perform bias correction. However, no bias formulae are available when interest quantities are the parameters in either general diffusion processes or the prices of contingent claims, such as bonds and options. This section introduces two bias-correction methods that work well without knowing the bias formula: the jackknife method and the indirect inference method. Both methods can effectively reduce bias. The jackknife technique is easy to implement. In comparison, the indirect inference approach can simultaneously reduce bias and variance, at least in some situations.

4.4.1 Jackknife Method

The jackknife method was proposed by Quenouille (1956) to reduce the finite sample bias in parametric estimation problems. It has many applications in discrete time models; see, for example, Efron (1982), Shao and Tu (1995), and Hahn and Newey (2004). Phillips and Yu (2005) implement this method in estimating continuous-time diffusion processes and contingent claims prices.

To illustrate the idea of the jackknife technique, let us consider the OU process (4.4) as an example. The exact ML estimator $\widehat{\kappa}_n^{ML}$ has been defined in (4.12), where $n = T/\Delta$ represents the sample size. Formula (4.13) describes the finite-sample bias of $\widehat{\kappa}_n^{ML}$, which is rewritten here for convenience:

$$E\left(\widehat{\kappa}_n^{ML}\right) = \kappa + \frac{c}{T} + O\left(n^{-2}\right) = \kappa + \frac{c}{n\Delta} + O\left(n^{-2}\right),$$

where $c = 5/2 + e^{\kappa\Delta} + e^{2\kappa\Delta}/2$. Now, decompose the whole sample into m consecutive subsamples, each of which has $l = n/m$ observations. Let $\widehat{\kappa}_{li}^{ML}$ denote the ML estimator of κ by using the observations in the ith subsample, for $i = 1, 2, \ldots, m$. From the formula (4.13), $\widehat{\kappa}_{li}^{ML}$ has the finite-sample bias

$$E\left(\widehat{\kappa}_{li}^{ML}\right) = \kappa + \frac{m}{n\Delta}c + O\left(\left(\frac{n}{m}\right)^{-2}\right).$$

Define the jackknife estimator as

$$\widehat{\kappa}_{jack} = \frac{m}{m-1}\widehat{\kappa}_n^{ML} - \frac{\sum_{i=1}^m \widehat{\kappa}_{li}^{ML}}{m^2 - m}. \tag{4.29}$$

The expectation of the jackknife estimator is

$$E\left(\widehat{\kappa}_{jack}\right) = \frac{m}{m-1}\left(\kappa + \frac{c}{n\Delta}\right) - \frac{\sum_{i=1}^{m}\left(\kappa + \frac{m}{n\Delta}c\right)}{m^2 - m} + O\left(n^{-2}\right)$$
$$= \kappa + O\left(n^{-2}\right).$$

The preceding formula clearly shows that the leading term of the bias of $\widehat{\kappa}_n^{ML}$ is canceled out by the counterparts of $\widehat{\kappa}_{li}^{ML}$. As a result, the bias of the jackknife estimator $\widehat{\kappa}_{jack}$ is reduced to the order of $O\left(n^{-2}\right)$.

To apply the jackknife technique, people often choose $m=2$ for simplicity. However, choosing larger values of m can help reduce the finite-sample variance of the jackknife estimator. The variance of $\widehat{\kappa}_{jack}$ with small values of m is often greater than that of the ML estimator $\widehat{\kappa}_n^{ML}$. However, under broad conditions, these two estimators can have the same asymptotic variance. For the stationary OU process with $\kappa > 0$, Tang and Chen (2009) prove that $\sqrt{n}\left(\widehat{\kappa}_n^{ML} - \kappa\right)$ converges to a normally distributed random variable as $n \to \infty$ with a fixed Δ. From the formula in (4.29), we have

$$\sqrt{n}\left(\widehat{\kappa}_{jack} - \kappa\right) = \frac{m\sqrt{n}\left(\widehat{\kappa}_n^{ML} - \kappa\right)}{m-1} - \frac{1}{m-1}\left\{\frac{1}{\sqrt{m}}\sum_{i=1}^{m}\sqrt{l}\left(\widehat{\kappa}_{li}^{ML} - \kappa\right)\right\}.$$

The stationarity of the OU process makes $\widehat{\kappa}_{li}^{ML}$, for $i = 1, 2, \ldots, m$, a weakly dependent sequence. Hence, when $n \to \infty$ with $m \to \infty$ and $1/l + m/l \to 0$, the second term in the preceding equation goes to zero, making $\widehat{\kappa}_{jack}$ have the same limiting distribution as $\widehat{\kappa}_n^{ML}$.

When the quantity of interest becomes the price of the contingent claims, as in the case of bonds and options, plugging the jackknife estimator $\widehat{\kappa}_{jack}$ into the corresponding pricing formula may not lead to a better estimate of the price than the ML estimate in terms of finite-sample bias. This is because, as shown by Equation (4.24), both the bias and the MSE of $\widehat{\kappa}_{jack}$ contribute to the bias of the price estimation. The MSE part is critically important for pricing bias when price formulae have strong nonlinearity. The jackknife estimator $\widehat{\kappa}_{jack}$ has a smaller bias but a greater variance than $\widehat{\kappa}_n^{ML}$. More often than not, $\widehat{\kappa}_{jack}$ has a larger MSE than $\widehat{\kappa}_n^{ML}$. Accordingly, the plug-in estimator $P\left(\widehat{\kappa}_{jack}\right)$ may have a greater bias than the ML estimator $P\left(\widehat{\kappa}_n^{ML}\right)$.

To obtain a bias-reduced estimator for the contingent claims price, Phillips and Yu (2005) recommend applying the jackknife technique directly to the price estimation through the following procedure:

1. Obtain the ML estimate $\widehat{\kappa}_n^{ML}$ using the entire sample;
2. Calculate the price estimate $P\left(\widehat{\kappa}_n^{ML}\right)$;
3. Use subsamples to obtain the estimates $\left\{\widehat{\kappa}_{li}^{ML}\right\}_{i=1}^{m}$;
4. Calculate the price estimates $P\left(\widehat{\kappa}_{li}^{ML}\right)$, for $i = 1, \ldots, m$;

Table 4.3 *Comparison of alternative estimators in option pricing. Data are simulated from the OU process in (4.4) with* $\kappa = 0.02$. *A two-year call option written on a discount bond that expires in three years with the terminal payoff* $L = 100$ *is considered. The* $\widehat{OP}_n^{ML}$, $\widehat{OP}_n^{Jack}$, *and* $\widehat{OP}_n^{SM}$ *columns are the ML estimator, the jackknife estimator with* $m = 2$, *and the indirect inference estimator, respectively.*

True value: $OP = 5.5098$			
Estimation Method	$\widehat{OP}_n^{ML}$	$\widehat{OP}_n^{Jack}$	$\widehat{OP}_n^{II}$
Mean	5.0944	5.2386	5.3923
Bias (in %)	−7.54	−4.9226	−2.134
Std err	0.7712	0.8517	0.7434
RMSE	0.8760	0.8939	0.7526

5. Obtain the final estimate of the price by using the jackknife estimator

$$\widehat{P}_{jack} = \frac{m}{m-1} P\left(\widehat{\kappa}_n^{ML}\right) - \frac{\sum_{i=1}^{m} P\left(\widehat{\kappa}_{li}^{ML}\right)}{m^2 - m}. \tag{4.30}$$

The estimation procedure presented here reveals another merit of the jackknife method: Implementing the jackknife technique does not require any knowledge of the analytical form of the bias. Moreover, provided that the bias of $P\left(\widehat{\kappa}_n^{ML}\right)$ can be expanded asymptotically in a series of increasing powers of n^{-1}, it can be proved that the jackknife estimator $\widehat{P}_{jack}$ has a bias of order $O\left(n^{-2}\right)$, not $O\left(n^{-1}\right)$.

Table 4.3 summarizes certain simulation results to reveal the performance of the jackknife technique in reducing the bias of option pricing. The simulation settings are the same as in Table 4.2. Again, we use OP to denote the price of a two-year call option written on a discount bond that expires in three years with the terminal payoff $L = \$100$. The $\widehat{OP}_n^{ML}$ represents the ML estimator of the option price, and $\widehat{OP}_n^{Jack}$ is the jackknife estimator with $m = 2$. $\widehat{OP}_n^{II}$ is the indirect-inference estimator that will be introduced in Subsection 4.4.2.

Table 4.3 clearly shows that the jackknife technique can significantly reduce the estimation bias compared with the ML approach. The bias percentage of the ML estimator $\widehat{OP}_n^{ML}$ is −7.54 percent. The jackknife estimator $\widehat{OP}_n^{Jack}$ reduces that percentage to −4.92 percent. However, Table 4.3 also shows that the jackknife estimator has a greater standard error than the ML estimator and slightly increases the MSE.

4.4.2 Indirect Inference Method

Many models in economics and finance are too complex to permit the likelihood function to be constructed analytically, but they can readily be simulated. To estimate these models effectively, Smith (1993) and Gouriéroux et al. (1993) develop a simulation-based estimation method that is called the indirect inference (II) approach. This technique can also be applied to perform bias correction in estimation. Among many other applications, the II technique is used by Phillips and Yu (2009) to correct the bias in pricing contingent claims, Gouriéroux et al. (2010) to reduce bias in estimating dynamic panel models, and Jiang et al. (2018) to reduce bias in structural change-point estimation.

This subsection takes the OU process defined in (4.4), with κ being the only unknown parameter, as an example to introduce the idea of the II method. We first consider the estimation of κ and then study the estimation of contingent claims prices.

Assume n is the number of observations available. Then, $\widehat{\kappa}_n^{ML}$ defined in (4.12) gives the ML estimate of κ. Empirical studies in the asset pricing literature suggest that reasonable values of κ fall into the interval $[0,3]$. For any possible choice of $\kappa \in [0,3]$, we can simulate data straightforwardly from the exact discretization of the OU process given in (4.11). Replicating the simulation K times generates K simulated data sets, denoted by $\widetilde{R}^{(j)} = \left\{\widetilde{r}_1^{(j)}, \widetilde{r}_2^{(j)}, \ldots, \widetilde{r}_n^{(j)}\right\}$, for $j = 1, 2, \ldots, K$. For the jth simulated data set, an ML estimate $\widetilde{\kappa}_n^{ML,j}$ can be obtained by using the same formula as in (4.12). Then, the indirect inference estimator of κ is defined as

$$\widehat{\kappa}_n^{II} = \arg\min_{\kappa \in [0,3]} \left| \widehat{\kappa}_n^{ML} - \frac{1}{K}\sum_{j=1}^{K} \widetilde{\kappa}_n^{ML,j} \right|. \tag{4.31}$$

The logic behind the indirect inference estimator is as follows. By construction, $\widetilde{\kappa}_n^{ML,j}$ should have the same finite sample properties as $\widehat{\kappa}_n^{ML}$. The sample mean of $\widetilde{\kappa}_n^{ML,j}$ can serve as a good approximation to the population expectation of $\widehat{\kappa}_n^{ML}$. In the case where $K \to \infty$, the law of large numbers implies that

$$\frac{1}{K}\sum_{j=1}^{K} \widetilde{\kappa}_n^{ML,j} \xrightarrow{p} E\left(\widetilde{\kappa}_n^{ML,j}\right) := b_n(\kappa),$$

where $\xrightarrow{p}$ denotes convergence in probability and $b_n(\kappa)$ is called the binding function. For each value of $\kappa \in [0,3]$, $b_n(\kappa)$ gives the expectation of the ML estimator of κ. When $b_n(\kappa)$ is invertible, the II estimator becomes

$$\widehat{\kappa}_n^{II} = \arg\min_{\kappa \in [0,3]} \left| \widehat{\kappa}_n^{ML} - b_n(\kappa) \right| = b_n^{-1}\left(\widehat{\kappa}_n^{ML}\right).$$

This means that the II estimator aims at finding one value of κ that minimizes the distance between the ML estimate $\widehat{\kappa}_n^{ML}$ and its expectation. Note that any bias occurring in $\widehat{\kappa}_n^{ML}$ also happens in the binding function $b_n(\kappa)$. Hence, $\widehat{\kappa}_n^{II}$ can correct the bias appearing in $\widehat{\kappa}_n^{ML}$.

Moreover, the II estimator is possible to possess a smaller finite-sample variance than $\widehat{\kappa}_n^{ML}$. The Taylor expansion of $b_n^{-1}\left(\widehat{\kappa}_n^{ML}\right)$ about the point $b_n(\kappa)$ takes the form of

$$\begin{aligned}\widehat{\kappa}_n^{II} &= b_n^{-1}\left(\widehat{\kappa}_n^{ML}\right)\\ &= \kappa + \left(\left.\frac{\partial b_n(\kappa)}{\partial \kappa}\right|_{\kappa=b_n(\kappa)}\right)^{-1}\left(\widehat{\kappa}_n^{ML} - b_n(\kappa)\right) + o_p\left(\left(\widehat{\kappa}_n^{ML} - b_n(\kappa)\right)\right),\end{aligned}$$

which leads to the approximation

$$Var\left(\widehat{\kappa}_n^{II}\right) \approx \left(\left.\frac{\partial b_n(\kappa)}{\partial \kappa}\right|_{\kappa=b_n(\kappa)}\right)^{-2} Var\left(\widehat{\kappa}_n^{ML}\right).$$

Therefore, when $|\partial b_n(\kappa)/\partial\kappa| > 1$, the slope of the binding function being greater than unity, we can have $Var\left(\widehat{\kappa}_n^{II}\right) < Var\left(\widehat{\kappa}_n^{ML}\right)$.

In addition to improving the finite-sample performance, the II estimator $\widehat{\kappa}_n^{II}$ can have the same good asymptotic properties as $\widehat{\kappa}_n^{ML}$. When $\widehat{\kappa}_n^{ML}$ is asymptotically unbiased with $\lim_{n\to\infty} E\left(\widehat{\kappa}_n^{ML}\right) = \kappa$, it has $\lim_{n\to\infty} b_n(\kappa) = \kappa$. Hence, $\widehat{\kappa}_n^{II}$ is asymptotically equivalent to $\widehat{\kappa}_n^{ML}$ as $n \to \infty$.

When the quantity of interest is either the bond price or the option price, constructing the II estimator needs to first set an interval containing possible price values. For any given price value in the interval, take the inverse of the pricing formula to obtain the corresponding value of the parameter in the diffusion process, then generate data by simulations. The concrete steps of applying the II technique to estimate the contingent claims price are as follows:

1. Obtain the ML estimate of the price $\widehat{P}_n^{ML} = P\left(\widehat{\kappa}_n^{ML}\right)$ by using the real observations available.
2. Based on the estimate $\widehat{P}_n^{ML}$, set an interval for possible price values, denoted by Λ.
3. For any given choice of $p \in \Lambda$, invert the pricing formula, Formula (4.9) for the bond price and (4.10) for the option price, to obtain the corresponding value of the parameter $\kappa = P^{-1}(p)$.
4. Simulate data from the OU process in (4.4) with $\kappa = P^{-1}(p)$ to get the simulated sample paths $\widetilde{R}^{(j)} = \left\{\widetilde{r}_1^{(j)}, \widetilde{r}_2^{(j)}, \ldots, \widetilde{r}_n^{(j)}\right\}$, for $j = 1, 2, \ldots, K$.

   For each simulated sample path, obtain the ML estimate $\widetilde{\kappa}_n^{ML,j}$ and $\widetilde{P}_n^{ML,j}(p) = P\left(\widetilde{\kappa}_n^{ML,j}\right)$.

5. Calculate the sample average of $\widetilde{P}_n^{ML,j}(p)$ as a simulated binding function

$$\widetilde{b}_n(p) = \frac{1}{K}\sum_{j=1}^{K} \widetilde{P}_n^{ML,j}(p). \tag{4.32}$$

6. Obtain the II estimate of P by

$$\widehat{P}_n^{II} = \arg\min_{p\in\Lambda} \left|\widehat{P}_n^{ML} - \widetilde{b}_n(p)\right|. \tag{4.33}$$

Simulation results reported in Table 4.3 demonstrate the finite-sample performance of the II estimator in pricing bond options. As in Table 4.2, a two-year call option written on a discount bond that expires in three years with the terminal payoff $L = 100$ is considered. We use $\widehat{OP}_n^{II}$ to denote the II estimator of the option price, and replicate the simulation 5,000 times to calculate the binding function.

Three features are clear in Table 4.3. First, compared to the ML estimator $\widehat{OP}_n^{ML}$, the II estimator $\widehat{OP}_n^{II}$ significantly reduces the bias, from -7.54 to -2.13 percent. Second, the finite-sample variance and the RMSE of $\widehat{OP}_n^{II}$ are also smaller than those of the ML estimator $\widehat{OP}_n^{ML}$. The variance of $\widehat{OP}_n^{ML}$ is 0.7712. In contrast, the variance of $\widehat{OP}_n^{II}$ is only 0.7434. Third, $\widehat{OP}_n^{II}$ performs better than the jackknife estimator $\widehat{OP}_n^{Jack}$ in terms of both finite-sample bias and variance. It is noticeable that the bias of $\widehat{OP}_n^{II}$ is less than half of the bias of $\widehat{OP}_n^{Jack}$.

To better understand the second feature mentioned above, namely, that $\widehat{OP}_n^{II}$ has a smaller finite-sample variance than $\widehat{OP}_n^{ML}$, Figure 4.5 plots the simulated binding function $\widetilde{b}_n(p)$ as defined in (4.31). It is clearly shown that the bonding function is nonlinear in the upper-right corner. The upper-right corner corresponds to a range of small values of κ, a region suggested by most empirical studies in the term structure literature. More importantly, the slope of the binding function in the upper-right corner is greater than unity. When the replication number increases, that is, $K \to \infty$, it has

$$\lim_{K\to\infty} \widetilde{b}_n(p) = \lim_{K\to\infty} \frac{1}{K}\sum_{j=1}^{K} \widetilde{P}_n^{ML,j}(p) = E\left(\widetilde{P}_n^{ML,j}(p)\right) := b_n(p),$$

and

$$\widehat{OP}_n^{II} = \arg\min_{p\in\Lambda} \left|\widehat{OP}_n^{ML} - b_n(p)\right| = b_n^{-1}\left(\widehat{OP}_n^{ML}\right).$$

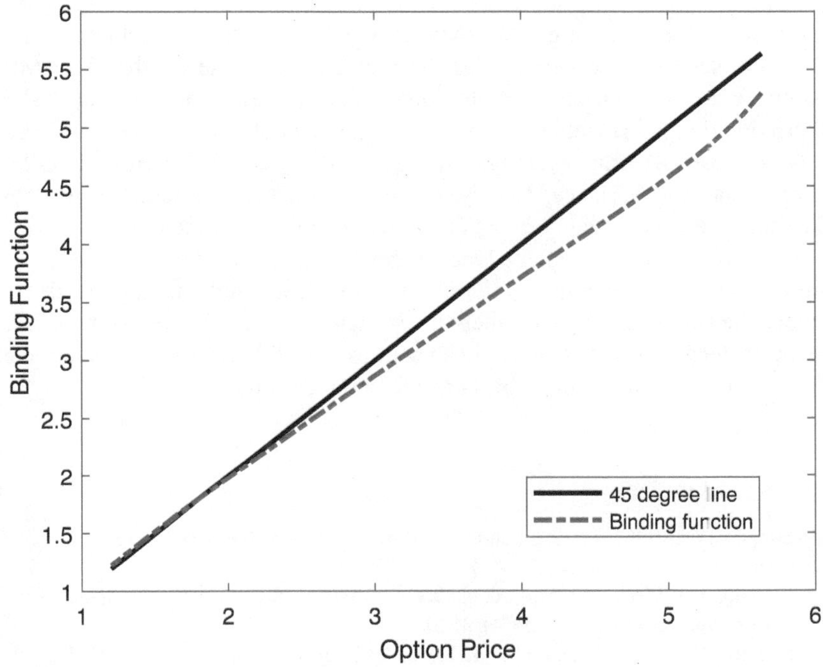

Figure 4.5 Binding function of the II estimator of the option price. The blue dash-dotted line draws the binding function $\widetilde{b}_n(p)$ defined in (4.31). The 45° solid line is plotted for comparison.

The Delta method implies that

$$Var\left(\widehat{OP}_n^{II}\right) \approx \left(\left.\frac{\partial b_n(p)}{\partial p}\right|_{p=b_n(p)}\right)^{-2} Var\left(\widehat{OP}_n^{ML}\right).$$

Hence, the slope of the binding function being larger than unity makes the variance of $\widehat{OP}_n^{II}$ smaller than that of $\widehat{OP}_n^{ML}$.

4.5 Conclusion

This chapter briefly reviews recent developments in the finite-sample theory of continuous-time models. It consists of three main parts. The first part introduces the applications of univariate diffusion processes in modeling short-term interest rates. Taking the OU process as an example, this part builds up the connections between the diffusion process and the prices of contingent claims, including both bonds and bond options.

The second part studies the finite-sample properties of the estimation of diffusion processes. We focus on the persistency parameter in the OU process and note that although it enjoys asymptotic efficiency, the ML estimator suffers from severe finite-sample bias. Various bias formulae for the exact ML estimator are introduced. Then, the quasi-ML estimator based on the Euler approximation is presented, along with an explanation of why this quasi-ML approach can perform better than the exact ML method in terms of finite-sample bias and variance. Finally, the bias problems in estimating general diffusion processes and in pricing contingent claims are discussed.

The third part of the chapter advocates two bias-correction methods: the jackknife method and the indirect inference method. Both methods can effectively reduce the finite-sample bias when the explicit bias formula is unknown. The jackknife technique is easy to apply. In contrast, the indirect inference approach may reduce the finite-sample bias and the variance simultaneously.

Bibliography

Aït-Sahalia, Y. (1996). Testing continuous-time models of the spot interest rate. *The Review of Financial Studies 9*(2), 385–426.

Aït-Sahalia, Y. (1999). Transition densities for interest rate and other nonlinear diffusions. *Journal of Finance 54*(4), 1361–1395.

Aït-Sahalia, Y. (2002). Maximum likelihood estimation of discretely sampled diffusions: A closed-form approximation approach. *Econometrica 70*(1), 223–262.

Aït-Sahalia, Y. (2008). Closed-form likelihood expansions for multivariate diffusions. *Annals of Statistics 36*(2), 906–937.

Aït-Sahalia, Y., J. Fan, and D. Xiu (2010). High-frequency covariance estimates with noisy and asynchronous financial data. *Journal of the American Statistical Association 105*(492), 1504–1517.

Aït-Sahalia, Y. and R. Kimmel (2007). Maximum likelihood estimation of stochastic volatility models. *Journal of Financial Economics 83*(2), 413–452.

Andersen, T. G. and J. Lund (1997). Estimating continuous-time stochastic volatility models of the short-term interest rate. *Journal of Econometrics 77*(2), 343–377.

Ball, C. A. and W. N. Torous (1996). Unit roots and the estimation of interest rate dynamics. *Journal of Empirical Finance 3*(2), 215–238.

Bartlett, M. S. (1946). On the theoretical specification and sampling properties of autocorrelated time-series. *Supplement to the Journal of the Royal Statistical Society 8*(1), 27–41.

Bergstrom, A. R. (1966). Nonrecursive models as discrete approximations to systems of stochastic differential equations. *Econometrica 34*(1), 173–182.

Bergstrom, A. R. (1990). *Continuous Time Econometric Modelling*. Oxford University Press.

Black, F. and M. Scholes (1973). The pricing of options and corporate liabilities. *Journal of Political Economy 81*(3), 637–654.

Brennan, M. J. and E. S. Schwartz (1980). Analyzing convertible bonds. *Journal of Financial and Quantitative Analysis 15*(4), 907–929.

Chan, K. C., G. A. Karolyi, F. A. Longstaff, and A. B. Sanders (1992). An empirical comparison of alternative models of the short-term interest rate. *Journal of Finance 47*(3), 1209–1227.

Chapman, D. A. and N. D. Pearson (2000). Is the short rate drift actually nonlinear? *The Journal of Finance 55*(1), 355–388.

Cox, J. C., J. E. Ingersoll, and S. A. Ross (1980). An analysis of variable rate loan contracts. *The Journal of Finance 35*(2), 389–403.

Cox, J. C., J. E. Ingersoll Jr, and S. A. Ross (1985). A theory of the term structure of interest rates. *Econometrica 53*(2), 385–407.

Duffie, D. and R. Kan (1996). A yield-factor model of interest rates. *Mathematical Finance 6*(4), 379–406.

Duffie, D., J. Pan, and K. Singleton (2000). Transform analysis and asset pricing for affine jump-diffusions. *Econometrica 68*(6), 1343–1376.

Durham, G. B. (2003). Likelihood-based specification analysis of continuous-time models of the short-term interest rate. *Journal of Financial Economics 70*(3), 463–487.

Durham, G. B. and A. R. Gallant (2002). Numerical techniques for maximum likelihood estimation of continuous-time diffusion processes. *Journal of Business & Economic Statistics 20*(3), 297–338.

Efron, B. (1982). *The Jackknife, the Bootstrap and other Resampling Plans*. SIAM.

Elerian, O., S. Chib, and N. Shephard (2001). Likelihood inference for discretely observed nonlinear diffusions. *Econometrica 69*(4), 959–993.

Eraker, B. (2001). MCMC analysis of diffusion models with application to finance. *Journal of Business & Economic Statistics 19*(2), 177–191.

Florens-Zmirou, D. (1989). Approximate discrete-time schemes for statistics of diffusion processes. *Statistics: A Journal of Theoretical and Applied Statistics 20*(4), 547–557.

Gallant, A. R. and G. Tauchen (1996). Which moments to match? *Econometric Theory 12*(4), 657–681.

Gallant, A. R. and G. Tauchen (1998). Reprojecting partially observed systems with application to interest rate diffusions. *Journal of the American Statistical Association 93*(441), 10–24.

Gouriéroux, C., A. Monfort, and E. Renault (1993). Indirect inference. *Journal of Applied Econometrics 8*(S1), S85–S118.

Gouriéroux, C., P. C. B. Phillips, and J. Yu (2010). Indirect inference for dynamic panel models. *Journal of Econometrics 157*(1), 68–77.

Gouriéroux, C. and R. Sufana (2006). A classification of two-factor affine diffusion term structure models. *Journal of Financial Econometrics 4*(1), 31–52.

Hahn, J. and W. Newey (2004). Jackknife and analytical bias reduction for nonlinear panel models. *Econometrica 72*(4), 1295–1319.

Hansen, L. P. and J. A. Scheinkman (1995). Back to the future: Generating moment implications for continuous-time Markov processes. *Econometrica 63*(4), 767–804.

Heston, S. L. (1993). A closed-form solution for options with stochastic volatility with applications to bond and currency options. *The Review of Financial Studies 6*(2), 327–343.

Hull, J. and A. White (1987). The pricing of options on assets with stochastic volatilities. *The Journal of Finance 42*(2), 281–300.

Hurvicz, L. (1950). Least square bias in time series. In *Statistical Inference in Dynamic Economic Models*, pp. 365–383. New York, Wiley.

Jamshidian, F. (1989). An exact bond option formula. *The Journal of Finance 44*(1), 205–209.

Jiang, L., X. Wang, and J. Yu (2018). New distribution theory for the estimation of structural break point in mean. *Journal of Econometrics 205*(1), 156–176.

Kendall, M. G. (1954). Note on bias in the estimation of autocorrelation. *Biometrika 41*(3–4), 403–404.

Knight, J. L. and J. Yu (2002). Empirical characteristic function in time series estimation. *Econometric Theory 18*(3), 691–721.

Li, C. (2013). Maximum-likelihood estimation for diffusion processes via closed-form density expansions. *The Annals of Statistics 41*(3), 1350–1380.

Lo, A. W. (1988). Maximum likelihood estimation of generalized Itô processes with discretely sampled data. *Econometric Theory 4*(2), 231–247.

Marriott, F. and J. Pope (1954). Bias in the estimation of autocorrelations. *Biometrika 41*(3/4), 390–402.

Merton, R. C. (1973). Theory of rational option pricing. *The Bell Journal of Economics and Management Science 4*(1), 141–183.

Merton, R. C. (1992). *Continuous Time Finance*. Basel: Blackwell.

Nowman, K. B. (1997). Gaussian estimation of single-factor continuous time models of the term structure of interest rates. *The Journal of Finance 52*(4), 1695–1706.

Pedersen, A. R. (1995). A new approach to maximum likelihood estimation for stochastic differential equations based on discrete observations. *Scandinavian Journal of Statistics 22*(1), 55–71.

Phillips, P. C. B. (1972). The structural estimation of a stochastic differential equation system. *Econometrica: Journal of the Econometric Society 40*(6), 1021–1041.

Phillips, P. C. B. and J. Yu (2005). Jackknifing bond option prices. *The Review of Financial Studies 18*(2), 707–742.

Phillips, P. C. B. and J. Yu (2009). Simulation-based estimation of contingent-claims prices. *The Review of Financial Studies 22*(9), 3669–3705.

Piazzesi, M. (2010). Affine term structure models. In *Handbook of Financial Econometrics: Tools and Techniques*, pp. 691–766. Elsevier.

Quenouille, M. H. (1956). Notes on bias in estimation. *Biometrika 43*(3/4), 353–360.

Santa-Clara, P. (1997). Simulated likelihood estimation of diffusions with an application to the short-term interest rate. *UCLA: Finance*. www.researchgate.net/publication/46440390.

Shao, J. and D. Tu (1995). Applications to time series and other dependent data. In *The Jackknife and Bootstrap*, pp. 386–415. Springer.

Shenton, L. and W. L. Johnson (1965). Moments of a serial correlation coefficient. *Journal of the Royal Statistical Society: Series B (Methodological) 27*(2), 308–320.

Shreve, S. E. (2004). *Stochastic Calculus for Finance II: Continuous-Time Models*. Springer.

Singleton, K. J. (2001). Estimation of affine asset pricing models using the empirical characteristic function. *Journal of Econometrics 102*(1), 111–141.

Smith, A. A. (1993). Estimating nonlinear time-series models using simulated vector autoregressions. *Journal of Applied Econometrics 8*(S1), S63–S84.

Sundaresan, S. M. (2000). Continuous-time methods in finance: A review and an assessment. *The Journal of Finance 55*(4), 1569–1622.

Tang, C. Y. and S. X. Chen (2009). Parameter estimation and bias correction for diffusion processes. *Journal of Econometrics 149*(1), 65–81.

Trolle, A. B. and E. S. Schwartz (2009). A general stochastic volatility model for the pricing of interest rate derivatives. *The Review of Financial Studies 22*(5), 2007–2057.

Vasicek, O. (1977). An equilibrium characterization of the term structure. *Journal of Financial Economics 5*(2), 177–188.

Vinod, H. D. and L. Shenton (1996). Exact moments for autoregressive and random walk models for a zero or stationary initial value. *Econometric Theory 12*(3), 481–499.

Wang, X., P. C. B. Phillips, and J. Yu (2011). Bias in estimating multivariate and univariate diffusions. *Journal of Econometrics 161*(2), 228–245.

White, J. S. (1961). Asymptotic expansions for the mean and variance of the serial correlation coefficient. *Biometrika 48*(1–2), 85–94.

Yamamoto, T. and N. Kunitomo (1984). Asymptotic bias of the least squares estimator for multivariate autoregressive models. *Annals of the Institute of Statistical Mathematics 36*(3), 419–430.

Yu, J. (2012). Bias in the estimation of the mean reversion parameter in continuous time models. *Journal of Econometrics 169*(1), 114–122.

Yu, J. and P. C. B. Phillips (2001). A Gaussian approach for continuous time models of the short-term interest rate. *The Econometrics Journal 4*(2), 210–224.

5 Infill Asymptotic Theory and Applications in Financial Econometrics

YIU LIM LUI *Dongbei University of Finance and Economics*

5.1 Introduction

Consider the following first-order autoregressive (AR (1)) model:

$$X_t = \rho X_{t-1} + \varepsilon_t,\ \varepsilon_t \sim_{iid} \left(0, \sigma^2\right), t = 1, 2, \ldots, T, X_0 = O_p(1), \quad (5.1)$$

where ρ is the AR coefficient, $\{\varepsilon_t\}$ is a sequence of an independent and identically distributed error term, T is the number of observations, and X_0 is the initialization of the time series.

Different values of ρ have a different implication for the dynamic behavior of the time series X_t. When $|\rho| < 1$, X_t is a stationary time series, which features a mean reversion; when $\rho = 1$, X_t is a unit root time series and follows a random walk; when $\rho > 1$, X_t is an explosive time series that can produce an upward trajectory. Not surprisingly, the model defined in (5.1) has elicited a wide range of interest in econometrics, with studies focusing on the estimation and inference of ρ. An incomplete list of references includes Phillips (1987a,b), Phillips and Perron (1988), and Kwiatkowski et al. (1992), where the authors test whether a time series is stationary or not. The studies reported in Andrews (1993), Andrews and Chen (1994), Hansen (1999), and Mikusheva (2015) consider how to construct a better estimate and inference of ρ via bootstrapping. On the other hand, Diba and Grossman (1988), Evans (1991), and Phillips and Yu (2011) and Phillips et al. (2015) explore the existence of explosiveness in the time series data.

Suppose ρ is estimated by least squares (LS) (denote as $\hat{\rho}$), the inference of ρ usually relies on asymptotic analysis where the number of observations T in model (5.1) is assumed to diverge to infinity. As discussed in Phillips (1987a), limiting distribution of $\hat{\rho}$ depends critically on the value of ρ. When $|\rho| < 1$, upon normalization, $\hat{\rho}$ asymptotically has a Gaussian distribution, while when $\rho = 1$, $\hat{\rho}$ asymptotically has a nonstandard Dickey–Fuller distribution. If $\rho > 1$ and ε_t follows a Gaussian distribution in (5.1), White (1958) showed a normalized $\hat{\rho}$ follows a Cauchy distribution.

Since the value of ρ is not known a priori, the usually used limiting Gaussian distribution which assumes $|\rho| < 1$ is not always valid. Likewise, the use of the Dickey–Fuller distribution, which assumes $\rho = 1$, is incorrect when $\rho \neq 1$. Clearly, the discontinuity in ρ of the limiting distributional function and ignoring the value of ρ make the inference of ρ difficult because we need some knowledge of ρ to carry out its inference. However, difficulties may arise even if $|\rho|$ is known to be less than 1. For example, when ρ is close to 1 (say $\rho = 0.98$), it is well known that the Dickey–Fuller distribution will provide a better finite sample approximation than the Gaussian distribution. However, as ρ moves further closer to the stationary region (say $\rho = 0.9$), Dickey–Fuller distribution starts to provide a less accurate finite sample approximation. Chan and Wei (1987) and Phillips (1987b) introduced a local to unit unity (LTU) model to cater the case where ρ is in the neighborhood of 1, and they assumed ρ has the form $\rho = 1 + c/T$ and $\rho = \exp(c/T)$, respectively, where c is a localizing constant. They found that the asymptotic distribution of $\hat{\rho}$ is nonstandard and continuous in c and provides a good finite sample performance when ρ is near 1. As expected, the LTU distribution outperforms the Gaussian distribution and the Dickey–Fuller distribution for the finite sample approximation of $\hat{\rho}$ when ρ is close to 1.

Although the LTU distribution has a good finite sample performance, it does share the same drawback as the limiting Gaussian distribution and the Dickey–Fuller distribution in that the initialization X_0 is not taken into account in the distributional functions. Since the finite sample distribution of $\hat{\rho}$ is dependent on X_0, none of the three asymptotic distributions of $\hat{\rho}$ may approximate the finite sample distribution well when the magnitude of X_0 is large.

In empirical studies, while we usually observe economic data at some discrete points (e.g., monthly and weekly data), we can think of the data series as a continuous time process being observed at some sampling interval Δ and over a time span N. More precisely, we assume a continuous time series $X(t)$ with T observations that are sampled in a discrete time interval at $[0, N]$ and therefore $t = 0, \Delta, 2\Delta \ldots, T\Delta = N$. Monthly data in one year is a special case with $\Delta = 1/12$, $N = 1$ and $T = 12$. This setting allows us to obtain limiting distributions with an increasing T under one of the following three asymptotic schemes:

1. (Long-span) Δ is fixed and $N \to \infty$.
2. (Infill) N is fixed and $\Delta \to 0$.
3. (Double) $N \to \infty$ and $\Delta \to 0$.

The long-span scheme assumes that the sampling interval is fixed and the time span increases. This scheme corresponds to the ones used by White (1958), Phillips (1987a,b), and Phillips and Perron (1988). The infill scheme assumes the time span is fixed and the sampling interval shrinks to zero. Finally, the double scheme assumes the span goes to infinity and the sampling interval shrinks to zero. Phillips (1987b), Perron (1991), and Zhou and Yu (2015) showed that the infill distributions of $\hat{\rho}$ under different AR(1) models provide a better finite sample approximation than the long-span distribution in three aspects. First, the infill distributions do not have a discontinuity in the value of ρ. Second, X_0 is preserved at the limit. Third, the infill distribution is not symmetric. Eventually, the infill distribution outperforms the long-span distribution by exhibiting these three features and they can also be found in finite sample distributions of $\hat{\rho}$.

We have just mentioned that under an AR model, the infill distribution of $\hat{\rho}$ can outperform those under the long-span scheme. Interestingly, the AR model is not the only example in which the infill scheme provides a better finite sample performance. Suppose that we have the following time series with a structural break in mean:

$$X_t = \begin{cases} \mu + u_t & \text{if } t \leq k_0 \\ \mu + \delta + u_t & \text{if } t > k_0 \end{cases}, t = 1, \ldots, T, u_t \sim_{iid} (0, \sigma^2),$$
$$1 \leq k_0 < T. \tag{5.2}$$

X_t has mean μ before the break date k_0, and the mean increases by δ after k_0. Suppose the goal is to estimate the structural break date k_0. Jiang et al. (2018) pointed out that when the break size δ is small, the finite sample distribution of the LS estimator of the break date is often asymmetric and has trimodality. These two features are not captured by the limiting distribution developed under the long-span asymptotic scheme. Consequently, the long-span asymptotic distribution might poorly approximate the finite sample distribution. Jiang et al. (2018) then constructed a continuous-time model equivalent to the structure break model in (5.2) and introduced an infill asymptotic scheme. They proved that their infill asymptotic distribution has asymmetry and trimodality similar to the finite sample distribution and can provide an excellent approximation. Jiang et al. (2021) extend the infill asymptotic theory to the AR(1) model with a structural break in the AR root.

This chapter is divided into two parts. In the first part, we examine the long-span distribution of the LS estimator in discrete time AR models. We also explore corresponding continuous time models and their discrete time representations, as well as infill theory for the LS estimator. Furthermore, we discuss the application of infill theory in unit root tests and double asymptotics for explosive time series. Finally, we highlight some challenges in implementing infill asymptotics and review the grid bootstrap confidence interval method, which can be used to infer the AR parameter.

In the second part of this chapter, we present two structural break models: one with a break in mean and the other with a break in the AR parameter. We start by examining the finite sample distribution and its long-span distribution of the break point estimator. We then explore corresponding continuous time models and the infill asymptotic distribution of the break date estimator. Finally, we demonstrate that the infill theory provides superior finite sample approximation to the long-span theory for both the AR and structural break models.

Although we introduce continuous time models in studying infill asymptotics, our primary interest is still in the estimation and inference of the parameters in the discrete time models. The continuous time models are only used to obtain infill distributions that provide better finite sample approximations. Section 5.2 reviews the unit root tests in the literature under continuous-time models, Section 5.3 reviews the structural break models, and Section 5.4 concludes the chapter.

5.2 The AR Model

Consider the following model:

$$X_t = d + \rho X_{t-1} + \varepsilon_t, \varepsilon_t \sim_{iid} \left(0, \sigma^2\right), t = 1, 2, \ldots, T, X_0 = O_p(1), \tag{5.3}$$

and the following two regressions:

$$X_t = \hat{\rho} X_{t-1} + \hat{e}_t, \tag{5.4}$$
$$X_t = \hat{d} + \tilde{\rho} X_{t-1} + \tilde{e}_t, \tag{5.5}$$

where $\tilde{\rho}$ and $\hat{\rho}$ are the LS estimators of ρ with and without intercept, respectively, $\hat{d}$ is the LS estimator of the intercept d in (5.3), and $\hat{e}_t$ and $\tilde{e}_t$ are LS residuals. In this section, we analyze the limiting distribution of the LS estimators based on different asymptotic schemes.

5.2.1 Long-Span Asymptotics

The asymptotic distributions of $\hat{\rho}$ and $\tilde{\rho}$ where we let $T \to \infty$ are listed in the following theorems. Later, when we introduce the discrete time representation of a continuous time model, it will be clear that the long-span distribution where the $N \to \infty$ with a fixed Δ corresponds to $T \to \infty$ under model (5.3). For the moment, we will just call the asymptotic distributions of $\hat{\rho}$ and $\tilde{\rho}$ under model (5.3) the long-span asymptotic distribution. As will be shown, the long-span distributions of the LS estimators are crucially dependent on the value of AR parameter ρ.

The long-span distribution of the LS estimator $\hat{\rho}$ from regression (5.4) is summarized as follows.

Theorem 5.2.1 *Under model (5.3) with $d = 0$, the LS estimator $\hat{\rho}$ has the following limits as $T \to \infty$.*

(a) If $|\rho| < 1$,

$$\sqrt{T}(\hat{\rho} - \rho) \Rightarrow N\left(0, 1 - \rho^2\right), \tag{5.6}$$

(b) If $\rho = 1$,

$$T(\hat{\rho} - 1) \Rightarrow \frac{\int_0^1 W(r)dW(r)}{\int_0^1 W^2(r)dr}, \tag{5.7}$$

where $W(r)$ *is a standard Brownian motion (BM).*

(c) If $\rho > 1$, $\varepsilon_t \sim_{iid} N\left(0, \sigma^2\right)$, *and* $X_0 = 0$,

$$\frac{\rho^T}{\rho^2 - 1}(\hat{\rho} - \rho) \Rightarrow C, \tag{5.8}$$

where C *is a standard Cauchy variate.*

We also summarize the long-span distribution of the LS estimator of ρ from regression (5.5) as follows.

Theorem 5.2.2 *Under model (5.3), the LS estimator* $\tilde{\rho}$ *has the following limit as* $T \to \infty$.

(a) If $|\rho| < 1$,

$$\sqrt{T}(\tilde{\rho} - \rho) \Rightarrow N\left(0, 1 - \rho^2\right). \tag{5.9}$$

(b) If $\rho = 1$ *and* $d = 0$,

$$T(\tilde{\rho} - 1) \Rightarrow \frac{\int_0^1 \bar{W}(r)dW(r)}{\int_0^1 \bar{W}^2(r)dr}, \tag{5.10}$$

where $\bar{W}(r) = W(r) - \int_0^1 W(s)ds$ *is the demeaned BM.*

(c) If $\rho > 1$, $\varepsilon_t \sim$ *i.i.d.*$N\left(0, \sigma^2\right)$,

$$\frac{\rho^T}{\rho^2 - 1}(\tilde{\rho} - \rho) \Rightarrow \frac{y}{z + \rho d/(\rho - 1)}, \tag{5.11}$$

where $y = N\left(0, \rho^2\sigma^2/(\rho^2 - 1)\right)$, $z = N\left(0, \rho^2\sigma^2/(\rho^2 - 1)\right) + \rho X_0$, *and* y *and* z *are independently distributed.*

The results (5.6) and (5.9) are standard. Equations (5.7) and (5.10), which can be obtained from Phillips (1987a), are usually called the Dickey–Fuller distributions. Equations (5.8) and (5.11) were derived by White (1958) and Wang and Yu (2015) respectively. The asymptotic results under $\rho > 1$ require that ε_t follows a Gaussian distribution. Therefore, (5.8) and (5.11) are not obtained from an invariance principle. Theorems 5.2.1 and 5.2.2 show that magnitude of ρ determines the form of the asymptotic distribution. When $|\rho| < 1$ the LS estimates are asymptotically Gaussian. When $\rho = 1$, the Dickey–Fuller distribution shows up at the limit. When $\rho > 1$, $\hat{\rho}$ asymptotically follow a Cauchy distribution and the limiting distribution of $\tilde{\rho}$ is nonstandard. Clearly, the asymptotic distributional functions of the LS estimators are not continuous in ρ.

Aside from the settings in Theorems 5.2.1 and 5.2.2, Phillips (1987b) and Chan and Wei (1987) introduced the local to unity (LTU) AR model where ρ is in the vicinity of 1. Phillips (1987b) assumed $\rho = \exp\left(\frac{c}{T}\right), -\infty < c < \infty$, and it is called LTU because $\rho = \exp\left(\frac{c}{T}\right) = 1 + \frac{c}{T} + O(T^{-2}) \to 1$ as $T \to \infty$, and if $c = 0$, the AR model reduces to a unit root model. Under model (5.3) with $d = 0$ and $\rho = \exp\left(\frac{c}{T}\right)$, using repeated backward substitution, X_t can be expressed as a partial sum:

$$X_t = \sum_{j=1}^{t} \exp\left(\frac{c}{T}\right)^{t-j} \varepsilon_j + \exp\left(\frac{c}{T}\right)^{t} X_0.$$

Suppose $t = [Tr]$ with $r \in [0, 1]$, $W_n(r) = T^{-1/2} \sum_{j=1}^{[Tr]} \varepsilon_j$, and premultiply X_t by $T^{-1/2}$. Phillips (1987b) showed that as $T \to \infty$,

$$\begin{aligned} T^{-1/2} X_{[Tr]} &= \sum_{j=1}^{[Tr]} \exp\left(\frac{c}{T}\right)^{[Tr]-j} \frac{\varepsilon_j}{T^{1/2}} + \exp\left(\frac{c}{T}\right)^{[Tr]} \frac{X_0}{T^{1/2}} \\ &= \sigma \sum_{j=1}^{[Tr]} \exp\left(\frac{c}{T}\right)^{[Tr]-j} \int_{(j-1)/T}^{j/T} dW_n(s) + O_p(T^{-1/2}) \\ &= \sigma \int_0^r \exp(c(r-s)) dW_n(s) + O_p(T^{-1/2}) \\ &\Rightarrow \sigma \int_0^r \exp\left(c(r-s)\right) dW(s) := J_c(r), \end{aligned} \tag{5.12}$$

where we have applied the functional central limit theorem $W_n(s) \Rightarrow W(s)$[1] to obtain the convergence (5.12), and $J_c(r) = \int_0^r e^{c(r-s)} dW(r)$ is called an Ornstein–Uhlenbeck (OU) process that can also be defined by

$$dJ_c(r) = cJ_c(r)dr + dW(r),$$

with $J_c(r) = 0$.

It is noteworthy that the way in which we normalize $X_{[Tr]}$ makes the initial condition X_0 irrelevant asymptotically because $X_0/T^{-1/2} = O_p(T^{-1/2})$. Consequently, the LTU distributions of $\hat{\rho}$ and $\tilde{\rho}$ do not include the initialization.

[1] The functional central limit theorem ensures that $W_n(r)$ converges weakly to $W(r)$. For a detailed explanation, please see Phillips (1987a,b) and chapter 17 in Davidson (1994).

We are now ready to discuss the following asymptotic distributions for the LS estimators of ρ under the LTU model.

Theorem 5.2.3 *Under (5.3) with $d = 0$, $\rho = \exp\left(\frac{c}{T}\right)$, and $-\infty < c < \infty$, the LS estimators $\hat{\rho}$ and $\tilde{\rho}$ have the following limits as $T \to \infty$,*

$$T(\hat{\rho} - \rho) \Rightarrow \frac{\int_0^1 J_c(r)dW(r)}{\int_0^1 J_c^2(r)dr}, \tag{5.13}$$

$$T(\tilde{\rho} - \rho) \Rightarrow \frac{\int_0^1 \bar{J}_c(r)dW(r)}{\int_0^1 \bar{J}_c^2(r)dr}, \tag{5.14}$$

where $\bar{J}_c(r) = \bar{J}_c(r) - \int_0^1 \bar{J}_c(s)ds$ is the demean OU process.

The proofs of (5.13) and (5.14) can be found in Phillips (1987b) and Mikusheva (2007), respectively, and are called the LTU distributions. When $c = 0$, LTU asymptotic distributions of $\hat{\rho}$ and $\tilde{\rho}$ become the Dickey–Fuller distributions. The limit distributions of $\hat{\rho}$ and $\tilde{\rho}$ under an LTU model are nonstandard, dependent on the localizing parameter c and the Ornstein–Uhlenbeck (OU) process $J_c(r)$. Phillips (1987b) showed the LTU distribution (5.13) is continuous in c, and when $c \to -\infty$ and $c \to +\infty$, the LTU asymptotic distribution of a suitably normalized $\hat{\rho}$ becomes the limiting Gaussian distribution and Cauchy distribution, respectively. Therefore, LTU asymptotic theory bridges the limiting Gaussian distribution, Dickey–Fuller distribution, and Cauchy distribution.

From Theorems 5.2.1, 5.2.2 and 5.2.3, it can be seen that all asymptotic distributions except (5.11) are independent of the initial condition X_0, and the distributions are discontinuous in ρ except those under the LTU models. In simulations, Zhou and Yu (2015) showed that the asymmetry of the distribution of $\hat{\rho}$, the dependence on X_0, and the continuity of ρ can be seen in the finite sample. Since these three features are not captured by these asymptotic distributions, they may not provide a good finite sample approximation of the distributional functional of $\hat{\rho}$ and $\tilde{\rho}$ when ρ is close to 1 and X_0 is large.

5.2.2 Continuous Time Model and Infill Asymptotics

We now introduce a continuous time model that is closely related to the discrete time model (5.1). Consider the following stochastic differential equation:

$$dX(t) = -\kappa X(t)dt + \sigma dW(t),\ X(0) = X_0 = O_p(1), t \in [0, N], \tag{5.15}$$

where $\kappa \in (-\infty, +\infty)$ measures the persistence of $X(t)$, $\sigma > 0$ measures the spot volatility, and $W(t)$ is a standard BM.

Given a sampling interval Δ, Equation (5.15) has an exact discrete time first order autoregressive (AR(1)) representation:

$$X_{t\Delta} = \rho_\kappa X_{(t-1)\Delta} + \varepsilon_{t\Delta},\ t = 1, 2, \ldots, T = N/\Delta, \tag{5.16}$$

where $\rho_\kappa = \exp(-\kappa\Delta)$, $\varepsilon_{t\Delta} = \sigma \int_{(t-1)\Delta}^{t\Delta} \exp(-\kappa(t\Delta - s))dW(s) \sim_{iid} N\left(0, \sigma_\kappa^2\right)$, and $\sigma_\kappa^2 = \sigma^2 \frac{1-\exp(-2\kappa\Delta)}{2\kappa}$.

Equation (5.16) shows that the sign of κ (or equivalently ρ_κ) determines the dynamics of $X(t)$: if $\kappa > 0$, $\rho_\kappa < 1$, and $X(t)$ is a stationary time series; if $\kappa = 0$, $X(t)$ follows a random walk; if $\kappa < 0$, $\rho_\kappa > 1$, and $X(t)$ is an explosive time series.

When Δ is fixed, model (5.16) is equivalent to model (5.1) with $\rho = \rho_\kappa, X_t = X_{t\Delta}$, and σ in (5.1) becomes σ_κ. Therefore, the limiting results in Theorem 5.2.1 correspond to those under long-span schemes in model (5.16).

Under the infill asymptotic scheme, model (5.15) and Equation (5.16) are closely related to the LTU model studied in Phillips (1987b). To see this, since $T = N/\Delta$, $T \to \infty$ when $\Delta \to 0$, letting $c = -\kappa N$ gives

$$\rho_\kappa = \exp\left(\frac{c}{T}\right) = 1 + \frac{c}{T} + O(T^{-2}) \to 1 \text{ as } \Delta \to 0.$$

Dividing both sides of (5.16) by σ_κ and letting $Y_{t\Delta} = X_{t\Delta}/\sigma_\kappa$ and $\varepsilon_{t\Delta} = \varepsilon_{t\Delta}/\sigma_\kappa$ give a discrete time representation:

$$\begin{aligned} Y_{t\Delta} &= \rho_\kappa Y_{(t-1)\Delta} + \varepsilon_{t\Delta}, t = 1, 2, \ldots, T, \\ Y_0 &= X_0/\sigma_\kappa = O_p(\sigma_\kappa^{-1}), \\ \varepsilon_{t\Delta} &\sim {}_{iid}N(0, 1). \end{aligned} \tag{5.17}$$

Model (5.17) therefore shows that $\{Y_{t\Delta}\}_{t=1}^{T}$ is an LTU model with an AR coefficient ρ_κ that has a localizing parameter $c = -\kappa N$. When $X_0 = 0$, Phillips (1987b) showed the convergence (5.12) holds for $Y_{t\Delta}$ upon normalization by $T^{-1/2}$.

However, when $X_0 = O_p(1)$, the initial condition in model (5.17) is diverging since $Y_0 = O_p(\sigma_\kappa^{-1})$ and

$$\begin{aligned} \sigma_\kappa^{-1} &= \left(\frac{2\kappa}{\sigma\left(1 - \exp(-2\kappa\Delta)\right)}\right)^{-1} = \left(\frac{2\kappa}{\sigma(2\kappa\Delta + o(1))}\right)^{-1} \\ &= O\left(\frac{1}{\sqrt{\Delta}}\right) \to \infty \text{ as } \Delta \to 0. \end{aligned}$$

Perron (1991) generalized the results of Phillips (1987b) by allowing for a nonzero X_0. Since $Y_0 = O_p(1/\sqrt{\Delta})$, upon a suitable normalization, the initial condition appears at the infill limit unlike that under the LTU model and we have

$$\exp\left(\frac{c}{T}\right)^{[Tr]} \frac{Y_0}{T^{1/2}} = \exp\left(\frac{c}{T}\right)^{[Tr]} \frac{X_0}{T^{1/2}\sigma_\kappa^2} \to e^{cr}\gamma_0,$$

where $\gamma_0 = \frac{X_0}{\sigma\sqrt{N}}$.

The following theorem gives the limit expression of $Y_{t\Delta}$ and its sample moments.

Theorem 5.2.4 *Under model (5.16), suppose* $X_0 = 0$, *as* $\Delta \to 0$,

$$T(\hat{\rho}_\kappa - \rho_\kappa) \Rightarrow \frac{\int_0^1 J_c(r)dW(r)}{\int_0^1 J_c^2(r)dr}. \tag{5.18}$$

Suppose $X_0 = O_p(1)$, *as* $\Delta \to 0$,

$$T(\hat{\rho}_\kappa - \rho_\kappa) \Rightarrow \frac{A(\gamma_0, c)}{B(\gamma_0, c)}, \tag{5.19}$$

where $\hat{\rho}_\kappa$ *is the LS estimator of* ρ_κ,

$$A(\gamma_0, c) = \int_0^1 J_c(r)dW(r) + \gamma_0 \int_0^1 e^{cr} dW(r),$$

$$B(\gamma_0, c) = \int_0^1 J_c^2(r)dr + 2\gamma_0 \int_0^1 e^{cr} J_c(r)dr + \gamma_0^2 \frac{e^{2c} - 1}{2c},$$

and $c = -\kappa N$.

Results in (5.17) and (5.18) were proven in Phillips (1987b) and Perron (1991), respectively. Theorem 5.2.4 shows that the infill distribution of $\hat{\rho}_\kappa$ is the same as the LTU distribution (5.13) when the initialization $X_0 = 0$, and the infill distribution contains the initialization X_0 via γ_0 when $X_0 = O_p(1)$.

Zhou and Yu (2015) later generalized the model (5.14) in Phillips (1987b) and Perron (1991) by adding an additional parameter $\mu \in (-\infty, \infty)$ such that

$$dX(t) = \kappa\left(\mu - X(t)\right) dt + \sigma dW(t), X(0) = X_0 = O_p(1). \tag{5.20}$$

Under model (5.19), when $\kappa > 0$, $X(t)$ is stationary and mean-reverting, μ is the long-run mean of the model. Analogous to (5.15), Zhou and Yu (2015) used the exact discrete time representation of (5.19), which has the following form:

$$X_{t\Delta} = \rho_\kappa X_{(t-1)\Delta} + g_\kappa + \varepsilon_{t\Delta},\ t = 1, 2, \ldots, T,\ g_\kappa = \mu(1 - e^{-\kappa\Delta}). \tag{5.21}$$

This is analogous to model (5.3).

Similar to (5.16), dividing both sides of (5.20) by σ_κ gives

$$Y_{t\Delta} = \rho_\kappa Y_{(t-1)\Delta} + \tilde{g}_\kappa + \varepsilon_{t\Delta},\ t = 1, 2, \ldots, T,\ \breve{g}_\kappa = g_\kappa/\sigma_\kappa. \tag{5.22}$$

Under the infill asymptotic scheme, the intercept term $\breve{g}_\kappa$ is not asymptotically negligible upon normalization. To see this, using backward substitution, $Y_{t\Delta}$ can be expressed as

$$Y_{t\Delta} = \rho_\kappa^t Y_0 + \breve{g}_\kappa \sum_{j=1}^{t} \rho_\kappa^{t-j} + \sum_{j=1}^{t} \rho_\kappa^{t-j} \varepsilon_{j\Delta}.$$

Note that $\sum_{j=1}^{t} \rho_\kappa^{t-j} \varepsilon_{j\Delta} = O_p(T^{1/2})$ for $t = [Tr]$ from (5.12), $\sum_{j=1}^{t} \rho_\kappa^{t-j} = \frac{\rho_\kappa^{t+1}-1}{\rho_\kappa-1} = \frac{\exp\left(\frac{c(t+1)}{T}\right)-1}{\exp(\frac{c}{T})-1}$. If $t = [Tr]$ with $r \in [0, 1]$, we can see $\frac{\exp\left(\frac{c(t+1)}{T}\right)-1}{T[\exp(\frac{c}{T})-1]} \to \frac{e^{cr}-1}{c}$ as $T \to 0$. Consequently, $\sum_{j=1}^{t} \rho_\kappa^{t-j} = O(T) = O(\Delta^{-1})$. Moreover, as $\Delta \to 0, N/T = \Delta$

$$\begin{aligned}
\breve{g}_\kappa = g_\kappa/\sigma_\kappa &= \mu(1 - e^{-\kappa\Delta}) \times \left(\frac{2\kappa}{\sigma^2 (1 - \exp(-2\kappa\Delta))}\right)^{1/2} \\
&= \mu(\kappa\Delta) \times \left(\frac{1}{\sigma^2\Delta}\right)^{1/2} + o(1) \\
&= \frac{\mu\kappa}{\sigma}\sqrt{\Delta} + o(1) \\
&= \frac{\mu\kappa}{\sigma}\sqrt{\frac{N}{T}} + o(1).
\end{aligned} \tag{5.23}$$

This implies $\breve{g}_\kappa \sum_{j=1}^{t} \rho_\kappa^{t-j} = O(T^{-1/2})O(T) = O(T^{1/2})$, and $T^{-1/2}\breve{g}_\kappa \sum_{j=1}^{t} \rho_\kappa^{t-j} \to \frac{\mu\kappa\sqrt{N}}{\sigma}\frac{e^{cr}-1}{c}$ which is dependent on μ.

Zhou and Yu (2015) showed that the introduction of $\mu \neq 0$ in (5.19) produces an infill asymptotic expression of $T^{-1/2}Y_{(t-1)\Delta}$ which consists of μ, γ_0 and the OU process $J_c(r)$. Additionally, the LS estimator of ρ_κ has the infill asymptotic distribution stated in the following theorem.

Theorem 5.2.5 *Under model (5.21), the LS estimator* $\tilde{\rho}_\kappa = \frac{\sum_{t=1}^{T}(Y_{(t-1)\Delta}-\bar{Y})(Y_{t\Delta}-\bar{Y})}{\sum_{t=1}^{T}(Y_{t\Delta}-\bar{Y})^2}$ *where* $\bar{Y} = \frac{1}{T}\sum_{t=1}^{T} Y_{(t-1)\Delta}$ *has the following asymptotic distribution as* $\Delta \to 0$,

$$T(\tilde{\rho}_\kappa - \rho_\kappa) \Rightarrow \frac{A_2(\gamma_0, c)}{B_2(\gamma_0, c)}, \tag{5.24}$$

where

$$\begin{aligned}
A_2(\gamma_0, c) = &\ \frac{b}{c}\int_0^1 c_1 dW(r) \\
&+ \int_0^1 J_c(r)dW(r) + \gamma_0 \int_0^1 e^{cr} dW(r) - W(1)\left(c_2 b + \int_0^1 J_c(r)dr + c_4\gamma_0\right),
\end{aligned}$$

Table 5.1 *Percentiles of* $T(\tilde{\rho}_\kappa - \rho_\kappa)$ *when* $\kappa = -0.01$ *and* $\rho_\kappa = 1.0008$.

Percentile	1%	5%	10%	50%	90%	95%	99%
Finite sample	−19.26	−13.28	−10.70	−4.29	−0.83	−0.12	1.30
Infill	−21.96	−13.66	−10.82	−3.92	−0.81	0.00	1.10
Long-span	−3.25	−0.59	−0.29	0.00	0.28	0.57	3.10

Table 5.2 *Percentiles of* $T(\tilde{\rho}_\kappa - \rho_\kappa)$ *when* $\kappa = 0.01$ *and* $\rho_\kappa = 0.9992$.

Percentile	1%	5%	10%	50%	90%	95%	99%
Finite sample	−18.75	−13.28	−10.78	−4.31	−0.82	−0.09	1.31
Infill	−22.03	−14.91	−11.13	−4.12	−0.77	−0.02	1.06
Long-span	−0.74	−0.52	−0.41	0.00	0.41	0.52	0.74

$$B_2(\gamma_0, c) = c_3 b^2 + \frac{2b}{c}\int_0^1 c_1 J_c(r)dr + \int_0^1 J_c^2(r)dr + c_4^2 b\gamma_0 + 2\gamma_0 \int_0^1 e^{cr} J_c(r)dr$$
$$+ \gamma_0^2 \frac{e^{2c} - 1}{2c} - \left(c_2 b + \int_0^1 J_c(r)dr + c_4\gamma_0\right)^2,$$

$c_1 = e^{rc} - 1, c_2 = \frac{e^c - c - 1}{c^2}, c_3 = \frac{e^{2c} - 4e^c + 2c + 3}{2c^3}, c_4 = \frac{e^c - 1}{c}$ *and* $b = \mu\frac{\sqrt{-c\kappa}}{\sigma}$.

Some interesting findings can be seen from the limit (5.7) and Theorem 5.2.1. First, the limit expressions of the long-span asymptotic distributions are critically dependent on the value of the AR coefficient, while the infill distribution has a uniform expression for any ρ_κ. Second, unlike the long-span asymptotics, the initial condition always shows up at the infill limit.

To know which limiting distributions produce the most accurate finite sample approximation, following Zhou and Yu (2015), we conduct a small-scale Monte Carlo simulation.

Tables 5.1 and 5.2 report the simulated percentiles of the finite sample distribution and the limiting distribution of $T(\tilde{\rho}_\kappa - \rho_\kappa)$ under the infill and long-span asymptotic schemes and model (5.20) with the following parameters: $N = 5, \Delta = 1/12, \mu = 0.1, X_0 = 5$. We set $\kappa = -0.01$ and $\rho_\kappa = 1.0008$ in Table 5.1 and $\kappa = 0.01$ and $\rho_\kappa = 0.9992$ in Table 5.2. The number of replications is set to 2,500. This parameter setting allows us to compare the finite sample performance of the limiting distributions (5.9) or (5.11) with (5.23).

From Table 5.2, it can be seen that the percentiles of the finite sample distribution and the infill distribution of $T(\tilde{\rho}_\kappa - \rho_\kappa)$ do not vary much when we slightly change the value of ρ_κ. However, for the long-span distribution, the percentiles change drastically. Moreover, the percentiles of the infill distribution are very close to those of the finite sample distribution, while the long-span asymptotic distributions do not approximate the finite sample very well. Third, both the finite sample distribution and infill distribution are not symmetric. These simulation results echo the findings of Yu (2014), Zhou and Yu (2015), and Bao et al. (2017). They showed that in simulations, the infill distribution approximates the finite sample percentile the best among the two schemes. They attributed the superiority of the infill distribution to the inclusion of the initial condition via γ_0 for all values of ρ_κ, the continuity in ρ_κ of the infill distribution, and the asymmetry of the infill distribution. All these three features can be seen in the finite sample distribution but are lost under the long-span asymptotics.

Dickey–Fuller t statistic $t_T(\tilde{\rho}) = \frac{\tilde{\rho}-1}{se(\tilde{\rho})}$ is often used to detect unit roots in time series. Laurent and Shi (2022) derived the infill distribution of the Dickey–Fuller t statistic $t_T(\tilde{\rho})$ under the model (5.19) in Zhou and Yu (2015). They showed that the test statistic $t_T(\tilde{\rho})$ has the following infill distribution:

Theorem 5.2.6 *Under the model (5.19) and (5.20) in Zhou and Yu (2015), let* $t_T(\tilde{\rho}) = \frac{\tilde{\rho}-1}{se(\tilde{\rho})}$*, as* $\Delta \to 0$*, we have*

$$t_T(\tilde{\rho}) \Rightarrow \begin{cases} \dfrac{\frac{1}{2}((W(1))^2-1)-W(1)\int_0^1 W(s)ds}{\left(\int_0^1 (W(s))^2 ds - \left(\int_0^1 W(s)ds\right)^2\right)^{1/2}} & \text{if } \rho_\kappa = 1, \text{ or equivalently } \kappa = 0 \\ \dfrac{-\Xi_2 W(1) - \Xi_1}{(\Xi_3 - \Xi_2^2)^{1/2}} + c\left(\Xi_3 - \Xi_2^2\right)^{1/2} & \text{if } \rho_\kappa \neq 1, \text{ or equivalently } \kappa \neq 0 \end{cases} \tag{5.25}$$

where

$$\Xi_1 \equiv \frac{b}{c}\int_0^1 (e^{cr}-1)dW(r) + \int_0^1 J_c(r)dW(r) + \gamma_0 \int_0^1 e^{cr} dW(r)$$

$$\Xi_2 \equiv \frac{e^c - c - 1}{c^2} b + \int_0^1 J_c(r)dr + \gamma_0 \frac{e^c - 1}{c},$$

$$\Xi_3 \equiv \frac{e^{2c} - 4e^c + 2c + 3}{2c^3} b^2 + \frac{2b}{c}\int_0^1 (e^{cr}-1)J_c(r)dr + \int_0^1 J_c^2(r)dr + \frac{e^{2c} - 2e^c + 1}{c^2} b\gamma_0 + 2\gamma_0 \int_0^1 e^{cr} J_c(r)dr + \gamma_0^2 \frac{e^{2c}-1}{2c}.$$

The infill distribution (5.25) shows that imposing the condition $\rho_\kappa = 1$ removes the parameters c, μ, and γ_0 in the limiting distribution. Therefore, (5.24) provides a feasible test under the unit root hypothesis. The authors show in simulation that the test has bad asymptotic power against the mean reversion alternative $\rho_\kappa < 1$ when the time span N is small and ρ_κ is close to 1 but generally has good asymptotic power against the explosive alternative $\rho_\kappa > 1$.

5.2.3 Double Asymptotics

Aside from performing unit root tests, the infill theory can also be used to obtain the double asymptotic distribution when we first let $\Delta \to 0$ followed by $N \to \infty$. Wang and Yu (2016a) derived the sequential asymptotics for the centered LS estimator under the model (5.16) with $\kappa < 0$.[2] Note that under this parameter setting, the model has an explosive AR parameter as $\rho_\kappa = \exp(-\kappa\Delta) > 1$. More precisely, they showed

$$\lim_{N\to\infty}\lim_{\Delta\to 0}\frac{e^{-\kappa N}(\hat{\rho}-\rho_\kappa)}{-2\kappa\Delta} = \lim_{c\to\infty}\frac{(2c)e^{-c}A(\gamma_0,c)}{(2c)^2e^{-2c}B(\gamma_0,c)} = \frac{\xi}{\lambda_0+\eta}, \tag{5.26}$$

where $\lambda_0 = Y_0\sqrt{-2\kappa}/\sigma$, ξ and η are two independent $N(0,1)$ random variables, and $A(\gamma_0, c)$ and $B(\gamma_0, c)$ are defined in (5.19).

Similar to the infill distribution (5.19) and the long span distribution (5.11), the double asymptotic distribution preserves the initial condition via λ_0. Using the double asymptotic distribution, Wang and Yu (2016a) constructed a confidence interval for ρ_κ, which indicates the evidence of explosiveness in the monthly log Nasdaq real price data between 1990 and 2000.

5.2.4 Grid Bootstrap Confidence Interval

The infill asymptotic theory is shown to approximate the finite sample distribution well but it does have an obvious drawback. As the localizing parameter c is not consistently estimable under the infill scheme, this feature prevents us from directly inferring the AR coefficient based on the LTU distributions (5.13), (5.14), the infill distributions (5.17), (5.18), and (5.23).

Hansen (1999) proposed the grid bootstrap confidence interval (CI) method to perform a feasible inference for ρ under the discrete time LTU model. This method first defines a set of $G \equiv [\rho_L, \rho_R]$, generates bootstrap samples at each $\rho \in G$ under the hypothesis that ρ is the true value,[3] and the coefficient-based statistic or test statistic is inverted to obtain an q-level grid bootstrap CI

$$CI_q = \{\rho \in R : c_T^*(q_1|\rho) \le t_T(\hat{\rho},\rho) \le c_T^*(q_2|\rho)\}, \tag{5.27}$$

where $t_T(\hat{\rho},\rho)$ can be $T(\hat{\rho}-\rho)$ or $(\hat{\rho}-\rho)/se(\hat{\rho})$ and the qth quantile of the bootstrap distribution of $t_T(\hat{\rho},\rho)$ is $c_T^*(q|\rho)$.

Hansen showed that the grid bootstrap CI in (5.27) produces a valid inference under the local-to-unit-root model by showing the coverage probability is asymptotically correct as $T \to \infty$,

[2] Wang and Yu (2016b) also derived the double asymptotic distribution where $\Delta \to 0$ and $N \to \infty$ simultaneously.

[3] A fine grid for ρ containing 200 grid points is used by Hansen (1999).

$$\Pr\{\rho_0 \in CI_q\} \to q_2 - q_1, \tag{5.28}$$

where ρ_0 is the true value of ρ.

The key idea to obtain (5.28) is that, given the value of the localized parameter c, the bootstrap data have the same limiting distribution as the original LTU model so that the analog of (5.12) holds:

$$T^{-1/2} Y^*_{[Tr]} = \sum_{j=1}^{[Tr]} \exp\left(\frac{c}{T}\right)^{[Tr]-j} \frac{\varepsilon^*_j}{T^{1/2}} \Rightarrow J_c(r), \tag{5.29}$$

where $Y^*_t = \sum_{j=1}^{t} \exp\left(\frac{c}{T}\right)^{t-j} \varepsilon^*_j$, $\{\varepsilon^*_j\}_{j=1}^{T}$ is the usual LS nonparametric bootstrap residuals, and $J_c(r)$ is defined in (5.12). Mikusheva (2007, 2015) later showed that Hansen's method is uniformly valid and provide a second-order refinement to the LTU distribution.

Noting the similarity between the local to unit root model and the discrete time representation (5.17) under an infill asymptotic scheme, Lui et al. (2022) proposed constructing a grid bootstrap CI in the spirit of Hansen's method. Since the initial condition shows up at the infill limit, they modified the grid bootstrap procedure by letting the bootstrap initialization X^*_0 be equal to the initial condition X_0 in (5.20). They showed that the modified approach can produce a CI that is asymptotically and uniformly valid for any $\kappa \geq 0$ under the infill scheme. Moreover, they found that the modified grid bootstrap CI provides a second-order refinement to the infill distribution. Therefore, this method provides a valid CI under model (5.20). The authors used the CI to check the stationarity of the daily log realized volatility and the monthly nominal interest rate data under different maturities and concluded that log realized volatility is stationary while the stationarity of nominal interest rates are inconclusive.

5.3 Structural Break Models

Structural break models are widely used to study unit root problems and the parameter instability in models. Perron (1989, 1997) and Perron and Vogelsang (1992) studied the unit root test problem when a structural break is allowed in the model and the estimation of the break date. In empirical studies, Stock and Watson (1996) found evidence of nonconstant parameters in commodity prices and interest rates. Bai (1997b) showed interest rate response to the change in the discount rate has a structural break. Paye and Timmermann (2006) showed that the instability of the parameters has implications for return prediction models. How to locate the break time and make statistical inferences about the break time is therefore crucial. Hence, it is well studied in the literature. Among all the possible estimations methods, the LS method of the break date was popularized by Bai (1994, 1997a,b) and Chong (2001). These authors derived the long-span asymptotic distributions of the LS estimator and showed that they are pivotal and symmetric. Consequently, structural break tests based on LS can be easily applied.

Recent studies by Jiang et al. (2018, 2021) (hereafter JWYa and JWYb) showed that the finite sample distribution of the LS estimator is not symmetric and has three modes. As a result, they suggested that the inference based on the popularly used long-span distribution, which has a single mode and is symmetric, can potentially be misleading. However, the infill distribution of the LS estimator displays trimodality and asymmetry. Therefore, it offers a better finite sample approximation than that under the long-span scheme.

In this section, we review two structural break models. The first model allows for a structural break in the mean, while the second model allows for a break in the AR parameter. The organization of this section closely follows the previous one. We first introduce the discrete time models followed by the continuous time models and their discrete time representations. We then show that the infill asymptotic provides a more reliable approximation than the long-span asymptotic to the finite sample distribution of the LS estimator.

5.3.1 Structural Break in Mean

Hinkley (1970), Hawkins et al. (1986), Yao (1987), and Bai (1994, 1997a,b) studied time series models with a structural break and developed the asymptotic theory for the estimator of the break date under long-span scheme. Consider the structural break in the mean model (5.2),

$$X_t = \begin{cases} \mu + u_t & \text{if } t \leq k_0 \\ \mu + \delta + u_t & \text{if } t > k_0 \end{cases}, t = 1, \ldots, T, u_t \sim_{iid} (0, \sigma^2),$$
$$1 \leq k_0 < T. \tag{5.30}$$

We call k_0 and δ the structural break point and the break size, respectively.

Yao (1987) assumed that the error term u_t follows a Gaussian process and proposed to estimate k_0 by maximum likelihood estimation (MLE). We will focus on the LS method proposed by Bai (1994), as he showed that the LS method provided the same limit distribution as that obtained by MLE in Yao (1987). However, unlike Yao, Bai did not impose the Gaussian assumption on u_t.

Let $\tau_0 = k_0/T$ be the fractional break point and $\hat{k}_T^{LS}$ and $\hat{\tau}_T^{LS}$ be the LS estimators of k_0 and τ_0, respectively, such that

$$\hat{k}_T^{LS} = \arg \min_{k=1,\ldots,T-1} \{S_k^2\},$$
$$S_k^2 = \sum_{t=1}^{k} (X_t - \bar{X}_t)^2 + \sum_{t=k+1}^{T} \left(X_t - \tilde{X}_t\right)^2, \tag{5.31}$$
$$\hat{\tau}_T^{LS} = \hat{k}_T^{LS}/T,$$

where $\bar{X}_t$ and $\tilde{X}_t$ are the sample averages of the first k observations and last $T-k$ observations, respectively.

Bai (1994) assumed $\delta = \delta_T \to 0$ as $T \to \infty$, with the condition $\frac{\sqrt{T}\delta}{\sqrt{\log T}} \to \infty$, and showed that the limit of $\hat{\tau}_T^{LS}$ does not depend on the distributional function of u_t[4] and has the following asymptotic distribution.

Theorem 5.3.1 *Under model (5.30) with the conditions $\delta \to 0$ as $T \to \infty$ and $\frac{\sqrt{T}\delta}{\sqrt{\log T}} \to \infty$,*

$$T\frac{\delta_T^2}{\sigma^2}\left(\hat{\tau}_T^{LS} - \tau_0\right) \Rightarrow \arg\max_{u\in(-\infty,\infty)} \left\{W_2(u) - \frac{1}{2}|u|\right\}, \tag{5.32}$$

where $W_2(u)$ is a two-sided BM such that

$$W_2(u) = \begin{cases} W_a(-u) = W(\tau_0) - W(\tau_0 - (-u)) & \text{if } u \leq 0 \\ W_b(-u) = W(\tau_0) - W(\tau_0 + u) & \text{if } u > 0 \end{cases},$$

where $W_a(-u)$ and $W_b(-u)$ are two independent BMs.

Theorem 5.3.1 suggests the long-span distribution of $\hat{\tau}_T^{LS} - \tau_0$ is symmetric. JWYa argued that the finite sample distribution of $\hat{\tau}_T^{LS} - \tau_0$ is not symmetric when $\tau_0 \neq 0.5$ as the number of observations before and after the break are unequal. To see the finite sample performance of the long-span limiting distribution (5.32), we follow JWYa and conduct a Monte Carlo simulation with $\delta = 0.3$, $u_t \sim_{iid} N(0,1)$, $\tau_0 = 0.75$, $T = 100$. The number of replications is set to 10,000.

Figure 5.1 shows the simulated density of the finite sample distribution of $T\frac{\delta_T^2}{\sigma^2}\left(\hat{\tau}_T^{LS} - \tau_0\right)$ and long-span limiting distribution (5.32) in solid and dotted lines, respectively. From Figure 5.1, it can be seen that the long-span distribution (5.32) is symmetric, has a single mode centered at 0, and suggests that the estimator is unbiased. On the other hand, the finite sample distribution is asymmetric, has three modes with the centered mode not around zero when $\tau_0 \neq 0.5$, and suggests that the estimator is seriously biased. Therefore, the long-span distribution does not provide a good finite sample approximation. This unsatisfactory performance of the long-span theory motivated JWYa to seek a limit distribution under the infill asymptotic scheme, which can provide a better finite sample approximation. To obtain an infill distribution, as in the AR(1) models, we need a continuous time model and its discrete time representation, which are closely related to model (5.30).

[4] In contrast, if δ is fixed, Hinkley (1970) showed that the limit distribution of $\hat{\tau}_T^{LS}$ depends on the distributional function of u_t and hence there is no invariance principle.

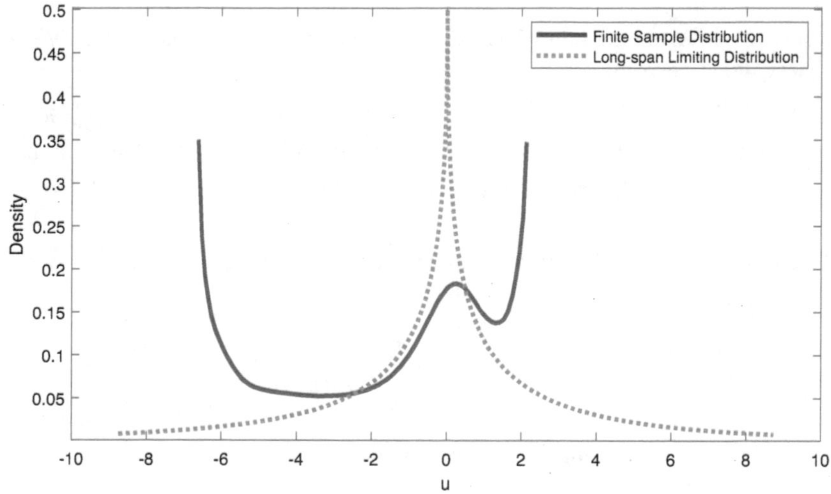

Figure 5.1 The density of $\arg\max_{u\in(-\infty,\infty)}\left\{W_2(u)-\frac{1}{2}|u|\right\}$ and the finite sample distribution of $T\frac{\delta_T^2}{\sigma^2}\left(\hat{\tau}_T^{LS}-\tau_0\right)$.

Consider the following continuous time model:

$$dX(t)=\left(\mu+\left(\frac{\delta}{\varepsilon}\right)1(t>\tau_0)\right)dt+\sigma dW(t) \tag{5.33}$$

where $t\in[0,1]$, $1(t>\tau_0)$ is an indicator function, $\sigma>0$ is the spot volatility, μ,δ,ε, and τ_0 are constants. Model (5.33) has a structural break at τ_0 for the drift function with the break size δ/ε.

We now introduce the discrete time representation that is used to elicit the infill asymptotics. Let $\{X_{t\Delta}\}_{t=1}^{T}$ be the discrete time observations; JWYa showed that the continuous time model (5.33) has the following exact discrete time representation:

$$X_{t\Delta}-X_{(t-1)\Delta}=\begin{cases}\mu\Delta+\sqrt{\Delta}\varepsilon_t & \text{if } t=1,\dots,k_0,\\ [\mu+\delta/\varepsilon]\,\Delta+\sqrt{\Delta}\varepsilon_t & \text{if } t=k_0+1,\dots,T,\end{cases} \tag{5.34}$$

$$\varepsilon_t\sim{}_{iid}N(0,\sigma^2).$$

Let $Z_{t\Delta}=\left(X_{t\Delta}-X_{(t-1)\Delta}\right)/\sqrt{\Delta}$; Equation (5.34) becomes

$$Z_{t\Delta}=\begin{cases}\mu\sqrt{\Delta}+\varepsilon_t & \text{if } t=1,\dots,k_0,\\ [\mu+\delta/\varepsilon]\sqrt{\Delta}+\varepsilon_t & \text{if } t=k_0+1,\dots,T.\end{cases} \tag{5.35}$$

When Δ is fixed, the discrete time model (5.35) is the same as model (5.30) with the break size equal to $\frac{\delta}{\varepsilon}\sqrt{\Delta}$.

Theorem 5.3.2 *(a) Under model (5.34), the LS estimator in (5.31) has the following limit distribution when* $\Delta \to 0$ *:*

$$T\left(\frac{\delta}{\sigma\varepsilon}\sqrt{\Delta}\right)^2\left(\hat{\tau}_T^{LS}-\tau_0\right) \Rightarrow \left(\frac{\delta}{\sigma\varepsilon}\right)^2 \arg\max_{u\in(-\tau_0,(1-\tau_0))}\left\{\tilde{W}(u)\right\}^2, \tag{5.36}$$

where

$$\tilde{W}(u) = \begin{cases} \frac{W(\tau_0+u)-(\tau_0+u)W(1)}{\sqrt{(\tau_0+u)(1-\tau_0-u)}} - \frac{(1-\tau_0)\sqrt{\tau_0+u}}{\sqrt{1-\tau_0-u}}\frac{\delta}{\sigma\varepsilon} & \text{if } u \le 0 \\ \frac{W(\tau_0+u)-(\tau_0+u)W(1)}{\sqrt{(\tau_0+u)(1-\tau_0-u)}} - \frac{\tau_0\sqrt{1-\tau_0-u}}{\sqrt{\tau_0+u}}\frac{\delta}{\sigma\varepsilon} & \text{if } u > 0 \end{cases}.$$

(b) Furthermore, when $\Delta \to 0$, $\varepsilon \to 0$ *with* $\frac{\delta}{\varepsilon}\sqrt{\Delta} \to 0$ *simultaneously,*

$$\left(\frac{\delta}{\sigma\varepsilon}\sqrt{\Delta}\right)^2\left(\hat{\tau}_T^{LS}-\tau_0\right) \Rightarrow \arg\max_{u\in(-\infty,+\infty)}\left\{W_2(u)-\frac{1}{2}|u|\right\}. \tag{5.37}$$

Theorem 5.3.2, which gives the infill distribution (5.35) of the LS estimator, was proven in JWYa. It shows that the infill distribution shares two important features. First, it has three modes and is asymmetric. The similarity between the infill distribution and the finite sample distribution suggests that the infill asymptotic distribution tends to outperform the long-span distribution (5.32) in approximating the finite sample distribution of $\hat{\tau}_T^{LS}$. Note that the interval to locate the argmax is $(-\infty,\infty)$ in the long-span distribution, while it is $u \in (-\tau_0, 1-\tau_0)$ under the infill distribution. This difference, as discussed in detail in JWYa, gives the infill distribution the additional two modes at the left and right ends and yields the trimodality. The result (5.37) shows that the small ε distribution coincides with the distribution (5.32) obtained by Yao (1987) and Bai (1994), respectively.

Using the same data generating process as in Figure 5.1, we report the simulated density of the distribution (5.36).

Figure 5.2 complements Figure 5.1 by adding the simulated density of the infill distribution (5.36) in the dash-dotted line. The infill distribution has three modes and is asymmetric. It suggests that the LS estimator is biased at the infill limit. This distribution therefore provides a significantly better finite sample approximation than the long-span distribution.

5.3.2 Structural Break in Autoregressions

Consider the following AR(1) model:

$$X_t = \begin{cases} \theta_1 X_{t-1} + u_t & \text{if } t \le k_0 \\ \theta_2 X_{t-1} + u_t & \text{if } t > k_0 \end{cases}, t = 1,\ldots,T, u_t \sim_{iid} (0,\sigma^2). \tag{5.38}$$

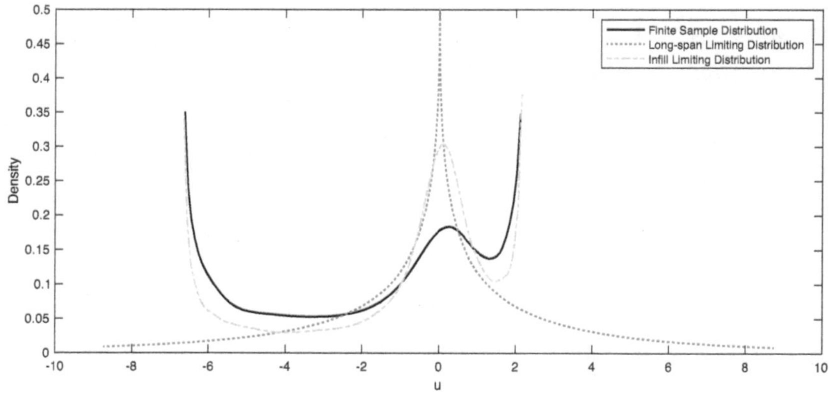

Figure 5.2 The densities of $\left(\frac{\delta}{\sigma\varepsilon}\right)^2 \arg\max_{u\in(-\tau_0,(1-\tau_0))}\left\{\tilde{W}(u)\right\}^2$ and $\arg\max_{u\in(-\infty,\infty)}\left\{W_2(u)-\frac{1}{2}|u|\right\}$ and the finite sample distribution of $T\frac{\delta_T^2}{\sigma^2}\left(\hat{\tau}_T^{LS}-\tau_0\right)$.

Assuming $\theta_1 \neq \theta_2$, model (5.38) is a model with a structural break in the AR(1) parameter at k_0 with break size $|\theta_2 - \theta_1|$.

Let the LS estimator for k_0 be

$$\hat{k}_T^{LS} = \arg\min_{k=1,\ldots,T-1}\{S_k^2\},$$

$$S_k^2 = \sum_{t=1}^{k}\left(X_t - \hat{\theta}_1(k)X_{t-1}\right)^2 + \sum_{t=k+1}^{T}\left(X_t - \hat{\theta}_2(k)X_{t-1}\right)^2, \quad (5.39)$$

$$\hat{\theta}_1(k) = \frac{\sum_{t=1}^{k} X_t X_{t-1}}{\sum_{t=1}^{k} X_{t-1}^2}, \hat{\theta}_2(k) = \frac{\sum_{t=k+1}^{T} X_t X_{t-1}}{\sum_{t=k+1}^{T} X_{t-1}^2},$$

and the LS estimator of the fractional break point is $\hat{\tau}_T^{LS} = \hat{k}_T^{LS}/T$.

Chong (2001), Pang et al. (2014), and Liang et al. (2018) derived the long-span asymptotic distributions of the LS estimator $\hat{\tau}_T^{LS}$ under various assumptions of θ_1, θ_2, break size, and the initialization X_0. Their results showed that the long-span distributions are critically dependent on these assumptions. We summarize their results in the following theorem.

Theorem 5.3.3 *Under model (5.38), $\hat{\tau}_T^{LS}$ has the following limits under different sets of assumptions.*

(a) Suppose that $|\theta_1| < 1, |\theta_2| < 1, \theta_2 = \theta_{2,T}, \theta_{2,T} - \theta_1 \to 0, \sqrt{T}|\theta_{2,T} - \theta_1| \to \infty$, *and* $X_0 = O_p(1)$, *as* $T \to \infty$:

$$\frac{T(\theta_{2,T} - \theta_1)^2}{1 - \theta_1^2}\left(\hat{\tau}_T^{LS} - \tau_0\right) \Rightarrow \arg \max_{u \in (-\infty,+\infty)} \left\{W_2(u) - \frac{1}{2}|u|\right\}. \tag{5.40}$$

(b) Suppose that $|\theta_1| < 1, \theta_2 = 1, \theta_1 = \theta_{1,T}, 1 - \theta_{1,T} \to 0$ *with* $T(1 - \theta_{1,T}) \to \infty$ *and* $X_0 = O_p(1)$, *as* $T \to \infty$:

$$T(1 - \theta_{1,T})(\hat{\tau}_T^{LS} - \tau_0) \Rightarrow \arg \max_{u \in (-\infty,+\infty)} \left\{\frac{W_a^*(u)}{R_1} - \frac{1}{2}|u|\right\}, \tag{5.41}$$

where

$$W_a^*(u) = \begin{cases} W_a(-u) & \text{if } u \le 0 \\ -W_b(u) - \int_0^u \frac{W_b(s)}{R_1} dW_b(s) - \int_0^u \left(\frac{W_b(s)}{2R_1} + 1\right) W_b(s) ds & \text{if } u > 0 \end{cases},$$

where $W_a(u)$ *and* $W_b(u)$ *are two independent BMs, and* $R_1 = \int_0^\infty \exp(-s) dW(s)$.

(c) Suppose that $\theta_1 = 1, |\theta_2| < 1, \theta_2 = \theta_{2,T}, \sqrt{T}(1 - \theta_{2,T}) \to \infty, T^{3/4}(1 - \theta_{2,T}) \to \infty$, *and* $X_0 = O_p(1)$, *as* $T \to \infty$,

$$T^2(\theta_{2,T} - 1)^2 \left(\hat{\tau}_T^{LS} - \tau_0\right) \Rightarrow \arg \max_{u \in (-\infty,+\infty)} \left\{\frac{W_2(u)}{W_c(u)} - \frac{1}{2}|u|\right\}, \tag{5.42}$$

where $W_c(u)$ *is an independent BM.*

(d) Suppose that $\theta_1 = \theta_{1,T}, |\theta_{1,T}| < 1, \theta_2 = \theta_{2,T} = 1 + c/T, |\theta_{2,T} - \theta_1| \to 0, T(\theta_{2,T} - \theta_1) \to \infty$, *and* $X_0 = o_p(\sqrt{T})$, *as* $T \to \infty$,

$$T(\theta_{2,T} - \theta_1)\left(\hat{\tau}_T^{LS} - \tau_0\right) \Rightarrow \arg \max_{u \in (-\infty,+\infty)} \left\{\frac{W_d^*(u)}{R_1} - \frac{1}{2}|u|\right\},$$

where

$$W_d^*(u) = \begin{cases} W_a(-u) & \text{if } u \le 0 \\ -I(W_b, c, \tau_0, u) - \int_0^u \frac{I(W_b, c, \tau_0, u)}{R_1} dI(W_b, c, \tau_0, u) \\ \quad - \int_0^u \left(\frac{I(W_b, c, \tau_0, s)}{2R_1} + 1\right) I(W_b, c, \tau_0, s) ds & \text{if } u > 0 \end{cases}, \tag{5.43}$$

and

$$I(W_b, c, \tau_0, u) = W_b(\tau_0 + u) - W_b(\tau_0) \\ - c \int_{\tau_0}^{\tau_0 + u} e^{-c(\tau_0 + u - r)} (W_b(u) - W_b(\tau_0)) du.$$

(e) Suppose $\theta_1 = \theta_{1,T} = 1 + c/T, \theta_2 = \theta_{2,T}, |\theta_{2,T}| < 1, \sqrt{T}(\theta_{2,T} - \theta_{1,T}) \to 0, T^{3/4}(\theta_{2,T} - \theta_{1,T}) \to \infty$, *and* $X_0 = o_p(\sqrt{T})$, *as* $T \to \infty$,

$$T^2(\theta_{2,T} - \theta_{1,T})^2 \left(\hat{\tau}_T^{LS} - \tau_0\right) \Rightarrow \arg \max_{u \in (-\infty,+\infty)} \left\{ \frac{W_2(u)}{\exp(c(1-\tau_0))G(W_a, c, \tau_0)} - \frac{1}{2}|u| \right\}, \tag{5.44}$$

where $G(W_a, c, \tau_0) = \exp(-c(1-\tau_0))W_a(\tau_0) - c\int_0^{\tau_0} \exp(-c(1-s))W_a(s)ds$.

(f) Suppose $\theta_1 = \theta_{1,T} = 1 - c/k_T, c > 0, \theta_2 = 1, k_T \to \infty, k_T/T \to 0$, *and* $X_0 = o_p(\sqrt{k_T})$, *as* $T \to \infty$,

$$\frac{cT}{k_T}\left(\hat{\tau}_T^{LS} - \tau_0\right) \Rightarrow \arg \max_{u \in (-\infty,+\infty)} \left\{ \frac{W_e^*(u)}{R_c} - \frac{1}{2}|u| \right\}, \tag{5.45}$$

where

$$W_e^*(u) = \begin{cases} W_a(-u) & \text{if } u \le 0 \\ -W_b(-u) - \int_0^u \frac{W_b(s)}{R_c} dW_b(s) - \int_0^u \left(\frac{W_b(s)}{2R_c} + 1\right) W_b(s)ds & \text{if } u > 0 \end{cases},$$

and $R_c = \sqrt{c}\int_0^\infty \exp(-cs)dW_a(s)$.

(g) Suppose $\theta_1 = 1, \theta_2 = \theta_{2,T} = 1 - c/k_T, k_T \to \infty, k_T/T \to 0, T^{1/2}/k_T \to 0, T^{3/4}/k_T \to \infty$ *and* $X_0 = o_p(\sqrt{k_T})$, *as* $T \to \infty$,

$$\frac{c^2T^2}{k_T^2}\left(\hat{\tau}_T^{LS} - \tau_0\right) \Rightarrow \arg \max_{u \in (-\infty,+\infty)} \left\{ \frac{W_2(u)}{W_c(\tau_0)} - \frac{1}{2}|u| \right\}. \tag{5.46}$$

Theorem 5.3.3 shows that when the AR parameters are strictly stationary before and after the break, the limit has the form given by (5.40). When one of the AR parameters suggests stationarity and the other is unity, (5.41) and (5.42) become applicable. When one of the AR parameters is local to unity and the other suggests stationarity, (5.43) and (5.44) apply. When one of the AR parameters is unity, the other is in the further vicinity of unity, and (5.45) and (5.46) are valid. It can be clearly seen that there is no uniform expression for the long-span asymptotic distribution since the limiting distribution varies across different assumptions regarding the AR parameters, the break size, and the initial condition.

The results show several weaknesses of long-span asymptotics. First, since the long-span distribution has a discontinuity in the values θ_1 and θ_2, and the AR parameters are not known a priori, it is unclear which limit distribution should be used in practice. Second, the long-span distribution does not approximate the finite sample distribution well. Under the case where limit (5.40) is applicable, the long-span distribution is symmetric and has only one mode, while trimodality and asymmetry can be observed in a finite sample distribution under general parameter settings. Third, as in the AR(1) model in Section 5.2, the finite sample distribution also depends on the initial condition X_0, while X_0 is missing in the limit distributions in various settings of Theorem 5.3.3. Finally, when θ_1 and θ_2 are both less than 1, for example, $\theta_1 = 0.85$ and $\theta_2 = 0.90$. It is not clear whether θ_2 is local to unity or not. Consequently, which result ((a), (d) or (g)) under Theorem 5.3.3 should be applied becomes debatable.

JWYb performed extensive simulations to showcase the significant differences between the long-span distributions (5.40) to (5.46) and the finite sample distributions. They found that long-span distributions (5.40) to (5.46) only have a single mode, unlike that under finite sample which displays trimodality. These significant differences motivate them to study the infill distribution of $\hat{\tau}_T^{LS}$.

To elicit the infill asymptotic, we now introduce a continuous time model. Consider the following model:

$$
\begin{aligned}
& dX(t) = -(\kappa + \delta 1(t > \tau_0))X(t)dt + \sigma dW(t), t \in [0, 1], \\
& X(0) = X_0 = O_p(1).
\end{aligned} \tag{5.47}
$$

JWYb showed the exact discrete time representation of model (5.47) with sampling interval Δ has the following form:

$$
\begin{aligned}
X_{t\Delta} &= \left(\theta_1 1\left(t \leq k_0\right) + \theta_2 1\left(t > k_0\right)\right) X_{(t-1)\Delta} \\
&\quad + \sqrt{\frac{1 - e^{-2(\kappa + \delta 1(t\Delta > \tau_0))\Delta}}{2(\kappa + \delta 1(t\Delta > \tau_0)}}\varepsilon_t, t = 1, \ldots, T, \\
\theta_1 &= \exp\left(-\kappa/T\right), \theta_2 = \exp\left(-\left(\kappa + \delta\right)/T\right), \varepsilon_t \sim_{iid} N(0, \sigma^2), \\
\Delta &= 1/T, \\
X_0 &= O_p(1),
\end{aligned} \tag{5.48}
$$

and the fractional break date is $\tau_0 = k_0/T$.

Clearly, the continuous time model (5.47) with the exact discrete time representation (5.48) generalizes (5.15) and (5.16) with time span $N = 1$, and both models (5.16) and (5.48) have local to unit root coefficients as $\Delta \to 0$ with a variance of the error term that is asymptotically equal to Δ.[5] To generalize the Gaussian assumption of the error term in (5.48), JWYb studied the following discrete time model:

$$
X_t = \left(\theta_1 1\left(t \leq k_0\right) + \theta_2 1\left(t > k_0\right)\right) X_{t-1} + \sqrt{\Delta}\varepsilon_t, t = 1, \ldots, T, \varepsilon_t \sim_{iid} (0, \sigma^2), \tag{5.49}
$$

where $\theta_1, \theta_2, \Delta$, and X_0 are the same as those in (5.48).

5 $\frac{1-e^{-2\kappa\Delta}}{2\kappa} = \Delta + O(\Delta^2)$ and $\frac{1-e^{-2(\kappa+\delta)\Delta}}{2(\kappa+\delta)} = \Delta + O(\Delta^2)$ as $\Delta \to 0$.

If we let $Y_t = X_t/\sqrt{\Delta}$, we can write

$$Y_t = (\theta_1 1 (t \le k_0) + \theta_2 1 (t > k_0)) Y_{t-1} + \varepsilon_t, t = 1, \ldots, T,$$
$$Y_0 \doteq X_0/\sqrt{\Delta} = O_p(T^{1/2}). \tag{5.50}$$

Clearly, when Δ is fixed, model (5.50) is the same as model (5.38). While under the infill asymptotic, the initial condition Y_0 diverges with rates $T^{1/2}$ and θ_1 and θ_2 are both local to unit root AR coefficients in model (5.50). Consequently, these two features allow us to obtain the infill distribution, which has a uniform expression for different values of κ and an initial condition as $\Delta \to 0$. We list the infill asymptotic distribution of $\hat{\tau}_T^{LS}$ in the following theorem.

Theorem 5.3.4 *Suppose the LS estimator is $\hat{\tau}_T^{LS} = \hat{k}_T^{LS}/T$, with $\hat{k}_T^{LS}$ being defined in (5.39). Under model (5.49), as $\Delta \to 0$, we have*

$$\hat{\tau}_T^{LS} \Rightarrow$$
$$\arg\max_{\tau\in(0,1)} \left\{ \frac{\left\{ \left(\tilde{J}_{\tau_0}(\tau)\right)^2 - \left(\tilde{J}_{\tau_0}(0)\right)^2 - \tau \right\}^2}{\int_0^\tau \left(\tilde{J}_{\tau_0}(r)\right)^2 dr} + \frac{\left\{ \left(\tilde{J}_{\tau_0}(1)\right)^2 - \left(\tilde{J}_{\tau_0}(\tau)\right)^2 - (1-\tau) \right\}^2}{\int_\tau^1 \left(\tilde{J}_{\tau_0}(r)\right)^2 dr} \right\}, \tag{5.51}$$

where $\tilde{J}_{\tau_0}(r), r \in (0,1)$ is defined by

$$d\tilde{J}_{\tau_0}(r) = -(\kappa + \delta 1(t > \tau_0))\tilde{J}_{\tau_0}(r)dr + dW(r),$$

with $\tilde{J}_{\tau_0}(0) = X(0)/\sigma$.

Let $\tau = \tau_0 + u$,. We can also obtain an alternative expression for the centered estimator $\hat{\tau}^{ML} - \tau_0$:

$$\hat{\tau}^{ML} - \tau_0 \overset{d}{=}$$
$$\arg\max_{u\in(-\tau_0,1-\tau_0)} \left\{ \begin{array}{ll} \delta\left\{ \left(\tilde{J}_{\tau_0}(\tau_0+u)\right)^2 - u - (2\kappa+\delta)\int_{\tau_0+u}^{\tau_0} \left(\tilde{J}_{\tau_0}(r)\right)^2 dr \right\} & \text{if } u \le 0 \\ \delta\left\{ \left(\tilde{J}_{\tau_0}(\tau_0+u)\right)^2 - u + (2\kappa+\delta)\int_{\tau_0}^{\tau_0+u} \left(\tilde{J}_{\tau_0}(r)\right)^2 dr \right\} & \text{if } u > 0 \end{array} \right. . \tag{5.52}$$

Theorem 5.3.4 was proven in JWYb. Several observations can be made based on the theorem. First, from the expression (5.52), the asymmetry is from the interval to locate the argmax $(-\tau_0, 1-\tau_0)$, and $\tilde{J}_{\tau_0}(\tau)$. Second, the initial condition X_0 enters the infill limit via $\tilde{J}_{\tau_0}(\tau)$. Finally, for all values of κ and δ, the limit (5.51) is valid. From the simulation, JWYb also showed that the infill distribution (5.51) displays trimodality.

From Theorem 5.3.4, we can see that the infill theory has two major advantages over the long-span theory. First, it is a unified theory where the infill distributional form (5.51) is valid regardless of the sign and values of κ and δ.

This is in sharp contrast to the long-span theory, where the values of θ_1 and θ_2 determine the form of the limiting distribution. These findings indeed echo the results in the AR models, where the infill distributions are continuous in the localizing parameter c. These features allow the infill distribution to provide a better approximation to the finite sample distribution than those of the long-span distribution. Second, the infill theory provides distributions with trimodality in both structural break in the mean and AR coefficient models. It thus provides a better finite sample approximation.

Remark 5.3.5 *The trimodality in the infill distribution makes the use of confidence intervals invalid. Therefore, JWYb suggested the use of the highest density region (HDR) to construct an inference for* τ.

Remark 5.3.6 *To avoid the trimodality in the infill distribution, Baek (2023) proposed a modified LS estimator, which removes the modes at the two ends of the unit interval. She showed that if the LS objective function is premultiplied by an inverse U-shaped weighting function, one can obtain a modified LS estimator, and the infill distribution of the modified estimator has a single mode.*

5.4 Conclusion

This chapter provides a review of discrete time AR(1) models and structural break models, as well as the asymptotic theory. We have examined the asymptotic results in Baek (2023), Perron (1991), Zhou and Yu (2015), and Wang and Yu (2015). These results provide the limit distributions of LS estimators under long-span asymptotics. However, we have shown that these long-span distributions do not provide an accurate approximation of the finite sample distribution. In simulation, we have demonstrated that the finite sample distribution is continuous in the autoregressive parameter, asymmetric, and dependent on the initial condition. These three essential features are typically absent in the long-span distributions, leading to poor finite sample performance.

Phillips (1987b), Perron (1991), and Zhou and Yu (2015) have shown that continuous time models and their discrete time representations can be used to obtain infill asymptotics, where the sampling interval approaches zero. Infill distributions provide a much better finite sample approximation as they are continuous in the AR parameter and preserve the initial condition under the infill limit. The infill theory can also be applied to unit root tests, as shown by Laurent and Shi (2022). Infill asymptotics provide an intermediate tool to obtain sequential double asymptotics that first shrink the sampling interval to zero, followed by an increasing time span, as shown by Wang and Yu (2016a).

Although the infill distribution generally provides a good finite sample approximation, it is not directly implementable due to an inconsistently estimable localizing parameter that appears in the limit. To infer the autoregressive parameter, Lui et al. (2022) proposed a grid bootstrap method, a modified version of Hansen (1999), to obtain a feasible and asymptotically correct confidence interval under the infill asymptotic scheme.

In addition to AR(1) models, this chapter also reviews two structural break models. The first model has a break in the mean, and Bai (1994) has shown that the long-span distribution of the LS estimator of the break date is symmetric and has one mode. However, the finite sample distribution can be significantly different and has been shown to be asymmetric and have three modes. Therefore, JWYa developed an infill theory using the continuous time model with the discrete time representation. JWYa has shown that the infill asymptotic distribution of the LS estimator well approximates the finite sample distribution and displays trimodality.

The second structural break model has a break in the AR parameter. Similar to the first model, JWYb has shown that the long-span distribution cannot well approximate the finite sample, whereas the infill distribution of the LS estimator of the break date has trimodality, incorporates the initial condition, is asymmetric, and is valid across all values of the AR coefficients. These features of the infill distribution are similar to those found in the finite sample distribution of the LS estimator. Therefore, the infill distribution outperforms the long-span distribution in approximating the finite sample. Due to the nonstandard infill distribution with three modes, JWYb suggests using the highest density region (HDR) to construct an inference for the break date.

Bibliography

Andrews, D. W. K. (1993). Exactly median-unbiased estimation of first order autoregressive/unit root models. *Econometrica 61*(1), 139–165.

Andrews, D. W. K. and H.-Y. Chen (1994). Approximately median-unbiased estimation of autoregressive models. *Journal of Business & Economic Statistics 12*(2), 187–204.

Baek, Y. (2023). Estimation of a Structural Break Point in Linear Regression Models. *Journal of Business & Economic Statistics*, *42*(1), 95–108.

Bai, J. (1994). Least squares estimation of a shift in linear processes. *Journal of Time Series Analysis 15*(5), 453–472.

Bai, J. (1997a). Estimating multiple breaks one at a time. *Econometric Theory 13*(3), 315–352.

Bai, J. (1997b). Estimation of a change point in multiple regression models. *Review of Economics and Statistics 79*(4), 551–563.

Bao, Y., A. Ullah, and Y. Wang (2017). Distribution of the mean reversion estimator in the Ornstein–Uhlenbeck process. *Econometric Reviews 36*(6–9), 1039–1056.

Chan, N. H. and C. Z. Wei (1987). Asymptotic inference for nearly nonstationary AR(1) processes. *The Annals of Statistics 15*(3), 1050–1063.

Chong, T. T.-L. (2001). Structural change in AR(1) models. *Econometric Theory 17*(1), 87–155.

Davidson, J. (1994). *Stochastic limit theory: An introduction for econometricians.* Oxford: Oxford University Press.

Diba, B. T. and H. I. Grossman (1988). Explosive rational bubbles in stock prices? *The American Economic Review 78*(3), 520–530.

Evans, G. W. (1991). Pitfalls in testing for explosive bubbles in asset prices. *The American Economic Review 81*(4), 922–930.

Hansen, B. E. (1999). The grid bootstrap and the autoregressive model. *Review of Economics and Statistics 81*(4), 594–607.

Hawkins, D., A. Gallant, and W. Fuller (1986). A simple least squares method for estimating a change in mean. *Communications in Statistics - Simulation and Computation 15*(3), 523–530.

Hinkley, D. V. (1970). Inference about the change-point in a sequence of random variables. *Biometrika 57*(1), 1–17.

Jiang, L., X. Wang, and J. Yu (2018). New distribution theory for the estimation of structural break point in mean. *Journal of Econometrics 205*(1), 156–176.

Jiang, L., X. Wang, and J. Yu (2021). In-fill asymptotic theory for structural break point in autoregressions. *Econometric Reviews 40*(4), 359–386.

Kwiatkowski, D., P. C. Phillips, P. Schmidt, and Y. Shin (1992). Testing the null hypothesis of stationarity against the alternative of a unit root: How sure are we that economic time series have a unit root? *Journal of Econometrics 54*(1), 159–178.

Laurent, S. and S. Shi (2022). Unit root test with high-frequency data. *Econometric Theory 38*(1), 113–171.

Liang, Y., T. Pang, D. Zhang, and T. Chong (2018). Structural change in mildly integrated AR(1) models. *Econometric Theory 34*(5), 985–1017.

Lui, Y. L., W. Xiao, and J. Yu (2022). The grid bootstrap for continuous time models. *Journal of Business & Economic Statistics 40*(3), 1390–1402.

Mikusheva, A. (2007). Uniform inference in autoregressive models. *Econometrica 75*(5), 1411–1452.

Mikusheva, A. (2015). Second order expansion of the t-statistic in AR(1) models. *Econometric Theory 31*(3), 426–448.

Pang, T., D. Zhang, and T. T.-L. Chong (2014). Asymptotic inferences for an AR(1) model with a change point: Stationary and nearly non-stationary cases. *Journal of Time Series Analysis 35*(2), 133–150.

Paye, B. S. and A. Timmermann (2006). Instability of return prediction models. *Journal of Empirical Finance 13*(3), 274–315.

Perron, P. (1989). The great crash, the oil price shock, and the unit root hypothesis. *Econometrica: Journal of the Econometric Society 57*(6), 1361–1401.

Perron, P. (1991). A continuous time approximation to the unstable first-order autoregressive process: The case without an intercept. *Econometrica: Journal of the Econometric Society 59*(1), 211–236.

Perron, P. (1997). Further evidence on breaking trend functions in macroeconomic variables. *Journal of Econometrics 80*(2), 355–385.

Perron, P. and T. J. Vogelsang (1992). Nonstationarity and level shifts with an application to purchasing power parity. *Journal of Business & Economic Statistics 10*(3), 301–320.

Phillips, P. C. B. (1987a). Time series regression with a unit root. *Econometrica: Journal of the Econometric Society 55*(2), 277–301.

Phillips, P. C. B. (1987b). Towards a unified asymptotic theory for autoregression. *Biometrika 74*(3), 535–547.

Phillips, P. C. B. and P. Perron (1988). Testing for a unit root in time series regression. *Biometrika 75*(2), 335–346.

Phillips, P. C. B., S. Shi, and J. Yu (2015). Testing for multiple bubbles: Historical episodes of exuberance and collapse in the S&P 500. *International Economic Review 56*(4), 1043–1078.

Phillips, P. C. B. and J. Yu (2011). Warning signs of future asset bubbles.

Stock, J. H. and M. W. Watson (1996). Evidence on structural instability in macroeconomic time series relations. *Journal of Business & Economic Statistics 14*(1), 11–30.

Wang, X. and J. Yu (2015). Limit theory for an explosive autoregressive process. *Economics Letters 126*, 176–180.

Wang, X. and J. Yu (2016a). Double asymptotics for explosive continuous time models. *Journal of Econometrics 193*(1), 35–53.

Wang, X. and J. Yu (2016b). Double asymptotics for explosive continuous time models. *Journal of Econometrics 193*(1), 35–53.

White, J. S. (1958). The limiting distribution of the serial correlation coefficient in the explosive case. *The Annals of Mathematical Statistics 29*(4), 1188–1197.

Yao, Y.-C. (1987). Approximating the distribution of the maximum likelihood estimate of the change-point in a sequence of independent random variables. *The Annals of Statistics 15*(3), 1321–1328.

Yu, J. (2014). Econometric analysis of continuous time models: A survey of Peter Phillips's work and some new results. *Econometric Theory 30*(4), 737–774.

Zhou, Q. and J. Yu (2015). Asymptotic theory for linear diffusions under alternative sampling schemes. *Economics Letters 128*, 1–5.

6 Econometric Analysis of Nonstationary Continuous-Time Models

YE CHEN *Capital University of Economics and Business*

6.1 Introduction

A covariance stationary process is a stochastic process whose mean, variance, and covariance do not change when shifted in time. In contrast, a nonstationary process has a time-varying mean, variance, or covariance. It may exhibit a trend, a structural break, cycles, or some combination thereof. While stationarity makes the econometric analysis of time series simpler, many economic and financial time series are nonstationary.

In finance, stock prices, earning-price ratios, and dividend-price ratios are commonly believed to be integrated of order one (Alessi and Kerssenfischer, 2019; Stambaugh, 1999; Welch and Goyal, 2008; Cai et al., 2015; Phillips, 2015). The time series properties of those data series are fundamental to the efficient market hypothesis (Lo and MacKinlay (1988)) and have been of significant interest. In the housing market, in addition to housing prices, some fundamentals such as price-to-income ratios and rent-to-price ratios are generally found to be nonstationary (Case and Shiller, 2003; McCarthy et al., 2004; Ambrose et al., 2013). In particular, house prices follow an explosive process in the presence of speculative bubbles. Evidence of bubble presence has been documented for many housing markets; see, for example, Greenaway-McGrevy and Phillips (2016); Shi et al. (2016); Hu and Oxley (2018); Pan (2019); Chen et al. (2023). When analyzing long-run purchasing power parity, the nonstationarity of exchange rates is studied. For example, Boswijk and Zu (2022) investigated the cointegration hypothesis of exchanges rates for the United Kingdom, Germany, and Japan relative to the United States. Furthermore, many macroeconomic variables such as GDP, inflation, money demand, and interest rates are commonly believed to be nonstationary (Zivot and Andrews, 2002; Henry and Shields, 2004; Bae and De Jong, 2007). Hence, it is of great importance to take nonstationarity into consideration in modeling.

We can model nonstationary time series in both discrete time and continuous time. While discrete-time models are more popular in practical applications, there are several advantages of using continuous-time models in econometric modeling. First, continuous-time models enable us to sample discretely at any frequency; hence, parameters are not subject to the time-aggregation problem. Due to the cost of collecting and measuring variables, data are usually collected at different frequencies (Ghysels and Miller, 2015). Hence, the frequency of these nonstationary data can vary considerably. For example, the DGP is usually collected at a quarterly frequency, and stock returns can be sampled yearly, quarterly, monthly, daily, and even every second. Second, the continuous-time model enables the convenient handling of not only stock variables (CPI, population, and money supply) but also flow variables such as GDP, income, and exports by simple time aggregation. Last, the continuous-time model enables us to study the impact of the initial conditions on parameter estimation and inference, which is one of focuses of this chapter. In particular, the initial value enters into the limiting distribution of each estimated parameter. By taking into account the initial values, test statistics that are based on the new limiting distributions are expected to result in better finite sample performance.

This chapter discusses nonstationary continuous-time models, including models with unit root regressors and explosive regressors. Many empirical works in finance and economics have identified the I(1) property and explosiveness in time series data. Hence, the continuous-time models that are introduced in this chapter provide basic econometric tools for modeling, inference, and forecasting economic and finance time series. In particular, we aim to provide a selective review of estimation methods and inferential theory and to present an empirical example that demonstrates the usefulness of nonstationary continuous-time models. For both unit root and explosive processes, we begin our discussions with the univariate analysis framework, followed by multivariate models for generality.

The remainder of this chapter is organized as follows. Section 6.2 presents an overview. Section 6.3 introduces univariate continuous-time models, including stationary, unit root, and explosive Ornstein–Uhlenbeck (OU hereafter) models, and discusses the estimation method and the limit theory. Section 6.4 introduces multivariate continuous-time models and discusses the estimation method and the limit theory. Section 6.5 presents Monte Carlo simulations. Section 6.6 provides an empirical study. Section 6.7 presents the conclusions of this chapter.

6.2 Overview

The random process that is studied in this chapter is the OU process. The OU process has a wide range of empirical applications in the practice. Vasicek (1977) assumes the spot rate process follows the OU process. Burgess (2014) provides an overview of the Vasicek model and its advantages and extensions. Barndorff-Nielsen and Shephard (2001) consider the non-Gaussian processes of OU type, where the deviation from Gaussianity allows for flexibility in modeling the dependence structures in the data. The model has been applied to study the instantaneous volatility of exchange rates (Barndorff-Nielsen and Shephard, 2003) and stock returns (Roberts et al., 2004).

The OU process is the solution of the following stochastic differential equation:

$$dx(t) = \kappa(\mu - x(t))\, dt + dB_x(t), \tag{6.1}$$

with $B_x(t) = \sigma_{xx} W_x(t)$, where W_x is a standard Brownian motion. In a more general case, we allow $B_x(t)$ to be a Lévy process. The initial value is set to $x(0) = x_0 = O_p(1)$.

Parameter μ is the drift of the process. Parameter κ determines the level of persistence in $x(t)$. For $\kappa > 0$, the process $x(t)$ is stationary when the initial condition comes from the infinite past ($x(0) = \int_{-\infty}^{0} e^{\kappa s} dB_x(s)$). In this case, μ is the unconditional mean of $x(t)$ and κ determines the speed of mean-reversion. $x(t)$ is a Brownian motion when $\kappa = 0$ and explosive when $\kappa < 0$. For data over a large time span, several different regimes of κ might be contemplated, possibly with break points separating the regimes. In this chapter, we focus on cases with $\kappa = 0$ and $\kappa < 0$.

6.2.1 Exact Discrete-Time Representation

When only discrete observations are available, discretization of the continuous-time model is necessary for estimating the parameters of interest, namely, the persistence parameter κ (defined in Equation (6.1)) and the co-movement parameters B (defined in Equation (6.19) for cointegration models) and β (defined in equation (6.26) for coexplosive models).

Suppose data are recorded at N equally spaced points over a time interval $[0, T]$. Denote the sampling interval by Δ such that we have $N = T/\Delta$ observations. In practical applications in economics, T measures the number of years. Typical values for T are not very large (between 1 and 50). In some cases, even if T is large, a smaller value for T may be used to avoid possible structural breaks (e.g., Zhou and Yu, 2015). In empirical studies, three sampling intervals are often considered, namely, $\Delta = 1/12, 1/52, 1/252$, which correspond to monthly, weekly, and daily frequencies.

Following Phillips (1972), the exact discrete-time representation of (6.1) is as follows:

$$x_{t\Delta} = a_\Delta(\kappa) x_{(t-1)\Delta} + g_\Delta + u_{x,t\Delta}, \tag{6.2}$$

where

$$\begin{aligned} a_\Delta(\kappa) &= \exp(-\kappa\Delta), \\ g_\Delta &= \mu\left(1 - e^{-\kappa\Delta}\right), \\ u_{x,t\Delta} &= \sigma_{xx} \int_{(t-1)\Delta}^{t\Delta} e^{-\kappa(t\Delta - s)} dB_x(s) \overset{d}{=} \mathcal{N}\left(0, \frac{\sigma_{xx}^2}{2\kappa}\left(1 - e^{-2\kappa\Delta}\right)\right). \end{aligned}$$

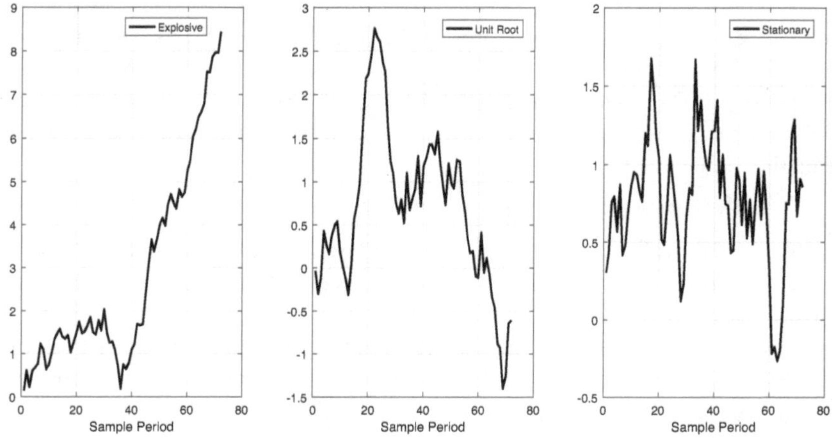

Figure 6.1 A typical realization of the data-generating process (6.1).

The initial value is $x_{0\Delta} = x_0 = O_p(1)$. The autoregressive parameter $a_\Delta(\kappa)$ depends directly on the sampling frequency Δ and persistency parameter κ. Note that Δ is related to the sample size N. The standard error of $u_{x,t\Delta}$ is $\lambda_\Delta = \sqrt{\frac{\sigma_{xx}^2}{2\kappa}\left(1 - e^{-2\kappa\Delta}\right)} \sim \sigma_{xx}\sqrt{\Delta} \to 0$ as $\Delta \to 0$.

Restandardizing Equation (6.2) by λ_Δ, Equation (6.2) becomes

$$\widetilde{x}_{t\Delta} = a_\Delta(\kappa)\widetilde{x}_{(t-1)\Delta} + \widetilde{g}_\Delta + \widetilde{u}_{x,t\Delta}, \tag{6.3}$$

where $\widetilde{x}_{t\Delta} = x_{t\Delta}/\lambda_\Delta$, $\widetilde{g}_\Delta = g_\Delta/\lambda_\Delta$ and $\widetilde{u}_{x,t\Delta} = u_{x,t\Delta}/\lambda_\Delta$. In addition, we have

$$a_\Delta(\kappa) = 1 - \kappa\Delta + O\left(\Delta^2\right) \to 1,$$
$$\widetilde{g}_\Delta \sim O\left(\sqrt{\Delta}\right),$$
$$\widetilde{u}_{x,t\Delta} \sim_{iid} \mathcal{N}(0,1),$$

as $\Delta \to 0$. The initial value then become $\widetilde{x}_{0\Delta} = x_{0\Delta}/\lambda_\Delta = O_p\left(\Delta^{-1/2}\right)$.

Figure 6.1 presents one typical simulated path of the data-generating process (6.1) using the exact discrete-time representation of (6.3). The parameter configuration is $T = 6$, $\Delta = 1/12$, $\mu = 1$, and $\sigma_{xx} = 1$. It corresponds to monthly data for a six-year time span. From the left to the right panel, the parameter κ is set to -0.3, 0, and 3. These values correspond to $a_\Delta(\kappa) = 1.0253$, 1, and 0.7788, respectively. The initial value x_0 is set to 0. Figure 6.1 shows that the explosive series demonstrates a rapid escalation, the unit root process wanders around and demonstrates a stochastic trend, and the stationary series exhibits a mean-reversion behavior.

6.2.2 Estimator and Test Statistic

For the OU process, the parameters of interest are g_Δ and $a_\Delta(\kappa)$ (a_Δ hereafter). The corresponding least squares (LS) estimators are as follows:

$$\begin{bmatrix} \widehat{g}_\Delta \\ \widehat{a}_\Delta \end{bmatrix} = \begin{bmatrix} T & \sum_{t=1}^N x_{(t-1)\Delta} \\ \sum_{t=1}^N x_{(t-1)\Delta} & \sum_{t=1}^N x_{(t-1)\Delta}^2 \end{bmatrix}^{-1} \begin{bmatrix} \sum_{t=1}^N x_{t\Delta} \\ \sum_{t=1}^N x_{t\Delta} x_{(t-1)\Delta} \end{bmatrix}, \tag{6.4}$$

and hence,

$$\begin{bmatrix} \widehat{g}_\Delta - g_\Delta \\ \widehat{a}_\Delta - a_\Delta \end{bmatrix} = \begin{bmatrix} T & \sum_{t=1}^N \widetilde{x}_{(t-1)\Delta} \\ \sum_{t=1}^N \widetilde{x}_{(t-1)\Delta} & \sum_{t=1}^N \widetilde{x}_{(t-1)\Delta}^2 \end{bmatrix}^{-1} \begin{bmatrix} \sum_{t=1}^N \widetilde{u}_{x,t\Delta} \\ \sum_{t=1}^N \widetilde{x}_{(t-1)\Delta} \widetilde{u}_{x,t\Delta} \end{bmatrix}. \tag{6.5}$$

The LS estimator of κ, which is denoted by $\hat{\kappa}$, is $-\frac{1}{\Delta}\ln(\widehat{a}_\Delta)$.

Defining $s_x^2 = N^{-1}\sum_{t=1}^N \widehat{u}_{x,t\Delta}^2$, we have

$$s_{a_\Delta}^2 = s_x^2 \left(\sum_{t=1}^N \widetilde{x}_{(t-1)\Delta}^2 \sigma_{xx}^2 \Delta - \frac{1}{N}\left(\sum_{t=1}^N \widetilde{x}_{(t-1)\Delta} \sigma_{xx} \sqrt{\Delta} \right)^2 \right)^{-1}.$$

The t statistic for $\widehat{a}_\Delta$ is

$$\begin{aligned} t_{a_\Delta} &= \frac{\widehat{a}_\Delta - a_\Delta}{s_{a_\Delta}} \\ &= \frac{a_\Delta^N/\Delta\,(\widehat{a}_\Delta - a_\Delta)}{\left\{ s_x^2 \left(a_\Delta^{-2N}\Delta^2 \sum_{t=1}^N \widetilde{x}_{(t-1)\Delta}^2 \sigma_{xx}^2 \Delta - \frac{1}{N}\left(a_\Delta^{-N}\Delta \sum_{t=1}^N \widetilde{x}_{(t-1)\Delta}\sigma_{xx}\sqrt{\Delta} \right)^2 \right)^{-1} \right\}^{1/2}}. \end{aligned} \tag{6.6}$$

Similarly, given $a_\Delta = \exp(-k\Delta)$, we have

$$\Delta s_\kappa = s_{a_\Delta} + o_p(\Delta),$$

and the t statistic for $\widehat{\kappa}$ is

$$\begin{aligned} t_\kappa &= \frac{\widehat{\kappa} - \kappa}{s_\kappa} \\ &= \frac{a_\Delta^N(\widehat{\kappa} - \kappa)}{\left\{ s_x^2 \left(\frac{1}{a_\Delta^{2N}/\Delta^2} \sum_{t=1}^N x_{(t-1)\Delta}^2 - \frac{1}{N}\left(\frac{1}{a_\Delta^N/\Delta} \sum_{t=1}^N x_{(t-1)\Delta} \right)^2 \right)^{-1} \right\}^{1/2}}. \end{aligned} \tag{6.7}$$

6.2.3 Asymptotics

Three sampling schemes are considered in this chapter:

1. the long-span asymptotics: $T \to \infty$, Δ is fixed, and hence, $N \to \infty$;
2. the double asymptotics: $T \to \infty$, $\Delta \to 0$, and hence, $N \to \infty$;
3. the infill asymptotics: $\Delta \to 0$, T is fixed, and hence, $N \to \infty$.

The first scheme (the long-span asymptotics) assumes that the sampling interval Δ is fixed and the time span $T \to \infty$ and hence the sample size N goes to infinity as $T \to \infty$. This is the usual asymptotic scheme that is considered in the discrete-time literature. The limiting distribution is not continuous in κ (Tang and Chen, 2009; Yu, 2012; and Yu, 2014), and hence, disjoint pieces of the confidence interval are generated.

The third scheme (the infill asymptotics) enables the sample size to go to infinity by decreasing the sampling interval but keeping the time span fixed. Perron (1991a) provides the infill asymptotics regarding the persistence parameter κ for the OU process (6.1) without an intercept. The limiting distribution is continuous in κ for all values of κ, and hence, it provides a unified framework for making inferences regarding parameter κ. In addition, the limiting distribution of κ depends on the initial values, and it provides a good approximation of the finite sample distribution. In addition, the infill asymptotic theory with a known intercept is presented in Yu (2014), and the infill asymptotic theory with a more general initial condition is provided in Perron, 1991b.

The second scheme (the double asymptotics) combines the long-span scheme and the infill scheme and is referred to as the double asymptotics. There is a discontinuity of the limiting distribution of the persistence parameter κ (Zhou and Yu, 2015).

6.3 Univariate Continuous-Time Models

In this section, we discuss univariate continuous-time models. We start with the univariate OU process with $\kappa > 0$ under three sampling schemes. Among the three asymptotics, the infill asymptotics provide the best approximation to the finite sample distribution (Zhou and Yu, 2015). However, the infill distribution depends on unknown parameters that cannot be consistently estimated. Lui et al. (2022) suggested using the new grid bootstrap for inference. Hence, we further discuss the local-to-unity model under the infill scheme since the discretized model is closely related to the local-to-unity model under the infill sampling scheme as $\Delta \to 0$. We also discuss the unit root continuous-time model. Finally, we consider the univariate OU process with $\kappa < 0$ (the explosive case). The use of a continuous-time framework with double asymptotics readily accommodates initial condition and drift effects, with a limit theory that is easy to implement in practice with no nuisance parameters

(Wang and Yu, 2016; Chen et al., 2017). In contrast, discrete-time models with local-to-unity and mildly integrated or mildly explosive autoregressive parameters typically involve localizing coefficients that enter the limit theory as nuisance parameters and are not generally consistently estimable, thereby complicating inference.

6.3.1 Univariate OU Process with $\kappa > 0$

When $\kappa > 0, x(t)$ as defined in (6.1) is a stationary process. Zhou and Yu (2015) summarized the limiting distribution of the LS estimator of $\widehat{\kappa}$ under the three sampling schemes as follows.

The long-span asymptotics of $\widehat{\kappa}$ are

$$T(\widehat{\kappa} - \kappa) \overset{d}{\to} N\left(0, \frac{e^{2\kappa\Delta} - 1}{\Delta}\right), \tag{6.8}$$

as T goes to ∞.

Under the double asymptotics, as $T \to \infty$ and $\Delta \to 0$, the limiting result is

$$T(\widehat{\kappa} - \kappa) \overset{d}{\to} N(0, 2\kappa),$$

as $T \to \infty$ and $\Delta \to 0$.

For model (6.1), if $\kappa < 0$, the infill asymptotic distribution of $\widehat{\kappa}$ is

$$T(\widehat{\kappa} - \kappa) \overset{d}{\to} \frac{A(\gamma_0, c)}{B(\gamma_0, c)},$$

where $c = -\kappa T$, $c_1 = e^{rc} - 1$, $c_2 = \frac{e^c - c - 1}{c^2}$, $c_3 = \frac{e^{2c} - 4e^c + 2c + 3}{2c^3}$, $c_4 = \frac{e^c - 1}{c}$, $J_c(r) = \int_0^r e^{c(r-s)} dW(s)$, $b = \mu\sqrt{-c\kappa}/\sigma_{xx}$, $\gamma_0 = X_0/\left(\sigma_{xx}\sqrt{T}\right)$, and

$$A(\gamma_0, c) = \frac{b}{c}\int_0^1 c_1 dW(r) + \int_0^1 J_c(r)\, dW(r) + \gamma_0 \int_0^1 e^{rc} dW(r) - \left(\int_0^1 dW(r)\right)\left(c_2 b + \int_0^1 J_c(r)\, dr + c_4\gamma_0\right),$$

$$B(\gamma_0, c) = c_3 b^2 + \frac{2b}{c}\int_0^1 c_1 J_c(r)\, dr + \int_0^1 J_c(r)^2\, dr + c_4^2 b\gamma_0 + 2\gamma_0 \int_0^1 e^{rc} J_c(r)\, dr + \gamma_0^2 \frac{e^{2c} - 1}{2c} - \left(c_2 b + \int_0^1 J_c(r)\, dr + c_4\gamma_0\right).$$

The infill asymptotics apply for all values of κ. Zhou and Yu (2015) showed that the infill asymptotic distribution provides much more accurate approximations to the finite sample distribution in a simulation study. In an empirical application, they applied the three alternative asymptotic theories to real monthly short-term interest rates from July 1954 to June 2002. The confidence intervals using all three alternative sampling schemes suggested a unit root in both the 90 percent and 95 percent confidence intervals. However, the confidence intervals that were implied by both the long-span asymptotics and the double asymptotics suggested that there was no unit root in the series.

6.3.2 Local-to-Unity Model under the Infill Scheme

When $\kappa \neq 0$, the autoregressive parameter in the exact discrete-time representation of (6.1) is $a_\Delta = \exp(-\kappa\Delta)$. We rewrite it as

$$a_\Delta = \exp(-\kappa\Delta) = \exp\left(\frac{-\kappa T}{N}\right).$$

Under the infill asymptotic scheme ($\Delta \to 0$, T is fixed, and hence, $N \to \infty$), the discretized model has a root that is local-to-unity (Phillips, 1987b). Correspondingly, Phillips (1987b) studied a near-integrated random process whose autoregressive parameter is defined by $\exp(c/N)$, where c is the local-to-unity parameter and measures the deviation from the unit root case and N is the sample size. When $c > 0$, the process is said to be locally explosive, and when $c < 0$, the process is said to be locally stationary.

The asymptotics of the estimated autoregressive parameter in discrete time are provided in Phillips (1987b). For continuous-time models, the infill asymptotic theory with a more general initial condition is provided in Perron (1991b). The infill asymptotic theory with a known intercept is presented in Yu (2014). There is a discontinuity in the long-span asymptotics and the double asymptotics of $\widehat{\kappa}$ as κ passes through zero. However, the infill asymptotic distribution is continuous in κ. Hence, it provides a unified framework for statistical inference about κ.

Lui et al. (2022) considered the infill asymptotic distribution of $\widehat{\kappa}$. Since there are unknown parameters in the limiting result of $\widehat{\kappa}$ (Lemma 3.2 in Lui et al., 2022), the CIs are infeasible. In particular, Lui et al. (2022) studied the following Lévy-driven models:

$$dx(t) = \kappa(\mu - x(t))\,dt + \sigma dL(t), x(0) = x_0 = O_p(1), \tag{6.9}$$

where $L(t)$ is a Lévy process that is defined on a filtered probability space $\left(\Omega, \mathcal{F}, \{\mathcal{F}_t\}_{t\geqslant 0}, P\right)$ with $L(0) = 0$ a.s.. $F_t = \sigma\left\{[x(s)]_{s=0}^{t}\right\}$ and satisfies the following three properties:

1. Independent increments: for every increasing sequence of times $t_0, \ldots .t_N$, the random variables $L(t_0)$, $L(t_1) - L(t_0)$, ..., $L(t_N) - L(t_{N-1})$ are independent;
2. Stationary increments: the law of $L(t + \Delta) - L(t)$ is independent of t;

3. Stochastic continuity: for any $\varepsilon > 0$ and $t \geqslant 0$, $\lim_{\Delta \to 0} P\left(|L(t+\Delta) - L(t)| \geqslant \varepsilon\right) = 0$. The characteristic function of $L(t)$ takes the form $E\left(isL(t)\right) = \exp\left\{-t\psi\left(s\right)\right\}$, where i is the imaginary unit and the function $\psi\left(\cdot\right) \mathbb{R} \to \mathbb{C}$ is the Lévy exponent of $L(t)$.

The initial value x_0 is assumed to be independent of $L\left(t\right)$. The exact discrete-time representation of (6.9) is

$$x_{t\Delta} = a_\Delta x_{(t-1)\Delta} + g_\Delta + \lambda_\Delta u_{x,t\Delta},\ x_{0\Delta} = x_0 = O_p\left(1\right), \tag{6.10}$$

or

$$\widetilde{x}_{t\Delta} = a_\Delta \widetilde{x}_{(t-1)\Delta} + \widetilde{g}_\Delta + u_{x,t\Delta},\ \widetilde{x}_{0\Delta} = x_0/\lambda_\Delta, \tag{6.11}$$

where

$$\begin{aligned}
a_\Delta &= \exp\left(-\kappa\Delta\right), \\
g_\Delta &= \left(\mu + \frac{\sigma i\psi'\left(0\right)}{\kappa}\right)\left(1 - e^{-\kappa\Delta}\right), \\
\lambda_\Delta &= \sigma\sqrt{\psi''\left(0\right)\left(1 - e^{-2\kappa\Delta}\right)/2\kappa}, \\
u_{x,t\Delta} &= \lambda_\Delta^{-1}\left(\sigma\int_{(t-1)\Delta}^{t\Delta} e^{-\kappa(t\Delta - s)}dL\left(s\right) - \sigma i\psi'\left(0\right)\frac{1 - e^{-\kappa\Delta}}{\kappa}\right).
\end{aligned}$$

Lemma 3.1 of Lui et al. (2022) provides the infill asymptotic theory that is stated in what follows:

Lemma 6.3.1 *For model (6.9), as $\Delta \to 0$,*

$$N\left(\widehat{\kappa} - \kappa\right) \Rightarrow -\frac{\Upsilon_3 - \Upsilon_2 W(1)}{\Upsilon_1 - \Upsilon_2^2}, \tag{6.12}$$

where

$$\begin{aligned}
\Upsilon_1 = {} & \frac{\exp(2c) - 4\exp(c) + 2c + 3}{2c^3}b^2 + \frac{2b}{c}\int_0^1 (\exp(rc) - 1)J_c(r)dr \\
& + \int_0^1 J_c^2(r)dr \\
& + \frac{\exp(2c) - 2\exp(c) + 1}{c^2}b\gamma_0 + 2\gamma_0\int_0^1 \exp(rc)J_c(r)dr \\
& + \gamma_0^2\frac{\exp(2c) - 1}{2c}; \\
\Upsilon_2 = {} & \frac{\exp(c) - c - 1}{c^2}b + \int_0^1 J_c(r)dr + \frac{\exp(c) - 1}{c}\gamma_0;
\end{aligned}$$

$$\Upsilon_3 = \frac{b}{c}\int_0^1 (\exp(rc) - 1)dW(r) + \int_0^1 J_c(r)dW(r) + \gamma_0 \int_0^1 \exp(rc)dW(r),$$

with

$$J_c(r) = \int_0^r \exp(c(r-s))dW(s);\ \gamma_0 = \frac{x_0}{\sigma_\psi \sqrt{N}};\ \sigma_\psi^2 = \sigma^2 \psi''(0);$$

$$b = \left(\mu + \frac{\sigma i \psi'(0)}{\kappa}\right)\frac{\sqrt{-c\kappa}}{\sigma_\psi};\ c = -\kappa N.$$

The limiting result facilitates the inversion of the coefficient-based statistic and the construction of confidence intervals (CIs) for κ. Since there are unknown parameters that cannot be consistently estimated in the limiting result, the CIs are infeasible. Hence, Lui et al. (2022) suggested using the new grid bootstrap for inference.

According to Lui et al. (2022), the following steps are needed to construct a grid bootstrap CI for κ:

1. Given the data $\{x_{t\Delta}\}_{t=0}^N$, the LS estimates of $\widehat{g}_\Delta$ and $\widehat{a}_\Delta$ are computed, and the residual,
$$\widehat{u}_{x,t\Delta} = x_{t\Delta} - \widehat{a}_\Delta x_{(t-1)\Delta} - \widehat{g}_\Delta,$$
and its variance estimator $s_x^2 = N^{-1}\sum_{t=1}^N \widehat{u}_{x,t\Delta}^2$ are obtained;
2. A grid of a_Δ, $A_G = \{a_{\Delta 1}, a_{\Delta 2}, \ldots, a_{\Delta G}\}$ that is centered at $\widehat{a}_\Delta$ is constructed, with the first and last grid points being calculated from $\widehat{a}_\Delta \pm 7 \times s.e.(\widehat{a}_\Delta)$. Lui et al. (2022) set $G = 50$ in the simulation;
3. Given a point in the grid ($a_{\Delta G} \in A_G$), a second regression is performed:
$$x_{t\Delta} - a_{\Delta G} x_{(t-1)\Delta} = \widetilde{g}_\Delta + v_t,$$
where v_t is the residual of the second regression and $\widetilde{g}_\Delta$ is a function of $a_{\Delta G}$;
4. $u_{x,t\Delta}^*$ (independently drawn from the empirical distribution of $\left\{\widehat{u}_{x,t\Delta}\right\}_{t=0}^N$) is an *i.i.d.* random variable for $t = 1, \ldots, N$. Bootstrap data $\left\{x_{t\Delta}^*\right\}_{t=1}^N$ are generated based on $\left\{u_{x,t\Delta}^*\right\}_{t=1}^N$ and the same initial condition as that of the observed data, namely,
$$x_{t\Delta}^* = a_{\Delta G} x_{(t-1)\Delta}^* + \widetilde{g}_\Delta + s_x \lambda_\Delta u_{x,t\Delta}^*, x_{0\Delta}^* = x_0;$$
5. B sets of bootstrap data of $\left\{\left\{x_{t\Delta}^{*B}\right\}_{t=0}^N\right\}_{b=1}^B$ are generated. For every set of bootstrap data, the LS estimator of κ (denoted by $\widehat{\kappa}^*$) is obtained, and the

bootstrap coefficient-based statistic $T(\widehat{\kappa}^* - \kappa_G)$, where $\kappa_G = -\frac{\ln(a_{\Delta G})}{\Delta}$, is calculated. The $y^{t\Delta}$ quantile of the bootstrap statistic $T(\widehat{\kappa}^* - \kappa_G)$ is determined, which is denoted by $c_N^*(y|\kappa_G)$. Lui et al. (2022) set $B = 399$ in the simulation;

6. Following Hansen (1999), the quantile function $c_N^*(y|\kappa)$ is estimated by applying kernel regression:

$$c_N^*(y|\kappa) = \frac{\sum_{g=1}^{G} K\left(\frac{\kappa-\kappa_G}{\delta}\right) c_N^*(y|\kappa_G)}{\sum_{g=1}^{G} K\left(\frac{\kappa-\kappa_G}{\delta}\right)},$$

where $K(\cdot)$ is a kernel function and δ is the bandwidth. Lui et al. (2022) suggested using the Epanechnokov kernel such that $K(x) = \frac{3}{4}\left(1 - x^2 1(|x| \leqslant 1)\right)$ and choosing the bandwidth by LS cross-validation;

7. The CI for κ is obtained by inverting

$$CI_q^B = \left\{\kappa \in R\colon c_N^*(y_1|\kappa) \leqslant T(\widehat{\kappa} - \kappa_G) \leqslant c_N^*(y_2|\kappa)\right\}.$$

Step 4 is critically different from that in Hansen (1999), as the initial condition in the bootstrap samples is always set to $x_{0\Delta}^* = x_0$.

The grid bootstrap procedure that was proposed in Lui et al. (2022), is different from the standard grid bootstrap procedure that was proposed by Hansen (1999), which was developed for the local-to-unity AR(1) model when the initial condition is $O_p(1)$. In the procedure of Hansen (1999), the bootstrap initialization x_0^* is set to 0 when the AR coefficient is not smaller than one and to the fitted value of x_0 that is based on the LS estimates when the AR coefficient is smaller than one. This choice of initialization is made to avoid dependence on the initialization. Since under the infill scheme the initial condition explicitly enters the infill asymptotic distribution, the initialization is needed when generating the bootstrapped samples. As a result, Lui et al. (2022) modified the grid bootstrap procedure when generating bootstrap samples by setting $x_0^* = x_0$ regardless of the AR coefficient. The modified grid bootstrap leads to uniform inferences on the persistence parameter. Simulation studies showed that this improves the infill asymptotics in terms of empirical coverage.

6.3.3 Unit Root Models in Continuous Time

When $\kappa = 0$, $x(t)$ as defined in (6.1) is an $I(1)$ process. Zhou and Yu (2015) summarized the limiting distribution of the LS estimator of $\widehat{\kappa}$ under the three sampling schemes as follows.

The long-span asymptotics of $\widehat{\kappa}$ are

$$T(\widehat{\kappa}-0) \xrightarrow{d} -\frac{\int_0^1 W(r)\,dW(r) - W(1)\int_0^1 W(r)\,dr}{\int_0^1 W(r)^2\,dr - \left(\int_0^1 W(r)\,dr\right)^2}, \tag{6.13}$$

as T goes to ∞. The result in (6.13) was developed in Phillips (1987a) and Phillips (1987b).

Under the double asymptotics, as $T \to \infty$ and $\Delta \to 0$, the obtained limiting result is the same as the long-span asymptotics, as stated in (6.13).

6.3.4 *Explosive Continuous-Time Models*

Explosive OU processes are able to capture market exuberance in financial time series. In empirical work, the value of the autoregressive coefficient is also often taken to depend on the frequency of observation. This is because the use of higher-frequency data typically leads to a more persistent autoregressive coefficient estimate and expectations do not change over short time horizons as much as they do over long horizons. For these reasons, dependence of the autoregressive parameter on the sampling frequency often provides greater realism in empirical work where it is necessary to model near-unit root phenomena in continuous time.

Link with the Discrete-Time Models

When $\kappa < 0$, model (6.1) is an explosive OU model. Its standardized discrete model (6.3) corresponds to the model of Phillips and Magdalinos (2007). In particular, Phillips and Magdalinos (2007) analyzed the following triangular model:

$$x_t = R_N x_{t-1} + u_{xt}, \quad x_0 = o_p(N^{\alpha/2}), \tag{6.14}$$

The autoregressive coefficient has the form $R_N = I_K + \frac{C}{N^\alpha}$, $\alpha \in (0,1)$, and $C = \text{diag}\,(c_1, \ldots c_K)$, where $N^\alpha \to \infty$ when $N \to \infty$. Hence x_t is a moderately integrated time series, as R_N involves moderate deviations from a unit root in the sense of Phillips and Magdalinos (2007). Moreover, since $C > 0$, x_t is a mildly explosive time series. The vector (u_{xt}) is a sequence of random variables with zero mean and a finite second moment.

Justification of the moderate deviations from a unit root from the double asymptotic scheme in continuous-time systems is stated in Chen et al. (2017). First, the autoregressive setup with $R_N = I_K + \frac{C}{N^\alpha}$, $\alpha \in (0,1)$ corresponds to the scheme of $\Delta \to 0$ and $T \to \infty$. In a similar way of justification, Boswijk (2001) and Phillips et al. (2001) introduce the block-local-to-unity concept. They formulate the block-local-to-unity model using $1 + c/m$, where m denotes the number of observations such that $m = \frac{N}{M}$ for M blocks. When M is fixed and $m \to \infty$, the autoregressive coefficient parameter corresponds to the standard local-to-unity model, where $1 + \frac{c}{m}$ has the same order of magnitude as the local-to-unity parameter. When $m \to \infty$ and then $M \to \infty$, the autoregressive coefficient parameter is further from unity compared with the standard local-to-unity model. By setting $m = N^{\gamma}$ and $M = N^{1-\gamma}$, $\gamma \in (0,1)$, the latter case corresponds to the standard local-to-unity model. In this case, both m and M are decided by N and γ. By setting $\Delta = \frac{1}{m}$, and $T = M$, the latter case corresponds to the model of Wang and Yu (2016) and Chen et al. (2017). However, unlike in Phillips et al. (2001) and Boswijk (2001), N is not predetermined in Wang and Yu (2016) or Chen et al. (2017) because N is determined after Δ and T are chosen in the setup.

By setting $\Delta = \frac{1}{m}$, and $T = M$, links between the notations (m, M, N) in Boswijk (2001) and those in Wang and Yu (2016) and Chen et al. (2017) (Δ, T, N) are established. Clearly, the double asymptotics ($T \to \infty$ and $\Delta \to 0$) correspond to case (2) in Phillips et al. (2001) and Boswijk (2001). However, unlike in Phillips et al. (2001) and Boswijk (2001), N is not predetermined in Wang and Yu (2016) or Chen et al. (2017) because N is determined after Δ and T are chosen in our setup.

Asymptotics

Consider the following modified model of (6.14):

$$x_t = \mu + R_N x_{t-1} + u_{xt}, x_0 = O_p\left(N^{\alpha/2}\right), \mu = O_p\left(N^{-\alpha/2}\right). \quad (6.15)$$

The error u_{xt} is an *iid* sequence with mean zero and variance σ_{xx}^2. Compared to the model in Phillips and Magdalinos (2007), the model of (6.14) allows for a larger initial condition and a local (to zero) drift. The limit distribution of $\widehat{\mu}$, which is the LS estimator of the intercept parameter μ, follows simply as

$$\begin{aligned}
&\sqrt{N}(\widehat{\mu} - \mu) \\
&= \sqrt{N}\frac{\left[\begin{array}{c}\left(R_N^N N^{\alpha}\right)^{-2} \sum_{t=1}^N x_{t-1}^2 \left(\frac{1}{N}\sum_{t=1}^N u_{xt}\right) - \\ \frac{1}{N}\left\{\left(R_N^N N^{\alpha}\right)^{-1} \sum_{t=1}^N x_{t-1}\right\}\left\{\left(R_N^N N^{\alpha}\right)^{-1} \sum_{t=1}^N x_{t-1} u_{xt}\right\}\end{array}\right]}{\left(R_N^N N^{\alpha}\right)^{-2} \sum_{t=1}^N x_{t-1}^2 - \frac{1}{N}\left\{\left(R_N^N N^{\alpha}\right)^{-1} \sum_{t=1}^N x_{t-1}\right\}^2} \\
&= \frac{1}{\sqrt{N}}\sum_{t=1}^{N} u_{xt} + o_p(1) \xrightarrow{d} \mathcal{N}\left(0, \sigma_{xx}^2\right). \qquad (6.16)
\end{aligned}$$

This result is useful in testing for $\mu = 0$ in the model of (6.14).

We let $\widetilde{x}_0 = x_0 N^{-\alpha/2} \Rightarrow X^*$, $\widetilde{\mu} = N^{\alpha/2}\mu \Rightarrow \mu^*$, and $D = X^* + \frac{\mu^*}{c}$. The LS estimator of R_N is denoted by $\widehat{R}_N$, and hence, $\widehat{c} = N^{\alpha}\left(\widehat{R}_N - 1\right)$. The limit theory for $\widehat{R}_N$ follows from the proof of Theorem 2.1 in Chen et al. (2017):

$$R_N^N N^{\alpha}\left(\widehat{R}_N - R_N\right) \xrightarrow{d} 2c\frac{\sigma_{xx} U_x}{\sigma_{xx} U_x + (2c)^{1/2} D}, \quad (6.17)$$

where $U_x \stackrel{d}{=} \mathcal{N}(0,1)$. Given $\widehat{c}-c=\left(\widehat{R}_N-R_N\right)N^{\alpha}$, the limit theory for $\widehat{c}$ is

$$R_N^N(\widehat{c}-c) \xrightarrow{d} 2c\frac{\sigma_{xx}U_x}{\sigma_{xx}U_x+(2c)^{1/2}D}.$$

Defining the regression residuals $\hat{u}_{xt}=x_t-\widehat{R}_N x_{t-1}-\widehat{\mu}$ and considering that the residual variance estimate satisfies $s_x^2=N^{-1}\sum_{t=1}^N \hat{u}_{xt}^2 \xrightarrow{p} \sigma_{xx}^2$, the associated t statistic is as follows:

$$t_{R_N}=\frac{\widehat{R}_N-R_N}{s_{R_N}}=\frac{R_N^N N^{\alpha}\left(\widehat{R}_N-R_N\right)}{\left\{s_x^2\left(\frac{1}{R_N^{2N}N^{2\alpha}}\sum_{t=1}^N x_{t-1}^2-\frac{1}{N}\left(\frac{1}{R_N^N N^{\alpha}}\sum_{t=1}^N x_{t-1}\right)^2\right)^{-1}\right\}^{1/2}}$$

$$\xrightarrow{d} \frac{2c\frac{\sigma_{xx}U_x}{\sigma_{xx}U_x+(2c)^{1/2}D}}{\sigma_{xx}\left\{\left(\frac{1}{2c}\right)^2\left(\sigma_{xx}U_x+(2c)^{1/2}D\right)^2\right\}^{-1/2}}=U_x\stackrel{d}{=}\mathcal{N}(0,1).$$

Similarly, given $R_N=1+\frac{c}{N^{\alpha}}$($\alpha$ is known), we have $s_c=N^{\alpha}s_{R_N}$, and the associated t test statistic is

$$t_c=\frac{\widehat{c}-c^0}{s_c}=\left(\widehat{R}_N-R_N\right)N^{\alpha}N^{-\alpha}s_{R_N}^{-1}\xrightarrow{d} U_x\stackrel{d}{=}\mathcal{N}(0,1).$$

From the mappings

$$\sigma_{xx}^2\mapsto 1, R_{\mathcal{N}}\mapsto a_\Delta=e^{-\kappa\Delta}, X^*\mapsto\frac{x_0}{\sigma_{xx}}, \mu\mapsto\frac{\mu\kappa}{\sigma_{xx}}\Delta^{1/2}, \mu^*\mapsto\frac{\mu\kappa}{\sigma_{xx}},$$
$$D_{\mathcal{N}}\mapsto D_\Delta=\tilde{x}_{0\Delta}\Delta^{1/2}-\frac{\Delta^{-1/2}\tilde{g}_\Delta}{\kappa}\to D^*=\frac{x_0}{\sigma_{xx}}-\frac{\mu}{\sigma_{xx}};$$

with $\Delta=1/N^{\alpha}$, it follows that

$$\frac{a_\Delta^N}{\sqrt{\Delta}}\left(\widehat{a}_\Delta-a_\Delta\right)\xrightarrow{d}(-2\kappa)\frac{\sigma_{xx}U_x}{U_x+(-2\kappa)^{1/2}D^*} \tag{6.18}$$

and

$$a_\Delta^N(\widehat{\kappa}-\kappa)\xrightarrow{d}2\kappa\frac{\sigma_{xx}U_x}{\sigma_{xx}U_x+(-2\kappa)^{1/2}D}.$$

Defining $s_x^2=N^{-1}\sum_{t=1}^N\widehat{u}_{x,t\Delta}^2$, which satisfies $\Delta^{-1}s_x^2\xrightarrow{p}\sigma_{xx}^2$, the t statistic for $\widehat{a}_\Delta$ is

$$\begin{aligned}
t_{a_\Delta} &= \frac{\widehat{a}_\Delta - a_\Delta}{s_{a_\Delta}} \\
&= \frac{a_\Delta^N/\Delta\left(\widehat{a}_\Delta - a_\Delta\right)}{\left\{s_x^2\left(a_\Delta^{-2N}\Delta^2\sum_{t=1}^N \widetilde{x}_{(t-1)\Delta}^2\sigma_{xx}^2\Delta - \frac{1}{N}\left(a_\Delta^{-N}\Delta\sum_{t=1}^N \widetilde{x}_{(t-1)\Delta}\sigma_{xx}\sqrt{\Delta}\right)^2\right)^{-1}\right\}^{1/2}} \\
&\overset{d}{\to} \frac{-2\kappa\frac{\sigma_{xx}Ux}{\sigma_{xx}U_x+(-2\kappa)^{1/2}D}}{\sigma_{xx}\left\{\left(\frac{1}{-2\kappa}\right)^2\left(\sigma_{xx}U_x+(-2\kappa)^{1/2}D\right)^2\right\}^{-1/2}} = U_x \overset{d}{=} \mathcal{N}(0,1),
\end{aligned}$$

and the t statistic for $\widehat{\kappa}$ is

$$\begin{aligned}
t_\kappa = \frac{\widehat{\kappa} - \kappa}{s_\kappa} &= \frac{a_\Delta^N\left(\widehat{\kappa} - \kappa\right)}{\left\{s_x^2\left(\frac{1}{a_\Delta^{2N}/\Delta^2}\sum_{t=1}^N x_{(t-1)\Delta}^2 - \frac{1}{N}\left(\frac{1}{a_\Delta^N/\Delta}\sum_{t=1}^N x_{(t-1)\Delta}\right)^2\right)^{-1}\right\}^{1/2}} \\
&\overset{d}{\to} \frac{-2\kappa\frac{\sigma_{xx}Ux}{\sigma_{xx}U_x+(-2\kappa)^{1/2}D}}{\sigma_{xx}\left\{\left(\frac{1}{-2\kappa}\right)^2\left(\sigma_{xx}U_x+(-2\kappa)^{1/2}D\right)^2\right\}^{-1/2}} = U_x \overset{d}{=} \mathcal{N}(0,1),
\end{aligned}$$

where $\Delta s_\kappa = s_{a_\Delta} + o_p(\Delta)$ given $a_\Delta = \exp(-k\Delta)$. Clearly, t_κ is a feasible statistic, in contrast to the discrete-time case, where the test statistic relies on the unknown rate parameter α. Notably, if α is unknown, then both the estimate $\widehat{c}$ and the standard error $s_c = N^\alpha s_{R_N}$ are unavailable, and inference using this limit theory for $\widehat{c}$ is infeasible.

There are also important differences between the discrete-time model (6.3) and the MP model (6.14). First, the autoregressive coefficient in (6.3) is determined by the sampling interval Δ. However, the autoregressive coefficient in (6.14) is formulated as a function of the overall sample size N. Second, the initial condition for x_t is assumed to be $o_p(N^{\alpha/2}) = o_p\left(\Delta^{-1/2}\right)$ in (6.14). However, in (6.3), it has a larger order of magnitude of $O_p\left(\Delta^{-1/2}\right)$. This result corresponds to a distant past initialization introduced in Phillips and Magdalinos (2009). These initializations do affect the limit theory due to its larger order property. Third, the presence of the constant intercept in (6.14) dominates the asymptotics. However, the intercept in (6.3),

$$\begin{aligned}
\widetilde{g}_\Delta = g_\Delta/\lambda_\Delta &= \mu\left(1 - e^{-\kappa\Delta}\right)/\lambda_\Delta \\
&= \frac{\mu\left(1 - e^{-\kappa\Delta}\right)}{\sigma_{xx}\sqrt{\left(1 - e^{-2\kappa\Delta}\right)/2\kappa}} \\
&= \frac{\mu\kappa\Delta}{\sigma_{xx}\Delta^{1/2}}\left\{1 + o(\Delta)\right\} = O\left(\sqrt{\Delta}\right),
\end{aligned}$$

is asymptotically negligible as $\Delta \to 0$; hence, it does not affect the double asymptotics for the model.

Lévy-Driven Models

Wang and Yu (2016) studied Lévy-driven models (6.9) with $\kappa < 0$. The LS estimator of $a_\Delta(\kappa)$ and g_Δ is presented in (6.4). Wang and Yu (2016) developed the simultaneous double asymptotics for the estimator $\widehat{a}_\Delta(\kappa)$ and $\widehat{g}_\Delta$. The result is

$$\frac{a_\Delta^N}{a_\Delta(\kappa)^2 - 1}\left(\widehat{a}_\Delta - a_\Delta\right) \xrightarrow{d} \frac{\xi}{\eta + D},$$

$$\sqrt{T\kappa}\left(\widehat{g}_\Delta - g_\Delta\right) \xrightarrow{d} \sigma\sqrt{\psi''(0)}Z,$$

where $D = \sqrt{2}\left(\kappa\mu + \sigma i\psi'(0) - \kappa x_0\right) / \left(\sigma\sqrt{-\kappa\psi''(0)}\right)$ and (ξ, η, Z) are independent standard normal random variables. They also considered two types of sequential double asymptotics: (i) $T \to \infty$ followed by $\Delta \to 0$ and (ii) $\Delta \to 0$ followed by $T \to \infty$. The two sequential asymptotics are the same as the simultaneous double asymptotics.

6.4 Multivariate Continuous-Time Models

This section is the multivariate counterpart of Section 6.3. In particular, we discuss both the cointegration and coexplosive systems.

6.4.1 Cointegration System and Error-Correction Models

One of the most researched relationships for empirical work is cointegration. The model measures the long-run relationship, namely, equilibrium, between underlying variables. When the underlying variables deviate from the long-run relationship in the short-term dynamics, we use an error correction model to measure the deviation. In discrete time, Granger (1981) and Engle and Granger (1987) studied the connection between cointegration systems and error correction models. Later, Phillips (1991) showed how to formulate a cointegration system and error correction models in continuous time and proposed an inferential procedure for such systems based on frequency-domain techniques.

Let $y(t)$ be an $m \times 1$ $I(1)$ process in continuous time and $u(t)$ be an $m \times 1$ stationary time series. $y(t)$ is further partitioned into two subvectors: an $m_1 \times 1$ vector $y_1(t)$ and an $m_2 \times 1$ vector $y_2(t)$. $u(t)$ is further partitioned into two subvectors: an $m_1 \times 1$ vector $u_1(t)$ and an $m_2 \times 1$ vector $u_2(t)$. We let $D = d/dt$ represent the mean square differential operator with respect to continuous time. The model that Phillips (1991) studied is as follows:

$$y_1(t) = By_2(t) + u_1(t), \tag{6.19}$$

$$Dy_2(t) = u_2(t), \tag{6.20}$$

where B is an $m_1 \times m_2$ matrix of unknown coefficients. Equation (6.19) expresses the long-run equilibrium relationship between variables $y_1(t)$ and $y_2(t)$. This long-run relationship is perturbed by a stationary deviation $u_1(t)$. The error-correction model (ECM hereafter) of the system (6.19)–(6.20) is of the form

$$Dy_1(t) = -[I, -B]\,y(t) + u_1(t) + Bu_2(t) + Du_1(t). \tag{6.21}$$

Combining equations (6.20) and (6.21), the error correction model (6.22) is obtained for the cointegration system (6.19)–(6.20):

$$Dy(t) = -EAy(t) + w(t), \tag{6.22}$$

where

$$E = \begin{bmatrix} I_{m_1 \times m_1} \\ 0_{m_1 \times m_2} \end{bmatrix}, A = \left[I_{m_1 \times m_1}, -B\right],$$
$$w(t) = \begin{bmatrix} u_1(t) + Bu_2(t) + Du_1(t) \\ u_2(t) \end{bmatrix}.$$

The exact discrete model of (6.22) is

$$y(n) = \exp(-EA)\,y(n-1) + \varepsilon(n), \tag{6.23}$$
$$\varepsilon(n) = \int_0^1 \exp(-sEA)\,w(n-s)\,ds.$$

Since $AE = I$ and $\exp(-EA) = I - \frac{e-1}{e}EA$, (6.23) can be rewritten in the following triangular system ECM format:

$$\Delta y(n) = -EAy(n-1) + x(n), \tag{6.24}$$
$$x(n) = \varepsilon(n) + (1/e)\,EAy(n-1),$$

where $x(n) = I(0)$.

The coefficient matrix B, which is a submatrix of A, is to be estimated. Phillips (1991) suggested the Hannan efficient and band spectral estimators for estimating the coefficient matrix B under the following assumptions:

1. The residual process $x(n)$ is stationary with spectral matrix $f_{xx}^{d}(\lambda) > 0$ that is continuous at the origin $\lambda = 0$.
2. We set $\Omega = 2\pi\, f_{xx}^{d}(\lambda)$, decompose the long-run covariance matrix as $\Omega = \Sigma + \Lambda + \Lambda'$, where $\Sigma = E\left(x(0)\,x(0)'\right)$ and $\Lambda = \sum_{k=1}^{\infty} E\left(x(0)\,x(k)'\right)$, and define $\Delta = \Sigma + \Lambda$. Ω is partitioned as $\begin{bmatrix} \Omega_{11} & \Omega_{21}' \\ \Omega_{21} & \Omega_{22} \end{bmatrix}$, and the dimensions of Ω_{11}, Ω_{21}, and Ω_{21} are $m_1 \times m_1$, $m_2 \times m_1$, and $m_2 \times m_2$, respectively. We define $\Omega_{11\cdot 2} = \Omega_{11} - \Omega_{21}'\Omega_{22}^{-1}\Omega_{21}$.

In addition, we define

$$y_*(n)' = \left(y_1(n)', \Delta y_2(n)'\right), \; w_*(\lambda)' = (2\pi T)^{-1/2} \sum_{n=1}^{T} y_*(n) e^{in\lambda},$$

$$w_2(\lambda) = (2\pi T)^{-1/2} \sum_{n=1}^{T} y_2(n) e^{in\lambda} \text{ for } \lambda \in [-\pi, \pi].$$

We let $\widehat{B}$ denote the LS estimator of B and let $\omega_j = \pi j/M$ for $j = -M+1, \ldots, M$, where M is an integer (this requires $M = o\left(T^{1/2}\right)$). The smoothed periodogram estimate is

$$\widehat{f}_{xx}\left(\omega_j\right) = \frac{M}{T} \sum_{\lambda_s \in \mathcal{B}_j} \left[w_*(\lambda_s) - E\widehat{B}w_2(\lambda_s)\right]\left[w_*(\lambda_s) - E\widehat{B}w_2(\lambda_s)\right]$$

with

$$\lambda_s = 2\pi s/T,$$
$$\mathcal{B}_j = \left(\omega_j - \pi/2M < \lambda \leqslant \omega_j + \pi/2M\right).$$

Hence, the Hannan efficient estimator of B is

$$vec\left(\widetilde{B}\right) = \left[\frac{1}{2M} \sum_{j=-M+1}^{M} E'\widehat{f}_{xx}\left(\omega_j\right)^{-1} E \otimes \widehat{f}_{22}\left(\omega_j\right)\right]^{-1} \times \left[\frac{1}{2M} \sum_{j=-M+1}^{M} \left(E'\widehat{f}_{xx}\left(\omega_j\right)^{-1} \otimes I_{m_2}\right) vec\left(\widehat{f}_{*2}\left(\omega_j\right)\right)\right], \tag{6.25}$$

where

$$\widehat{f}_{22}\left(\omega_j\right) = l^{-1} \sum_{\mathcal{B}_j} w_2(\lambda_2) w_2(\lambda_s)^*,$$

$$\widehat{f}_{*2}\left(\omega_j\right) = l^{-1} \sum_{\mathcal{B}_j} w_*(\lambda_2) w_2(\lambda_s)^*,$$

for $l = [T/M]$. The band spectral estimator $\widetilde{B}_0$ is similarly defined but based on the spectral estimates at the origin.

Phillips (1991) also considered the subsystem band spectral estimator of B, which is expressed as follows:

$$B_0^+ = \left[\widehat{f}_{12}(0) - \widehat{f}_{1\Delta}(0)\widehat{f}_{\Delta\Delta}(0)^{-1}\widehat{f}_{\Delta 2}(0)\right] \left[\widehat{f}_{22}(0) - \widehat{f}_{2\Delta}(0)\widehat{f}_{\Delta\Delta}(0)^{-1}\widehat{f}_{\Delta 2}(0)\right]^{-1},$$

where $\widehat{f}_{\Delta\Delta}(0)$ denotes the estimated spectral matrix of $\Delta y_2(n)$ and $\widehat{f}_{12}(0)$, $\widehat{f}_{1\Delta}(0)$ and $\widehat{f}_{2\Delta}(0)$ denote the estimated cross spectral matrices of $(y_1(n), y_2(n))$, $(y_1(n), \Delta y_2(n))$, and $(y_2(n), \Delta y_2(n))$, respectively.

Following the approach in Phillips and Perron (1988), the three estimators $\widetilde{B}$, $\widetilde{B}_0$, and B_0^+ are asymptotically equivalent, and the following limiting result is obtained:

$$T\left(\widetilde{B}-B\right), T\left(\widetilde{B}_0-B\right), T\left(B_0^+-B\right) \xrightarrow{d} \left(\int_0^1 dS_{1\cdot 2}S_2'\right)\left(\int_0^1 S_2S_2'\right)^{-1},$$

where

$$\begin{bmatrix} S_{1\cdot 2} \\ S_2 \end{bmatrix} = BM\left(\begin{bmatrix} \Omega_{11\cdot 2} & 0 \\ 0 & \Omega_{22} \end{bmatrix}\right).$$

The finite sample performance of the Hannan efficient estimator (6.25) was evaluated in Chambers (2001). Simulation studies in Chambers (2001) showed that the choices of bandwidth parameter and kernel function impact the finite sample performance. In particular, in terms of mean squared error, they found that the band spectral estimator $\widetilde{B}_0$ with the Parzen kernel performed the best in the studied cases.

6.4.2 Explosive Continuous-Time Systems

Chen et al. (2017) studied the following scalar continuous-time model in two variates, $y(t)$ and $x(t)$. Here, $x(t)$ follows an Ornstein–Uhlenbeck process, and the stochastic process $y(t)$ co-moves with $x(t)$ as

$$y(t) = \beta x(t) + u_0(t), \tag{6.26}$$

$$dx(t) = \kappa(\mu - x(t))\,dt + dB_x(t),\ x(0) = x_0 = O_p(1),\ \kappa < 0, \tag{6.27}$$

where $u_0(t)$ is Gaussian pure noise – a generalized stochastic process in continuous time (see Hannan (1970) and Phillips (1991)), and $B_x(t) = \sigma_{xx}W_x(t)$ with W_x being a standard Brownian motion that may be correlated with W_0. The parameter of central interest for inference is the coefficient β, which captures the co-movement between $y(t)$ and $x(t)$.

Let $u_0(t) = DB_0(t)$, where $B_0(t) = \sigma_{00}W_0(t)$ with W_0 being the standard Brownian motion, and $D = d/dt$ is the mean square differential operator. Consider the case where $u_0(t)$ is unrealizable as a covariance stationary stochastic process, and the corresponding discrete-time process of $y(t)$ is realizable. In particular, $y(t)$ takes the form of a pure noise process of independent identically distributed (*iid*) $\mathrm{N}\left(0, \sigma_{00}^2\right)$ errors. This formulation is extensively used in modeling microstructure noise effects in the measurement of efficient financial asset prices. This formulation corresponds to the discrete-time system (6.30). Phillips and Yu (2006) discussed such models with standard formulation of an efficient price subject to unobserved microstructure noise. Alternate specifications are to set $u_0(t) = 0$ a.s.. This corresponds to the limit form of a discrete-time cointegrated system, as discussed in Remark 12 of Chen et al. (2017).

The continuous-time system (6.26)–(6.27) is related to the market microstructure literature. For example, Zhang et al. (2005), Aït-Sahalia et al. (2005)(AMZ, hereafter), and Bandi and Russell (2006) assume that the observed transaction price is equal to the sum of the efficient price and an *iid* noise component. In particular, AMZ assumes that the observed logarithmic price of a security follows

$$\widetilde{X}(t\Delta) = X(t\Delta) + U(t\Delta), \tag{6.28}$$

where the logarithmic efficient price $X(t)$ is

$$dX(t) = \mu\,(X(t))\,dt + \sigma\,(X(t))\,dW(t), \tag{6.29}$$

and the *iid* error $\{U(t\Delta)\}$ has a zero mean and a finite variance σ_u^2. $U(t\Delta)$ is independent of $X(t\Delta)$. Formulating of systems (6.28)–(6.29) in continuous time have been discussed in the market microstructure noise literature, see Hansen and Lunde (2006) and Phillips and Yu (2006).

The Exact Discrete-Time Representation

Following Phillips (1972), the exact discrete time representation of (6.26)–(6.27) is

$$y_{t\Delta} = \beta x_{t\Delta} + u_{0,t\Delta}, \tag{6.30}$$

$$x_{t\Delta} = a_\Delta(\kappa)\, x_{(t-1)\Delta} + g_\Delta + u_{x,t\Delta},\ x_{0\Delta} = x_0 = O_p(1), \tag{6.31}$$

where

$$\begin{aligned} a_\Delta(\kappa) &= \exp(-\kappa\Delta), \\ g_\Delta &= \mu\left(1 - e^{-\kappa\Delta}\right), \\ u_{x,t\Delta} &= \sigma_{xx} \int_{(t-1)\Delta}^{t\Delta} e^{-\kappa(t\Delta - s)}\, dB_x(s) \overset{d}{=} \mathcal{N}\left(0, \frac{\sigma_{xx}^2}{2\kappa}\left(1 - e^{-2\kappa\Delta}\right)\right), \\ u_{0,t\Delta} &\overset{d}{=} \mathcal{N}\left(0, \sigma_{00}^2\right). \end{aligned}$$

The autoregressive parameter $a_\Delta(\kappa)$ is determined by the sampling frequency Δ, and hence both Δ and $a_\Delta(\kappa)$ are related to the sample size N. The standard error of $u_{x,t\Delta}$ is $\lambda_\Delta \sim \sigma_{xx}\sqrt{\Delta} \to 0$. But the variance of $u_{0,t\Delta}$ does not depend on the sampling interval Δ. $u_{0,t\Delta}$ in discrete time corresponds to the generalized stochastic process $u_0(t)$ in continuous time. Gaussianity follows from the Brownian motion driver processes in (6.26)–(6.27).

Standardizing the equation (6.31) by λ_Δ gives

$$y_{t\Delta} = \beta x_{t\Delta} + u_{0,t\Delta}, \tag{6.32}$$

$$\widetilde{x}_{t\Delta} = a_{\Delta}(\kappa)\widetilde{x}_{(t-1)\Delta} + \widetilde{g}_{\Delta} + \widetilde{u}_{x,t\Delta},\ \widetilde{u}_{x,t\Delta} \sim_{iid} \mathcal{N}(0,1), \tag{6.33}$$

where $\widetilde{x}_{t\Delta} = x_{t\Delta}/\lambda_{\Delta}$ ($\widetilde{x}_{0\Delta} = x_{0\Delta}/\lambda_{\Delta}$), $\widetilde{g}_{\Delta} = g_{\Delta}/\lambda_{\Delta}$ as $\Delta \to 0$. Clearly, we have $\frac{1}{N\Delta} = \frac{1}{T} \to 0$, and $a_{\Delta}(\kappa) = 1 - \kappa\Delta + O(\Delta^2) \to 1$ when $T \to \infty$ and $\Delta \to 0$.

Since $\kappa < 0$, $\widetilde{x}_{t\Delta}$ in (6.33) is a mildly explosive process, as defined in Phillips and Magdalinos (2007). Further as $\Delta \to 0$, it follows that $\widetilde{x}_{0\Delta} = x_{0\Delta}/\lambda_{\Delta} = O_p(\Delta^{-1/2})$. Thus, in the standardized discrete system (6.32)–(6.33), the initial condition is $\widetilde{x}_{0\Delta} \sim O_p(\Delta^{-1/2})$, while in the original system (6.26)–(6.27), it is $x_0 \sim O_p(1)$. In addition, the order of magnitude of the drift is $O\left(\sqrt{\Delta}\right)$ in model (6.33) but is $O_p(1)$ in (6.27).

The standardized discrete system (6.32)–(6.33) corresponds to the modified MP model

$$y_t = Ax_t + u_{0t}, \tag{6.34}$$

$$x_t = \mu + R_N x_{t-1} + u_{xt}, x_0 = x_{0\mathcal{N}} = O_p\left(\mathcal{N}^{\alpha/2}\right), \mu = O_p\left(\mathcal{N}^{-\alpha/2}\right). \tag{6.35}$$

where the error $u_t = [u_{0t}, u_{xt}]'$ is an *iid* sequence with mean zero and covariance $\begin{bmatrix} \sigma_{00}^2 & \sigma_{0x} \\ \sigma_{0x} & \sigma_{xx}^2 \end{bmatrix}$. This model extends systems in MP by allowing for a larger initial condition and a (local to zero) drift.

Double Asymptotics for the Coexplosive System

The LS estimator $\widehat{\beta}$ of the slope coefficient in the continuous-time model (6.26) is

$$\begin{aligned}\widehat{\beta} - \beta &= \left(\sum_{t=1}^{N} x_{t\Delta}^2\right)^{-1} \left(\sum_{t=1}^{N} x_{t\Delta} u_{0,t\Delta}\right) \\ &= \frac{1}{\lambda_{\Delta}} \left(\sum_{t=1}^{N} \widetilde{x}_{t\Delta}^2\right)^{-1} \left(\sum_{t=1}^{N} \widetilde{x}_{t\Delta} u_{0,t\Delta}\right).\end{aligned} \tag{6.36}$$

Chen et al. (2017) presents the associated limit theory, according to which

$$\frac{a_{\Delta}^N}{\sqrt{\Delta}}\left(\widehat{\beta} - \beta\right) \xrightarrow{d} (-2\kappa) \frac{\sigma_{00} U_0}{\sigma_{xx} U_x + (-2\kappa)^{1/2}(x_0 - \mu)}, \tag{6.37}$$

under the condition that $\Delta^{1-\alpha} T^{\alpha} \to 1$ as $T \to \infty$. The limit result can be extended to the case where $u_0(t)$ is weakly dependent.

Next, we let the residual variance estimate be $s_0^2 = N^{-1}\sum_{t=1}^N \widehat{u}_{0,t\Delta}^2$, which satisfies $s_0^2 \xrightarrow{p} \sigma_{00}^2$. The usual t statistic is

$$t_\beta = \frac{\widehat{\beta}-\beta}{s_\beta} = \frac{\left(\widehat{\beta}-\beta\right) a_\Delta^N/\sqrt{\Delta}}{\left\{s_0^2\left(a_\Delta^{-2N}\Delta\sum_{t=1}^N \widetilde{x}_{t\Delta}^2\sigma_{xx}^2\Delta\right)^{-1}\right\}^{1/2}}$$

$$\xrightarrow{d} \frac{(-2\kappa)\frac{\sigma_{00}U_0}{\sigma_{xx}U_x+(-2\kappa)^{1/2}(x_0-\mu)}}{\sigma_{00}\left\{\left(\frac{1}{-2\kappa}\right)^2\left(U_x+(-2\kappa)^{1/2}D^*\right)^2\sigma_{xx}^2\right\}^{-1/2}} = U_0 \overset{d}{=} \mathcal{N}(0,1),$$

where $D^* = X^* - \mu^*$ with $\widetilde{x}_0 = x_{0N}N^{-\alpha/2} \Rightarrow X^*$ and $\widetilde{\mu} = N^{\alpha/2}\mu \Rightarrow \mu^*$. This result leads to feasible inference concerning the slope coefficient β in continuous time.

When the errors are weakly dependent such that $u_{0,t\Delta}$ is a sequence of zero mean and weakly dependent errors, the limiting result of (6.37) holds. In particular, we assume $u_{0,t\Delta}$ satisfying Assumption LP as defined in MP, such that

$$N^{-1/2}\sum_{t=1}^N u_{0,t\Delta}^2 \Rightarrow \mathcal{N}\left(0,\omega_{00}^2\right).$$

where the long-run variance ω_{00}^2 can be decomposed as

$$\omega_{00}^2 = \sigma_{00}^2 + 2\lambda_{00},$$

with variance component σ_{00}^2 and one-sided long-run variance

$$\lambda_{00} := \sum_{i=1}^{\infty} E\left(u_{0,t\Delta}u_{0,(t-i)\Delta}\right).$$

Then we obtain

$$\frac{a_\Delta^N}{\sqrt{\Delta}}\left(\widehat{\beta}-\beta\right) \xrightarrow{d} (-2\kappa)\frac{\omega_{00}U_0}{\sigma_{xx}U_x + (-2\kappa)^{1/2}(x_0-\mu)}.$$

follows the limit results from Theorem 4.1 in MP and (6.37).

Alternatively, we set $u_0(t) \overset{a.s.}{=} 0$ in (6.26). This formulation corresponds to a discrete system (6.32) with $u_{0,t\Delta} \sim_{iid} \mathcal{N}\left(0,\sigma_{00}^2\Delta\right)$. Hence, the relationship between $x(t)$ and $y(t)$ is exact in the limit, which is analogous to the relationship of limit Brownian motion processes $\left(B_y, B_x\right)$ of cointegrated discrete series (y_t, x_t) where $x_t = x_{t-1} + u_{xt}$ and $y_t = \beta x_t + u_{0t}$ with (u_{0t}, u_{xt}) stationary and limiting linear relation $B_y(t) = \beta B_x(t)$. In this case, it follows that the limit distribution of $\widehat{\beta}$ is

$$\frac{a_{\Delta}^{N}}{\Delta}\left(\widehat{\beta}-\beta\right)\xrightarrow{d}(-2\kappa)\frac{\sigma_{00}U_0}{\sigma_{xx}U_x+(-2\kappa)^{1/2}(x_0-\mu)}, \tag{6.38}$$

when $\Delta\to 0$ and $T\to\infty$. In view of the scaling effect in the discrete time error, there is a faster rate of convergence in the estimation of β.

Double Asymptotics for the Cointegration System When $\kappa=0$, the model (6.26)–(6.27) corresponds to the cointegration system in continuous time. Its discretized system corresponds to the following cointegration model:

$$y_t = Ax_t + u_{0t}, \tag{6.39}$$

$$x_t = Rx_{t-1} + u_{xt}, x_0 = O_p\left(N^{1/2}\right), \tag{6.40}$$

where the error $u_t=[u_{0t},u_{xt}]'$ is an *iid* sequence with mean zero and covariance $\begin{bmatrix}\sigma_{00}^2 & \sigma_{0x}\\ \sigma_{0x} & \sigma_{xx}^2\end{bmatrix}$. We have assumed that $x_0 N^{-\frac{1}{2}}\Rightarrow X^*$.

We have the following asymptotics.

Theorem 6.4.1 *For the discrete time system (6.39)–(6.40) with $R=1$, when $N\to\infty$,*

(i)

$$N\left(\widehat{R}-1\right)\Rightarrow\frac{X^*\sigma_{xx}W_x(1)+\sigma_{xx}^2\int_0^1W_x(r)\,dW_x(r)}{X^{*2}+\sigma_{xx}^2\int_0^1W_x(r)^2\,dr+2X^*\sigma_{xx}\int_0^1W_x(r)\,dr}$$

(ii)

$$N\left(\widehat{A}-A\right)\Rightarrow\frac{X^*\sigma_{00}W_0(1)+\sigma_{xx}\sigma_{00}\int_0^1W_x(r)\,dW_0(r)}{X^{*2}+\sigma_{xx}^2\int_0^1W_x(r)^2\,dr+2X^*\sigma_{xx}\int_0^1W_x(r)\,dr}.$$

Corollary 6.4.2 provides the asymptotics for the LS estimates of β for the continuous-time system (6.26)–(6.27) with $\kappa=0$.

Corollary 6.4.2 *We let $\Delta=N^{-\alpha}$, where $\alpha\in(0,1)$. For the continuous-time system (6.26)–(6.27) with $\kappa=0$, we assume that there exists $\alpha\in(0,1)$ such that $h^{1-\alpha}T^{\alpha}\to 1$ as $T\to\infty$. Then, we have*

(i)

$$N\sqrt{\Delta}\left(\widehat{a}_{\Delta}-1\right)\Rightarrow\frac{\frac{x_0}{\sigma_{xx}}W_x(1)+\int_0^1W_x(r)\,dW_x(r)}{\sigma_{xx}\left(\left(\frac{x_0}{\sigma_{xx}}\right)^2+\int_0^1W_x(r)^2\,dr+2\frac{x_0}{\sigma_{xx}}\int_0^1W_x(r)\,dr\right)}.$$

(ii)

$$N\sqrt{\Delta}\left(\widehat{\beta}-\beta\right) \Rightarrow \frac{\frac{\sigma_{00}}{\sigma_{xx}}\left(\frac{x_0}{\sigma_{xx}}W_0\left(1\right)+\int_0^1 W_x\left(r\right)dW_0\left(r\right)\right)}{\left(\left(\frac{x_0}{\sigma_{xx}}\right)^2+\int_0^1 W_x\left(r\right)^2 dr+2\frac{x_0}{\sigma_{xx}}\int_0^1 W_x\left(r\right)dr\right)}.$$

Multivariate Coexplosive Systems in Continuous Time

In continuous-time systems with more than one mildly explosive regressor, two cases are examined in Chen et al. (2017): (i) when all the regressors have distinct explosive roots and (ii) when all the regressors share the same explosive root. The limit behavior is different for these two cases.

The multivariate continuous-time system is

$$y(t) = \beta x(t) + u_0(t), \tag{6.41}$$

$$dx\left(t\right) = \kappa\left(\mu - x\left(t\right)\right)dt + \Omega_{xx}^{1/2}dB_x(t), x\left(0\right) = x_0 = O_p\left(1\right), \kappa < 0, \tag{6.42}$$

where $u_0(t) \sim \mathcal{N}\left(0, \Omega_{00}\right)$ is Gaussian noise. The driver process $x(t)$ is a multivariate Ornstein–Uhlenbeck process with persistence matrix κ, where $\kappa = diag\left(\kappa_1, \kappa_2, \ldots \kappa_K\right)$ is a $K \times K$ diagonal matrix and $\kappa_i < 0$ for $i = 1, \ldots, K$. In addition, $B_x(t) = \Omega_{xx}^{1/2}W_x\left(t\right)$, where W_x is standard vector Brownian motion that may be correlated with W_0. Our interest is the co-movement coefficient matrix β, which is an $m \times K$ matrix.

The exact discrete time representation of (6.41)–(6.42) is (see Phillips (1972))

$$\begin{aligned} y_{t\Delta} &= \beta x_{t\Delta} + u_{0,t\Delta}, \\ x_{t\Delta} &= a_\Delta\left(\kappa\right)x_{(t-1)\Delta} + g_\Delta + u_{x,t\Delta},\ x_{0\Delta} = x_0 = O_p\left(1\right), \end{aligned} \tag{6.43}$$

where

$$\begin{aligned} a_\Delta\left(\kappa\right) &= \exp\left(-\kappa\Delta\right), \\ g_\Delta &= \kappa^{-1}\left(I_K - e^{-\kappa\Delta}\right)\kappa\mu, \\ u_{x,t\Delta} &= \int_{(t-1)\Delta}^{t\Delta} e^{-\kappa(t\Delta-s)}\Omega_{xx}dB_x\left(s\right) \overset{d}{=} \mathcal{N}\left(0, \Omega_{xx}\Delta\right), \\ u_{0,t\Delta} &\overset{d}{=} \mathcal{N}\left(0, \Omega_{00}\right), \end{aligned}$$

since

$$\mathbb{E}\left(u_{x,t\Delta}u_{x,t\Delta}'\right) = \int_{(t-1)\Delta}^{t\Delta} e^{-2\kappa(t\Delta-s)}\Omega_{xx}ds = \frac{1}{2}\kappa^{-1}\left(I_K - e^{-2\kappa\Delta}\right)\Omega_{xx}.$$

Restandardized it by $\sqrt{\Delta}$, the system becomes

$$y_{t\Delta} = \beta x_{t\Delta} + u_{0,t\Delta}, \tag{6.44}$$

$$\widetilde{x}_{t\Delta} = a_{\Delta}(\kappa)\widetilde{x}_{(t-1)\Delta} + \widetilde{g}_{\Delta} + \widetilde{u}_{x,t\Delta}, \widetilde{x}_{0\Delta} = \Delta^{-1/2}x_{0\Delta}, \widetilde{u}_{x,t\Delta} \sim_{iid} \mathcal{N}(0, \Omega_{xx}), \tag{6.45}$$

where $\widetilde{x}_{t\Delta} = \Delta^{-1/2}x_{t\Delta}$, $\widetilde{g}_{\Delta} = \Delta^{-1/2}g_{\Delta}$ and $\widetilde{u}_{x,t\Delta} = \Delta^{-1/2}u_{x,t\Delta} \stackrel{d}{=} \mathcal{N}(0, \Omega_{xx})$. The order of the initial value $\widetilde{x}_{0\Delta} = \Delta^{-1/2}x_{0\Delta}$ is $O_p(\Delta^{-1/2})$, and the order of the drift term $\widetilde{g}_{\Delta}$ is $O_p(\Delta^{1/2})$.

Distinct Explosive Roots We let $U_x \stackrel{d}{=} \mathcal{N}(0, I_K)$, $\widetilde{U}_x = \left(\int_0^\infty e^{p\kappa}\Omega_{xx}e^{p\kappa}dp\right)^{1/2} U_x$, and $D = x_0 - \mu$. For the continuous-time system (6.44)–(6.45), the double asymptotic theory for the LS estimator of the coefficient matrix β when κ has distinct diagonal elements ($\kappa_i \neq \kappa_j$ for $i \neq j$) is expressed as follows:

$$vec\left\{\frac{1}{\sqrt{\Delta}}\left(\widehat{\beta} - \beta\right)a_{\Delta}^{N}\right\} \stackrel{d}{\to} \left[\left(\int_0^\infty e^{p\kappa}\left(D + \widetilde{U}_x\right)\left(D + \widetilde{U}_x\right)' e^{p\kappa}dp\right)^{-1} \otimes \Omega_{00}\right]^{1/2} \times \mathcal{N}(0, I_{mK}), \tag{6.46}$$

assuming that there exists $\alpha \in (0, 1)$ such that $\Delta^{1-\alpha}T^{\alpha} \to 1$ as $T \to \infty$.

The LS estimator of κ is consistent since Δ is known. We let $S_{00} = N^{-1}\sum_{t=1}^{N}\widehat{u}_{0,t\Delta}\widehat{u}_{0,t\Delta}'$, which satisfies

$$S_{00} \stackrel{p}{\to} \Omega_{00},$$

and the corresponding estimate of the covariance matrix of $\widehat{\beta}_j$ is

$$S_{\beta_j\beta_j} = \left(\sum_{t=1}^{N} x_{j,t\Delta}^2\right)^{-1} S_{00}.$$

Then, the Wald statistic for testing the full rank restrictions $\mathbb{H}_0: Q_j\beta_j = r_j$ is

$$W_{\beta_j} = \left\{Q_j\left(\widehat{\beta}_j - \beta_j\right)\right\}'\left(Q_jS_{\beta_j\beta_j}Q_j'\right)^{-1}\left\{Q_j\left(\widehat{\beta}_j - \beta_j\right)\right\} \stackrel{d}{\to} \chi_g^2,$$

which leads to feasible inference about β_j in the continuous-time framework.

Let a_j be the jth column of $a_{\Delta}(\kappa)$. The Wald statistic for testing the full rank restrictions $\mathbb{H}_0: Q_ja_j = q_j$ for given (Q_j, q_j) has the following chi-squared limit:

$$W_{a_j} := \left\{Q_j\left(\widehat{a}_j - a_j\right)\right\}'\left(Q_jS_{a_ja_j}Q_j'\right)^{-1}\left\{Q_j\left(\widehat{a}_j - a_j\right)\right\} \stackrel{d}{\to} \chi_g^2,$$

where $S_{a_ja_j} = \left(\sum_{t=1}^{N} x_{j(t-1)\Delta}^2 - \frac{1}{N}\left(\sum_{t=1}^{N} x_{j(t-1)\Delta}\right)^2\right)^{-1} S_{xx}$, with $S_{xx} = N^{-1}\sum_{t=1}^{N}\widehat{u}_{x,t\Delta}\widehat{u}_{x,t\Delta}'$ satisfying $\Delta^{-1}S_{xx} \stackrel{p}{\to} \Omega_{xx}$, where $\widehat{u}_{x,t\Delta} = x_{t\Delta} - \widehat{a}_{\Delta}x_{(t-1)\Delta} - \hat{g}_{\Delta}$ are regression residuals. We let κ^j denote the jth column of κ. Given the matrix exponential relation, we have the covariance matrix of $\widehat{\kappa^j}$, which satisfies $\Delta^2 S_{\kappa^j \kappa^j} = S_{a_j a_j} + o(\Delta)$. Thus,

$$\left(\widehat{\kappa^j} - \kappa^j\right) e^{-k_j N} \xrightarrow{d} MN\left(0, \left(\int_0^\infty e^{2p\kappa_j} \left(D_j + \widetilde{U}_{jx}\right)^2 dp\right)^{-1} \Omega_{xx}\right)$$

$$\overset{d}{=} MN\left(0, \frac{-2\kappa_j \Omega_{xx}}{\left(D_j + \widetilde{U}_{jx}\right)^2}\right).$$

Then, the Wald statistic for testing the (full rank) restrictions $\mathbb{H}_0 \colon Q_j \kappa^j = q_j$ satisfies

$$W_{\kappa^j} := \{Q_j \widehat{\kappa^j} - q_j\}' \left(Q_j S_{\kappa_j \kappa_j} Q_j'\right)^{-1} \{Q_j \widehat{\kappa^j} - q_j\} \xrightarrow{d} \chi^2_g.$$

Common Explosive Roots Now we consider the case where the localizing explosive coefficients are identical, namely, $\kappa_i = \kappa$ for $i = 1, \ldots, K$. Let $H_\perp$ be the $K \times (K-1)$ random matrix that is an orthogonal complement to

$$X_c = \left(D + \tilde{U}_x\right) / \left\{\left(D + \tilde{U}_x\right)' \left(D + \tilde{U}_x\right)\right\}^{1/2}, \qquad (6.47)$$

satisfying $H_\perp H_\perp' = I_K - X_c X_c'$ and with

$$\widetilde{U}_x \equiv \left(\int_0^\infty e^{p\kappa} \Omega_{xx} e^{p\kappa} dp\right)^{1/2} U_x = \Omega_{xx}^{1/2} U_x / (2c)^{1/2},$$

$$U_x \overset{d}{=} \mathcal{N}(0, I_K), \text{ and } D = x_0 - \mu.$$

The LS estimator of the coefficient matrix β when κ has common diagonal elements ($\kappa_i = \kappa$ for $i = 1, \ldots, K$) is expressed as follows:

$$vec\left\{\sqrt{N}\left(\widehat{\beta} - \beta\right)\right\} \xrightarrow{d} \left[H_\perp \left\{H_\perp' \left(\mu\mu' + \frac{1}{-2\kappa}\Omega_{xx}\right) H_\perp\right\}^{-1/2}\right.$$

$$\left. \otimes \Omega_{00}^{1/2}\right] \times \mathcal{N}(0, I_{mK}), \qquad (6.48)$$

assuming that there exists $\alpha \in (0,1)$, such that $\Delta^{1-\alpha} T^\alpha \to 1$ as $T \to \infty$.

Then, the Wald statistic for testing $\mathbb{H}_0 \colon Q\left[vec\left(\beta\right)\right] = q$ for full row rank (Q, q) is

$$W_\beta := \{Q\widehat{\beta} - q\}' \left(QS_{\beta\beta}Q'\right)^{-1} \{Q\widehat{\beta} - q\} \xrightarrow{d} \chi^2_g,$$

which leads to feasible inference about the matrix coefficient β in the continuous-time framework. Inference about the full matrix β is possible in this case because of the common factorization convergence rate in (6.48). The Wald statistics for testing full rank restrictions on a_Δ and κ such as

$\mathbb{H}_0: Q[vec(a_\Delta)] = q$ and $\mathbb{H}_0: Q[vec(\kappa)] = q$ are defined in a similar way and have the following chi-squared limits:

$$W_{a_\Delta} := \{Q[vec(\widehat{a}_\Delta)] - q\}' \left(QS_{aa}Q'\right)^{-1} \{Q[vec(\widehat{a}_\Delta)] - q\} \xrightarrow{d} \chi^2_g,$$

and

$$W_\kappa := \{Q[vec(\widehat{\kappa})] - q\}' \left(QS_{\kappa\kappa}Q'\right)^{-1} \{Q[vec(\widehat{\kappa})] - q\} \xrightarrow{d} \chi^2_g,$$

which again lead to feasible inference on a_Δ and κ because of the common factorization convergence rate. When x_t has a common explosive root, LS estimation by $\widehat{a}_\Delta$ and $\widehat{\kappa}$ produces biased estimates due to endogeneity in the regressor, as shown in Phillips and Magdalinos (2013). The bias distorts the Wald test statistics, and the distortion will be demonstrated in the Monte Carlo simulation in the following section.

6.5 Monte Carlo Studies

This section examines the performance of the double asymptotic limit theory for both cointegration ($\kappa = 0$) and coexplosive ($\kappa = -2$) systems in simulations.

Data are generated from the model (6.30)–(6.31) with $\sigma_{00} = \sigma_{xx} = 1$ and $\mu = 0$, and three sampling intervals are considered, namely, $\Delta = 1/12,\ 1/52, 1/252$, which correspond to monthly, weekly, and daily frequencies, respectively. The initial value x_0 is set to 3.5, and time spans of $T = 4$ and $T = 10$ years are considered. The percentiles at levels $\{1\%, 2.5\%, 10\%, 90\%, 97.5\%, 99\%\}$ are reported in the limit distribution (6.37) and the finite sample distribution of the coefficient-based test (called the C test hereafter) for both the cointegration ($N\sqrt{\Delta}\,(\widehat{\beta} - \beta)$) and coexplosive systems ($\frac{a^N}{-2\kappa\sqrt{\Delta}}\,(\widehat{\beta} - \beta)$). In addition, the densities of the limit distributions and finite sample distributions of the C test statistic are compared. The number of replications is 10,000.

Table 6.1[1] reports the percentiles when $x_0 = 3.5$ by using the true values of κ and μ. Both the double asymptotic distribution and the finite sample distribution are sensitive to changes in the initial condition for the C test. In all cases, the double asymptotic limit distribution provides a good approximation to the finite sample distribution.

Figure 6.2 plots the densities of the C test statistic when $T = 4$. The first row corresponds to the C test for cointegration cases. The second row corresponds to the C test for coexplosive cases. These plots show that the limit distribution well approximates the finite sample distribution for C tests.

[1] The results in Table 6.1 for the coexplosive system are similar to those of Chen et al. (2017).

Table 6.1 *Comparison of the finite sample and double asymptotic distributions of $\hat{\beta}$ when the initial value is $x_0 = 3.5$.*

	Time Span	T = 4						T = 10					
$\kappa = -2$	C test	1%	2.50%	10%	90%	97.50%	99%	1%	2.50%	10%	90%	97.50%	99%
Daily (h=1/252)	Double Asymptotics	−1.081	−0.932	−0.663	0.668	1.365	1.803	−2.194	−1.796	−1.194	0.551	1.287	1.723
	Finite Sample	−1.091	−0.937	−0.662	0.661	1.354	1.780	−2.182	−1.722	−1.163	0.578	1.317	1.817
Weekly (h=1/52)	Double Asymptotics	−1.104	−0.968	−0.681	0.711	1.445	1.936	−2.088	−1.724	−1.188	0.612	1.374	1.862
	Finite Sample	−1.091	−0.937	−0.662	0.661	1.354	1.780	−2.182	−1.722	−1.163	0.578	1.317	1.817
Monthly (h=1/12)	Double Asymptotics	−1.116	−0.960	−0.682	0.670	1.332	1.814	−2.100	−1.746	−1.205	0.591	1.353	1.906
	Finite Sample	−1.091	−0.937	−0.662	0.661	1.354	1.780	−2.182	−1.722	−1.163	0.578	1.317	1.817
$\kappa = 0$	C test												
Daily (h=1/252)	Double Asymptotics	−0.354	−0.294	−0.187	0.187	0.295	0.356	−0.354	−0.294	−0.187	0.187	0.295	0.356
	Finite Sample	−0.358	−0.282	−0.183	0.182	0.290	0.356	−0.375	−0.302	−0.189	0.187	0.292	0.349
Weekly (h=1/52)	Double Asymptotics	−0.354	−0.294	−0.187	0.187	0.295	0.356	−0.354	−0.294	−0.187	0.187	0.295	0.356
	Finite Sample	−0.350	−0.287	−0.183	0.183	0.292	0.346	−0.339	−0.286	−0.186	0.183	0.286	0.351
Monthly (h=1/12)	Double Asymptotics	−0.354	−0.294	−0.187	0.187	0.295	0.356	−0.354	−0.294	−0.187	0.187	0.295	0.356
	Finite Sample	−0.332	−0.283	−0.177	0.171	0.267	0.319	−0.316	−0.260	−0.169	0.178	0.274	0.334

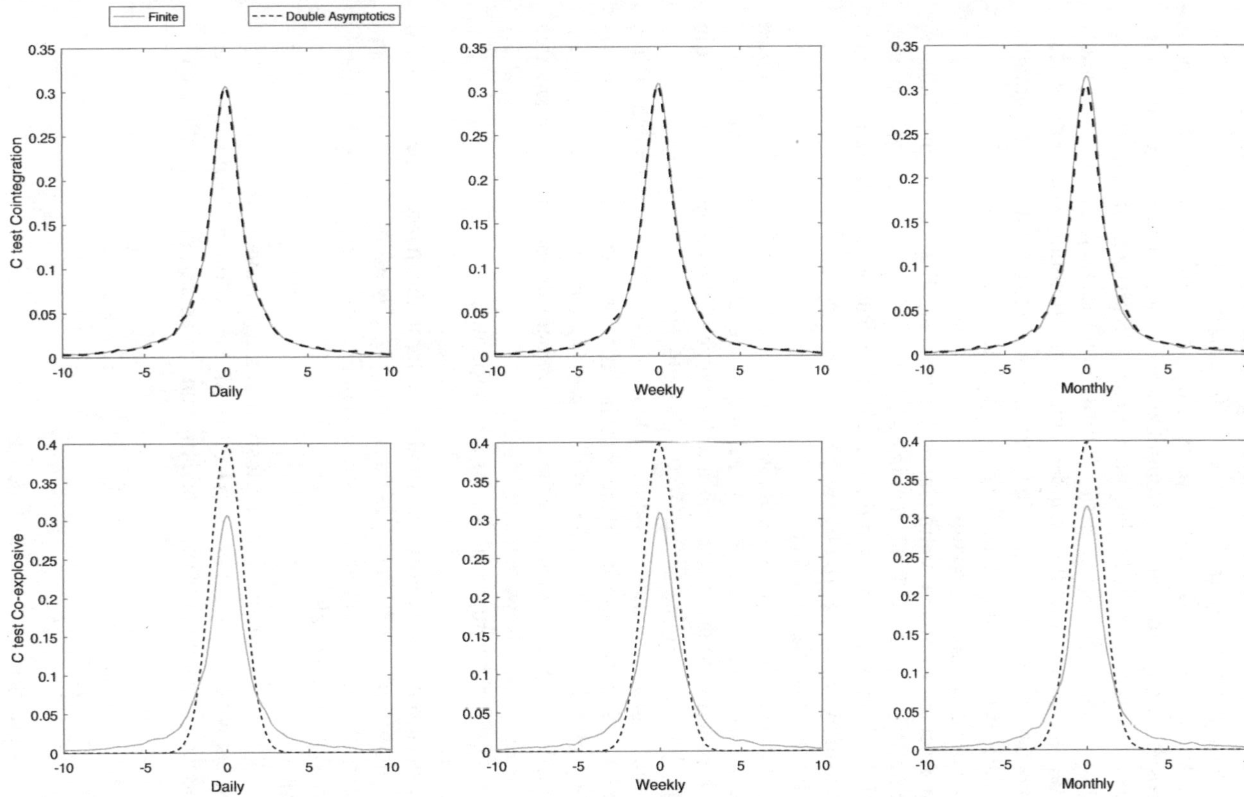

Figure 6.2 Density comparison of the C test for both finite sample and limit distributions when the initial value is $x_0 = 3.5$.

6.6 Empirical Illustrations

We conduct an empirical study of the relationship between the US nationwide real estate market and metropolitan real estate markets during an explosive period and a normal period by applying the limit theory for univariate co-moving systems (6.26)–(6.27) for $\kappa < 0$ (coexplosive period) and $\kappa = 0$ (cointegration period) to real estate data using the S&P/Case-Shiller home price composite 20-city index and metropolitan area indices. The S&P/Case-Shiller home price indices are the leading measures of US residential real estate prices and track changes in the value of residential real estate nationwide. Monthly data for the composite 20-city index and 20 metropolitan area indices were downloaded from the St. Louis Fed.[2] We apply the logarithmic transformation to all data. With monthly data, the sampling interval is set to $\Delta = 1/12$.

Coexplosive Sample Period:

The selected explosive sample period is from April 2000 to April 2006. In this case, $N = 73$, $\Delta = 1/12$, and hence, $T = 5.25$. The initial value in each equation of the system is set to the value of the composite 20 index in January 2000, namely, $x_0 = \log(162.01) = 5.0877$.

Cointegration Sample Period:

The selected cointegration sample period is from August 2008 to August 2014. In this case, $N = 73$, $\Delta = 1/12$, and hence, $T = 5.25$. The initial value in each equation of the system is set to the value of the composite 20 index in August 2008, namely, $x_0 = \log(104) = 4.6444$.

A multiequation continuous-time system (6.26)–(6.27) is estimated with x_t as the logarithmic composite 20 index (called the countrywide index in the present paper) and each y_t being one of the logarithmic metropolitan area indices. The coefficient β then measures the co-movement of each metropolitan area index with the countrywide index.

The steps for the empirical studies are as follows:

Step 1:

The occurrence of explosive/normal behavior in the market index ($x_{t\Delta}$) and in the individual area indices ($y_{t\Delta}$) is investigated by estimating κ and κ_y and obtaining the 99 percent and 90 percent confidence intervals based on the C test confidence intervals.

Step 2:

For the areas that exhibit explosive/normal behavior, the possible co-movement with the market index is studied further. Allowing for possible weak dependence in u_{0t}, the variance and long-run variances of u_{0t} are estimated by

$$\widehat{\sigma}_{00}^2 = \frac{1}{N}\sum_{\Delta=1}^{N} \widehat{u}_{0t}\widehat{u}_{0t}', \quad \widehat{\varpi}_{00}^2 = \widehat{\sigma}_{00}^2 + 2\widehat{\lambda}_{00}^2,$$

[2] http://research.stlouisfed.org/fred2/release?rid=199

$$\widehat{\lambda}_{00}^{2} = \frac{1}{N} \sum_{\Delta=1}^{M_n} \left(1 - \frac{\Delta}{M_n + 1}\right) \sum_{t=\Delta+1}^{N} \widehat{u}_{0t}\widehat{u}_{0t-\Delta}',$$

with truncation lag $M_n = N^{1/3}$.

Results from Step 1 are reported in Table 6.2.[3] First, in the explosive period, for the countrywide index, the LS estimate of κ is -0.1184. Its 90 percent confidence interval is $[-0.1202, -0.1168]$ based on the C test. The results confirm explosive behavior in $x_{t\Delta}$ over this period. For all individual area indices, explosive behavior is found based on both the 90 percent and the 99 percent confidence intervals by the C test. Second, in the normal period, for the countrywide index, the LS estimate of κ is -0.0088. Its 90 percent confidence interval is $[-0.0144, -0.0022]$ based on the C test. The results confirm unit root behavior in $x_{t\Delta}$ over this period. The unit root behavior is found for all individual area indices based on both the 90 percent and the 99 percent confidence intervals by the C test.

Now we study the possible co-movement with the market index. Based on the C test, Table 6.3 reports the LS estimates of β and the 99 percent and 90 percent confidence intervals. The null hypothesis $H_0: \beta = 0$ is comfortably rejected in all cases. The confidence intervals can also be used to assess whether $\beta = 1$ versus $\beta < 1$ or $\beta > 1$. If $\beta > 1$ (respectively, $\beta < 1$), we claim that the index of the associated metropolitan area moves faster (slower) than the national index, which provides a useful perspective on the relationships of different metropolitan area indices to the national index. The results show that cities such as Los Angeles, Miami, SanDiego, Washington DC, Boston, and New York have more "aggressive" real estate markets than the whole United States in both the explosive sample period and the normal sample period.

6.7 Conclusions

This chapter reviewed recent developments in nonstationary continuous-time models. For I(1) continuous-time models, the main focus has been on the I(1) OU process, the associated cointegrated system, and the error correction model. Several estimators have been introduced in the literature, and their finite sample performance and the applications have been reported. For explosive continuous-time systems, the focus has been on the explosive OU model and the coexplosive model. The limit distributions of the parameters of interest depend explicitly on the initial conditions. This dependence mimics a corresponding property in the finite sample distribution and, thus, improves the quality of the double asymptotic limit theory as a finite sample approximation. The localized coefficient c in a discrete time explosive model, whose counterpart in continuous time is $-\kappa$, is consistently estimable in continuous time

3 The results in Table 6.2 for the coexplosive system are from Chen et al. (2017).

Table 6.2 *Estimated persistence parameter values in y_{th} and x_{th} and confidence intervals for the persistence parameter of the US logarithmic real estate prices.*

	Coexplosive Periods					Cointegration Periods				
Place	κ or κ_y	C test 99% CI		C test 90% CI		κ or κ_y	C test 99% CI		C test 90% CI	
Market	−0.1184	−0.1212	−0.1159	−0.1202	−0.1168	−0.0088	−0.0172	0.0025	−0.0144	−0.0022
SF	−0.0024	−0.0044	−0.0017	−0.0034	−0.0019	−0.0011	−0.0150	0.0213	−0.0106	0.0112
LA	−0.0036	−0.0050	−0.0029	−0.0043	−0.0031	−0.0007	−0.0115	0.0147	−0.0080	0.0082
Las Vegas	−0.0031	−0.0119	−0.0020	−0.0056	−0.0023	0.0006	−0.0135	0.0235	−0.0090	0.0132
Miami	−0.0040	−0.0053	−0.0034	−0.0047	−0.0036	−0.0001	−0.0109	0.0155	−0.0074	0.0089
Phoenix	−0.0036	−0.0083	−0.0027	−0.0054	−0.0029	−0.0001	−0.0142	0.0228	−0.0097	0.0125
San Diego	−0.0027	−0.0055	−0.0019	−0.0040	−0.0021	−0.0008	−0.0114	0.0143	−0.0080	0.0079
Denver	−0.0009	−0.0012	−0.0008	−0.0011	−0.0008	−0.0006	−0.0064	0.0063	−0.0045	0.0036
DC	−0.0032	−0.0044	−0.0025	−0.0038	−0.0027	−0.0003	−0.0076	0.0090	−0.0052	0.0053
Chicago	−0.0017	−0.0019	−0.0015	−0.0018	−0.0016	0.0007	−0.0077	0.0118	−0.0049	0.0072
Boston	−0.0016	−0.0023	−0.0012	−0.0020	−0.0013	−0.0003	−0.0061	0.0067	−0.0041	0.0040
Charlotte	−0.0007	−0.0008	−0.0006	−0.0008	−0.0006	0.0001	−0.0078	0.0104	−0.0051	0.0062
Portland	−0.0022	−0.0031	−0.0017	−0.0027	−0.0019	0.0001	−0.0085	0.0115	−0.0057	0.0068
Dallas	−0.0006	−0.0007	−0.0005	−0.0007	−0.0006	−0.0006	−0.0065	0.0066	−0.0045	0.0038
Detroit	−0.0007	−0.0008	−0.0006	−0.0008	−0.0007	−0.0002	−0.0125	0.0186	−0.0086	0.0103
Atlanta	−0.0009	−0.0010	−0.0008	−0.0009	−0.0009	0.0003	−0.0110	0.0168	−0.0074	0.0097
Seattle	−0.0021	−0.0027	−0.0017	−0.0025	−0.0018	0.0002	−0.0084	0.0116	−0.0056	0.0069
Minneapolis	−0.0017	−0.0020	−0.0015	−0.0019	−0.0015	0.0001	−0.0114	0.0170	−0.0077	0.0096
Tampa	−0.0035	−0.0048	−0.0028	−0.0042	−0.0030	0.0004	−0.0094	0.0140	−0.0062	0.0083
Cleveland	−0.0006	−0.0007	−0.0006	−0.0007	−0.0006	0.0001	−0.0058	0.0073	−0.0038	0.0045
NY	−0.0026	−0.0029	−0.0023	−0.0028	−0.0024	0.0004	−0.0048	0.0065	−0.0030	0.0042

Table 6.3 *Estimated β coefficients and confidence intervals for β of the US logarithmic real estate prices.*

	Coexplosive Periods					Cointegration Periods				
City	β	C test 99% CI		C test 90% CI		β	C test 99% CI		C test 90% CI	
SF	1.0697	1.0684	1.0710	1.0688	1.0705	0.9863	0.9856	0.9871	0.9858	0.9869
LA	1.1731	1.1683	1.1781	1.1700	1.1763	1.2134	1.2129	1.2139	1.2131	1.2138
Las Vegas	1.0467	1.0420	1.0515	1.0436	1.0497	0.7354	0.7348	0.7360	0.7350	0.7358
Miami	1.1329	1.1284	1.1376	1.1300	1.1359	1.0371	1.0368	1.0374	1.0369	1.0373
Phoenix	0.9341	0.9304	0.9380	0.9317	0.9366	0.7993	0.7987	0.7999	0.7989	0.7996
San Diego	1.2087	1.2048	1.2127	1.2062	1.2112	1.1099	1.1094	1.1104	1.1096	1.1102
Denver	0.8288	0.8237	0.8339	0.8255	0.8320	0.8856	0.8854	0.8859	0.8855	0.8858
DC	1.1350	1.1318	1.1383	1.1329	1.1371	1.2530	1.2526	1.2534	1.2527	1.2533
Chicago	0.8843	0.8818	0.8868	0.8826	0.8859	0.8129	0.8124	0.8134	0.8126	0.8132
Boston	1.0058	1.0029	1.0088	1.0039	1.0076	1.0510	1.0508	1.0513	1.0509	1.0512
Charlotte	0.7220	0.7174	0.7266	0.7190	0.7249	0.7905	0.7902	0.7908	0.7903	0.7907
Portland	0.8285	0.8263	0.8307	0.8271	0.8298	0.9888	0.9885	0.9891	0.9886	0.9889
Dallas	0.7481	0.7430	0.7533	0.7448	0.7514	0.8135	0.8133	0.8136	0.8134	0.8136
Detroit	0.7676	0.7629	0.7724	0.7646	0.7706	0.5244	0.5241	0.5247	0.5242	0.5246
Atlanta	0.7732	0.7688	0.7777	0.7704	0.7760	0.7014	0.7010	0.7018	0.7011	0.7016
Seattle	0.8450	0.8427	0.8474	0.8436	0.8465	0.9917	0.9914	0.9920	0.9915	0.9919
Minneapolis	0.9437	0.9408	0.9468	0.9418	0.9456	0.8289	0.8287	0.8290	0.8288	0.8290
Tampa	1.0154	1.0131	1.0177	1.0139	1.0168	0.9442	0.9439	0.9446	0.9440	0.9444
Cleveland	0.7441	0.7396	0.7487	0.7412	0.7469	0.6867	0.6864	0.6871	0.6865	0.6870
NY	1.0483	1.0475	1.0492	1.0478	1.0489	1.1363	1.1357	1.1370	1.1359	1.1367

using the LS estimator, thereby facilitating the use of a coefficient-based test for mildly explosive behavior. The coexplosive model is useful in studying the co-movement behavior in different financial markets. These constitute promising directions for future empirical research. For future theoretical research, the development of nonstationary continuous-time models with mixed frequency data is a possible direction.

6.8 Appendix

This Online Supplement provides proofs of the main results in this chapter.

6.8.1 *Proof of Theorem 6.4.2*

Proof (i) We start by expressing x_t in (6.40) as

$$x_t = x_0 + \sum_{j=1}^{t} u_{xj}. \tag{6.49}$$

Then, the standardized numerator can be decomposed as

$$N^{-1} \sum_{t=1}^{N} x_t u_{xt} = N^{-1} \sum_{t=1}^{N} u_{xt} x_0 + N^{-1} \sum_{t=1}^{N} u_{xt} \left(\sum_{j=1}^{t} u_{xj} \right). \tag{6.50}$$

For the first term on the right-hand side of (6.50), since $x_0 N^{\frac{-1}{2}} \Rightarrow X^*$, we have

$$N^{-1} \sum_{t=1}^{N} u_{xt} x_0 \Rightarrow X^* \sigma_{xx} W_x(1), \tag{6.51}$$

from Hamilton (2020) (Proposition 17.1 (a)). For the second term on the right-hand side of (6.50),

$$N^{-1} \sum_{t=1}^{N} u_{xt} \left(\sum_{j=1}^{t} u_{xj} \right) \Rightarrow \sigma_{xx}^2 \int_0^1 W_x(r)\, dW_x(r), \tag{6.52}$$

from Hamilton (2020) (Proposition 17.1 (b)). Combining the results of (6.51) and (6.52) yields

$$N^{-1} \sum_{t=1}^{N} x_t u_{xt} \Rightarrow X^* \sigma_{xx} W_x(1) + \sigma_{xx}^2 \int_0^1 W_x(r)\, dW_x(r).$$

Next, we consider the standardized denominator

$$N^{-2}\sum_{t=1}^{N}x_t^2 = N^{-1}x_0^2+N^{-2}\sum_{t=1}^{N}\left(\sum_{j=1}^{t}u_{xj}\right)^2+2N^{-2}x_0\sum_{t=1}^{N}\left(\sum_{j=1}^{t}u_{xj}\right). \tag{6.53}$$

For the first term on the right-hand side of (6.53), since $\widetilde{x}_0 = x_{0N}N^{-1/2} \Rightarrow X^*$, we have

$$N^{-1}x_0^2 \Rightarrow X^{*2}. \tag{6.54}$$

For the second term on the right-hand side of (6.53), we then have

$$N^{-2}\sum_{t=1}^{N}\left(\sum_{j=1}^{t}u_{xj}\right)^2 \Rightarrow \sigma_{xx}^2\int_0^1 W_x(r)^2\,dr, \tag{6.55}$$

from Hamilton (2020) (Proposition 17.1 (e)). For the third term on the right-hand side of (6.53), we have

$$2N^{-2}x_0\sum_{t=1}^{N}\left(\sum_{j=1}^{t}u_{xj}\right) \Rightarrow 2X^*\sigma_{xx}\int_0^1 W_x(r)\,dr, \tag{6.56}$$

from Hamilton (2020) (Proposition 17.1 (d)). Combining the results of (6.54)–(6.56) yields

$$N^{-2}\sum_{t=1}^{N}x_t^2 \Rightarrow X^{*2}+\sigma_{xx}^2\int_0^1 W_x(r)^2\,dr+2X^*\sigma_{xx}\int_0^1 W_x(r)\,dr.$$

Hence, we obtain

$$N\left(\widehat{R}-1\right) \Rightarrow \frac{X^*\sigma_{xx}W_x(1)+\sigma_{xx}^2\int_0^1 W_x(r)\,dW_x(r)}{X^{*2}+\sigma_{xx}^2\int_0^1 W_x(r)^2\,dr+2X^*\sigma_{xx}\int_0^1 W_x(r)\,dr}$$

(ii) By the same argument, we obtain

$$N\left(\widehat{A}-A\right) \Rightarrow \frac{X^*\sigma_{00}W_0(1)+\sigma_{xx}\sigma_{00}\int_0^1 W_x(r)\,dW_0(r)}{X^{*2}+\sigma_{xx}^2\int_0^1 W_x(r)^2\,dr+2X^*\sigma_{xx}\int_0^1 W_x(r)\,dr}.$$

■

6.8.2 *Proof of Corollary 6.4.2*

The proof follows from Theorem 6.4.2 by considering the mappings

$$\sigma_{00}^2 \mapsto \sigma_{00}^2, \sigma_{xx}^2 \mapsto 1, X^* \mapsto \frac{\widetilde{x}^*}{\sigma_{xx}},$$

with $\Delta = N^{-\alpha}$.

For (i), it follows that

$$N^{-1}\sum_{t=1}^{N}\tilde{x}_{t\Delta}u_{x,t\Delta} \Rightarrow \frac{\widetilde{x}^{*}}{\sigma_{xx}}W_x(1)+\int_0^1 W_x(r)\,dW_x(r),$$

$$N^{-2}\sum_{t=1}^{N}\tilde{x}_{t\Delta}^{2} \Rightarrow \left(\frac{\widetilde{x}^{*}}{\sigma_{xx}}\right)^2+\int_0^1 W_x(r)^2\,dr+2\frac{\widetilde{x}^{*}}{\sigma_{xx}}\int_0^1 W_x(r)\,dr,$$

and hence

$$\begin{aligned} &N\sqrt{\Delta}\left(\widehat{a}_{\Delta}(\kappa)-1\right)\\ &=\sqrt{\Delta}\frac{N^{-1}\sum_{t=1}^{N}x_{t\Delta}u_{x,t\Delta}}{N^{-2}\sum_{t=1}^{N}x_{t\Delta}^{2}}=\frac{N^{-1}\sum_{t=1}^{N}\tilde{x}_{t\Delta}u_{x,t\Delta}}{N^{-2}\sum_{t=1}^{N}\tilde{x}_{t\Delta}^{2}}\frac{\sqrt{\Delta}}{\lambda_{\Delta}}\\ &\Rightarrow\frac{\frac{\widetilde{x}^{*}}{\sigma_{xx}}W_x(1)+\int_0^1 W_x(r)\,dW_x(r)}{\sigma_{xx}\left(\left(\frac{\widetilde{x}^{*}}{\sigma_{xx}}\right)^2+\int_0^1 W_x(r)^2\,dr+2\frac{\widetilde{x}^{*}}{\sigma_{xx}}\int_0^1 W_x(r)\,dr\right)}. \end{aligned}$$

For (ii), it follows that

$$N^{-1}\sum_{t=1}^{N}\tilde{x}_{t\Delta}u_{0,t\Delta} \Rightarrow \frac{\widetilde{x}^{*}}{\sigma_{xx}}\sigma_{00}W_0(1)+\sigma_{00}\int_0^1 W_x(r)\,dW_0(r),$$

and hence

$$\begin{aligned} &N\sqrt{\Delta}\left(\widehat{\beta}-\beta\right)\\ &=\sqrt{\Delta}\frac{N^{-1}\sum_{t=1}^{N}x_{t\Delta}u_{0,t\Delta}}{N^{-2}\sum_{t=1}^{N}x_{t\Delta}^{2}}=\frac{N^{-1}\sum_{t=1}^{N}\tilde{x}_{t\Delta}u_{0,t\Delta}}{N^{-2}\sum_{t=1}^{N}\tilde{x}_{t\Delta}^{2}}\frac{\sqrt{\Delta}}{\lambda_{\Delta}}\\ &\Rightarrow\frac{\frac{\sigma_{00}}{\sigma_{xx}}\left(\frac{\widetilde{x}^{*}}{\sigma_{xx}}W_0(1)+\int_0^1 W_x(r)\,dW_0(r)\right)}{\left(\left(\frac{\widetilde{x}^{*}}{\sigma_{xx}}\right)^2+\int_0^1 W_x(r)^2\,dr+2\frac{\widetilde{x}^{*}}{\sigma_{xx}}\int_0^1 W_x(r)\,dr\right)}. \end{aligned}$$

Bibliography

Aït-Sahalia, Y., P. A. Mykland, and L. Zhang (2005). How often to sample a continuous-time process in the presence of market microstructure noise. *The Review of Financial Studies 18*(2), 351–416.

Alessi, L. and M. Kerssenfischer (2019). The response of asset prices to monetary policy shocks: Stronger than thought. *Journal of Applied Econometrics 34*(5), 661–672.

Ambrose, B. W., P. Eichholtz, and T. Lindenthal (2013). House prices and fundamentals: 355 years of evidence. *Journal of Money, Credit and Banking 45*(2–3), 477–491.

Bae, Y. and R. M. De Jong (2007). Money demand function estimation by nonlinear cointegration. *Journal of Applied Econometrics 22*(4), 767–793.

Bandi, F. M. and J. R. Russell (2006). Separating microstructure noise from volatility. *Journal of Financial Economics 79*(3), 655–692.

Barndorff-Nielsen, O. E. and N. Shephard (2001). Non-Gaussian Ornstein–Uhlenbeck-based models and some of their uses in financial economics. *Journal of the Royal Statistical Society: Series B (Statistical Methodology) 63*(2), 167–241.

Barndorff-Nielsen, O. E. and N. Shephard (2003). Integrated OU processes and non-Gaussian OU-based stochastic volatility models. *Scandinavian Journal of Statistics 30*(2), 277–295.

Boswijk, H. P. (2001). Block local to unity and continuous record asymptotics. Tinbergen Institute Discussion Paper, No. 01-078/4.

Boswijk, H. P. and Y. Zu (2022). Adaptive testing for cointegration with nonstationary volatility. *Journal of Business & Economic Statistics 40*(2), 744–755.

Burgess, N. (2014). An overview of the vasicek short rate model. Available at SSRN 2479671.

Cai, Z., Y. Wang, and Y. Wang (2015). Testing instability in a predictive regression model with nonstationary regressors. *Econometric Theory 31*(5), 953–980.

Case, K. E. and R. J. Shiller (2003). Is there a bubble in the housing market? *Brookings Papers on Economic Activity 2003*(2), 299–362.

Chambers, M. J. (2001). Temporal aggregation and the finite sample performance of spectral regression estimators in cointegrated systems: A simulation study. *Econometric Theory 17*(3), 591–607.

Chen, Y., P. C. B. Phillips, and S. Shi (2023). Common bubble detection in large dimensional financial systems. *Journal of Financial Econometrics 21*(4), 989–1063.

Chen, Y., P. C. B. Phillips, and J. Yu (2017). Inference in continuous systems with mildly explosive regressors. *Journal of Econometrics 201*(2), 400–416.

Engle, R. F. and C. W. Granger (1987). Co-integration and error correction: Representation, estimation, and testing. *Econometrica: Journal of the Econometric Society 55*(2), 251–276.

Ghysels, E. and J. I. Miller (2015). Testing for cointegration with temporally aggregated and mixed-frequency time series. *Journal of Time Series Analysis 36*(6), 797–816.

Granger, C. W. (1981). Some properties of time series data and their use in econometric model specification. *Journal of Econometrics 16*(1), 121–130.

Greenaway-McGrevy, R. and P. C. B. Phillips (2016). Hot property in New Zealand: Empirical evidence of housing bubbles in the metropolitan centres. *New Zealand Economic Papers 50*(1), 88–113.

Hamilton, J. D. (2020). *Time series analysis*. Princeton, NJ: Princeton University Press.

Hannan, E. J. (1970). *Multiple time series*. New York: Wiley.

Hansen, B. E. (1999). The grid bootstrap and the autoregressive model. *Review of Economics and Statistics 81*(4), 594–607.

Hansen, P. R. and A. Lunde (2006). Realized variance and market microstructure noise. *Journal of Business and Economic Statistics 24*(2), 127–161.

Henry, O. T. and K. Shields (2004). Is there a unit root in inflation? *Journal of Macroeconomics 26*(3), 481–500.

Hu, Y. and L. Oxley (2018). Bubbles in US regional house prices: Evidence from house price–income ratios at the state level. *Applied Economics 50*(29), 3196–3229.

Lo, A. W. and A. C. MacKinlay (1988). Stock market prices do not follow random walks: Evidence from a simple specification test. *The Review of Financial Studies 1*(1), 41–66.

Lui, Y. L., W. Xiao, and J. Yu (2022). The grid bootstrap for continuous time models. *Journal of Business & Economic Statistics 40*(3), 1390–1402, 1–13.

McCarthy, J. et al. (2004). Are home prices the next bubble? *Economic Policy Review 10*(3), 1–17.

Pan, W.-F. (2019). Detecting bubbles in China's regional housing markets. *Empirical Economics 56*(4), 1413–1432.

Perron, P. (1991a). A continuous time approximation to the unstable first-order autoregressive process: The case without an intercept. *Econometrica: Journal of the Econometric Society 59*(1), 211–236.

Perron, P. (1991b). A continuous time approximation to the unstable first-order autoregressive process: The case without an intercept. *Econometrica: Journal of the Econometric Society 59*(1), 211–236.

Phillips, P. C. B. (1972). The structural estimation of a stochastic differential equation system. *Econometrica: Journal of the Econometric Society 40*(6), 1021–1041.

Phillips, P. C. B. (1987a). Time series regression with a unit root. *Econometrica: Journal of the Econometric Society 55*(2), 277–301.

Phillips, P. C. B. (1987b). Towards a unified asymptotic theory for autoregression. *Biometrika 74*(3), 535–547.

Phillips, P. C. B. (1991). Error correction and long-run equilibrium in continuous time. *Econometrica 59*(4), 967–980.

Phillips, P. C. B. (2015). Halbert White Jr. Memorial JFEC Lecture: Pitfalls and possibilities in predictive regression. *Journal of Financial Econometrics 13*(3), 521–555.

Phillips, P. C. B. and T. Magdalinos (2007). Limit theory for moderate deviations from a unit root. *Journal of Econometrics 136*(1), 115–130.

Phillips, P. C. B. and T. Magdalinos (2009). Unit root and cointegrating limit theory when initialization is in the infinite past. *Econometric Theory 25*(06), 1682–1715.

Phillips, P. C. B. and T. Magdalinos (2013). Inconsistent VAR regression with common explosive roots. *Econometric Theory 29*(4), 808–837.

Phillips, P. C. B., H. R. Moon, and Z. Xiao (2001). How to estimate autoregressive roots near unity. *Econometric Theory 17*(1), 29–69.

Phillips, P. C. B. and P. Perron (1988). Testing for a unit root in time series regression. *Biometrika 75*(2), 335–346.

Phillips, P. C. B. and J. Yu (2006). Comments on "Realized Variance and Market Microstructure Noise" by P. R. Hansen and A. Lunde. *Journal of Business and Economic Statistics 24*, 202–208.

Roberts, G. O., O. Papaspiliopoulos, and P. Dellaportas (2004). Bayesian inference for non-Gaussian Ornstein–Uhlenbeck stochastic volatility processes. *Journal of the Royal Statistical Society: Series B (Statistical Methodology) 66*(2), 369–393.

Shi, S., A. Valadkhani, R. Smyth, and F. Vahid (2016). Dating the timeline of house price bubbles in Australian capital cities. *Economic Record 92*(299), 590–605.

Stambaugh, R. F. (1999). Predictive regressions. *Journal of Financial Economics 54*(3), 375–421.

Tang, C. Y. and S. X. Chen (2009). Parameter estimation and bias correction for diffusion processes. *Journal of Econometrics 149*(1), 65–81.

Vasicek, O. (1977). An equilibrium characterization of the term structure. *Journal of Financial Economics 5*(2), 177–188.

Wang, X. and J. Yu (2016). Double asymptotics for explosive continuous time models. *Journal of Econometrics 193*(1), 35–53.

Welch, I. and A. Goyal (2008). A comprehensive look at the empirical performance of equity premium prediction. *The Review of Financial Studies 21*(4), 1455–1508.

Yu, J. (2012). Bias in the estimation of the mean reversion parameter in continuous time models. *Journal of Econometrics 169*(1), 114–122.

Yu, J. (2014). Econometric analysis of continuous time models: A survey of Peter Phillips's work and some new results. *Econometric Theory 30*(4), 737–774.

Zhang, L., P. A. Mykland, and Y. Aït-Sahalia (2005). A tale of two time scales: Determining integrated volatility with noisy high-frequency data. *Journal of the American Statistical Association 100*(472), 1394–1411.

Zhou, Q. and J. Yu (2015). Asymptotic theory for linear diffusions under alternative sampling schemes. *Economics Letters 128*, 1–5.

Zivot, E. and D. W. K. Andrews (2002). Further evidence on the great crash, the oil-price shock, and the unit-root hypothesis. *Journal of Business & Economic Statistics 20*(1), 25–44.

7 Fractional Brownian Motions in Financial Econometrics

WEILIN XIAO *Zhejiang University*
Xili Zhang *Zhejiang University*

7.1 Introduction

Continuous-time processes driven by the standard Brownian motion are widely used to describe the price dynamics of financial assets or portfolios since the celebrated works of Black and Scholes (1973) and Merton (1973). Even though the option pricing model from Black and Scholes (1973) remains one of the most successful methods for pricing European options, the assumptions of the independence of asset returns (e.g., Greene and Fielitz (1977); Willinger et al. (1999)) and the constant volatility of stock returns (e.g., Comte and Renault (1998); Corlay et al. (2014)) are too strong to be true.

To explain the dependence properties of asset returns, Mandelbrot and Van Ness (1968) introduced fractional Brownian motion (fBm) that models the dynamics of stock prices. If the standard Brownian motion is replaced with the fBm in the Black–Scholes model, the resulting model is a geometric fractional Brownian motion (gfBm) that was shown to be more in line with the behavior of stock markets in Cont (2001). Unfortunately, fBm is considered inadequate for modeling stock returns because it is not a semimartingale when the Hurst parameter $H \neq \frac{1}{2}$. Consequently, the arbitrage opportunity in the fBm-driven Black–Scholes model and approaches to remove arbitrage in the context of fBm have been extensively investigated in the literature, including Rogers (1997); Sottinen (2001); Cheridito et al. (2003); Elliott and Van Der Hoek (2003); Björk and Hult (2005); Rostek (2009). Additionally, when using the fBm in financial modeling, one must define an Itô-type formula and a risk-neutral measure, which is also true for Brownian motion.

Dedicated to fBm, Duncan et al. (2000) is the first study that proposed the Wick product approach to defining fractional stochastic integrals with respect to fBm, called the Wick–Itô integral. Hu and Øksendal (2003), Elliott and Van Der Hoek (2003), and Hu et al. (2003) extended the idea of the Wick product and developed a fractional white noise calculus that can be applied to option pricing and portfolio optimization. However, at the same time, severe critiques arose concerning the economic meaning of the Wick products (e.g., Björk and Hult (2005)).

To explain the stylized facts in the implied volatility surface (e.g., volatility smile and skew), many stochastic volatility models have been developed in the literature, including Hull and White (1987), Scott (1987), Stein and Stein (1991), Heston (1993), Bates (1996), Duffie et al. (2000), and Schöbel and Zhu (1999). More details regarding these stochastic volatility models can be found in Fouque et al. (2000). Both academics and practitioners have recognized the importance of the stochastic volatility models mentioned above for pricing options; see Bakshi et al. (1997) for an example. Nevertheless, none of these stochastic volatility models are problem-free. One of the key disadvantages among all the aforementioned stochastic volatility models is that the volatility process is driven by the standard Brownian motion. Therefore, the autocorrelation function of the volatility exponentially decays. However, many empirical studies argue that the decay in the autocorrelation function is better modeled by a power function. Unsurprisingly, in the discrete-time volatility literature, Baillie (1996), Baillie et al. (1996), Andersen et al. (2003), and Shi and Yu (2023) proposed the autoregressive fractionally integrated moving average model for volatility. In the continuous-time volatility literature, Comte and Renault (1998), Aït-Sahalia and Mancini (2008), Comte et al. (2012), Bayer et al. (2016), Gatheral et al. (2018), Bennedsen et al. (2022), and Liu et al. (2024) proposed models based on the fBm for volatility.

As a nonstationary process, the fBm is not suitable for modeling stationary time series. Consequently, the fractional Ornstein–Uhlenbeck process (fOUp) and the fractional Vasicek model (fVm) were developed to model stationary financial time series such as volatility and interest rates (see, for example, Comte and Renault (1998), Fink et al. (2013), Aït-Sahalia and Mancini (2008), Comte et al. (2012), Bayer et al. (2016), Gatheral et al. (2018), Bennedsen et al. (2022), and Bolko et al. (2023)). Recently, an econometric analysis of the fOUp and fVm has received considerable attentions, including parameter estimation and asymptotic theory.

This chapter first introduces the basic properties of fractional Brownian motion and then reviews the fOUp, fVm, and stochastic volatility models driven by the fBm. We also review the parameter estimation methods proposed in the literature and the associated asymptotic theory. The estimation methods are based on either continuous-time observations or discrete-time observations.

The rest of this chapter is organized as follows: Section 7.2 reviews some basic properties of the fBm, fOUp, and fVm and discusses their application when modeling financial time series. Section 7.3 summarizes some well-known stochastic volatility models driven by Brownian motion and by the fBm.

Section 7.4 reviews alternative estimators of the drift parameters in the fVm based on continuous-time observations. Section 7.5 reviews the generalized method of moments (GMM) for the fVm based on discrete-time observations. Section 7.6 provides conclusions.

7.2 Fractional Brownian Motion and Related Stochastic Processes

7.2.1 Fractional Brownian Motion

It is well known that standard Brownian motion has independent increments that are normally distributed. As a generalization of standard Brownian motion, the fBm is self-similar and its increments are normally distributed and stationarity.[1] In this subsection, we present the definition of the fBm and introduce some of its basic properties by comparing it with standard Brownian motion.

The fBm was first introduced by Kolmogorov (1940) in 1940, and then Mandelbrot and Van Ness (1968) provided its stochastic integral (moving average) representation and obtained many of its properties. The definition of the fBm is as follows:

Definition 7.2.1 *Consider the probability space* $(\Omega, \mathcal{F}, \mathbb{P})$ *and let* B^H *be an fBm in this space. Then, a standard fBm is a centered and continuous Gaussian process with the Hurst parameter* $H \in (0, 1)$*, which has stationary increments and the following covariance function:*

$$\mathbb{E}\left(B_t^H B_s^H\right) = R_H(s,t) \equiv \frac{1}{2}\left(|t|^{2H} + |s|^{2H} - |t-s|^{2H}\right), \tag{7.1}$$

with $t,\ s > 0$.

From Samorodnitsky and Taqqu (1994), we can see that the variance-covariance matrix implied by Equation (7.1) is nonnegative definite, and hence, Equation (7.1) is a proper covariance function. In Equation (7.1), the coefficient H is known as the Hurst parameter and is named for British climatologist H. E. Hurst, who proposed the classical test to detect the long-memory phenomenon of reservoir control near the Nile River Dam (see Hurst (1951)). We can obtain the standard Brownian motion by setting $H = \frac{1}{2}$, and in this case, the covariance function becomes $\min\{t, s\}$, which is the covariance function of the standard Brownian motion. Some important properties of the fBm are provided by the following proposition.

Proposition 7.2.1 *The fBm has the following properties:*

(i) $B_t^H \sim \mathcal{N}\left(0, t^{2H}\right)$.

[1] A process $X = (X_t)_{t\geq 0}$ has stationary increments if we have $X_{t+h} - X_t \overset{d}{=} X_h - X_0$ for every $h, t \geq 0$.

(ii) $\mathbb{E}\left(B_t^H - B_s^H\right)^2 = |t-s|^{2H}$ *for* $t, s > 0$;

(iii) *In particular, the fBm has* δ*-Hölder continuous paths for any* $\delta < H$.[2]

(iv) *The fBm is not a Markov process except that* $H = \frac{1}{2}$.[3]

(v) *The fBm exhibits long-range dependence if* $H > \frac{1}{2}$ *and is a short-memory process if* $H < \frac{1}{2}$.[4]

(vi) *Let* $\pi_n = \left\{t_k = \frac{k}{2^n} : k = 0, \ldots, 2^n\right\}$ *be a partition of* $[0, 1]$ *and* $n \in \mathbb{N}$. *Then, we have*

$$\lim_{n\to\infty} \sum_{k=1}^{n} \left|B_{t_k}^H - B_{t_{k-1}}^H\right|^p = \begin{cases} \infty, & \text{if} \quad pH < 1, \\ \mathbb{E}\left|B_1^H\right|^p, & \text{if} \quad pH = 1, \\ 0, & \text{if} \quad pH > 1, \end{cases} \tag{7.2}$$

in probability.

(vii) *The fBm is not a semimartingale expect that* $H = 1/2$.

(viii) *The fBm is nowhere differentiable. That is, for every* $s \in [0, \infty]$, *we have*

$$\mathbb{P}\left(\limsup_{t\to s}\left|\frac{B_t^H - B_s^H}{t-s}\right| = \infty\right) = 1.$$

Using the properties provided in Proposition 7.2.1, the fBm can be represented as an integral of a deterministic kernel with respect to standard Brownian motion. In the literature, there exist several representations of the fBm as a Wiener integral, which can be described as follows:

(i) Mandelbrot and Van Ness (1968):

$$\begin{aligned} B_t^H &= \int_{-\infty}^{\infty} \left\{(t-u)_+^{H-\frac{1}{2}} - (-u)_+^{H-\frac{1}{2}}\right\} dB_u \\ &= \frac{1}{c_H}\left\{\int_{-\infty}^{0} \left[(t-u)^{H-\frac{1}{2}} - (-u)^{H-\frac{1}{2}}\right] dB_u + \int_0^t (t-u)^{H-\frac{1}{2}} dB_u\right\}, \end{aligned}$$

where $(x)_+ = \max(x, 0)$, $c_H = \left[\frac{1}{2H} + \int_0^\infty \left((1+s)^{H-1/2} - s^{H-\frac{1}{2}}\right)^2 ds\right]^{\frac{1}{2}}$ and B_u is a standard Brownian motion.

[2] For a process X: $[0, +\infty) \times \Omega \to \mathbb{R}$ if for all $T > 0$, there exist $\alpha, \beta, C > 0$ such that $\mathbb{E}\left[|X_t - X_s|^\alpha\right] \le C|t-s|^{1+\beta}, \forall 0 \le t, s \le T$, then there exists a version of X, which is Hölder continuous of order $\gamma \in \left[0, \frac{\beta}{\alpha}\right)$ almost surely.

[3] A Gaussian process X with covariance function $R(s,t)$ is Markovian if and only if $R(s,u) = \frac{R(s,t)R(t,u)}{R(t,t)}$ for every $s \le t \le u$.

[4] A process X exhibits long-range dependence (or it is a long-memory process) if $\sum_{n\ge0} \mathbb{E}\left(X_1 - X_0\right)\left(X_{n+1} - X_n\right) = \infty$. Otherwise, if $\sum_{n\ge0} \mathbb{E}\left(X_1 - X_0\right)\left(X_{n+1} - X_n\right) < \infty$, we can state that X is a short-memory process.

(ii) Samorodnitsky and Taqqu (1994):

$$B_t^H = \left(\frac{1}{C_2(H)} \int_{\mathbb{R}} \frac{e^{itx} - 1}{ix} |x|^{-\left(H - \frac{1}{2}\right)} dB_x \right)_{t \in \mathbb{R}},$$

where $i = \sqrt{-1}$, $C_2(H) = \sqrt{\frac{\pi}{H\Gamma(2H)\sin(H\pi)}}$ and $\Gamma(\cdot)$ denotes the gamma function.

(iii) Norros et al. (1999):

$$B_t^H = \int_0^t z_H(t,s) dB_s,$$

where B_s is a standard Brownian motion and the deterministic kernel is

$$z_H(t,s) = \begin{cases} \alpha_H\Big(-\left(H - \frac{1}{2}\right) s^{\frac{1}{2}-H} \int_s^t u^{H-\frac{3}{2}} (u-s)^{H-\frac{1}{2}} du \\ \qquad + \left(\frac{t}{s}\right)^{H-\frac{1}{2}} (t-s)^{H-\frac{1}{2}} \Big) \ for\ H \in (0, \frac{1}{2}) \\ (H - \frac{1}{2})\alpha_H s^{\frac{1}{2}-H} \int_s^t (v-s)^{H-\frac{3}{2}} v^{H-\frac{1}{2}} dv \ for\ H \in (\frac{1}{2}, 1) \end{cases},$$

and $\alpha_H = \left(\frac{2H\Gamma(\frac{3}{2}-H)}{\Gamma(H+\frac{1}{2})\Gamma(2-2H)} \right)^{\frac{1}{2}}$.

A more detailed description of the representations can be found in Nourdin (2012). It is well known that the Hurst index H determines the main properties of the fBm such as memory, self-similarity, regularity of sample paths and so on. Therefore, the fBm has been employed in different fields exhibiting long-range dependence and antipersistence, including hydrology, biology, medicine, traffic networks, economics, and finance, among others. In financial mathematics, the fBm was first introduced to model stock price since a large number of empirical studies of financial time series have found long-range dependence properties in asset returns (e.g., Greene and Fielitz (1977), Lo and MacKinlay (1988), Willinger et al. (1999), and Cont (2005)). It has been suggested as a replacement for Brownian motion in the geometric Brownian motion model for stock prices. Consequently, some option pricing models have been proposed to extend the classical Black–Scholes model, such as Hu and Øksendal (2003), Elliott and Van Der Hoek (2003), Elliott and Chan (2004), Mishura (2008), and Rostek (2009). However, when the Hurst parameter $H \neq \frac{1}{2}$, the fBm is not a semimartingale. Hence, there exists an arbitrage opportunity in the fractional Black–Scholes model. In the literature, Rogers (1997) first stated that the fBm is an inappropriate candidate for usage in financial models. In fact, for Hurst parameters $H \neq \frac{1}{2}$, Rogers (1997) proved that a fractional Bachelier-type model can admit arbitrage possibilities. Then, Sottinen (2001), Cheridito

(2001), Bender and Elliott (2004), and Björk and Hult (2005) demonstrated that the fractional Black–Scholes model, which replaces the driving Brownian motion in the Black–Scholes model by a fBm, allows arbitrage in a number of ways.

To exclude arbitrage, a new stochastic integral of the fBm, namely the Wick integral, can be used (see Duncan et al. (2000), Hu and Øksendal (2003), and Hu et al. (2003)). From a purely mathematical point of view, the Wick integral, which was proposed by Hu and Øksendal (2003) and Hu et al. (2003), is formally correct and accurate. However, until now, a reasonable economic interpretation for the Wick integral has not been provided yet.

Fractional Gaussian noise (fGn), which is the stationary increment of the fBm with mean zero, can be defined as $G_t^H = B_{t+1}^H - B_t^H$ with $t \in \mathbb{Z}^+$. Using (7.1), we can easily obtain that the covariance of G_t^H and G_{t+k}^H is

$$\mathrm{Cov}\left(G_t^H, G_{t+k}^H\right) = \gamma_G(k) = \frac{1}{2}\left(|k+1|^{2H} + |k-1|^{2H} - 2|k|^{2H}\right), \quad k \in \mathbb{Z}, \tag{7.3}$$

where $H \in (0,1)$ is referred to as the Hurst exponent and is a measure of the long-term correlation between the discrete time points. Using the Taylor expansion, we can obtain the asymptotic behavior of $\gamma_G(k)$. Let $\gamma_G(k) = \frac{1}{2}k^{2H}g\left(k^{-1}\right)$ with $g(x) = (1+x)^{2H} - 2 + (1-x)^{2H}$. If $0 < H < 1$ and $H \neq \frac{1}{2}$, then the first nonzero term in the Taylor expansion of $g(x)$, expanded at the origin, is equal to $2H(2H-1)x^2$. Therefore, as k tends to infinity, $\gamma_G(k)$ is equivalent to $H(2H-1)k^{2H-2}$, which implies that the covariance function of the fGn has a power-law decay. The result of (7.3) implies that fGn becomes uncorrelated white Gaussian noise when $H = \frac{1}{2}$. When $H > \frac{1}{2}$, the fGn has a positive correlation with a persistent autocorrelation structure. Similarly, the covariance is negative when $H < \frac{1}{2}$, and the resulting process is then referred to as being antipersistent. Note that, when $H = 1$, (7.3) implies $\gamma_G(k) \equiv 1$. Thus, all these correlations of fGn are equal to 1 no matter how big k is. Hence, this case is hardly of any practical significance. When $H > 1$, we can see that $g\left(k^{-1}\right)$ diverges to infinity. This behavior contradicts the fact that correlation coefficients must be in $(-1, 1)$. As a consequence, if covariances exist and $\lim_{k\to\infty}\gamma_G(k) = 0$, then $0 < H < 1$. For $H = \frac{1}{2}$, the observations are uncorrelated; for $\frac{1}{2} < H < 1$, the process has long-range dependence; and for $0 < H < \frac{1}{2}$, the process has short-range dependence and the correlations sum to zero. Some important properties of the fGn are provided by the following proposition, whose proofs can be found in Beran (1994).

Proposition 7.2.2 *The fGn has the following properties:*

(i) *The spectral density is*

$$f_G(\lambda; H) = \frac{\sin(\pi H)\,\Gamma(2H+1)\,(1-\cos(\lambda))}{\pi} \sum_{j\in\mathbb{Z}} |\lambda+2j\pi|^{-2H-1},$$

which has a pole at $\lambda = 0$ *and asymptotic behavior*

$$f_G(\lambda; H) \sim \mathcal{O}\left(|\lambda|^{1-2H}\right) \quad \text{as} \quad \lambda \to 0\,.$$

In particular, if $H \in (0, 1/2)$*, then* $f_G(\lambda; H) \to 0$ *as* $\lambda \to 0$ *and if* $H \in (\frac{1}{2}, 1)$, $f_G(\lambda; H) \to \infty$ *as* $\lambda \to 0$.

(ii) *For large lags k, the behavior of the autocorrelation function (7.3) is*

$$\gamma_G(k) \sim H(2H-1)\,k^{2H-2} \tag{7.4}$$

as $k \to \infty$*, which implies that*

$$\sum_{k\in\mathbb{Z}} \gamma_G(k) = \infty$$

for $H \in (\frac{1}{2}, 1)$.

(iii) *For all* $H \in (0, 1)$*, we have* $G_t^H \sim N(0, 1)$ *and*

$$G_t^H - G_0^H \sim \mathcal{N}\left(0, 2 - |t-1|^{2H} - |t+1|^{2H} + 2|t|^{2H}\right).$$

Moreover, we have $G_t^H - G_0^H \Rightarrow \mathcal{N}(0, 2)$ *as* $t \to \infty$.

7.2.2 The Fractional Ornstein–Uhlenbeck Process and the Fractional Vasicek Model

Based on the discussion in the preceding subsection, we can see that difficulties arise when using the fBm to model financial asset returns. However, using the fBm to model the time series of volatility or interest rates is fruitful. In fact, a popular statistical model is the fVm, which extends the fOUp. Both the fOUp and fVm are driven by the fBm.

As a solution to the Langevin stochastic differential equation with the fBm, the fOUp was proposed by Cheridito et al. (2003) and can be defined as follows:

$$dX_t = -\kappa X_t dt + \sigma dB_t^H, \tag{7.5}$$

where $\kappa, \sigma > 0$.

Using the pathwise Riemann–Stieltjes integral, Cheridito et al. (2003) obtained a unique path-wise solution to Model (7.5) as

$$X_t = e^{-\kappa t} X_0 + \sigma \int_0^t e^{-\kappa(t-s)} dB_s^H, \tag{7.6}$$

where $\int_0^t e^{-\kappa(t-s)} dB_s^H$ is a Wiener integral with respect to the fBm. One can also rewrite the unique solution to (7.5) as

$$X_t = X_0 e^{-\kappa t} + \sigma \kappa e^{-\kappa t} \int_0^t e^{\kappa s} B_s^H ds + \sigma B_t^H. \tag{7.7}$$

The representation is obtained via integration by parts, that is, $\int_0^t e^{\kappa s} dB_s^H = -\kappa \int_0^t e^{\kappa s} B_s^H ds + e^{\kappa t} B_t^H$.

Here, we review some important properties of the fOUp.

Proposition 7.2.3 *The fOUp has the following properties:*

(i) X_t is Holder continuous with Holder exponents $\gamma \in (0, H)$.

(ii) Let $\mathfrak{Z}$ be the class of nonnegative random variables ζ. Then there exists $C > 0$ independent of t such that $\mathbb{E} \exp\left\{x\zeta^2\right\} < \infty$ for any $0 < x < C$ such that $\sup_{0 \le s \le t} |X_s| \le \left(Ce^{\alpha s} + s^H \log^2 s\right) \zeta$.

(iii) The random variable X_t has a normal distribution with mean $X_0 e^{-\kappa t}$ and variance $\operatorname{Var} X_t = H \int_0^t s^{2H-1} \left(e^{-\kappa s} + e^{-\kappa(2t-s)}\right) ds$. Moreover, if $\kappa < 0$, then $\operatorname{Var} X_t \sim \frac{H\Gamma(2H)}{(-\kappa)^{2H}} e^{-2\kappa t}$ as $t \to \infty$. If $\kappa > 0$, then $\operatorname{Var} X_t \to \frac{H\Gamma(2H)}{\kappa^{2H}}$ as $t \to \infty$. When $\kappa = 0$, $\operatorname{Var} X_t = t^{2H}$ for $t \ge 0$.

(iv) For $\kappa < 0$, $e^{\kappa t} X_t \to X_0 - \kappa \int_0^\infty e^{\theta s} B_s^H ds \simeq \mathcal{N}\left(X_0, \frac{H\Gamma(2H)}{(-\kappa)^{2H}}\right)$ a.s. as $t \to \infty$. For $\kappa > 0$, $\frac{1}{T} \int_0^T X_t^2 dt \to \frac{H\Gamma(2H)}{\kappa^{2H}}$ a.s. as $T \to \infty$.

(v) Let $\kappa > 0$. Then, for any $p \ge 1$, there exist some positive constants c_p and C_p such that $\mathbb{E}|X_t|^p \le c_p$ for $t \ge 0$ and $\mathbb{E}|X_t - X_s|^p \le C_p |t-s|^{pH}$ for $|t-s| \le 1$. Moreover, for any $s, t \in [0, T]$, we have $\mathbb{E} X_t X_s \le C|t-s|^{2H-2}$.

(vi) Let $H \in (0, 1)$ and $t \ge s \ge 0$. Then, the covariance function of the fOUp can be written as

$$\begin{aligned}
\operatorname{Cov}(X_t, X_s) = \frac{H\sigma^2}{2}\Big(&- e^{-\kappa t + \kappa s} \int_0^{t-s} e^{\kappa z} z^{2H-1} dz + e^{\kappa t - \kappa s} \int_{t-s}^t e^{-\kappa z} z^{2H-1} dz \\
&- e^{-\kappa t - \kappa s} \int_s^t e^{\kappa z} z^{2H-1} dz + e^{-\kappa t + \kappa s} \int_0^s e^{-\kappa z} z^{2H-1} dz \\
&+ 2e^{-\kappa t - \kappa s} \int_0^t e^{\kappa z} z^{2H-1} dz\Big).
\end{aligned}$$

(vii) For $H \ne \frac{1}{2}$, $N = 1, 2 \ldots$ and $s \ge 0$, the asymptotic relation for the covariance function is provided by

$$\begin{aligned}
\operatorname{Cov}(X_s, X_{s+t}) = \frac{\sigma^2}{2} &\sum_{n=1}^{N} (-\theta)^{-2n} \left(\prod_{k=0}^{2n-1} (2H-k)\right) \left(t^{2H-2n} - e^{\theta s}(s+t)^{2H-2n}\right) \\
&+ O\left(t^{2H-2N-2}\right), \quad \text{as } t \to \infty.
\end{aligned}$$

Now, we consider the stationary fOUp. When $\kappa > 0$, under the assumption of the initial condition

$$X_0 = \mu + \sigma \int_{-\infty}^{0} e^{\kappa s} d\widetilde{B}_s^H \text{ with } \widetilde{B}_s^H = \begin{cases} B_s^H & \text{for } s \geq 0 \\ W_{|s|}^H & \text{for } s \leq 0 \end{cases}, \quad (7.8)$$

where $W_{|s|}^H$ is another fBm that is independent of B_s^H, and $\widetilde{B}_s^H$ is a two-sided fBm. In this situation, we obtain

$$Y_t = \mu + \sigma \int_{-\infty}^{t} e^{-\kappa(t-s)} dB_s^H = X_t - \left(1 - e^{-\kappa t}\right)\mu - X_0 e^{-\kappa t} + e^{-\kappa t} Y_0 . \quad (7.9)$$

A standard but tedious calculation yields

$$\begin{aligned} \operatorname{Cov}(Y_t, Y_s) = \frac{H\sigma^2}{2}\Bigg(& \frac{\Gamma(2H)}{\kappa^{2H}} e^{-\kappa(t-s)} - e^{-\kappa(t-s)} \int_0^{t-s} e^{\kappa z} z^{2H-1} dz \\ & + e^{\kappa(t-s)} \int_{t-s}^{+\infty} e^{-\kappa z} z^{2H-1} dz \Bigg), \end{aligned} \quad (7.10)$$

which implies the stationarity of the process Y_t.

Let $\tau = t - s$. To show the ergodicity of the Gaussian stationary process Y_t, it suffices to show that its covariance function $\operatorname{Cov}(Y_t, Y_s)$ vanishes as τ tends to infinity. According to (7.10), the change of variables, and integration by parts, we have

$$\begin{aligned} \operatorname{Cov}(Y_t, Y_s) &= \frac{H\sigma^2}{2\kappa^{2H}} \Bigg(\Gamma(2H) e^{-\kappa\tau} - e^{-\kappa\tau} \int_0^{\kappa\tau} e^{y} y^{2H-1} dy \\ &\quad + e^{\kappa\tau} \int_{\kappa\tau}^{+\infty} e^{-y} y^{2H-1} dy \Bigg) \\ &\leq \frac{H(2H-1)\sigma^2}{2\kappa^{2H}} \left(e^{\frac{-\kappa\tau}{2}} + \left(\frac{\kappa\tau}{2}\right)^{2H-2} + (\kappa\tau)^{2H-2} \right) + O\left(e^{-\kappa\tau}\right), \end{aligned}$$

which converges to zero as $\tau \to \infty$ and implies the ergodicity of the Gaussian stationary process Y_t.

In fact, when $\kappa > 0$, Cheridito et al. (2003) have shown that when $H \neq \frac{1}{2}$, Y_t in Model (7.9) is an ergodic stationary Gaussian process where the autocorrelation function is

$$\operatorname{Cov}(Y_t, Y_{t+s}) = \frac{1}{2}\sigma^2 \sum_{n=1}^{N} \kappa^{-2n} \left(\prod_{k=0}^{2n-1} (2H - k) \right) s^{2H-2n} + O\left(s^{2H-2N-2}\right), \quad (7.11)$$

for fixed $t \in \mathbb{R}$, $s \to \infty$, and $N = 1, 2, \ldots$.

From Equation (7.11), we can see that the decay of the covariance function of a stationary fOUp when $H \neq \frac{1}{2}$ is like that of a power function. Equation (7.11) also shows that for $H \in \left(0, \frac{1}{2}\right) \cup \left(\frac{1}{2}, 1\right)$, the decay of the stationary fOUp is very similar to the decay of the fGn defined by (7.4). In particular, for $H \in \left(\frac{1}{2}, 1\right)$, $(Y_t)_{t\in\mathbb{R}}$ is ergodic and exhibits long-range dependence.

Since a stationary fOUp has a mean of zero, to construct a good candidate model for volatility and interest rates, a natural extension of the fOUp is the fVm, which adds the long-term mean to the fOUp:

$$dX_t = \kappa\,(\mu - X_t)\,dt + \sigma\,dB_t^H, \tag{7.12}$$

where $\sigma \in \mathbb{R}^+$, $\kappa \in \mathbb{R}$, $\mu \in \mathbb{R}$, the initial condition is set at X_0, and B_t^H is an fBm with Hurst index $H \in (0, 1)$.

The key difference between Model (7.12) and Model (7.5) is that μ is assumed to be zero and known in Model (7.5), while μ is unknown in Model (7.12). The fVm inherits all the important properties of the fOUp reviewed in Proposition 7.2.3.

7.3 Fractional Stochastic Volatility Models

Model (7.12) has been used to model realized volatility (RV) in the literature (e.g., Gatheral et al. (2018) and Wang et al. (2023)). However, when the volatility is latent, Model (7.12) alone cannot be a complete model and an observation equation is needed. This modeling strategy leads to a class of fractional stochastic volatility models.

This class of fractional stochastic volatility models extends the class of standard stochastic volatility models driven by standard Brownian motion in the volatility equation. Before discussing the fractional stochastic volatility models, we first review some famous stochastic volatility models driven by Brownian motion.

A general representation of the continuous-time stochastic volatility model driven by standard Brownian motion may be written as

$$\begin{cases} dS_t/S_t = \mu dt + S_t^{\gamma} f(V_t)[\sqrt{1-\rho^2}dW_t + \rho dZ_t], \\ dV_t/V_t = \beta(V_t)dt + g(V_t)dZ_t, \end{cases} \tag{7.13}$$

with independent standard Brownian motions W_t and Z_t. The probability space for both W_t and Z_t is denoted as before by $(\Omega, \mathcal{F}, \mathbb{P})$. Here, $S_t > 0$ denotes the price of the (traded) asset and $V_t > 0$ denotes the (nontraded) stochastic local return variance. Model (7.13) allows for level (also known as scale) dependence ($\gamma = 0$) and correlation between returns and variance ($\rho = 0$). As shown in Table 7.1, Model (7.13) is the generalization of the most commonly used models (without the jump component) in research as well as in practice.

Table 7.1 *Specification of stochastic volatility models for Model (7.13)*

Author(s) (year)	Specification	Remarks
Hull and White (1987)	$f(\upsilon)=v$, $\beta(\upsilon)=0$, $g(\upsilon)=\sigma$, $\rho=0,\gamma=0$.	Instantaneous variance: Geometric Brownian motion. Pricing options by mixing.
Wiggins (1987)	$f(\upsilon)=e^{\frac{\upsilon}{2}}$, $\beta(v)=\frac{\kappa(\theta-\upsilon)}{\upsilon}$, $g(\upsilon)=\sigma,\rho=0,\gamma=0$.	Instantaneous volatility: The Ornstein–Uhlenbeck process in logarithms.
Stein and Stein (1991)	$f(\upsilon)=\|\upsilon\|$, $\beta(v)=\frac{\kappa(\theta-\upsilon)}{\upsilon}$, $g(\upsilon)=\frac{\sigma}{\upsilon},\rho=0,\gamma=0$.	The instantaneous volatility: Reflected Ornstein–Uhlenbeck.
Heston (1993)	$f(\upsilon)=\sqrt{\upsilon}$, $\beta(v)=\frac{\kappa(\theta-\upsilon)}{\upsilon}$, $g(\upsilon)=\frac{\sigma}{\sqrt{\upsilon}}$, $\rho\in[-1,1],\gamma=0$.	Instantaneous volatility: CIR process. First model with correlation. Pricing options by the Fourier inversion.
Romano and Touzi (1997)	f,β and g free, $\rho\in[-1,1],\gamma=0$.	Extension of mixing to correlation
Schöbel and Zhu (1999)	$f(\upsilon)=\|\upsilon\|$, $\beta(v)=\frac{\kappa(\theta-\upsilon)}{\upsilon}$, $g(\upsilon)=\frac{\sigma}{\upsilon}$, $\rho\in[-1,1],\gamma=0$.	Stein and Stein model with correlation. Pricing options by the Fourier inversion.
Hagan et al. (2002)	$f(\upsilon)=v$, $\beta(\upsilon)=0$, $g(\upsilon)=\sigma$, $\rho\in[-1,1],\gamma\in[-1,1]$.	Level dependence in returns. Pricing options by the perturbation technique.

One of the key assumptions among all the aforementioned stochastic volatility models is that the drivers are standard Brownian motions. As irregular as the paths might look, Brownian motion has independent increments. As a result, the autocorrelation function (ACF) of V_t decays at an exponential rate. To generate the power function for the ACF that is not absolutely summable, Comte and Renault (1998) proposed the first fractional stochastic volatility model in continuous-time

$$\begin{cases} dS_t = rS_t dt + \sigma_t S_t dW_t, \\ d\ln(\sigma_t) = \kappa(\mu - \ln(\sigma_t))\,dt + \sigma\, dB_t^H, \end{cases} \tag{7.14}$$

where B_t^H is an fBm with the Hurst parameter H. To ensure the ACF of $\ln(\sigma_t^2)$ is not absolutely summable, Comte and Renault (1998) assumed $H \in (\frac{1}{2}, 1)$.

Comte and Renault (1998) considered the option pricing problem in the long-memory volatility framework of Model (7.14). Since the closed-form solution for option pricing does not exist, Comte and Renault (1998) provided discrete approximation to fVm Model (7.14) and computed option prices based on Monte Carlo simulation. Comte et al. (2012) investigated the option pricing model by introducing a long-memory extension of the Heston model, which is a usual square root volatility process with the fractional integration and has the power decay feature in the large-time limit for the autocovariance function of the volatility process. Both models in Comte and Renault (1998) and Comte et al. (2012) assume that the return process is independent of the volatility process. Due to the complex structures of long-memory stochastic volatility models, Comte and Renault (1998) and Comte et al. (2012) cannot provide the analytical formulae for pricing standard options but introduce some discretization schemes and price options using some Monte Carlo simulations.

Moreover, Chronopoulou and Viens (2012a,b) introduced the following fractional stochastic models:

$$\begin{cases} \mathrm{d}S_t/S_t = r\mathrm{d}t + \sigma\,(X_t)\,\mathrm{d}W_t, \\ \mathrm{d}X_t = \alpha\,(m - X_t)\,\mathrm{d}t + \beta dB_t^H, \end{cases} \tag{7.15}$$

where $\sigma\,(X_t) = \sqrt{X_t}$, $\sigma\,(X_t) = |X_t|$, $\sigma\,(X_t) = e^{X_t}$, and $H > \frac{1}{2}$. In the long-memory volatility framework, Chronopoulou and Viens (2012a) used an interacting particle stochastic filtering algorithm to estimate the fractional stochastic volatility model of Comte and Renault (1998) and constructed a multinomial recombining tree to price options. Chronopoulou and Viens (2012b) implemented a particle filtering algorithm to estimate the fractional stochastic volatility model of Comte and Renault (1998) and constructed a multinomial recombining tree to price options.

Recently, some empirical studies have documented the roughness of volatility both in realized volatility and implied volatility (e.g., Bayer et al. (2016), Gatheral et al. (2018), Livieri et al. (2018), El Euch and Rosenbaum (2019), and Bennedsen et al. (2022)). More precisely, Gatheral et al. (2018) calibrated the parameters in the fVm using the implied volatility surface of options based on the S&P 500, showing that the Hurst parameter of the volatility is close to 0.1. This result indicates extremely rough paths for the volatility process; these paths are much more irregular than those of the standard stochastic volatility models driven by Brownian motion. Livieri et al. (2018) found that at-the-money short-term volatility from the S&P 500 options is also rough. More empirical studies confirmed that the roughness of the log volatility for thousands of stocks was investigated by Bennedsen et al. (2022). Therefore, both the realized volatility and the option-implied volatility have recently been shown to be rough. Thus, modeling the roughness of the volatility is becoming increasingly popular and has important applications in finance because rough volatility models can describe the volatility skew, which is defined as the derivative of the implied volatility surface with respect to the log-strike price evaluated at-the-money under the Black–Scholes–Merton model.

Model (7.12) can describe both the mean reverting property and the roughness of the volatility. Consequently, the fVm has become the usual candidate for capturing some phenomena of the volatility of financial assets (e.g., Comte and Renault (1998), Aït-Sahalia and Mancini (2008), Comte et al. (2012), Bayer et al. (2016), Gatheral et al. (2018), Bennedsen et al. (2022), and Bolko et al. (2023)). The fVm is an extension of the Vasicek process with the fBm driving term. In finance, it has been used as a one-factor short-term interest rate model (e.g., Fink et al. (2013)) or financial asset volatility model (e.g., Comte and Renault (1998)) for more than two decades. In Model (7.12), $\kappa\,(\mu - X_t)$ is the drift function which contains two unknown parameters, μ and κ. The persistence in X_t is determined by the parameter κ. Model (7.12) can capture stationary, explosive, and null recurrent behavior with the different sign of κ. The fVm has been used to describe the dynamics of volatility in a large set. The development of the application for the fVm naturally led to statistical inference for this model. Consequently, estimating the drift parameter in the fVm has been of great interest in the past decade, and it is a challenging theoretical problem. In the following two sections, we consider parameter estimation for the fVm based on continuous observations and discrete-time observations individually.

7.4 Estimation Methods Based on Continuous-Time Observations

Despite the many applications of the fVm in practice, the statistic inference for the fVm has received little attention. For the special case of the fVm, the so-called fOUp provided by Model (7.5), we try to summarize the techniques proposed to estimate κ during the past two decades based on the continuous record of observations, which are listed as follows:

(i) The maximum likelihood estimator (MLE) was originally proposed by Kleptsyna and Le Breton (2002) for $\kappa > 0$ with $H \in (\frac{1}{2}, 1)$, in which the estimator of the drift parameter in the fOUp was constructed based on the Girsanov transforms for an fBm, and the strong consistency of the MLE was also established. Tudor and Viens (2007) addressed the problem of estimating the drift parameter in nonlinear stochastic differential equations driven by the fBm with a Hurst parameter range of $H \in (0, 1)$. The strong consistency of the MLE was investigated, but the asymptotic distribution was not investigated. Then, the asymptotic law of MLE was proposed by Tanaka (2013) with $H \in (\frac{1}{2}, 1)$. In fact, the asymptotic law is also valid for $H \in (0, \frac{1}{2})$. For $\kappa = 0$, Kleptsyna and Le Breton (2002) investigated the bias of the MLE. For $\kappa \leq 0$, the asymptotic theory was investigated by Tanaka (2015) with a Hurst parameter range of $H \in (0, 1)$. In particular, the MLE has three celebrated features that are clearly attractive: consistency, asymptotic normality, and the absence of stochastic integration with respect to the fBm. However, the MLE depends on the properties of the deterministic fractional operators (determined by the Hurst parameter) related to the fBm and relies on its ability to compute stochastic integrals with respect to fBm. Moreover, approximating pathwise integrals with respect to the fBm, if they exist, is challenging. Therefore, an actual implementation of the MLE is not easily computable.

(ii) The least squares estimator (LSE) was proposed by Hu and Nualart (2010) for $\kappa > 0$ with $H \in (\frac{1}{2}, 1)$ and by Hu et al. (2019) with $H \in (0, \frac{1}{2})$. For $\kappa < 0$, the LSE was investigated by Belfadli et al. (2011) in the case of $H \in (0, \frac{1}{2})$ and by El Machkouri et al. (2016) for a Hurst parameter range of $H \in (0, 1)$.

(iii) The method of moment estimator (MME) for $\kappa > 0$ was proposed by Hu and Nualart (2010) with $H \in (\frac{1}{2}, 1)$ and by Hu et al. (2019) with $H \in (0, \frac{1}{2})$ for practical purposes. It is worth emphasizing that the MLE involves deterministic fractional operators and that the LSE relies on an unobservable Skorohod integral. Therefore, an actual implementation of the MLE or the LSE is problematic. For the sake of practice, Hu and Nualart (2010) and Hu et al. (2019) proposed the MME and studied asymptotical properties for the MME.

(iv) The minimum contrast estimator (MCE) was developed by Bishwal (2011) for $\kappa > 0$ with $H \in (\frac{1}{2}, 1)$ and by Tanaka (2013) for a Hurst parameter range of $H \in (0, 1)$. Note that the MCE does not involve stochastic integrals, unlike the MLE. Bishwal (2011) studied the accuracy of normal approximation for the MCE based on uniform equally spaced sampling of the fOUp. When $\kappa = 0$, the MCE was also considered by Tanaka (2013).

Prakasa Rao (2010) proposed some alternative methods and the asymptotic theory for the fOUp. A survey of parametric estimation and inference procedures for statistical models driven by the fBm has been provided in a recent monograph, Kubilius et al. (2017).

In most of the empirically relevant cases, parameter μ in the drift function of Model (7.12) is unknown. Thus, it is important to estimate both κ and μ in the fVm. When a continuous record of observations is available for X_t with $t \in [0, T]$, there are three general methods of parameter estimation: the MLE, LSE, and MME. For a general Hurst parameter $H \in (0, 1)$, the asymptotic theory of the MLE and LSE is provided for $\kappa \in \mathbb{R}$ while the asymptotic theory of the MME is considered for $\kappa > 0$. The three estimators of κ and μ are reviewed and their asymptotic distributions are developed under the scheme of $T \to \infty$.[5]

[5] When a continuous record of observations is available, the unknown parameters of both H and σ can be recovered without estimation errors.

7.4.1 MLE

The MLE perhaps is the most popular method for estimating a parametric model because it has many desirable properties, including sufficiency, consistency, efficiency, and functional invariance.

For illustration purposes, we extend Model (7.12) to be a slightly more general form as follows:

$$dX_t = (\alpha - \kappa X_t)\, dt + \sigma\, dB_t^H . \tag{7.16}$$

From Model (7.16), the drift term is αdt and does not vanish, even when $\kappa = 0$. This alternative specification for the drift term was used in Chan et al. (1992) and Yu and Phillips (2001). When α in Model (7.16) is known (without loss of generality, it is assumed to be zero), Model (7.16) terms to the fOUp. A unique pathwise solution to the stochastic differential equation in Model (7.16) is

$$X_t = e^{-\kappa t} X_0 + \frac{\alpha}{\kappa}\left(1 - e^{-\kappa t}\right) + \sigma \int_0^t e^{-\kappa(t-s)} dB_s^H, \tag{7.17}$$

where the stochastic integral, $\int_0^t e^{-\kappa(t-s)} dB_s^H$, is the pathwise Riemann-Stieltjes integral, and the solution is unique (Proposition A.1 in Cheridito et al. (2003)).

When $H \in (\frac{1}{2}, 1)$, the MLEs of κ and α have been investigated by Lohvinenko and Ralchenko (2017) with $\kappa > 0$ and Lohvinenko and Ralchenko (2019) with $\kappa < 0$. Consequently, we aim to develop the asymptotic distributions for the MLE of κ and α under the following scenarios: (i) $\kappa < 0$ and $H \in (0, 1)$, (ii) $\kappa = 0$ and $H \in (0, 1)$, and (iii) $\kappa > 0$ and $H \in (0, \frac{1}{2}]$. Therefore, together with Lohvinenko and Ralchenko (2017, 2019), a complete coverage of asymptotic theory for all possible cases is obtained for the MLE with κ and α. Although the assumption of a continuous-time record is practically too strong, it allows us to obtain the MLE in a closed form. Furthermore, these results provided here will serve as the benchmark for those based on discrete-time data.

Following Kleptsyna et al. (2000), by applying the Girsanov theorem for the fBm developed in Norros et al. (1999), we can see that the continuous-record log-likelihood function for Model (7.16) can be written as follows:

$$\ell(\kappa, \alpha) = \int_0^T Q_H(t) dM_t^H + \frac{1}{2}\int_0^T (Q_H(t))^2\, d\omega_t^H,$$

where

$$Q_H(t) = \frac{1}{\sigma}\frac{d}{d\omega_t^H}\int_0^t k_H(t,s)\,(\alpha - \kappa X_s)\, ds, \tag{7.18}$$

$$k_H(t,s) = \frac{1}{k_H}\left(s\,(t-s)\right)^{\frac{1}{2}-H}, \; k_H = 2H\Gamma\left(\frac{3}{2} - H\right)\Gamma\left(H + \frac{1}{2}\right), \tag{7.19}$$

$$\omega_t^H = \frac{1}{\lambda_H} t^{2-2H}, \tag{7.20}$$

$$\lambda_H = \frac{2H\Gamma(3-2H)\Gamma\left(H+\frac{1}{2}\right)}{\Gamma\left(\frac{3}{2}-H\right)}, \tag{7.21}$$

$$M_t^H = \int_0^t k_H(t,s) dB_s^H. \tag{7.22}$$

Taking the derivatives of the log-likelihood function with respect to α and κ and setting them to zero, Lohvinenko and Ralchenko (2017) provided the following MLE estimators for α and κ:

$$\tilde{\alpha}_T = \frac{S_T \int_0^T P_H^2(t)\, d\omega_t^H - \int_0^T P_H(t)\, dS_t \int_0^T P_H(t)\, d\omega_t^H}{\omega_T^H \int_0^T P_H^2(t)\, d\omega_t^H - \left(\int_0^T P_H(t)\, d\omega_t^H\right)^2} \sigma, \tag{7.23}$$

$$\tilde{\kappa}_T = \frac{S_T \int_0^T P_H(t)\, d\omega_t^H - \omega_T^H \int_0^T P_H(t)\, dS_t}{\omega_T^H \int_0^T P_H^2(t)\, d\omega_t^H - \left(\int_0^T P_H(t)\, d\omega_t^H\right)^2}, \tag{7.24}$$

where

$$S_t = \frac{1}{\sigma} \int_0^t k_H(t,s)\, dX_s, \tag{7.25}$$

$$P_H(t) = \frac{1}{\sigma} \frac{d}{d\omega_t^H} \int_0^t k_H(t,s)\, X_s ds, \tag{7.26}$$

Combining Model (7.16) with Equations (7.19) and (7.26), we have

$$P_H(t) = \frac{1}{\sigma}\frac{\alpha}{\kappa} + \frac{1}{\sigma}\left(X_0 - \frac{\alpha}{\kappa}\right) V_H(t) + \tilde{P}_H(t), \tag{7.27}$$

where

$$V_H(t) = \frac{d}{d\omega_t^H} \int_0^t k_H(t,s)\, e^{-\kappa s} ds, \tag{7.28}$$

$$\tilde{P}_H(t) = \frac{d}{d\omega_t^H} \int_0^t k_H(t,s)\, U_s ds, \tag{7.29}$$

$$U_t = \int_0^t e^{-\kappa(t-s)} dB_s^H. \tag{7.30}$$

Using the idea of Kleptsyna and Le Breton (2002), Lohvinenko and Ralchenko (2017) provided the following results:

$$Q_H(t) = \frac{\alpha}{\sigma} - \kappa P_H(t)\,, \tag{7.31}$$

$$S_t = \int_0^t Q_H(s)\, d\omega_s^H + M_t^H = \frac{\alpha}{\sigma}\omega_t^H - \kappa \int_0^t P_H(s)\, d\omega_s^H + M_t^H\,, \tag{7.32}$$

$$dS_t = \frac{\alpha}{\sigma} d\omega_t^H - \kappa P_H(t)\, d\omega_t^H + dM_t^H\,. \tag{7.33}$$

The fundamental martingale, M_t^H, is a Gaussian process with variance ω_t^H. Moreover, the natural filtration of the martingale M^H coincides with the natural filtration of the fBm. Based on Models (7.32) and (7.33), the MLE of α and κ can be represented as

$$\tilde{\alpha}_T = \alpha + \frac{M_T^H \int_0^T P_H^2(t)\, d\omega_t^H - \int_0^T P_H(t)\, dM_t^H \int_0^T P_H(t)\, d\omega_t^H}{\omega_T^H \int_0^T P_H^2(t)\, d\omega_t^H - \left(\int_0^T P_H(t)\, d\omega_t^H\right)^2}\sigma\,, \tag{7.34}$$

$$\tilde{\kappa}_T = \kappa + \frac{M_T^H \int_0^T P_H(t)\, d\omega_t^H - \omega_T^H \int_0^T P_H(t)\, dM_t^H}{\omega_T^H \int_0^T P_H^2(t)\, d\omega_t^H - \left(\int_0^T P_H(t)\, d\omega_t^H\right)^2}\,, \tag{7.35}$$

When a continuous record of observations of X_t is available, Lohvinenko and Ralchenko (2017) considered the consistency and the asymptotic normality of the MLE as defined by Equations (7.23) and (7.24) when $H > \frac{1}{2}$ and $\kappa > 0$. From Tanaka et al. (2020), we can obtain the asymptotic theory for the MLE of α and κ for all other cases, including $H \in (0, 1)$ and $\kappa = 0$, $H < \frac{1}{2}$ and $\kappa > 0$, and $H \in (0, 1)$ and $\kappa < 0$. Table 7.2 summarizes the asymptotic distributions of $\tilde{\alpha}_T$ and $\tilde{\kappa}_T$ for different ranges of H and κ, where $\lambda_H = \frac{2H\Gamma(3-2H)\Gamma\left(H+\frac{1}{2}\right)}{\Gamma\left(\frac{3}{2}-H\right)}$, $\rho_H = \lambda_H(3-2H)^2$, $\phi_H = \frac{32H(1-H)(2-H)\Gamma(3-2H)\Gamma(H+\frac{1}{2})}{\Gamma(\frac{3}{2}-H)}$, ξ_∞, η_∞ are two independent $\mathcal{N}(0, -\sigma^2/(2\kappa))$ random variables, and X and Y are two independent $\mathcal{N}(0, 1)$ random variables. Moreover, we assume $X_0 = \alpha/\kappa$ for $\kappa < 0$ and $H \in (0, \frac{1}{2}) \cup (\frac{1}{2}, 1)$.

7.4.2 LSE

Based on Model (7.12) and borrowing the idea of Hu and Nualart (2010), Belfadli et al. (2011), and El Machkouri et al. (2016), we denote the LSE of κ and μ to be the minimizers of the following (formal) quadratic Function:

$$L(\kappa, \mu) = \int_0^T \left(\dot{X}_t - \kappa(\mu - X_t)\right)^2 dt\,, \tag{7.36}$$

Table 7.2 *The asymptotic laws of $\tilde{\alpha}_T$ and $\tilde{\kappa}_T$ for different ranges of H and κ.*

	$1/2 < H < 1$	$H = 1/2$	$0 < H < 1/2$
$\kappa < 0$	$T^{1-H}(\tilde{\alpha}_T - \alpha) \Rightarrow \mathcal{N}\left(0, \lambda_H \sigma^2\right)$	$\sqrt{T}(\tilde{\alpha}_T - \alpha) \Rightarrow \mathcal{N}\left(0, \sigma^2\right)$	$T^{1-H}(\tilde{\alpha}_T - \alpha) \Rightarrow \mathcal{N}\left(0, \lambda_H \sigma^2\right)$
	$\frac{e^{-\kappa T}}{2\kappa}(\tilde{\kappa}_T - \kappa) \Rightarrow \frac{X\sqrt{\sin(\pi H)}}{Y}$	$\frac{e^{-\kappa T}}{2\kappa}(\tilde{\kappa}_T - \kappa) \Rightarrow \frac{\eta_\infty}{X_0 - \frac{\alpha}{\kappa} + \xi_\infty}$	$\frac{e^{-\kappa T}}{2\kappa}(\tilde{\kappa}_T - \kappa) \Rightarrow \frac{X\sqrt{\sin(\pi H)}}{Y}$
$\kappa = 0$	$T^{1-H}(\tilde{\alpha}_T - \alpha) \Rightarrow \mathcal{N}\left(0, \sigma^2 \rho_H\right)$	$\sqrt{T}(\tilde{\alpha}_T - \alpha) \Rightarrow \mathcal{N}\left(0, 4\sigma^2\right)$	$T^{1-H}(\tilde{\alpha}_T - \alpha) \Rightarrow \mathcal{N}\left(0, \sigma^2 \rho_H\right)$
	$T^{2-H}(\tilde{\kappa}_T - \kappa) \Rightarrow \mathcal{N}\left(0, \frac{\sigma^2}{\alpha^2}\phi_H\right)$	$T^{3/2}(\tilde{\kappa}_T - \kappa) \Rightarrow \mathcal{N}\left(0, \frac{12\sigma^2}{\alpha^2}\right)$	$T^{2-H}(\tilde{\kappa}_T - \kappa) \Rightarrow \mathcal{N}\left(0, \frac{\sigma^2}{\alpha^2}\phi_H\right)$
$\kappa > 0$	$\sqrt{T}(\tilde{\alpha}_T - \alpha) \Rightarrow \mathcal{N}\left(0, \lambda_H \sigma^2\right)$	$\sqrt{T}(\tilde{\alpha}_T - \alpha) \Rightarrow \mathcal{N}\left(0, \sigma^2 + \frac{2\alpha^2}{\kappa}\right)$	$T^{1-H}(\tilde{\alpha}_T - \alpha) \Rightarrow \mathcal{N}\left(0, \frac{2\alpha^2}{\kappa}\right)$
	$\sqrt{T}(\tilde{\kappa}_T - \kappa) \Rightarrow \mathcal{N}(0, 2\kappa)$	$\sqrt{T}(\tilde{\kappa}_T - \kappa) \Rightarrow \mathcal{N}(0, 2\kappa)$	$\sqrt{T}(\tilde{\kappa}_T - \kappa) \Rightarrow \mathcal{N}(0, 2\kappa)$

where $\dot{X}_t$ denotes the differentiation of X_t with respect to t, although $\int_0^T \dot{X}_t^2 dt$ does not exist. Consequently, we obtain the following analytical expressions for the LSE of κ and μ, which are denoted by $\hat{\kappa}_{LS}$ and $\hat{\mu}_{LS}$, respectively.

$$\hat{\kappa}_{LS} = \frac{(X_T - X_0)\int_0^T X_t dt - T\int_0^T X_t dX_t}{T\int_0^T X_t^2 dt - \left(\int_0^T X_t dt\right)^2}, \tag{7.37}$$

$$\hat{\mu}_{LS} = \frac{(X_T - X_0)\int_0^T X_t^2 dt - \int_0^T X_t dX_t \int_0^T X_t dt}{(X_T - X_0)\int_0^T X_t dt - T\int_0^T X_t dX_t}. \tag{7.38}$$

When $H = \frac{1}{2}$, the stochastic integral $\int_0^T X_t dX_t$ can be interpreted as an Itô integral. When $H \in (\frac{1}{2}, 1)$, X_t is not a semimartingale. In this case, for $\hat{\kappa}_{LS}$ and $\hat{\mu}_{LS}$ to consistently estimate κ and μ, the stochastic integral $\int_0^T X_t dX_t$ should be interpreted carefully. In fact, we interpret $\int_0^T X_t dX_t$ differently when the sign of κ is different. If $\kappa > 0$, we interpret it as an Itô–Skorohod integral; if $\kappa < 0$, we use a Young integral; and if $\kappa = 0$, we can interpret it as either an Itô–Skorohod integral or a Young integral. In the case of a Lévy process–driven or a Brownian motion-driven Vasicek model, from Wang and Yu (2016), we know that the asymptotic theory for κ depends on the sign of κ.

In the case of the fVm, here, we review the idea that the asymptotic theory for κ continues to depend on the sign of κ. The asymptotic distributions of $\hat{\kappa}_{LS}$ are different across these three cases. From Xiao and Yu (2019a,b), we can obtain the following asymptotic distributions of $\hat{\kappa}_{LS}$ and $\hat{\mu}_{LS}$, which are provided in Table 7.3. Here, $\overline{B}_u^H = B_u^H - \int_0^1 B_t^H dt$, $\delta_{LS}^2 = (4H-1) + \frac{2\Gamma(2-4H)\Gamma(4H)}{\Gamma(2H)\Gamma(1-2H)}$, $C_H = (4H-1)\left(1 + \frac{\Gamma(3-4H)\Gamma(4H-1)}{\Gamma(2H)\Gamma(2-2H)}\right)$, ν and ω are two independent standard normal variables, and $R(H)$ is the Rosenblatt random variable whose characteristic function is expressed as

$$c(s) = \exp\left(\frac{1}{2}\sum_{k=2}^{\infty}\left(2\sqrt{-1}s\sigma(H)\right)^k \frac{a_k}{k}\right), \tag{7.39}$$

with $\sigma(H) = \sqrt{H(H-\frac{1}{2})}$ and

$$a_k = \int_0^1 \cdots \int_0^1 |x_1 - x_2|^{H-1} \cdots |x_{k-1} - x_k|^{H-1} |x_k - x_1|^{H-1} dx_1 \cdots dx_k.$$

From Table 7.3, we can see that the LSEs of μ and κ are strongly consistent regardless of the sign of the persistence coefficient κ. Moreover, the asymptotic distribution of the LSE of κ critically depends on the sign of κ, while the asymptotic distribution of the LSE of μ is asymptotically normal regardless of the sign of κ. In particular, when $\kappa > 0$ and $H \in (0, 3/4)$, we can see that

Table 7.3 *The asymptotic laws of $\hat{\kappa}_T$ and $\hat{\mu}_T$ for different ranges of H and κ.*

	$\kappa > 0$	$\kappa = 0$	$\kappa < 0$
$0 < H < \frac{1}{2}$	$\sqrt{T}\left(\hat{\kappa}_{LS} - \kappa\right) \Rightarrow \mathcal{N}\left(0, \kappa\delta_{LS}^2\right)$	$T\hat{\kappa}_{LS} \stackrel{d}{=} -\frac{\int_0^1 \overline{B}_u^H dB_u^H}{\int_0^1 \left(\overline{B}_u^H\right)^2 du}$	$\frac{e^{-\kappa T}}{2\kappa}\left(\hat{\kappa}_{LS} - \kappa\right) \Rightarrow \frac{\sigma \frac{\sqrt{H\Gamma(2H)}}{\lvert\kappa\rvert^H} \nu}{X_0 - \mu + \sigma \frac{\sqrt{H\Gamma(2H)}}{\lvert\kappa\rvert^H} \omega}$
	$T^{1-H}\left(\hat{\mu}_{LS} - \mu\right) \Rightarrow \mathcal{N}\left(0, \frac{\sigma^2}{\kappa^2}\right)$	——	$T^{1-H}\left(\hat{\mu}_{LS} - \mu\right) \Rightarrow \mathcal{N}\left(0, \frac{\sigma^2}{\kappa^2}\right)$
$\frac{1}{2} \le H < 3/4$	$\sqrt{T}\left(\hat{\kappa}_{LS} - \kappa\right) \Rightarrow \mathcal{N}\left(0, \kappa C_H\right)$	$T\hat{\kappa}_{LS} \stackrel{d}{=} -\frac{\int_0^1 \overline{B}_u^H dB_u^H}{\int_0^1 \left(\overline{B}_u^H\right)^2 du}$	$\frac{e^{-\kappa T}}{2\kappa}\left(\hat{\kappa}_{LS} - \kappa\right) \Rightarrow \frac{\sigma \frac{\sqrt{H\Gamma(2H)}}{\lvert\kappa\rvert^H} \nu}{X_0 - \mu + \sigma \frac{\sqrt{H\Gamma(2H)}}{\lvert\kappa\rvert^H} \omega}$
	$T^{1-H}\left(\hat{\mu}_{LS} - \mu\right) \Rightarrow \mathcal{N}\left(0, \frac{\sigma^2}{\kappa^2}\right)$	——	$T^{1-H}\left(\hat{\mu}_{LS} - \mu\right) \Rightarrow \mathcal{N}\left(0, \frac{\sigma^2}{\kappa^2}\right)$
$H = 3/4$	$\frac{\sqrt{T}}{\sqrt{\log(T)}}\left(\hat{\kappa}_{LS} - \kappa\right) \Rightarrow \mathcal{N}\left(0, \frac{4\kappa}{\pi}\right)$	$T\hat{\kappa}_{LS} \stackrel{d}{=} -\frac{\int_0^1 \overline{B}_u^H dB_u^H}{\int_0^1 \left(\overline{B}_u^H\right)^2 du}$	$\frac{e^{-\kappa T}}{2\kappa}\left(\hat{\kappa}_{LS} - \kappa\right) \Rightarrow \frac{\sigma \frac{\sqrt{H\Gamma(2H)}}{\lvert\kappa\rvert^H} \nu}{X_0 - \mu + \sigma \frac{\sqrt{H\Gamma(2H)}}{\lvert\kappa\rvert^H} \omega}$
	$T^{1-H}\left(\hat{\mu}_{LS} - \mu\right) \Rightarrow \mathcal{N}\left(0, \frac{\sigma^2}{\kappa^2}\right)$	——	$T^{1-H}\left(\hat{\mu}_{LS} - \mu\right) \Rightarrow \mathcal{N}\left(0, \frac{\sigma^2}{\kappa^2}\right)$
$3/4 < H < 1$	$T^{2-2H}\left(\hat{\kappa}_{LS} - \kappa\right) \Rightarrow \frac{-\kappa^{2H-1}}{H\Gamma(2H)} R(H)$	$T\hat{\kappa}_{LS} \stackrel{d}{=} -\frac{\int_0^1 \overline{B}_u^H dB_u^H}{\int_0^1 \left(\overline{B}_u^H\right)^2 du}$	$\frac{e^{-\kappa T}}{2\kappa}\left(\hat{\kappa}_{LS} - \kappa\right) \stackrel{d}{\to} \frac{\sigma \frac{\sqrt{H\Gamma(2H)}}{\lvert\kappa\rvert^H} \nu}{X_0 - \mu + \sigma \frac{\sqrt{H\Gamma(2H)}}{\lvert\kappa\rvert^H} \omega}$
	$T^{1-H}\left(\hat{\mu}_{LS} - \mu\right) \Rightarrow \mathcal{N}\left(0, \frac{\sigma^2}{\kappa^2}\right)$	——	$T^{1-H}\left(\hat{\mu}_{LS} - \mu\right) \Rightarrow \mathcal{N}\left(0, \frac{\sigma^2}{\kappa^2}\right)$

the asymptotic distribution of the LSE of κ is a normal distribution with a rate of convergence of $\sqrt{T}$. When $\kappa > 0$ and $H = 3/4$, the asymptotic distribution of the LSE of κ is also a normal distribution with a rate of convergence of $\sqrt{T/\log(T)}$. However, a noncentral limit theorem for the LSE of κ is obtained for $H \in (3/4, 1)$. In this situation, the asymptotic law as a Rosenblatt random variable is obtained. When $\kappa < 0$, we can see that the limiting distribution is a Cauchy type with a rate of convergence of $e^{-\kappa T}$. If μ equals the initial condition, the limiting distribution becomes the standard Cauchy distribution. When $\kappa = 0$, the asymptotic distribution is a Dickey–Fuller–Phillips type of distribution with the convergence rate T, which is neither normal nor a mixture of normal.

7.4.3 MME

In this subsection, we consider an alternative estimation technique by exploiting the ergodic property of the fVm when $\kappa > 0$. Borrowing the idea from Xiao and Yu (2019a,b), the asymptotic properties of the MME are compared.

Using the initial condition of (7.8), we can show that X_t in Model (7.12) is covariance stationary with

$$\lim_{t\to\infty} \mathbb{E}(X_t) = \mu \quad \text{and} \quad \lim_{t\to\infty} Var(X_t) = \sigma^2\kappa^{-2H} H\Gamma(2H)\,. \tag{7.40}$$

Moreover, X_t can be identically represented as

$$X_t = \mu + \sigma \int_{-\infty}^{t} e^{-\kappa(t-s)} d\widetilde{B}_s^H\,. \tag{7.41}$$

If $\kappa > 0$, under a general initial condition $X_0 = O_p(1)$, X_t is asymptotically covariance stationary. In this situation, motivated by Hu and Nualart (2010), we can consider alternative estimators of κ and μ (denoted by $\hat{\kappa}_{HN}$ and $\hat{\mu}_{HN}$, respectively). The strong solution for the fVm in Model (7.12) is expressed as

$$X_t = \mu + (X_0 - \mu)\exp(-\kappa t) + \sigma \int_{-\infty}^{t} e^{-\kappa(t-s)} dB_s^H\,. \tag{7.42}$$

Moreover, when $\kappa > 0$, we can easily obtain

$$\frac{1}{T}\int_0^T X_t dt \to_{a.s.} \mu\,, \tag{7.43}$$

$$\frac{1}{T}\int_0^T X_t^2 dt \to_{a.s.} \sigma^2\kappa^{-2H} H\Gamma(2H) + \mu^2\,. \tag{7.44}$$

According to the ergodic theorem and using Equations (7.43) and (7.44), the MME of μ and $\kappa > 0$ was introduced by Xiao and Yu (2019a,b):

$$\hat{\mu}_{HN} = \frac{1}{T}\int_0^T X_t dt\,. \tag{7.45}$$

$$\hat{\kappa}_{HN} = \left(\frac{T \int_0^T X_t^2 dt - \left(\int_0^T X_t dt \right)^2}{T^2 \sigma^2 H \Gamma(2H)} \right)^{-\frac{1}{2H}}. \tag{7.46}$$

Compared with the LSE in Equations (7.37) and (7.38), which involve the stochastic integral $\int_0^T X_t dX_t$, the MME $\hat{\mu}_{HN}$ and $\hat{\kappa}_{HN}$ in Equations (7.45) and (7.46) do not contain any stochastic integrals with respect to the fBm but only involve quadratic integral functionals. Therefore, they are conceptually easier to understand and numerically easier to compute than the LSE and MLE.

From Xiao and Yu (2019a,b), we can obtain the consistency of $\hat{\kappa}_{HN}$ and $\hat{\mu}_{HN}$, which is shown by the following theorem:

Theorem 7.4.1 *Let $H \in (0,1)$, $X_0/\sqrt{T} = o_{a.s.}(1)$ and $\kappa > 0$ in Model (7.12). Then, we have $\hat{\kappa}_{HN} \to_{a.s.} \kappa$ and $\hat{\mu}_{HN} \to_{a.s.} \mu$.*

Using the asymptotic distributions of $\hat{\kappa}_{LS}$ and $\hat{\mu}_{LS}$, the asymptotic distributions of $\hat{\kappa}_{HN}$ and $\hat{\mu}_{HN}$ can be developed as follows:

Theorem 7.4.2 *Let $X_0/\sqrt{T} = o_p(1)$ and $\kappa > 0$ in (7.12). Then, we have*

$$T^{1-H}\left(\hat{\mu}_{HN} - \mu\right) \Rightarrow \mathcal{N}\left(0, \frac{\sigma^2}{\kappa^2}\right). \tag{7.47}$$

Moreover, let $X_0/\sqrt{T} = o_p(1)$ and $\kappa > 0$ in Model (7.12). Then, the following convergence results hold true:

(i) For $H \in (0, 3/4)$, we have

$$\sqrt{T}\left(\hat{\kappa}_{HN} - \kappa\right) \Rightarrow \mathcal{N}\left(0, \kappa \rho_H\right), \tag{7.48}$$

where $\rho_H = \frac{4H-1}{4H^2}\left(1 + \frac{\Gamma(3-4H)\Gamma(4H-1)}{\Gamma(2H)\Gamma(2-2H)}\right) = \frac{C_H}{4H^2}$.

(ii) For $H = 3/4$, we have

$$\frac{\sqrt{T}}{\sqrt{\log(T)}}\left(\hat{\kappa}_{HN} - \kappa\right) \Rightarrow \mathcal{N}\left(0, \frac{16\kappa}{9\pi}\right). \tag{7.49}$$

(iii) For $H \in (3/4, 1)$, we have

$$T^{2-2H}\left(\hat{\kappa}_{HN} - \kappa\right) \Rightarrow \frac{-\kappa^{2H-1}}{H\Gamma(2H+1)} R(H), \tag{7.50}$$

where $R(H)$ is the Rosenblatt random variable defined in (7.39).

7.5 Estimation Method Based on Discrete-Time Observations

In the previous section, the estimators $\tilde{\alpha}_T$, $\tilde{\kappa}_T$, $\hat{\kappa}_{LS}$, $\hat{\mu}_{LS}$, $\hat{\mu}_{HN}$, and $\hat{\kappa}_{HN}$ were developed based on continuous-time observations. In practice, observations of X_t are available only at discrete-time points, for example, at $n(:= T/\Delta)$ equally spaced points $\{i\Delta\}_{i=0}^{n}$ over time interval $[0, T]$ where Δ is the sampling interval and T denotes the time span. When X_t is annualized and observed daily (weekly or monthly), then $\Delta = 1/252$ ($1/52$ or $1/12$). We now consider Model (7.12), where $\kappa \in \mathbb{R}^+$, $\sigma \in \mathbb{R}^+$, $\mu \in \mathbb{R}$, and $H \in (0, 1)$ are constants. Let $\{X_{i\Delta}\}_{i=0}^{n}$ denote the discrete-time observations of X_t. From Equation (7.42), the exact discrete-time model of $\{X_{i\Delta}\}_{i=0}^{n}$ is obtained as

$$X_{i\Delta} = e^{-\kappa\Delta} X_{(i-1)\Delta} + \left(1 - e^{-\kappa\Delta}\right)\mu + \varepsilon_{i\Delta}\,, \tag{7.51}$$

where $\varepsilon_{i\Delta} = \sigma \int_{(i-1)\Delta}^{i\Delta} e^{-\kappa(i\Delta - s)} dB_s^H$.

We now review the two-stage approach of Wang et al. (2023) for estimating all of the unknown parameters in Model (7.12) based on discrete-time observations of X_t. In the first stage, following Lang and Roueff (2001) and Barndorff-Nielsen et al. (2013), we estimate H using the ratio of the squared summations of the second-order differences of X_t at different frequencies. In the second stage, we estimate the other parameters in Model (7.12) based on method of moments where the true parameter Closed-form expressions can be established for all the proposed estimators using this two-stage method. We next review a large sample theory for the proposed estimators. In particular, we review two asymptotic frameworks: (i) the fixed-domain asymptotic framework under which the sampling interval Δ goes to zero with a fixed time span T and (ii) increasing-domain asymptotic framework in which $\Delta \to 0$ and $T \to \infty$ simultaneously. Under both frameworks, both $\widehat{H}$ and $\widehat{\sigma}$ are consistent and asymptotically normal for all $H \in (0, 1)$ under some mild regularity conditions. Furthermore, the asymptotic variance of $\widehat{H}$, which depends only on the value of H, is proposed in a closed-form expression. Under the double (or increasing-domain asymptotic) scheme, we proposed the consistency and the asymptotic distributions of $\widehat{\kappa}$ and $\widehat{\mu}$. The convergence rate of $\widehat{\mu}$ depend crucially on H. Both the asymptotic distribution and the convergence rate of $\widehat{\kappa}$ depend crucially on H.

7.5.1 The Two-Stage Approach

To estimate the parameters in Model (7.12) with discrete-time data, it is difficult to use the MLE to estimate the four unknown parameters simultaneously because the errors $\{\varepsilon_{t\Delta}\}$ in Equation (7.51) have a complicated dependent structure when $H \neq \frac{1}{2}$. Following Phillips and Yu (2009), we review the two-stage estimation approach introduced by Wang et al. (2023).

In the first stage, following Lang and Roueff (2001) and Barndorff-Nielsen et al. (2013), Wang et al. (2023) estimated the Hurst parameter H by using the change-of-frequency (COF) estimator based on the second-order differences of X_t.

$$\widehat{H} = \frac{1}{2}\log_2\left(\frac{\sum_{i=1}^{n-4}\left(X_{(i+4)\Delta} - 2X_{(i+2)\Delta} + X_{i\Delta}\right)^2}{\sum_{i=1}^{n-2}\left(X_{(i+2)\Delta} - 2X_{(i+1)\Delta} + X_{i\Delta}\right)^2}\right), \tag{7.52}$$

where $\log_2(\cdot)$ is the base-2 logarithm, $\left\{X_{(i+4)\Delta} - 2X_{(i+2)\Delta} + X_{i\Delta}\right\}_{i=1}^{n-4}$, and $\left\{X_{(i+2)\Delta} - 2X_{(i+1)\Delta} + X_{i\Delta}\right\}_{i=1}^{n-2}$ are second-order differences of $\{X_{i\Delta}\}_{i=1}^{n}$ taken at two different frequencies.

In the second stage, Wang et al. (2023) proposed using the following method-of-moments estimators to estimate the other parameters (i.e., σ, μ, and κ):

$$\widehat{\sigma} = \sqrt{\frac{\sum_{i=1}^{n-2}\left(X_{(i+2)\Delta} - 2X_{(i+1)\Delta} + X_{i\Delta}\right)^2}{n\left(4 - 2^{2\widehat{H}}\right)\Delta^{2\widehat{H}}}}, \tag{7.53}$$

$$\widehat{\mu} = \frac{1}{n}\sum_{i=1}^{n} X_{i\Delta}, \tag{7.54}$$

$$\widehat{\kappa} = \left(\frac{n\sum_{i=1}^{n} X_{i\Delta}^2 - \left(\sum_{i=1}^{n} X_{i\Delta}\right)^2}{n^2\widehat{\sigma}^2\widehat{H}\Gamma\left(2\widehat{H}\right)}\right)^{-1/(2\widehat{H})}. \tag{7.55}$$

Note that $\widehat{\sigma}$ is a function of $\widehat{H}$, which is obtained in the first stage, and $\widehat{\kappa}$ is a function of both $\widehat{\sigma}$ and $\widehat{H}$.

The estimators $\widehat{\mu}$ and $\widehat{\kappa}$ can be regarded as the discrete-time versions of the ergodic-type estimators of κ and μ of Xiao and Yu (2019a,b). However, since Xiao and Yu (2019a,b) assumed that σ^2 and H are known and a continuous record of $\{X_t\}$ is observed, we have to modify their estimators by (i) replacing σ and H with $\widehat{\sigma}$ and $\widehat{H}$ and (ii) replacing the Riemann integrals with the summations. When discrete-time observations of $\{X_t\}$ are available, the MLE, MCE, LSE, and MME have previously been studied by Tudor and Viens (2007), Ludeña (2004), Hu et al. (2019), respectively. A critical difference from these studies is that the estimator reviewed in this section does not assume H is known when estimating κ. The asymptotic distribution of the LSE of κ has been derived in the O-U model (H is assumed to be $\frac{1}{2}$). For example, assuming $\kappa > 0$, both the long-span and double asymptotic distributions of the MLE of κ are discussed by Tang and Chen (2009). Assuming $\kappa < 0$, the double asymptotic distribution of the LSE of κ is investigated by Wang and Yu (2016). We review the asymptotics of κ from the standard O-U model to the fVm.

7.5.2 Asymptotic Theory

In this subsection, we first review the consistency of $\widehat{H}$ and $\widehat{\sigma}$ when $T\Delta \to 0$ and $n = T/\Delta \to \infty$, which is satisfied under either (i) the infill asymptotic scheme where $\Delta \to 0$ with a fixed T or (ii) the double asymptotic scheme where $\Delta \to 0$ and $T \to \infty$ simultaneously while T diverges at a lower rate than that of $1/\Delta$.[6] Then, we review the results from Wang et al. (2023). Thus, $T \to \infty$ is a necessary condition for the consistency of $\widehat{\mu}$ and $\widehat{\kappa}$ as proposed in Equations (7.54) and (7.55). We also review the double asymptotic theory from $\widehat{\mu}$ and $\widehat{\kappa}$ using the results from Wang et al. (2023).

Theorem 7.5.1 *Let $\widehat{H}$ and $\widehat{\sigma}$ denote the MME defined in Equations (7.52) and (7.53) for Model (7.12). Then, if $T\Delta \to 0$ and $n = T/\Delta \to \infty$, for all $H \in (0, 1)$, we have*
(a) $\widehat{H} \to_p H$, and

$$\sqrt{n}\left(\widehat{H} - H\right) \Rightarrow \mathcal{N}\left(0, \frac{\Sigma_{11} + \Sigma_{22} - 2\Sigma_{12}}{(2\log 2)^2}\right); \tag{7.56}$$

(b) $\widehat{\sigma} \to_p \sigma$, and

$$\frac{\sqrt{n}}{\log(\Delta)}\left(\widehat{\sigma} - \sigma\right) \Rightarrow \mathcal{N}\left(0, \frac{\Sigma_{11} + \Sigma_{22} - 2\Sigma_{12}}{(2\log 2)^2}\sigma^2\right), \tag{7.57}$$

where

$$\Sigma_{11} = 2 + 2^{2-4H}\sum_{j=1}^{\infty}\left(\rho_{j+2} + 4\rho_{j+1} + 6\rho_j + 4\rho_{|j-1|} + \rho_{|j-2|}\right)^2, \tag{7.58}$$

$$\Sigma_{12} = 2^{1-2H}\left(4(\rho_1 + 1)^2 + 2\sum_{j=0}^{\infty}\left(\rho_{j+2} + 2\rho_{j+1} + \rho_j\right)^2\right), \tag{7.59}$$

$$\Sigma_{22} = 2 + 4\sum_{j=1}^{\infty}\rho_j^2, \tag{7.60}$$

[6] The consistency of $\widehat{H}$ requires $\Delta \to 0$ only. That is to say, even when T diverges faster than $1/\Delta$, violating the condition $T\Delta \to 0$, $\widehat{H}$ is still consistent as long as $\Delta \to 0$.

with

$$\rho_j = \frac{-\left|j+2\right|^{2H} + 4\left|j+1\right|^{2H} - 6\left|j\right|^{2H} + 4\left|j-1\right|^{2H} - \left|j-2\right|^{2H}}{2\left(4-2^{2H}\right)}. \tag{7.61}$$

Remark 7.5.2 *The asymptotics of $\widehat{H}$ and $\widehat{\sigma}$ hold for all $H \in (0, 1)$. It is clear that the asymptotics of $\widehat{H}$ and $\widehat{\sigma}$ can apply to all values of κ, including $\kappa < 0$, $\kappa = 0$ and $\kappa > 0$.*

Remark 7.5.3 *Let us observe that the asymptotic variance of $\widehat{H}$ only depends on H, while the asymptotic variance of $\widehat{\sigma}$ depends on both H and σ. Neither depends on κ and μ. This feature plays an important role in statistical inference about H and σ because, when T is fixed, we can obtain consistent estimators for both H and σ, while we cannot estimate κ and μ consistently. If we use an alternative estimator for H, which has a rate of convergence $\sqrt{n}$, then we can see that $\sqrt{n}\left(\widehat{H}-H\right)$ and $\sqrt{n}\left(\widehat{\sigma}-\sigma\right)/\left(\sigma\log\left(\Delta\right)\right)$ should share the same limiting distribution.*

It is worth mentioning that, for all $H \in (0, 1)$ and all κ, including $\kappa > 0$, $\kappa = 0$, and $\kappa < 0$, the asymptotics of $\widehat{H}$ and $\widehat{\sigma}$ always hold. When $H = \frac{1}{2}$, Model (7.12) becomes the standard O-U model and enjoys the Markov property, whereas Model (7.12) does not have the Markov property once $H \neq \frac{1}{2}$. To test the hypothesis $H = \frac{1}{2}$, the following Corollary 7.5.4 provides the asymptotic variance of $\sqrt{n}\left(\widehat{H}-\frac{1}{2}\right)$. By substituting $H = \frac{1}{2}$ into the formulae provided in Theorem 7.5.1, we obtain that $\rho_0 = 1$, $\rho_1 = -1/2$, $\rho_j = 0$ for $j \geq 2$, $\Sigma_{11} = 7/2$, $\Sigma_{12} = 3/2$, and $\Sigma_{22} = 3$. Consequently, we can obtain Corollary 7.5.4 directly.

Corollary 7.5.4 *Let $H = \frac{1}{2}$, $T\Delta \to 0$, and $n = T/\Delta \to \infty$. Then, we obtain*

$$\sqrt{n}\left(\widehat{H}-\frac{1}{2}\right) \Rightarrow \mathcal{N}\left(0, \frac{7}{8\left(\log 2\right)^2}\right).$$

The asymptotic theory of $\widehat{\mu}$ and $\widehat{\kappa}$ defined in Equations (7.54) and (7.55) can be obtained under the double asymptotic scheme where $T \to \infty$ and $\Delta \to 0$. Under the condition of $\kappa > 0$, Wang et al. (2023) proposed a condition that governs the relative divergence/convergence rates of T and Δ.

Theorem 7.5.5 *Let $\widehat{\mu}$ be the estimator of μ defined in Equation (7.54). Then, when $T \to \infty$ and $\Delta \to 0$, we can obtain $\widehat{\mu} \to_p \mu$ for all $H \in (0, 1)$. Moreover, if $T^{1-H}\Delta^H \to 0$, then we have*

$$T^{1-H}\left(\widehat{\mu}-\mu\right) \Rightarrow \mathcal{N}\left(0, \sigma^2/\kappa^2\right). \tag{7.62}$$

Theorem 7.5.6 *Let $\widehat{\kappa}$ be the estimator of κ defined in Equation (7.55). Then, when $T \to \infty$ and $\Delta \to 0$, we have $\widehat{\kappa} \to_p \kappa$. Moreover, (a) for $H \in (0, 3/4)$ and $\sqrt{T}\Delta^H \to 0$, then*

$$\sqrt{T}(\widehat{\kappa} - \kappa) \Rightarrow (0, \kappa\phi_H), \tag{7.63}$$

with

$$\phi_H = \begin{cases} \frac{1}{4H^2}\left[(4H-1) + \frac{2\Gamma(2-4H)\Gamma(4H)}{\Gamma(2H)\Gamma(1-2H)}\right] & \text{if } H \in (0, \frac{1}{2}) \\ \frac{4H-1}{4H^2}\left[1 + \frac{\Gamma(3-4H)\Gamma(4H-1)}{\Gamma(2-2H)\Gamma(2H)}\right] & \text{if } H \in [\frac{1}{2}, \frac{3}{4}) \end{cases};$$

(b) for $H = 3/4$ and $\sqrt{T}\Delta^H / \log(T) \to 0$, then

$$\frac{\sqrt{T}}{\log(T)}(\widehat{\kappa} - \kappa) \Rightarrow \mathcal{N}\left(0, \frac{16\kappa}{9\pi}\right);$$

(c) for $H \in (3/4, 1)$ and $T^{2-2H}\Delta^H \to 0$, then

$$T^{2-2H}(\widehat{\kappa} - \kappa) \Rightarrow \frac{-\kappa^{2H-1}}{H\Gamma(2H+1)}R(H),$$

where $R(H)$ is the Rosenblatt random variable defined by (7.39).

Let us observe that the double asymptotic distribution of the MLE of κ is known to be $\mathcal{N}(0, 2\kappa)$ if $H = \frac{1}{2}$ (see, for example, Tang and Chen (2009)). Obviously, $\phi_H = 2$ when $H = \frac{1}{2}$. Therefore, the MME $\widehat{\kappa}$ has the same limiting distribution as the MLE for $H = \frac{1}{2}$, and $\widehat{\kappa}$ is asymptotically efficient when $H = \frac{1}{2}$.

7.6 Conclusions

Stochastic models have played an important role in the development of financial markets. The first mathematical model in finance was introduced by Bachelier (1900), who used the normal distribution to describe the behavior of asset prices. An obvious deficiency in Bachelier's model (Bachelier (1900)) is that stock prices can be negative at any time $t \in [0, T]$. To overcome this obstacle, Osborne (1959) introduced the geometric Brownian motion to describe stock prices. In parallel, Itô (1951) developed the stochastic integral method with respect to Brownian motion and a stochastic differential equation driven by Brownian motion. In 1973, Black and Scholes (1973) and Merton (1973) proposed the celebrated Black–Scholes option pricing formula in two separate papers, which were awarded the Nobel Prize for Economics in 1997. To date, previous work has addressed pricing equity options, but little attention has been paid to interest rates. Vasicek (1977) developed a framework for pricing interest rate options. This model was the first to use geometric Brownian motion for short-term interest rates. Similar to the well-known Black–Scholes model, the bond pricing equation was postulated as a parabolic partial differential equation in Vasicek (1977). Moreover, the risk-neutral pricing formula, which is an essential tool of stochastic calculus, was introduced by Harrison and Pliska (1981) using the martingale theory.

From an empirical point of view, a basic requirement for any good model is its ability to capture the main features in the observed data. However, the assumptions of the independence of asset returns and the constant volatility in the Black–Scholes model are clearly contrary to the empirical data, which reveal that there exists a strong dependence of asset returns and implied volatility driven by financial derivatives.

First, to consider the dependence of asset returns, the fBm, which allows for dependent increments and memory property, was introduced into finance. In fact, Delbaen and Schachermayer (1994) showed that no-arbitrage pricing is only possible in semimartingale stochastic processes. Therefore, the basic ideas of mathematical finance in Delbaen and Schachermayer (1994) already imply that the fBm allows a certain kind of arbitrage since the fBm is not a semimartingale.

Second, to exclude the constant volatility assumption, some stochastic volatility models driven by Brownian motion that allow the volatility parameter to vary in a random fashion are provided in finance (e.g., Gatheral (2006)). These stochastic volatility models are useful since they can describe empirical observations, namely, options with different strike prices and expirations have different values of implied volatility. However, the main drawback of stochastic volatility models driven by Brownian motion is that they fail to produce decent results for short maturities. To perform well, some fractional stochastic volatility models with the long-memory property were proposed by Comte and Renault (1998). Gatheral et al. (2018) showed that the log RV is rough and behaves as an fBm where H has a value of around 0.1 at any reasonable time scale. This observation motivated them to examine the performance of the fVm for modeling the RV relative to other models. In fact, the fVm has been the subject of active research for the last two decades because this model seems to be one of the most suitable tools for capturing the phenomenon of long-range dependence (e.g., Comte and Renault (1998); Aït-Sahalia and Mancini (2008)) or the roughness of the volatility (e.g., Bayer et al. (2016); Gatheral et al. (2018)) in financial asset volatility. The development of the application for the fVm naturally led to its statistical inference. Consequently, estimating the unknown parameters in the fVm has been the subject of active research for the last decade and is a challenging theoretical problem.

This chapter considers the development and the application of the fBm in finance. First, we discussed the advantages and disadvantages of using the fBm to describe the fluctuations in financial asset returns. Then, we considered the application of the fVm in stochastic volatility models and discussed the free arbitrage property of stochastic volatility models driven by the fBm. Furthermore, we discussed the problem of estimating unknown parameters in the fVm based on both continuous-time observations and discrete-time observations. Our study considered three well-known methods for estimating the drift parameters in the fVm from a continuous record of observations, including the MLE, LSE, and MME. Our study also contributes to the literature by developing an estimation method for all parameters in the fVm based on discrete-time observations for all ranges of the Hurst parameter. The application and statistic inference of the fVm with jumps are important directions for future research.

7.7 Appendix

7.7.1 Proof of Proposition 7.2.1

Proof From Definition 7.2.1, we can see that the fBm is centered. Moreover, using Model (7.1), we can easily obtain $\operatorname{Var}(B_t^H) = \mathbb{E}\left((B_t^H)^2\right) = t^{2H}$.

For any $c > 0$ and $s, t \geq 0$, the process B_{ct}^H is a centered Gaussian process with covariance

$$\begin{aligned}\mathbb{E}\left(B_{cs}^H B_{ct}^H\right) &= \frac{1}{2}\left[|ct|^{2H} + |cs|^{2H} - c^{2H}|t-s|^{2H}\right] \\ &= c^{2H}\mathbb{E}\left(B_t^H B_s^H\right) \\ &= \mathbb{E}\left[\left(c^H B_t^H\right)\left(c^H B_s^H\right)\right]. \qquad (7.64)\end{aligned}$$

Since all processes are centered and Gaussian, Equation (7.64) implies that $(B_{ct}^H) \overset{d}{=} (|c|^H B_t^H)$. Then, we show that the fBm has stationary increments. Note that for $h > 0$, we have

$$\begin{aligned}&\mathbb{E}\left[\left(B_{t+h}^H - B_h^H\right)\left(B_{s+h}^H - B_h^H\right)\right] \\ &= \mathbb{E}\left[\left(B_{t+h}^H B_{s+h}^H\right)\right] - \mathbb{E}\left[\left(B_{t+h}^H B_h^H\right)\right] - \mathbb{E}\left[\left(B_{s+h}^H B_h^H\right)\right] + \mathbb{E}\left[\left(B_h^H\right)^2\right] \\ &= \frac{1}{2}\Big[\left((t+h)^{2H} + (s+h)^{2H} - |t-s|^{2H}\right) - \left((t+h)^{2H} + h^{2H} - t^{2H}\right) \\ &\quad - \left((s+h)^{2H} + h^{2H} - s^{2H}\right) + 2h^{2H}\Big] \\ &= \frac{1}{2}\left[t^{2H} + s^{2H} - |t-s|^{2H}\right] \\ &= \mathbb{E}\left(B_t^H B_s^H\right),\end{aligned}$$

which implies $(B_{t+h}^H - B_h^H) \overset{d}{=} B_t^H$.

For $s, t \geq 0$, we have

$$\begin{aligned}\mathbb{E}\left|B_t^H - B_s^H\right|^2 &= \mathbb{E}\left|B_t^H\right|^2 - 2\mathbb{E}\left[B_t^H B_s^H\right] + \mathbb{E}\left|B_s^H\right|^2 \\ &= t^{2H} - 2R_H(t,s) + s^{2H} \\ &= |t-s|^{2H}.\end{aligned}$$

Since for any $s \leq t$, the random variable $B_t^H - B_s^H$ is a normal distribution with zero mean and $|t-s|^H$ variance, we obtain that, for any $p \geq 1$,

$$\mathbb{E}\left|B_t^H - B_s^H\right|^p = \mathbf{E}|Z|^p |t-s|^{Hp}. \tag{7.65}$$

The Hölder continuity follows from Equation (7.65) and the Kolmogorov continuity theorem.

We can see that if $H \neq \frac{1}{2}$, B_H does not satisfy the condition of $R_H(s,u)R_H(t,t) = R_H(s,t)R_H(t,u)$.

Indeed, the covariance of its increments, also known as fGn, is given by

$$\begin{aligned}\rho_H(n) &= \mathbb{E}\left(\left(B_i^H - B_{i-1}^H\right)\left(B_{i+n}^H - B_{i-1+n}^H\right)\right) \\ &= \frac{1}{2}\left((n+1)^{2H} + (n-1)^{2H} - 2n^{2H}\right) \\ &\sim H(2H-1)n^{2H-2} \quad \text{as } n \to \infty.\end{aligned} \tag{7.66}$$

From Equation (7.66), we have $\rho_H(n) = 0$ for $H = \frac{1}{2}$, suggesting that B_t^H becomes a standard Brownian motion with independent increments and is therefore uncorrelated. When $H \in \left(\frac{1}{2}, 1\right)$, it can be seen that $\rho_H(n) > 0$, which means that the increments of B_t^H are positively correlated to each other, making $\sum_{n=1}^{\infty} \rho_H(n) = \infty$ as $n \to \infty$. However, when $H \in \left(0, \frac{1}{2}\right)$, the increments of B_t^H are negatively correlated to each other and have the short-range dependence property, namely, $\sum_{n=1}^{\infty} \rho_H(n) < \infty$.

Set $Y_n := (2^n)^{pH-1} \sum_{k=1}^{2^n} \left|B_{t_k}^H - B_{t_{k-1}}^H\right|^p$. By self-similarity, we have

$$Y_n \sim (2^n)^{pH-1} \sum_{k=1}^{2^n} |t_k - t_{k-1}|^{pH} \left|B_k^H - B_{k-1}^H\right|^p = 2^{-n} \sum_{k=1}^{2^n} \left|B_k^H - B_{k-1}^H\right|^p.$$

The sequence of one-step increments of $B_k^H - B_{k-1}^H$ is a stationary, centered Gaussian with covariance function $\rho_H(n)$, which tends to zero. Therefore, the fGn is ergodic. According to Birkhof's Ergodic Theorem,[7]

[7] Birkhof's Ergodic Theorem: Let $\{\xi_n\}$ be a stationary (strict sense), ergodic random sequence with $\mathbb{E}|\xi_1| < \infty$. Then, $\lim_{n\to\infty} \frac{1}{n} \sum_{k=1}^{n} \xi_k(\omega) = \mathbb{E}(\xi_1)$ almost surely and in L^1.

$$2^{-n}\sum_{k=1}^{2^n}\left|B_k^H - B_{k-1}^H\right|^p \to \mathbb{E}\left|B_1^H\right|^p \to_{a.s} C.$$

Therefore, $Y_n \to_p C$. Because $\left|B_{t_k}^H - B_{t_{k-1}}^H\right|^p = \left(2^{-n}\right)^{pH-1} Y_n$, we obtain Equation (7.2).

From Equation (7.2), we can see that the index of the p-variation of the fBm is $\frac{1}{H}$. However, for a semimartingale, the index must be either in [0, 1] or equal to 2, namely, $\frac{1}{H} \in [0,1] \cup \{2\}$. Since $H \in (0,1), H^{-1} \notin [0,1]$, the fBm is a semimartingale only for $H = \frac{1}{2}$.

Using the self-similarity property, we have

$$\frac{B_t^H - B_{t_0}^H}{t - t_0} \stackrel{d}{=} (t - t_0)^{H-1} B_1^H.$$

Let us consider the event $A(t) = \left\{\sup_{t_0 \le s \le t}\left|\frac{B_s^H - B_{t_0}^H}{s - t_0}\right| > d\right\}$. Then, for any sequence t_n decreasing to t_0, we have $A(t_n) \supset A(t_{n+1})$ and $A(t_n) \supset \left\{\left|\frac{B_{t_n}^H - B_{t_0}^H}{t_n - t_0}\right| > d\right\}$. Thus, we have

$$\mathbb{P}\left(\left\{\left|\frac{B_{t_n}^H - B_{t_0}^H}{t_n - t_0}\right| > d\right\}\right) = \mathbb{P}\left(\left\{\left|B_1^H\right| > (t_n - t_0)^{1-H} d\right\}\right) \to 1, \text{ as } n \to \infty.$$

Note that there is a stronger form since here we prove the assertion locally. ■

7.7.2 *Proof of Proposition 7.2.2*

Proof From Sinai (1976), we can easily obtain that the spectral density of the fGn can be written as

$$f_G(\lambda; H) = F(H)(1 - \cos\lambda)\sum_{j\in\mathbb{Z}}|\lambda + 2j\pi|^{-2H-1},$$

where $F(H)$ is a normalizing factor designated to ensure $\int_{-\pi}^{\pi} f_G(\lambda; H)\, d\lambda = 1$.

Consequently, we have

$$f_G(\lambda; H) = \frac{\sigma^2}{\pi}\sin(\pi H)\Gamma(2H+1)(1 - \cos\lambda)\sum_{j\in\mathbb{Z}}|\lambda + 2j\pi|^{-2H-1}.$$

The behavior of $f_G(\lambda; H)$ near the origin is followed by a Taylor expansion of $(1 - \cos\lambda)$ at zero, and it can be shown that

$$f_G(\lambda; H) \sim \mathcal{O}\left(|\lambda|^{1-2H}\right) \quad \text{as} \quad \lambda \to 0.$$

The asymptotic behavior of $\gamma_G(k)$ is followed by the Taylor expansion. Let $\gamma_G(k) = \frac{1}{2}k^{2H}g\left(k^{-1}\right)$ with $g(x) = (1+x)^{2H} - 2 + (1-x)^{2H}$. If $0 < H < 1$ and $H \neq \frac{1}{2}$, then expanding $g(x)$ at the origin, we can see that the first nonzero term in the Taylor expansion of $g(x)$ is equal to $2H(2H-1)x^2$. Therefore, as k tends to infinity, we have (7.4). For $\frac{1}{2} < H < 1$, the fGn has long memory. For $0 < H < \frac{1}{2}$, we can see that $\sum_{k=-\infty}^{\infty} \gamma_G(k) = 0$, which implies that the process is antipersistent. For $H = \frac{1}{2}$, all the correlations at nonzero lags are zero, namely, the observations are uncorrelated, and the process has short memory. A standard calculation yields

$$\begin{aligned}
\mathbb{E}\left[G_t^H - G_0^H\right] &= \mathbb{E}\left[G_t^H\right] - \mathbb{E}\left[G_0^H\right] = 0 \\
\operatorname{Var}\left(G_t^H - G_0^H\right) &= \mathbb{E}\left(Y_H(n) - Y_H(0)\right)^2 \\
&= 2 - |t-1|^{2H} - |t+1|^{2H} + 2t^{2H}
\end{aligned}$$

as

$$\begin{aligned}
\mathbb{E}\left[G_t^H G_0^H\right] &= \mathbb{E}\left[\left(G_{t+1}^H - G_t^H\right)\left(G_1^H - G_0^H\right)\right] \\
&= \frac{1}{2}\left[|t-1|^{2H} + |t+1|^{2H} - 2t^{2H}\right].
\end{aligned}$$

Moreover, $\left(G_t^H, G_0^H\right)$ has a bivariate Gaussian distribution with the correlation matrix given by

$$\begin{pmatrix} 1 & \frac{1}{2}\left[|t-1|^{2H} + |t+1|^{2H} - 2t^{2H}\right] \\ \frac{1}{2}\left[|t-1|^{2H} + |t+1|^{2H} - 2t^{2H}\right] & 1 \end{pmatrix}. \tag{7.67}$$

Thus, $G_t^H - G_0^H$ has a Gaussian distribution with zero mean and the variance $2 - |t-1|^{2H} - |t+1|^{2H} + 2|t|^{2H}$. Of course, for $t=0$, we have a degenerated distribution with zero variance. Moreover, using $\lim_{t\to\infty}\left(|t-1|^{2H} + |t+1|^{2H} - 2t^{2H}\right) = 0$, we have $\operatorname{Var}\left(G_t^H - G_0^H\right) \longrightarrow 2$ as $t \to \infty$. Therefore, $G_t^H - G_0^H \Rightarrow \mathcal{N}(0,2)$ as $t \to \infty$. ∎

Bibliography

Aït-Sahalia, Y. and L. Mancini (2008). Out of sample forecasts of quadratic variation. *Journal of Econometrics 147*(1), 17–33.

Andersen, T. G., T. Bollerslev, F. X. Diebold, and P. Labys (2003). Modeling and forecasting realized volatility. *Econometrica 71*(2), 579–625.

Bachelier, L. (1900). Théorie de la spéculation. In *Annales scientifiques de l'École normale supérieure*, Volume 17, pp. 21–86.

Baillie, R. T. (1996). Long memory processes and fractional integration in econometrics. *Journal of Econometrics 73*(1), 5–59.

Baillie, R. T., T. Bollerslev, and H. O. Mikkelsen (1996). Fractionally integrated generalized autoregressive conditional heteroskedasticity. *Journal of Econometrics 74*(1), 3–30.

Bakshi, G., C. Cao, and Z. Chen (1997). Empirical performance of alternative option pricing models. *Journal of Finance 52*(5), 2003–2049.

Barndorff-Nielsen, O. E., J. M. Corcuera, and M. Podolskij (2013). Limit theorems for functionals of higher order differences of brownian semi-stationary processes. In *Prokhorov and Contemporary Probability Theory: In Honor of Yuri V. Prokhorov*, Volume 33, pp. 69–96. Springer Science & Business Media.

Bates, D. S. (1996). Jumps and stochastic volatility: Exchange rate processes implicit in deutsche mark options. *Review of Financial Studies 9*(1), 69–107.

Bayer, C., P. Friz, and J. Gatheral (2016). Pricing under rough volatility. *Quantitative Finance 16*(6), 887–904.

Belfadli, R., K. Es-Sebaiy, and Y. Ouknine (2011). Parameter estimation for fractional Ornstein–Uhlenbeck processes: Non-ergodic case. *Frontiers in Science and Engineering (An International Journal Edited by Hassan II Academy of Science and Technology) 1*(1), 1–16.

Bender, C. and R. J. Elliott (2004). Arbitrage in a discrete version of the Wick-fractional Black–Scholes market. *Mathematics of Operations Research 29*(4), 935–945.

Bennedsen, M., A. Lunde, and M. S. Pakkanen (2022). Decoupling the short-and long-term behavior of stochastic volatility. *Journal of Financial Econometrics 20*(5), 961–1006.

Beran, J. (1994). *Statistics for long-memory processes*. New York: CRC Press.

Bishwal, J. (2011). Minimum contrast estimation in fractional Ornstein–Uhlenbeck process: Continuous and discrete sampling. *Fractional Calculus and Applied Analysis 14*(3), 375–410.

Björk, T. and H. Hult (2005). A note on Wick products and the fractional Black–Scholes model. *Finance and Stochastics 9*(2), 197–209.

Black, F. and M. Scholes (1973). The pricing of options and corporate liabilities. *Journal of Political Economy 81*(3), 637–654.

Bolko, A. E., K. Christensen, M. S. Pakkanen, and B. Veliyev (2023). A GMM approach to estimate the roughness of stochastic volatility. *Journal of Econometrics 235*(2), 745–778.

Chan, K. C., G. A. Karolyi, F. A. Longstaff, and A. B. Sanders (1992). An empirical comparison of alternative models of the short-term interest rate. *Journal of Finance 47*(3), 1209–1227.

Cheridito, P. (2001). Mixed fractional Brownian motion. *Bernoulli 7*(6), 913–934.

Cheridito, P., H. Kawaguchi, and M. Maejima (2003). Fractional Ornstein–Uhlenbeck processes. *Electronic Journal of Probability 8*(3), 1–14.

Chronopoulou, A. and F. G. Viens (2012a). Estimation and pricing under long-memory stochastic volatility. *Annals of Finance 8*(2–3), 379–403.

Chronopoulou, A. and F. G. Viens (2012b). Stochastic volatility and option pricing with long-memory in discrete and continuous time. *Quantitative Finance 12*(4), 635–649.

Comte, F., L. Coutin, and É. Renault (2012). Affine fractional stochastic volatility models. *Annals of Finance 8*(2–3), 337–378.

Comte, F. and E. Renault (1998). Long memory in continuous-time stochastic volatility models. *Mathematical Finance 8*(4), 291–323.

Cont, R. (2001). Empirical properties of asset returns: Stylized facts and statistical issues. *Quantitative Finance 1*(2), 223–236.

Cont, R. (2005). Long range dependence in financial markets. In *Fractals in Engineering: New Trends in Theory and Application*. Lutton, E. and Vehel, J., (Eds.), pp. 159–179. Springer, New York.

Corlay, S., J. Lebovits, and J. L. Véhel (2014). Multifractional stochastic volatility models. *Mathematical Finance 24*(2), 364–402.

Delbaen, F. and W. Schachermayer (1994). A general version of the fundamental theorem of asset pricing. *Mathematische Annalen 300*(1), 463–520.

Duffie, D., J. Pan, and K. Singleton (2000). Transform analysis and asset pricing for affine jump-diffusions. *Econometrica 68*(6), 1343–1376.

Duncan, T., Y. Hu, and B. Pasik-Duncan (2000). Stochastic calculus for fractional Brownian motion I. theory. *SIAM Journal on Control and Optimization 38*(2), 582–612.

El Euch, O. and M. Rosenbaum (2019). The characteristic function of rough Heston models. *Mathematical Finance 29*(1), 3–38.

El Machkouri, M., K. Es-Sebaiy, and Y. Ouknine (2016). Least squares estimator for non-ergodic Ornstein–Uhlenbeck processes driven by Gaussian processes. *Journal of the Korean Statistical Society 45*(3), 329–341.

Elliott, R. and L. Chan (2004). Perpetual American options with fractional Brownian motion. *Quantitative Finance 4*(2), 123–128.

Elliott, R. and J. Van Der Hoek (2003). A general fractional white noise theory and applications to finance. *Mathematical Finance 13*(2), 301–330.

Fink, H., C. Klüppelberg, and M. Zähle (2013). Conditional distributions of processes related to fractional Brownian motion. *Journal of Applied Probability 50*(1), 166–183.

Fouque, J.-P., G. Papanicolaou, and K. R. Sircar (2000). *Derivatives in financial markets with stochastic volatility*. Cambridge University Press.

Gatheral, J. (2006). *The volatility surface: A practitioner's guide*. John Wiley & Sons.

Gatheral, J., T. Jaisson, and M. Rosenbaum (2018). Volatility is rough. *Quantitative Finance 18*(6), 933–949.

Greene, M. T. and B. D. Fielitz (1977). Long-term dependence in common stock returns. *Journal of Financial Economics 4*(3), 339–349.

Hagan, P. S., D. Kumar, A. S. Lesniewski, and D. E. Woodward (2002). Managing smile risk. *The Best of Wilmott 1*, 249–296.

Harrison, J. M. and S. R. Pliska (1981). Martingales and stochastic integrals in the theory of continuous trading. *Stochastic Processes and Their Applications 11*(3), 215–260.

Heston, S. L. (1993). A closed-form solution for options with stochastic volatility with applications to bond and currency options. *Review of Financial Studies 6*(2), 327–343.

Hu, Y. and D. Nualart (2010). Parameter estimation for fractional Ornstein–Uhlenbeck processes. *Statistics and Probability Letters 80*(11), 1030–1038.

Hu, Y., D. Nualart, and H. Zhou (2019). Parameter estimation for fractional Ornstein–Uhlenbeck processes of general Hurst parameter. *Statistical Inference for Stochastic Processes 22*(1), 111–142.

Hu, Y. and B. Øksendal (2003). Fractional white noise calculus and applications to finance. *Infinite Dimensional Analysis Quantum Probability and Related Topics 6*(1), 1–32.

Hu, Y., B. Øksendal, and A. Sulem (2003). Optimal consumption and portfolio in a Black–Scholes market driven by fractional Brownian motion. *Infinite Dimensional Analysis, Quantum Probability and Related Topics 6*(4), 519–536.

Hull, J. and A. White (1987). The pricing of options on assets with stochastic volatilities. *Journal of Finance 42*(2), 281–300.

Hurst, H. E. (1951). Long-term storage capacity of reservoirs. *Transactions of the American Society of Civil Engineers 116*, 770–799.

Itô, K. (1951). *On stochastic differential equations*. American Mathematical Society.

Kleptsyna, M. and A. Le Breton (2002). Statistical analysis of the fractional Ornstein–Uhlenbeck type process. *Statistical Inference for Stochastic Processes 5*(3), 229–248.

Kleptsyna, M. L., A. Le Breton, and M.-C. Roubaud (2000). Parameter estimation and optimal filtering for fractional type stochastic systems. *Statistical Inference for Stochastic Processes 3*(1), 173–182.

Kolmogorov, A. N. (1940). Wienersche spiralen und einige andere interessante Kurven in Hilbertscen Raum, C.R. (doklady). *Comptes rendus de l'Académie des sciences de l'URSS (NS) 26*, 115–118.

Kubilius, K., Y. Mishura, and K. Ralchenko (2017). *Parameter estimation in fractional diffusion models*. Springer.

Lang, G. and F. Roueff (2001). Semi-parametric estimation of the hölder exponent of a stationary Gaussian process with minimax rates. *Statistical Inference for Stochastic Processes 4*(3), 283–306.

Liu, X., S. Shi, and Y. Jun (2024). Fractional stochastic volatility model. Journal of Time Series Analysis. DOI: https://doi.org/10.1111/jtsa.12749

Livieri, G., S. Mouti, A. Pallavicini, and M. Rosenbaum (2018). Rough volatility: Evidence from option prices. *IISE Transactions 50*(9), 767–776.

Lo, A. W. and A. C. MacKinlay (1988). Stock market prices do not follow random walks: Evidence from a simple specification test. *Review of Financial Studies 1*(1), 41–66.

Lohvinenko, S. and K. Ralchenko (2017). Maximum likelihood estimation in the fractional Vasicek model. *Lithuanian Journal of Statistics 56*(1), 77–87.

Lohvinenko, S. and K. Ralchenko (2019). Maximum likelihood estimation in the non-ergodic fractional Vasicek model. *Modern Stochastics: Theory and Applications 6*(3), 377–395.

Ludeña, C. (2004). Minimum contrast estimation for fractional diffusions. *Scandinavian Journal of Statistics 31*(4), 613–628.

Mandelbrot, B. B. and J. W. Van Ness (1968). Fractional Brownian motions, fractional noises and applications. *SIAM Review 10*(4), 422–437.

Merton, R. C. (1973). Theory of rational option pricing. *Bell Journal of Economics and Management Science 4*(1), 141–183.

Mishura, Y. (2008). *Stochastic calculus for fractional Brownian motion and related processes*. Springer.

Norros, I., E. Valkeila, and J. Virtamo. (1999). An elementary approach to a Girsanov formula and other analytical results on fractional Brownian motions. *Bernoulli 5*(4), 571–587.

Nourdin, I. (2012). *Selected aspects of fractional Brownian motion*, Volume 4. Springer.

Osborne, M. F. (1959). Brownian motion in the stock market. *Operations Research 7*(2), 145–173.

Phillips, P. C. B. and J. Yu (2009). A two-stage realized volatility approach to estimation of diffusion processes with discrete data. *Journal of Econometrics 150*(2), 139–150.

Prakasa Rao, B. (2010). *Statistical Inference for Fractional Diffusion Processes*. Wiley, Chichester.

Rogers, L. C. G. (1997). Arbitrage with fractional Brownian motion. *Mathematical Finance 7*(1), 95–105.

Romano, M. and N. Touzi (1997). Contingent claims and market completeness in a stochastic volatility model. *Mathematical Finance 7*(4), 399–412.

Rostek, S. (2009). *Option pricing in fractional Brownian markets*. Springer.

Samorodnitsky, G. and M. Taqqu (1994). *Stable non-Gaussian random processes*. Chapman & Hall, New York.

Schöbel, R. and J. Zhu (1999). Stochastic volatility with an Ornstein–Uhlenbeck process: An extension. *European Finance Review 3*(1), 23–46.

Scott, L. O. (1987). Option pricing when the variance changes randomly: Theory, estimation, and an application. *Journal of Financial and Quantitative Analysis 22*(04), 419–438.

Shi, S. and J. Yu (2023). Volatility puzzle: Long memory or antipersistency. *Management Science 69*(7), 3861–3883.

Sinai, Y. G. (1976). Self-similar probability distributions. *Theory of Probability & Its Applications 21*(1), 64–80.

Sottinen, T. (2001). Fractional Brownian motion, random walks and binary market models. *Finance and Stochastics 5*(3), 343–355.

Stein, E. M. and J. C. Stein (1991). Stock price distributions with stochastic volatility: An analytic approach. *Review of Financial Studies 4*(4), 727–752.

Tanaka, K. (2013). Distributions of the maximum likelihood and minimum contrast estimators associated with the fractional Ornstein–Uhlenbeck process. *Statistical Inference for Stochastic Processes 16*(3), 173–192.

Tanaka, K. (2015). Maximum likelihood estimation for the non-ergodic fractional Ornstein–Uhlenbeck process. *Statistical Inference for Stochastic Processes 18*(3), 315–332.

Tanaka, K., W. Xiao, and J. Yu (2020). Maximum likelihood estimation for the fractional Vasicek model. *Econometrics 8*(3), 32.

Tang, C. Y. and S. X. Chen (2009). Parameter estimation and bias correction for diffusion processes. *Journal of Econometrics 149*(1), 65–81.

Tudor, C. and F. Viens (2007). Statistical aspects of the fractional stochastic calculus. *Annals of Statistics 35*(3), 1183–1212.

Vasicek, O. (1977). An equilibrium characterization of the term structure. *Journal of Financial Economics 5*(2), 177–188.

Wang, X., W. Xiao, and J. Yu (2023). Modeling and forecasting realized volatility with the fractional Ornstein–Uhlenbeck process. *Journal of Econometrics 232*(2), 389–415.

Wang, X. and J. Yu (2016). Double asymptotics for explosive continuous time models. *Journal of Econometrics 193*(1), 35–53.

Wiggins, J. B. (1987). Option values under stochastic volatility: Theory and empirical estimates. *Journal of Financial Economics 19*(2), 351–372.

Willinger, W., M. S. Taqqu, and V. Teverovsky (1999). Stock market prices and long-range dependence. *Finance and Stochastics 3*(1), 1–13.

Xiao, W. and J. Yu (2019a). Asymptotic theory for estimating drift parameters in the fractional Vasicek model. *Econometric Theory 35*(1), 198–231.

Xiao, W. and J. Yu (2019b). Asymptotic theory for rough fractional Vasicek models. *Economics Letters 177*, 26–29.

Yu, J. and P. C. B. Phillips (2001). A Gaussian approach for continuous time models of the short-term interest rate. *Econometrics Journal 4*(2), 210–224.

8 Estimation of Integrated Covariance Matrix Using High-Frequency Data with Applications in Portfolio Choice

CHENG LIU *Wuhan University*

8.1 Introduction

Due to advances in the financial market and technology, high-frequency data have become readily available. We can download data in milliseconds from the Trade and Quote (TAQ) database, including the transaction data of all equities in New York Stock Exchange, American Stock Exchange, NASDAQ National Market System and SmallCap issues as introduced on the website of Wharton research data services. Compared with low-frequency data such as daily and weekly data, high-frequency data, which are usually referred to as intraday data in finance, contain more information from a statistical point of view. Due to the availability of high-frequency data, new methods for analyzing high-frequency data have mushroomed over the past twenty years. Additionally, applications of the new methods can be found in portfolio allocations, risk management, asset pricing, and so on.

At least two textbooks addressing high-frequency data are available, namely Jacod and Protter (2012) and Aït-Sahalia and Jacod (2014). These two excellent books focus on the mathematical foundation for analyzing high-frequency data in the univariate context. In contrast to these two books, this chapter focuses on the analysis of multivariate high-frequency data by providing a selective review of alternative estimation methods of the integrated covariance matrix (ICM). We separate the methods into two classes: the first assumes the dimension of the ICM is fixed, while the second assumes the dimension of the ICM goes to infinity with the sample size.

To study the properties of the alternative estimators of the ICM, we assume prices are generated from a very flexible continuous-time model whose spot covariance matrix is time-variant. The ICM is an integration of covariance matrices in many infinitely small intervals. Estimating the ICM is therefore different from estimating the covariance matrix based on independent and identically distributed (i.i.d.) samples, which is a core research topic in statistics, especially when the dimension of a covariance matrix is high; see for example Bickel and Levina (2008a), Bickel and Levina (2008b), Ledoit and

Wolf (2004), Ledoit and Wolf (2017), Bai and Ng (2002), Bai (2003), and a review in Fan et al. (2016). However, the difficulties encountered in the estimation of a covariance matrix also apply to estimating the ICM and are even more challenging, as the samples are usually assumed to be nonindependent, nonidentically distributed, and associated with measurement errors (usually called microstructure noises in high-frequency data studies).

In this chapter, we provide explicit forms or detailed estimating procedures for several popular and simple estimators of the ICM using high-frequency data. In terms of data, we assume that they are contaminated with microstructure noise and nonsynchronous, which are common characteristics of high-frequency data. Therefore, some estimators, which are not robust to microstructure noises, are not included. For example, Andersen et al. (2003), Barndorff-Nielsen and Shephard (2004), and Hayashi and Yoshida (2005) study the estimation of the covariance without considering the effect of microstructure noise. The estimators that are extensions of some popular estimators are also not included. For example, instead of introducing Varneskov (2016), which extends a generalized flat-top realized kernel estimator and provides a finite sample correction for a symmetric matrix to ensure the estimator is positive definite, we give the explicit form of the realized kernel estimator proposed in Barndorff-Nielsen et al. (2011). The Fourier transformation-based estimators, including Mancino and Sanfelici (2008), Malliavin and Mancino (2009), and Park et al. (2016), are also not provided. However, we give the explicit form of the local method of moments estimation developed in Bibinger et al. (2014), whose main idea is to use a representation of localized Fourier coefficients.

This chapter is organized as follows. We first present the commonly used continuous-time model in high-frequency data literature, and then discuss the specific characteristics of high-frequency data in Section 8.2. Estimations of the ICM are introduced in Section 8.3. In Section 8.4, we apply some estimations of the ICM to constructing portfolio allocations with real stocks and compare their performances with some popular portfolio strategies in the literature that relied on low-frequency data. A discussion is provided in Section 8.5.

8.2 The Integrated Covariance Matrix and Data

The logarithmic prices of p assets at time t are denoted by $\boldsymbol{X}_t = (X_{1t}, \ldots, X_{pt})'$. Following the common assumptions in the literature (see, for example, Aït-Sahalia et al. (2010), Barndorff-Nielsen et al. (2011), Liu and Tang (2014), and Shephard and Xiu (2017)), we model $\boldsymbol{X}_t$ by a Brownian semimartingale defined on some filtered probability space $(\Omega, \mathcal{F}, \mathcal{F}_t, \mathbb{P})$,

$$d\boldsymbol{X}_t = \boldsymbol{\mu}_t dt + \boldsymbol{\sigma}_t d\boldsymbol{W}_t, \tag{8.1}$$

where $\boldsymbol{\mu}_t = (\mu_{1t}, \ldots, \mu_{pt})'$ is a p-dimensional drift process and is often assumed to be locally bounded and progressively measurable; $\boldsymbol{\sigma}_t$ is the $p \times p$

covolatility process with each element assumed to be càdlàg; and $\boldsymbol{W}_t$ is a p-dimensional standard independent Brownian motion.

The spot covariance matrix of $\boldsymbol{X}_t$ at time t is $\boldsymbol{\Sigma}_t = \boldsymbol{\sigma}_t\boldsymbol{\sigma}_t'$ and the ICM over the interval $[0, T]$ with a fixed T is denoted by

$$\boldsymbol{C}_T = \int_0^T \boldsymbol{\Sigma}_t dt,$$

and when $p = 1$, $C_T = \int_0^T \sigma_t^2 dt$ is called the integrated volatility (IV). Our goal is to estimate ICM – $\boldsymbol{C}_T$ based on the discrete observed prices. In the simplest case that we have equally spaced observations of the price process $\boldsymbol{X}_t$, namely, $\boldsymbol{X}_{t_0}, \ldots, \boldsymbol{X}_{t_n}$ with $t_j = j\Delta$ and $\Delta = T/n$ being the time length between two observations, Protter (2004, pp. 66–27) and Barndorff-Nielsen et al. (2011) show that

$$\boldsymbol{C}_T = \lim_{n\to\infty} \sum_{j=1}^{n} (\boldsymbol{X}_{t_j} - \boldsymbol{X}_{t_{j-1}})(\boldsymbol{X}_{t_j} - \boldsymbol{X}_{t_{j-1}})' \tag{8.2}$$

when p is finite, which means the realized covariance matrix is a consistent estimator of the ICM. However, empirical results show that the realized volatility, which is the summation of squared log-returns, goes to ∞ as Δ reduces to zero; see Hansen and Lunde (2006). This is due to microstructure noise contamination in high-frequency data. We now introduce some specific characteristics of high-frequency data.

8.2.1 Characteristics of High-Frequency Data

Three main specific characteristics of high-frequency data have been discussed frequently in the literature and practice. First, the observations for each asset are not always equally spaced. The time interval between two consecutive observations of an asset can be random and may depend on the movements of prices. As mentioned in Aït-Sahalia and Jacod (2014), the time between observations may be informative for the price process since the trades may depend on the news flows. In addition, the trading frequency itself can also be a kind of news flow. Engle and Russell (1998) propose an autoregressive conditional duration (ACD) model to study irregular spaced data. Tse and Yang (2012) use the ACD model to estimate the volatility based on high-frequency data. The second characteristic is the data for different assets are usually nonsynchronous. This is because in the financial market different stocks usually have different trading patterns, such as different trading volumes, frequencies and so on. Third, data are always contaminated with microstructure noise. We now discuss those characteristics in detail.

Nonsynchronicity

As the trading activity of an asset may depend on news flows, price changes, and other factors, the time interval between two consecutive observations of an asset can be random. Therefore, it is common for different assets to have distinct observation times in real high-frequency data. To study the nonsynchronicity of data, we use

$$\mathcal{G}_k = \left\{t_0^k, t_1^k, \ldots, t_{n_k}^k\right\}$$

to denote the grid of time points where the prices of the kth asset are observed, where $0 \leq t_0^k < t_1^k \cdots < t_{n_k}^k \leq T$ and $k = 1, \ldots, p$.

It is obvious that the nonsynchronicity of data may introduce bias in the estimation of the integrated covariance. For example,

$$E\left\{\sum_{j=1}^{n_1 \wedge n_2}\left(X_{t_j^1}^1 - X_{t_{j-1}^1}^1\right)\left(X_{t_j^2}^2 - X_{t_{j-1}^2}^2\right)\right\} = \int_{I_{12}} \Sigma_t(1,2)dt$$

$$\neq \int_{t_0^1 \vee t_0^2}^{t_n^1 \wedge t_n^2} \Sigma_t(1,2)dt$$

unless $t_j^1 = t_j^2$ for all $j = 1, \ldots, n_1 \wedge n_2$, where $I_{12} = \bigcup_{j=1}^{n_1 \wedge n_2}\left\{(t_{j-1}^1, t_j^1] \cap (t_{j-1}^2, t_j^2]\right\}$. For any fixed numbers a and b, $a \wedge b$ and $a \vee b$ are equal to the smaller and larger values between a and b, respectively.

To control the impact of nonsynchronicity in the ICM estimation, two varieties of methods have been developed in the literature. The first one is synchronizing original nonsynchronous data before estimation. The other type of method estimates the ICM based on a state space model and considers the nonsynchronous data as a data set with missing values; in this way, the method estimates the ICM and addresses the data nonsynchronicity simultaneously. We now introduce the first type of method in detail, and the second type of method will be introduced in Section 8.3.

In general, there are three popular synchronization methods in the literature: the refresh time scheme developed in Barndorff-Nielsen et al. (2011), the previous-tick method provided in Zhang (2011), and the generalized synchronization method proposed in Aït-Sahalia et al. (2010).

The refresh time scheme for $\mathcal{G}_k$ $(k = 1, \ldots, p)$ is defined as following:

Definition 8.2.1 *Refresh Time for $t \in [0, T]$. The first refresh time is defined as $\tau_0 = \max(t_0^1, \ldots, t_0^p)$. The subsequent refresh times are then defined as*

$$\tau_{j+1} = \max\left(t^1_{N^1_{\tau_j}+1}, \ldots, t^p_{N^p_{\tau_j}+1}\right), \quad j = 0, 1, \ldots, n-1,$$

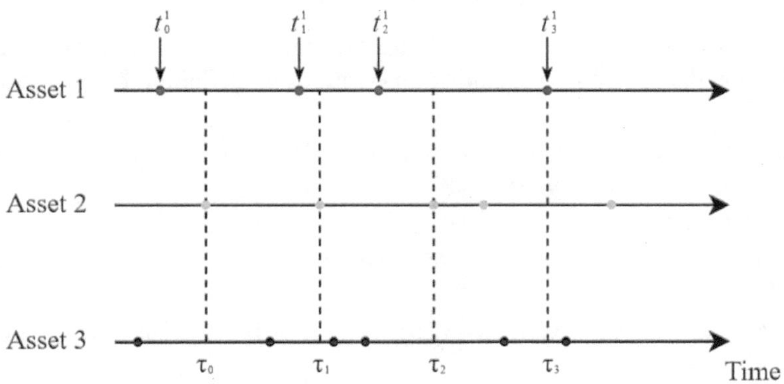

Figure 8.1 The Refresh Time scheme
Note: The dots in color represent the observation time points $\{t_j^k, k = 1, 2, 3; j = 0, 1, 2, \ldots\}$. In this example, the refresh times are $\tau_0 = t_0^2, \tau_1 = t_1^2, \tau_2 = t_2^2, \tau_3 = t_3^1$.

where the selected $(j+1)$*th observation time for the kth asset is*

$$t^k_{N^k_{\tau_j}} = \max\{t \in \mathcal{G}_k \colon t \le \tau_j\},$$

which is the time point in $\mathcal{G}_k$*, smaller or equal to* τ_j *and closest to* τ_j *for* $j = 0, 1, \ldots, n$*. Time point* $t^k_{N^k_{\tau_j}}$ *is the* $(N^k_{\tau_j} + 1)$*th observation time of the kth asset.*

An example of the refresh time scheme with three assets is shown in Figure 8.1. In this example, we find that $t^1_{N^1_{\tau_0}} = t^1_0, \ldots, t^1_{N^1_{\tau_3}} = t^1_3, t^2_{N^2_{\tau_3}} = t^2_3, t^3_{N^3_{\tau_3}} = t^3_4$. To simplify the notation, we use τ_j^k instead of $t^k_{N^k_{\tau_j}}$ to refer to the $(j+1)$th observation time point of the kth asset in synchronized data. Based on the preceding definition, the refresh time scheme would keep the data for the kth asset at time points $\{\tau_0^k, \ldots, \tau_n^k\}$, which is a subset of $\mathcal{G}_k$. It's clear that n depends on the frequencies of all p assets and may be determined by the least frequent asset. The refresh times $\{\tau_0, \tau_1, \ldots, \tau_n\}$ are usually unequally spaced.

The previous-tick method tries to construct equally spaced data by first choosing a sequence of time points $\{\Delta, 2\Delta, \ldots, [T/\Delta]\Delta\}$, where $[x]$ denote the integer part of $x \in \mathbb{R}^+$. Time point τ_j^k is then selected to be

$$\tau_j^k = \max\{t \in \mathcal{G}_k \colon t \le (j+1)\Delta\}, j = 0, \ldots, [T/\Delta] - 1.$$

As mentioned in Zhang (2011), typical Δ in financial applications includes 5 minutes, 15 minutes, 30 minutes, and 1 hour. We find that large Δ results in a large part of data being dropped and small Δ results in many zero returns in the synchronized data. Therefore, Δ should be chosen based on the frequencies of assets that need to be synchronized.

The third method is more general than the preceding two approaches and is built upon the generalized sampling time defined in Definition 8.2.2.

Definition 8.2.2 *A sequence of time points* $\{\tau_0, \tau_1, \tau_2, \ldots, \tau_n\}$ *is called the generalized sampling time if*
(1) $0 < \tau_0 < \tau_1 < \cdots < \tau_{n-1} < \tau_n \leq T$.
(2) Any asset contains at least one observation between two consecutive τ_j*s for* $j = 1, \ldots, n$ *and* $(0, \tau_0]$.
(3) The time intervals $\{\Delta_j = \tau_j - \tau_{j-1}; j = 1, \ldots, n\}$ *satisfy* $\sup_j \Delta_j \xrightarrow{p} 0$.

For each $1 \leq k \leq p$, the τ_j^k is then selected to be an arbitrary time point in $\mathcal{G}_k$ which is between $(\tau_{j-1}, \tau_j]$ for $1 \leq j \leq n$ and between $(0, \tau_0]$ for $j = 0$, respectively. As mentioned in Aït-Sahalia et al. (2010), the generalized synchronization method includes the refresh time scheme and previous-tick method as special cases. In addition, the refresh time scheme retains most of the data.

Microstructure Noise
It is well known that intraday high-frequency data are contaminated with microstructure noises which could significantly affect the estimation accuracy of market risks. Hansen and Lunde (2006) show that due to microstructure noises the realized volatility goes to ∞ when the sample frequency increases. Aït-Sahalia and Xiu (2019) develop Hausman tests for testing whether high-frequency data can be safely considered as free of noise. Their empirical results show that even the five-minute returns cannot be considered as noise-free for some constituent stocks in S&P 500 after 2009. Jacod et al. (2017) study the statistical properties of microstructure noises, and their empirical results show positive autocorrelations of time series of noises in the stock prices of Citigroup Inc. The sources of noise are summarized in Aït-Sahalia et al. (2011). They declare that the noise may come from the market microstructure effects such as the bid-ask bounces, discreteness of price changes and rounding, trades occurring on different markets or networks, inventory control effects, data recording error, and so on.

We model the actual observed data contaminated with microstructure noise by

$$Y^k_{t^k_j} = X^k_{t^k_j} + U^k_{t^k_j} \quad (k = 1, \ldots, p; j = 0, \ldots, n_k).$$

Four different noise structures are discussed in Aït-Sahalia and Jacod (2014) which are additive white noises, additive colored noises, pure rounding noises, and rounded white noises. For additive white noises, $U^k_{t^k_j}$s are assumed to be i.i.d. with mean 0 and finite variance for each k and $j = 0, 1, \ldots, n_k$, and $\boldsymbol{X}_t$ and

$\boldsymbol{U}_t$ are independent. If $U^k_{t^k_j}$s are realizations of a stationary process independent of the process $\boldsymbol{X}_t$, then they are additive colored noise.

The prices are always multiples of a tick size in finance. For tick size β, we observe

$$Y^k_{t^k_j} = \beta[X^k_{t^k_j}/\beta],$$

such that the pure rounding error is $\beta[X^k_{t^k_j}/\beta] - X^k_{t^k_j}$ for the process X^k_t at time t^k_j. To model the rounded white noise, the observation $Y^k_{t^k_j}$ is denoted by

$$Y^k_{t^k_j} = \beta\left[\left(X^k_{t^k_j} + \chi^k_{t^k_j}\right)/\beta\right],$$

where processes χ_t^k and X_t^k are independent and χ_t^k is white noise. For more detailed discussions about noises, we refer to Aït-Sahalia and Jacod (2014).

8.3 Estimations of the ICM

The ICM plays a key role in many financial applications such as portfolio allocation, asset pricing, risk management, and other applications. Many methods for estimating the ICM have been developed in the past ten years, where the dimension of the ICM is assumed to be finite or go to ∞ with the sample size. Before introducing the estimators, we first discuss the assumptions regarding noises and the nonsynchronicity of data. Assumption 8.3.1 is the commonly made assumption for synchronization times and frequencies of different assets; see, for example, Zhang (2011) and Liu and Tang (2014).

Assumption 8.3.1 *The synchronization times τ_js ($j = 0, \ldots, n$) are independent of $\boldsymbol{X}_t$, σ_t, and $\boldsymbol{U}_t$. In addition,* $\sup_j|\tau_j - \tau_{j-1}| = O\left(\frac{1}{n}\right)$ *and* $\sup_j|t^k_j - t^k_{j-1}| = O\left(\frac{1}{n_k}\right)$.

The preceding assumption generally requires that all assets have the same order of numbers of observations, and each asset cannot have dense observations at any small interval. For the noises, some articles assume that the noises are i.i.d.

Assumption 8.3.2 *The noises $\boldsymbol{U}_t$s are i.i.d. p-dimensional vectors with mean $\boldsymbol{0}$, covariance matrix $\boldsymbol{\Sigma}^U$, and have a finite fourth moment. $\boldsymbol{U}_t$ is independent of the latent process $\boldsymbol{X}_t$ for any $t \in [0, T]$.*

This assumption has been used in Aït-Sahalia et al. (2010), Christensen et al. (2010), Liu and Tang (2013), Liu and Tang (2014), and Shephard and Xiu (2017). Some articles assume the additive noise process to be stationary, for example, in Barndorff-Nielsen et al. (2011), Zhang (2011), and Varneskov (2016).

8.3.1 Estimate the ICM with a Finite Dimension

We denote the synchronized data by $\{\boldsymbol{Y}_{\tau_0}, \boldsymbol{Y}_{\tau_1}, \ldots, \boldsymbol{Y}_{\tau_n}\}$, where

$$\boldsymbol{Y}_{\tau_j} = \left(Y^1_{\tau_j^1}, \ldots, Y^p_{\tau_j^p}\right)', \quad j = 0, \ldots, n,$$

and $\tau_j^k \in \mathcal{G}_k$ are selected by some synchronization method introduced in Subsection 8.2.1.

We now give a selective review and introduce some popular estimators of the ICM. Most of those estimators are constructed based on the synchronized data $\{\boldsymbol{Y}_{\tau_0}, \boldsymbol{Y}_{\tau_1}, \ldots, \boldsymbol{Y}_{\tau_n}\}$. The other estimators are elementwise estimators of which each element is estimated separately.

Modulated Realized Covariance Estimation

To deal with microstructure noise, Christensen et al. (2010) propose using preaveraging returns, which is defined as

$$\bar{y}_i = \sum_{j=1}^{k_n-1} g\left(\frac{j}{k_n}\right)(\boldsymbol{Y}_{\tau_{i+j}} - \boldsymbol{Y}_{\tau_{i+j-1}}) \tag{8.3}$$

for a given k_n and $i = 0, \ldots, n-k_n+1$, where $g(x)$ is a continuous, differentiable function on [0, 1] with a piecewise Lipschitz derivative g', and satisfies

$$g(0) = g(1) = 0, \quad \int_0^1 g^2(s)ds > 0.$$

The ICM is then estimated by the modulated realized covariance (MRC):

$$\widehat{\boldsymbol{C}}_T^{\text{MRC}} = \frac{n}{n-k_n+2}\frac{1}{\psi_2 k_n}\sum_{i=0}^{n-k_n+1} \bar{y}_i \bar{y}_i', \tag{8.4}$$

where $\psi_2 = \phi_2(0), \phi_2(s) = \int_s^1 g(u)g(u-s)du$. The choice of $g(x)$ commonly used in the literature is

$$g(x) = x \wedge (1-x).$$

See, for example, Jacod et al. (2009), Xia and Zheng (2018), and Dai, Lu, and Xiu (2019). For such a $g(x)$, we have $\psi_2 = 1/12$ and for an even number k_n,

$$\bar{y}_i = \frac{1}{k_n}\left(\sum_{j=k_n/2}^{k_n-1} \boldsymbol{Y}_{\tau_{i+j}} - \sum_{j=0}^{k_n/2-1} \boldsymbol{Y}_{\tau_{i+j}}\right).$$

To mute the influence of noises and ensure that the estimator is positive semidefinite, Christensen et al. (2010) choose $k_n = \theta n^{1/2+\delta} + o(n^{1/4+3\delta/2})$ for some $\theta > 0$ and $0 < \delta < 0.5$ instead of setting $k_n = \theta n^{1/2}$ which is the optimal preaveraging window length such that the estimator can achieve the optimal convergence rate $n^{-1/4}$. Christensen et al. (2010) prove that under Assumption 8.3.2, $\widehat{\boldsymbol{C}}_T^{\text{MRC}}$ converges to $\boldsymbol{C}_T$ with rate $n^{-1/4+\delta/2}$ and without any bias when $\delta > 0.1$, and with convergence rate $n^{-1/5}$ but with an ignorable bias when $\delta = 0.1$ and the sample size n is large. Christensen et al. (2010) declare that getting the theoretical optimal θ is not easy in practice, as it relies on other estimations, which may be quite difficult to obtain. Based on their simulation and empirical studies, they suggest choosing $\delta = 0.1$ and $\theta = 1$ in practice.

The MRC $\widehat{\boldsymbol{C}}_T^{\text{MRC}}$ is constructed from synchronized data. To handle the nonsynchronicity of data, Christensen et al. (2010) propose a preaveraging Hayashi–Yoshida estimator for each element of $\boldsymbol{C}_T$,

$$\hat{C}_T^{\text{PAHY}}(k,l) = \frac{1}{(\psi_{\text{HY}} k_n)^2} \sum_{i=0}^{n_k-k_n+1} \sum_{j=0}^{n_l-k_n+1} \bar{Y}_i^k \bar{Y}_j^l 1_{\{(t_i^k, t_{i+k_n}^k] \cap (t_j^l, t_{j+k_n}^l] \neq \emptyset\}}, \tag{8.5}$$

where $1_{\{A\}}$ is the indicator function that equals 1 if A is true and 0 otherwise, $\psi_{\text{HY}} = \int_0^T g(x)dx$, and $\bar{Y}_i^k$ is a preaveraging return defined as

$$\bar{Y}_i^k = \sum_{j=1}^{k_n-1} g\left(\frac{j}{k_n}\right)(Y_{t_{i+j}}^k - Y_{t_{i+j-1}}^k) = \frac{1}{k_n}\left(\sum_{j=k_n/2}^{k_n-1} Y_{t_{i+j}}^k - \sum_{j=0}^{k_n/2-1} Y_{t_{i+j}}^k\right).$$

When $g(x) = x \wedge (1-x)$, $\bar{Y}_j^l$ are defined similarly. They prove that $\hat{C}_T^{\text{PAHY}}(k,l)$ is a consistent estimator of $C_T(k,l)$ with optimal convergence rate $n^{-1/4}$, where $C_T(k,l)$ is the (k,l)th element of $\boldsymbol{C}_T$. It is easy to find that the matrix estimator $\widehat{\boldsymbol{C}}_T^{\text{PAHY}} = \left(\hat{C}_T^{\text{PAHY}}(k,l)\right)_{k,l}$ may not be positive semidefinite.

Realized Kernel Estimation

Barndorff-Nielsen et al. (2011) propose estimating $\boldsymbol{C}_T$ by a realized kernel estimator,

$$\widehat{\boldsymbol{C}}_T^{\text{RK}} = \sum_{h=-\tilde{n}}^{\tilde{n}} k\left(\frac{h}{H}\right)\left\{\sum_{j=h+1}^{\tilde{n}} \boldsymbol{y}_j \boldsymbol{y}_{j-h}'\right\}, \tag{8.6}$$

for a given positive integer H, where $k(\cdot)$ is a kernel function, $\boldsymbol{y}_j = \widetilde{\boldsymbol{Y}}_{\tau_j} - \widetilde{\boldsymbol{Y}}_{\tau_{j-1}}$ for $j = 0, 1, 2 \ldots, \tilde{n}$ with $\tilde{n} = n - 2m + 2$,

$$\widetilde{\boldsymbol{Y}}_{\tau_0} = \frac{1}{m}\sum_{j=0}^{m-1} \boldsymbol{Y}_{\tau_j}, \quad \widetilde{\boldsymbol{Y}}_{\tau_{\tilde{n}}} = \frac{1}{m}\sum_{j=1}^{m} \boldsymbol{Y}_{\tau_{n-m+j}},$$

and $\widetilde{Y}_{\tau_j} = Y_{\tau_{j+m-1}}$ for $j = 1, 2 \ldots, \tilde{n} - 1$, where $\{Y_{\tau_1}, \ldots, Y_{\tau_n}\}$ are data synchronized by the refresh time scheme. Here, averaging m data at the very beginning and at the end is required for deriving the consistency of the estimator. Barndorff-Nielsen et al. (2011) prove that under some assumptions for the kernel function $k(\cdot)$ and the endogenous noises, $\widehat{C}_T^{\text{RK}}$ converges to C_T with rate $\tilde{n}^{-1/5}$ if $H = c_0\tilde{n}^{3/5}$ for some $c_0 > 0$ and $m^{-1} = o(\tilde{n}^{-1/5})$.

There are some practical issues for $\widehat{C}_T^{\text{RK}}$. The first is the kernel function. Many kernel functions can be chosen for $k(\cdot)$ such as the Parzen kernel function defined as

$$k(x) = \begin{cases} 1 - 6x^2 + 6x^3 & 0 \leq x \leq 1/2, \\ 2(1 - x)^3 & 1/2 \leq x \leq 1, \\ 0 & x > 1, \end{cases}$$

and the quadratic spectral kernel function defined as

$$k(x) = \frac{3}{x^2}\left(\frac{\sin x}{x} - \cos x\right)$$

for $x \geq 0$. Another issue is how to choose H. Barndorff-Nielsen et al. (2011) suggest choosing

$$H = p^{-1}\sum_{l=1}^{p} c^* \left\{\hat{A}(l,l)/\hat{C}_T(l,l)\right\}^{2/5} \tilde{n}^{3/5},$$

where $c^* = (k''(0)^2/k_\bullet^{0,0})^{1/5}$ with $k_\bullet^{0,0} = \int_0^\infty k^2(x)dx$, $\widehat{A}(l,l)$ and $\widehat{C}_T(l,l)$ are estimators of the long-run variance of noises contaminated in the observed prices of the lth asset and the integrated volatility of the latent prices of the lth asset, respectively. To obtain applicable $\widehat{A}(l,l)$ and $\widehat{C}_T(l,l)$, Barndorff-Nielsen et al. (2011) suggest using the realized variance of the lth asset based on all n_l data divided by $2n_l$ and the realized variance of the lth asset based on 15-minute returns divided by T, respectively; c^* equals 3.51 and 0.46 for the Parzen and quadratic spectral functions, respectively. The last practical issue is choosing m, which can be chosen as small integers such as 1 or 2. See the discussion about the subtlety of end effects in section 6.4 of Barndorff-Nielsen et al. (2011).

Covariance Estimation of the Two Scales

Zhang (2011) proposes estimating the ICM element by element. The integrated volatility and covariance are estimated by the two scales variance/covariance estimators defined as

$$\widehat{C}_T^{\text{TSE}}(k,l) = [Y^k, Y^l]_T^{(K)} - \frac{\bar{n}_K}{\bar{n}_J}[Y^k, Y^l]_T^{(J)}, \tag{8.7}$$

where

$$[Y^k, Y^l]_T^{(K)} = \frac{1}{K}\sum_{j=K}^{n}\left(Y^k_{\tau^k_j} - Y^k_{\tau^k_{j-K}}\right)\left(Y^l_{\tau^l_j} - Y^l_{\tau^l_{j-K}}\right),$$

$\bar{n}_K = (n-K+1)/K$, and similarly for $[Y^k, Y^l]_T^{(J)}$ and $\bar{n}_J$. Here J should satisfy $1 \le J \ll K$, and $K = O(n^{2/3})$. If $J = 1$, then it is the classical two scales setting. Zhang (2011) prove that under Assumption 8.3.1 and some assumptions for the stationary and exponentially α-mixing noises, $\widehat{C}_T^{\mathrm{TSE}}(k,l)$ converges to $C_T(k,l)$ in probability with convergence rate $n^{-1/6}$. The ICM is then estimated by

$$\widehat{\boldsymbol{C}}_T^{\mathrm{TSE}} = \left(\widehat{C}_T^{\mathrm{TSE}}(k,l)\right)_{k,l}.$$

Polarization with Quasi-Maximum Likelihood Estimation
Aït-Sahalia et al. (2010) utilize a polarization identity and estimate the integrated covariance of any two assets X_t^k and X_t^l during $[0,T]$ by

$$\widehat{C}_T^{\mathrm{POL}}(k,l) = \frac{1}{4}\left\{\widehat{\mathrm{var}}(X^k + X^l) - \widehat{\mathrm{var}}(X^k - X^l)\right\}, \tag{8.8}$$

where $\widehat{\mathrm{var}}(X^k + X^l)$ and $\widehat{\mathrm{var}}(X^k - X^l)$ are the quasi-maximum likelihood estimation (QMLE) of the IVs of processes $X_t^k + X_t^l$ and $X_t^k - X_t^l$ obtained based on the observations

$$\left\{Y^k_{\tau^k_0} + Y^l_{\tau^l_0}, \ldots, Y^k_{\tau^k_n} + Y^l_{\tau^l_n}\right\} \text{ and } \left\{Y^k_{\tau^k_0} - Y^l_{\tau^l_0}, \ldots, Y^k_{\tau^k_n} - Y^l_{\tau^l_n}\right\},$$

respectively.

The QMLE of the IV of a continuous time Itô process has been studied in Xiu (2010). Suppose a log-price process $\widetilde{X}_t$ satisfies

$$d\widetilde{X}_t = \tilde{\mu}_t dt + \tilde{\sigma}_t d\widetilde{W}_t,$$

with $\tilde{\sigma}_t$ being a positive and locally bounded Itô semimartingale, and $\tilde{\mu}_t$ being a locally bounded and progressively measurable process. Suppose the discrete observations of the process $\widetilde{X}_t$ are contaminated with microstructure noises such that

$$\widetilde{Y}_{\tau_j} = \widetilde{X}_{\tau_j} + \widetilde{U}_{\tau_j},$$

where $\widetilde{U}_{\tau_j}$, $j = 0, 1, \ldots, n$ are assumed to be i.i.d. with mean 0, variance $\tilde{a}^2$, and finite fourth moment.

The QMLE of the IV (i.e., $\int_0^T \tilde{\sigma}_t^2 dt$) is constructed from a model with two potential misspecifications: (1) $d\widetilde{X}_t = \tilde{\sigma}\, d\widetilde{W}_t$; (2) the noises $\{\widetilde{U}_j, j = 0, 1, 2, \ldots\}$

are i.i.d. Gaussian distributed with mean 0 and variance $\tilde{a}^2$. The QMLE of $(\tilde{a}^2, \int_0^T \tilde{\sigma}_t^2 dt)$ is the maximizer of the following log-likelihood function

$$l(\tilde{a}^2, \tilde{\sigma}^2) = -\frac{1}{2}\log\det(\widetilde{\boldsymbol{\Omega}}) - \frac{n}{2}\log(2\pi) - \frac{1}{2}\widetilde{\boldsymbol{Y}}'\widetilde{\boldsymbol{\Omega}}^{-1}\widetilde{\boldsymbol{Y}},$$

where

$$\widetilde{\boldsymbol{\Omega}} = \begin{pmatrix} \tilde{\sigma}^2\Delta + 2\tilde{a}^2 & -\tilde{a}^2 & 0 & \cdots & 0 \\ -\tilde{a}^2 & \tilde{\sigma}^2\Delta + 2\tilde{a}^2 & -\tilde{a}^2 & \ddots & \vdots \\ 0 & -\tilde{a}^2 & \tilde{\sigma}^2\Delta + 2\tilde{a}^2 & \ddots & 0 \\ \vdots & \ddots & \ddots & \ddots & -\tilde{a}^2 \\ 0 & \cdots & 0 & -\tilde{a}^2 & \tilde{\sigma}^2\Delta + 2\tilde{a}^2 \end{pmatrix},$$

and $\Delta = T/n$. The data are assumed to be equally spaced. Xiu (2010) proves that the QMLE of $\int_0^T \tilde{\sigma}_t^2 dt$ is a consistent estimator with convergence rate $n^{-1/4}$. Aït-Sahalia et al. (2010) show that under Assumptions 8.3.1 and 8.3.2 with diagonal $\boldsymbol{\Sigma}^U$, and when the time intervals $\{\Delta_j = \tau_j - \tau_{j-1}, j = 1, \ldots, n\}$ are i.i.d. with mean $\bar{\Delta}$, then the integrated covariance estimator $\widehat{C}_T^{\text{POL}}(k,l)$ satisfies

$$\widehat{C}_T^{\text{POL}}(k,l) - C_T(k,l) = O_p(\bar{\Delta}^{1/4}).$$

We refer to Aït-Sahalia et al. (2010) for the proof of the preceding result. The matrix $\boldsymbol{C}_T$ is estimated by

$$\widehat{\boldsymbol{C}}_T^{\text{POL}} = \left(\widehat{C}_T^{\text{POL}}(k,l)\right)_{k,l}.$$

The advantages of this approach include: (1) it has no tuning parameter; (2) each $\widehat{C}_T^{\text{POL}}(k,l)$ can achieve the optimal convergence rate $n^{-1/4}$.

It is obvious that the elementwise estimators $\widehat{\boldsymbol{C}}^{\text{POL}}$ and $\widehat{\boldsymbol{C}}^{\text{TSE}}$ may not be positive semidefinite. However, $\boldsymbol{C}_T$ must be positive semidefinite. To make any symmetric matrix $\boldsymbol{M}$ positive semidefinite, Fan et al. (2012) suggest using the following two projections. Suppose $\boldsymbol{M}$ has eigen-decomposition: $\boldsymbol{M} = \boldsymbol{\Gamma}\text{diag}(\lambda_1, \ldots, \lambda_p)\boldsymbol{\Gamma}'$, where $\lambda_1, \ldots, \lambda_p$ are eigenvalues and the kth column of $\boldsymbol{\Gamma}$ is the eigenvector corresponding to λ_k; then

$$\begin{aligned} \boldsymbol{M}_1^+ &= \boldsymbol{\Gamma}\text{diag}(\lambda_1^+, \ldots, \lambda_p^+)\boldsymbol{\Gamma}', \\ \boldsymbol{M}_2^+ &= (\boldsymbol{M} + \lambda_{\min}^- \boldsymbol{I}_p)/(1 + \lambda_{\min}^-), \end{aligned} \tag{8.9}$$

are both positive semidefinite and equal to $\boldsymbol{M}$ when $\boldsymbol{M}$ is positive semidefinite, where $\lambda_k^+ = \lambda_k \vee 0$, and $\lambda_{\min}^- = -(0 \wedge \min(\lambda_1, \ldots, \lambda_p))$. The preceding two projections may bring estimation biases, but they are necessary for the covariance matrix estimation.

Another issue for estimating the ICM element by element is how to synchronize the data. Instead of synchronizing data of all p assets together before estimation, we can also choose to synchronize the data pairwise and then estimate the nondiagonal element of ICM. This method can keep more data for the estimation, but the matrix estimator is more likely to be negative definite such that the projection (8.9) may distort the accuracy caused by more information used in the estimation process. The matrix estimator is more likely to be positive semidefinite if we synchronize the data of p assets. However, this may cause a large part of data to be dropped if p is large. We refer to Fan et al. (2012) for more discussions and comparisons of the preceding two projection methods and two synchronization choices. For the notation convenience, (8.7) and (8.8) use the data obtained by synchronizing the data of p assets together.

Multivariate Quasi-maximum Likelihood Estimation

Liu and Tang (2014) propose extending the quasi-maximum likelihood approach for the IV estimation studied in Xiu (2010) to the estimation of the ICM. By assuming time-invariant parameters, that is, $\boldsymbol{\sigma}_t = \boldsymbol{\sigma}$ and $\boldsymbol{\Sigma}_t = \boldsymbol{\sigma}_t\boldsymbol{\sigma}_t' = \boldsymbol{\Sigma}$, and assuming $\boldsymbol{U}_{\tau_0}, \boldsymbol{U}_{\tau_1}, \cdots, \boldsymbol{U}_{\tau_n}$ follow the normal distribution with mean $\mathbf{0}$ and covariance matrix $\boldsymbol{A}$, a quasi-likelihood function can be constructed as

$$l(\boldsymbol{\Sigma}, \boldsymbol{A}) = -\frac{1}{2}\log\det(\boldsymbol{\Omega}) - \frac{np}{2}\log(2\pi) - \frac{1}{2}\boldsymbol{y}'\boldsymbol{\Omega}^{-1}\boldsymbol{y}, \tag{8.10}$$

where $\boldsymbol{y} = (\boldsymbol{y}_1', \ldots, \boldsymbol{y}_n')'$, $\boldsymbol{y}_j = (y_{1j}, \ldots, y_{pj})' \equiv \boldsymbol{Y}_{\tau_j} - \boldsymbol{Y}_{\tau_{j-1}}$ for $j = 1, \ldots, n$. $\boldsymbol{\Sigma}$ and $\boldsymbol{A}$ are time-invariant covariance matrices,

$$\boldsymbol{\Omega} = \boldsymbol{I}_n \otimes (\boldsymbol{\Sigma}\Delta + 2\boldsymbol{A}) - (\boldsymbol{L}_n + \boldsymbol{L}_n') \otimes \boldsymbol{A}. \tag{8.11}$$

The notation $\otimes$ denotes the Kronecker product, and $\boldsymbol{I}_n$ is the n-dimensional identity matrix, $\boldsymbol{L}_n = (L(i,j))_{i,j=1,\ldots,n}$ is a n-dimensional one-lag subdiagonal matrix with $L(i-1, i) = 1$ $(i = 2, \ldots, n)$ and all other elements being 0. Here, Δ is set to be T/n. This means that one more misspecification, namely, that the synchronized data are equally spaced, is imposed for the QML estimation. The QML estimator of $(\boldsymbol{\Sigma}, \boldsymbol{A})$ is defined as the maximizer of (8.10).

We find that optimizing (8.10) is quite difficult, as $\boldsymbol{\Omega}$ is not a diagonal matrix, and its size is $np \times np$, which could be very large in practice. Liu and Tang (2014) develop a novel device to connect the model to a lower-dimensional multivariate moving average time series of order 1 (i.e., MA(1) model),

$$\boldsymbol{y}_j = \boldsymbol{v}_j - \boldsymbol{\Theta}\boldsymbol{v}_{j-1}, \tag{8.12}$$

where $\boldsymbol{\Theta}$ is a $p \times p$ invertible parameter matrix, $\{\boldsymbol{v}_j\}_{j=1}^n$ is a series of i.i.d. normal random vectors with mean $\mathbf{0}$ and invertible covariance matrix $\boldsymbol{\Gamma}$. Clearly, if $p \geq 2$, the unrestricted support of $(\boldsymbol{\Theta}, \boldsymbol{\Gamma})$ is actually larger than that of $(\boldsymbol{\Sigma}, \boldsymbol{A})$ because there are fewer free parameters in the latter due to the restriction that $\boldsymbol{\Sigma}$ and $\boldsymbol{A}$ must be symmetric. This is the main difficulty for using MA(1) model as a device to study the QML approach for multivariate cases because a general MA(1) model is not yet exactly equivalent to that of the QML approach without appropriate restriction on the support of $(\boldsymbol{\Theta}, \boldsymbol{\Gamma})$. Therefore, Liu and Tang (2014) first establish that there exists a one-to-one mapping from a restricted support of $(\boldsymbol{\Theta}, \boldsymbol{\Gamma})$ to the entire support of $(\boldsymbol{\Sigma}, \boldsymbol{A})$.

Proposition 8.3.1 *For any positive definite matrices* $\boldsymbol{\Sigma}$ *and* $\boldsymbol{A}$*, the square root matrix* $\boldsymbol{B} = \{(\boldsymbol{\Sigma}\boldsymbol{A}^{-1}\Delta + 4\boldsymbol{I}_p)\boldsymbol{\Sigma}\boldsymbol{A}^{-1}\Delta\}^{1/2}$ *exists and the following mapping from* $(\boldsymbol{\Sigma}, \boldsymbol{A})$ *to* $(\boldsymbol{\Theta}, \boldsymbol{\Gamma})$ *exists:*

$$\boldsymbol{\Theta} = (\boldsymbol{\Sigma}\boldsymbol{A}^{-1}\Delta + 2\boldsymbol{I}_p - \boldsymbol{B})/2 \quad \text{and} \quad \boldsymbol{\Gamma} = \boldsymbol{\Theta}^{-1}\boldsymbol{A}. \tag{8.13}$$

Define $\mathcal{S}$ *to be the set of all pairs* $(\boldsymbol{\Theta}, \boldsymbol{\Gamma})$ *such that* $\boldsymbol{\Theta} = \boldsymbol{Q}\boldsymbol{D}\boldsymbol{Q}^{-1}$ *and* $\boldsymbol{\Gamma} = \boldsymbol{\Theta}^{-1}\boldsymbol{A}$ *where* $\boldsymbol{Q} = \boldsymbol{A}^{1/2}\boldsymbol{T}$*,* $\boldsymbol{T} \in \mathbb{R}^{p\times p}$ *is a p-dimensional orthogonal matrix such that* $\boldsymbol{T}\boldsymbol{T}' = \boldsymbol{I}_p$*,* $\boldsymbol{A}$ *is a positive definite matrix, and* $\boldsymbol{D} = diag(\delta_1, \ldots, \delta_p)$ *where* $0 < \delta_k < 1$ $(k = 1, \ldots, p)$*. Then,* $(\boldsymbol{\Theta}, \boldsymbol{\Gamma})$ *in (8.13) is in* $\mathcal{S}$*, and the inverse mapping of (8.13) exists for any* $(\boldsymbol{\Theta}, \boldsymbol{\Gamma}) \in \mathcal{S}$*:*

$$\boldsymbol{\Sigma} = \{(\boldsymbol{\Theta} - \boldsymbol{I}_p)^2\boldsymbol{\Gamma}\}/\Delta \quad \text{and} \quad \boldsymbol{A} = \boldsymbol{\Theta}\boldsymbol{\Gamma}. \tag{8.14}$$

Based on the preceding proposition, the model (8.12) can be reexpressed as an auto-regressive form:

$$\boldsymbol{v}_j = \boldsymbol{\Theta}\boldsymbol{v}_{j-1} + \boldsymbol{y}_j = \boldsymbol{y}_j + \boldsymbol{\Theta}\boldsymbol{y}_{j-1} + \boldsymbol{\Theta}^2\boldsymbol{y}_{j-2} + \cdots,$$

such that methods developed for multivariate time series can be applied to obtain the QML estimators $\widehat{\boldsymbol{\Sigma}}^{\text{QML}}$ and $\widehat{\boldsymbol{A}}^{\text{QML}}$. An efficient algorithm based on the methods in Tsay (2010) is provided:

- **Step 1.** (Conditional MLE) By writing the model as $\boldsymbol{v}_j = \boldsymbol{y}_j + \boldsymbol{\Theta}\boldsymbol{v}_{j-1}$ and taking $\boldsymbol{v}_0 = \boldsymbol{0}$, we can obtain the conditional likelihood function as

$$f(\boldsymbol{y}_1, \ldots, \boldsymbol{y}_n | \boldsymbol{\Sigma}, \boldsymbol{A}) = \prod_{j=1}^{n} \frac{1}{(2\pi)^{p/2}|\boldsymbol{\Gamma}|^{1/2}} \exp\left(-\frac{1}{2}\boldsymbol{v}_j'\boldsymbol{\Gamma}^{-1}\boldsymbol{v}_j\right). \tag{8.15}$$

  Then, maximizing (8.15) with respect to $\boldsymbol{\Sigma}$ and $\boldsymbol{A}$ yields the initial estimators, and then using the connection in (8.13) gives the initial estimators for $\boldsymbol{\Gamma}$ and $\boldsymbol{\Theta}$.
- **Step 2.** Given the initial values from the previous step, we compute $\boldsymbol{v}_i$ recursively as

$$\boldsymbol{v}_1 = \boldsymbol{y}_1 + \boldsymbol{\Theta}\boldsymbol{v}_0, \ \ldots, \ \boldsymbol{v}_n = \boldsymbol{y}_n + \boldsymbol{\Theta}\boldsymbol{y}_{n-1} + \cdots + \boldsymbol{\Theta}^{n-1}\boldsymbol{y}_1 + \boldsymbol{\Theta}^n\boldsymbol{v}_0. \tag{8.16}$$

We note that (8.16) is equivalent to

$$y_1^* = -\boldsymbol{\Theta}\boldsymbol{\nu}_0 + \boldsymbol{\nu}_1, \ \ldots, y_n^* = -\boldsymbol{\Theta}^n\boldsymbol{\nu}_0 + \boldsymbol{\nu}_n, \tag{8.17}$$

where $y_j^* = y_j + \boldsymbol{\Theta}y_{j-1} + \cdots + \boldsymbol{\Theta}^{j-1}y_1$ for $j = 1, \ldots, n$. Given the initial estimator of $\boldsymbol{\Theta}$, and by left-multiplying each of the preceding equations by $\boldsymbol{\Gamma}^{-1/2}$, the resulting system becomes a multiple linear regression with $-\boldsymbol{\Gamma}^{-1/2}\boldsymbol{\Theta}, \ldots, -\boldsymbol{\Gamma}^{-1/2}\boldsymbol{\Theta}^n$ as the explanatory variables and $\boldsymbol{\Gamma}^{-1/2}y_1^*, \ldots, \boldsymbol{\Gamma}^{-1/2}y_n^*$ as the dependent variables. Therefore, we can use the ordinary least squares method to obtain an estimator of $\boldsymbol{\nu}_0$, denoted by $\hat{\boldsymbol{\nu}}_0$.

- **Step 3.** (Exact MLE) By replacing $\boldsymbol{\nu}_0$ in (8.16) with $\hat{\boldsymbol{\nu}}_0$, we obtain new $(\boldsymbol{\nu}_0, \boldsymbol{\nu}_1, \ldots, \boldsymbol{\nu}_n)$. Using the new data, we can construct the exact likelihood function by changing the lower bound of j in (8.15) from 1 to 0. We then update estimators for $\boldsymbol{\Sigma}$ and $\boldsymbol{A}$ by maximizing the likelihood function.
- **Step 4.** Repeat Steps 2–3 until convergence, and obtain the final estimators $\widehat{\boldsymbol{\Sigma}}^{\text{QML}}$ and $\widehat{\boldsymbol{A}}^{\text{QML}}$.

The QML estimator of $\boldsymbol{C}_T$ is defined as

$$\widehat{\boldsymbol{C}}_T^{\text{QML}} = T\widehat{\boldsymbol{\Sigma}}^{\text{QML}}.$$

Liu and Tang (2014) prove that under Assumptions 8.3.1 and 8.3.2, the $\widehat{\boldsymbol{\Sigma}}^{\text{QML}}$ satisfies $\|\widehat{\boldsymbol{\Sigma}}^{\text{QML}} - \boldsymbol{C}_T/T\|_F = O_p(n^{-1/4})$. In addition, we ensure $\widehat{\boldsymbol{\Sigma}}^{\text{QML}}$ are positive definite by implementing alternative parameterizations of $\boldsymbol{\Sigma}$ and $\boldsymbol{A}$ via using their Cholesky-type decomposition, which means we optimize (8.15) with respect to the Cholesky decomposition of $\boldsymbol{\Sigma}$ and $\boldsymbol{A}$ instead of directly. We find that this approach has no tuning parameter, consistent with ICM with an optimal convergence rate, and can ensure the estimator to be positive definite.

QMLE with a State Space Model

The preceding four methods need to synchronize original nonsynchronous data before estimation such that a large part of the data may be dropped. To obtain higher statistical efficiency, Liu and Tang (2013) and Shephard and Xiu (2017) propose using all observations and estimate the ICM by constructing a Gaussian state space model and applying the EM algorithm. By doing this, a nonsynchronous data set is considered as a data set with missing values.

The state space model is constructed by imposing two not necessarily correct assumptions, which are the same for obtaining $\widehat{\boldsymbol{\Sigma}}^{\text{QML}}$ in Subsection 8.3.1; then

$$\begin{aligned}
\boldsymbol{X}_{t_j} - \boldsymbol{X}_{t_{j-1}} &= \boldsymbol{\sigma}(\boldsymbol{W}_{t_j} - \boldsymbol{W}_{t_{j-1}}) \sim \mathcal{N}(0, \boldsymbol{\Sigma}\Delta_j),\\
\boldsymbol{Y}_{t_j} - \boldsymbol{Y}_{t_{j-1}} &= \boldsymbol{X}_{t_j} - \boldsymbol{X}_{t_{j-1}} + \boldsymbol{U}_{t_j} - \boldsymbol{U}_{t_{j-1}} \sim \mathcal{N}(0, \boldsymbol{\Sigma}\Delta_j + 2\boldsymbol{A}),
\end{aligned}$$

where $\Delta_j = t_j - t_{j-1}$ and $0 \le t_0 < t_1 < \cdots < t_N \le T$. Here, $\{t_j, j = 0, 1, \ldots, N\}$ are the distinct time points of $\bigcup_{k=1}^p \mathcal{G}_k$, where at least one asset has one trading record at each t_j. We treat the components with no record at time t_j as missing, and assume that there are p_j ($p_j \geq 1$) assets that have trade records at time t_j for $j = 0, \ldots, N$. Let $\boldsymbol{B}_j = \begin{pmatrix} \boldsymbol{B}_j^{(1)} \\ \boldsymbol{B}_j^{(2)} \end{pmatrix}$ be a permutation matrix such that $\widetilde{\boldsymbol{Y}}_j = \boldsymbol{B}_j(Y_{1j}, Y_{2j}, \ldots, Y_{pj})' = \left(\boldsymbol{Y}_j^{(1)'}, \boldsymbol{Y}_j^{(2)'}\right)'$ where $\boldsymbol{Y}_j^{(1)} \in \mathbb{R}^{p_j}$ collects the observed asset prices, and $\boldsymbol{Y}_j^{(2)} \in \mathbb{R}^{p-p_j}$ contains the missing components. Hence the role of $\boldsymbol{B}_j$ is such that the first p_j components in $\widetilde{\boldsymbol{Y}}_j$ are observed. Then we can write the state space model as

$$\widetilde{\boldsymbol{Y}}_j = \boldsymbol{B}_j\boldsymbol{X}_j + \widetilde{\boldsymbol{U}}_j, \qquad \boldsymbol{X}_j = \boldsymbol{X}_{j-1} + \boldsymbol{V}_j, \tag{8.18}$$

where $\widetilde{\boldsymbol{U}}_j$ is the reordered p-dimensional random vector with mean zero and variance $\boldsymbol{A}_j = \boldsymbol{B}_j\boldsymbol{A}\boldsymbol{B}_j'$, and $\boldsymbol{V}_j \sim \mathcal{N}(\boldsymbol{0}, \boldsymbol{\Sigma}\Delta_j)$.

The EM algorithm, see, for example, Dempster et al. (1977), is then applied to obtain the estimations of $\boldsymbol{\Sigma}$ and $\boldsymbol{A}$, where the conditional expectations in the EM algorithm can be conveniently evaluated by the Kalman filtering method; see, for example, Shumway and Stoffer (2011). To save space, we refer to Liu and Tang (2013) and Shephard and Xiu (2017) for the details of the EM algorithm. This method has used all the data and has no tuning parameter. Therefore, it can achieve higher efficiency.

Shephard and Xiu (2017) have proved that the estimation of the ICM is a consistent estimator with convergence rate $n^{-1/4}$ if the data are synchronous with sample size n and the covariance matrix of noise is a diagonal matrix. However, neither Liu and Tang (2013) nor Shephard and Xiu (2017) discussed the impact of nonsynchronicity of data theoretically.

Local Method of Moments Estimation

Another kind of procedure to deal with data nonsynchronicity is using Fourier transformations. Bibinger et al. (2014) propose using all high-frequency data available and develop a local method of moments (LMM) to estimate the ICM, which relies on an asymptotically equivalent continuous-time observation model. The main idea of LMM is to use a representation of localized Fourier coefficients.

Let vec($\cdot$) be the column stacking operator of a matrix. For example, for an $p \times p$ matrix $\boldsymbol{M}$,

$$\text{vec}(\boldsymbol{M}) := (M_{11}, M_{21}, \cdots, M_{p1}, M_{12}, M_{22}, \cdots, M_{p2}, \cdots, M_{p(p-1)}, M_{pp})',$$

where $M(i,j)$ is the (i,j)th element of matrix $\boldsymbol{M}$. The first step for obtaining the LMM estimation is to split the time interval $[0, T]$ into small blocks $[kh, (k+1)h)$, $k = 0, \ldots, [T/h] - 1$ with $h = O(n_{\max}^{-1/4})$ and $n_{\max} = \max(n_1, \ldots, n_p)$. Under Assumption 8.3.2 with diagonal matrix $\boldsymbol{\Sigma}^U$, the LMM estimator of $\text{vec}(\boldsymbol{C}_T)$ is defined as the weighted summations across all blocks and frequencies:

$$\widehat{\text{vec}(\boldsymbol{C}_T)}^{\text{LMM}} = \sum_{k=0}^{[T/h]-1} h \sum_{j=1}^{\infty} \widehat{\boldsymbol{W}}_{jk} \text{vec}\left(\boldsymbol{S}_{jk}\boldsymbol{S}'_{jk} - \pi^2 j^2 h^{-2} \text{diag}((\widehat{H}_{n,l}^{kh})^2)_l\right), \tag{8.19}$$

where $\widehat{\boldsymbol{W}}_{jk}$s are $p^2 \times p^2$ weight matrices, $\text{diag}((\widehat{H}_{n,l}^{kh})^2)_l$ is a $p \times p$ diagonal matrix with the lth diagonal element being $(\widehat{H}_{n,l}^{kh})^2$, and $\boldsymbol{S}_{jk}$ is a p-dimensional column vector with the lth element being

$$S_{jk}(l) = \pi j h^{-1} \left(\sum_{v=1}^{n_l} \left(Y_{t_v^l}^l - Y_{t_{v-1}^l}^l \right) \Phi_{jk} \left(\frac{t_{v-1}^l + t_v^l}{2} \right) \right)$$

and

$$\Phi_{jk}(t) = \frac{\sqrt{2h}}{j\pi} \sin\left(j\pi h^{-1}(t - kh) \right) 1_{\{t \in [kh,(k+1)h)\}}.$$

Here, $\widehat{H}_{n,l}^{kh}$ is an estimator of variance of U_t^l around time $t = kh$, which can be chosen as

$$\widehat{H}_{n,l}^{kh} = \frac{1}{2n_l^k} \sum_{t_{v-1}^l, t_v^l \in [kh,(k+1)h)} \left(Y_{t_v^l}^l - Y_{t_{v-1}^l}^l \right)^2$$

as suggested in Zhang et al. (2005), with n_l^k being the number of points in the set $\{v \colon t_{v-1}^l, t_v^l \in [kh, (k+1)h)\}$. The estimated weight matrix $\widehat{\boldsymbol{W}}_{jk}$ is obtained based on the Fisher information calculus that

$$\widehat{\boldsymbol{W}}_{jk} = \widehat{\boldsymbol{I}}_k^{-1} \widehat{\boldsymbol{I}}_{jk}, \ \widehat{\boldsymbol{I}}_k = \sum_{j=1}^{\infty} \widehat{\boldsymbol{I}}_{jk}, \ \widehat{\boldsymbol{I}}_{jk} = \widehat{\boldsymbol{C}}_{jk}^{-1} \otimes \widehat{\boldsymbol{C}}_{jk}^{-1},$$

$$\widehat{\boldsymbol{C}}_{jk} = \widehat{\boldsymbol{\Sigma}}^{kh} + \pi^2 j^2 h^{-2} \text{diag}(\widehat{H}_{n,l}^{kh})_l^2,$$

where $\widehat{\boldsymbol{\Sigma}}^{kh}$ can be set as the average of estimators of spot covariance $\boldsymbol{\Sigma}_t$ around $t = kh$. To obtain a uniformly consistent estimation of spot covariance $\boldsymbol{\Sigma}_t$, Bibinger and Reiß (2014) suggest using

$$\widehat{\boldsymbol{\Sigma}}_t = K^{-1} \sum_{k \in \mathcal{K}_t} J^{-1} \sum_{j=1}^{J} \left(\boldsymbol{S}_{jk}\boldsymbol{S}'_{jk} - \pi^2 j^2 h^{-2} \text{diag}((\widehat{H}_{n,l}^{kh})^2)_l \right),$$

where $\mathcal{K}_t$ is an adjacent block containing t, and $K = O(n^{\alpha/(2\alpha+1)})$ for some $\alpha > 1/2$ is the number of adjacent blocks that contain t. Bibinger et al. (2014) show that under Assumptions 8.3.1 and 8.3.2 with diagonal $\boldsymbol{\Sigma}^U$, $\widehat{\text{vec}(\boldsymbol{C}_T)}^{\text{LMM}}$

converges to $\mathrm{vec}(\boldsymbol{C}_T)$ with rate $n_{\min}^{-1/4}$ under some conditions for the observation times of asset prices, where $n_{\min} = \min(n_1, \ldots, n_p)$. For the tuning parameters, Bibinger and Reiß (2014) choose $h = 1/10$, $J = 30$, and $K = 8$ in their simulation study.

All the preceding methods are designed for estimating the ICM with finite dimension p, where their asymptotic properties rely on the fact that p is a fixed number. Although the elementwise estimators $\widehat{\boldsymbol{C}}_T^{\mathrm{TSE}}$, $\widehat{\boldsymbol{C}}_T^{\mathrm{POL}}$, and $\widehat{\boldsymbol{C}}_T^{\mathrm{PAHY}}$ can be used to estimate a large-dimensional ICM, their consistencies are constructed only for each element of the ICM.

8.3.2 Estimate the ICM with a Large Dimension

It is well known that estimating a large-dimensional covariance matrix is quite difficult even with i.i.d. samples. The main reason is that when the matrix dimension p goes to ∞ with the sample size n, even if the estimation of each element of the covariance matrix is consistent, the estimation of the whole matrix may not be consistent. For example, if the bias of the estimation of each element is of order $O_p(n^{-1/2})$, then the accumulation of biases of the whole matrix is $O_p(n^{-1/2}p^2)$ such that when $p = O(n^{1/4+\alpha})$ for $\alpha \geq 0$, the estimation of the whole matrix is not consistent with the true covariance matrix. However, when p is finite, then the matrix estimator is consistent when the estimator of each element is consistent. To obtain a consistent estimator for a large-dimensional covariance matrix, some structure constraints are needed, such as sparsity, bandability, or a factor structure. Estimating a large-dimensional ICM is even more difficult, as the samples are dependent and non-identically distributed because of microstructure noises and time-variant spot covariance.

Three types of estimations for a large-dimensional ICM have been studied in literature. The first one estimates the ICM elementwise and thresholding the nondiagonal elements, for example, Tao et al. (2011), Tao et al. (2013a), and Tao et al. (2013b). The second one estimates the ICM based on a factor model with known factors, unknown factors, or known loadings; see Aït-Sahalia and Xiu (2017), Dai et al. (2019), and Aït-Sahalia et al. (2020). The third one estimates the ICM relying on the random matrix theory; see Zheng and Li (2011), Xia and Zheng (2018), Lam et al. (2017), and Lam and Feng (2018). In contrast to the estimators in Subsection 8.3.1, which assume the dimension of ICM p is finite, those three types of estimators assume $p \to \infty$ asymptotically.

Threshold Multiscale Realized Volatility Matrix

Tao et al. (2013b) propose estimating ICM elementwise using multiscale realized volatility matrix (MSRVM) with thresholding. Let $\bar{n} = \frac{1}{p}\sum_{k=1}^{p}(n_k+1)$. The estimator is constructed through four steps.

- **Step 1** Construct the realized covariance of X_t^k and X_t^l based on a subsample of the data. Denote m and h as two fixed positive integers.
  - Set regular grids as follows:

    $$\boldsymbol{\tau}^{(h)} = \{T(r-1)/m, r = 1, \ldots, m\} + Th/\bar{n} = \{T\tau_r^{(h)}, r = 1, \ldots, m\},$$

    with $\tau_r^{(h)} = (r-1)/m + h/\bar{n}$. We find that for each h, there are m time points in $\boldsymbol{\tau}^{(h)}$, and the time length between any two consecutive points is T/m.
  - For each time point in $\boldsymbol{\tau}^{(h)}$, we use the previous-tick method to select one trading record for each asset. The previous-tick time of $\tau_r^{(h)}$ for the kth asset is

    $$t_r^{(h),k} = \max\{t_j^k \leq T\tau_r^{(h)}, j = 0, \ldots, n_k\},$$

    for $r \in \{1, \ldots, m\}$. Similar for the lth asset. Therefore, the data for constructing the realized covariance are $\left\{Y^k_{t_r^{(h),k}}, r = 1, \ldots, m\right\}$ and $\left\{Y^l_{t_r^{(h),l}}, r = 1, \ldots, m\right\}$.
  - The realized covariance of X_t^k and X_t^l is then defined as

    $$\widetilde{C}_T^{(h)}(k,l) = \sum_{r=1}^{m} \left(Y^k_{t_r^{(h),k}} - Y^k_{t_{r-1}^{(h),k}}\right)\left(Y^l_{t_r^{(h),l}} - Y^l_{t_{r-1}^{(h),l}}\right). \tag{8.20}$$

- **Step 2** Average H_m realized volatility matrices. Let $h = 1, \ldots, H_m$; then, we can obtain H_m realized volatility matrices based on Step 1. The average realized volatility matrix is defined as

  $$\widehat{\boldsymbol{C}}_T^{H_m} = \left(\widehat{C}_T^{H_m}(k,l)\right)_{k,l}, \quad \widehat{C}_T^{H_m}(k,l) = \frac{1}{H_m}\sum_{h=1}^{H_m} \widetilde{C}_T^{(h)}(k,l).$$

- **Step 3** Repeat Steps 1–2 M times. The MSRVM is set to be

  $$\widehat{\boldsymbol{C}}^{\text{MSRVM}} = \sum_{m=1}^{M} a_m \widehat{\boldsymbol{C}}_T^{H_m} + \zeta(\widehat{\boldsymbol{C}}_T^{H_1} - \widehat{\boldsymbol{C}}_T^{H_M}), \tag{8.21}$$

  where

  $$a_m = \frac{12(m+M)(m - M/2 - 1/2)}{M(M^2-1)},$$
  $$H_m = m + M, \ \zeta = \frac{2M(M+1)}{(\bar{n}+1)(M-1)}.$$

  Tao et al. (2013) set $M = O(\sqrt{\bar{n}})$.

- **Step 4** Threshold the MSRVM. To consistently estimate the large-dimensional ICM, Tao et al. (2013b) propose to threshold the MSRVM estimator by

$$\widehat{C}_T^{\text{TMSRVM}} = \left(\widehat{C}^{\text{MSRVM}}(k,l)1_{\{|\widehat{C}^{\text{MSRVM}}(k,l)|\geq \varpi\}}\right)_{k,l}, \tag{8.22}$$

where $\varpi = O(\bar{n}^{-1/4}p^{2/\beta}h_{n,p})$ with $\beta > 2$ and $h_{n,p}$ goes to infinity slowly, for example $h_{n,p} = \log\log(\bar{n} \wedge p)$.

Under Assumption 8.3.2 with $\mathbf{\Sigma}^U$ being a diagonal matrix, some moment conditions for the noises and $\boldsymbol{X}_t$, and assumptions for nonsynchronicity of the data, Tao et al. (2013a) prove that the convergence rate of each element of $\widehat{\boldsymbol{C}}_T^{\text{MSRVM}}$ is $\bar{n}^{-1/4}$ and $\widehat{\boldsymbol{C}}_T^{\text{TMSRVM}}$ converges to $\boldsymbol{C}_T$ in L_2 norm with rate $\pi(p)[\bar{n}^{-1/4}p^{2/\beta}]^{1-\delta}$ under the sparse structure assumption for $\boldsymbol{C}_T$, where $0 \leq \delta < 1$ calibrates the magnitude level of significantly large elements and is used to control the sparsity of a large-dimensional matrix. The sparsity of the ICM in Tao et al. (2013a, b) is defined by assuming

$$\sum_{l=1}^{p} |C_T(k,l)|^\delta \leq \Theta\pi(p), \quad k = 1,\ldots,p, \quad E(\Theta) \leq c,$$

with c being a positive constant, $\Theta > 0$ being a random variable, and $\pi(p)$ being a deterministic function of p, which grows very slowly with p.

Tao et al. (2011) propose a similar threshold average realized volatility for each day,

$$\widehat{\boldsymbol{C}}_T^{\text{TARV}} = \widehat{\boldsymbol{C}}_T^{H} - 2m\text{diag}(\hat{\boldsymbol{\eta}}),\ \hat{\boldsymbol{\eta}} = (\hat{\eta}_1,\ldots,\hat{\eta}_p),\ \hat{\eta}_k = \frac{1}{2n_k}\sum_{j=1}^{n_k}(Y_{t_j^k} - Y_{t_{j-1}^k})^2,$$

where $\hat{\eta}_k$ is the estimator of variance of noises contaminated in the kth asset price. To address the dimensionality problem, Tao et al. (2011) then propose a factor model for each day's ICM such that the final estimator for the ICM is a combination of thresholding and the factor structure. Tao et al. (2011) prove that $\widehat{\boldsymbol{C}}_T^{\text{TARV}}$ is a consistent estimator with convergence rate $\pi(p)[\bar{n}^{-1/6}p^{2/\beta}]^{1-\delta}$, which is much slower than the convergence rate of $\widehat{\boldsymbol{C}}_T^{\text{TMSRVM}}$.

Preaveraging Time-Variation-Adjusted Realized Covariance

The first estimator of the ICM relied on the random matrix theory, called time-variation adjusted realized covariance (TVARCV), is developed in Zheng and Li (2011) without considering microstructure noises but assuming that the spot covariance of $\boldsymbol{X}_t$ varies over time and the observation durations $\Delta_j := \tau_j - \tau_{j-1}$ $(j = 1,\ldots,n)$ may be different. Xia and Zheng (2018) then extend TVARCV to the preaveraging time-variation adjusted realized covariance (PA-TVARCV) estimator. This PA-TVARCV estimator addresses the microstructure noises with the preaveraging technique and is defined as

$$\widehat{\boldsymbol{C}}_T^{\text{PA-TVARCV}} = 3\frac{\sum_{i=1}^{m}|\Delta\overline{\boldsymbol{Y}}_{2i}|^2}{m}\sum_{i=1}^{m}\frac{\Delta\overline{\boldsymbol{Y}}_{2i}(\Delta\overline{\boldsymbol{Y}}_{2i})'}{|\Delta\overline{\boldsymbol{Y}}_{2i}|^2}, \tag{8.23}$$

where $m = \lfloor n/(2k) \rfloor$ and

$$\Delta\overline{\boldsymbol{Y}}_{2i} = \frac{1}{k}\sum_{j=0}^{k-1}\left(\boldsymbol{Y}_{\tau_{(2i-1)k+j}} - \boldsymbol{Y}_{\tau_{(2i-2)k+j}}\right)$$

is the preaveraging returns. Divided $\Delta\overline{\boldsymbol{Y}}_{2i}(\Delta\overline{\boldsymbol{Y}}_{2i})'$ by $|\Delta\overline{\boldsymbol{Y}}_{2i}|^2$ adjusts the time variation of the spot covariance.

Xia and Zheng (2018) prove that if $\boldsymbol{X}_t$ belongs to the class $\mathcal{C}$, then, under some conditions, the limit spectral distributions of $\widehat{\boldsymbol{C}}_T^{\text{PA-TVARCV}}$ and $\boldsymbol{C}_T$ are related via the standard Marčenko–Pastur equation such that the empirical spectral distribution of $\boldsymbol{C}_T$ can be consistently estimated based on the empirical spectral distribution of $\widehat{\boldsymbol{C}}_T^{\text{PA-TVARCV}}$. Here, $\boldsymbol{X}_t$ belongs to the class $\mathcal{C}$, which means that $\boldsymbol{X}_t$ satisfies (8.1), and almost surely, there exists a $\gamma_t \in D([0,T];\mathbb{R})$ such that

$$\boldsymbol{\sigma}_t = \gamma_t\boldsymbol{\Lambda} \text{ with } \operatorname{tr}(\boldsymbol{\Lambda}\boldsymbol{\Lambda}') = p. \tag{8.24}$$

Rotation-Equivalent Estimators

It is well known that when the dimension of the covariance matrix is close to the sample size, the sample covariance matrix is ill-conditioned such that the largest and smallest eigenvalues of the sample covariance matrix are much larger and smaller than the corresponding eigenvalues of the population covariance matrix, respectively; see the simulation in Tao et al. (2011). To address this problem, Abadir et al. (2014) first split the data into two parts and estimate the eigenvectors of the covariance matrix based on the first part of the sample and then use them to transform the second part of the data into approximately orthogonal series. Because orthogonal matrices are never ill-conditioned, they then estimate the eigenvalues of the covariance matrix by the diagonal elements of the sample covariance matrix of the transformed data such that the matrix estimator is now well conditioned. This actually shrinks the eigenvalues of the sample covariance matrix constructed based on the first part of the sample. The estimator developed in Abadir et al. (2014) belongs to the class of rotation-equivalent estimators, which are introduced in Stein (1975) and Stein (1986) and satisfy the requirement that rotating the original variables results in the same rotation being applied to the covariance matrix estimator, as demonstrated in Ledoit and Wolf (2017).

Lam et al. (2017) use the idea in Abadir et al. (2014) to estimate the ICM with high-frequency data. They propose a nonlinear shrinkage time variation-adjusted realized covariance (NS-TVARCV) estimation for the large-dimensional ICM based on sparsely sampled data such that the impacts of nonsynchronicity and noises are not significant. Suppose $\boldsymbol{Y}_{\tau_0}, \ldots, \boldsymbol{Y}_{\tau_n}$ are sparsely sampled data, which can be obtained by synchronizing data using the previous-tick method with large Δ. Denote $\boldsymbol{y}_j = \boldsymbol{Y}_{\tau_j} - \boldsymbol{Y}_{\tau_{j-1}}$, $j = 1, \ldots, n$. Lam et al. (2017) first permute the returns into two parts for K times. For the kth permutation, denote $\boldsymbol{y}^{(k)} = (\boldsymbol{y}^{(k,1)}, \boldsymbol{y}^{(k,2)})$ where $\boldsymbol{y}^{(k,v)}$ is a $p \times m_v$ matrix containing m_v returns for $v = 1, 2$. Denoting $\boldsymbol{\Phi}_v^{(k)} = m_v^{-1} \sum_{j \in I_{k,v}} \boldsymbol{y}_j \boldsymbol{y}_j'$ with $I_{k,v} = \{j : \boldsymbol{y}_j \in \boldsymbol{y}^{(k,v)}\}$, and writing the eigen-decomposition of $\boldsymbol{\Phi}_1^{(k)}$ as $\boldsymbol{\Phi}_1^{(k)} = \boldsymbol{P}_1^{(k)} \boldsymbol{D}_1^k \left(\boldsymbol{P}_1^{(k)}\right)'$, then the NS-TVARCV is defined as

$$\widehat{\boldsymbol{C}}_T^{\text{NS-TVARCV}} = \frac{\operatorname{tr}(\sum_{j=1}^n \boldsymbol{y}_j \boldsymbol{y}_j')}{pK} \sum_{k=1}^K \boldsymbol{P}_1^{(k)} \operatorname{diag}\left\{(\boldsymbol{P}_1^{(k)})' \boldsymbol{\Phi}_2^{(k)} \boldsymbol{P}_1^{(k)}\right\} \left(\boldsymbol{P}_1^{(k)}\right)'. \tag{8.25}$$

Lam et al. (2017) show that under some conditions, if $\boldsymbol{X}_t$ belongs to class $\mathcal{C}$ defined in Xia and Zheng (2018), then $\widehat{\boldsymbol{C}}_T^{\text{NS-TVARCV}}$ is asymptotically almost surely positive definite and close to the so-called ideal but not applicable estimator $\int_0^T \gamma_t^2 dt \boldsymbol{P} \operatorname{diag}(\boldsymbol{P}' \breve{\boldsymbol{\Phi}} \boldsymbol{P}) \boldsymbol{P}'$, where $\boldsymbol{P}$ is a matrix satisfying the following eigen-decomposition:

$$\breve{\boldsymbol{\Phi}} := \frac{p}{n} \sum_{j=1}^n \frac{\boldsymbol{x}_j \boldsymbol{x}_j'}{\|\boldsymbol{x}_j\|^2} = \boldsymbol{P} \breve{\boldsymbol{D}} \boldsymbol{P}'.$$

Here, $\breve{\boldsymbol{\Phi}}$ is an estimator of $\boldsymbol{\Lambda}\boldsymbol{\Lambda}'$ and $\boldsymbol{x}_j$s are the returns of process $\boldsymbol{X}_t$, which are not observable.

Lam and Feng (2018) extend the work of Lam et al. (2017) and consider the estimation of the ICM with high-frequency data contaminated with noise. They first divide the time interval $(0, T]$ into L small intervals $(v_l, v_{l+1}]$ for $l = 1, \ldots, L$ with $v_1 = 0$ and $v_{L+1} = T$. For the lth interval, they first estimate ICM during $(v_l, v_{l+1}]$ by two scales of covariance estimator – $\widehat{\boldsymbol{C}}_{(l)}^{\text{TSE}}$ with data of p assets synchronized together by the refresh time scheme. Let $\widehat{\boldsymbol{C}}_{(-j)} = \sum_{l \neq j} \widehat{\boldsymbol{C}}_{(l)}^{\text{TSE}}$ and suppose it has the eigen-decomposition $\widehat{\boldsymbol{C}}_{(-j)} = \boldsymbol{P}_{(-j)} \boldsymbol{D}_{(-j)} \boldsymbol{P}_{(-j)}'$, then the new estimator developed in Lam and Feng (2018), called the nonparametrically eigenvalue-regularized integrated covariance matrix estimator (NERIVE), is defined as

$$\widehat{\boldsymbol{C}}_T^{\text{NERIVE}} = \sum_{l=1}^L \boldsymbol{P}_{(-l)} \operatorname{diag}\left\{\boldsymbol{P}_{(-l)}' \widehat{\boldsymbol{C}}_{(l)}^{TSE} \boldsymbol{P}_{(-l)}\right\} \boldsymbol{P}_{(-l)}'. \tag{8.26}$$

Lam and Feng (2018) prove that under some conditions for the noises and the nonsynchronicity of data, $\widehat{\boldsymbol{C}}_T^{\text{NERIVE}}$ is consistent with the idea of, but not applicable to rotation-equivalent estimator $\sum_{l=1}^{L} \boldsymbol{P}_{(-l)}\text{diag}\left\{\boldsymbol{P}'_{(-l)}\boldsymbol{C}_{(l)}\boldsymbol{P}_{(-l)}\right\}\boldsymbol{P}'_{(-l)}$, where $\boldsymbol{C}_{(l)} = \int_{v_l}^{v_{l+1}} \boldsymbol{\Sigma}_t dt$. In addition, $\widehat{\boldsymbol{C}}_T^{\text{NERIVE}}$ is positive definite with probability one when all $\boldsymbol{C}_{(1)}, \ldots, \boldsymbol{C}_{(L)}$ are positive definite. We refer to Lam and Feng (2018) for the detailed asymptotic properties of $\widehat{\boldsymbol{C}}_T^{\text{NERIVE}}$.

Factor-Model-Based Estimators

Factor-model-based estimators for the large-dimensional ICM have been developed in a few articles. Fan et al. (2016) assume the high-frequency factors are observable and estimate the ICM based on sparse sampled data where the impacts of noises are ignorable. Aït-Sahalia and Xiu (2017) propose to estimate the ICM by principal component analysis (PCA) and without considering the noise and nonsynchronicity of high-frequency data. Dai et al. (2019) extend the preceding approaches and make them more applicable in practice by considering that data are nonsynchronous and contaminated with noises. They first synchronize data by the refresh time scheme and then use the preaveraging returns to estimate ICM. Kong and Liu (2018) and Kong et al. (2021) also study the high-frequency factor model but focus on testing whether the factor loadings and factor spaces are time-invariant or not, respectively.

We now introduce estimators developed in Dai et al. (2019). Assume that the latent process $\boldsymbol{X}_t$ follows the factor model,

$$\boldsymbol{X}_t = \boldsymbol{\beta}\boldsymbol{F}_t + \boldsymbol{Z}_t,$$

where $\boldsymbol{F}_t$ is an r-dimensional factor process and

$$\boldsymbol{F}_t = \int_0^t \boldsymbol{h}_s ds + \int_0^t \boldsymbol{\eta}_s d\boldsymbol{W}_s, \ \boldsymbol{Z}_t = \int_0^t \boldsymbol{f}_s ds + \int_0^t \boldsymbol{\gamma}_s d\boldsymbol{B}_s,$$

where $\boldsymbol{W}_s$ and $\boldsymbol{B}_s$ are independent Brownian motions, $\boldsymbol{h}_s$ and $\boldsymbol{f}_s$ satisfy the same condition as $\boldsymbol{\mu}_t$ in (8.1), and $\boldsymbol{\eta}_s$ and $\boldsymbol{\gamma}_s$ satisfy the same condition as $\boldsymbol{\sigma}_t$ in (8.1). Denote $\boldsymbol{\Gamma} = \frac{1}{T}\int_0^T \boldsymbol{\gamma}_s\boldsymbol{\gamma}_s' ds$, and define the degree of its sparsity by

$$m_p = \max_{k\leq p} \sum_{l\leq p} |\Gamma(k,l)|^q \ \text{ for some } q \in [0, 1).$$

We assume the observations of assets are synchronized by the refresh time scheme and denoted by $\boldsymbol{Y}_{\tau_0}, \ldots, \boldsymbol{Y}_{\tau_n}$. To decrease the impact of microstructure noises, Dai et al. (2019) propose using the preaveraging returns,

$$\bar{y}_i = \sum_{j=1}^{k_n-1} g\left(\frac{j}{k_n}\right)(\boldsymbol{Y}_{\tau_{i+j}} - \boldsymbol{Y}_{\tau_{i+j-1}}),$$

$$\bar{\boldsymbol{f}}_i = \sum_{j=1}^{k_n-1} g\left(\frac{j}{k_n}\right)(\boldsymbol{F}_{\tau_{i+j}} - \boldsymbol{F}_{\tau_{i+j-1}}), \tag{8.27}$$

and $\bar{\boldsymbol{v}}_i = (\bar{\boldsymbol{y}}_i', \bar{\boldsymbol{f}}_i')'$ for $i = 0, \ldots, n - k_n + 1$. Here, the definition of the preaveraging returns is the same as that for $\widehat{\boldsymbol{C}}_T^{\text{MRC}}$, $g(x)$ can be chosen as $x \wedge (1 - x)$, and k_n satisfies $\frac{k_n}{n^{1/2+\delta}} = \theta + o(n_\delta^{-1/2})$ with $n_\delta^{-1/2} := n^{-1/4+\delta/2} + n^{-2\delta}$ for some $\theta > 0$ and $\delta > 0$.

Assuming that the factor process has observations $\boldsymbol{F}_{\tau_0}, \ldots, \boldsymbol{F}_{\tau_n}$, the estimator for the ICM with known factors is defined as

$$\widehat{\boldsymbol{C}}_T^{\text{FactorK}} = \widehat{\boldsymbol{\beta}}\widehat{\boldsymbol{E}}\widehat{\boldsymbol{\beta}}' + \widehat{\boldsymbol{\Gamma}}^S, \tag{8.28}$$

where

$$\widehat{\boldsymbol{\beta}} = \widehat{\boldsymbol{\Pi}}^{12}(\widehat{\boldsymbol{\Pi}}^{22})^{-1},\ \widehat{\boldsymbol{E}} = \widehat{\boldsymbol{\Pi}}^{22},\ \widehat{\boldsymbol{\Gamma}} = \widehat{\boldsymbol{\Pi}}^{11} - \widehat{\boldsymbol{\Pi}}^{12}(\widehat{\boldsymbol{\Pi}}^{22})^{-1}\widehat{\boldsymbol{\Pi}}^{21},\ \widehat{\boldsymbol{\Gamma}}^S = \left(\widehat{\Gamma}^S(k,l)\right)_{k,l},$$

$$\widehat{\boldsymbol{\Pi}} = \frac{n}{n - k_n + 2}\frac{1}{\psi_2 k_n T}\sum_{i=0}^{n-k_n+1} \bar{\boldsymbol{v}}_i\bar{\boldsymbol{v}}_i' = \begin{pmatrix} \widehat{\boldsymbol{\Pi}}^{11} & \widehat{\boldsymbol{\Pi}}^{12} \\ \widehat{\boldsymbol{\Pi}}^{21} & \widehat{\boldsymbol{\Pi}}^{22} \end{pmatrix},$$

and $\widehat{\boldsymbol{\Gamma}}^S = s(\widehat{\boldsymbol{\Gamma}})$, which is defined as $\widehat{\boldsymbol{\Gamma}}^S := \left(\widehat{\Gamma}^S(k,l)\right)_{k,l}$ with $\widehat{\Gamma}^S(k,l) = \widehat{\Gamma}(k,l)$ if $k = l$ and $\widehat{\Gamma}^S(k,l) = s_{\lambda_{kl}}(\widehat{\Gamma}(k,l))$ if $k \neq l$ where $s_\lambda(z)$ is a thresholding function. $\psi_2 = 1/12$ when $g(x) = x \wedge (1 - x)$.

When the factors are unobservable, the estimator for the ICM based on PCA is constructed as

$$\widehat{\boldsymbol{C}}_T^{\text{FactorUK}} = \sum_{r=1}^{\hat{r}} \widehat{\lambda}_r \widehat{\boldsymbol{\xi}}_r \widehat{\boldsymbol{\xi}}_r' + \widetilde{\boldsymbol{\Gamma}}^S, \tag{8.29}$$

where $\widehat{\lambda}_1 \geq \widehat{\lambda}_2 \cdots \geq \widehat{\lambda}_p$ are eigenvalues of

$$\widehat{\boldsymbol{C}} = \frac{n}{n - k_n + 2}\frac{1}{\psi_2 k_n T}\sum_{i=0}^{n-k_n+1} \bar{\boldsymbol{y}}_i\bar{\boldsymbol{y}}_i'$$

and $\widehat{\boldsymbol{\xi}}_r$ is the eigenvector corresponding to the eigenvalue $\widehat{\lambda}_r$. $\widetilde{\boldsymbol{\Gamma}}^S := \left(\widetilde{\Gamma}^S(k,l)\right)_{k,l} = s(\widetilde{\boldsymbol{\Gamma}})$ with $\widetilde{\boldsymbol{\Gamma}} = \sum_{r=\hat{r}+1}^{p} \widehat{\lambda}_r \widehat{\boldsymbol{\xi}}_r \widehat{\boldsymbol{\xi}}_r'$ and the estimated number of factors $\hat{r}$ is chosen by

$$\hat{r} = \arg\min_{1 \leq r \leq r_{\max}} (p^{-1}\lambda_r(\widehat{\boldsymbol{C}}) + r \times g(n,p)) - 1,$$

where $\lambda_r(\widehat{\boldsymbol{C}})$ is the rth largest eigenvalue of $\boldsymbol{C}$ and the penalty function $g(n,p)$ satisfies

$$g(n,p)\left((n_\delta^{-1/2}\log p)^{1/2} + p^{-1}m_p\right)^{-1} \to \infty.$$

Dai et al. (2019) also discuss the case that the factor-loading matrix $\boldsymbol{\beta}$ is known and propose a Cross-Section Regression (CSR)-based estimator

$$\widehat{\boldsymbol{C}}_T^{\mathrm{CSR}} = \boldsymbol{\beta}\widehat{\boldsymbol{E}}^*\boldsymbol{\beta}' + \breve{\boldsymbol{\Gamma}}^S, \tag{8.30}$$

where

$$\widehat{\boldsymbol{E}}^* = \frac{1}{T}\widehat{\boldsymbol{F}}\widehat{\boldsymbol{F}}', \ \widehat{\boldsymbol{F}} = (\boldsymbol{\beta}'\boldsymbol{\beta})^{-1}\boldsymbol{\beta}'\bar{\boldsymbol{y}}^*, \ \bar{\boldsymbol{y}}^* = (\bar{\boldsymbol{y}}_0, \ldots, \bar{\boldsymbol{y}}_{n-k_n+1}),$$

$$\breve{\boldsymbol{\Gamma}}^S := \left(\breve{\Gamma}^S(k,l)\right)_{k,l} = s(\breve{\boldsymbol{\Gamma}}), \quad \breve{\boldsymbol{\Gamma}} = \frac{1}{T}(\bar{\boldsymbol{y}}^* - \boldsymbol{\beta}\widehat{\boldsymbol{F}})(\bar{\boldsymbol{y}}^* - \boldsymbol{\beta}\widehat{\boldsymbol{F}})'.$$

Now, we discuss some practical issues. To threshold $\widehat{\boldsymbol{\Gamma}}$, Dai et al. (2019) suggest two approaches. The first assumption is that $\widehat{\boldsymbol{\Gamma}}^S$ to be a block diagonal matrix. As introduced in Fan et al. (2016), there is an eight-digit global industrial classification standard (GICS) code for each company, where digits 1–2 describe the company's sector, digits 3–4 describe the industry group, digits 5–6 describe the industry, and digits 7–8 describe the subindustry. By first sorting the companies based on their GICS codes, $\widehat{\Gamma}^S(k,l)$ is assumed to be one if the kth and lth companies belong to the same block, and zero otherwise such that $\widehat{\boldsymbol{\Gamma}}^S$ is a block diagonal matrix.

The second choice for $s_{\lambda_{kl}}(\widehat{\Gamma}(k,l))$ is first setting

$$\lambda_{kl} = \theta\sqrt{\widehat{\Gamma}(k,k)\widehat{\Gamma}(l,l)},$$

for some $\theta > 0$ and then applying the popular thresholding methods such as hard thresholding, soft thresholding, smoothly clipped absolute deviation (SCAD) (Fan and Li, 2001), and adaptive lasso (AL) (Zou, 2006). Here, θ can be obtained through a grid search algorithm. We refer to Dai et al. (2019) for the details. The same threshold approaches can be applied for $\widetilde{\boldsymbol{\Gamma}}$ and $\breve{\boldsymbol{\Gamma}}$.

For the penalty function $g(n,p)$, Dai et al. (2019) suggest choosing

$$g(n,p) = \mu\left((n_\delta^{-1}\log p)^{1/2} + p^{-1}m_p\right)^\kappa \operatorname{median}(\hat{\lambda}_1, \ldots, \hat{\lambda}_p),$$

with μ and $0 < \kappa < 1$ being positive constants. The size of each block k_n for constructing preaveraging returns is chosen to satisfy

$$\frac{k_n}{n^{1/2+\delta}} = \tilde{\theta} + o(n_\delta^{-1/2}).$$

To balance the bias and variance, Dai et al. (2019) suggest choosing $\delta = 0.1$. k_n is then determined by $\tilde{\theta}$ whose value is not crucial to the accuracy of the ICM estimate. Dai et al. (2019) choose $\tilde{\theta} = 0.08$ in their simulation study.

Dai et al. (2019) prove that under some general assumptions for the noises and the nonsynchronicity of data, the three factor-based estimators are consistent with $\boldsymbol{C}_T$ with convergence rate depending on the sample size n, the dimension p, the choice of δ, and also m_p.

8.4 Applications in Portfolio Allocation

In this section, we apply some of the preceding estimations of the ICM on the global minimum variance (GMV) portfolio problem with a L_1 norm constraint based on real stock prices, which is trying to solve the following optimization problem:

$$\min \boldsymbol{w}'\boldsymbol{\Sigma}\boldsymbol{w} \quad \text{s.t.} \quad \boldsymbol{w}'\mathbf{1} = 1 \quad \text{and} \quad |\boldsymbol{w}| \leq c, \tag{8.31}$$

where $\boldsymbol{\Sigma}$ is the covariance matrix of stock returns and needs to be estimated. We consider two kinds of estimations. The first one assumes the stock returns are i.i.d., which is a common assumption in portfolio studies with low-frequency data; see, for example, Jagannathan and Ma (2003), Tu and Zhou (2011), Ledoit and Wolf (2017), and so on. The second one assumes time-varying covariance matrices and estimates the integrated covariance matrix based on high-frequency data.

We randomly selected 90 constituent stocks of S&P 500 and downloaded their intraday data starting from the first trading day in 2016 and ending at the last trading day of 2018 from the TAQ database. The trading days on which the NASDAQ Stock Exchange closed at 1 pm were deleted such that there are 251, 249, and 248 trading days in 2016, 2017, and 2018, respectively. For the high-frequency data, the data cleaning procedure in Barndorff-Nielsen et al. (2011) was applied to preprocess the data by: (1) deleting entries with 0 or negative prices; (2) deleting entries with negative values in the column of "correction indicator"; (3) deleting entries with a letter code in the column of "COND", except for "E" or "F"; (4) deleting entries outside the period 9:30 am to 4 pm; and (5) using the median price if there were multiple entries at the same second. We found that there are 9,005 observations on average of 90 stocks and 748 days. The highest and lowest frequency stocks had 19, 190, and 4,585 observations on average of 748 days, respectively. After synchronizing all 90 stocks together by the refresh time scheme, there were on average 1,349 observations in one day. The highest and the lowest averaged numbers of observations on different days were 3,054 and 835, respectively. We found that, on average, there were only approximately 15 percent (1349/9005) of data that were retained after synchronizing 90 stocks together.

The starting investment day was set to be the first trading day of 2009, such that there were 497 investment days. The portfolio weights were updated daily or weekly (five days). We compared the performances of portfolio strategies constructed based on the following ICM/covariance matrix estimations. These estimators included three popular estimators constructed with low-frequency data and four estimators obtained based on high-frequency data with three different kinds of methods to solve the dimensionality problem, where two of them were estimated elementwise, and the other two relied on the shrinkage technique and the factor model.

- **1/N**: The equal-weight portfolio, which can be viewed as the covariance matrix of returns estimated by the $p \times p$ identity matrix.
- **SCV**: $\boldsymbol{\Sigma}$ in (8.31) is replaced by the sample covariance (SCV) matrix of daily returns of the previous N_l days.
- **LS**: $\boldsymbol{\Sigma}$ in (8.31) is replaced by $\widehat{\boldsymbol{\Sigma}}_{\text{LS}}$ – the linear shrinkage of the SCV of the previous N_l days' daily returns, which is developed in Ledoit and Wolf (2004).
- **NLS**: $\boldsymbol{\Sigma}$ in (8.31) is replaced by $\widehat{\boldsymbol{\Sigma}}_{\text{NLSF}}$ – the single-factor-preconditioned nonlinear shrinkage of SCV of the previous N_l days' daily returns, which is developed in Ledoit and Wolf (2017).
- **POL**: $\boldsymbol{\Sigma}$ in (8.31) is replaced by the average of N_h days' $\widehat{\boldsymbol{C}}_T^{\text{POL}}$.
- **TSE**: $\boldsymbol{\Sigma}$ in (8.31) is replaced by the average of N_h days' $\widehat{\boldsymbol{C}}_T^{\text{TSE}}$.
- **NER**: $\boldsymbol{\Sigma}$ in (8.31) is replaced by the average of N_h days' $\widehat{\boldsymbol{C}}_T^{\text{NERIVE}}$.
- **PCA**: $\boldsymbol{\Sigma}$ in (8.31) is replaced by the average of N_h days' $\widehat{\boldsymbol{C}}_T^{\text{PCA}}$.

For the PCA, we used the GICS code and assume $\widetilde{\boldsymbol{\Gamma}}^S$ in (8.29) to be a block diagonal matrix and set $\widetilde{\Gamma}^S(k,l) = 1$ if the kth and lth assets were in the same sector, meaning the first two numbers of their GICS codes were the same, and $\widetilde{\Gamma}^S(k,l) = 0$ otherwise. For estimators relying on daily returns, we set $N_l = 250$, which means we used the previous 250 days' daily returns to construct the portfolio weights. We set $N_h = 10$ and used the average of the previous N_h days' ICM estimations to replace $\boldsymbol{\Sigma}$ in (8.31). We also tried $N_h = 5$ and found that the results were similar to those with $N_h = 10$. The following three out-of-sample measures for each portfolio are reported. The AV and SD are in percentages.

- AV: The annualized average of out-of-sample returns during the investment period.
- SD: The annualized standard deviation of out-of-sample returns during the investment period.
- SR: The Sharpe ratio is the AV/SD ratio.

Tables 8.1 and 8.2 are results with different values for the L_1 norm constraint c for daily and weekly updated portfolios, respectively. In general, a high AV and a high SR with a low SD are expected for a good portfolio. Since the GMV portfolio is designed to minimize the variance of a portfolio, the most important performance measure for GMV is SD. Therefore, we first compared the standard deviations of different methods and then compare the Sharp ratios and the average returns.

The number in boldface represents the lowest SD. We found, in general, the portfolios that relied on high-frequency data performed better than the ones that relied on low-frequency data for all cases, except the PCA constructed based

Table 8.1 *The out-of-sample performances of different daily rebalanced strategies for the GMV portfolio with different L_1 norm constraint c.*

$c = 1.2$	1/N	SP	LS	NLS	POL	TSE	NER	PCA
	Investment Periods: Years 2017–2018							
AV	3.88	3.79	3.06	3.23	7.60	10.06	9.08	10.25
SD	11.96	9.28	9.26	9.10	8.87	8.86	**8.81**	9.41
SR	0.32	0.41	0.33	0.36	0.86	1.14	1.03	1.09
	Investment Periods: Year 2017							
AV	13.48	12.26	10.75	11.23	14.54	16.96	16.14	19.81
SD	6.37	5.81	5.74	5.65	**5.10**	5.20	5.23	5.25
SR	2.12	2.11	1.87	1.99	2.85	3.26	3.08	3.78
	Investment Periods: Year 2018							
AV	−5.76	−4.71	−4.65	−4.80	0.63	3.15	2.00	0.64
SD	15.68	11.77	11.77	11.56	11.47	11.41	**11.31**	12.22
SR	−0.37	−0.40	−0.40	−0.42	0.06	0.28	0.18	0.05

$c = 1.5$	1/N	SP	LS	NLS	POL	TSE	NER	PCA
	Investment Periods: Years 2017–2018							
AV	3.88	2.86	2.69	2.91	8.04	10.16	9.25	12.13
SD	11.96	9.45	9.32	9.13	8.81	8.78	**8.73**	9.52
SR	0.32	0.30	0.29	0.32	0.91	1.16	1.06	1.27
	Investment Periods: Year 2017							
AV	13.48	10.14	9.40	10.12	14.58	16.50	15.79	20.43
SD	6.37	6.21	5.95	5.82	**5.12**	5.23	5.25	5.33
SR	2.12	1.63	1.58	1.74	2.85	3.16	3.01	3.84
	Investment Periods: Year 2018							
AV	−5.76	−4.46	−4.05	−4.33	1.47	3.80	2.69	3.80
SD	15.68	11.84	11.77	11.53	11.37	11.28	**11.19**	12.37
SR	−0.37	−0.38	−0.34	−0.38	0.13	0.34	0.24	0.31

on high-frequency data. In terms of Sharp ratios, we found that the portfolios with high-frequency data have much higher Sharp ratios than those with low-frequency data. In particular, the achievements for using high-frequency data were significant in 2018, as the Sharp ratios were positive for all portfolios with high-frequency data but negative for those constructed based on low-frequency data. These findings suggest that high-frequency data can achieve significant improvements for constructing portfolio allocations.

8.5 Discussion

Estimating the ICM is difficult due to the microstructure noises contaminated in observations, nonsynchronicity of data, curse of dimensionality, and positive

Table 8.2 *The out-of-sample performances of different weekly rebalanced strategies for the GMV portfolio with different L_1 norm constraint c.*

$c = 1.2$	1/N	SP	LS	NLS	POL	TSE	NER	PCA
	Investment Periods: Years 2017–2018							
AV	3.88	3.50	2.90	2.77	7.76	10.48	9.86	10.88
SD	11.96	9.15	9.14	8.98	8.91	8.87	**8.86**	9.09
SR	0.32	0.38	0.32	0.31	0.87	1.18	1.11	1.20
	Investment Periods: Year 2017							
AV	13.48	11.50	10.13	10.44	13.64	15.65	14.98	16.89
SD	6.37	5.63	5.59	5.47	**5.16**	5.27	5.32	5.22
SR	2.12	2.04	1.81	1.91	2.64	2.97	2.81	3.24
	Investment Periods: Year 2018							
AV	−5.76	−4.53	−4.35	−4.94	1.87	5.29	4.73	4.85
SD	15.68	11.66	11.66	11.47	11.51	11.40	**11.36**	11.75
SR	−0.37	−0.39	−0.37	−0.43	0.16	0.46	0.42	0.41
$c = 1.5$	1/N	SP	LS	NLS	POL	TSE	NER	PCA
	Investment Periods: Years 2017–2018							
AV	3.88	2.33	2.29	2.25	8.29	10.84	10.26	12.25
SD	11.96	9.29	9.18	8.98	8.85	8.81	**8.79**	9.15
SR	0.32	0.25	0.25	0.25	0.94	1.23	1.17	1.34
	Investment Periods: Year 2017							
AV	13.48	9.13	8.54	8.97	13.61	15.38	14.81	16.84
SD	6.37	6.02	5.80	5.65	**5.17**	5.29	5.31	5.30
SR	2.12	1.52	1.47	1.59	2.63	2.91	2.79	3.18
	Investment Periods: Year 2018							
AV	−5.76	−4.50	−3.99	−4.49	2.95	6.28	5.70	7.64
SD	15.68	11.68	11.62	11.39	11.42	11.31	**11.26**	11.83
SR	−0.37	−0.39	−0.34	−0.39	0.26	0.56	0.51	0.65

semidefinite requirement. For the noises, there are many thorough studies in the literature, for example, in Aït-Sahalia and Jacod (2014) and Jacod et al. (2017). In general, four methods are commonly used to handle the effect of noise. One is the sparse sampling method, but its drawback is that it deletes a large part of the data. The second method uses the preaveraging returns, for example, the MRC in Christensen et al. (2010) and factor-based estimators in Dai et al. (2019). The third method constructs a model for the noise such as in Xiu (2010), Liu and Tang (2013), Liu and Tang (2014) and Shephard and Xiu (2017). The last one uses Fourier transformations; see, for example, Malliavin and Mancino (2009) and Park et al. (2016), and so on. For the curse of dimensionality, it is more difficult to estimate the ICM than to estimate a general covariance matrix with i.i.d. samples due to the nonsynchronicity of high-frequency data. If the dimension is large, synchronizing data together may result in the loss of a large part of the data. If the data are synchronized pairwise, it may result in a negative definite ICM estimator. For example, the pairwise estimators – $\widehat{C}_T^{\mathrm{TSE}}$ and $\widehat{C}_T^{\mathrm{POL}}$ may be not positive semidefinite if the dimension of the ICM is large. However, those two estimators are simple and can be easily implemented for estimating a high-dimensional ICM.

There are still some open questions in the area of estimating the ICM. For example, although a few synchronization methods and state space models have been developed to deal with nonsynchronous data, the theoretical analysis of the impact of nonsynchronicity has not been addressed in the literature to the best of our knowledge. Another interesting open question is how to derive the finite sample properties of the estimators for the ICM. Almost all studies for high-frequency data focus on the asymptotic properties of the estimators. Li et al. (2020) discuss the finite sample performances of IV estimators and propose to improve the performances by a multistep approach that corrects the finite sample bias. However, to the best of our knowledge, there are few discussions of finite performances in estimating the ICM. We emphasize that this may be crucial in application. For example, when we use preaveraging returns to construct an estimator for the ICM and the dimension is large, the sample size may not be large for one day, as we need to synchronize data first and then construct preaveraging returns, as in Dai et al. (2019).

Although there are still many unsolved problems regarding estimating the ICM with high-frequency data, we believe that high-frequency data are extremely useful in the financial market, especially when the market is volatile, such as in financial crisis periods.

Bibliography

Abadir, K. M., W. Distaso, and F. Žikeš (2014). Design-free estimation of variance matrices. *Journal of Econometrics 181*(2), 165–180.

Aït-Sahalia, Y., J. Fan, and D. Xiu (2010). High frequency covariance estimates with noisy and asynchronous financial data. *Journal of the American Statistical Association 105*(492), 1504–1517.

Aït-Sahalia, Y. and J. Jacod (2014). *High-Frequency Financial Econometrics*. Princeton University Press.

Aït-Sahalia, Y., I. Kalnina, and D. Xiu (2020). High-frequency factor models and regressions. *Journal of Econometrics 216*(1), 86–105.

Aït-Sahalia, Y., P. A. Mykland, and L. Zhang (2011). Ultra high frequency volatility estimation with dependent microstructure noise. *Journal of Econometrics 160*(1), 160–175.

Aït-Sahalia, Y. and D. Xiu (2017, Dec.). Using principal component analysis to estimate a high dimensional factor model with high-frequency data. *Journal of Econometrics 201*(2), 384–399.

Aït-Sahalia, Y. and D. Xiu (2019). A Hausman test for the presence of market microstructure noise in high frequency data. *Journal of Econometrics 211*(1), 176–205.

Andersen, T. G., T. Bollerslev, F. X. Diebold, and P. Labys (2003). Modeling and forecasting realized volatility. *Econometrica 71*(2), 579–625.

Bai, J. (2003). Inferential theory for factor models of large dimensions. *Econometrica 71*(1), 135–171.

Bai, J. and S. Ng (2002). Determining the number of factors in approximate factor models. *Econometrica 70*(1), 191–221.

Barndorff-Nielsen, O. E., P. R. Hansen, A. Lunde, and N. Shephard (2011). Multivariate realised kernels: Consistent positive semi-definite estimators of the covariation of equity prices with noise and non-synchronous trading. *Journal of Econometrics 162*(2), 149–169.

Barndorff-Nielsen, O. E. and N. Shephard (2004). Econometric analysis of realized covariation: High frequency based covariance, regression, and correlation in financial economics. *Econometrica 72*(3), 885–925.

Bibinger, M., N. Hautsch, P. Malec, and M. Reiß (2014). Estimating the quadratic covariation matrix from noisy observations: Local method of moments and efficiency. *The Annals of Statistics 42*(4), 1312–1346.

Bibinger, M. and M. Reiß (2014). Spectral estimation of covolatility from noisy observations using local weights. *Scandinavian Journal of Statistics 41*(1), 23–50.

Bickel, P. J. and E. Levina (2008a, dec). Covariance regularization by thresholding. *The Annals of Statistics 36*(6), 2577–2604.

Bickel, P. J. and E. Levina (2008b). Regularized estimation of large covariance matrices. *The Annals of Statistics 36*(1), 199–227.

Christensen, K., S. Kinnebrock, and M. Podolskij (2010). Pre-averaging estimators of the ex-post covariance matrix in noisy diffusion models with non-synchronous data. *Journal of Econometrics 159*(1), 116–133.

Dai, C., K. Lu, and D. Xiu (2019). Knowing factors or factor loadings, or neither? Evaluating estimators of large covariance matrices with noisy and asynchronous data. *Journal of Econometrics 208*(1), 43–79.

Dempster, A. P., N. M. Laird, and D. B. Rubin (1977). Maximum likelihood from incomplete data via the em algorithm. *Journal of the Royal Statistical Society: Series B (Methodological) 39*(1), 1–22.

Engle, R. F. and J. R. Russell (1998, Sept.). Autoregressive conditional duration: a new model for irregularly spaced transaction data. *Econometrica 66*(5), 1127–1162.

Fan, J., A. Furger, and D. Xiu (2016). Incorporating global industrial classification standard into portfolio allocation: A simple factor-based large covariance matrix estimator with high-frequency data. *Journal of Business & Economic Statistics 34*(4), 489–503.

Fan, J. and R. Li (2001). Variable selection via nonconcave penalized likelihood and its oracle properties. *Journal of the American Statistical Association 96*(456), 1348–1360.

Fan, J., Y. Li and K. Yu (2012). Vast volatility matrix estimation using high-frequency data for portfolio selection. *Journal of the American Statistical Association 107*(497), 412–428.

Fan, J., Y. Liao and H. Liu (2016, Feb.). An overview of the estimation of large covariance and precision matrices. *The Econometrics Journal 19*(1), C1–C32.

Hansen, P. R. and A. Lunde (2006, Apr.). Realized variance and market microstructure noise. *Journal of Business & Economic Statistics 24*(2), 127–161.

Hayashi, T. and N. Yoshida (2005). On covariance estimation of non-synchronously observed diffusion processes. *Bernoulli 11*(2), 359–379.

Jacod, J., Li, Y., Mykland, P. A., Podolskij, M., & Vetter, M. (2009). Microstructure noise in the continuous case: The pre-averaging approach. *Stochastic Processes and Their Applications 119*(7), 2249–2276.

Jacod, J., Y. Li, and X. Zheng (2017). Statistical properties of microstructure noise. *Econometrica 85*(4), 1133–1174.

Jacod, J. and P. Protter (2012). *Discretization of Processes*, Volume 67. Springer, New York.

Jagannathan, R. and T. Ma (2003). Risk reduction in large portfolios: Why imposing the wrong constraints helps. *The Journal of Finance 58*(4), 1651–1683.

Kong, X.-B., J.-G. Lin, C. Liu, and G.-Y. Liu (2021). Discrepancy between global and local principal component analysis on large-panel high-frequency data. Technical report, School of Economics and Economics, Wuhan University (China).

Kong, X.-B. and C. Liu (2018). Testing against constant factor loading matrix with large panel high-frequency data. *Journal of Econometrics 204*(2), 301–319.

Lam, C. and P. Feng (2018). A nonparametric eigenvalue-regularized integrated covariance matrix estimator for asset return data. *Journal of Econometrics 206*(1), 226–257.

Lam, C., P. Feng, and C. Hu (2017). Nonlinear shrinkage estimation of large integrated covariance matrices. *Biometrika 104*(2), 481–488.

Ledoit, O. and M. Wolf (2004, Feb.). A well-conditioned estimator for large-dimensional covariance matrices. *Journal of Multivariate Analysis 88*(2), 365–411.

Ledoit, O. and M. Wolf (2017, June). Nonlinear shrinkage of the covariance matrix for portfolio selection: Markowitz meets Goldilocks. *The Review of Financial Studies 30*(12), 4349–4388.

Li, Z. M., R. J. Laeven, and M. H. Vellekoop (2020). Dependent microstructure noise and integrated volatility estimation from high-frequency data. *Journal of Econometrics 215*(2), 536–558.

Liu, C. and C. Y. Tang (2013). A state space model approach to integrated covariance matrix estimation with high frequency data. *Statistics and Its Interface 6*(4), 463.

Liu, C. and C. Y. Tang (2014). A quasi-maximum likelihood approach for integrated covariance matrix estimation with high frequency data. *Journal of Econometrics 180*, 217–232.

Malliavin, P. and M. E. Mancino (2009). A Fourier transform method for nonparametric estimation of multivariate volatility. *The Annals of Statistics 37*(4), 1983–2010.

Mancino, M. E. and S. Sanfelici (2008). Covariance estimation via Fourier method in the presence of asynchronous trading and microstructure noise. Technical report, Department of Economics, Parma University (Italy).

Park, S., S. Y. Hong, and O. Linton (2016). Estimating the quadratic covariation matrix for asynchronously observed high frequency stock returns corrupted by additive measurement error. *Journal of Econometrics 191*(2), 325–347.

Protter, P. (2004). *Stochastic Integration and Differential Equations*, Volume 21. Springer, New York.

Shephard, N. and D. Xiu (2017). Econometric analysis of multivariate realised QML: Estimation of the covariation of equity prices under asynchronous trading. *Journal of Econometrics 201*(1), 19–42.

Shumway, R. H. and D. S. Stoffer (2011). *Time series analysis and its applications: With R examples*. Springer.

Stein, C. (1975). *Estimation of a covariance matrix, Rietz Lecture*. Unpubished lecture notes.

Stein, C. (1986). Lectures on the theory of estimation of many parameters. *Journal of Soviet Mathematics 34*(1), 1373–1403.

Tao, M., Y. Wang, and X. Chen (2013a). Fast convergence rates in estimating large volatility matrices using high-frequency financial data. *Econometric Theory 29*(4), 838–856.

Tao, M., Y. Wang, Q. Yao, and J. Zou (2011). Large volatility matrix inference via combining low-frequency and high-frequency approaches. *Journal of the American Statistical Association 106*(495), 1025–1040.

Tao, M., Y. Wang, and H. Zhou (2013b). Optimal sparse volatility matrix estimation for high dimensional Itô processes with measurement errors. *Annals of Statistics 41*(4), 1816–1864.

Tsay, R. S. (2010). *Analysis of financial time series: Third edition*. Wiley, New York.

Tse, Y.-K. and T. T. Yang (2012). Estimation of high-frequency volatility: An autoregressive conditional duration approach. *Journal of Business & Economic Statistics 30*(4), 533–545.

Tu, J. and G. Zhou (2011). Markowitz meets Talmud: A combination of sophisticated and naive diversification strategies. *Journal of Financial Economics 99*(1), 204–215.

Varneskov, R. T. (2016). Flat-top realized kernel estimation of quadratic covariation with nonsynchronous and noisy asset prices. *Journal of Business & Economic Statistics 34*(1), 1–22.

Xia, N. and X. Zheng (2018). On the inference about the spectral distribution of high-dimensional covariance matrix based on high-frequency noisy observations. *The Annals of Statistics 46*(2), 500–525.

Xiu, D. (2010). Quasi-maximum likelihood estimation of volatility with high frequency data. *Journal of Econometrics 159*(1), 235–250.

Zhang, L. (2011). Estimating covariation: Epps effect, microstructure noise. *Journal of Econometrics 160*(1), 33–47.

Zhang, L., P. A. Mykland, and Y. Aït-Sahalia (2005). A tale of two time scales: Determining integrated volatility with noisy high frequency data. *Journal of the American Statistical Association 100*, 1394–1411.

Zheng, X. and Y. Li (2011). On the estimation of integrated covariance matrices of high dimensional diffusion processes. *The Annals of Statistics 39*(6), 3121–3151.

Zou, H. (2006). The adaptive lasso and its oracle properties. *Journal of the American Statistical Association 101*(476), 1418–1429.

Part III

Bayesian Estimation and Inferences

9 Methods for Estimating Discrete-Time Stochastic Volatility Models

XIAOBIN LIU *Sun Yat-sen University*

9.1 Introduction

For an asset, when only returns are available, measuring the volatility of the asset at the same frequency (for example, daily) is challenging. While the square of the return can be used to measure volatility, it is widely recognized as a very noisy estimator. To better estimate the volatility, one approach is to use returns at a higher frequency to construct the so-called realized volatility. This approach has been very popular in the last twenty years. The literature was excellently reviewed in Andersen and Benzoni (2010) and a good textbook review of the approach is given in Aït-Sahalia and Jacod (2012).

However, information about the returns of assets is not always available at a higher frequency than the intended frequency for estimating the volatility. In this case, can the volatility be better estimated than by the use of the squared return? The answer is yes. There are two popular approaches in the literature. Both are motivated by the fact that the volatilities of financial assets tend to cluster over time.

The first approach uses a class of models called generalized autoregressive conditional heteroskedasticity (GARCH). The other adopts models from the stochastic volatility (SV) class. The GARCH-type models, initially proposed by Bollerslev (1986), are extensions of the autoregressive conditional heteroscedasticity (ARCH) model of Engle (1982). The properties of the GARCH model have been well studied. In addition to the basic model, many specifications have been developed to accommodate important features, such as leverage effects and fat-tails in return distributions. In the GARCH-type models, the current volatility is a deterministic function of past returns and past volatilities. In other words, in the appropriately defined probability space, the volatility at period t is measurable given the information set at period t. This assumption makes the estimation of the model easier as the likelihood function of the model can be decomposed as the product of a sequence of univariate conditional densities, thus facilitating the maximum likelihood estimation.

Unlike GARCH-type models, the SV models assume volatilities evolve as a random process and hence, are latent. The first SV model allowing for volatility clustering was proposed by Taylor (1986), who suggested modeling the log-volatilities as a first-order autoregressive process. The properties of the SV model have been investigated thoroughly (Ghysels et al., 1996). The advantages of the SV model relative to GARCH-type models are now well understood (see, for example, Broto and Ruiz (2004) and Kim et al. (1998)). For example, compared with GARCH-type models, the SV model fits the asset return series better. Moreover, it has a stronger connection to the continuous-time SV models widely used for pricing options. Consequently, many methods have been developed to estimate the SV models. We classify them into two categories: frequentist and Bayesian.

In the frequentist domain, all methods rely on carefully specifying a criterion function and then maximizing or minimizing that criterion function. The frequentist methods reviewed include generalized method of moments (GMM), quasi-maximum likelihood (QML), empirical characteristic function (ECF), efficient method of moments (EMM), and simulated maximum likelihood (SML). GMM, QML, ECF, and EMM avoid calculating the full likelihood function, whereas SML relies on the likelihood information by employing a simulation-based method to approximate the value of likelihood given the parameter values. The asymptotic behaviors of those estimators depend on the properties of the targeted model and the criterion function. They are usually asymptotically normally distributed. Unfortunately, since volatilities of most financial assets are highly persistent, asymptotic normality may not work well in finite samples (Wang and Yu, 2022), especially for the persistency parameter. Therefore, the asymptotic theory-based statistical inference may be misleading.

Unlike the asymptotic theory-based inference used by frequentist methods, with a Bayesian approach, finite-sample inference is conducted via posterior analysis. There are several Bayesian methods available in the literature for estimating SV models. We discuss two classes of Bayesian methods based on whether the data augmentation technique is used. Data augmentation treats the latent variables (or the log-volatilities) as parameters to estimate. In this case, the complete data likelihood function for both the parameters and latent variables has a closed-form expression. Therefore, we can use the classic Markov chain Monte Carlo method (MCMC) to sample from the posterior distribution (see, e.g., Jacquier et al. (2002), Shephard and Pitt (1997), Kim et al. (1998), Chib et al. (2002), Liesenfeld and Richard (2003), and Omori et al. (2007)). Specifically, we review two MCMC algorithms. The first is the single-move MCMC, which updates the latent volatility step by step. The other is the multimove MCMC, which updates the volatility in a block and is more efficient than the single-move MCMC. A smoothed estimate of volatility is obtained as a by-product in both algorithms.

Without data augmentation, we can use a Bayesian parameter learning algorithm that consists of the so-called sequential Monte Carlo (SMC) method and a marginal resample-move step. The SMC method is used to filter the hidden state (log-volatility). We can use it to approximate the likelihood given the values of parameters by marginalizing the hidden states. The resample-move step keeps the parameter from being static all the time and hence avoids particle depletion (Fulop and Li, 2013). The algorithm is sequential compared to the particle MCMC (PMCMC, see Andrieu et al. (2010)) and it is more suitable for financial time-series applications since the belief is updated recursively as new data become available. The filtered estimate of volatility is obtained as a by-product in the algorithm.

However, Bayesian methods require sampling from the posterior. Consequently, the computation is very intensive, especially for latent variable models. In addition, the model must be fully specified since the likelihood function is required.

The rest of this chapter proceeds as follows. Section 9.2 introduces the SV model of Taylor (1986) to illustrate alternative estimation methods. This section also discusses some basic properties of the model. In Section 9.3, the methods in the frequentist domain are reviewed and the motivations and details of each method are presented. Section 9.4 provides a review of the methods in the Bayesian domain and explains the motivations and limitations of each method. A conclusion is provided in Section 9.5.

9.2 The Basic Model

Let y_t be the observed return at period t. In the literature, the log-normal SV model proposed by Taylor (1986) is defined as

$$y_t = \varepsilon_t \exp\left(\frac{1}{2}h_t\right), \tag{9.1}$$

$$h_t = \mu + \phi\left(h_{t-1} - \mu\right) + \sigma_\eta \eta_t, \tag{9.2}$$

where $t = 1, \ldots, T$, h_t is the log-volatility and $|\phi| < 1$, $\eta_t \overset{i.i.d}{\sim} \mathcal{N}(0,1)$, $\varepsilon_t \overset{i.i.d}{\sim} \mathcal{N}(0,1)$, η_t and ε_t are independent, and $h_1 \sim \mathcal{N}\left(0, \frac{\sigma_\eta^2}{1-\phi^2}\right)$. The parameters of interest are $\boldsymbol{\theta} = \left(\mu, \phi, \sigma_\eta\right)' \in \boldsymbol{\Theta} \subset \mathbb{R}^3$, where $\boldsymbol{\Theta}$ is a compact parameter space. For the simplicity of notation, we use the subscript $1:t$ to represent the data ranging from period 1 to period t, that is, $y_{1:t} = (y_1, y_2, \ldots, y_t)'$. Denote the information set up to period t as $\mathcal{I}_t$, the model defined in Eq. (9.1)–(9.2) has the following properties.

Theorem 9.2.1 *The conditional variance and kurtosis of* y_{t+1} *are*

$$Var\left(y_{t+1} \mid \mathcal{I}_t\right) = \exp\left(\mu + \phi\left(h_t - \mu\right) + \frac{1}{2}\sigma_\eta^2\right). \tag{9.3}$$

$$Kurt\left(y_t\right) = 3\exp\left(\frac{\sigma_\eta^2}{1-\phi}\right) \tag{9.4}$$

Theorem 9.2.2 *The moments of* y_t *and* $|y_t|$ *satisfy*

$$\mathbb{E}\left(|y_t|^m\right) = 2^{\frac{m}{2}} \frac{\Gamma\left(\frac{m+1}{2}\right)}{\Gamma\left(\frac{1}{2}\right)} \exp\left[\frac{m\mu}{2\left(1-\phi\right)} + \frac{m^2\sigma_\eta^2}{8\left(1-\phi^2\right)}\right], \textit{for } m > -1,$$

$$\mathbb{E}\left(y_t^m\right) = \begin{cases} 0 & m \textit{ is odd,} \\ (m-1)!!\exp\left(\frac{m}{2}\mu + \frac{m^2\sigma_\eta^2}{8(1-\phi^2)}\right) & m \textit{ is even,} \end{cases}$$

where $n!!$ *denotes the double factorial.*

Corollary 9.2.3 *The model given by Eq. (9.1)–(9.2) has the following properties,*

$$\mathbb{E}\left(|y_t y_{t-k}|\right) = \frac{2}{\pi}\exp\left[\mu + \frac{\left(1+\phi^k\right)\sigma_\eta}{4\left(1-\phi^2\right)}\right],$$

$$\mathbb{E}\left(y_t^2 y_{t-k}^2\right) = \exp\left[2\mu + \frac{\left(1+\phi^k\right)\sigma_\eta}{1-\phi^2}\right].$$

Theorem 9.2.1 shows that the simple SV model can capture the fat tail and volatility clustering properties that are common in return time series. Theorem 9.2.2 and Corollary 9.2.3 imply that the moments of powers of both y_t and $|y_t|$ are finite when some restrictions of the powers m are satisfied, which is helpful for developing various tools to estimate the parameters. However, the simple structure raises a challenge to use the maximum likelihood estimation directly. Specifically, the complete-data likelihood of the model including the unobservable log-volatility $h_{1:T}$ is

$$\begin{aligned} p\left(y_{1:T}, h_{1:T} | \boldsymbol{\theta}\right) = & \prod_{t=1}^{T} \frac{1}{\sqrt{2\pi} e^{\frac{h_t}{2}}} \exp\left[-\frac{y_t^2}{2e^{h_t}}\right] \prod_{t=2}^{T} \frac{1}{\sqrt{2\pi}\sigma_\eta} \\ & \exp\left[-\frac{\left(h_t - \mu - \phi\left(h_{t-1}-\mu\right)\right)^2}{2\sigma_\eta^2}\right] \\ & \times \sqrt{\frac{1-\phi^2}{2\pi\sigma_\eta^2}} \exp\left[-\frac{\left(1-\phi^2\right)\left(h_1-\mu\right)^2}{2\sigma_\eta^2}\right], \end{aligned} \tag{9.5}$$

which implies the likelihood of the observed data and the associated maximum likelihood estimator (MLE) is

$$L(\boldsymbol{\theta}) = \int p(y_{1:T}, h_{1:T}|\boldsymbol{\theta})\, dh_{1:T} = \int p(y_{1:t}|h_{1:T}, \boldsymbol{\theta})\, p(h_{1:T}|\boldsymbol{\theta})\, dh_{1:T}, \tag{9.6}$$

$$\widehat{\boldsymbol{\theta}}_{MLE} = \arg\max_{\theta \in \Theta} \log L(\boldsymbol{\theta}). \tag{9.7}$$

where $\log L(\boldsymbol{\theta})$ is not analytically available since the integration is very complicated and suffers from the curse of dimensionality. The larger the sample size is, the greater the computational challenge faced by MLE. Therefore, one cannot directly compute MLE.

Lastly, the model is closely related to the well-known state-space model since it can be rewritten as

$$\log\left(y_t^2\right) = h_t + \log\left(\varepsilon_t^2\right), \tag{9.8}$$
$$h_t = \mu + \phi(h_{t-1} - \mu) + \sigma_\eta \eta_t.$$

where $\log\left(\varepsilon_t^2\right)$ is the logarithm of a chi-squared random variable with 1 degree of freedom. Therefore, the model belongs to the nonnormal state-space models. One can refer to Durbin (2000) for more discussion of the state-space model. Even though we cannot apply the usual Kalman filter and smooth technique, the model expression (9.8) inspires some innovative alternative estimation approaches. Those approaches for the log-normal SV model shed new light on the estimation of other types of SV models.

9.3 Methods in the Frequentist Domain

As mentioned previously, the frequentist estimators are all based on minimizing or maximizing a carefully designed criterion function. We define the estimator as the one minimizing a distance measure closely related to the criterion function,

$$\widehat{\boldsymbol{\theta}}_{freq} = \arg\min_{\theta \in \Theta} Dist(\boldsymbol{\theta}), \tag{9.9}$$

where $Dist(\boldsymbol{\theta})$ is the distance measure defined in different estimation approaches. The asymptotic behavior of the estimators depends on this distance measure and the properties of the model, and they are usually asymptotically normally distributed.

9.3.1 Generalized Method of Moments

Hansen and Singleton (1982) firstly formalized the generalized method of moments (GMM). GMM has become one of the most widely used econometric methods in economics and finance. Unlike MLE, which requires full knowledge of the distribution of the data, GMM only uses a set of moment conditions. Classic GMM estimation proceeds relying on the convergence of the sample moments to their population counterparts. Following Hansen and Singleton (1982) and Andersen and Sørensen (1996), by denoting the true value of parameters as $\boldsymbol{\theta}_0$, we define the GMM estimator as

$$\begin{aligned}\widehat{\boldsymbol{\theta}}_{GMM} &= \arg\min_{\boldsymbol{\theta}\in\boldsymbol{\Theta}} Dist^{GMM}(\boldsymbol{\theta}) \\ &= \arg\min_{\boldsymbol{\theta}\in\boldsymbol{\Theta}} \left[\widehat{M}(\boldsymbol{\theta}) - A(\boldsymbol{\theta})\right]' W^{-1}\left[\widehat{M}(\boldsymbol{\theta}) - A(\boldsymbol{\theta})\right], \end{aligned} \tag{9.10}$$

where the function in the right-hand side of the equation is the criterion function, $\widehat{M}(\boldsymbol{\theta}) = \left(\widehat{M}_1(\boldsymbol{\theta}), \ldots, \widehat{M}_q(\boldsymbol{\theta})\right)'$, $\widehat{M}_i(\boldsymbol{\theta}) = \sum_{t=j+1}^{T} \frac{\widehat{m}_{it}(\boldsymbol{\theta})}{T-j}$ for $j = 1, \ldots, q$, $\widehat{m}_{it}(\boldsymbol{\theta})$ is the sample realization of the moments at time t, q is the number of selected moments, which is usually larger than the number of parameters, $A(\boldsymbol{\theta})$ are the analytical moments corresponding to the sample counterparts, $\widehat{M}(\boldsymbol{\theta})$, and W is the weighting matrix. The optimal choice of W minimizing the asymptotic covariance matrix of $\boldsymbol{\theta}$ is given by

$$W = \lim_{T\to\infty} E\left[\sum_{t,\tau=1}^{T} \frac{(m_t(\boldsymbol{\theta}_0) - A(\boldsymbol{\theta}_0))(m_\tau(\boldsymbol{\theta}_0) - A(\boldsymbol{\theta}_0))'}{T}\right],$$

where $m_t(\boldsymbol{\theta}_0) = \left(m_{1t}(\boldsymbol{\theta}_0), \ldots, m_{qt}(\boldsymbol{\theta}_0)\right)'$. When a model satisfies some regular conditions, the associated GMM estimator $\widehat{\boldsymbol{\theta}}_{GMM}$ is consistent and asymptotically normal.

For the SV model, the implementation of GMM is straightforward as the moments have closed-form expressions. Furthermore, GMM is advantageous compared with MLE since the computation of the latter is very burdensome (Melino and Turnbull, 1990). However, there are many challenges to GMM. One issue is that the finite sample and large sample properties of GMM depend on the selected moments but in general we do not know which or how many moments should be used.

Jacquier et al. (2002) and Andersen and Sørensen (1996) investigated the performance of GMM for the log-normal SV model defined in Eq. (9.1) and (9.2). The basic set of moments they used was inspired by Melino and Turnbull (1990), that is,

$$\left\{\left\{\mathbb{E}\left(|y_t|^m\right)\right\}_{m=1}^{4}, \left\{\mathbb{E}\left(|y_t y_{t-k}|\right)\right\}_{k=1}^{10}, \left\{\mathbb{E}\left(y_t^2 y_{t-k}^2\right)\right\}_{k=1}^{10}\right\}, \tag{9.11}$$

among which the moments of the marginal distribution serve to identify μ, and the autocovariance of the squares and absolute values help to identify ϕ. Thanks to Theorem 9.2.2 and Corollary 9.2.3, these moments have analytical expressions. The weighting matrix recommended is the kernel estimator of the spectral density matrix,

$$\widehat{W} = \sum_{j=-T+1}^{T+1} \mathcal{K}(j)\,\widehat{\Gamma}(j),$$

$$\widehat{\Gamma}(j) = \frac{1}{T}\sum_{t=j+1}^{T} \left[m_t(\widehat{\theta}) - A(\widehat{\theta})\right]\left[m_{t-j}(\widehat{\theta}) - A(\widehat{\theta})\right]', \tag{9.12}$$

where $\mathcal{K}(j)$ is a weighted kernel function.

Jacquier et al. (2002) used the full set of (9.11) and found that the GMM estimators of the parameters were substantially biased. Andersen and Sørensen (1996) investigated the finite sample performance of GMM extensively. They reported several interesting findings. First, the selection of moments was limited due to the requirement for analytical expression. Second, they postulated that the number of moments used should depend on the sample size. When the sample size is small, an excessive number of moments may introduce more bias and a larger root mean square error (RMSE) since the highly correlated moments can result in a poor estimate for the weighting matrix in the criterion function. Third, when the sample is large, a fairly large number of lags (L_T) in the kernel function should be used. Fourth, the paper recommends using lower-order moments of y_t because the higher-order moments can cause erratic finite sample behavior. Based on the work of Andersen and Sørensen (1996), one may use the Bartlett kernel function with fixed bandwidth $L_T = 1.2T^{\frac{1}{3}}$,

$$\mathcal{K}(j) = \begin{cases} 1 - \frac{j}{L_T}, & j \le L_T, \\ 0, & j > L_T, \end{cases}$$

and define another two sets of moments for estimation as follows:

$$\mathcal{M}9 = \left\{ \left\{\mathbb{E}\left(|y_t|^m\right)\right\}_{m=1}^{4}, \left\{\mathbb{E}\left(|y_t y_{t-k}|\right)\right\}_{k=1,3,5}, \left\{\mathbb{E}\left(y_t^2 y_{t-k}^2\right)\right\}_{k=2,4} \right\},$$

$$\mathcal{M}14 = \left\{ \left\{\mathbb{E}\left(|y_t|^m\right)\right\}_{m=1}^{4}, \left\{\mathbb{E}\left(|y_t y_{t-k}|\right)\right\}_{k=2,4,6,8,10}, \left\{\mathbb{E}\left(y_t^2 y_{t-k}^2\right)\right\}_{k=1,3,5,7,9} \right\}.$$

We can summarize the estimation procedure in Algorithm 1.

9.3.2 Quasi-Maximum Likelihood

The quasi-maximum likelihood (QML) is another popular estimation approach for SV models. The advantage of the QML approach is its speed and adaptability to various situations. Specifically, we use an approximated model instead of the true one to obtain the MLE,

Algorithm 1 GMM estimation

1: Initialize $\boldsymbol{\theta}^{(0)}$.

2: Select the moments to use. When $T \geq 1000$, adopt the moments $\mathcal{M} = \mathcal{M}14$. Otherwise adopt $\mathcal{M} = \mathcal{M}9$.

3: Compute

$$\boldsymbol{\theta}^{(1)} = \arg\min_{\boldsymbol{\theta}\in\boldsymbol{\Theta}} \left[\widehat{M}(\boldsymbol{\theta}) - A(\boldsymbol{\theta})\right]' \left[\widehat{M}(\boldsymbol{\theta}) - A(\boldsymbol{\theta})\right].$$

4: Define $L_T = 1.2T^{\frac{1}{3}}$ and compute

$$\mathcal{K}(j) = \begin{cases} 1 - \frac{j}{L_T}, & j \leq L_T, \\ 0, & j > L_T. \end{cases}$$

5: Compute the weighting matrix

$$\widehat{W} = \sum_{j=-T+1}^{T+1} \mathcal{K}(j)\,\widehat{\Gamma}(j),$$

$$\widehat{\Gamma}(j) = \frac{1}{T}\sum_{t=j+1}^{T} \left[m_t\left(\boldsymbol{\theta}^{(1)}\right) - A\left(\boldsymbol{\theta}^{(1)}\right)\right]\left[m_{t-j}\left(\boldsymbol{\theta}^{(1)}\right) - A\left(\boldsymbol{\theta}^{(1)}\right)\right]',$$

where the moments used are from $\mathcal{M}$.

6: Compute

$$\widehat{\boldsymbol{\theta}}_{GMM} = \arg\min_{\boldsymbol{\theta}\in\boldsymbol{\Theta}} \left[\widehat{M}(\boldsymbol{\theta}) - A(\boldsymbol{\theta})\right]' \widehat{W}^{-1} \left[\widehat{M}(\boldsymbol{\theta}) - A(\boldsymbol{\theta})\right],$$

where the moments used are from $\mathcal{M}$.

$$\widehat{\boldsymbol{\theta}}_{QML} = \arg\min_{\boldsymbol{\theta}\in\boldsymbol{\Theta}} Dist^{QML}(\boldsymbol{\theta}) = \arg\min_{\boldsymbol{\theta}\in\boldsymbol{\Theta}} \left[-\log L^{quasi}(\boldsymbol{\theta})\right],$$

where $\log L^{quasi}(\boldsymbol{\theta})$ is the likelihood function of the approximated model. This is why we call it quasi-likelihood and the estimator is denoted as $\widehat{\boldsymbol{\theta}}_{QML}$. Although the QML method is inefficient, it leads to consistent estimators and is easy to implement numerically since the quasi-likelihood function is easy to evaluate.

In this section we discuss how to use QML to estimate the log-normal SV model. According to the properties of the log-normal SV model discussed in Section 9.2, the likelihood is intractable and hence the MLE is difficult to obtain. Thanks to the close relation to the linear state-space model as shown in Section 9.2, Ruiz (1994) proposed to estimate the SV model using QML based on the Kalman filter. To see how it works, following the derivation in Section 9.2, the model (9.1)–(9.2) can be rewritten as

$$\log\left(y_t^2\right) = h_t + \log\left(\varepsilon_t^2\right),$$
$$h_t = \mu + \phi\left(h_{t-1} - \mu\right) + \sigma_\eta \eta_t,$$

where $\log\left(\varepsilon_t^2\right)$ is the logarithm of the chi-squared random variable with one degree of freedom.

If $\log\left(\varepsilon_t^2\right)$ is indeed normally distributed, the preceding model is the state-space model widely used in economics and finance. We can obtain the MLE of state-space models with Gaussian error terms via the Kalman filter. However, we know that $\log\left(\varepsilon_t^2\right)$ does not follow a Gaussian white noise process, therefore, the Kalman filter can only approximate the outcome of the true nonlinear optimal filter. Specifically, in the QML method, we use a normal distribution to approximate $\log\left(\varepsilon_t^2\right)$. However, as pointed out by Harvey et al. (1994) and Ruiz (1994), the performance of QML depends on the magnitude of σ_η. If σ_η is large, the $\log\left(h_t\right)$ will dominate the error term $\log\left(\varepsilon_t^2\right)$ in the measurement equation. As a result, a normal approximation may be adequate and the Kalman filter may be close to the optimal filtering. However, for small values of σ_η, the normal approximation may break down and the QML method may perform poorly compared to the full-likelihood-based approach. Jacquier et al. (2002) also showed that the QML estimator has similar performance relative to the GMM estimator only for high values of σ_η. Following the steps in Yu (2002), we use a normal distribution with mean -1.27 and variance $\pi^2/2$ to approximate $\log\left(\varepsilon_t^2\right)$ and rewrite the model as

$$y_t = A + B\tilde{h}_t + \tilde{\varepsilon}_t, \tilde{\varepsilon}_t \sim \mathcal{N}\left(0, R\right),$$
$$\tilde{h}_{t+1} = \phi\tilde{h}_t + v_{t+1}, v_{t+1} \sim \mathcal{N}\left(0, Q\right),$$

where $A = -1.27 + \mu$, $B = 1$, $R = \pi^2/2$, $\tilde{h}_t = h_t - \mu$, $Q = \sigma_\eta^2$. We describe the algorithm employing the Kalman filter to evaluate the quasi-likelihood of the log-normal SV model in Algorithm 2.

9.3.3 Empirical Characteristic Function

There is a one-to-one correspondence between the cumulative distribution function (CDF) and the characteristic function (CF). As a result, the empirical CF (ECF) should incorporate the same information as the empirical cumulative distribution (ECDF). Therefore, we can use the ECF to estimate parameters for a model. Essentially, the method approximates the likelihood by the product of joint densities of overlapping blocks with a fixed size. We briefly outline the ECF method in what follows for general models. For more details, one can refer to Knight and Yu (2002) and Knight et al. (2002).

Given a random variable X and its realization x, we assume the cumulative distribution function (CDF) as $F\left(x|\boldsymbol{\theta}\right)$, which depends on a parameter $\boldsymbol{\theta}$. The CF is defined as

Algorithm 2 Computation of $\log L^{quasi}(\boldsymbol{\theta})$

1: Initialization: $\widehat{\tilde{h}}_{1|0} = 0$, $\tilde{\Sigma}_{1|0} = \sigma_\eta^2 / \left(1 - \phi^2\right)$.

2: Sequential updating:

$$\widehat{\tilde{h}}_{t|t} = \widehat{\tilde{h}}_{t|t-1} + \tilde{\Sigma}_{t|t-1} \frac{y_t - A - \widehat{\tilde{h}}_{t|t-1}}{\tilde{\Sigma}_{t|t-1} + R},$$

$$\tilde{\Sigma}_{t|t} = \tilde{\Sigma}_{t|t-1} - \tilde{\Sigma}_{t|t-1} \left(\tilde{\Sigma}_{t|t-1} + R\right)^{-1} \tilde{\Sigma}_{t|t-1}.$$

3: In-sample sequential prediction

$$\widehat{\tilde{h}}_{t+1|t} = \phi \widehat{\tilde{h}}_{t|t-1} + \phi \frac{y_t - A - \widehat{\tilde{h}}_{t|t-1}}{1 + R \tilde{\Sigma}_{t|t-1}^{-1}},$$

$$\tilde{\Sigma}_{t+1|t} = \phi^2 \tilde{\Sigma}_{t|t} + \sigma_\eta^2.$$

4: Compute the quasi-likelihood

$$\log L^{quasi}(\boldsymbol{\theta}) = -\frac{1}{2} \sum_{t=1}^{T} \log\left(\tilde{\Sigma}_{t|t-1} + R\right) - \frac{1}{2} \sum_{t=1}^{T} \frac{\left(y_t - A - \widehat{\tilde{h}}_{t|t-1}\right)^2}{\tilde{\Sigma}_{t|t-1} + R}.$$

$$C(m, \boldsymbol{\theta}) = \mathbb{E}\left(e^{imx}\right) = \int e^{imx} dF(x|\boldsymbol{\theta}), \tag{9.13}$$

and the ECF is

$$C_T(m) = \frac{1}{T} \sum_{t=1}^{T} e^{imx_t} = \int e^{imx} dF_T(x), \tag{9.14}$$

where $F_T(x)$ is the ECDF and m is the transform variable. Apparently, Eq. (9.13) only involves the parameter $\boldsymbol{\theta}$ and Eq. (9.14) contains only data. Hence we can estimate $\boldsymbol{\theta}$ by minimizing the distance between the CF and ECF, namely, given a grid of transform variable $m_1, \ldots, m_q$ and the weight function $w(\cdot)$, the ECF estimator minimizes

$$\sum_{j=1}^{q} \left|C_T(m_j) - C(m_j, \boldsymbol{\theta})\right|^2 w(m_j),$$

or we can minimize the distance given the continuous transformation m,

$$\int |C_T(m) - C(m, \boldsymbol{\theta})|^2 w(m)\, dm.$$

The marginal ECDF cannot capture the structure of dependence in time-series data. Knight and Yu (2002) and Knight et al. (2002) recommended to use the joint ECF involving moving blocks of data. Given the observations $\{x_1, \ldots, x_T\}$, the overlapping blocks are

$$\boldsymbol{r}_j = \left(x_j, \ldots, x_{j+p}\right) \quad (j = 1, \ldots, T-p),$$

which imply that each block has p periods overlapping with its adjacent blocks. The CF of each block is basically a joint CF and is defined as

$$C(\boldsymbol{m}, \boldsymbol{\theta}) = \mathbb{E}\left(e^{i\boldsymbol{m}'\boldsymbol{r}_j}\right), \tag{9.15}$$

where the transformation variable $\boldsymbol{m} = \left(m_1, \ldots, m_{p+1}\right)'$. Hence, the joint ECF is

$$C_n(\boldsymbol{m}) = \frac{1}{n}\sum_{j=1}^{n} e^{i\boldsymbol{m}'\boldsymbol{r}_j}, \text{ where } n = T - p. \tag{9.16}$$

It is obvious that $\boldsymbol{r}_j$ is dependent since it is a sequence of overlapping moving blocks. Feuerverger (1990) proved that under standard regularity conditions, $C_n(\boldsymbol{m})$ converges almost surely to $C(\boldsymbol{m}, \boldsymbol{\theta})$ for any $\boldsymbol{m}$. Matching the joint CF in Eq. (9.15) with the ECF in Eq. (9.16) over a grid of discrete points is an alternative method for MLE (Knight and Satchell (1997)). Knight et al. (2002) defined the estimator for time-series data as

$$\begin{aligned} \widehat{\boldsymbol{\theta}}_{ECF} &= \arg\min_{\boldsymbol{\theta}\in\Theta} Dist^{ECF}(\boldsymbol{\theta}) \\ &= \arg\min_{\boldsymbol{\theta}\in\Theta} \int |C(\boldsymbol{m}, \boldsymbol{\theta}) - C_n(\boldsymbol{m})|^2 w(\boldsymbol{m})\, d\boldsymbol{m}, \end{aligned} \tag{9.17}$$

or equivalently, the parameter that solving

$$\int \left[C(\boldsymbol{m}, \widehat{\boldsymbol{\theta}}_{ECF}) - C_n(\boldsymbol{m})\right] g\left(\boldsymbol{m}, \widehat{\boldsymbol{\theta}}_{ECF}\right) d\boldsymbol{m} = 0,$$

where $C(\boldsymbol{m}, \boldsymbol{\theta})$ and $C_n(\boldsymbol{m})$ are from Eq. (9.15) and (9.16), respectively. $g(\boldsymbol{m}, \boldsymbol{\theta})$ and $w(\boldsymbol{m})$ are weighted functions. In fact, if $\boldsymbol{m}$ is a discrete grid of points (discrete ECF, DECF), the estimation is equivalent to matching a finite number of moments like GMM. Knight and Yu (2002) and Knight et al. (2002) proposed minimizing the integral in Eq. (9.17), namely, matching all the moments continuously. To do this, the weight function should be continuous and hence we do not need to choose the transform variable, $\boldsymbol{m}$, which will be integrated out in Eq. (9.17). One appropriate proposal for the weight function is the exponential function, $\exp\left(-\boldsymbol{m}'\boldsymbol{m}\right)$. The exponential function can put more weight on the interval around the origin and also has the advantage of convenient computation of the integration. Specifically, we can use the Hermitian quadrature or Monte Carlo integration to calculate the integral in Eq. (9.17). Theoretically, an optimal choice for the weight function $\omega\left(\boldsymbol{m},\boldsymbol{\theta}\right)$ is

$$\omega^*\left(\boldsymbol{m},\boldsymbol{\theta}\right) = \int \exp\left(-i\boldsymbol{m}'\boldsymbol{r}_j\right) \frac{\partial \log p\left(x_{j+p}|x_{j:j+p-1},\boldsymbol{\theta}\right)}{\partial\boldsymbol{\theta}} dx_{j:j+p},$$

which is not available for some time-series models where the conditional score function does not have an analytical expression (Knight and Yu, 2002).

The estimator in Eq. (9.17) is consistent and asymptotically normal for strictly stationary processes under some mild assumptions (Knight and Yu, 2002). For the log-normal SV model, we firstly transform the return data following the logarithm operation in Eq. (9.8),

$$x_t = \log\left(y_t\right) = h_t + \log\left(\varepsilon_t^2\right), \tag{9.18}$$

and then plug the transformed data into the general estimation procedure. Specifically, the joint CF for $x_{t:t+p-1}$ is

$$\begin{aligned} C\left(m_1,\ldots,m_{p+1},\boldsymbol{\theta}\right) = \exp&\left[i\mu\sum_{j=1}^{p+1} m_j - \frac{\sigma_\eta^2}{2\left(1-\phi^2\right)}\right. \\ &\left.\left(\sum_{j=1}^{p+1} m_j^2 + 2\phi\sum_{l=1}^{p+1}\sum_{j=l+1}^{p+1}\phi^{j-l-1}m_l m_j\right)\right] \\ &\times \frac{\prod_{j=1}^{p+1}\Gamma\left(\frac{1}{2}+im_j\right)}{\Gamma\left(\frac{1}{2}\right)^k} 2^{i\sum_{j=1}^{p+1}m_j}. \end{aligned} \tag{9.19}$$

As pointed out by Knight et al. (2002), the autocorrelation for kth lag for $\{x_t\}_{t=1}^T$ is

$$\varrho_k = \phi^k \frac{\sigma_\eta^2/\left(1-\phi^2\right)}{\sigma_\eta^2/\left(1-\phi^2\right)+c}, k = 1,2,\ldots, \text{ and}$$

$$c = \frac{\Gamma''\left(\frac{1}{2}\right)}{\Gamma\left(\frac{1}{2}\right)} - \left[\frac{\Gamma'\left(\frac{1}{2}\right)}{\Gamma\left(\frac{1}{2}\right)}\right]^2 \approx 0.4948.$$

Therefore, we only need $k=1$ to identify the parameter ϕ. We briefly summarize the evaluation of criterion function in Algorithm 3.

Algorithm 3 Computation of $Dist^{ECF}(\boldsymbol{\theta})$

1: Compute

$$C(m_1, m_2, \boldsymbol{\theta}) = \exp\left[i\mu(m_1 + m_2) - \frac{\sigma_\eta^2}{2(1-\phi^2)}\left(m_1^2 + 2\phi m_1 m_2 + m_2^2\right)\right] \times \frac{\Gamma\left(\frac{1}{2} + im_1\right)\Gamma\left(\frac{1}{2} + im_2\right)}{\Gamma\left(\frac{1}{2}\right)^2} 2^{im_1 + im_2}$$

by extracting the real and imaginary parts $Re(C(m_1, m_2|\boldsymbol{\theta}))$ and $Im(C(m_1, m_2|\boldsymbol{\theta}))$.

2: Compute

$$C_n(m_1, m_2) = \frac{1}{n}\sum_{j=1}^{n} \exp\left(im_1 x_j + im_2 x_{j+1}\right)$$

by extracting the real and imaginary parts $Re(C_n(m_1, m_2))$ and $Im(C_n(m_1, m_2))$, where $n = T - 1$. Specifically

$$Re(C_n(m_1, m_2)) = \frac{1}{n}\sum_{j=1}^{n} \cos\left(m_1 x_j + m_2 x_{j+1}\right),$$

$$Im(C_n(m_1, m_2)) = \frac{1}{n}\sum_{j=1}^{n} \sin\left(m_1 x_j + m_2 x_{j+1}\right).$$

3: Compute the criterion function

$$Dist^{ECF}(\boldsymbol{\theta}) = \int\int \left\{[Re(C(m_1, m_2|\boldsymbol{\theta})) - Re(C_n(m_1, m_2))]^2 + [Im(C(m_1, m_2|\boldsymbol{\theta})) - Im(C_n(m_1, m_2))]^2\right\} \exp\left(-m_1^2 - m_2^2\right) dm_1 dm_2.$$

9.3.4 Efficient Method of Moments

Unless the moment conditions correspond to the scores, GMM leads to, in general, an inefficient estimator. The efficient method of moments (EMM) provides more efficient estimators than GMM. Specifically, EMM relies on an auxiliary quasi-likelihood to generate a set of moments. Like GMM, EMM accommodates a variety of models, and its asymptotic property has been studied in Gallant and Tauchen (1996).

Following Andersen et al. (1999), the estimation procedure includes two major steps. In the first step, we choose an auxiliary model and estimate it by QML. Denote the conditional density of the auxiliary model as $f(y_t \mid \mathcal{I}_{t-1}, \boldsymbol{\vartheta})$, where $\mathcal{I}_{t-1}$ is the information set up to time $t-1$ and $\boldsymbol{\vartheta}$ is the parameter. EMM firstly obtains the QML estimator for $\boldsymbol{\vartheta}$, $\widehat{\boldsymbol{\vartheta}}$, which satisfies the first-order condition based on the quasi-score function $s(y_t, \boldsymbol{\vartheta}) = \frac{\partial \log f(y_t \mid \mathcal{I}_{t-1}, \boldsymbol{\vartheta})}{\partial \boldsymbol{\vartheta}'}$, that is,

$$\frac{1}{T}\sum_{t=1}^{T} \frac{\partial}{\partial \boldsymbol{\vartheta}} \log f\left(y_t \mid \mathcal{I}_{t-1}, \widehat{\boldsymbol{\vartheta}}\right) = \frac{1}{T}\sum_{t=1}^{T} s\left(y_t, \widehat{\boldsymbol{\vartheta}}\right) = 0. \tag{9.20}$$

After that, we use GMM to estimate the original parameter $\boldsymbol{\theta}$. The moment conditions used to identify $\boldsymbol{\theta}$ are denoted as

$$m(\boldsymbol{\theta}, \boldsymbol{\vartheta}_0) = \mathbb{E}_{\boldsymbol{\theta}}\left[s(y_t, \boldsymbol{\vartheta}_0)\right] = \int s(y_t, \boldsymbol{\vartheta}_0)\, dP(y_t, \boldsymbol{\theta}) \tag{9.21}$$

$$= \int \frac{\partial \log f(y_t \mid \mathcal{I}_{t-1}, \boldsymbol{\vartheta}_0)}{\partial \boldsymbol{\vartheta}} dP(y_t, \boldsymbol{\theta}), \tag{9.22}$$

where the number of moment conditions should be larger than $\dim(\boldsymbol{\theta})$ for identification and $P(y_{1:t}, \boldsymbol{\theta})$ is the probability measure induced by the targeted model.

However, the presence of the latent log-volatility makes the moment condition analytically intractable. Following Duffie and Singleton (1993), the corresponding sample moments for Eq. (9.22) at the fixed QML estimate $\widehat{\boldsymbol{\vartheta}}$ are

$$\widehat{m}_S\left(\boldsymbol{\theta}, \widehat{\boldsymbol{\vartheta}}\right) = \frac{1}{S}\sum_{s=1}^{S} \frac{\partial}{\partial \boldsymbol{\vartheta}} \log f\left(\widehat{y}_s(\boldsymbol{\theta}) \mid \mathcal{I}_{s-1}(\boldsymbol{\theta}), \widehat{\boldsymbol{\vartheta}}\right), \tag{9.23}$$

where $\widehat{y}_s(\boldsymbol{\theta})$ is the simulated data from the targeted model given the value of $\boldsymbol{\theta}$, S is the sample size. As $S \to \infty$, $m_S\left(\boldsymbol{\theta}, \widehat{\boldsymbol{\vartheta}}\right) \to m\left(\boldsymbol{\theta}, \widehat{\boldsymbol{\vartheta}}\right)$ almost surely. Conditional on Eq. (9.23),

$$\widehat{\boldsymbol{\theta}}_{EMM} = \arg\min_{\boldsymbol{\theta} \in \Theta} Dist^{EMM}(\boldsymbol{\theta}) = \arg\min_{\boldsymbol{\theta} \in \Theta} \left[\widehat{m}\left(\boldsymbol{\theta}, \widehat{\boldsymbol{\vartheta}}\right)' \widehat{W}^{-1} \widehat{m}\left(\boldsymbol{\theta}, \widehat{\boldsymbol{\vartheta}}\right)\right], \tag{9.24}$$

where the weighting matrix $\widehat{W}$ is one of the remaining problems. Andersen et al. (1999) proposed to use the quasi-information matrix

$$\widehat{W} = \frac{1}{T}\sum_{t=1}^{T} \frac{\partial}{\partial \boldsymbol{\vartheta}} \log f\left(y_t \mid \mathcal{I}_{t-1}, \widehat{\boldsymbol{\vartheta}}\right) \frac{\partial}{\partial \boldsymbol{\vartheta}'} \log f\left(y_t \mid \mathcal{I}_{t-1}, \widehat{\boldsymbol{\vartheta}}\right), \tag{9.25}$$

which can be obtained directly from the QML step. Clearly, the second step is simulation-based.

EMM uses the scores as moment conditions. However, the scores do not come from the original model since those are analytically intractable. Instead, the moment conditions are based on the quasi-score of the auxiliary model. Clearly, the choice of the auxiliary model determines the efficiency of the EMM estimator and hence, is critical. If the quasi-score of the auxiliary model asymptotically spans the true score vector, the estimation achieves the full asymptotic efficiency. In other words, as the score generator gets close to the true one, the covariance matrix estimated converges that of the MLE.

Gallant et al. (1997) proposed using EMM to estimate stochastic volatility models. Andersen et al. (1999) performed an extensive Monte Carlo study of the performance of EMM to estimate the log-normal SV model. Specifically, they examined the sensitivity to different choices of the auxiliary model such as ARCH, GARCH, and EGARCH models for the score and found that the inference is sensitive to the choice of the auxiliary model when the sample size is small but robust in large samples. They further showed that the efficiency of EMM approaches that of MLE as the sample size increased. Following Andersen et al. (1999), one may choose GARCH(1,1) as the auxiliary model given by

$$y_t = \sigma_t \varepsilon_t,$$
$$\sigma_t^2 = \omega + \alpha \sigma_{t-1}^2 + \beta \varepsilon_{t-1}^2.$$

where we denote the parameters of the GARCH(1,1) as $\boldsymbol{\vartheta} = (\omega, \alpha, \beta)'$. We describe the details of evaluating the criterion function of EMM to estimate the log-normal SV model in Algorithm 4.

9.3.5 Simulated Maximum Likelihood

The GMM, QML, ECF, and EMM methods reviewed earlier are alternative approaches to the classic MLE when the likelihood of the model does not have an analytical expression. These methods lead to estimators that are consistent but less efficient compared to the MLE. With careful design, ECF and EMM can approach the efficiency of the MLE for only a limited set of models. Under mild regularity conditions, the MLE is consistent, asymptotically normal, and efficient. Further, due to the invariance principle, any function of the MLE is still an MLE, inheriting all its asymptotic properties. Therefore, it is worthwhile to obtain the MLE. One popular approach to resolve the intractable likelihood function is to use simulation-based methods. Shephard and Pitt (1997) and Durbin and Koopman (1997) introduced SML methods for nonlinear non-Gaussian state-space models. Durham (2006), Durham (2007), Koopman et al. (2009), Skaug and Yu (2009), and Yu (2012a) used the SML method to estimate SV models and showed its reliable performance in different cases. There

Algorithm 4 Computation of $Dist^{EMM}(\boldsymbol{\theta})$

1: Estimate the parameters of GARCH(1,1) model given the data $y_{1:T}$

$$\widehat{\boldsymbol{\vartheta}} = \arg\max_{\boldsymbol{\vartheta}} \log \tilde{L}(\boldsymbol{\vartheta}),$$

where

$$\log \tilde{L}(\boldsymbol{\vartheta}) = -\frac{T-1}{2}\log 2\pi - \frac{1}{2}\sum_{t=2}^{T}\log\sigma_t^2 - \sum_{t=2}^{T}\frac{y_t^2}{2\sigma_t^2}.$$

2: Compute

$$\widehat{W} = \frac{1}{T}\sum_{t=1}^{T}\frac{\partial}{\partial\boldsymbol{\vartheta}}\log f\left(y_t \mid \mathcal{I}_{t-1}, \widehat{\boldsymbol{\vartheta}}\right)\frac{\partial}{\partial\boldsymbol{\vartheta}'}\log f\left(y_t \mid \mathcal{I}_{t-1}, \widehat{\boldsymbol{\vartheta}}\right),$$

where

$$\frac{\partial \log f(y_t \mid \mathcal{I}_{t-1}, \boldsymbol{\vartheta})}{\partial\boldsymbol{\vartheta}} = \begin{pmatrix} \frac{1}{\sigma_t^2} + \frac{y_t^2}{2\sigma_t^4} \\ \frac{\sigma_{t-1}^2}{\sigma_t^2} + \frac{y_t^2\sigma_{t-1}^2}{2\sigma_t^4} \\ \frac{\varepsilon_{t-1}^2}{\sigma_t^2} + \frac{y_t^2\varepsilon_{t-1}^2}{2\sigma_t^4} \end{pmatrix}$$

3: Simulate data from the log-normal SV model given $\boldsymbol{\theta}$ with $S = 20{,}000$. The first one uses the simulated $\{\widehat{\varepsilon}_t, \widehat{\eta}_t\}$ to construct the $\left\{\widehat{y}_t^1\right\}_{t=1}^S$, while the latter uses the simulated $\{-\widehat{\varepsilon}_t, -\widehat{\eta}_t\}$ to generate the $\left\{\widehat{y}_t^2\right\}_{t=1}^S$.

4: Compute

$$\widehat{m}\left(\boldsymbol{\theta}, \widehat{\boldsymbol{\vartheta}}\right) = \frac{1}{2}\left[\frac{1}{S}\sum_{s=1}^{S}\frac{\partial}{\partial\boldsymbol{\vartheta}}\log f\left(\widehat{y}_s^1(\boldsymbol{\theta}) \mid \mathcal{I}_{s-1}(\boldsymbol{\theta}), \widehat{\boldsymbol{\vartheta}}\right)\right.$$
$$\left. + \frac{1}{S}\sum_{s=1}^{S}\frac{\partial}{\partial\boldsymbol{\vartheta}}\log f\left(\widehat{y}_s^2(\boldsymbol{\theta}) \mid \mathcal{I}_{s-1}(\boldsymbol{\theta}), \widehat{\boldsymbol{\vartheta}}\right)\right].$$

5: Compute

$$Dist^{EMM}(\boldsymbol{\theta}) = \widehat{m}\left(\boldsymbol{\theta}, \widehat{\boldsymbol{\vartheta}}\right)'\widehat{W}^{-1}\widehat{m}\left(\boldsymbol{\theta}, \widehat{\boldsymbol{\vartheta}}\right).$$

are other variations, like the Monte Carlo likelihood (MCL) method proposed by Durbin and Koopman (2000) and the efficient importance sampler (EIS) of Richard and Zhang (2007). For more details, one can refer to Yu (2012b). In the section, following Yu (2012b), we focus on how to use the simulated maximum likelihood (SML) to estimate the log-normal SV model. The methodology can also accommodate other complex models.

Recall the discussion in Section 9.2, the likelihood function for the log-normal SV model does not have a closed-form expression. By treating the log-volatility $h_{1:T}$ as missing data, the so-called "complete-data likelihood" is

$$p(y_{1:T}, h_{1:T}|\boldsymbol{\theta}) = \prod_{t=1}^{T} \frac{1}{2\pi e^{\frac{h_t}{2}}} \exp\left[-\frac{y_t^2}{2e^{h_t}}\right]$$
$$\prod_{t=2}^{T} \frac{1}{2\pi\sigma_\eta} \exp\left[-\frac{(h_t - \mu - \phi(h_{t-1} - \mu))^2}{2\sigma_\eta^2}\right]$$
$$\times \sqrt{\frac{1-\phi^2}{2\pi\sigma_\eta^2}} \exp\left[-\frac{\left(1-\phi^2\right)(h_1 - \mu)^2}{2\sigma_\eta^2}\right],$$

which implies that the likelihood of the observed data is

$$L(\boldsymbol{\theta}) = \int p(y_{1:T}, h_{1:T}|\boldsymbol{\theta})\, dh_{1:T} = \int p(y_{1:T}|h_{1:T}, \boldsymbol{\theta})\, p(h_{1:T}|\boldsymbol{\theta})\, dh_{1:T}.$$

Although the integration cannot be solved analytically, the integral can be approximated by the Monte Carlo integration, that is,

$$L^{SML}(\boldsymbol{\theta}) = \frac{1}{S}\sum_{s=1}^{S} p\left(y_{1:T}|h_{1:T}^{(s)}, \boldsymbol{\theta}\right), \tag{9.26}$$

where $h_{1:T}^{(s)}$ is the sth sample generated from the targeted model given $\boldsymbol{\theta}$. The associated SML estimator is

$$\widehat{\boldsymbol{\theta}}_{SML} = \arg\min_{\boldsymbol{\theta}\in\boldsymbol{\Theta}} Dist^{SML}(\boldsymbol{\theta}) = \arg\min_{\boldsymbol{\theta}\in\boldsymbol{\Theta}} \left[-L^{SML}(\boldsymbol{\theta})\right]. \tag{9.27}$$

In practice, the direct simple average in Eq. (9.26) is not efficient and very hard for convergence. Therefore, we need to find a proposal distribution $q(h_{1:T}|\boldsymbol{\theta})$ to replace the original one and then based on importance sampling, the integral can be approximated by

$$L^{SML}(y_{1:T}|\boldsymbol{\theta}) = \frac{1}{S}\sum_{s=1}^{S} p\left(y_{1:T}|h_{1:T}^{(s)}, \boldsymbol{\theta}\right) \frac{p\left(h_{1:T}^{(s)}|\boldsymbol{\theta}\right)}{q\left(h_{1:T}^{(s)}|\boldsymbol{\theta}\right)}$$
$$= \frac{1}{S}\sum_{s=1}^{S} p\left(y_{1:T}|h_{1:T}^{(s)}, \boldsymbol{\theta}\right)\omega^{(s)}, \tag{9.28}$$

where $h_{1:T}^{(s)}$ is now the sth sample generated from proposal distribution $q(h_{1:T}|\boldsymbol{\theta})$ and the weights $\omega^{(s)}$ compensate for discrepancy between $p\left(h_{1:T}^{(s)}|\boldsymbol{\theta}\right)$ and $q\left(h_{1:T}^{(s)}|\boldsymbol{\theta}\right)$. Apparently, as $S \to \infty$,

$$\frac{1}{S}\sum_{s=1}^{S} p\left(y_{1:T}|h_{1:T}^{(s)},\boldsymbol{\theta}\right)\omega^{(s)} \to \int p\left(y_{1:T}|h_{1:T},\boldsymbol{\theta}\right)\frac{p\left(h_{1:T}|\boldsymbol{\theta}\right)}{q\left(h_{1:T}|\boldsymbol{\theta}\right)}q\left(h_{1:T}|\boldsymbol{\theta}\right)dh_{1:T}.$$

In the following, we discuss one of the popular approaches to specify a "good" proposal distribution, $q\left(h_{1:T}|\boldsymbol{\theta}\right)$. Here we introduced a multivariate normal distribution based on the Laplace approximation. We then draw a sequence of independent variables from the multivariate normal distribution and approximate the integral by the sample mean of a function of the independent draws. Here the carefully selected multivariate normal distribution is served as the proposal distribution in the importance sampler. This method is called the Laplace-based importance sampler.

The Laplace approximation is to choose a multivariate normal distribution as the proposal distribution given the values of parameter $\boldsymbol{\theta}$, namely $\mathcal{MN}\left(\boldsymbol{h}_{\theta}^{*}, -\Omega_{\theta}^{*-1}\right)$. To select the desired multivariate normal density, we need to pin down the mean and the covariance matrix, which can be achieved by

$$\boldsymbol{h}_{\theta}^{*} = \arg\max_{\boldsymbol{h}\in\mathbb{R}^{T}} \log p\left(y_{1:T}|\boldsymbol{h},\boldsymbol{\theta}\right), \tag{9.29}$$

where $p\left(y_{1:T},\boldsymbol{h}|\boldsymbol{\theta}\right)$ is defined in Eq. (9.5) and $\boldsymbol{h} = h_{1:T}$. Besides, the covariance matrix can be obtained by

$$\Omega_{\theta}^{*} = \left.\frac{\partial^{2}\log p\left(y_{1:T}|\boldsymbol{h},\boldsymbol{\theta}\right)}{\partial\boldsymbol{h}\partial\boldsymbol{h}'}\right|_{\boldsymbol{h}=\boldsymbol{h}_{\theta}^{*}}. \tag{9.30}$$

The SV model in Eq. (9.1)–(9.2) does not have analytical expressions for $\boldsymbol{h}_{\theta}^{*}$ and hence numerical methods are needed. Following Shephard and Pitt (1997), Durham (2006), and Hans and Yu (2014), we can use Newton's method for calculation, which is very straightforward to use in widely available programming languages such as MATLAB, Python, and R. In particular, the evaluation of $L^{SML}\left(y_{1:T}|\boldsymbol{\theta}\right)$ can be summarized in Algorithm 5.

Under the assumption of finite variance, Kolmogorov's strong law of large numbers ensures the convergence of Eq. (9.31) to the true likelihood as $S \to \infty$. By the central limit theorem, the square root rate of convergence is achieved if

$$Var\left[\frac{p\left(y_{1:T}|\boldsymbol{h}^{(s)},\boldsymbol{\theta}\right)}{q\left(\boldsymbol{h}^{(s)}|\boldsymbol{\theta}\right)}\right] < \infty, \forall s.$$

Hence, we can apply Eq. (9.31) to compute the likelihood value given parameter value $\boldsymbol{\theta}$. The Laplace approximation is straightforward to implement, but it will result in approximation errors. The magnitude of errors is determined not only by the distance between the true distribution and the proposal but also the value of S. The approximation error decreases as S increases. To ensure that the likelihood surface is smooth, when simulating the random samples over the parameter space, the same set of random seeds should be used.

Algorithm 5 SML estimation based on Laplace approximation

1: Initialize $\boldsymbol{h}^0$.

2: Calculate the $\boldsymbol{h}_{\boldsymbol{\theta}}^*$ according to the first-order condition

$$\frac{\partial}{\partial \boldsymbol{h}} \log p\left(y_{1:T} | \boldsymbol{h}, \boldsymbol{\theta}\right) = \boldsymbol{0},$$

which can be achieved by the Newton method in a recursive algorithm. For $j = 1$ to J

a: $\boldsymbol{h}^j = \boldsymbol{h}^{j-1} - \left[\Omega(\boldsymbol{h}^{j-1})\right]^{-1} \boldsymbol{h}^{j-1}$, where $\Omega(\cdot)$ is defined as follows:

$$\Omega\left(\boldsymbol{h}\right) = \begin{pmatrix} -\frac{1}{\sigma_\eta^2} - \frac{1}{2}\varepsilon_1^2 & \frac{\phi}{\sigma_\eta^2} & \cdots & 0 & 0 \\ \frac{\phi}{\sigma_\eta^2} & -\frac{1+\phi^2}{\sigma_\eta^2} - \frac{1}{2}\varepsilon_2^2 & \cdots & 0 & 0 \\ \vdots & \vdots & \ddots & \vdots & \vdots \\ 0 & 0 & \cdots & \frac{1+\phi^2}{\sigma_\eta^2} - \frac{1}{2}\varepsilon_{T-1}^2 & \frac{\phi}{\sigma_\eta^2} \\ 0 & 0 & \cdots & \frac{\phi}{\sigma_\eta^2} & -\frac{1}{\sigma_\eta^2} - \frac{1}{2}\varepsilon_T^2 \end{pmatrix},$$

and $\varepsilon_t = y_t \exp\left(-\frac{h_t}{2}\right)$, for $t = 1, \ldots, T$.

b: Stop when $\left|\boldsymbol{h}^j - \boldsymbol{h}^{j-1}\right| < \delta$, and $\boldsymbol{h}_{\boldsymbol{\theta}}^* = \boldsymbol{h}^j$, where δ is some stop criterion otherwise $\boldsymbol{h}_{\boldsymbol{\theta}}^* = \boldsymbol{h}^j$.

3: Calculate $\Omega_{\boldsymbol{\theta}}^* = \Omega\left(\boldsymbol{h}_{\boldsymbol{\theta}}^*\right)$ and obtain $q\left(h_{1:T}|\boldsymbol{\theta}\right)$, which is $\mathcal{MN}\left(\boldsymbol{h}_{\boldsymbol{\theta}}^*, -\Omega_{\boldsymbol{\theta}}^{*-1}\right)$.

4: Simulate $h_{1:T}^{(s)} = \boldsymbol{h}^{(s)} \sim \mathcal{MN}\left(\boldsymbol{h}_{\boldsymbol{\theta}}^*, -\Omega_{\boldsymbol{\theta}}^{-1}\right)$ for $s = 1, \ldots, S$, and compute

$$L^{SML}\left(\boldsymbol{\theta}\right) = \frac{1}{S}\sum_{s=1}^{S} p\left(y_{1:T}|\boldsymbol{h}^{(s)}, \boldsymbol{\theta}\right)\omega^{(s)}, \omega^{(s)} = \frac{p\left(\boldsymbol{h}^{(s)}|\boldsymbol{\theta}\right)}{q\left(\boldsymbol{h}^{(s)}|\boldsymbol{\theta}\right)}. \quad (9.31)$$

For the estimators discussed earlier, the inference relies on the asymptotic normality properties of the estimators. The asymptotic behavior of the estimators may not work well in finite samples, especially when the time series is highly persistent. Therefore, inference based on asymptotic theory may lead to a misleading conclusion.

9.4 Methods in the Bayesian Domain

In the Bayesian paradigm, when we combine the likelihood function $p\left(y|\boldsymbol{\theta}\right)$ with prior information, which is expressed as a probability distribution with density $\pi\left(\boldsymbol{\theta}\right)$, we obtain the posterior, which is another probability distribution, $\pi\left(\boldsymbol{\theta}|y\right)$. The posterior is obtained by the Bayes formula,

$$\pi(\boldsymbol{\theta} \mid y) = \frac{p(y|\boldsymbol{\theta})\,\pi(\boldsymbol{\theta})}{p(y)},$$

where $p(y)$ is the marginal density of y (see, e.g., Robert (2007)).

In the Bayesian domain, the estimation of the parameter $\boldsymbol{\theta}$ is based on the decision theory framework. To achieve this we firstly need to specify a loss function $\rho(\boldsymbol{\delta}, \boldsymbol{\theta})$, which represents the loss caused by choosing the estimates of $\boldsymbol{\theta}$ as $\boldsymbol{\delta}$. The Bayesian estimator is the one minimizing posterior risk defined as follows:

$$\widehat{\boldsymbol{\theta}}^{Bayes} = \arg\min_{\boldsymbol{\delta}\in\boldsymbol{\Theta}} \int \int \rho(\boldsymbol{\delta}, \boldsymbol{\theta})\,\pi(\boldsymbol{\theta}|y)\,d\boldsymbol{\theta}\,dy. \tag{9.32}$$

Specifically, we usually choose the quadratic loss function

$$\rho(\boldsymbol{\delta}, \boldsymbol{\theta}) = \|\boldsymbol{\theta} - \boldsymbol{\delta}\|^2.$$

Then the Bayes estimator is the posterior mean $\widehat{\boldsymbol{\theta}}^{Bayes} = \bar{\boldsymbol{\theta}} = \mathbb{E}(\boldsymbol{\theta}|y)$.

Unlike frequentist methods, Bayesian approaches estimate the parameter by performing posterior analysis. Given the likelihood function $p(y|\boldsymbol{\theta})$ and the prior $\pi(\boldsymbol{\theta})$ for parameters, the posterior distribution $\pi(\boldsymbol{\theta}|y)$ is also available. If we can obtain random samples from the posterior distribution, we can use sample moments to estimate parameters and make statistical inference about parameters. For example, we can use the sample mean (the posterior mean) and the sample quantiles (the posterior quantiles) to calculate the point estimate and credible intervals, respectively.

While the inference of frequentist methods often relies on asymptotic theory that may or may not provide accurate approximations to the finite sample distribution, Bayesian inference is based on the posterior distribution. The exact finite sample inference provided by $\pi(\boldsymbol{\theta}|y)$ can be performed in the Bayesian domain via posterior analysis. However, the Bayesian approach always requires numerical integration or sampling techniques. Consequently, the computational cost is generally high. Besides, the model must be fully specified since the likelihood function is required.

The log-normal SV model belongs to the class of latent variable models. For latent variable models, one way to implement Bayesian estimation is to treat the unobserved variables $h_{1:T}$ as additional parameters to estimate. This technique is known as data augmentation. Another way is to directly calculate the likelihood function without data augmentation, which can be achieved by applying the sequential Monte Carlo method (SMC). We discuss how to estimate the parameters in the log-normal SV model with and without data augmentation. The procedures can accommodate other types of latent variable models. Specifically, when using data augmentation, we can estimate the model either through the single-move Markov chain Monte Carlo method (single-move MCMC, see, Jacquier et al. (2002)) or multimove MCMC method (multimove MCMC).

In the former, only one variable at one time is updated and in the latter, the latent vector $\boldsymbol{h}$ is sampled in a single block, which is more efficient (see, e.g., Shephard and Pitt (1997), Kim et al. (1998), Chib et al. (2002), Liesenfeld and Richard (2003), and Omori et al. (2007)).

9.4.1 Single-Move MCMC

When applying data augmentation for the log-normal SV model, we treat the unobserved log-volatility $\boldsymbol{h} = h_{1:T}$ as a parameter vector. By doing this, we avoid the problem of intractable likelihood function. Instead, according to the discussion in Section 9.2, the analytical expression for $(\boldsymbol{h}, \boldsymbol{\theta})$, the so-called complete-data likelihood, is given by

$$
\begin{aligned}
p\left(y_{1:T}|\boldsymbol{h}, \boldsymbol{\theta}\right) = & \prod_{t=1}^{T} \frac{1}{\sqrt{2\pi e^{\frac{h_t}{2}}}} \exp\left[-\frac{y_t^2}{2e^{h_t}}\right] \prod_{t=2}^{T} \frac{1}{\sqrt{2\pi}\sigma_\eta} \\
& \exp\left[-\frac{\left(h_t - \mu - \phi\left(h_{t-1} - \mu\right)\right)^2}{2\sigma_\eta^2}\right] \\
& \times \sqrt{\frac{1-\phi^2}{2\pi\sigma_\eta^2}} \exp\left[-\frac{\left(1-\phi^2\right)\left(h_1 - \mu\right)^2}{2\sigma_\eta^2}\right].
\end{aligned}
$$

To perform Bayesian estimation, the prior for $\boldsymbol{\theta}$ is specified as

$$
\pi\left(\boldsymbol{\theta}\right) = \pi\left(\mu\right)\pi\left(\phi\right)\pi\left(\sigma_\eta^2\right).
$$

Therefore, the joint posterior density function is

$$
\pi\left(\boldsymbol{\theta}, \boldsymbol{h}|y_{1:T}\right) \propto \pi\left(\mu\right)\pi\left(\phi\right)\pi\left(\sigma_\eta^2\right) p\left(y_{1:T}|\boldsymbol{h}, \boldsymbol{\theta}\right). \tag{9.33}
$$

which implies that we only need to focus on the posterior of $(\boldsymbol{\theta}, \boldsymbol{h})$ and the next step is to draw samples of $(\boldsymbol{\theta}, \boldsymbol{h})$ from the posterior distribution in Eq. (9.33).

How to draw samples from the targeted posterior distribution is the key problem in Bayesian estimation. MCMC is one of the popular approaches in practice. Essentially, MCMC is a category of algorithms which generate a correlated sample from a Markov chain with stationary distribution being the same as the posterior distribution. The single-move MCMC was first proposed by Jacquier et al. (2002) and Kim et al. (1998) summarized the algorithm clearly. Here we use the priors in Kim et al. (1998) to illustrate how the single-move MCMC works. In the following, s indicates the sth MCMC draws and we define the notation $h_{-t}^{(s-1)} = \left(h_1^{(s)}, \ldots, h_{t-1}^{(s)}, h_{t+1}^{(s-1)}, h_{t+2}^{(s-1)}, \ldots, h_T^{(s-1)}\right)'$. The Gibbs sampler with Metropolis–Hasting step is illustrated in Algorithm 6.

We discuss the posterior distributions used in Algorithm 6 in detail.

Algorithm 6 The single-move MCMC algorithm

```
Initialize $\boldsymbol{\theta}^{(1)} = \left(\mu^{(1)}, \phi^{(1)}, \sigma_\eta^{2(1)}\right)$ and $h_t = 0$ for $t = 1, \ldots, T$.
Prespecify the number of effective samples $S$ and the burn-in samples $S_{burnin}$.
for $s = 2$ to $S + S_{burnin}$ do
    Draw $h_t^{(s)} \sim \pi\left(h_t | h_{-t}^{(s-1)}, y_{1:T}, \boldsymbol{\theta}^{(s-1)}\right)$, for $t = 1, \ldots, T$.
    Draw $\sigma_\eta^{2(s)} \sim \pi\left(\sigma_\eta^2 | h_{1:T}^{(s)}, \phi^{(s-1)}, \mu^{(s-1)}\right)$.
    Draw $\phi^{(s)} \sim \pi\left(\phi | h_{1:T}^{(s)}, \mu^{(s-1)}, \sigma_\eta^{2(s)}\right)$.
    Draw $\mu^{(s)} \sim \pi\left(\mu | h_{1:T}^{(s)}, \phi^{(s)}, \sigma_\eta^{2(s)}\right)$.
Collect $\left\{h_{1:T}^{(s)}, \phi^{(s)}, \mu^{(s)}, \sigma_\eta^{2(s)}\right\}_{s=S_{burnin}+1}^{S+S_{burnin}}$ as the effective samples.
```

The Posterior for h_t, $\pi(h_t|\cdot)$
The posterior density function has the following property,

$$\pi\left(h_t | h_{-t}^{(s-1)}, y_{1:T}, \boldsymbol{\theta}^{(s-1)}\right) \propto f_{\mathcal{N}}\left(h_t | h_t^{*(s)}, \upsilon^{2(s)}\right) p\left(y_t | h_t, \boldsymbol{\theta}^{(s-1)}\right),$$

where $f_{\mathcal{N}}$ is the normal density function with mean and variance as

$$h_t^{(s)*} = \mu^{(s-1)} + \frac{\phi^{(s-1)}\left[\left(h_{t-1}^{(s)} - \mu^{(s-1)}\right) + \left(h_{t+1}^{(s-1)} - \mu^{(s-1)}\right)\right]}{\left(1 + \phi^{(s-1)2}\right)},$$

$$\upsilon^{2(s)} = \frac{\sigma_\eta^{2(s-1)}}{1 + \phi^{(s-1)2}}.$$

Besides, since

$$\begin{aligned}\log p\left(y_t | h_t, \boldsymbol{\theta}\right) &= -\log 2\pi - \frac{h_t}{2} - \frac{y_t}{2e^{h_t}} \\ &\leq -\log 2\pi - \frac{1}{2}h_t - \frac{y_t^2}{2}\left[\exp\left(-h_t^*\right)\left(1 + h_t^*\right) - h_t \exp\left(-h_t^*\right)\right],\end{aligned}$$

we can find

$$\pi\left(h_t | h_{-t}^{(s-1)}, y_{1:T}, \boldsymbol{\theta}^{(s-1)}\right) \leq f_{\mathcal{N}}\left(h_t | \mu_t^{*(s)}, \upsilon^{2(s)}\right),$$

where

$$\mu_t^{*(s)} = h_t^{*(s)} + \frac{\upsilon^{2(s)}}{2}\left[y_t^2 \exp\left(-h_t^{*(s)}\right) - 1\right].$$

One may say that it is possible to directly sample the latent variable h_t from the normal proposal distribution and implement the Reject/Accept algorithm to obtain the samples. However, in practice, we usually use the Metropolis–Hasting step to ensure the effectiveness of samples. The sampling of $h_t^{(s)}$ is performed as follows.

1. Draw $\tilde{h} \sim \mathcal{N}\left(\mu_t^{*(s)}, \upsilon^{2(s)}\right)$.
2. Compute

$$\alpha = \min\left\{1, \frac{f_{\mathcal{N}}\left(h_t^{(s-1)}|\mu_t^{*(s)}, \upsilon^{2(s)}\right)}{f_{\mathcal{N}}\left(\tilde{h}|\mu_t^{*(s)}, \upsilon^{2(s)}\right)}\right.$$
$$\left.\times \frac{f_{\mathcal{N}}\left(\tilde{h}|h_t^{*(s)}, \upsilon^{2(s)}\right) p\left(y_t|\tilde{h}, \boldsymbol{\theta}^{(s-1)}\right)}{f_{\mathcal{N}}\left(h_t^{(s-1)}|h_t^{*(s)}, \upsilon^{2(s)}\right) p\left(y_t|h_t^{(s-1)}, \boldsymbol{\theta}^{(s-1)}\right)}\right\}.$$

3. Generate $u \sim U(0, 1)$,

$$h_t^{(s)} = \begin{cases} \tilde{h}, & \text{if } u \leq \alpha, \\ h_t^{(s-1)}, & \text{if } u > \alpha. \end{cases}$$

The Posterior for σ_η, $\pi\left(\sigma_\eta|\cdot\right)$

Following Kim et al. (1998), we impose a conjugate prior

$$\sigma_\eta^2 \mid \phi, \mu \sim \mathcal{IG}\left(s_r/2, S_\sigma/2\right),$$

then σ_η^2 is sampled from an inverse-Gamma distribution,

$$\sigma_\eta^2 \mid y_{1:T}, h_{1:T}^{(s)}, \phi^{(s-1)}, \mu^{(s-1)}$$
$$\sim \mathcal{IG}\left\{\frac{T+s_r}{2}, \frac{S_\sigma + \left(h_1^{(s)} - \mu^{(s-1)}\right)^2\left(1-\phi^{(s-1)2}\right)}{2}\right.$$
$$\left. + \frac{\sum_{t=1}^{T-1}\left(\left(h_{t+1}^{(s)} - \mu^{(s-1)}\right) - \phi^{(s-1)}\left(h_t^{(s)} - \mu^{(s-1)}\right)\right)^2}{2}\right\},$$

where $\mathcal{IG}$ denotes the inverse-gamma distribution. Here we set $\sigma_r = 5$ and $S_\sigma = 0.01 \times \sigma_r$.

The Posterior for ϕ, $\pi(\phi|\cdot)$
For ϕ, denote $\phi = 2\phi^* - 1$, where ϕ^* follows a Beta distribution with parameters (γ_1, γ_2). Hence, the prior used for ϕ is

$$\pi(\phi) \propto \left[\frac{(1+\phi)}{2}\right]^{\gamma_1 - 1} \left[\frac{(1-\phi)}{2}\right]^{\gamma_2 - 1}, \quad \gamma_1, \gamma_2 > \frac{1}{2}$$

and has support on the interval $(-1, 1)$. Here we set $\gamma_1 = 20$ and $\gamma_2 = 1.5$. Then the posterior of ϕ is

$$\pi\left(\phi|y_{1:T}, h_{1:T}^{(s)}, \mu^{(s-1)}, \sigma_\eta^{2(s)}\right) \propto \pi(\phi)\, p\left(h_{1:T}^{(s)}|\mu^{(s-1)}, \phi, \sigma_\eta^{2(s)}\right).$$

The Metropolis–Hasting sampling procedure is illustrated as follows:

1. Draw $\tilde{\phi} \sim \mathcal{N}\left(\phi^{*(s)}, S_\phi^{(s)}\right)$, where

$$\phi^{*(s)} = \frac{\sum_{t=1}^{T-1}\left(h_{t+1}^{(s)} - \mu^{(s-1)}\right)\left(h_t^{(s)} - \mu^{(s-1)}\right)}{\sum_{t=1}^{T-1}\left(h_t^{(s)} - \mu^{(s-1)}\right)^2},$$

$$S_\phi^{(s)} = \sigma_\eta^{2(s)}\left[\sum_{t=1}^{T-1}\left(h_t^{(s)} - \mu^{(s-1)}\right)^2\right]^{-1}.$$

2. Compute

$$\alpha_\phi = \min\left\{1, \frac{f_{\mathcal{N}}\left(\phi^{(s-1)}|\phi^{*(s)}, S_\phi^{(s)}\right)}{f_{\mathcal{N}}\left(\tilde{\phi}|\phi^{*(s)}, S_\phi^{(s)}\right)} \times \frac{\pi\left(\tilde{\phi}\right) p\left(h_{1:T}^{(s)}|\mu^{(s-1)}, \tilde{\phi}, \sigma_\eta^{2(s)}\right)}{\pi\left(\phi^{(s-1)}\right) p\left(h_{1:T}^{(s)}|\mu^{(s-1)}, \phi^{(s-1)}, \sigma_\eta^{2(s)}\right)}\right\}.$$

3. Generate $u \sim U(0, 1)$,

$$\phi^{(s)} = \begin{cases} \tilde{\phi}, & \text{if } u \le \alpha_\phi, \\ \phi^{(s-1)}, & \text{if } u > \alpha_\phi. \end{cases}$$

The Posterior for μ, $\pi(\mu|\cdot)$
We can impose a normal prior for μ ,

$$\pi\left(\mu|h_{1:T}^{(s)}, \phi^{(s)}, \sigma_\eta^{2(s)}\right) \propto \pi\left(h_{1:T}^{(s)}|\mu, \phi^{(s)}, \sigma_\eta^{2(s)}\right)\pi(\mu),$$

where $\pi(\mu)$ is the prior $\mathcal{N}\left(0, \upsilon_\mu^2\right)$. It can be derived that

$$\mu|h_{1:T}^{(s)}, \phi^{(s)}, \sigma_\eta^{2(s)} \sim \mathcal{N}\left(\mu^{*(s)}, \sigma_\mu^{2(s)}\right),$$

where

$$\mu^{*(s)} = \sigma_\mu^{2(s)} \left\{ \frac{\left(1-\phi^{(s)2}\right)}{\sigma_\eta^{2(s)}} h_1^{(s)} + \frac{\left(1-\phi^{(s)}\right)}{\sigma_\eta^{2(s)}} \sum_{t=1}^{T-1} \left(h_{t+1}^{(s)} - \phi^{(s)} h_t^{(s)} \right) \right\},$$

$$\sigma_\mu^{2(s)} = \frac{\upsilon_\mu^2 \sigma_\eta^{2(s)}}{\sigma_\eta^{2(s)} + \upsilon_\mu^2 \left[(T-1)(1-\phi^{(s)})^2 + \left(1-\phi^{(s)2}\right) \right]}.$$

There we can directly sample μ from the normal distribution.

After iterating until $S + S_{burnin}$ we can obtain a series of correlated samples from the posterior. To remove the impact of initial values, we must perform the burn-in step, that is, remove the first S_{burnin} samples. The final remaining samples are treated as the effective samples from the posterior distribution and can be used for inference. In particular, we can directly compute the estimator according to Eq. (9.32). If we choose the quadratic loss function, the estimator is the posterior mean, that is,

$$\bar{\boldsymbol{\theta}} = \frac{\sum_{s=1}^{S} \boldsymbol{\theta}^{(s)}}{S}, \tag{9.34}$$

and we can use the posterior samples to construct posterior intervals for parameters.

9.4.2 Multimove MCMC

As pointed out by Kim et al. (1998), the samples generated by single-move MCMC have high correlation and hence, are not efficient. Multimove algorithms are more efficient. Shephard and Pitt (1997), Kim et al. (1998), Chib et al. (2002), Liesenfeld and Richard (2003), and Omori et al. (2007) have developed various multimove algorithms to estimate univariate and multivariate SV models. Essentially, the multimove algorithms sample the latent volatility $h_{1:T}$ in a single block. Here we use the algorithm in Kim et al. (1998) for illustration.

As discussed in Section 9.2, the observation equation can be rewritten as

$$\log\left(y_t^2\right) = h_t + \log\left(\varepsilon_t^2\right), \tag{9.35}$$

where $\log\left(\varepsilon_t^2\right)$ is the logarithm of the chi-squared random variable with 1 degree of freedom and hence, the Kalman filter cannot be applied. In Section 9.3.2, we use a normal distribution with mean -1.27 and variance $\pi^2/2$ to approximate $\log\left(\varepsilon_t^2\right)$ and the Kalman filter to conduct the QML estimation. However, a better approximation of the logarithm of the chi-squared distribution is a mixture of normal distributions given by

Table 9.1 *Selection of* $\{w_i, m_i, v_i^2\}$

i	w_i	m_i	v_i^2
1	0.00730	−10.12999	5.79596
2	0.10556	−3.97281	2.61369
3	0.00002	−8.56686	5.17950
4	0.04395	2.77786	0.16735
5	0.34001	0.61942	0.64009
6	0.24566	1.79518	0.34023
7	0.25750	−1.08819	1.26261

$$\sum_{i=1}^{K} w_i f_{\mathcal{N}}\left(\varepsilon_t \mid m_i, v_i^2\right),$$

which is a mixture of K normal densities $f_{\mathcal{N}}$ with component weights w_i. The constants $\{w_i, m_i, v_i^2\}$ are predetermined (see, e.g., Kim et al. (1998)) and summarized in Table 9.1.

We then rewrite the density of the mixture of normal distributions in terms of a component indicator variable q_t at each time t, such that Eq. (9.35) is now

$$\log\left(y_t^2\right) = h_t + \tilde{\varepsilon}_t, \tag{9.36}$$

$$\tilde{\varepsilon}_t | q_t = i \sim \mathcal{N}\left(m_i - 1.2704, v_i^2\right), i = 1, \ldots, K, \tag{9.37}$$

$$P\left(q_t = i\right) = w_i. \tag{9.38}$$

Therefore, by introducing the indicator vector $\boldsymbol{q} = (q_1, \ldots, q_T)'$ and the mixture normal distribution, we can directly use the Kalman filter and smoother since we can use a normal random variable to replace the $\log \varepsilon_t^2$ at every time t given the values of q_t. The log-volatility $h_{1:T}$ can now be treated as state variables in a Gaussian state-space model and updated in a block. In other words, we only need to add the updating of indicator vector $\boldsymbol{q}$ and use the Kalman filter and smoother to update $h_{1:T}$ in the single-move MCMC. By doing this, the samples obtained are much more efficient relative to those obtained as in Section 9.4.1. The algorithm is summarized in Algorithm 7.

In the following, we discuss how to sample $\boldsymbol{h}$ and $\boldsymbol{q}$.

The Posterior for $\boldsymbol{h}$*,* $\pi\left(\boldsymbol{h}|\cdot\right)$

The posterior for $\boldsymbol{h}$ conditional on $\boldsymbol{q}$ can be sampled by the Kalman filter. Specifically, given $\boldsymbol{q}$, the state-space model is

$$\tilde{x}_t - \mu^{(s)} = z_t + \tilde{\varepsilon}_t,$$

$$z_t = \phi^{(s)} z_{t-1} + \sigma_\eta^{(s)} \eta_t.$$

Algorithm 7 The multimove MCMC algorithm

```
Initialize θ^(1) = (μ^(1), φ^(1), σ_η^2(1)) and q_t^(1) = 1 for t = 1, ..., T.
Prespecify the number of effective samples S and the burn-in samples S_burnin.
for s = 2 to S + S_burnin do
    Draw h^(s) ~ π(h | x̃, q^(s−1), θ^(s−1)).
    Draw q^(s) ~ π(q | x̃, h^(s)).
    Draw σ_η^2(s) ~ π(σ_η^2 | h^(s), φ^(s−1), μ^(s−1)).
    Draw φ^(s) ~ π(φ | h^(s), μ^(s−1), σ_η^2(s)).
    Draw μ^(s) ~ π(μ | h^(s), φ^(s), σ_η^2(s)).
Collect {h^(s), φ^(s), μ^(s), σ_η^2(s)}_{s=S_burnin+1}^{S+S_burnin} as the effective samples.
```

Therefore, conditional on $\boldsymbol{q}$, we can sample $\boldsymbol{h}^{(s)}$ at the sth sampling as follows.

1. At the sth sampling, initialize $\boldsymbol{h} = \mu^{(s)}$, namely, $z_t = 0$, for $t = 1, \ldots T$.
2. Kalman filter: let $z_t | y_{1:t-1} \sim \mathcal{N}(c_{t-1}, C_{t-1})$, conditional on $q_t = i$, $\tilde{\varepsilon}_t \sim \mathcal{N}\left(m_i, v_i^2\right)$,
$$a_t = \phi^{(s)} m_{t-1}, R_t = \phi^{(s)2} C_{t-1} + \sigma_\eta^{2(s)},$$
$$f_t = a_t + m_i - 1.2704, Q_t = R_t + v_i^2,$$
$$c_t = a_t + R_t Q_t^{-1}\left(\tilde{x}_t - \mu^{(s)} - f_t\right), C_t = R_t - R_t^2 / Q_t.$$
3. Smoother: let $z_t | y_{1:T} \sim \mathcal{N}(d_t, D_t)$, conditional on $q_t = i$, $\tilde{\varepsilon}_t \sim \mathcal{N}\left(m_i, v_i^2\right)$,
$$d_t = c_t + \phi^{(s)} C_t \left(c_{t+1} - a_{t+1}\right) / R_{t+1}, D_t = C_t - \phi^{(s)2} C_t^2 \left(R_{t+1} - D_{t+1}\right) / R_{t+1}^2.$$
4. Draw $z_t \sim \mathcal{N}(d_t, D_t)$ for $t = 1, \ldots, T$.
5. Recover $h_t^{(s)} = z_t + \mu^{(s)}$.

The Posterior for $\boldsymbol{q}$, $\pi(\boldsymbol{q}|\cdot)$
The posterior for q_t has the property,
$$Pr\left(q_t^{(s)} = i \middle| \tilde{x}_t, h_t^{(s)}\right) \propto w_i f_{\mathcal{N}}\left(\tilde{x}_t | h_t^{(s)} + m_i, v_i^2\right), i = 1, \ldots, K.$$
Therefore, it can be sampled by using the probability mass function.

In summary, the above-reviewed MCMC methods perform well in estimating the SV model. Moreover, the posterior mean of $\boldsymbol{h}$ is easy to obtain, which serves as the smooth estimate of log-volatility as it is conditional on $\boldsymbol{y}$. However, these MCMC methods require full knowledge of the likelihood function and are time-consuming. Besides, we must usually design the Gibbs MCMC estimation procedure case-by-case for a specific data-generating process.

9.4.3 Parameter Learning via Sequential Monte Carlo Methods

The single-move MCMC and multimove MCMC algorithms are all based on data augmentation, which makes the complete-data likelihood function analytically tractable. A class of alternative Bayesian approaches uses the particle filter, or the sequential Monte Carlo (SMC) method. SMC is mainly used to analyze state-space models, in which there is a hidden state of interest. Inference regarding the states depends on the known parameter $\boldsymbol{\theta}$ and the noisy observations $\boldsymbol{y}$. Different from the classic Kalman filter, which is optimally designed for linear and Gaussian state-space models, the particle filter also works well for nonlinear and non-Gaussian state-space models. Essentially, the particle filter uses a set of random samples ("particles") with associated weights to represent the density in the prediction and updating steps.

However, the target here is to estimate the parameter $\boldsymbol{\theta}$ instead of $\boldsymbol{h}$. To estimate parameters, the particle MCMC (PMCMC) proposed by Andrieu et al. (2010) combines the MCMC method and SMC. They provided a generic solution to estimate parameters for a variety of models. While it is flexible, Fulop and Li (2013) and Fulop et al. (2015) emphasized that sequential learning (i.e., filtering as opposed to smoothing) is preferred in financial and economic applications, in which the states and parameters are updated as new observations arrive. Therefore, we explain how to use the sequential learning algorithm combined with the SMC method. For convenience, we divide the estimation procedure into two parts. The first is the bootstrap filter (see, e.g., Gordon (1993), Kitagawa (1996)) for the inference of hidden state $\boldsymbol{h}$, the other is the parameter learning as in Fulop and Li (2013). Estimates are computed based on the particles and weights. As the number of samples generated becomes large, this simulation-based empirical distribution is equivalent to the true distribution.

Sequential Monte Carlo Method

In this section, we show how to use the sequential Monte Carlo method, or particle filter to filter the log-volatility in the log-normal SV model. This filter necessitates simulation from the transition density $p\left(h_{t+1}|h_t, y_t\right)$ and computation of the measurement density $p\left(y_t|h_t\right)$. Suppose we have a set of "particles," $h_t^{(1)}, \ldots, h_t^{(M)}$ with associated discrete probability masses $w_t^{(1)}, \ldots, w_t^{(M)}$. Based on the Bayes rule, SMC algorithms propagate and update particles to yield a sample from $p\left(h_t|y_{1:t}, \boldsymbol{\theta}\right)$ according to the following filter density,

$$p\left(h_t|y_{1:t}, \boldsymbol{\theta}\right) \propto p\left(y_t|h_t, \boldsymbol{\theta}\right) \int p\left(h_t|h_{t-1}, \boldsymbol{\theta}\right) p\left(h_{t-1}|y_{1:t-1}, \boldsymbol{\theta}\right) dh_{t-1}.$$

Following Chopin and Papaspiliopoulos (2020), the bootstrap particle filter algorithm is outlined in Algorithm 8. For the log-normal SV model Eqs. (9.1)–(9.2), we can define

$$p(h_1|\boldsymbol{\theta}) \equiv \mathcal{N}\left(0, \frac{1}{1-\phi^2}\sigma_\eta^2\right),$$

$$p(h_t|h_{t-1}, \boldsymbol{\theta}) \equiv \mathcal{N}\left(\mu + \phi(h_{t-1} - \mu), \sigma_\eta^2\right),$$

$$p(y_t|h_t, \boldsymbol{\theta}) \equiv \frac{1}{\sqrt{2\pi}e^{\frac{h_t}{2}}} \exp\left[-\frac{y_t^2}{2e^{h_t}}\right].$$

The estimator for the log-likelihood is

$$\log \widehat{L}_{SMC}(\boldsymbol{\theta}) = \sum_{t=1}^{T} \log \widehat{p}(y_t|y_{1:t-1}, \boldsymbol{\theta}) = \sum_{t=1}^{T} \log\left(\sum_{i=1}^{M} \frac{\tilde{\omega}_t^{(i)}}{\sum_{i=1}^{M} \tilde{\omega}_{t-1}^{(i)}}\right),$$

where $\tilde{\omega}_t^{(i)}$ are the weights for the particles at time t.

The particle filter is flexible for a variety of models. However, the accuracy depends on the number of particles (M). The larger M is, the better the approximation. Given M, if the sample size is large, the computation will be intensive. There are many other variations of the particle filter, which are similar to the bootstrap particle filter, like the sampling importance resampling filter of Gordon et al. (1993), the auxiliary sampling importance resampling filter of Pitt and Shephard (1999), and the regularized particle filter of Smith (2013). They can improve certain aspects of the performance, but face some trade-offs between the computational burden and restricted model forms.

Parameter Learning via Marginal Resample-Move

SMC for state filtering is relatively straightforward, but the goal of drawing $\boldsymbol{\theta}$ from $\pi(\boldsymbol{\theta}|\boldsymbol{y})$ sequentially is still difficult. If we simply apply a particle filter over $\pi(\boldsymbol{\theta}|\boldsymbol{y})$ while keeping $\boldsymbol{\theta}$ invariant, the algorithm will quickly fail and result in particle depletion. Following Fulop and Li (2013), by approximately integrating out the states using a SMC as in Section 9.4.3, we can break up the interdependence of the log-volatility $\boldsymbol{h}$ and the static parameters $\boldsymbol{\theta}$. In what follows, we apply a Bayesian resample-move algorithm according to Gilks and Berzuini (2001) and Chopin (2002) after the marginalization. For more details, one can also refer to Chopin et al. (2013).

Conditional on $\boldsymbol{\theta}$, we denote the particles for the log-volatility h_t at time t as $\mathcal{S}_t = \left\{h_t^{(i)}, \omega_t^{(i)}, \tilde{\omega}_t^{(i)}, i = 1, \ldots, M\right\}$. We denote $\mathcal{S}_t$ associated with the nth particles $\boldsymbol{\theta}^{(n)}$ as $\mathcal{S}_t^{(n)}$ and outline the procedure in Algorithm 9. In the algorithm, the proposal distribution $q_t\left(\boldsymbol{\theta} \mid \tilde{\boldsymbol{\theta}}^{(n)}\right)$ is used to keep the particles

Algorithm 8 The Bootstrap Particle Filter

Draw $h_1^{(i)} \sim p(h_1|\boldsymbol{\theta})$ for $i = 1, \ldots, M$ and initialize

$$\omega_1^{(i)} = \frac{\tilde{\omega}_1^{(i)}}{\sum_{i=1}^{M} \tilde{\omega}_1^{(i)}}, \quad \tilde{\omega}_1^{(i)} = p\left(y_1|\widetilde{h}_1^{(i)}, \boldsymbol{\theta}\right)$$

for $t = 2$ to T **do**

Calculate the effective sample size (ESS),

$$ESS_h = \frac{1}{\sum_{i=1}^{M} \omega_{t-1}^{(i)2}},$$

if $ESS_h < c_h$ **then**

Draw $h_{t-1}^{(i)}$ by resampling according to $\omega_{t-1} = \left(\omega_{t-1}^{(1)}, \ldots, \omega_{t-1}^{(M)}\right)$.

Change

$$\tilde{\omega}_{t-1}^{(i)} = 1, \omega_{t-1}^{(i)} = \frac{1}{M},$$

else

$h_{t-1}^{(i)}, \omega_{t-1}^{(i)}$ and $\tilde{\omega}_{t-1}^{(i)}$ are unchanged.

Draw $\widetilde{h}_t^{(i)} \sim p\left(h_t|h_{t-1}^{(i)}, \boldsymbol{\theta}\right)$, for $i = 1, \ldots, M$.

Calculate normalized weights,

$$\omega_t^{(i)} = \frac{\tilde{\omega}_t^{(i)}}{\sum_{i=1}^{M} \tilde{\omega}_t^{(i)}}, \quad \tilde{\omega}_t^{(i)} = p\left(y_t|\widetilde{h}_t^{(i)}, \boldsymbol{\theta}\right) \tilde{\omega}_{t-1}^{(i)}.$$

Calculate

$$\widehat{p}\left(y_t|y_{1:t-1}, \boldsymbol{\theta}\right) = \sum_{i=1}^{M} f\left(y_t|\widetilde{h}_t^{(i)}, \boldsymbol{\theta}\right) \frac{\tilde{\omega}_{t-1}^{(i)}}{\sum_{i=1}^{M} \tilde{\omega}_{t-1}^{(i)}} = \sum_{i=1}^{M} \frac{\tilde{\omega}_t^{(i)}}{\sum_{i=1}^{M} \tilde{\omega}_{t-1}^{(i)}}.$$

$\boldsymbol{\theta}^{(n)}$ away from being static all the time. In practice, following Fulop and Li (2013), we can define $q_t\left(\boldsymbol{\theta} \mid \tilde{\boldsymbol{\theta}}^{(n)}\right) \equiv \mathcal{MN}(\boldsymbol{\mu}, \Sigma)$ where $\boldsymbol{\mu} = \frac{1}{N}\sum_{n=1}^{N} \tilde{\boldsymbol{\theta}}^{(n)}$, $\Sigma = \frac{1}{N}\sum_{n=1}^{N}\left(\tilde{\boldsymbol{\theta}}^{(n)} - \boldsymbol{\mu}\right)\left(\tilde{\boldsymbol{\theta}}^{(n)} - \boldsymbol{\mu}\right)'$.

Finally we can collect the joint particles from $p(\boldsymbol{\theta}, \boldsymbol{h}|y_{1:T})$, namely, $\{\boldsymbol{h}^{(n,i)}, \boldsymbol{\theta}^{(n)}\}_{n=1,\ldots,N, i=1,\ldots,M}$. For any function $g(\boldsymbol{\theta}, \boldsymbol{h})$, its posterior expectation can be approximated by

$$\mathbb{E}\left(g(\boldsymbol{\theta}, \boldsymbol{h})\,|y_{1:t}\right) \approx \sum_{n=1}^{N}\sum_{i=1}^{M} W_t^{(n)} \omega_t^{(n,i)} g\left(\boldsymbol{\theta}^{(n)}, \boldsymbol{h}^{(n,i)}\right). \tag{9.39}$$

Algorithm 9 Bayesian Parameter Learning

Draw $\boldsymbol{\theta}^{(n)} \sim \pi(\boldsymbol{\theta})$, for $n = 1, \ldots, N$ and initialize the particle weights $\tilde{W}_1^{(n)} = 1$.
Conditional on y_1, run Algorithm 8 to obtain $\mathcal{S}_1^{(n)}$, $n = 1, \ldots, N$.
for $t = 2$ to T **do**
  At the beginning, $\left\{\boldsymbol{\theta}^{(n)}, \mathcal{S}_{t-1}^{(n)}, \tilde{W}_{t-1}^{(n)}, W_{t-1}^{(n)}\right\}$ are known for $n = 1, \ldots N$.
  Run Algorithm 8 to obtain $\mathcal{S}_t^{(n)}$.
  Calculate

$$\tilde{W}_t^{(n)} = \tilde{W}_{t-1}^{(n)} \widehat{p}\left(y_t | y_{1:t-1}, \boldsymbol{\theta}^{(n)}\right), W_t^{(n)} = \frac{\tilde{W}_t^{(n)}}{\sum_{n=1}^N \tilde{W}_t^{(n)}},$$

$$\widehat{p}\left(y_{1:t} | \boldsymbol{\theta}^{(n)}\right) = \widehat{p}\left(y_{1:t-1} | \boldsymbol{\theta}^{(n)}\right) \widehat{p}\left(y_t | y_{1:t-1}, \boldsymbol{\theta}^{(n)}\right).$$

  Calculate the effective sample size

$$ESS_{\theta,t} = \frac{1}{\sum_{n=1}^N W_t^{(n)2}}.$$

  if $ESS_{\theta,t} < B_1$ **then**
    Resample the particles proportional to $W_t^{(n)}$, denoted as $\tilde{\boldsymbol{\theta}}^{(n)}$.
    Update the weights $\tilde{W}_t^{(n)} = 1$, for $n = 1, \ldots, N$.
    Move the particles via the Metropolis–Hasting step:
    for $n = 1$ to N **do**
      Draw $\boldsymbol{\theta}^{(n)*} \sim q_t\left(\boldsymbol{\theta} \mid \tilde{\boldsymbol{\theta}}^{(n)}\right)$.
      Calculate

$$\alpha = \min\left\{1, \frac{p\left(\boldsymbol{\theta}^{(n)*}\right) \hat{p}\left(y_{1:t} \mid \boldsymbol{\theta}^{(n)*}\right) q_t\left(\tilde{\boldsymbol{\theta}}^{(n)} \mid \boldsymbol{\theta}^{(n)*}\right)}{p\left(\tilde{\boldsymbol{\theta}}^{(n)}\right) \hat{p}\left(y_{1:t} \mid \tilde{\boldsymbol{\theta}}^{(n)}\right) q_t\left(\boldsymbol{\theta}^{(n)*} \mid \tilde{\boldsymbol{\theta}}^{(n)}\right)}\right\}.$$

      Generate $u \sim U(0,1)$,

$$\boldsymbol{\theta}^{(n)} = \begin{cases} \boldsymbol{\theta}^{(n)*}, & \text{if } u \le \alpha, \\ \tilde{\boldsymbol{\theta}}^{(n)}, & \text{if } u > \alpha. \end{cases}$$

Therefore, based on Eq. (9.39), given the quadratic loss function, the Bayesian estimator of parameters is

$$\bar{\boldsymbol{\theta}} = \sum_{n=1}^N W_T^{(n)} \boldsymbol{\theta}^{(n)}.$$

9.5 Conclusion

In this chapter, we reviewed and illustrated several methods for estimating the discrete-time SV model. The methods reviewed were either in the frequentist domain or in the Bayesian domain.

Due to the intractable likelihood function, classic MLE estimation is difficult, and many alternatives have been proposed in the literature. The frequentist methods include GMM, QML, ECF, EMM, and SML. The frequentist estimators are extreme estimates obtained by minimizing a distance measure function. Additionally, inference regarding frequentist estimators relies on the asymptotic normality. Among these methods, GMM, QML, ECF, and EMM avoid calculating the likelihood. They generally suffer from a loss of efficiency. The SML method instead approximates the likelihood via simulation. The asymptotic normality of the frequentist methods may not hold in finite samples, especially when the volatility process is highly persistent.

In contrast to frequentist methods, Bayesian inference is conducted based on the posterior distribution. We reviewed three Bayesian methods for estimating the log-normal SV model. The first two methods use the data augmentation technique and the third one applies SMC. Data augmentation treats the log-volatility as parameters and hence, the likelihood is analytically tractable, facilitating posterior sampling via MCMC. Specifically, we reviewed two types of data-augmentation-based MCMC methods. One updates the log-volatility step-by-step and is referred to as single-move MCMC. The other draws the log-volatility in a block and is known as multimove MCMC. Without data augmentation, we introduced the Bayesian parameter learning algorithm combining the SMC for the hidden states (log-volatility) and a marginal resample-move step for the parameters. Bayesian parameter learning is recursive and generic and hence is suitable for financial time series. However, compared with frequentist methods, the computation of Bayesian estimation is always very intensive.

Although we reviewed methods that estimate volatility using return observed at low frequency, many of the reviewed methods are applicable when we use realized volatility to estimate integrated volatility or spot volatility. This is because log realized volatility is an estimate of log integrated volatility and hence, a nonlinear state-space model is needed.

Bibliography

Aït-Sahalia, Y. and J. Jacod (2012). Analyzing the spectrum of asset returns: Jump and volatility components in high frequency data. *Journal of Economic Literature 50*(4), 1007–1050.

Andersen, T. G. and L. Benzoni (2010). Stochastic volatility. *CREATES Research Paper* (2010-10).

Andersen, T. G., H.-J. Chung, and B. E. Sørensen (1999). Efficient method of moments estimation of a stochastic volatility model: A Monte Carlo study. *Journal of Econometrics 91*(1), 61–87.

Andersen, T. G. and B. E. Sørensen (1996). GMM estimation of a stochastic volatility model: A Monte Carlo study. *Journal of Business & Economic Statistics 14*(3), 328–352.

Andrieu, C., A. Doucet, and R. Holenstein (2010). Particle Markov chain Monte Carlo methods. *Journal of the Royal Statistical Society: Series B (Statistical Methodology) 72*(3), 269–342.

Bollerslev, T. (1986). Generalized autoregressive conditional heteroskedasticity. *Journal of Econometrics 31*(3), 307–327.

Broto, C. and E. Ruiz (2004). Estimation methods for stochastic volatility models: A survey. *Journal of Economic Surveys 18*(5), 613–649.

Chib, S., F. Nardari, and N. Shephard (2002). Markov chain Monte Carlo methods for stochastic volatility models. *Journal of Econometrics 108*(2), 281–316.

Chopin, N. (2002). A sequential particle filter method for static models. *Biometrika 89*(3), 539–552.

Chopin, N., P. E. Jacob, and O. Papaspiliopoulos (2013). SMC^2: An efficient algorithm for sequential analysis of state space models. *Journal of the Royal Statistical Society Series B 75*(3), 397–426.

Chopin, N. and O. Papaspiliopoulos (2020). *An Introduction to Sequential Monte Carlo*. Springer Series in Statistics.

Duffie, D. and K. J. Singleton (1993). Simulated moments estimation of Markov models of asset prices. *Econometrica 61*(4), 929–952.

Durbin, J. (2000). The Foreman lecture: The state space approach to time series analysis and its potential for official statistics (with discussion). *Australian & New Zealand Journal of Statistics 42*(1), 1–23.

Durbin, J. and S. J. Koopman (1997). Monte Carlo maximum likelihood estimation for non-Gaussian state space models. *Biometrika 84*(3), 669–684.

Durbin, J. and S. J. Koopman (2000). Time series analysis of non-Gaussian observations based on state space models from both classical and Bayesian perspectives. *Journal of the Royal Statistical Society: Series B (Statistical Methodology) 62*(1), 3–56.

Durham, G. B. (2006). Monte Carlo methods for estimating, smoothing, and filtering one- and two-factor stochastic volatility models. *Journal of Econometrics 133*(1), 273–305.

Durham, G. B. (2007). SV mixture models with application to S&P 500 index returns. *Journal of Financial Economics 85*(3), 822–856.

Engle, R. F. (1982). Autoregressive conditional heteroscedasticity with estimates of the variance of United Kingdom inflation. *Econometrica: Journal of the Econometric Society 50*(4), 987–1007.

Feuerverger, A. (1990). An efficiency result for the empirical characteristic function in stationary time-series models. *The Canadian Journal of Statistics/La Revue Canadienne de Statistique 18*(2), 155–161.

Fulop, A. and J. Li (2013). Efficient learning via simulation: A marginalized resample-move approach. *Journal of Econometrics 176*(2), 146–161.

Fulop, A., J. Li, and J. Yu (2015). Self-exciting jumps, learning, and asset pricing implications. *The Review of Financial Studies 28*(3), 876–912.

Gallant, A. R., D. Hsieh, and G. Tauchen (1997). Estimation of stochastic volatility models with diagnostics. *Journal of Econometrics 81*(1), 159–192.

Gallant, A. R. and G. Tauchen (1996). Which moments to match? *Econometric Theory 12*, 657–681.

Ghysels, E., A. C. Harvey, and E. Renault (1996). 5 stochastic volatility. *Handbook of Statistics 14*, 119–191.

Gilks, W. R. and C. Berzuini (2001). Following a moving target: Monte Carlo inference for dynamic Bayesian models. *Journal of the Royal Statistical Society: Series B (Statistical Methodology) 63*(1), 127–146.

Gordon, N. (1993). *Bayesian methods for tracking*. Doctoral dissertation, Imperial College London (University of London).

Gordon, N. J., D. J. Salmond, and A. F. Smith (1993). Novel approach to nonlinear/non-Gaussian Bayesian state estimation. *IEE Proceedings F-Radar and Signal Processing 140*(2), 107–113.

Hans, S. and J. Yu (2014). A flexible and automatic likelihood based framework for inference in stochastic volatility models. *Computational Statistics and Data Analysis 76*, 642–654.

Hansen, L. P. and K. J. Singleton (1982). Generalized instrumental variables estimation of nonlinear rational expectations models. *Econometrica: Journal of the Econometric Society 50*(5), 1269–1286.

Harvey, A., E. Ruiz, and N. Shephard (1994). Multivariate stochastic variance models. *The Review of Economic Studies 61*(2), 247–264.

Jacquier, E., N. G. Polson, and P. E. Rossi (2002). Bayesian analysis of stochastic volatility models. *Journal of Business & Economic Statistics 20*(1), 69–87.

Kim, S., N. Shephard, and S. Chib (1998). Stochastic volatility: Likelihood inference and comparison with arch models. *The Review of Economic Studies 65*(3), 361–393.

Kitagawa, G. (1996). Monte Carlo filter and smoother for non-Gaussian nonlinear state space models. *Journal of Computational and Graphical Statistics 5*(1), 1–25.

Knight, J. L. and S. E. Satchell (1997). The cumulant generating function estimation method: Implementation and asymptotic efficiency. *Econometric Theory 13*, 170–184.

Knight, J. L., S. E. Satchell, and J. Yu (2002). Estimation of the stochastic volatility model by the empirical characteristic function method. *Australian & New Zealand Journal of Statistics 44*(3), 319–335.

Knight, J. L. and J. Yu (2002). Empirical characteristic function in time series estimation. *Econometric Theory 18*, 691–721.

Koopman, S. J., N. Shephard, and D. Creal (2009). Testing the assumptions behind importance sampling. *Journal of Econometrics 149*(1), 2–11.

Liesenfeld, R. and J.-F. Richard (2003). Univariate and multivariate stochastic volatility models: estimation and diagnostics. *Journal of Empirical Finance 10*(4), 505–531.

Melino, A. and S. M. Turnbull (1990). Pricing foreign currency options with stochastic volatility. *Journal of Econometrics 45*(1–2), 239–265.

Omori, Y., S. Chib, N. Shephard, and J. Nakajima (2007). Stochastic volatility with leverage: Fast and efficient likelihood inference. *Journal of Econometrics 140*(2), 425–449.

Pitt, M. K. and N. Shephard (1999). Filtering via simulation: Auxiliary particle filters. *Journal of the American Statistical Association 94*(446), 590–599.

Richard, J.-F. and W. Zhang (2007). Efficient high-dimensional importance sampling. *Journal of Econometrics 141*(2), 1385–1411.

Robert, C. (2007). *The Bayesian choice: From decision-theoretic foundations to computational implementation*, Volume 2. Springer Science & Business Media.

Ruiz, E. (1994). Quasi-maximum likelihood estimation of stochastic volatility models. *Journal of Econometrics 63*(1), 289–306.

Shephard, N. and M. K. Pitt (1997). Likelihood analysis of non-Gaussian measurement time series. *Biometrika 84*(3), 653–667.

Skaug, H. and J. Yu (2009). Automated likelihood based inference for stochastic volatility models. Working Paper.

Smith, A. (2013). *Sequential Monte Carlo methods in practice*. Springer Science & Business Media.

Taylor, S. J. (1986). *Modelling financial time series*. New York: John Wiley & Sons.

Wang, X. and J. Yu (2022). Latent local-to-unity models. Working Paper, Singapore Management University.

Yu, J. (2002). Forecasting volatility in the New Zealand stock market. *Applied Financial Economics 12*(3), 193–202.

Yu, J. (2012a). A semiparametric stochastic volatility model. *Journal of Econometrics 167*(2), 473–482.

Yu, J. (2012b). Simulation-based estimation methods for financial time series models. In *Handbook of Computational Finance*, pp. 401–435. Research Collection School of Economics.

10 Hypothesis Testing Statistics Based on Posterior Output with Applications in Financial Econometrics

YONG LI *Renmin University of China*

10.1 Introduction

In economics and finance, a fundamental aspect of statistical inference revolves around hypothesis testing. Typically, economic theories are translated into hypotheses that can be empirically tested. Therefore, the evaluation of a point null hypothesis is crucial for determining whether statistical data corroborates or contradicts a specific economic theory. This chapter focuses on addressing the key question of how to conduct a point null hypothesis test using available posterior output.

In Bayesian hypothesis testing, the literature identifies three primary posterior-based methods. The first is the Bayes factor (BF), a widely recognized approach that evaluates the marginal likelihoods of competing models for null and alternative hypotheses (Kass and Raftery, 1995). However, BFs encounter several theoretical and practical challenges. Firstly, they are undefined with improper priors. Secondly, BFs are prone to the Jeffreys–Lindley–Bartlett paradox, often favoring the null hypothesis under extremely noninformative priors for parameters within the null hypothesis (refer to Kass and Raftery (1995), Poirier (1995), and Chapter 4 in Wakefield (2013)). Thirdly, calculating marginal likelihoods can be complex. To mitigate these issues, various solutions have been proposed. For the first two issues, one approach is to employ data-dependent priors in BF calculations. This involves dividing the data into a training set for prior updating (which could be improper) and another set for analysis, thus forming a proper prior for the latter (see O'Hagan (1995) for fractional BF and Berger (1985) for intrinsic BF). To overcome computational challenges associated with BFs, methods from Friel and Pettitt (2008), Li et al. (2023), and Chib (1995) are recommended.

The second method, gaining traction among econometricians and statisticians, involves the use of credible intervals or sets, as highlighted in works by Chernozhukov and Hong (2003), Moon and Schorfheide (2012), Kline and Tamer (2016), Liao and Simoni (2019), and Chen et al. (2018).

The third approach is rooted in statistical decision theory, originating from the ideas of Bernardo and Rueda (2002, BR). They illustrated that the Bayes factor can be interpreted as a decision-making problem with a binary loss function in point hypothesis testing. This binary loss function is the source of the Jeffreys–Lindley–Bartlett paradox. BR also proposed replacing this with the continuous Kullback–Leibler (KL) divergence function as the loss function. Further developments in this area, involving alternative loss functions, have been made by Li and Yu (2012), Li et al. (2014), Li et al. (2015), Liu et al. (2024), and Li et al. (2022).

By focusing on the third line of approaches, the goal of this chapter is to review the literature on hypothesis testing based on posterior output. Posterior output can be achieved via some advanced posterior simulation techniques such as Markov chain Monte Carlo (MCMC) or sequential Monte Carlo (SMC). The posterior test statistics developed for hypothesis testing when posterior output is available can be justified in a frequentist setup in the same way as testing methods based on the maximum likelihood (ML) estimator are justified.

With posterior output, it is not immediately obvious how to make statistical inference in the frequentist framework. For the point-null hypothesis testing problem, this chapter describes how the posterior test statistics for hypothesis testing are developed under the decision framework. In this chapter, three posterior test statistics for hypothesis testing that were developed in recent years are reviewed. They can be viewed as the Bayesian version of the "trinity" of test statistics based on ML, namely, the likelihood ratio (LR) test, the Lagrange multiplier (LM) test, and the Wald test. Under repeated sampling, the asymptotic distributions of these posterior test statistics are discussed. Simulated data are also used to examine the finite sample properties of the test statistics and real data to show of their usefulness.

This chapter is organized as follows. Section 10.2 reviews the Bayesian inference based on posterior output. Inferential approaches that are typically used in the Bayesian literature are also briefly explained. Section 10.3 reviews several statistics for hypothesis testing based on decision theory, and Section 10.4 reviews the posterior statistics. Section 10.5 describes various simulation studies, and Section 10.6 provides the empirical illustrations. Finally, Section 10.7 concludes the chapter.

10.2 Bayesian Inference Based on Posterior Distributions

Without loss of generality, let $\mathbf{y} = (y_1, \ldots, y_n)'$ denote the data generated from a probability measure P_0 on the probability space (Ω, F, P_0), and $p(\mathbf{y}|\boldsymbol{\vartheta})$ is denoted as the likelihood function. To perform Bayesian inference about $\boldsymbol{\vartheta}$, let

$p(\boldsymbol{\vartheta})$ be the prior distribution of $\boldsymbol{\vartheta}$. Then, the posterior distribution is obtained via the Bayesian theorem:

$$p(\boldsymbol{\vartheta}|\mathbf{y}) = \frac{p(\mathbf{y}|\boldsymbol{\vartheta})p(\boldsymbol{\vartheta})}{p(\mathbf{y})} \propto p(\mathbf{y}|\boldsymbol{\vartheta})p(\boldsymbol{\vartheta}), \tag{10.1}$$

where $p(\mathbf{y}) = \int p(\mathbf{y}|\boldsymbol{\vartheta})p(\boldsymbol{\vartheta})d\boldsymbol{\vartheta}$ is the marginal likelihood.

Frequentist inference is based on the likelihood function $p(\mathbf{y}|\boldsymbol{\vartheta})$, and the Bayesian statistical inference is based on the posterior distribution $p(\boldsymbol{\vartheta}|\mathbf{y})$. The posterior distribution $p(\boldsymbol{\vartheta}|\mathbf{y})$, when it is not analytically tractable, can be obtained via some advanced posterior simulation techniques such as MCMC or SMC. Gamerman and Lopes (2006) and Chopin and Papaspiliopoulos (2020) provide details about these simulation techniques.

Samples obtained from the posterior simulation can be used for statistical inference. Bayesian estimates of $\boldsymbol{\vartheta}$ can be obtained easily via sampling means of random samples. Specifically, let $\{\boldsymbol{\vartheta}^{(j)}, j = 1, 2, \cdots, J\}$ be the effective random samples generated from the joint posterior distribution $p(\boldsymbol{\vartheta}|\mathbf{y})$. Then, the Bayesian estimates of $\boldsymbol{\vartheta}$ can be obtained as follows:

$$\bar{\boldsymbol{\vartheta}} = E[\boldsymbol{\vartheta}|\mathbf{y}] = \int \boldsymbol{\vartheta} p(\boldsymbol{\vartheta}|\mathbf{y})d\boldsymbol{\vartheta} \approx \frac{1}{J}\sum_{j=1}^{J} \boldsymbol{\vartheta}^{(j)}. \tag{10.2}$$

Clearly, these Bayesian estimates are consistent estimates of the corresponding posterior means (Geyer, 1992). A consistent estimate of $Var(\boldsymbol{\vartheta}|y)$ can be described as follows:

$$\widehat{Var(\boldsymbol{\vartheta}|\mathbf{y})} = \frac{1}{J}\sum_{j=1}^{J}(\boldsymbol{\vartheta}^{(j)} - \bar{\boldsymbol{\vartheta}}_J)(\boldsymbol{\vartheta}^{(j)} - \bar{\boldsymbol{\vartheta}}_J)',$$

where $\bar{\boldsymbol{\vartheta}}_J = \frac{1}{J}\sum_{j=1}^{J} \boldsymbol{\vartheta}^{(j)}$.

Under some regularity conditions, when $p(\boldsymbol{\vartheta}) = O_p(1)$, Li et al. (2024) showed that the relationship between the posterior mean $\bar{\boldsymbol{\vartheta}}$ and the posterior mode $\hat{\boldsymbol{\vartheta}}$ can be expressed as follows:

$$\bar{\boldsymbol{\vartheta}} = \hat{\boldsymbol{\vartheta}} + O_p(n^{-1}), \tag{10.3}$$

$$Var(\boldsymbol{\vartheta}|\mathbf{y}) = \left[-\frac{\partial^2 \ln p(\mathbf{y}|\hat{\boldsymbol{\vartheta}})}{\partial\boldsymbol{\vartheta}\partial\boldsymbol{\vartheta}'}\right]^{-1} + O_p(n^{-2}). \tag{10.4}$$

The large sample properties in (10.3) and (10.4) provide the fountainhead from which all the methods reviewed in this chapter spring.

10.3 Hypothesis Testing Based on Posterior Output

10.3.1 Hypothesis Testing under Decision Theory

It is assumed that probability model $M \equiv \{p(\mathbf{y}|\boldsymbol{\vartheta})\}$ is used to fit data $\mathbf{y}$ where $\boldsymbol{\vartheta} = (\boldsymbol{\theta}', \boldsymbol{\psi}')' \in \Theta$. We are concerned with testing a point null hypothesis that may arise from the prediction of a particular theory. Let $\boldsymbol{\theta} \in \Theta_\theta$ denote a vector of q_θ-dimensional parameters of interest and $\boldsymbol{\psi} \in \Theta_\psi$ a vector of q_ψ-dimensional nuisance parameters so that $\Theta = \Theta_\theta \times \Theta_\psi$. The testing problem is given by the following:

$$\begin{cases} H_0: & \boldsymbol{\theta} = \boldsymbol{\theta}_0, \\ H_1: & \boldsymbol{\theta} \neq \boldsymbol{\theta}_0. \end{cases} \tag{10.5}$$

Within the statistical decision-making framework, hypothesis testing can be conceptualized as a choice between two distinct statistical actions: accepting the null hypothesis H_0 (referred to as d_0) or rejecting it (d_1). Let $\{\mathcal{L}(d_i, \boldsymbol{\theta}, \boldsymbol{\psi}), i = 0, 1\}$ be the loss function of the statistical decision associated with d_i. For the decision problem, the loss functions $\{\mathcal{L}(d_i, \boldsymbol{\theta}, \boldsymbol{\psi}), i = 0, 1\}$ can be used to measure the loss of accepting H_0 or rejecting H_0 as a function of the real value of the parameters $(\boldsymbol{\theta}, \boldsymbol{\psi})$.

Given the loss function and data $\mathbf{y}$, the optimal action is to reject the null hypothesis H_0 if, and only if, the expected loss from accepting H_0, as calculated using posterior expectations, exceeds the expected loss from rejecting H_0:

$$\int_{\Theta_\theta}\int_{\Theta_\psi} \mathcal{L}(d_0, \boldsymbol{\theta}, \boldsymbol{\psi}) p(\boldsymbol{\theta}, \boldsymbol{\psi}|\mathbf{y}) \mathrm{d}\boldsymbol{\theta} \mathrm{d}\boldsymbol{\psi} - \int_{\Theta_\theta}\int_{\Theta_\psi} \mathcal{L}(d_1, \boldsymbol{\theta}, \boldsymbol{\psi}) p(\boldsymbol{\theta}, \boldsymbol{\psi}|\mathbf{y}) \mathrm{d}\boldsymbol{\theta} \mathrm{d}\boldsymbol{\psi}$$
$$= \int_{\Theta_\theta}\int_{\Theta_\psi} \{\mathcal{L}(d_0, \boldsymbol{\theta}, \boldsymbol{\psi}) - \mathcal{L}(d_1, \boldsymbol{\theta}, \boldsymbol{\psi})\} p(\boldsymbol{\theta}, \boldsymbol{\psi}|\mathbf{y}) \mathrm{d}\boldsymbol{\theta} \mathrm{d}\boldsymbol{\psi} > 0.$$

Therefore, in practice, only the following net loss difference function is required to be specified:

$$\triangle\mathcal{L}(H_0, \boldsymbol{\theta}, \boldsymbol{\psi}) = \mathcal{L}(d_0, \boldsymbol{\theta}, \boldsymbol{\psi}) - \mathcal{L}(d_1, \boldsymbol{\theta}, \boldsymbol{\psi}). \tag{10.6}$$

This equation measures the evidence against H_0 as a function of $(\boldsymbol{\theta}, \boldsymbol{\psi})$.

For this prespecified net loss difference function $\triangle\mathcal{L}(H_0, \boldsymbol{\theta}, \boldsymbol{\psi})$, we can define a posterior-based statistic as follows:

$$\mathbf{T}_0(\mathbf{y}, \boldsymbol{\theta}_0) = \int_{\Theta_\theta}\int_{\Theta_\psi} \triangle\mathcal{L}(H_0, \boldsymbol{\theta}, \boldsymbol{\psi}) p(\boldsymbol{\theta}, \boldsymbol{\psi}|\mathbf{y}) \mathrm{d}\boldsymbol{\theta} \mathrm{d}\boldsymbol{\psi} = E_{\boldsymbol{\vartheta}|\mathbf{y}} \left(\triangle\mathcal{L}(H_0, \boldsymbol{\theta}, \boldsymbol{\psi})\right). \tag{10.7}$$

Following Berger (1985), any Bayesian admissible solution to the decision problem must satisfy the following condition:

$$\text{Reject } H_0 \text{ if and only if } \mathbf{T}_0(\mathbf{y}, \boldsymbol{\theta}_0) > 0. \tag{10.8}$$

BR shows that the net loss function can generally take the following form:

$$\Delta\mathcal{L}(H_0,\boldsymbol{\theta},\boldsymbol{\psi}) = m(\boldsymbol{\theta}_0,\boldsymbol{\theta},\boldsymbol{\psi}) - c,$$

where $m(\boldsymbol{\theta}_0,\boldsymbol{\theta},\boldsymbol{\psi})$ is a nonnegative discrepancy measure between model $p(\mathbf{y}|\boldsymbol{\theta} = \boldsymbol{\theta}_0,\boldsymbol{\psi})$ and model $p(\mathbf{y}|\boldsymbol{\theta},\boldsymbol{\psi})$, $c > 0$ is a context-dependent utility value that measures the advantage of being able to work with the simpler model when it is true. For this type of net loss function, a possible loss function for the decision can be given as follows:

$$\mathcal{L}(d_0,\boldsymbol{\theta},\boldsymbol{\psi}) = \begin{cases} c_0 & \text{if } \boldsymbol{\theta} = \boldsymbol{\theta}_0 \\ c_0 + \frac{1}{2}m(\boldsymbol{\theta}_0,\boldsymbol{\theta},\boldsymbol{\psi}) & \text{if } \boldsymbol{\theta} \neq \boldsymbol{\theta}_0 \end{cases} \tag{10.9}$$

$$\mathcal{L}(d_1,\boldsymbol{\theta},\boldsymbol{\psi}) = \begin{cases} c_1 & \text{if } \boldsymbol{\theta} = \boldsymbol{\theta}_0 \\ c_1 - \frac{1}{2}m(\boldsymbol{\theta}_0,\boldsymbol{\theta},\boldsymbol{\psi}) & \text{if } \boldsymbol{\theta} \neq \boldsymbol{\theta}_0 \end{cases} \tag{10.10}$$

where c_i measures the cost of action d_i and $c = c_1 - c_0 > 0$. Then, let $\mathbf{T}(\mathbf{y},\boldsymbol{\theta}_0)$ be defined as follows:

$$\mathbf{T}(\mathbf{y},\boldsymbol{\theta}_0) = E_{\boldsymbol{\vartheta}|\mathbf{y}}(m(\boldsymbol{\theta}_0,\boldsymbol{\theta},\boldsymbol{\psi})) = E_{\boldsymbol{\vartheta}|\mathbf{y}}(\Delta\mathcal{L}(H_0,\boldsymbol{\theta},\boldsymbol{\psi})) - c. \tag{10.11}$$

Then, $\mathbf{T}_0(\mathbf{y},\boldsymbol{\theta}_0) > 0$ is equivalent to $\mathbf{T}(\mathbf{y},\boldsymbol{\theta}_0) > c$. In this case, H_0 is rejected.

10.3.2 The Choice of Loss Function for Hypothesis Testing

This subsection delves into the various loss functions utilized in formulating hypothesis test statistics. It is demonstrated that BFs align with a binary loss function, assigning values of 0 and 1. To address the limitations inherent in BFs, the literature has introduced alternative continuous loss functions, enabling the creation of novel test statistics derived from MCMC output. These new test statistics differ fundamentally from BFs. They are validated within a frequentist framework by assuming that the data $\mathbf{y}$ is produced from a data generating process in repeated experiments. In contrast, BFs are grounded in a Bayesian framework, where decisions are made conditional on $\mathbf{y}$.

BFs and Zero-One Loss Function

If one uses the following zero-one loss functions:

$$\mathcal{L}(d_0,\boldsymbol{\theta},\boldsymbol{\psi}) = \begin{cases} 0 & if\, \boldsymbol{\theta} = \boldsymbol{\theta}_0 \\ 1 & if\, \boldsymbol{\theta} \neq \boldsymbol{\theta}_0 \end{cases}, \quad \mathcal{L}(d_1,\boldsymbol{\theta},\boldsymbol{\psi}) = \begin{cases} 1 & if\, \boldsymbol{\theta} = \boldsymbol{\theta}_0 \\ 0 & if\, \boldsymbol{\theta} \neq \boldsymbol{\theta}_0 \end{cases},$$

then, the net loss function $\Delta\mathcal{L}(H_0,\boldsymbol{\vartheta},\boldsymbol{\psi})$ is:

$$\Delta\mathcal{L}(H_0,\boldsymbol{\theta},\boldsymbol{\psi}) = \begin{cases} -1 & if\, \boldsymbol{\theta} = \boldsymbol{\theta}_0 \\ 1 & if\, \boldsymbol{\theta} \neq \boldsymbol{\theta}_0 \end{cases}.$$

Thus, the expected posterior loss is given by:

$$\int \triangle\mathcal{L}(H_0, \boldsymbol{\theta}, \boldsymbol{\psi})\, p(\boldsymbol{\theta}, \boldsymbol{\psi}|\mathbf{y})\mathrm{d}\boldsymbol{\theta}\mathrm{d}\boldsymbol{\psi} = \int \triangle\mathcal{L}(H_0, \boldsymbol{\theta}, \boldsymbol{\psi})\, p(\boldsymbol{\theta}|\mathbf{y})\mathrm{d}\boldsymbol{\theta}.$$

For point hypothesis testing, a reasonable prior for $\boldsymbol{\theta}$ requires a positive probability w being assigned to H_0. Let the prior $\boldsymbol{\theta}$ be a mixed random variable whose density is:

$$p(\boldsymbol{\theta}) = w\delta(\boldsymbol{\theta} - \boldsymbol{\theta}_0) + (1-w)\,\pi(\boldsymbol{\theta}),$$

where $\delta(\cdot)$ denotes the Dirac delta function and $\pi(\boldsymbol{\theta})$ is a proper density function. For more details about the mixed random variable and Dirac delta function, see Pishro-Nik (2016).

Thus, the joint posterior density of $\boldsymbol{\theta}$ and $\boldsymbol{\psi}$ is:

$$\begin{aligned} p(\boldsymbol{\theta}, \boldsymbol{\psi}|\mathbf{y}) &= \frac{p(\mathbf{y}|\boldsymbol{\theta}, \boldsymbol{\psi})p(\boldsymbol{\theta}, \boldsymbol{\psi})}{p(\mathbf{y})} \\ &= \frac{p(\mathbf{y}|\boldsymbol{\theta} = \boldsymbol{\theta}_0, \boldsymbol{\psi})p(\boldsymbol{\psi}|\boldsymbol{\theta} = \boldsymbol{\theta}_0)w\delta(\boldsymbol{\theta} - \boldsymbol{\theta}_0)}{p(\mathbf{y})} + \frac{p(\mathbf{y}|\boldsymbol{\theta}, \boldsymbol{\psi})p(\boldsymbol{\psi}|\boldsymbol{\theta})(1-w)\,\pi(\boldsymbol{\theta})}{p(\mathbf{y})}, \end{aligned}$$

where $p(y) = \int\int p(y|\boldsymbol{\theta}, \boldsymbol{\psi})p(\boldsymbol{\theta}, \boldsymbol{\psi})\mathrm{d}\boldsymbol{\theta}\mathrm{d}\boldsymbol{\psi}$ is the marginal likelihood that can be expressed as:

$$\begin{aligned} p(\mathbf{y}) = w &\int p(\mathbf{y}|\boldsymbol{\theta} = \boldsymbol{\theta}_0, \boldsymbol{\psi})p(\boldsymbol{\psi}|\boldsymbol{\theta} = \boldsymbol{\theta}_0)d\boldsymbol{\psi} \\ &+ (1-w)\int \pi(\boldsymbol{\theta}) \int p(\mathbf{y}|\boldsymbol{\theta}, \boldsymbol{\psi})p(\boldsymbol{\psi}|\boldsymbol{\theta})d\boldsymbol{\psi}\, d\boldsymbol{\theta}. \end{aligned} \tag{10.12}$$

Then, the posterior density of $\boldsymbol{\theta}$ is:

$$\begin{aligned} p(\boldsymbol{\theta}|\mathbf{y}) &= \int p(\boldsymbol{\theta}, \boldsymbol{\psi}|\mathbf{y})d\boldsymbol{\psi} \\ &:= w^*\delta(\boldsymbol{\theta} - \boldsymbol{\theta}_0) + \left(1 - w^*\right)\frac{\int p(\mathbf{y}|\boldsymbol{\theta}, \boldsymbol{\psi})p(\boldsymbol{\psi}|\boldsymbol{\theta})d\boldsymbol{\psi}\,\pi(\boldsymbol{\theta})}{\int \pi(\boldsymbol{\theta})\int p(\mathbf{y}|\boldsymbol{\theta}, \boldsymbol{\psi})p(\boldsymbol{\psi}|\boldsymbol{\theta})d\boldsymbol{\psi}\, d\boldsymbol{\theta}} \end{aligned} \tag{10.13}$$

where:

$$w^* = \frac{w\int p(\mathbf{y}|\boldsymbol{\theta} = \boldsymbol{\theta}_0, \boldsymbol{\psi})p(\boldsymbol{\psi}|\boldsymbol{\theta} = \boldsymbol{\theta}_0)d\boldsymbol{\psi}}{p(\mathbf{y})}, \tag{10.14}$$

which is the probability of the event $\{\boldsymbol{\theta} \in \Theta_\theta : \boldsymbol{\theta} = \boldsymbol{\theta}_0\}$. Equation (10.13) is the density of a mixed random variable. Under this posterior, $\triangle\mathcal{L}(H_0, \boldsymbol{\theta}, \boldsymbol{\psi})$ accounts for only two possible values, ± 1, and:

$$P_{\boldsymbol{\theta}|\mathbf{y}}(\triangle\mathcal{L}(H_0, \boldsymbol{\theta}, \boldsymbol{\psi}) = -1) = w^*, P_{\boldsymbol{\theta}|\mathbf{y}}(\triangle\mathcal{L}(H_0, \boldsymbol{\theta}, \boldsymbol{\psi}) = 1) = 1 - w^*.$$

Thus, the expected posterior net loss is:

$$\begin{aligned}E_{\boldsymbol{\theta}|\mathbf{y}}\left(\Delta\mathcal{L}\left(H_0,\boldsymbol{\theta},\boldsymbol{\psi}\right)\right) &= -w^* + 1 - w^*\\ &= -\frac{w\int p(\mathbf{y}|\boldsymbol{\theta}=\boldsymbol{\theta}_0,\boldsymbol{\psi})p(\boldsymbol{\psi}|\boldsymbol{\theta}=\boldsymbol{\theta}_0)d\boldsymbol{\psi}}{p(\mathbf{y})}\\ &\quad+\frac{(1-w)\int\pi(\boldsymbol{\theta})\int p(\mathbf{y}|\boldsymbol{\theta},\boldsymbol{\psi})p(\boldsymbol{\psi}|\boldsymbol{\theta})d\boldsymbol{\psi}\,d\boldsymbol{\theta}}{p(\mathbf{y})},\end{aligned}$$

where the second equality is due to (10.14).

The decision rule is as follows:

$$\begin{aligned}\text{reject } H_0 \text{ iff } w\int p(\mathbf{y}|\boldsymbol{\theta}=\boldsymbol{\theta}_0,\boldsymbol{\psi})p(\boldsymbol{\psi}|\boldsymbol{\theta}=\boldsymbol{\theta}_0)d\boldsymbol{\psi}&\\ < (1-w)\int\pi(\boldsymbol{\theta})\int p(\mathbf{y}|\boldsymbol{\theta},\boldsymbol{\psi})p(\boldsymbol{\psi}|\boldsymbol{\theta})d\boldsymbol{\psi}\,d\boldsymbol{\theta}.&\end{aligned}$$

To represent the prior ignorance, w is often set to $1/2$. In this case, the decision rule is:

$$\text{reject } H_0 \text{ if and only if } B_{01} = \frac{\int p(\mathbf{y}|\boldsymbol{\theta}=\boldsymbol{\theta}_0,\boldsymbol{\psi})p(\boldsymbol{\psi}|\boldsymbol{\theta}=\boldsymbol{\theta}_0)\mathrm{d}\boldsymbol{\psi}}{\int\int p(\mathbf{y}|\boldsymbol{\theta},\boldsymbol{\psi})p(\boldsymbol{\psi}|\boldsymbol{\theta})\pi(\boldsymbol{\theta})\mathrm{d}\boldsymbol{\theta}\mathrm{d}\boldsymbol{\psi}} = \frac{m_0}{m_1} < 1, \tag{10.15}$$

where $\{m_k, k = 0, 1\}$ are the marginal likelihoods for H_0 and H_1, respectively.

As the ratio of the marginal likelihoods, B_{01} is the well-known BF (Kass and Raftery, 1995). An important condition for BF to be valid in hypothesis testing is $w = P(\boldsymbol{\theta} = \boldsymbol{\theta}_0) > 0$, which means that H_0 must have a positive probability mass although $\boldsymbol{\theta}$ is a point in the parameter space. If this condition is not satisfied such that $p(\boldsymbol{\theta})$ is continuous, then:

$$\begin{aligned}&\int\Delta\mathcal{L}\left(H_0,\boldsymbol{\theta},\boldsymbol{\psi}\right)\frac{p(\mathbf{y}|\boldsymbol{\theta},\boldsymbol{\psi})p(\boldsymbol{\theta},\boldsymbol{\psi})}{p(\mathbf{y})}d\boldsymbol{\psi}\,d\boldsymbol{\theta}\\ &\quad=\int\Delta\mathcal{L}\left(H_0,\boldsymbol{\theta},\boldsymbol{\psi}\right)\frac{p(\mathbf{y}|\boldsymbol{\theta},\boldsymbol{\psi})p(\boldsymbol{\psi}|\boldsymbol{\theta})p(\boldsymbol{\theta})}{p(\mathbf{y})}d\boldsymbol{\psi}\,\mathrm{d}\boldsymbol{\theta}\\ &\quad=\int\frac{p(\mathbf{y}|\boldsymbol{\theta},\boldsymbol{\psi})p(\boldsymbol{\psi}|\boldsymbol{\theta})p(\boldsymbol{\theta})}{p(\mathbf{y})}d\boldsymbol{\psi}\,\mathrm{d}\boldsymbol{\theta}.\end{aligned}$$

This equation is always positive so that H_0 is always rejected.

Within Bayesian analysis, BF is considered the benchmark for comparing models once their posterior distributions have been established. Bayes factor is favored for its intuitive appeal and robust probabilistic foundation, yet it encounters certain theoretical and computational challenges. First, when a subjective prior $\pi(\boldsymbol{\theta})$ is not available, Jeffreys' prior or reference prior (Jeffreys, 1961; Bernardo and Smith, 2009) are often used to reflect the lack of prior information. These priors are typically improper. Thus, $\pi(\boldsymbol{\theta}) = Cf(\boldsymbol{\theta})$, where

$f(\boldsymbol{\theta})$ is a function that does not integrate to a finite value, and C is an arbitrary positive constant. In this case, the BF can be expressed as:

$$B_{01} = \frac{1}{C} \frac{\int_{\Psi} p(\mathbf{y}|\boldsymbol{\psi}, \boldsymbol{\theta}_0) p(\boldsymbol{\psi}|\boldsymbol{\theta}_0) \mathrm{d}\boldsymbol{\psi}}{\int_{\Theta} \int_{\Psi} p(\mathbf{y}|\boldsymbol{\theta}, \boldsymbol{\psi}) p(\boldsymbol{\psi}|\boldsymbol{\theta}) f(\boldsymbol{\theta}) \mathrm{d}\boldsymbol{\theta} \mathrm{d}\boldsymbol{\psi}}.$$

Clearly, the BF is ill-defined because it depends on the arbitrary constant, C.

Second, to remedy the issue of BF being ill-defined under an improper prior, the adoption of a proper prior $\pi(\boldsymbol{\theta})$ with substantial variance, representing a vague prior, has been suggested to encapsulate prior uncertainty. Although this approach renders the BF well-defined, it inadvertently biases the outcome toward the null hypothesis, even in instances where the null is incorrect. This bias gives rise to the well-known Jeffreys–Lindley–Bartlett's paradox, a phenomenon extensively discussed in literature such as Jeffreys (1961), Lindley (1957), Bartlett (1957), Poirier (1995), and Robert (1993, 2007).

To explain this statistical paradox, we use the example in Liu et al. (2022). Let $\mathbf{y}$ be an independent and identically distributed random sample from a normal distribution $N(\theta, \sigma^2)$ with a known variance σ^2. Suppose the null hypothesis is $H_0 : \theta = 0$ and the alternative is $H_1 : \theta \neq 0$. Suppose the prior distribution of θ is $N(\mu_0, \tau^2)$. The posterior odds are expressed as the ratio of the posterior probabilities of the alternative and null hypotheses:

$$PO_{10} = \frac{p(H_1|\bar{y})}{p(H_0|\bar{y})} = \frac{p(\bar{y}|H_1)}{p(\bar{y}|H_0)} \times \frac{p(H_1)}{p(H_0)} = BF_{10} \times \frac{p(H_1)}{p(H_0)}, \tag{10.16}$$

where $\bar{y} = \frac{1}{n}\sum_{i=1}^{n} y_i$, $p(H_0)$ and $p(H_1)$ are the prior probabilities of H_0 and H_1 respectively; and BF_{10} is the ratio of marginal densities of $\bar{y}$ under the null and alternative hypotheses. The posterior distribution under the alternative hypothesis is defined as follows:

$$\theta|\bar{y} \sim N\left(\mu^*, \sigma^{*2}\right),$$

where:

$$\mu^* = \sigma^{*2}\left(\frac{\mu_0}{\tau^2} + \frac{n\bar{y}}{\sigma^2}\right) = \frac{\mu_0\sigma^2 + n\tau^2\bar{y}}{\sigma^2 + n\tau^2}, \quad \sigma^{*2} = \frac{1}{\frac{\mu_0}{\tau^2} + \frac{n}{\sigma^2}} = \frac{\sigma^2\tau^2}{\sigma^2 + n\tau^2}.$$

The marginal densities under the different hypotheses are:

$$\bar{y}|H_0 \sim N\left(0, \sigma^2/n\right), \tag{10.17}$$

$$\bar{y}|H_1 \sim N\left(\mu_0, \sigma^2/n + \tau^2\right). \tag{10.18}$$

Then, the logarithm of BF can be written as:

$$2\log BF_{10} = (z(\bar{y}))^2 - \frac{1}{\sigma^2/n + \tau^2}\left(\frac{\sigma}{\sqrt{n}} z(\bar{y}) - \mu_0\right)^2 + \log\frac{\sigma^2}{\sigma^2 + n\tau^2}, \tag{10.19}$$

where $z(\bar{y}) = \sqrt{n}(\bar{y} - 0)/\sigma$ is the standard z-statistic. As noted by Bartlett (1957), for any fixed dataset, and hence, the fixed $\bar{y}$ and the fixed sample size n, (10.19) suggests that $\log BF_{10} \rightarrow -\infty$ as $\tau^2 \rightarrow \infty$. Even when the absolute value of $z(\bar{y})$ is sufficiently large so that H_0 is rejected in the frequentist inference, the BF favors H_0. This type of disagreement is due to the arbitrary value of τ which reflects some indeterminacy of the prior density.

Jeffreys–Lindley–Bartlett's paradox has prompted researchers to develop alternative forms of the BF. Notable examples include the *partial Bayes factor* (O'Hagan, 1991), the *intrinsic Bayes factor* (Berger and Pericchi, 1996), and the *fractional Bayes factor* (O'Hagan, 1995). These variations typically involve dividing the data $\mathbf{y}$ into a portion for training and another for testing. The training segment is utilized to transform an uninformative prior into an informative one. However, these methods are often criticized for their somewhat arbitrary selection of training samples, the weights assigned for averaging these samples, and the determination of fractions.

Finally, in latent variable models and several others, the computation of the marginal likelihoods $M_k, k = 0, 1$ frequently requires solving complex high-dimensional integrals, making the calculation of BFs a challenging task. For a comprehensive review of methods to compute BFs from MCMC output, see Han and Carlin (2001).

Bernardo and Rueda (2002) and the K-L Loss Function

Bernardo and Rueda (2002, BR) highlighted that in cases where $\boldsymbol{\theta}$ is a continuous parameter, hypothesis testing necessitates the adoption of a "sharp" prior that is nonregular (not absolutely continuous). This type of prior concentrates a positive probability mass, ensuring that the null hypothesis H_0 is assigned a strictly positive prior probability. Such a nonregular prior structure leads to the theoretical difficulties associated with BF. To address these challenges, Bernardo and Rueda (2002) proposed the use of a continuous loss function based on the Kullback–Leibler (KL) divergence, as an alternative to the discrete loss function:

$$KL[p(x), q(x)] = \int p(x) \ln \frac{p(x)}{q(x)} dx,$$

where $p(x)$ and $q(x)$ are any two regular probability density functions.

Based on the Kullback–Leibler (KL) divergence, BR takes the form of the net loss function as follows:

$$\Delta\mathcal{L}(H_0, \boldsymbol{\theta}, \boldsymbol{\psi}) = m(\boldsymbol{\theta}_0, \boldsymbol{\theta}, \boldsymbol{\psi}) - c,$$
$$m(\boldsymbol{\theta}_0, \boldsymbol{\theta}, \boldsymbol{\psi}) = \min\left\{KL\left[p(\mathbf{y}|\boldsymbol{\theta}, \boldsymbol{\psi}), p(\mathbf{y}|\boldsymbol{\theta}_0, \boldsymbol{\psi})\right], KL\left[p(\mathbf{y}|\boldsymbol{\theta}_0, \boldsymbol{\psi}), p(\mathbf{y}|\boldsymbol{\theta}, \boldsymbol{\psi})\right]\right\}.$$

As shown in Section 10.3.1, as to this type of net loss function, a possible loss function for decision making can be given by:

$$\mathcal{L}(d_0,\boldsymbol{\theta},\boldsymbol{\psi}) = \begin{cases} c_0 & \text{if } \boldsymbol{\theta} = \boldsymbol{\theta}_0 \\ c_0 + \frac{1}{2}\min\left\{KL\left[p(\mathbf{y}|\boldsymbol{\theta},\boldsymbol{\psi}), p(\mathbf{y}|\boldsymbol{\theta}_0,\boldsymbol{\psi})\right], KL\left[p(\mathbf{y}|\boldsymbol{\theta}_0,\boldsymbol{\psi}), p(\mathbf{y}|\boldsymbol{\theta},\boldsymbol{\psi})\right]\right\} & \text{if } \boldsymbol{\theta} \neq \boldsymbol{\theta}_0 \end{cases}$$

$$\mathcal{L}(d_1,\boldsymbol{\theta},\boldsymbol{\psi}) = \begin{cases} c_1 & \text{if } \boldsymbol{\theta} = \boldsymbol{\theta}_0 \\ c_1 - \frac{1}{2}\min\left\{KL\left[p(\mathbf{y}|\boldsymbol{\theta},\boldsymbol{\psi}), p(\mathbf{y}|\boldsymbol{\theta}_0,\boldsymbol{\psi})\right], KL\left[p(\mathbf{y}|\boldsymbol{\theta}_0,\boldsymbol{\psi}), p(\mathbf{y}|\boldsymbol{\theta},\boldsymbol{\psi})\right]\right\} & \text{if } \boldsymbol{\theta} \neq \boldsymbol{\theta}_0 \end{cases}$$

where c_i measures the cost of action d_i and $c = c_1 - c_0 > 0$. Then, the corresponding hypothesis test statistic can be given by:

$$\mathbf{T}_{BR}(\mathbf{y},\boldsymbol{\theta}_0) = E_{\boldsymbol{\vartheta}|\mathbf{y}}\left[m(\boldsymbol{\theta}_0,\boldsymbol{\theta},\boldsymbol{\psi})\right].$$

A Bayesian admissible solution to the decision problem should satisfy the following condition:

$$\text{Reject } H_0 \text{ iff } \mathbf{T}_{BR}(\mathbf{y},\boldsymbol{\theta}_0) > c.$$

The test statistic $\mathbf{T}BR(\mathbf{y},\boldsymbol{\theta}0)$, as proposed by Bernardo and Rueda (BR), remains well-defined even under improper priors due to its reliance on the Kullback–Leibler (KL) divergence function. However, the practical computation of $\mathbf{T}BR(\mathbf{y},\boldsymbol{\theta}0)$ poses challenges, particularly for latent variable models, as the KL divergence function often lacks a closed-form solution. Additionally, determining the constant c in this context is not straightforward. To implement their test, BR suggested the use of threshold values derived from the normal distribution for c. This recommendation likely stems from the observation that many test statistics tend toward a normal distribution asymptotically. However, it's important to note that BR's method does not align strictly with Bayesian principles, as it utilizes the sampling distribution of the test statistic. This approach is based on the concept of repeated sampling, rather than being conditional on $\mathbf{y}$.

For the normal mean hypothesis testing problem we have discussed before, $m(0,\theta)$ takes the following form:

$$m(0,\theta) = \int N\left(\bar{y}|\theta,\frac{\sigma^2}{n}\right)\log\frac{N\left(\bar{y}|\theta,\sigma^2/n\right)}{N\left(\bar{y}|0,\sigma^2/n\right)}d\bar{y} = \frac{1}{2}\frac{n\theta^2}{\sigma^2},$$

Then, we have:

$$\mathbf{T}_{BR}(\mathbf{y},\theta_0) = \frac{1}{2}\int\frac{n\theta^2}{\sigma^2}N\left(\theta|\mu^*,\sigma^{2*}\right)d\theta = \frac{1}{2}\frac{n}{\sigma^2}\left(\mu^{*2}+\sigma^{2*}\right).$$

It can be shown that:

$$\mathbf{T}_{BR}(\mathbf{y},\theta_0) = \frac{1}{2}\frac{n\tau^2}{\sigma^2+n\tau^2}\left(\frac{n\tau^2}{\sigma^2+n\tau^2}z(\bar{y})^2 + 2\frac{\sqrt{n}\mu_0\sigma}{\sigma^2+n\tau^2}z(\bar{y}) + \frac{\sigma^2\mu_0^2}{\tau^2\left(\sigma^2+n\tau^2\right)}+1\right),$$

which is immune to Jeffreys–Lindley–Bartlett's paradox. Under the condition that $\mu_0 = 0, \sigma = 1$, we have:

$$\mathbf{T}_{BR}(\mathbf{y}, \theta_0) = \frac{1}{2}\frac{n\tau^2}{1+n\tau^2}\left(\frac{n\tau^2}{1+n\tau^2}z(\bar{y})^2 + 1\right).$$

As $n \to \infty$, we can further obtain

$$\mathbf{T}_{BR}(\mathbf{y}, \theta_0) - \frac{1}{2}\left(z(\bar{y})^2 + 1\right) \xrightarrow{p} 0$$

under the null hypothesis.

Li and Yu (2012) and the $\mathcal{Q}$ Loss Function

In response to the computational challenges associated with $\mathbf{T}BR(\mathbf{y}, \theta 0)$, Li and Yu (2012, LY) introduced an alternative loss function. This new function is grounded in the $\mathcal{Q}$ function, which is a key component of the EM (Expectation-Maximization) algorithm, as detailed in Dempster et al. (1977). Their approach replaces the Kullback–Leibler (KL) divergence function to facilitate easier computation. For any two points such as $\boldsymbol{\vartheta}_1$ and $\boldsymbol{\vartheta}_2$ defined in the parameter space, the $\mathcal{Q}$ function can be expressed as:

$$\mathcal{Q}(\boldsymbol{\vartheta}_1|\boldsymbol{\vartheta}_2) = E_{\mathbf{z}|\mathbf{y},\boldsymbol{\vartheta}_2}\left[\ln p(\mathbf{y}, \mathbf{z}|\boldsymbol{\vartheta}_1)\right].$$

Compared with the observed data likelihood function $p(\mathbf{y}|\boldsymbol{\vartheta})$, the $\mathcal{Q}$ function is easier to evaluate for the latent variable model. Let $\boldsymbol{\vartheta}_0 = (\boldsymbol{\theta}_0, \boldsymbol{\psi})$, Li and Yu (2012) defined a new continuous net loss function as:

$$\begin{aligned} \triangle\mathcal{L}(\boldsymbol{\vartheta}, \boldsymbol{\vartheta}_0) &= m(\boldsymbol{\theta}_0, \boldsymbol{\theta}, \boldsymbol{\psi}) - c \\ m(\boldsymbol{\theta}_0, \boldsymbol{\theta}, \boldsymbol{\psi}) &= \{\mathcal{Q}(\boldsymbol{\vartheta}|\boldsymbol{\vartheta}) - \mathcal{Q}(\boldsymbol{\vartheta}_0|\boldsymbol{\vartheta})\} + \{\mathcal{Q}(\boldsymbol{\vartheta}_0|\boldsymbol{\vartheta}_0) - \mathcal{Q}(\boldsymbol{\vartheta}|\boldsymbol{\vartheta}_0)\} \end{aligned}$$

Correspondingly, for this type of net loss function, a possible loss function for decision making can be given by:

$$\mathcal{L}(d_0, \boldsymbol{\theta}, \boldsymbol{\psi}) = \begin{cases} c_0 & \text{if } \boldsymbol{\theta} = \boldsymbol{\theta}_0 \\ c_0 + \frac{1}{2}\{\mathcal{Q}(\boldsymbol{\vartheta}|\boldsymbol{\vartheta}) - \mathcal{Q}(\boldsymbol{\vartheta}_0|\boldsymbol{\vartheta})\} + \frac{1}{2}\{\mathcal{Q}(\boldsymbol{\vartheta}_0|\boldsymbol{\vartheta}_0) - \mathcal{Q}(\boldsymbol{\vartheta}|\boldsymbol{\vartheta}_0)\} & \text{if } \boldsymbol{\theta} \neq \boldsymbol{\theta}_0 \end{cases}$$

$$\mathcal{L}(d_1, \boldsymbol{\theta}, \boldsymbol{\psi}) = \begin{cases} c_1 & \text{if } \boldsymbol{\theta} = \boldsymbol{\theta}_0 \\ c_1 - \frac{1}{2}\{\mathcal{Q}(\boldsymbol{\vartheta}|\boldsymbol{\vartheta}) - \mathcal{Q}(\boldsymbol{\vartheta}_0|\boldsymbol{\vartheta})\} - \frac{1}{2}\{\mathcal{Q}(\boldsymbol{\vartheta}_0|\boldsymbol{\vartheta}_0) - \mathcal{Q}(\boldsymbol{\vartheta}|\boldsymbol{\vartheta}_0)\} & \text{if } \boldsymbol{\theta} \neq \boldsymbol{\theta}_0 \end{cases}$$

where c_i measures the cost of action d_i and $c = c_1 - c_0 > 0$. Thus, LY proposed a posterior-based test statistic as follows:

$$\mathbf{T}_{LY}(\mathbf{y}, \boldsymbol{\theta}_0) = E_{\boldsymbol{\vartheta}|\mathbf{y}}\left[m(\boldsymbol{\theta}_0, \boldsymbol{\theta}, \boldsymbol{\psi})\right]$$

Although $T_{LY}(\mathbf{y}, \boldsymbol{\theta}_0)$ is well-defined with improper priors and is easy to compute for the latent variable model, one still must specify some threshold values for c to make a decision. Again, these threshold values given by LY lack rigorous statistical justifications.

10.4 Bayesian Version of LR, LM, and Wald Test Statistics

To address the problem in choosing threshold values, Li et al. (2015, 2022) and Liu et al. (2022) introduce another three loss functions. The corresponding test statistics can be explained as the posterior version of LR, LM, and Wald test statistics, which are popular in the frequentist paradigm.

Assuming that $\mathbf{y}$ comes from a probability measure P_0 on the probability space (Ω, F, P_0), let $P_{\boldsymbol{\vartheta}}$ be a collection of candidate models indexed by parameters $\boldsymbol{\vartheta}$. Following White (1987), if there exists $\boldsymbol{\vartheta}$ such that $P_0 \in P_{\boldsymbol{\vartheta}}$, we say that the model $P_{\boldsymbol{\vartheta}}$ is correctly specified. If for any $\boldsymbol{\vartheta}$, $P_0 \notin P_{\boldsymbol{\vartheta}}$, we say the model $P_{\boldsymbol{\vartheta}}$ is misspecified. In this subsection, we assume that the model is correctly specified.

In this subsection, we establish large sample properties for $\mathbf{T}(\mathbf{y}, \boldsymbol{\theta}_0)$ under repeated sampling. Let $\mathbf{y}^t := (y_0, y_1, \ldots, y_t)$ for any $0 \le t \le n$ and $l_t\left(\mathbf{y}^t, \boldsymbol{\vartheta}\right) = \log p(\mathbf{y}^t|\boldsymbol{\vartheta}) - \log p(\mathbf{y}^{t-1}|\boldsymbol{\vartheta})$ be the conditional log-likelihood for the tth observation for any $1 \le t \le n$. When there is no confusion, we just write $l_t\left(\mathbf{y}^t, \boldsymbol{\vartheta}\right)$ as $l_t(\boldsymbol{\vartheta})$ so that the log-likelihood function $\mathcal{L}_n(\boldsymbol{\vartheta})$ $(= \log p(\mathbf{y}|\boldsymbol{\vartheta})$ conditional on the initial observation) can be written as $\sum_{t=1}^{n} l_t(\boldsymbol{\vartheta})$. Let $l_t^{(j)}(\boldsymbol{\vartheta})$ be the jth derivative of $l_t(\boldsymbol{\vartheta})$ and $l_t^{(0)}(\boldsymbol{\vartheta}) = l_t(\boldsymbol{\vartheta})$. Moreover, let:

$$
\begin{aligned}
\mathbf{s}(\mathbf{y}^t, \boldsymbol{\vartheta}) &= \frac{\partial \log p(\mathbf{y}^t|\boldsymbol{\vartheta})}{\partial \boldsymbol{\vartheta}} = \sum_{i=1}^{t} l_i^{(1)}(\boldsymbol{\vartheta}), \ \mathbf{h}(\mathbf{y}^t, \boldsymbol{\vartheta}) = \frac{\partial^2 \log p(\mathbf{y}^t|\boldsymbol{\vartheta})}{\partial \boldsymbol{\vartheta} \partial \boldsymbol{\vartheta}'} \\
&= \sum_{i=1}^{t} l_i^{(2)}(\boldsymbol{\vartheta}), \\
\mathbf{s}_t(\boldsymbol{\vartheta}) &= l_t^{(1)}(\boldsymbol{\vartheta}) = \mathbf{s}(\mathbf{y}^t, \boldsymbol{\vartheta}) - \mathbf{s}(\mathbf{y}^{t-1}, \boldsymbol{\vartheta}), \ \mathbf{h}_t(\boldsymbol{\vartheta}) = l_t^{(2)}(\boldsymbol{\vartheta}) \\
&= \mathbf{h}(\mathbf{y}^t, \boldsymbol{\vartheta}) - \mathbf{h}(\mathbf{y}^{t-1}, \boldsymbol{\vartheta}), \\
\bar{\mathbf{H}}_n(\boldsymbol{\vartheta}) &= \frac{1}{n} \sum_{t=1}^{n} \mathbf{h}_t(\boldsymbol{\vartheta}), \bar{\mathbf{J}}_n(\boldsymbol{\vartheta}) \\
&= \frac{1}{n} \sum_{t=1}^{n} \left[\mathbf{s}_t(\boldsymbol{\vartheta}) - \bar{\mathbf{s}}_t(\boldsymbol{\vartheta})\right] \left[\mathbf{s}_t(\boldsymbol{\vartheta}) - \bar{\mathbf{s}}_t(\boldsymbol{\vartheta})\right]', \bar{\mathbf{s}}_t(\boldsymbol{\vartheta}) = \frac{1}{n} \sum_{t=1}^{n} \mathbf{s}_t(\boldsymbol{\vartheta}), \\
\mathbf{B}_n(\boldsymbol{\vartheta}) &= Var\left[\frac{1}{\sqrt{n}} \sum_{t=1}^{n} l_t^{(1)}(\boldsymbol{\vartheta})\right], \mathbf{H}_n(\boldsymbol{\vartheta}) = \int \bar{\mathbf{H}}_n(\boldsymbol{\vartheta}) g(\mathbf{y})\, d\mathbf{y}, \ \mathbf{J}_n(\boldsymbol{\vartheta}) \\
&= \int \bar{\mathbf{J}}_n(\boldsymbol{\vartheta}) g(\mathbf{y})\, d\mathbf{y},
\end{aligned}
$$

where $g(\mathbf{y})$ is the data generating process (DGP). In the literature, $\mathbf{H}_n(\boldsymbol{\vartheta})$ and $\mathbf{J}_n(\boldsymbol{\vartheta})$ are generally known as the Hessian matrix and the Fisher information matrix; $\bar{\mathbf{H}}_n(\boldsymbol{\vartheta})$ and $\bar{\mathbf{J}}_n(\boldsymbol{\vartheta})$ are the empirical Hessian matrix and empirical Fisher information matrix.

In this subsection, to show the equivalence between the posterior test statistics and their frequentist versions, we introduce the following regularity conditions:

Assumption 1: For $q = q_\theta + q_\psi$, Θ is a compact subset of $\mathbb{R}^q$.

Assumption 2: For any $\varepsilon > 0$ and $r > 2$, the α-mixing condition with the coefficient $\alpha(m) = O\left(m^{\frac{-2r}{r-2}-\varepsilon}\right)$ is satisfied for $\{y_t\}_{t=1}^{\infty}$.

Assumption 3: For all t, $l_t(\boldsymbol{\vartheta})$ is three-times differentiable on $\boldsymbol{\Theta}$ almost surely.

Assumption 4: For any $\boldsymbol{\vartheta}, \boldsymbol{\vartheta}' \in \boldsymbol{\Theta}$, $\left\| l_t^{(j)}(\boldsymbol{\vartheta}) - l_t^{(j)}(\boldsymbol{\vartheta}') \right\| \le c_t^j(\mathbf{y}^t) \left\| \boldsymbol{\vartheta} - \boldsymbol{\vartheta}' \right\|$ in probability, where $c_t^j(\mathbf{y}^t) > 0$, $\sup_t E\left\| c_t^j(\mathbf{y}^t) \right\| < \infty$, $\frac{1}{n}\sum_{t=1}^n \left(c_t^j(\mathbf{y}^t) - E\left(c_t^j(\mathbf{y}^t)\right)\right) \xrightarrow{p} 0$, and $j = 0, 1, 2$.

Assumption 5: For all $\boldsymbol{\vartheta} \in \Theta$, there exists $M_t(\mathbf{y}^t) > 0$ such that $l_t^{(j)}(\boldsymbol{\vartheta})$ exists, $\sup_{\boldsymbol{\vartheta}\in\Theta} \left\| l_t^{(j)}(\boldsymbol{\vartheta}) \right\| \leqslant M_t(\mathbf{y}^t)$, and $\sup_t E\left\| M_t(\mathbf{y}^t) \right\|^{r+\delta} \le M$ for some $\delta > 0$ and $M < \infty$, where r is the same as that in Assumption 2, and $j = 0, 1, 2$.

Assumption 6: For $0 \leqslant j \leqslant 1$, $\left\{ l_t^{(j)}(\boldsymbol{\vartheta}) \right\}$ is L_2-near epoch dependent of size -1 and for $j = 2$, of size $-\frac{1}{2}$ uniformly on Θ.

Assumption 7: For any $\varepsilon > 0$:

$$\lim_{n\to\infty}\sup \sup_{\boldsymbol{\vartheta}\in\Theta\backslash N\left(\boldsymbol{\vartheta}^0,\varepsilon\right)} \frac{1}{n}\sum_{t=1}^{n} \left\{ E\left[l_t(\boldsymbol{\vartheta})\right] - E\left[l_t\left(\boldsymbol{\vartheta}^0\right)\right]\right\} < 0, \quad (10.20)$$

where $N\left(\boldsymbol{\vartheta}^0, \varepsilon\right)$ is the open ball of radius ε around the true value $\boldsymbol{\vartheta}^0$.

Assumption 8: The prior distribution $p(\boldsymbol{\vartheta})$ is assumed to be thrice continuously differentiable and $0 < p\left(\boldsymbol{\vartheta}_n^0\right) < \infty$ uniformly in n. For some n^*, when $n > n^*$, it is assumed that the posterior distribution $p(\boldsymbol{\vartheta}|\mathbf{y})$ is proper and $\int \|\boldsymbol{\vartheta}\|^2 p(\boldsymbol{\vartheta}|\mathbf{y})\, d\boldsymbol{\vartheta} < +\infty$.

Remark 10.4.1 *For dependent and heterogeneous data, Assumptions 1–7 are standard primitive conditions to develop the maximum likelihood theory (e.g., consistency and asymptotic normality). Assumption 1 is the compactness condition. Assumption 2 shows the weak dependence in y_t. Assumption 3 is the continuity condition. Assumption 4 is the Lipschitz condition for l_t. Assumption 5 is the domination condition for l_t. Assumption 6 shows weak dependence in l_t. Assumption 7 is the identification condition. Assumption 8 is the primitive condition on the prior distribution. More details about these regularity conditions* *can be found in Gallant and White (1988), Wooldridge (1994), Li et al. (2022, 2024), and Liu et al. (2022).*

10.4.1 Li et al. (2022) and LR-Type Loss Function

Spiegelhalter et al. (2002) defined the following Bayesian deviance function to measure the Bayesian model fit of a candidate model:

$$D(\mathbf{y}) = \int \ln p(\mathbf{y}|\boldsymbol{\theta}, \boldsymbol{\psi}) p(\boldsymbol{\theta}, \boldsymbol{\psi}|\mathbf{y}) \mathrm{d}\boldsymbol{\theta} \mathrm{d}\boldsymbol{\psi}. \tag{10.21}$$

Based on the Bayesian deviance function, we can develop a loss function for hypothesis testing as follows:

$$\mathcal{L}(d_0, \boldsymbol{\theta}, \boldsymbol{\psi}) = \begin{cases} c_0 & \text{if } \boldsymbol{\theta} = \boldsymbol{\theta}_0 \\ c_0 + \ln p(\mathbf{y}|\boldsymbol{\theta}, \boldsymbol{\psi}) - \ln p(\mathbf{y}|\boldsymbol{\theta}_0, \boldsymbol{\psi}) & \text{if } \boldsymbol{\theta} \neq \boldsymbol{\theta}_0 \end{cases},$$

$$\mathcal{L}(d_1, \boldsymbol{\theta}, \boldsymbol{\psi}) = \begin{cases} c_1 & \text{if } \boldsymbol{\theta} = \boldsymbol{\theta}_0 \\ c_1 + \ln p(\mathbf{y}|\boldsymbol{\theta}_0, \boldsymbol{\psi}) - \ln p(\mathbf{y}|\boldsymbol{\theta}, \boldsymbol{\psi}) & \text{if } \boldsymbol{\theta} \neq \boldsymbol{\theta}_0 \end{cases},$$

where c_i measures the cost of action d_i. Let $c = c_1 - c_0 > 0$ and we have:

$$\Delta\mathcal{L}(H_0, \boldsymbol{\theta}, \boldsymbol{\psi}) = 2\left(\ln p(\mathbf{y}|\boldsymbol{\theta}, \boldsymbol{\psi}) - \ln p(\mathbf{y}|\boldsymbol{\theta}_0, \boldsymbol{\psi})\right) - c.$$

According to the original definition given in (10.7), the corresponding test statistic can be established as:

$$\begin{aligned}\mathbf{T}_0(\mathbf{y}, \boldsymbol{\theta}_0) &= \int\int \Delta\mathcal{L}(H_0, \boldsymbol{\theta}, \boldsymbol{\psi}) p(\boldsymbol{\theta}, \boldsymbol{\psi}|\mathbf{y}) \mathrm{d}\boldsymbol{\theta} \mathrm{d}\boldsymbol{\psi} \\ &= \int\int \left[2\left(\ln p(\mathbf{y}|\boldsymbol{\theta}, \boldsymbol{\psi}) - \ln p(\mathbf{y}|\boldsymbol{\theta}_0, \boldsymbol{\psi})\right) - c\right] p(\boldsymbol{\theta}, \boldsymbol{\psi}|\mathbf{y}) \mathrm{d}\boldsymbol{\theta} \mathrm{d}\boldsymbol{\psi}.\end{aligned} \tag{10.22}$$

Let:

$$\mathbf{T}_1(\mathbf{y}, \boldsymbol{\theta}_0) = \int\int \left[2\left(\ln p(\mathbf{y}|\boldsymbol{\theta}, \boldsymbol{\psi}) - \ln p(\mathbf{y}|\boldsymbol{\theta}_0, \boldsymbol{\psi})\right)\right] p(\boldsymbol{\theta}, \boldsymbol{\psi}|\mathbf{y}) \mathrm{d}\boldsymbol{\theta} \mathrm{d}\boldsymbol{\psi}.$$

Then, $\mathbf{T}_0(\mathbf{y}, \boldsymbol{\theta}_0) > 0$ is equivalent to $\mathbf{T}_1(\mathbf{y}, \boldsymbol{\theta}_0) > c$. In this case, H_0 is rejected.

The posterior test statistic $\mathbf{T}_1(\mathbf{y}, \boldsymbol{\theta}_0)$ was first introduced by Li et al. (2014, LZY). To determine c for hypothesis testing, given some mild regularity conditions, Li et al. (2014) derived the asymptotic distribution of the test statistic as follows:

$$\mathbf{T}_1(\mathbf{y}, \boldsymbol{\theta}_0) + \left[p + q - \mathbf{tr}[-L_{0n}^{(2)}(\bar{\boldsymbol{\vartheta}}) V_{22}(\bar{\boldsymbol{\vartheta}})]\right] \overset{a}{\sim} \boldsymbol{\varepsilon}' \left[\mathbf{IJ}_{11}^{1/2}(\boldsymbol{\vartheta}_0) \mathbf{J}_{11}(\boldsymbol{\vartheta}_0) \mathbf{IJ}_{11}^{1/2}(\boldsymbol{\vartheta}_0)\right] \boldsymbol{\varepsilon},$$

where $\boldsymbol{\varepsilon}$ is a standard multivariate normal variate, $\boldsymbol{\vartheta}_0 = (\boldsymbol{\theta}_0, \boldsymbol{\psi}_0)'$ is the true value of $\boldsymbol{\vartheta}$, $\mathbf{J}(\boldsymbol{\vartheta}_0)$ is the Fisher information matrix given by

$$\mathbf{J}(\boldsymbol{\vartheta}_0) = \frac{1}{n} \int -L_n^{(2)}(\boldsymbol{\vartheta}_0) p(\mathbf{y}|\boldsymbol{\vartheta}_0) \mathrm{d}\mathbf{y},$$

with $\mathbf{IJ}(\boldsymbol{\vartheta}_0)$ being the inverse of $\mathbf{J}(\boldsymbol{\vartheta}_0)$, and $\mathbf{J}_{11}(\boldsymbol{\vartheta}_0)$ and $\mathbf{IJ}_{11}(\boldsymbol{\vartheta}_0)$ being the submatrices of $\mathbf{J}(\boldsymbol{\vartheta}_0)$ and $\mathbf{IJ}(\boldsymbol{\vartheta}_0)$, respectively, both corresponding to $\boldsymbol{\theta}$. Based on the asymptotic distribution, quantiles at certain probability levels can be chosen to make statistical inferences.

The asymptotic distribution is not pivotal. To overcome this disadvantage, Li et al. (2022, LWYZ) revised the loss function as follows:

$$\mathcal{L}(d_0, \boldsymbol{\theta}, \boldsymbol{\psi}) = \begin{cases} c_0 & \text{if } \boldsymbol{\theta} = \boldsymbol{\theta}_0 \\ c_0 + \left[2\ln p(\mathbf{y}, \hat{\boldsymbol{\vartheta}}) - \ln p(\mathbf{y}, \boldsymbol{\theta}, \boldsymbol{\psi}) - D_c(\mathbf{y}, \boldsymbol{\theta}_0)\right] & \text{if } \boldsymbol{\theta} \neq \boldsymbol{\theta}_0 \end{cases}, \tag{10.23}$$

$$\mathcal{L}(d_1, \boldsymbol{\theta}, \boldsymbol{\psi}) = \begin{cases} c_1 & \text{if } \boldsymbol{\theta} = \boldsymbol{\theta}_0 \\ c_1 - \left[2\ln p(\mathbf{y}, \hat{\boldsymbol{\vartheta}}) - \ln p(\mathbf{y}, \boldsymbol{\theta}, \boldsymbol{\psi}) - D_c(\mathbf{y}, \boldsymbol{\theta}_0)\right] & \text{if } \boldsymbol{\theta} \neq \boldsymbol{\theta}_0 \end{cases}, \tag{10.24}$$

where $D_c(\mathbf{y}, \boldsymbol{\theta}_0) = \int \ln p(\mathbf{y}, \boldsymbol{\theta}_0, \boldsymbol{\psi}) p(\boldsymbol{\psi}, \boldsymbol{\theta}_0 | \mathbf{y}) d\boldsymbol{\psi}$ is the Bayesian complete deviance function under the null hypothesis. It can be shown that

$$\Delta\mathcal{L}(H_0, \boldsymbol{\theta}, \boldsymbol{\psi}) = m(\boldsymbol{\theta}_0, \boldsymbol{\theta}, \boldsymbol{\psi}) - c,$$

where

$$m(\boldsymbol{\theta}_0, \boldsymbol{\theta}, \boldsymbol{\psi}) = 4\ln p(\mathbf{y}, \hat{\boldsymbol{\vartheta}}) - 2\ln p(\mathbf{y}, \boldsymbol{\theta}, \boldsymbol{\psi}) - 2D_c(\mathbf{y}, \boldsymbol{\theta}_0).$$

The corresponding test statistic is

$$\begin{aligned} \mathbf{T}_{LWYZ}(\mathbf{y}, \boldsymbol{\theta}_0) &= E_{\boldsymbol{\vartheta}|\mathbf{y}}\left[m(\boldsymbol{\theta}_0, \boldsymbol{\theta}, \boldsymbol{\psi})\right] \\ &= \int \left[4\ln p(\mathbf{y}, \hat{\boldsymbol{\vartheta}}) - 2\ln p(\mathbf{y}, \boldsymbol{\theta}, \boldsymbol{\psi}) - 2D_c(\mathbf{y}, \boldsymbol{\theta}_0)\right] p(\boldsymbol{\theta}, \boldsymbol{\psi} | \mathbf{y}) d\boldsymbol{\theta} d\boldsymbol{\psi}. \end{aligned}$$

We can show that we

$$\text{reject } H_0 \text{ if and only if } \mathbf{T}_{LWYZ}(\mathbf{y}, \boldsymbol{\theta}_0) > c. \tag{10.25}$$

Again, one can derive the asymptotic distribution of $\mathbf{T}_{LWYZ}(\mathbf{y}, \boldsymbol{\theta}_0)$ so that quantiles at certain probability levels can be chosen to make statistical inferences.

In many models, the MLE $\hat{\boldsymbol{\vartheta}}$ is not easy to find. Based on $\mathbf{T}_{LWYZ}(\mathbf{y}, \boldsymbol{\theta}_0)$, to avoid the use of $\hat{\boldsymbol{\vartheta}}$, Li et al. (2022) defined two test statistics:

$$\begin{aligned} \mathbf{T}_{1,LWYZ}(\mathbf{y}, \boldsymbol{\theta}_0) &= 2\left[D_c(\mathbf{y}) - D_c(\mathbf{y}, \boldsymbol{\theta}_0)\right], \\ \mathbf{T}_{2,LWYZ}(\mathbf{y}, \boldsymbol{\theta}_0) &= 2\left[\ln p(\mathbf{y}, \bar{\boldsymbol{\theta}}, \bar{\boldsymbol{\psi}}) - \ln p(\mathbf{y}, \boldsymbol{\theta}_0, \bar{\boldsymbol{\psi}}_0)\right], \end{aligned} \tag{10.26}$$

where $D_c(\mathbf{y})$, the Bayesian complete deviance function with the prior information, is given by

$$D_c(\mathbf{y}) = \int\int [\ln p(\mathbf{y}|\boldsymbol{\theta}, \boldsymbol{\psi}) + \ln p(\boldsymbol{\theta}, \boldsymbol{\psi})]\, p(\boldsymbol{\theta}, \boldsymbol{\psi}|\mathbf{y}) \mathrm{d}\boldsymbol{\theta} \mathrm{d}\boldsymbol{\psi},$$

and

$$\ln p(\mathbf{y}, \bar{\boldsymbol{\theta}}, \bar{\boldsymbol{\psi}}) = \ln p(\mathbf{y}|\bar{\boldsymbol{\theta}}, \bar{\boldsymbol{\psi}}) + \ln p(\bar{\boldsymbol{\theta}}, \bar{\boldsymbol{\psi}}),$$
$$\ln p(\mathbf{y}, \boldsymbol{\theta}_0, \bar{\boldsymbol{\psi}}_0) = \ln p(\mathbf{y}|\boldsymbol{\theta}_0, \bar{\boldsymbol{\psi}}_0) + \ln p(\boldsymbol{\theta}_0, \bar{\boldsymbol{\psi}}_0).$$

Under some regularity conditions, Li et al. (2022) showed that under the null and alternative hypotheses,

$$\mathbf{T}_{LWYZ}(\mathbf{y}, \boldsymbol{\theta}_0) = \mathbf{T}_{1,LWYZ}(\mathbf{y}, \boldsymbol{\theta}_0) + q_\theta + O_p(n^{-1/2}) = \mathbf{T}_{2,LWYZ}(\mathbf{y}, \boldsymbol{\theta}_0) + O_p(n^{-1/2}), \tag{10.27}$$

and under the null hypothesis,

$$\begin{aligned}\mathbf{T}_{1,LWYZ}(\mathbf{y}, \boldsymbol{\theta}_0) + q_\theta &= \mathbf{T}_{2,LWYZ}(\mathbf{y}, \boldsymbol{\theta}_0) + O_p(n^{-1/2}) \\ &= \mathbf{LR} + O_p(n^{-1/2}) \xrightarrow{d} \chi^2(q_\theta).\end{aligned}$$

Thus, we can obtain that

$$\mathbf{T}_{1,LWYZ}(\mathbf{y}, \boldsymbol{\theta}_0) + q_\theta \xrightarrow{d} \chi^2(q_\theta), \mathbf{T}_{2,LWYZ}(\mathbf{y}, \boldsymbol{\theta}_0) \xrightarrow{d} \chi^2(q_\theta).$$

Li et al. (2022) explained $\mathbf{T}_{1,LWYZ}(\mathbf{y}, \boldsymbol{\theta}_0)$ as the Bayesian version of the LR statistic, and $\mathbf{T}_{2,LWYZ}(\mathbf{y}, \boldsymbol{\theta}_0)$ as the Bayesian plug-in version of the LR statistic. In practice, one can use these posterior test statistics for hypothesis testing.

Using the normal mean hypothesis testing example shown earlier, we can show that

$$\mathbf{T}_{1,LWYZ}(\mathbf{y}, \theta_0) = \frac{n\tau^2}{\sigma^2 + n\tau^2} z(\bar{y})^2 + \frac{2\sqrt{n}\sigma\mu_0}{\sigma^2 + n\tau^2} z(\bar{y}) - 1 + \frac{\mu_0^2\sigma^2}{\tau^2(\sigma^2 + n\tau^2)},$$

$$\mathbf{T}_{2,LWYZ}(\mathbf{y}, \theta_0) = \frac{n\tau^2}{\sigma^2 + n\tau^2} z(\bar{y})^2 + \frac{2\sqrt{n}\sigma\mu_0}{\sigma^2 + n\tau^2} z(\bar{y}) + \frac{\mu_0^2\sigma^2}{\tau^2(\sigma^2 + n\tau^2)},$$

which is immune to Jeffreys–Lindley–Bartlett's paradox. If we set $\mu_0 = 0$ and $\sigma = 1$, the expression can be simplified as

$$\mathbf{T}_{1,LWYZ}(\mathbf{y}, \theta_0) = \frac{n\tau^2}{1 + n\tau^2} z(\bar{y})^2 - 1, \mathbf{T}_{2,LWYZ}(\mathbf{y}, \theta_0) = \frac{n\tau^2}{1 + n\tau^2} z(\bar{y})^2.$$

When $n \to \infty$, under the null hypothesis, we have

$$\mathbf{T}_{1,LWYZ}(\mathbf{y}, \theta_0) + 1 - z(\bar{y})^2 \xrightarrow{p} 0, \mathbf{T}_{2,LWYZ}(\mathbf{y}, \theta_0) - z(\bar{y})^2 \xrightarrow{p} 0.$$

10.4.2 Li et al. (2015) and LM-Type Loss Function

Let

$$m(\boldsymbol{\theta}_0, \boldsymbol{\theta}, \boldsymbol{\psi}) = (\boldsymbol{\theta} - \bar{\boldsymbol{\theta}})' C_{\theta\theta}(\bar{\boldsymbol{\vartheta}}_0)(\boldsymbol{\theta} - \bar{\boldsymbol{\theta}}), \tag{10.28}$$

where

$$C(\boldsymbol{\vartheta}) = s(\boldsymbol{\vartheta})s(\boldsymbol{\vartheta})', \mathrm{s}(\boldsymbol{\vartheta}) = \frac{\partial \ln p(\mathbf{y}|\boldsymbol{\vartheta})}{\partial \boldsymbol{\vartheta}},$$

where $s(\boldsymbol{\vartheta})$ is the score function of $\boldsymbol{\vartheta}$, $C_{\theta\theta}(\boldsymbol{\vartheta})$ is the submatrix of $C(\boldsymbol{\vartheta})$ corresponding to $\boldsymbol{\theta}$ and is semi-positive definite, $\bar{\boldsymbol{\vartheta}}_0 = (\boldsymbol{\theta}_0, \bar{\boldsymbol{\psi}}_0)$ is the posterior mean of $\boldsymbol{\vartheta}$ under H_0, and $\bar{\boldsymbol{\theta}}$ is the posterior mean of $\boldsymbol{\theta}$ under H_1.

Based on this quadratic loss, a possible loss function for hypothesis testing can be specified as

$$\mathcal{L}(d_0, \boldsymbol{\theta}, \boldsymbol{\psi}) = \begin{cases} c_0 & \text{if } \boldsymbol{\theta} = \boldsymbol{\theta}_0 \\ c_0 + \frac{1}{2}(\boldsymbol{\theta} - \bar{\boldsymbol{\theta}})' C_{\theta\theta}(\bar{\boldsymbol{\vartheta}}_0)(\boldsymbol{\theta} - \bar{\boldsymbol{\theta}}) & \text{if } \boldsymbol{\theta} \neq \boldsymbol{\theta}_0 \end{cases}, \tag{10.29}$$

$$\mathcal{L}(d_1, \boldsymbol{\theta}, \boldsymbol{\psi}) = \begin{cases} c_1 & \text{if } \boldsymbol{\theta} = \boldsymbol{\theta}_0 \\ c_1 - \frac{1}{2}(\boldsymbol{\theta} - \bar{\boldsymbol{\theta}})' C_{\theta\theta}(\bar{\boldsymbol{\vartheta}}_0)(\boldsymbol{\theta} - \bar{\boldsymbol{\theta}}) & \text{if } \boldsymbol{\theta} \neq \boldsymbol{\theta}_0 \end{cases}. \tag{10.30}$$

Thus, based on this loss function, a posterior test statistic proposed by Li et al. (2015, LLY) can be given by

$$\mathbf{T}_{LLY}(\mathbf{y}, \boldsymbol{\theta}_0) = E_{\vartheta|\mathbf{y}}\left[m(\boldsymbol{\theta}_0, \boldsymbol{\theta}, \boldsymbol{\psi})\right] = \int (\boldsymbol{\theta} - \bar{\boldsymbol{\theta}})' C_{\theta\theta}(\bar{\boldsymbol{\vartheta}}_0)(\boldsymbol{\theta} - \bar{\boldsymbol{\theta}}) p(\boldsymbol{\vartheta}|\mathbf{y}) d\boldsymbol{\vartheta}, \tag{10.31}$$

where $p(\boldsymbol{\vartheta}|\mathbf{y})$ is the posterior distribution of $\boldsymbol{\vartheta}$ under H_1. Thus, we can further show that

$$\text{Reject } H_0 \text{ if and only if } \mathbf{T}_{LLY}(\mathbf{y}, \boldsymbol{\theta}_0) > c. \tag{10.32}$$

The proposed test can be viewed as the Bayesian version of the LM test. To show this link, let the LM statistic (Breusch and Pagan, 1980) be

$$\mathbf{LM} = \frac{1}{n} s_\theta(\widehat{\boldsymbol{\vartheta}}_0) \left[-\bar{\mathbf{H}}_{n,\theta\theta}^{-1}\left(\widehat{\boldsymbol{\vartheta}}_0\right)\right] s_\theta(\widehat{\boldsymbol{\vartheta}}_0),$$

where $\widehat{\boldsymbol{\vartheta}}_0 = (\boldsymbol{\theta}_0, \widehat{\boldsymbol{\psi}}_0)$ is the MLE of $\boldsymbol{\vartheta}$ under the null hypothesis, $s_\theta(\boldsymbol{\vartheta})$ is the subvector of $s(\boldsymbol{\vartheta})$ corresponding to $\boldsymbol{\theta}$, and $\bar{\mathbf{H}}_{n,\theta\theta}(\boldsymbol{\vartheta})$ is the submatrix of $\bar{\mathbf{H}}_n(\boldsymbol{\vartheta})$ corresponding to $\boldsymbol{\theta}$. Under some regularity assumptions, when the null hypothesis is true and the likelihood dominates the prior, Li et al. (2015) showed that

$$\mathbf{T}_{LLY}(\mathbf{y}, \boldsymbol{\theta}_0) = \mathbf{LM} + o_p(1) \xrightarrow{d} \chi^2(q_\theta).$$

The test statistic $\mathbf{T}_{LLY}(\mathbf{y}, \boldsymbol{\theta}_0)$ has a few important properties. For example, the test statistic is well-defined under an improper prior and immune to Jeffreys–Lindley–Bartlett's paradox. In addition, for the latent variable model, it is not difficult to compute with the EM algorithm. Finally, it follows a pivotal $\chi^2(\cdot)$ asymptotically, and thus, it is easy to obtain threshold values.

For the normal mean hypothesis testing, we have

$$\mathbf{T}_{LLY}(\mathbf{y}, \theta_0) = \frac{n\tau^2}{\sigma^2 + n\tau^2} z(\bar{y})^2 .$$

which is immune to Jeffreys–Lindley–Bartlett's paradox. Under the condition that $\mu_0 = 0, \sigma = 1$, we have

$$\mathbf{T}_{LLY}(\mathbf{y}, \theta_0) = \frac{n\tau^2}{1 + n\tau^2} z(\bar{y})^2 .$$

As $n \to \infty$, we can further obtain

$$\mathbf{T}_{LLY}(\mathbf{y}, \theta_0) - z(\bar{y})^2 \xrightarrow{p} 0$$

under the null hypothesis.

10.4.3 Liu et al. (2022) and Wald-Type Loss Function

The test statistic developed by Li et al. (2015) is recognized for its ease of computation and advantageous properties. However, it necessitates the computation of the first-order derivative of the likelihood function, a task that can be challenging in many models, especially latent variable models, where the observed-data likelihood function might lack an analytical form.[1] Another feature of $\mathbf{T}_{LLY}(\mathbf{y}, \boldsymbol{\theta}_0)$ is that it requires estimating both the null model and the alternative model, although under H_0, it is shown to be asymptotically equivalent to the Lagrange Multiplier (LM) test that requires the estimation of the null model only. In a different approach, Liu et al. (2022, LLYZ) introduced a test statistic based on another quadratic loss function. This statistic is a derivative of the MCMC output under H_1, making it more straightforward to compute.

Let the posterior covariance matrix under the alternative hypothesis be

$$\mathbf{V}(\bar{\boldsymbol{\vartheta}}) = E\left[(\boldsymbol{\vartheta} - \bar{\boldsymbol{\vartheta}})(\boldsymbol{\vartheta} - \bar{\boldsymbol{\vartheta}})'|\mathbf{y}, H_1\right] = \int (\boldsymbol{\vartheta} - \bar{\boldsymbol{\vartheta}})(\boldsymbol{\vartheta} - \bar{\boldsymbol{\vartheta}})' p(\boldsymbol{\vartheta}|\mathbf{y}) d\boldsymbol{\vartheta},$$

[1] Advanced methods like automatic differentiation can aid in derivative evaluation. For instance, Skaug and Yu (2014) employed automatic differentiation in conjunction with the Laplace approximation to estimate the likelihood function in stochastic volatility models.

where $\bar{\boldsymbol{\vartheta}}$ is the posterior mean of $\boldsymbol{\vartheta}$ under the alternative hypothesis H_1. Liu et al. (2022) proposed the following net loss function for hypothesis testing:

$$m(\boldsymbol{\theta}_0, \boldsymbol{\theta}, \boldsymbol{\psi}) = (\boldsymbol{\theta} - \boldsymbol{\theta}_0)' \left[\mathbf{V}_{\theta\theta}(\bar{\boldsymbol{\vartheta}})\right]^{-1} (\boldsymbol{\theta} - \boldsymbol{\theta}_0),$$

where $\mathbf{V}_{\theta\theta}(\bar{\boldsymbol{\vartheta}})$ is the submatrix of $\mathbf{V}(\bar{\boldsymbol{\vartheta}})$ corresponding to $\boldsymbol{\theta}$, and $\left[\mathbf{V}_{\theta\theta}(\bar{\boldsymbol{\vartheta}})\right]^{-1}$ is the inverse matrix of $\mathbf{V}_{\theta\theta}(\bar{\boldsymbol{\vartheta}})$.

Based on this quadratic loss function, one can specify two possible loss functions for hypothesis testing:

$$\mathcal{L}(d_0, \boldsymbol{\theta}, \boldsymbol{\psi}) = \begin{cases} c_0 & \text{if } \boldsymbol{\theta} = \boldsymbol{\theta}_0 \\ c_0 + \frac{1}{2}(\boldsymbol{\theta} - \boldsymbol{\theta}_0)' \left[\mathbf{V}_{\theta\theta}(\bar{\boldsymbol{\vartheta}})\right]^{-1} (\boldsymbol{\theta} - \boldsymbol{\theta}_0) & \text{if } \boldsymbol{\theta} \neq \boldsymbol{\theta}_0 \end{cases}, \tag{10.33}$$

$$\mathcal{L}(d_1, \boldsymbol{\theta}, \boldsymbol{\psi}) = \begin{cases} c_1 & \text{if } \boldsymbol{\theta} = \boldsymbol{\theta}_0 \\ c_1 - \frac{1}{2}(\boldsymbol{\theta} - \boldsymbol{\theta}_0)' \left[\mathbf{V}_{\theta\theta}(\bar{\boldsymbol{\vartheta}})\right]^{-1} (\boldsymbol{\theta} - \boldsymbol{\theta}_0) & \text{if } \boldsymbol{\theta} \neq \boldsymbol{\theta}_0 \end{cases}. \tag{10.34}$$

Thus, Liu et al. (2022) proposed the following posterior-based test statistic:

$$\begin{aligned} \mathbf{T}_{LLYZ}(\mathbf{y}, \boldsymbol{\theta}_0) &= E_{\vartheta|y}\left[m(\boldsymbol{\theta}_0, \boldsymbol{\theta}, \boldsymbol{\psi})\right] \\ &= \int (\boldsymbol{\theta} - \boldsymbol{\theta}_0)' \left[\mathbf{V}_{\theta\theta}(\bar{\boldsymbol{\vartheta}})\right]^{-1} (\boldsymbol{\theta} - \boldsymbol{\theta}_0) p(\boldsymbol{\vartheta}|\mathbf{y}) d\boldsymbol{\vartheta}. \end{aligned} \tag{10.35}$$

Consequently, we can show:

$$\text{Reject } H_0 \text{ if and only if } \mathbf{T}_{LLYZ}(\mathbf{y}, \boldsymbol{\theta}_0) > c. \tag{10.36}$$

To show the link between $\mathbf{T}_{LLYZ}(\mathbf{y}, \boldsymbol{\theta}_0)$ and the Wald statistic, define the Wald statistic by (Engle, 1984):

$$\textbf{Wald} = n\left(\widehat{\boldsymbol{\theta}} - \boldsymbol{\theta}_0\right)' \left[-\bar{\mathbf{H}}_{n,\theta\theta}^{-1}\left(\widehat{\boldsymbol{\vartheta}}\right)\right]^{-1} \left(\widehat{\boldsymbol{\theta}} - \boldsymbol{\theta}_0\right), \tag{10.37}$$

where $\widehat{\boldsymbol{\vartheta}} := \left(\widehat{\boldsymbol{\theta}}, \widehat{\boldsymbol{\psi}}\right)$ is the ML estimate of $\boldsymbol{\vartheta}$. Under some regularity assumptions when the null hypothesis is true and the likelihood dominates the prior, Liu et al. (2022) showed that

$$\mathbf{T}_{LLYZ}(\mathbf{y}, \boldsymbol{\theta}_0) - q_\theta = \textbf{Wald} + o_p(1) \xrightarrow{d} \chi^2(q_\theta).$$

This result is why $\mathbf{T}_{LLYZ}(\mathbf{y}, \boldsymbol{\theta}_0)$ may be viewed as a Bayesian version of the Wald test.

Table 10.1 *Summary of posterior-based Trinity of Tests*

	$\mathbf{T}_{LYWZ}$	$\mathbf{T}_{LLY}$	$\mathbf{T}_{LLYZ}$
Expression	$2\left[D(\mathbf{y})-D(\mathbf{y},\boldsymbol{\theta}_0)\right]+q$	$\mathbf{tr}\left[C_{\theta\theta}(\bar{\boldsymbol{\vartheta}}_0)V_{\theta\theta}(\bar{\boldsymbol{\theta}})\right]$	$\left(\bar{\boldsymbol{\theta}}-\boldsymbol{\theta}_0\right)'\left[\mathbf{V}_{\theta\theta}(\bar{\boldsymbol{\vartheta}})\right]^{-1}\left(\bar{\boldsymbol{\vartheta}}-\boldsymbol{\theta}_0\right)$
Prior	Improper or proper	Improper or propers	Improper or proper
Jeffreys–Lindley's Paradox	No	No	No
Asymptotic Theory	$\chi^2(q)$	$\chi^2(q)$	$\chi^2(q)$
Asymptotic Pivotal	Yes	Yes	Yes

$\mathbf{T}_{LLYZ}(\mathbf{y},\boldsymbol{\theta}_0)$ shared some nice properties with the test statistic proposed by Li et al. (2015). First, this test statistic is well-defined under improper prior distributions and is immune to Jeffreys–Lindley–Bartlett's paradox. Second, the asymptotic distribution allows threshold values for c to be easily obtained from the $\chi^2(\cdot)$ distribution to make the decision.

An advantage of $\mathbf{T}_{LLYZ}(\mathbf{y},\boldsymbol{\theta}_0)$ compared to $\mathbf{T}_{LLY}(\mathbf{y},\boldsymbol{\theta}_0)$ is that $\mathbf{T}_{LLYZ}(\mathbf{y},\boldsymbol{\theta}_0)$ does not require evaluating the first-order derivative of the likelihood function. Another advantage of $\mathbf{T}_{LLYZ}(\mathbf{y},\boldsymbol{\theta}_0)$ over $\mathbf{T}_{LLY}(\mathbf{y},\boldsymbol{\theta}_0)$ is that $\mathbf{T}_{LLYZ}(\mathbf{y},\boldsymbol{\theta}_0)$ only must estimate the alternative model but $\mathbf{T}_{LLY}(\mathbf{y},\boldsymbol{\theta}_0)$ must estimate both the null model and alternative model.

For the normal mean hypothesis testing, we have

$$\mathbf{T}_{LLYZ}(\mathbf{y},\theta_0)=\frac{n\tau^2}{\sigma^2+n\tau^2}z(\bar{y})^2+\frac{2\sqrt{n}\mu_0\sigma}{\sigma^2+n\tau^2}z(\bar{y})+\frac{\mu_0^2\sigma^2}{(\sigma^2+n\tau^2)\tau^2}+1,$$

which is immune to Jeffreys–Lindley–Bartlett's paradox. Under the condition that $\mu_0=0,\sigma=1$, we have

$$\mathbf{T}_{LLYZ}(\mathbf{y},\theta_0)=\frac{n\tau^2}{\sigma^2+n\tau^2}z(\bar{y})^2+1.$$

As $n\to\infty$, we can further obtain:

$$\mathbf{T}_{LLYZ}(\mathbf{y},\theta_0)-1-z(\bar{y})^2\xrightarrow{p}0$$

under the null hypothesis.

Table 10.1 provides a comprehensive summary of the three posterior-based tests, along with their principal characteristics. Despite being derived from posterior outputs, which consist of random samples from the Bayesian posterior distribution, the statistical inferences drawn from these tests do not depend on the data. Rather, their validation is conducted within a frequentist context, necessitating repeated sampling from DGP and relying on asymptotic reasoning.

10.5 Simulation Studies

We designed two experiments to examine the finite-sample performance of the proposed test with simulated data. In the first experiment, we examine the finite performance of the proposed posterior statistics in terms of the empirical size and empirical power. In the second experiment, we consider a copula model in a similar manner.

10.5.1 Hypothesis Testing in a Linear Regression Model

In this subsection, we consider a simple linear regression model as follows:

$$y_i = \alpha + \beta x_i + \varepsilon_i, \quad \varepsilon_i \sim iidN(0, \sigma^2), \quad i = 1, 2, \cdots, n,$$

where x_i is randomly drawn from the standard normal distribution and then fixed under repeated sampling. For the point-null hypothesis testing problem, we test whether the slope coefficient is zero:

$$H_0 : \beta = 0 \quad \text{vs.} \quad H_1 : \beta \neq 0.$$

For the Bayesian analysis, we choose the prior distributions to be the natural conjugate Normal-Gamma priors:

$$(\alpha, \beta)' \sim N(\mu_0, \sigma^2 V_0) \text{ and } h = \frac{1}{\sigma^2} \sim G(a, b),$$

where $\mu_0 = (\mu_\alpha, \mu_\beta)'$, $V_0 = \text{diag}(V_\alpha, V_\beta)$, $G(a, b)$ denotes the gamma distribution with the shape parameter a and the rate parameter b. Let $\hat{\mu} = \left(X'X\right)^{-1} X'Y$ be the OLS estimator of $\mu = (\alpha, \beta)'$, where $Y = \begin{pmatrix} y_1 & \dots & y_n \end{pmatrix}'$, $X = \begin{pmatrix} 1 & \dots & 1 \\ x_1 & \dots & x_n \end{pmatrix}'$. Then, the posterior distributions of μ and h under H_1 are

$$\begin{aligned} \mu|\mathbf{y}, h; H_1 &\sim N(\mu_1, \sigma^2 V_1), \\ h|\mathbf{y}; H_1 &\sim G\left(a + \frac{n}{2}, b + \frac{1}{2}\left(\mathbf{y}'\mathbf{y} + \mu_0' V_0^{-1} \mu_0 - \mu_1' V_1^{-1} \mu_1\right)\right), \end{aligned}$$

where $V_1 = \left(X'X + V_0^{-1}\right)^{-1}$ and $\mu_1 = V_1(X'X\hat{\mu} + V_0^{-1}\mu_0) = V_1(X'\mathbf{y} + V_0^{-1}\mu_0)$.

Under H_0, $y_i = \alpha + \varepsilon_i$ and

$$\alpha|\mathbf{y}; H_0 \sim N(\mu_{\alpha 1}, \sigma^2 V_{\alpha 1}),$$

$$h|\mathbf{y}; H_0 \sim G\left(a + \frac{n}{2}, b + \frac{1}{2}\left(\mathbf{y}'\mathbf{y} + \frac{\mu_\alpha^2}{V_\alpha} - \frac{\mu_{\alpha 1}^2}{V_{\alpha 1}}\right)\right),$$

where $V_{\alpha 1} = \frac{V_\alpha}{nV_\alpha + 1}$ and $\mu_{\alpha 1} = V_{\alpha 1}\left(\sum_{i=1}^n y_i + \frac{\mu_\alpha}{V_\alpha}\right)$. We randomly draw 10,000 iid samples for each parameter. Based on these random samples, we calculate the posterior statistics.

Particularly, we set the true values for α^* and σ^{2*} to equal 1 and 1. We consider three different values for β^*, $\beta^* = 0.0, 0.1, 0.2$, and three different sample sizes, $n = 50$, 500, 2,000. For each case, we simulate data from the true DGP and perform hypothesis testing at the 5 percent significance level 1,000 times. We report the rejection rate of H_0 across the 1,000 replications.

We consider two types of priors, noninformative prior distributions (NP) and informative prior distributions (IP) of parameters of interest as follows:

$$NP: (\mu_\alpha, \mu_\beta, V_\alpha, V_\beta, a, b) = (\alpha^*, \beta^*, 10000, 10000, 1, 1),$$

$$IP: (\mu_\alpha, \mu_\beta, V_\alpha, V_\beta, a, b) = (\alpha^*, \beta^*, 10000, 0.001, 1, 1).$$

The empirical size and power of various statistics under different sample sizes are reported in Table 10.2 (under uninformative priors) and Table 10.3 (under informative priors).

The results in Table 10.2 show good finite sample performance of the proposed posterior statistics in terms of empirical size and empirical power under uninformative prior distributions (NP). For the empirical size, when the sample size is small (e.g., $n = 50$), the empirical sizes of different statistics reported in this study exhibit some variation, ranging from 4.5 to 6.5 percent. As the sample size increases, the empirical sizes of different statistics increasingly agree with each other and are all estimated to be around the nominal size of 5.0 percent. The results regarding size are consistent with our theoretical predictions. Regarding the empirical power, as the sample size increases, and β^* deviates from the hypothesized value under the null hypothesis, the empirical powers of all statistics reported in this study increase to 100.0 percent.

Table 10.3 shows the empirical size and power of these statistics in a linear regression model under informative prior distributions (IP). The performance of the frequentist *LR, Wald, LM* statistics remain the same as those under uninformative prior distributions (NP) reported in Table 10.2. For the posterior statistics, when informative prior information exists, the empirical size and power are strongly affected, particularly when the sample size is small. These results are easy to understand because the prior information matters for the posterior distribution of parameters when data information is insufficient (e.g., when the sample size is small). More specifically, when H_0 is true, the empirical size deviates markedly downwards from the nominal size of 5.0 percent

Table 10.2 *Empirical size and power of posterior statistics in a linear regression model (NP)*

	Empirical Size ($\beta^* = 0.0$)		
	$n = 50$	$n = 500$	$n = 2{,}000$
LR	5.2%	4.1%	4.6%
Wald	5.4%	4.1%	4.6%
LM	6.5%	4.3%	4.6%
$\mathbf{T}^1_{LYWZ}(\mathbf{y}, \boldsymbol{\theta}_0) + q_\theta$	4.9%	4.0%	4.6%
$\mathbf{T}^2_{LYWZ}(\mathbf{y}, \boldsymbol{\theta}_0)$	4.9%	4.1%	4.6%
$\mathbf{T}_{LLYZ}(\mathbf{y}, \boldsymbol{\theta}_0) - q_\theta$	5.3%	4.1%	4.6%
$\mathbf{T}_{LLY}(\mathbf{y}, \boldsymbol{\theta}_0)$	4.5%	4.0%	4.7%
	Empirical Power ($\beta^* = 0.1$)		
	$n = 50$	$n = 500$	$n = 2{,}000$
LR	9.2%	59.8%	99.4%
Wald	9.2%	59.8%	99.4%
LM	11.5%	60.3%	99.4%
$\mathbf{T}^1_{LYWZ}(\mathbf{y}, \boldsymbol{\theta}_0) + q_\theta$	8.8%	59.7%	99.4%
$\mathbf{T}^2_{LYWZ}(\mathbf{y}, \boldsymbol{\theta}_0)$	8.8%	59.6%	99.4%
$\mathbf{T}_{LLYZ}(\mathbf{y}, \boldsymbol{\theta}_0) - q_\theta$	9.2%	60.0%	99.4%
$\mathbf{T}_{LLY}(\mathbf{y}, \boldsymbol{\theta}_0)$	7.9%	59.4%	99.4%
	Empirical Power ($\beta^* = 0.2$)		
	$n = 50$	$n = 500$	$n = 2{,}000$
LR	25.5%	99.8%	100.0%
Wald	25.8%	99.8%	100.0%
LM	28.3%	99.8%	100.0%
$\mathbf{T}^1_{LYWZ}(\mathbf{y}, \boldsymbol{\theta}_0) + q_\theta$	23.9%	99.8%	100.0%
$\mathbf{T}^2_{LYWZ}(\mathbf{y}, \boldsymbol{\theta}_0)$	23.8%	99.8%	100.0%
$\mathbf{T}_{LLYZ}(\mathbf{y}, \boldsymbol{\theta}_0) - q_\theta$	25.7%	99.8%	100.0%
$\mathbf{T}_{LLY}(\mathbf{y}, \boldsymbol{\theta}_0)$	23.0%	99.8%	100.0%

(e.g., 0.0 percent when $n = 50, 500$; approximately 1.4 percent when $n =$ 2,000). However, as the sample size increases, and the data information begins to dominate the prior information, the empirical sizes of all the posterior statistics increase to be approximately 5.0 percent ($n =$ 20,000). When H_1 is true, the empirical powers of $\mathbf{T}^1_{LYWZ}(\mathbf{y}, \boldsymbol{\theta}_0) + q_\theta$, $\mathbf{T}^2_{LYWZ}(\mathbf{y}, \boldsymbol{\theta}_0)$, and $\mathbf{T}_{LLYZ}(\mathbf{y}, \boldsymbol{\theta}_0) - q_\theta$ increase markedly, equaling 100.0 percent even under a small sample size ($n = 50$). However, for $\mathbf{T}_{LLY}(\mathbf{y}, \boldsymbol{\theta}_0)$, the empirical power decreases sharply under small sample size, equaling 0 percent with $n = 50$, and gradually recovers to 100.0 percent as the sample size increases.

Table 10.3 *Empirical size and power of posterior statistics in a linear regression model (IP)*

	Empirical Size ($\beta^* = 0.0$)			
	$n = 50$	$n = 500$	$n = 2{,}000$	$n = 20{,}000$
LR	5.2%	4.1%	4.6%	4.8%
Wald	5.4%	4.1%	4.6%	4.8%
LM	6.5%	4.3%	4.6%	4.8%
$\mathbf{T}^1_{LYWZ}(\mathbf{y}, \boldsymbol{\theta}_0) + q_\theta$	0.0%	0.0%	1.4%	4.6%
$\mathbf{T}^2_{LYWZ}(\mathbf{y}, \boldsymbol{\theta}_0)$	0.0%	0.0%	1.5%	4.6%
$\mathbf{T}_{LLYZ}(\mathbf{y}, \boldsymbol{\theta}_0) - q_\theta$	0.0%	0.0%	1.4%	4.8%
$\mathbf{T}_{LLY}(\mathbf{y}, \boldsymbol{\theta}_0)$	0.0%	0.0%	1.4%	4.4%
	Empirical Power ($\beta^* = 0.1$)			
	$n = 50$	$n = 500$	$n = 2{,}000$	$n = 20{,}000$
LR	9.2%	59.8%	99.4%	100.0%
Wald	9.2%	59.8%	99.4%	100.0%
LM	11.5%	60.3%	99.4%	100.0%
$\mathbf{T}^1_{LYWZ}(\mathbf{y}, \boldsymbol{\theta}_0) + q_\theta$	100.0%	100.0%	100.0%	100.0%
$\mathbf{T}^2_{LYWZ}(\mathbf{y}, \boldsymbol{\theta}_0)$	100.0%	100.0%	100.0%	100.0%
$\mathbf{T}_{LLYZ}(\mathbf{y}, \boldsymbol{\theta}_0) - q_\theta$	100.0%	100.0%	100.0%	100.0%
$\mathbf{T}_{LLY}(\mathbf{y}, \boldsymbol{\theta}_0)$	0.0%	8.4%	97.8%	100.0%
	Empirical Power ($\beta^* = 0.2$)			
	$n = 50$	$n = 500$	$n = 2{,}000$	$n = 20{,}000$
LR	25.5%	99.8%	100.0%	100.0%
Wald	25.8%	99.8%	100.0%	100.0%
LM	28.3%	99.8%	100.0%	100.0%
$\mathbf{T}^1_{LYWZ}(\mathbf{y}, \boldsymbol{\theta}_0) + q_\theta$	100.0%	100.0%	100.0%	100.0%
$\mathbf{T}^2_{LYWZ}(\mathbf{y}, \boldsymbol{\theta}_0)$	100.0%	100.0%	100.0%	100.0%
$\mathbf{T}_{LLYZ}(\mathbf{y}, \boldsymbol{\theta}_0) - q_\theta$	100.0%	100.0%	100.0%	100.0%
$\mathbf{T}_{LLY}(\mathbf{y}, \boldsymbol{\theta}_0)$	0.0%	81.5%	100.0%	100.0%

10.5.2 Hypothesis Testing in Copula Models

In this subsection, we use the Gaussian copula model with a Gaussian margin to show the finite sample performance of the proposed posterior statistics. Let r_{1t}, r_{2t} be two time series random variables specified as follows:

$$
\begin{aligned}
r_{1t} &= \mu_1 + \sigma_1 z_{1t}, \\
r_{2t} &= \mu_2 + \sigma_2 z_{2t}, \\
C(F(r_{1t}), F(r_{2t}); \delta) &= \Phi(r_{1t}, r_{2t}; \rho),
\end{aligned}
$$

where μ_i and σ_i are the mean and the standard deviation of r_{it} and $C(\cdot)$ is the copula function $C(\cdot)$ with the dependence parameter ρ. This model is known to be the same as a bivariate normal distribution with the correlation coefficient being ρ. To simulate the data reasonably, we set $\mu^* = (0.02, 0.03)'$ and the true variance covariance matrix as

$$\Phi^* = \begin{pmatrix} 2 & 2\sqrt{2}\rho^* \\ 2\sqrt{2}\rho^* & 4 \end{pmatrix}, \tag{10.38}$$

where ρ^* is the true value of ρ. We thus test the following hypothesis:

$$H_0: \rho = 0 \quad \text{vs} \quad H_1: \rho \neq 0.$$

In this model, we have parameters $\boldsymbol{\vartheta} = (\mu_1, \mu_2, h_1, h_2, \rho)'$, where $(\mu_1, \mu_2)'$ and $(h_1, h_2)'$ are means and precision for the two random normally distributed variables, respectively, and ρ is of primary interest. The prior distributions for the parameters are set as follows:

$$\begin{aligned} \mu_1 &\sim N(\mu_{10}, \sigma_{10}^2), \quad \mu_2 \sim N(\mu_{20}, \sigma_{20}^2), \\ h_1 &\sim Gamma(s_{10}, r_{10}), \quad h_2 \sim Gamma(s_{20}, r_{20}), \\ \rho &\sim TN(\mu_\rho, \sigma_\rho^2, lb, ub), \end{aligned}$$

where $TN(\cdot)$ is the truncated normal distribution.

The uninformative prior distributions (NP) and informative prior distributions (IP) of the parameters of interest are set as follows:

$$\begin{aligned} &NP: (\mu_{10}, \mu_{20}, \sigma_{10}^2, \sigma_{20}^2, s_{10}, s_{20}, r_{10}, r_{20}, \mu_\rho, \sigma_\rho^2, lb, ub) \\ &= (\mu_1^*, \mu_2^*, 10000, 10000, 0.01, 0.01, 0.02, 0.04, \rho^*, 10000, -1, 1) \end{aligned}$$

$$\begin{aligned} &IP: (\mu_{10}, \mu_{20}, \sigma_{10}^2, \sigma_{20}^2, s_{10}, s_{20}, r_{10}, r_{20}, \mu_\rho, \sigma_\rho^2, lb, ub) \\ &= (\mu_1^*, \mu_2^*, 10000, 10000, 0.01, 0.01, 0.02, 0.04, \rho^*, 0.0009, -1, 1) \end{aligned}$$

To perform a simulation study, we consider three different ρ^* ($\rho^* = 0.0, 0.1, 0.2$) and three different sample sizes $n = 100, 500, 5{,}000$. For each case, we repeat the data generation process 1,000 times independently and report the rejection rate of H_0 based on different statistics at the 5 percent significance level across the 1,000 replications. The empirical size and power of the proposed statistics are reported in Table 10.4 (under uninformative priors) and Table 10.5 (under informative priors).

The results in Table 10.4 exhibit a similar pattern as those in Table 10.2. For the empirical size when the sample size is small (e.g., $n = 100$), marked disagreement among the empirical size of different statistics appears, and some are far away from the nominal size 5 percent (e.g., the empirical size of $\mathbf{T}_{LLYZ}(\mathbf{y}, \boldsymbol{\theta}_0) - q_\theta$ is as large as 13.6 percent, while the empirical size of

Table 10.4 *Empirical size and power of posterior statistics in a Gaussian copula model (NP)*

	Empirical Size ($\rho^* = 0.0$)		
	$n = 100$	$n = 500$	$n = 5{,}00$
LR	5.5%	6.0%	5.7%
Wald	6.3%	6.6%	5.7%
LM	5.5%	6.4%	5.7%
$\mathbf{T}^1_{LYWZ}(\mathbf{y}, \boldsymbol{\theta}_0) + q_\theta$	5.9%	6.4%	5.7%
$\mathbf{T}^2_{LYWZ}(\mathbf{y}, \boldsymbol{\theta}_0)$	5.8%	6.1%	5.5%
$\mathbf{T}_{LLYZ}(\mathbf{y}, \boldsymbol{\theta}_0) - q_\theta$	13.6%	9.4%	6.1%
$\mathbf{T}_{LLY}(\mathbf{y}, \boldsymbol{\theta}_0)$	2.7%	5.4%	5.1%
	Empirical Power ($\rho^* = 0.1$)		
	$n = 100$	$n = 500$	$n = 5{,}000$
LR	15.8%	58.0%	100.0%
Wald	17.0%	58.6%	100.0%
LM	16.1%	58.1%	100.0%
$\mathbf{T}^1_{LYWZ}(\mathbf{y}, \boldsymbol{\theta}_0) + q_\theta$	19.5%	58.9%	100.0%
$\mathbf{T}^2_{LYWZ}(\mathbf{y}, \boldsymbol{\theta}_0)$	15.9%	57.4%	100.0%
$\mathbf{T}_{LLYZ}(\mathbf{y}, \boldsymbol{\theta}_0) - q_\theta$	27.2%	59.2%	100.0%
$\mathbf{T}_{LLY}(\mathbf{y}, \boldsymbol{\theta}_0)$	7.0%	53.0%	100.0%
	Empirical Power ($\rho^* = 0.2$)		
	$n = 100$	$n = 500$	$n = 5{,}000$
LR	55.1%	99.4%	100.0%
Wald	57.4%	99.4%	100.0%
LM	56.3%	99.4%	100.0%
$\mathbf{T}^1_{LYWZ}(\mathbf{y}, \boldsymbol{\theta}_0) + q_\theta$	55.5%	99.4%	100.0%
$\mathbf{T}^2_{LYWZ}(\mathbf{y}, \boldsymbol{\theta}_0)$	53.5%	99.3%	100.0%
$\mathbf{T}_{LLYZ}(\mathbf{y}, \boldsymbol{\theta}_0) - q_\theta$	59.9%	99.3%	100.0%
$\mathbf{T}_{LLY}(\mathbf{y}, \boldsymbol{\theta}_0)$	34.8%	99.0%	100.0%

$\mathbf{T}_{LLY}(\mathbf{y}, \boldsymbol{\theta}_0)$ is as small as 2.7 percent). However, as the sample size increases, the empirical sizes of different statistics reported in this study converge toward each other, being approximately the nominal size of 5 percent. Regarding the empirical power, as the sample size increases, and as ρ^* deviates from the hypothesised value under the null hypothesis, the empirical powers of all statistics in this study approach 100 percent.

Table 10.5 shows the empirical size and power of these statistics in a Gaussian copula model under informative prior distributions (IP), which exhibit similar patterns to that in Table 10.3. The performance of the frequentist

Table 10.5 *Empirical size and power of posterior statistics in a Gaussian copula model (IP)*

	Empirical Size ($\rho^* = 0.0$)			
	$n = 100$	$n = 500$	$n = 5{,}000$	$n = 50{,}000$
LR	5.5%	6.0%	5.7%	5.0%
Wald	6.3%	6.6%	5.7%	5.0%
LM	5.5%	6.4%	5.7%	5.0%
$\mathbf{T}^1_{LYWZ}(\mathbf{y},\boldsymbol{\theta}_0) + q_\theta$	0.1%	0.1%	3.0%	4.7%
$\mathbf{T}^2_{LYWZ}(\mathbf{y},\boldsymbol{\theta}_0)$	0.1%	0.1%	3.3%	4.8%
$\mathbf{T}_{LLYZ}(\mathbf{y},\boldsymbol{\theta}_0) - q_\theta$	0.0%	0.1%	4.0%	5.8%
$\mathbf{T}_{LLY}(\mathbf{y},\boldsymbol{\theta}_0)$	0.0%	0.2%	2.8%	4.5%
	Empirical Power ($\rho^* = 0.1$)			
	$n = 100$	$n = 500$	$n = 5{,}000$	$n = 50{,}000$
LR	15.8%	58.0%	100.0%	100.0%
Wald	17.0%	58.6%	100.0%	100.0%
LM	16.1%	58.1%	100.0%	100.0%
$\mathbf{T}^1_{LYWZ}(\mathbf{y},\boldsymbol{\theta}_0) + q_\theta$	100.0%	100.0%	100.0%	100.0%
$\mathbf{T}^2_{LYWZ}(\mathbf{y},\boldsymbol{\theta}_0)$	100.0%	100.0%	100.0%	100.0%
$\mathbf{T}_{LLYZ}(\mathbf{y},\boldsymbol{\theta}_0) - q_\theta$	100.0%	99.9%	100.0%	100.0%
$\mathbf{T}_{LLY}(\mathbf{y},\boldsymbol{\theta}_0)$	0.0%	9.1%	100.0%	100.0%
	Empirical Power ($\rho^* = 0.2$)			
	$n = 100$	$n = 500$	$n = 5{,}000$	$n = 50{,}000$
LR	55.1%	99.4%	100.0%	100.0%
Wald	57.4%	99.4%	100.0%	100.0%
LM	56.3%	99.4%	100.0%	100.0%
$\mathbf{T}^1_{LYWZ}(\mathbf{y},\boldsymbol{\theta}_0) + q_\theta$	100.0%	100.0%	100.0%	100.0%
$\mathbf{T}^2_{LYWZ}(\mathbf{y},\boldsymbol{\theta}_0)$	100.0%	100.0%	100.0%	100.0%
$\mathbf{T}_{LLYZ}(\mathbf{y},\boldsymbol{\theta}_0) - q_\theta$	100.0%	100.0%	100.0%	100.0%
$\mathbf{T}_{LLY}(\mathbf{y},\boldsymbol{\theta}_0)$	0.0%	76.5%	100.0%	100.0%

LR, *Wald*, *LM* statistics remain the same as those under uninformative prior distributions (NP) reported in Table 10.4. For the posterior statistics, the empirical size and power are strongly affected by strong prior information, particularly under a relatively small sample size. When H_0 is true, the empirical size is distorted and nears 0.0 percent when $n = 100, 500$. As the sample size increases up to 50,000, the empirical sizes of all the posterior statistics increase to near the nominal size of 5.0 percent. When H_1 is true, the empirical powers of $\mathbf{T}^1_{LYWZ}(\mathbf{y},\boldsymbol{\theta}_0)+q_\theta$, $\mathbf{T}^2_{LYWZ}(\mathbf{y},\boldsymbol{\theta}_0)$, and $\mathbf{T}_{LLYZ}(\mathbf{y},\boldsymbol{\theta}_0)-q_\theta$ again increase to 100.0 percent, even with $n = 100$. However, for $\mathbf{T}_{LLY}(\mathbf{y},\boldsymbol{\theta}_0)$, the empirical power first decreases to 0.0 percent ($n = 100$), and then gradually increases to 100.0 percent as the sample size increases.

10.6 Empirical Illustrations

In this section, we demonstrate the application of the suggested test statistics through two prevalent examples in the fields of economics and finance. The initial example involves asset pricing models characterized by a t error distribution. These models not only possess likelihood functions with analytical expressions but can also be reformulated in terms of latent variables. The subsequent example focuses on a Gaussian copula model, which incorporates Gaussian margins.

10.6.1 Hypothesis Testing for Asset Pricing Models with Multivariate t Distribution

Asset pricing models hold significant relevance in contemporary finance, typically operating under the assumption that return distributions follow a normal pattern. However, substantial empirical evidence challenges this assumption, revealing that asset returns often deviate from normality and instead exhibit heavy-tailed characteristics. This discrepancy has prompted researchers to explore asset pricing models incorporating heavy-tailed distributions. Zhou (1993) and Kan and Zhou (2017) have proposed the adoption of the multivariate t distribution as an alternative to the conventional multivariate normal distribution. In line with the principles of efficient market theory, these models posit that the excess premium on assets should not exhibit statistically significant deviations from zero. Additionally, the multivariate t distribution can be reformulated into a scale-mixture format, thereby transforming it into a latent variable model. Thus, based on Zhang et al. (2019), we consider the following asset pricing model, which has two equivalent representations:

$$R_t = \boldsymbol{\alpha} + \boldsymbol{\beta}'\boldsymbol{F}_t + \varepsilon_t, \varepsilon_t \sim t[\mathbf{0}, \boldsymbol{\Sigma}, \nu];$$
$$R_t = \boldsymbol{\alpha} + \boldsymbol{\beta}'\boldsymbol{F}_t + \varepsilon_t, \varepsilon_t \sim N(\mathbf{0}, \boldsymbol{\Sigma}/\omega_t), \omega_t \sim \Gamma\left(\frac{\nu}{2}, \frac{\nu}{2}\right),$$

where R_t is the excess return of portfolio at period t with $N \times 1$ dimension, $\boldsymbol{F}_t$ a $K \times 1$ vector of factor portfolio excess returns, $\boldsymbol{\alpha}$ a $N \times 1$ vector of intercepts, $\boldsymbol{\beta}$ a $N \times K$ vector of scaled covariances, ε_t the random error, and $t = 1, 2, \cdots, n$. For convenience, we restrict $\boldsymbol{\Sigma}$ to be a diagonal matrix with diagonal elements $\sigma_{ii}^2, i = 1, 2, \cdots, N$, and ν to be a known constant as $\nu = 3$. The scale-mixture representation of t distribution is used to write the "model.txt" file that is passed to WinBUGS to generate MCMC outputs from the posterior distribution of parameters.

The data used in this study comprises monthly returns from 25 portfolios, which are formed at the end of each month. These portfolios are the product of intersecting five size-based portfolios (based on market equity, ME) with five portfolios organized according to the book equity to market equity ratio (BE/ME). The explanatory factors used in the study are Fama/French's five factors: market excess return, SMB (Small Minus Big), HML (High Minus Low), RMW (Robust Minus Weak), and CMA (Conservative Minus Aggressive), as detailed in Fama and French (2015). The timeframe for the sample extends from July 1963 to July 2021, resulting in $N = 25$ portfolios, $K = 5$ factors, and $n = 697$ monthly observations. These data are freely available from the data library of Kenneth French.[2]

The task of drawing inferences from asset pricing models has garnered significant interest within the empirical asset pricing research community. A comprehensive review of literature pertaining to Bayesian portfolio analysis has been provided by Avramov and Zhou (2010). In the context of Bayesian inference, it is essential to specify the prior distributions for the parameters involved. In this study, to represent the prior ignorance, we assign some vague conjugate prior distributions:

$$\alpha_i \sim N[0, 100], \beta_{ij} \sim N[0, 100], \sigma_{ii}^2 \sim IG[0.01, 0.0001].$$

In the R language, we use R2WinBUGS to obtain the MCMC outputs and draw 100,000 random observations from the posterior distributions in each model where the first 40,000 are used as the burn-in sample, and the next 60,000 iterations are collected with every third observation as an effective observation. Thus, 20,000 effective observations are considered.

In asset pricing theory, the efficient market theory suggests that the excess premium $\boldsymbol{\alpha}$ should be zero. Thus, we can write this problem as a hypothesis to be tested as:

$$H_0 : \boldsymbol{\alpha} = 0 \times 1_N, H_1 : \boldsymbol{\alpha} \neq 0 \times 1_N,$$

where 1_N is an N-dimensional vector with unit elements.

In section 10.3, we have shown that the threshold values from Bernardo and Rueda (2002) and Li and Yu (2012) are difficult to calibrate. Thus, in this study, we only consider the statistics developed by Li et al. (2015), Li et al. (2022), and Liu et al. (2024). Based on 20,000 MCMC samples, we calculate the four posterior test statistics, $\mathbf{T}_{LLY}(\mathbf{y}, \boldsymbol{\theta}_0)$, $\mathbf{T}_{LLYZ}(\mathbf{y}, \boldsymbol{\theta}_0)$, $\mathbf{T}^1_{LYWZ}(\mathbf{y}, \boldsymbol{\theta}_0)$, and $\mathbf{T}^2_{LYWZ}(\mathbf{y}, \boldsymbol{\theta}_0)$. For more details about computing these test statistics, see Li et al. (2015, 2022) and Liu et al. (2022). We report the results in Table 10.6.

[2] http://mba.tuck.dartmouth.edu/pages/faculty/ken.french/data_library.html

Table 10.6 *Asset pricing testing under a multivariate t distribution*

hypothesis	$\alpha = 0 \times 1_N$
$\mathbf{T}^1_{LYWZ}(\mathbf{y}, \boldsymbol{\theta}_0) + N$	72.23
$\mathbf{T}^2_{LYWZ}(\mathbf{y}, \boldsymbol{\theta}_0)$	72.45
$\mathbf{T}_{LLYZ}(\mathbf{y}, \boldsymbol{\theta}_0) - N$	71.59
$\mathbf{T}_{LLY}(\mathbf{y}, \boldsymbol{\theta}_0)$	71.61

From these results, according to the critical values (37.65) from $\chi^2(25)$ under the 5 percent significance level, all the test statistics reject the null hypothesis. Thus, we can conclude that the mean-variance efficiency does not hold in practice.

10.6.2 Hypothesis Testing for Copula Models

In this subsection, we use the Gaussian copula model with a Gaussian margin to fit real data and perform hypothesis testing based on the proposed posterior statistics. Recalling the simulation study in Section 10.5.2, the model is specified as:

$$\begin{aligned} r_{1t} &= \mu_1 + \sigma_1 z_{1t}, \\ r_{2t} &= \mu_2 + \sigma_2 z_{2t}, \\ C(F(r_{1t}), F(r_{2t}); \delta) &= \Phi(r_{1t}, r_{2t}; \rho), \end{aligned}$$

where r_{1t} and r_{2t} are now daily log returns on the S&P 100 and S&P 600 indices at time t, μ_i, σ_i are mean and standard deviation of r_{it}, respectively, $i = 1, 2$. $\Phi(\cdot)$ is the cumulative density function of bivariate normal distribution. The log likelihood function at time t is:

$$\ln L_t = -\ln 2\pi - \frac{1}{2}\ln\left(\frac{1-\rho^2}{h_1 h_2}\right) - \frac{z_{1t}^2 + z_{2t}^2 - 2\rho z_{1t} z_{2t}}{2(1-\rho^2)},$$

where $h_i = \frac{1}{\sigma_i^2}$ is the precision parameter, and $z_{it} = (r_{it} - \mu_i)h_i^{1/2}$. The required parameters are $\boldsymbol{\vartheta} = (\mu_1, h_1, \mu_2, h_2, \rho)'$; the first four are parameters related to the normal marginal distributions, and the last one is for the copula function.

The data used in this study are daily percentage returns on the S&P 100 and S&P 600 Indices from August 17, 1995 to September 22, 2021; thus, $T = 6{,}122$. We are interested in the dependence between the two series of index returns. Based on the Gaussian copula model with a Gaussian margin, the hypothesis testing problem can be formulated as:

$$H_0 : \rho = 0, H_1 : \rho \neq 0.$$

Table 10.7 *Posterior mean and standard error of parameters in a Gaussian copula model*

Parameters	μ_1	h_1	μ_2	h_2	ρ
Posterior Means	0.0361	0.6765	0.0475	0.4938	0.8354
SE	0.0158	0.0116	0.0184	0.0087	0.0036

Table 10.8 *Dependence testing based on a Gaussian copula model*

hypothesis	$\rho = 0$
$\mathbf{T}^1_{LYWZ}(\mathbf{y}, \boldsymbol{\theta}_0) + 1$	7333.372
$\mathbf{T}^2_{LYWZ}(\mathbf{y}, \boldsymbol{\theta}_0)$	7333.244
$\mathbf{T}_{LLYZ}(\mathbf{y}, \boldsymbol{\theta}_0) - 1$	53074.090
$\mathbf{T}_{LLY}(\mathbf{y}, \boldsymbol{\theta}_0)$	344.023

We assign the following prior distributions on parameters:

$$\mu_i \sim N(0, 25), \quad i = 1, 2,$$
$$h_i \sim Gamma(0.1, 1), \quad i = 1, 2,$$
$$\rho \sim TN[0, 100, -1, 1].$$

We iterate 100,000 times starting at the initial value $\theta_0 = (0, 1, 0, 1, 0)'$, and burn in the first 40,000 of the chain. For the remaining 60,000 observations, we take one of every three observations and finally obtain an effective MCMC output of sample size 20,000 for each parameter. Based on this MCMC output, we report the parameter estimation results based on the MCMC output in Table 10.6 and the values of the proposed posterior statistics in Table 10.7.

According to the posterior statistics shown in Table 10.7, all four posterior statistics strongly reject the null hypothesis that the two series of index returns are uncorrelated at the 5 percent significance level. This result is consistent with the expectations that the two indices (SP100, SP600) returns are naturally correlated with each other by construction. The estimation result for ρ in Table 10.6, which is 0.8354 with a relatively small standard error (0.0036), also provides strong evidence against the null hypothesis that assumes $\rho = 0$.

10.7 Discussion and Future Research

In this chapter, we review several statistics for hypothesis testing, which can be regarded as the Bayesian version of the "trinity" of test statistics widely used in the frequentist domain, the LR test, the LM test, and the Wald test.

Their asymptotic distributions are discussed based on a set of regular conditions. We show that these approaches have good theoretical properties and do not require tedious additional computations. We also demonstrate the methods using econometric models with simulation studies and real examples.

Bibliography

Avramov, D. and G. Zhou (2010). Bayesian portfolio analysis. *Annual Review of Financial Economics 2*(1), 25–47.

Bartlett, M. (1957). A comment on D. V. Lindley's statistical paradox. *Biometrika 44*, 533–534.

Berger, J. O. (1985). *Statistical decision theory and Bayesian analysis* (2 ed.). Springer Science & Business Media.

Berger, J. O. and L. R. Pericchi (1996). The intrinsic Bayes factor for model selection and prediction. *Journal of the American Statistical Association 91*(433), 109–122.

Bernardo, J. M. and R. Rueda (2002). Bayesian hypothesis testing: A reference approach. *International Statistical Review 70*(3), 351–372.

Bernardo, J. M. and A. F. Smith (2009). *Bayesian theory* (2 ed.), Volume 405. John Wiley & Sons Canada, Limited.

Breusch, T. S. and A. R. Pagan (1980). The Lagrange multiplier test and its applications to model specification in econometrics. *The Review of Economic Studies 47*(1), 239–253.

Chen, X., T. M. Christensen, and E. Tamer (2018). Monte Carlo confidence sets for identified sets. *Econometrica 86*(6), 1965–2018.

Chernozhukov, V. and H. Hong (2003). An MCMC approach to classical estimation. *Journal of Econometrics 115*(2), 293–346.

Chib, S. (1995). Marginal likelihood from the Gibbs output. *Journal of the American Statistical Association 90*(432), 1313–1321.

Chopin, N. and O. Papaspiliopoulos (2020). *An Introduction to Sequential Monte Carlo*. Springer Series in Statistics.

Dempster, A. P., N. M. Laird, and D. B. Rubin (1977). Maximum likelihood from incomplete data via the em algorithm. *Journal of the Royal Statistical Society: Series B (Methodological) 39*(1), 1–22.

Engle, R. F. (1984). Wald, likelihood ratio, and Lagrange multiplier tests in econometrics. *Handbook of Econometrics 2*, 775–826.

Fama, E. F. and K. R. French (2015). A five-factor asset pricing model. *Journal of Financial Economics 116*(1), 1–22.

Friel, N. and A. N. Pettitt (2008). Marginal likelihood estimation via power posteriors. *Journal of the Royal Statistical Society: Series B (Statistical Methodology) 70*(3), 589–607.

Gallant, A. R. and H. White (1988). *A unified theory of estimation and inference for nonlinear dynamic models*. Blackwell.

Gamerman, D. and H. F. Lopes (2006). *Markov Chain Monte Carlo: Stochastic Simulation for Bayesian Inference* (2 ed.). Taylor & Francis.

Geyer, C. J. (1992). Practical Markov chain Monte Carlo (with discussion). *Statistical Science 7*, 473–511.

Han, C. and B. P. Carlin (2001). Markov chain Monte Carlo methods for computing Bayes factors: A comparative review. *Journal of the American Statistical Association 96*(455), 1122–1132.

Jeffreys, H. (1961). *Theory of Probability* (3 ed.). Oxford University Press.

Kan, R. and G. Zhou (2017). Modelling non-normality using multivariate t: Implications for asset pricing. *China Finance Review International* 7(1), 2–32.

Kass, R. E. and A. E. Raftery (1995). Bayes factor. *Journal of the Americana Statistical Association 90*(430), 773–795.

Kline, B. and E. Tamer (2016). Bayesian inference in a class of partially identified models. *Quantitative Economics* 7(2), 329–366.

Li, Y., X. B. Liu, and J. Yu (2015). A Bayesian chi-squared test for hypothesis testing. *Journal of Econometrics 189*(1), 54–69.

Li, Y., N. Wang, and J. Yu (2023). Improved marginal likelihood estimation via power posteriors and importance sampling. *234*(1), 28–52

Li, Y., N. L. Wang, J. Yu, and Y. Zhang (2022). Hypothesis testing using posterior-test-based bayes factors. Working paper.

Li, Y. and J. Yu (2012). Bayesian hypothesis testing in latent variable models. *Journal of Econometrics 166*, 237–246.

Li, Y., S. K. Mallick, N. Wang, J. Yu and T. Zeng (2024). Deviance Information Criterion for Bayesian Model Selection: Theoretical Justification and Applications. Working Paper.

Li, Y., T. Zeng, and J. Yu (2014). A new approach to Bayesian hypothesis testing. *Journal of Econometrics 178*, 602–612.

Liao, Y. and A. Simoni (2019). Bayesian inference for partially identified smooth convex models. *Journal of Econometrics 211*(2), 338–360.

Lindley, D. V. (1957). A statistical paradox. *Biometrika 44*(1/2), 187–192.

Liu, X., Y. Li, J. Yu, and T. Zeng (2022). Posterior-based Wald-type statistics for hypothesis testing. *Journal of Econometrics 230*(1), 83–113.

Moon, H. R. and F. Schorfheide (2012). Bayesian and frequentist inference in partially identified models. *Econometrica 80*(2), 755–782.

O'Hagan, A. (1991). Discussion on posterior Bayes factors (by M. Aitkin). *Journal of Royal Statistic Society B 53*, 136.

O'Hagan, A. (1995). Fractional bayes factors for model comparison. *Journal of the Royal Statistical Society: Series B (Methodological) 57*(1), 99–118.

Pishro-Nik, H. (2016). *Introduction to probability, statistics, and random processes*. Kappa Research, LLC.

Poirier, D. J. (1995). *Intermediate statistics and econometrics: A comparative approach*. The Massachusetts Institute of Technology Press.

Robert, C. P. (1993). A note on Jeffreys–Lindley paradox. *Statistica Sinica 3*(2), 601–608.

Robert, C. P. (2007). *The Bayesian choice: From decision-theoretic foundations to computational implementation*, Volume 2. Springer.

Skaug, H. J. and J. Yu (2014). A flexible and automated likelihood based framework for inference in stochastic volatility models. *Computational Statistics and Data Analysis 76*, 642–654.

Spiegelhalter, D. J., N. G. Best, B. P. Carlin, and A. Van Der Linde (2002). Bayesian measures of model complexity and fit. *Journal of the Royal Statistical Society: Series B (Statistical Methodology) 64*(4), 583–639.

Wakefield, J. (2013). *Bayesian and frequentist regression Methods*, Volume 23. Springer Science & Business Media.

White, H. (1987). *Specification testing in dynamic models*, Volume 1. Cambridge University Press.

Wooldridge, J. M. (1994). Estimation and inference for dependent processes. *Handbook of Econometrics 4*, 2639–2738.

Zhang, H., N. Wang, Y. Li, and Y. Zhan (2019). Bayesian asset pricing testing under multivariate t-distribution. *Applied Economics Letters 26*(11), 898–901.

Zhou, G. (1993). Asset-pricing tests under alternative distributions. *The Journal of Finance 48*(5), 1927–1942.

11 Posterior-Based Specification Testing and Model Selection

TAO ZENG *Zhejiang University*

11.1 Introduction

In many models commonly used in economics and finance, obtaining maximum likelihood estimates (MLE) or constructing nonparametric estimates is not straightforward. These models include, but are not limited to, latent variable models and structural dynamic choice models. Due to the challenges in applying these frequentist methods, there's a growing interest in Bayesian posterior methods like Markov chain Monte Carlo (MCMC) and Sequential Monte Carlo (SMC) for posterior analysis of econometric models. With the rapid advancement in computing power, fitting increasingly complex models using MCMC or SMC has become more feasible. Once the MCMC and SMC outputs are available, two critical questions emerge. The first is about conducting specification tests of the model, and the second involves comparing alternative models, which may not be nested. Specification testing and model selection are crucial in empirical studies, making posterior-based responses to these questions vital in practice.

Li et al. (2018) introduced two novel specification tests based on posterior outputs. The first test, known as BIMT, is a posterior-based version of IOS_A from Presnell and Boos (2004), with a normal asymptotic null distribution. This test does not require specifying a model in the alternative hypothesis. The second test, named BMT, is inspired by the power enhancement technique from Fan et al. (2015), based on model expansion strategy. It combines a component (termed J_1) that tests a null point hypothesis in an expanded model and a power enhancement component (named J_0) derived from the first test. It's shown that J_0 converges to zero when the null model is correctly specified and diverges when it's misspecified. Also, J_1 is asymptotically χ^2-distributed, indicating that the test is asymptotically pivotal when the null model is correctly specified. The second test has several advantages: (i) its size distortion is small, eliminating the need for bootstrap methods; (ii) it's easy to compute from posterior outputs, making it applicable to a wide range of models, including latent variable models and structural dynamic choice models where ML and bootstrap methods are challenging; and (iii) it helps identify the source of misspecification when the test statistic rejects the null model specification and J_1 shows a large value.

For the purpose of model selection, there are two key metrics predominantly utilized within the Bayesian framework. The first metric is known as the Bayes factor (BF), which is instrumental in comparing the posterior probabilities of various proposed models, each conditioned on the observed data. While the Bayes factor is lauded for its statistical interpretability, it is not without its significant theoretical and computational challenges. A notable issue is its undefined nature in the context of improper priors. Additionally, the Bayes factor is vulnerable to the Jeffreys–Lindley–Bartlett's paradox, which manifests as a tendency to erroneously favor the null hypothesis, particularly when employing a vague prior. Furthermore, for numerous models, the calculation of posterior model probabilities, and consequently the Bayes factor, poses considerable computational difficulties.

The second method is the deviance information criterion (DIC) of Spiegelhalter et al. (2002). DIC has been interpreted as a Bayesian version of the well-known Akaike information criterion (AIC) of Akaike (1973). Like AIC, DIC is used to select a model that minimizes a plug-in predictive loss. Compared with the BF, DIC can be well defined under improper priors and immune to Jeffreys–Lindley–Bartlett's paradox. More importantly, DIC is easier to calculate from posterior output comparing to the BF, especially in the context of latent variable models. Hence, it has been used in many applications. For example, it has been widely applied to compare alternative specifications in stochastic volatility models (e.g. Chan and Grant (2016), and Berg et al. (2004)), and VAR models (e.g. Chan and Eisenstat (2018)). However, Spiegelhalter et al. (2014) pointed out that DIC lacks formal theoretical justification.

Li et al. (2024) offered a frequentist rationale for DIC, demonstrating its role as an asymptotically unbiased estimator for the expected Kullback–Leibler (KL) divergence. This divergence is measured between the data-generating process (DGP) and a predictive distribution that incorporates the posterior mean. The validation of this approach hinges on three critical conditions: the applicability of the Bernstein–von Mises theorem, the validity of standard maximum likelihood (ML) large sample theory (emphasizing consistency and asymptotic normality), and the correct specification of all candidate models, at least in an asymptotic sense. However, these conditions often fail to materialize in practical scenarios. Li et al. (2020) highlighted the limitations of the Bernstein–von Mises theorem and standard ML large sample theory, especially concerning latent variables in latent variable models, when DIC is computed using the conditional likelihood. This refers to the likelihood of observed data given the original model parameter and latent variables. Consequently, Li et al. (2020) introduced an alternative version of DIC, termed DIC_L, specifically for the comparison of latent variable models. Under certain regularity conditions, a frequentist justification for DIC_L was provided, paralleling the justification for DIC as presented in Li et al. (2024). Additionally, Li et al. (2020) proposed a different version of DIC, named DIC_M, for the comparison of misspecified models. DIC_M is posited as a Bayesian counterpart to the Takeuchi Information Criterion (TIC) as described in Takeuchi (1976).

The rest of the chapter is organized as follows. Section 11.2 reviews the posterior-based specification tests and their asymptotic properties. Section 11.3 presents an overview of the posterior-based model selection criteria, including the DIC method, the DIC_L for latent variable models, and the DIC_M for misspecified models. Section 11.4 summarizes and concludes.

11.2 Posterior-Based Specification Tests

It is well-known in the literature that, when the ML method is applied to estimate a candidate model, several specification tests may be used. These include the information matrix test (IMT) of White (1982)), the in-and-out likelihood ratio (IOS), and the IOS_A tests of Presnell and Boos (2004). Unfortunately, these tests are not directly applicable to estimates based on posterior output.

Recently, Li et al. (2018) proposed two posterior-based specification tests. One of them can be regarded as a posterior-based version of IOS. The other is constructed by the power enhancement technique of Fan et al. (2015) that can assess the validity of the model specification and identify the source of model misspecification if the null model is rejected.

First, we define some notation. Let $\mathbf{y} = (y_1, \ldots, y_n)'$ be the observed data from a probability measure Pr_0 on the probability space $(\Omega, F, \mathrm{Pr}_0)$. Let model Pr be a collection of candidate models indexed by parameters $\boldsymbol{\theta}$ whose dimension is P. Let $\mathrm{Pr}_{\boldsymbol{\theta}}$ denote Pr indexed by $\boldsymbol{\theta}$. Following White (1987), if there exists $\boldsymbol{\theta}$, such that $\mathrm{Pr}_0 \in \mathrm{Pr}_{\boldsymbol{\theta}}$, we say the model Pr is correctly specified. However, if for all $\boldsymbol{\theta}$, $\mathrm{Pr}_0 \notin \mathrm{Pr}_{\boldsymbol{\theta}}$, we say the model Pr is misspecified. We would like to test whether or not the model in question is correctly specified. Let $g(\mathbf{y})$ be the data-generating process (DGP) of $\mathbf{y}$.

Let $\mathbf{y}^t = (y_0, y_1, \ldots, y_t)$ for any $0 \le t \le n$ and $l_t\left(\mathbf{y}^t, \boldsymbol{\theta}\right) = \ln p(\mathbf{y}^t|\boldsymbol{\theta}) - \ln p(\mathbf{y}^{t-1}|\boldsymbol{\theta})$ be the log-likelihood for the tth observation for any $1 \le t \le n$. Often, we simply write $l_t\left(\mathbf{y}^t, \boldsymbol{\theta}\right)$ as $l_t(\boldsymbol{\theta})$ when there is no ambiguity so that $\ln p(\mathbf{y}|\boldsymbol{\theta}) = \sum_{t=1}^{n} l_t(\boldsymbol{\theta})$. It is important to note that in our definition of the log-likelihood, we ignore the initial condition $\ln p(y_0)$. For weakly dependent data, the impact of the initial condition is asymptotically negligible. We define $l_t^{(j)}(\boldsymbol{\theta})$ to be the jth derivative of $l_t(\boldsymbol{\theta})$ and $l_t^{(j)}(\boldsymbol{\theta}) = l_t(\boldsymbol{\theta})$ when $j = 0$. Additionally, we define

$$\begin{aligned} \mathrm{s}(\mathbf{y}^t, \boldsymbol{\theta}) &= \frac{\partial \ln p(\mathbf{y}^t|\boldsymbol{\theta})}{\partial \boldsymbol{\theta}} = \sum_{i=1}^{t} l_i^{(1)}(\boldsymbol{\theta}), \; \mathrm{s}_t(\boldsymbol{\theta}) = l_t^{(1)}(\boldsymbol{\theta}) \\ &= \mathrm{s}(\mathbf{y}^t, \boldsymbol{\theta}) - \mathrm{s}(\mathbf{y}^{t-1}, \boldsymbol{\theta}), \end{aligned}$$

$$\mathbf{h}(\mathbf{y}^t,\boldsymbol{\theta}) = \frac{\partial^2 \ln p(\mathbf{y}^t|\boldsymbol{\theta})}{\partial\boldsymbol{\theta}\partial\boldsymbol{\theta}'} = \sum_{i=1}^{t} l_i^{(2)}(\boldsymbol{\theta}),\ \mathbf{h}_t(\boldsymbol{\theta}) = l_t^{(2)}(\boldsymbol{\theta})$$
$$= \mathbf{h}(\mathbf{y}^t,\boldsymbol{\theta}) - \mathbf{h}(\mathbf{y}^{t-1},\boldsymbol{\theta}),$$
$$\bar{\mathbf{H}}_n(\boldsymbol{\theta}) = \frac{1}{n}\sum_{t=1}^{n}\mathbf{h}_t(\boldsymbol{\theta}), \mathbf{H}_n(\boldsymbol{\theta}) = \int \bar{\mathbf{H}}_n(\boldsymbol{\theta})g(\mathbf{y})\,dy, \bar{\mathbf{s}}(\boldsymbol{\theta}) = \frac{1}{n}\sum_{t=1}^{n}\mathbf{s}_t(\boldsymbol{\theta}),$$
$$\mathbf{B}_n(\boldsymbol{\theta}) = Var\left[\frac{1}{\sqrt{n}}\sum_{t=1}^{n} l_t^{(1)}(\boldsymbol{\theta})\right], L_n(\boldsymbol{\theta}) = \ln p(\boldsymbol{\theta}|\mathbf{y}), L_n^{(j)}(\boldsymbol{\theta})$$
$$= \partial^j \ln p(\boldsymbol{\theta}|\mathbf{y})/\partial\boldsymbol{\theta}^j,$$
$$\bar{\mathbf{J}}_n(\boldsymbol{\theta}) = \frac{1}{n}\sum_{t=1}^{n}[\mathbf{s}_t(\boldsymbol{\theta}) - \bar{\mathbf{s}}(\boldsymbol{\theta})][\mathbf{s}_t(\boldsymbol{\theta}) - \bar{\mathbf{s}}(\boldsymbol{\theta})]', \mathbf{J}_n(\boldsymbol{\theta}) = \int \bar{\mathbf{J}}_n(\boldsymbol{\theta})g(\mathbf{y})\,dy.$$

We impose the following regularity conditions which will be used throughout the chapter.

Assumption 1: $\boldsymbol{\Theta} \subset R^P$ is compact.

Assumption 2: $\{y_t\}_{t=1}^{\infty}$ satisfies the strong mixing condition with the mixing coefficient $\alpha(m) = O\left(m^{\frac{-2r}{r-2}-\varepsilon}\right)$ for some $\varepsilon > 0$ and $r > 2$.

Assumption 3: For all t, $l_t(\boldsymbol{\theta})$ satisfies the standard measurability and continuity condition, and the eight-times differentiability condition on $F_{-\infty}^t \times \boldsymbol{\Theta}$ where $F_{-\infty}^t = \sigma(y_t, y_{t-1}, \cdots)$.

Assumption 4: For $j = 0, 1, 2$, for any $\boldsymbol{\theta}, \boldsymbol{\theta}' \in \Theta$, $\left\| l_t^{(j)}(\boldsymbol{\theta}) - l_t^{(j)}(\boldsymbol{\theta}')\right\| \leq c_t^j(\mathbf{y}^t)\left\|\boldsymbol{\theta} - \boldsymbol{\theta}'\right\|$ in probability, where $c_t^j(\mathbf{y}^t)$ is a positive random variable with $\frac{1}{n}\sum_{t=1}^{n}\left(c_t^j(\mathbf{y}^t) - E\left(c_t^j(\mathbf{y}^t)\right)\right) \xrightarrow{p} 0$ and $\sup_t \left\|c_t^j(\mathbf{y}^t)\right\|_1 < \infty$.

Assumption 5: For $j = 0, 1, \ldots, 8$, there exists a function $M_t(\mathbf{y}^t)$ such that for all $\boldsymbol{\theta} \in \boldsymbol{\Theta}$, $l_t^{(j)}(\boldsymbol{\theta})$ exists, $\sup_{\theta\in\Theta}\left\|l_t^{(j)}(\boldsymbol{\theta})\right\| \leqslant M_t(\mathbf{y}^t)$, and $\sup_t \left\|M_t(\mathbf{y}^t)\right\|_{r+\delta} \leq M < \infty$ for some $\delta > 0$, where r is the same as that in Assumption 2.

Assumption 6: $\left\{l_t^{(j)}(\boldsymbol{\theta})\right\}$ is L_2-near epoch dependent with respect to $\{y_t\}$ of size -1 for $0 \leqslant j \leqslant 1$ and $-\frac{1}{2}$ for $j = 2$ uniformly on $\boldsymbol{\Theta}$.

Assumption 7: Let $\boldsymbol{\theta}_n^p$ be the pseudo-true value that minimizes the KL loss between the DGP and the candidate model

$$\boldsymbol{\theta}_n^p = \arg\min_{\boldsymbol{\theta}\in\Theta} \frac{1}{n}\int \ln\frac{g(\mathbf{y})}{p(\mathbf{y}|\boldsymbol{\theta})}g(\mathbf{y})d\mathbf{y},$$

where $\{\boldsymbol{\theta}_n^p\}$ is the sequence of minimizers interior to Θ uniformly in n and $\lim_{n\to\infty}\boldsymbol{\theta}_n^p \in \mathrm{Int}(\boldsymbol{\Theta})$. For all $\varepsilon > 0$,

$$\lim_{n\to\infty} \sup \sup_{\boldsymbol{\Theta}\backslash N\left(\boldsymbol{\theta}_{n}^{p},\varepsilon\right)} \frac{1}{n}\sum_{t=1}^{n} \left\{E\left[l_t\left(\boldsymbol{\theta}\right)\right] - E\left[l_t\left(\boldsymbol{\theta}_n^p\right)\right]\right\} < 0, \tag{11.1}$$

where $N\left(\boldsymbol{\theta}_n^p, \varepsilon\right)$ is the open ball of radius ε around $\boldsymbol{\theta}_n^p$.

Assumption 8: The sequence $\left\{\mathbf{H}_n\left(\boldsymbol{\theta}_n^p\right)\right\}$ is negative definite and the sequence $\left\{\mathbf{B}_n\left(\boldsymbol{\theta}_n^p\right)\right\}$ is positive definite, both uniformly in n.

Assumption 9: The prior density $p\left(\boldsymbol{\theta}\right)$ is thrice continuously differentiable and $0 < p\left(\boldsymbol{\theta}_n^p\right) < \infty$ uniformly in n. Moreover, there exists an n^* such that, for any $n > n^*$, the posterior distribution $p\left(\boldsymbol{\theta}\,|\mathbf{y}\right)$ is proper and $\int \|\boldsymbol{\theta}\|^2 p\left(\boldsymbol{\theta}\,|\mathbf{y}\right) d\boldsymbol{\theta} < \infty$.

Assumption 1 is the compactness condition of the parameter space. Assumption 2 implies weak dependence in y_t. Assumption 3 is the continuity and measurability condition for l_t. Assumption 4 is the Lipschitz condition for l_t first introduced in Andrews (1987) to develop the uniform law of large numbers for dependent and heterogeneous stochastic processes. Assumption 5 contains the dominance condition for l_t. Assumption 6 is the weak dependence condition for l_t, especially for the case where l_t is a measurable function of the distant past or future of a mixing process. Assumptions 4–6 imply that $\frac{1}{n}\sum_{t=1}^{n} E\left[l_t\left(\boldsymbol{\theta}\right)\right]$ is continuous on $\boldsymbol{\Theta}$ uniformly in n and the likelihood function $\frac{1}{n}\sum_{t=1}^{n} l_t\left(\boldsymbol{\theta}\right)$ converges to $\frac{1}{n}\sum_{t=1}^{n} E\left[l_t\left(\boldsymbol{\theta}\right)\right]$ uniformly on $\boldsymbol{\Theta}$. Assumption 7 is the identification condition used in Gallant and White (1988). Assumptions 1–7 are sufficient conditions for the consistency of the standard ML estimator, and the asymptotic normality can be ensured by adding Assumption 8. These assumptions are widely recognized as essential prerequisites for formulating ML theory, particularly for data that is dependent and heterogeneous; see, for example, Gallant and White (1988) and Wooldridge (1994). The first part of Assumption 9 ensures that when the sample size increases, the likelihood information dominates the prior information so that the prior information can be ignored asymptotically, the second part ensures the existence of the second-order posterior moment.

11.2.1 Posterior-Based IOS test

One of the earliest specification tests is proposed by White (1982) based on the information matrix equivalence. Under the null hypothesis that the model is correctly specified, it can be shown that $\mathbf{H}_n(\boldsymbol{\theta}_n^p) + \mathbf{J}_n(\boldsymbol{\theta}_n^p) = 0$. Let $d(y_t, \boldsymbol{\theta}) = vech\left[\mathbf{h}_t(\boldsymbol{\theta}) + \mathbf{s}_t(\boldsymbol{\theta})\mathbf{s}_t'(\boldsymbol{\theta})\right]$ where *vech* is the columnwise vectorization with the upper portion excluded. White (1982) proposed the following information matrix test

$$\mathrm{IMT} = nD_n\left(\hat{\theta}\right) U_n^{-1}\left(\hat{\theta}\right) D_n\left(\hat{\theta}\right), \tag{11.2}$$

where $\hat{\boldsymbol{\theta}}$ is the MLE of $\boldsymbol{\theta}$, and

$$D_n\left(\hat{\boldsymbol{\theta}}\right) = \frac{1}{n}\sum_{t=1}^{n} d\left(y_t, \hat{\boldsymbol{\theta}}\right), \quad \dot{D}_n = \frac{\partial D_n}{\partial \boldsymbol{\theta}},$$

$$U_n\left(\hat{\boldsymbol{\theta}}\right) = \frac{1}{n}\sum_{t=1}^{n} \nu_t\left(\hat{\boldsymbol{\theta}}\right)\nu_t\left(\hat{\boldsymbol{\theta}}\right)',$$

$$\nu_t\left(\hat{\boldsymbol{\theta}}\right) = d\left(y_t, \hat{\boldsymbol{\theta}}\right) - \dot{D}_n\left(\hat{\boldsymbol{\theta}}\right)\bar{\mathbf{H}}_n^{-1}\left(\hat{\boldsymbol{\theta}}\right)\mathbf{s}_t\left(\hat{\boldsymbol{\theta}}\right).$$

Under a set of regularity conditions, White (1982) demonstrated that IMT converges in distribution to a chi-squared (χ^2) distribution as the sample size n approaches infinity, provided the null hypothesis holds.

In a different approach, Presnell and Boos (2004) introduced the "in-and-out-of-sample" (IOS) likelihood ratio test test, an alternative testing method, designed for models with independent and identically distributed (i.i.d.) observations,

$$\mathrm{IOS} = \ln \frac{\prod_{t=1}^{n} p\left(y_t|\hat{\boldsymbol{\theta}}\right)}{\prod_{t=1}^{n} p\left(y_t|\hat{\boldsymbol{\theta}}^{(t)}\right)} = \sum_{t=1}^{n}\left[\ln p\left(y_t|\hat{\boldsymbol{\theta}}\right) - \ln p\left(y_t|\hat{\boldsymbol{\theta}}^{(t)}\right)\right],$$

where $\hat{\boldsymbol{\theta}}^{(t)}$ be the MLE of $\boldsymbol{\theta}$ when the tth observation, y_t, is deleted from the full sample. From the predictive perspective, the single likelihood $p\left(y_t|\hat{\boldsymbol{\theta}}^{(t)}\right)$ can be regarded as the predictive likelihood of y_t by all the other observations. It has been shown that the asymptotic form of IOS is

$$\mathrm{IOS}_A = \mathrm{tr}\left[-\bar{\mathbf{H}}_n^{-1}\left(\hat{\boldsymbol{\theta}}\right)\bar{\mathbf{J}}_n\left(\hat{\boldsymbol{\theta}}\right)\right], \tag{11.3}$$

and $\mathrm{IOS} - \mathrm{IOS}_A = o_p\left(n^{-1/2}\right)$. Like IMT, IOS_A also compares $\bar{\mathbf{H}}_n\left(\hat{\boldsymbol{\theta}}\right)$ with $\bar{\mathbf{J}}_n\left(\hat{\boldsymbol{\theta}}\right)$, but in a ratio form instead of in an additive form. Under the null hypothesis, $\mathrm{IOS}_A \xrightarrow{p} P$ and $n^{1/2}\left(\mathrm{IOS}_A - P\right)$ converges to a normal distribution with zero mean and finite variance.

IMT, IOS, and IOS_A are all prone to significant bias distortions when their test critical values are derived from asymptotic distributions. This issue arises due to the inadequate approximation of these asymptotic distributions to their finite sample equivalents. In an effort to mitigate the size distortion inherent in these tests, the implementation of bootstrap methods for acquiring critical values has been suggested. However, a notable drawback of these bootstrap methods is their computational intensity, which can be prohibitive in numerous instances.

Let $V\left(\bar{\theta}\right) = \int \left(\theta - \bar{\theta})(\theta - \bar{\theta}\right)' p(\theta|\mathrm{y})\,\mathrm{d}\theta$, a natural posterior-based informative matrix test statistic can be defined as:

$$\mathrm{BIMT} = \mathbf{tr}\left[nV\left(\bar{\theta}\right)\bar{\mathbf{J}}_n\left(\bar{\theta}\right)\right] = n\int \left(\theta - \bar{\theta}\right)'\bar{\mathbf{J}}_n\left(\bar{\theta}\right)\left(\theta - \bar{\theta}\right)p(\theta|\mathrm{y})\,\mathrm{d}\theta, \tag{11.4}$$

Based on Assumptions 1–10, Li et al. (2018) showed that under the null hypothesis,

$$\mathrm{BIMT} = \mathrm{IOS}_A + O_p\left(n^{-1}\right), \tag{11.5}$$

because

$$V\left(\bar{\theta}\right) = -\frac{1}{n}\bar{\mathbf{H}}_n^{-1}(\bar{\theta}) + O_p(n^{-2}),$$

see Li et al. (2020) for detailed proof. From (11.5), if the model is correctly specified,

$$\mathrm{BIMT} = P + O_p\left(n^{-1/2}\right) + O_p\left(n^{-1}\right) = P + O_p\left(n^{-1/2}\right),$$

since $n^{1/2}\left(\mathrm{IOS}_A - P\right)$ converges to a normal distribution Assumptions 1–8. Then it is straightforward to show that

$$n^{1/2}\left(\mathrm{BIMT}/P - 1\right) = n^{1/2}\left(\mathrm{IOS}_A/P - 1\right) + o_p(1),$$

so $n^{1/2}\left(\mathrm{BIMT}/P - 1\right)$ has the same asymptotic distribution as $n^{1/2}\left(\mathrm{IOS}_A/P - 1\right)$. Hence, BIMT may be regarded as the posterior-based version of IOS_A. Unfortunately but not surprisingly, BIMT inherits the size distortion problem of IOS_A and bootstrap methods must be used.

11.2.2 Posterior-Based Specification Test with Power Enhancement

To solve the size distortion and the computational problem of BIMT, Li et al. (2018) proposed a new posterior-based misspecification test (denoted as BMT) by using the power enhancement technique of Fan et al. (2015).

Power Enhancement Technique

Fan et al. (2015) addressed the hypothesis testing issue for $H_0 : \theta = \mathbf{0}$, where θ represents a high-dimensional vector. In this context, the alternative hypothesis H_1 is defined as sparse, meaning that only a few components are responsible for the deviation from the null hypothesis. They found that conventional tests, like the Wald test, exhibit limited power in this scenario. To counter this, they proposed an additional power enhancement component, which remains zero under the null hypothesis with a high probability but increases rapidly under sparse alternative conditions. The newly formulated test statistic, denoted as J, is expressed as

$$J = J_0 + J_1,$$

where J_1 is a standard asymptotically pivotal test statistic, such as the Wald test, and J_0 is the power enhancement component. The component J_0 must fulfill three criteria: (a) it should be non-negative almost surely; (b) under H_0, the probability of J_0 equalling zero should converge to 1; (c) under certain conditions within H_1, J_0 should diverge in probability. These properties ensure that J is at least as powerful as J_1 (property a), the asymptotic distribution of J under H_0 is primarily influenced by J_1, maintaining the size of J comparable to J_1 asymptotically (property b), and the power of J surpasses that of J_1 (property c).

Posterior-Based Specification Test with Power Enhancement
Similar to Fan et al. (2015), the BMT test incorporates two elements, J_1 and J_0. In the development of J_1, Li et al. (2018) expand $p(\mathbf{y}|\boldsymbol{\theta})$, the original model, to a larger model denoted by $p(\mathbf{y}|\boldsymbol{\theta}_L)$ where $\boldsymbol{\theta}_L = \left(\boldsymbol{\theta}', \boldsymbol{\theta}_E'\right)'$ with $\boldsymbol{\theta}_E$ being a P_E-dimensional vector. So the expanded model $p(\mathbf{y}|\boldsymbol{\theta}_L)$ nests the original model $p(\mathbf{y}|\boldsymbol{\theta})$. In this expanded framework, if the original model specification $p(\mathbf{y}|\boldsymbol{\theta})$ is correct, then the true value of the extension parameters $\boldsymbol{\theta}_E$ would be zero. Let

$$\mathbf{s}(\mathbf{y}, \boldsymbol{\theta}_L) = \frac{\partial \ln p(\mathbf{y}|\boldsymbol{\theta}_L)}{\partial \boldsymbol{\theta}_L}, \quad C(\mathbf{y}, \boldsymbol{\theta}_L) = \mathbf{s}(\mathbf{y}, \boldsymbol{\theta}_L)\, \mathbf{s}(\mathbf{y}, \boldsymbol{\theta}_L)',$$

$$\begin{aligned} V\left(\bar{\boldsymbol{\theta}}_L\right) &= E\left[\left(\boldsymbol{\theta}_L - \bar{\boldsymbol{\theta}}_L\right)\left(\boldsymbol{\theta}_L - \bar{\boldsymbol{\theta}}_L\right)' |\mathbf{y}\right] \\ &= \int \left(\boldsymbol{\theta}_L - \bar{\boldsymbol{\theta}}_L\right)\left(\boldsymbol{\theta}_L - \bar{\boldsymbol{\theta}}_L\right)' p(\boldsymbol{\theta}_L|\mathbf{y}) d\boldsymbol{\theta}_L, \end{aligned}$$

where $\bar{\boldsymbol{\theta}}_L$ is the posterior mean of $\boldsymbol{\theta}_L$ in the expanded model. Then the J_1 component is constructed as

$$J_1 = \mathbf{tr}\left\{C_E\left(\mathbf{y}, \left(\bar{\boldsymbol{\theta}}, \boldsymbol{\theta}_E = 0\right)\right) V_E\left(\bar{\boldsymbol{\theta}}_L\right)\right\}, \tag{11.6}$$

where $C_E\left(\mathbf{y}, \left(\bar{\boldsymbol{\theta}}, \boldsymbol{\theta}_E = 0\right)\right)$ is the submatrix of $C(\mathbf{y}, \boldsymbol{\theta}_L)$ corresponding to $\boldsymbol{\theta}_E$ evaluated at $\left(\bar{\boldsymbol{\theta}}, \boldsymbol{\theta}_E = 0\right)$ and $V_E\left(\bar{\boldsymbol{\theta}}_L\right)$ is the submatrix of $V(\boldsymbol{\theta}_L)$ corresponding to $\boldsymbol{\theta}_E$ evaluated at $\bar{\boldsymbol{\theta}}_L$. As shown in Li et al. (2015), J_1 is a posterior-version of LM test (Breusch and Pagan (1980)) designed to test the point null hypothesis $\boldsymbol{\theta}_E = 0$. They showed that $J_1 \xrightarrow{d} \chi^2(q_E)$ when $\boldsymbol{\theta}_E = 0$. Typically, J_1 has good size property as it is designed to test the point null hypothesis.

If J_1 leads to the rejection of the hypothesis that $\boldsymbol{\theta}_E = 0$, it implies the misspecification in the original model $p(\mathbf{y}|\boldsymbol{\theta})$, and highlights potential sources of error within it. However, the inability of J_1 to reject this hypothesis does not provide clarity on the validity of the original model $p(\mathbf{y}|\boldsymbol{\theta})$. This ambiguity arises due to the various avenues available for model expansion in practice. While J_1 may have sufficient power in some cases, it may have low power in others. This challenge mirrors the issues encountered with the Wald statistic when testing a high-dimensional vector against sparse alternatives, a topic thoroughly discussed in Fan et al. (2015). To deal with this problem of low power, Li et al. (2018) used BIMT to construct J_0, that is,

$$J_0 = \sqrt{n}(\mathrm{BIMT}/P - 1)^2. \tag{11.7}$$

Then from (11.6) and (11.7), the power enhancement posterior-based test for model misspecification is

$$\mathrm{BMT} = J_1 + J_0 = \mathbf{tr}\left\{C_E\left(\mathbf{y}, \left(\bar{\boldsymbol{\theta}}, \boldsymbol{\theta}_E = 0\right)\right) V_E\left(\bar{\boldsymbol{\theta}}_L\right)\right\} + \sqrt{n}(\mathrm{BIMT}/P - 1)^2. \tag{11.8}$$

Under some mild regularity conditions, when the model is correctly specified, Li et al. (2018) showed that

$$J_1 \overset{d}{\to} \chi^2(P_E), J_0 = o_p(1), \mathrm{BMT} \overset{d}{\to} \chi^2(P_E).$$

If the model is misspecified with $P^* \neq P$, the order of J_0 takes the form

$$J_0 = \sqrt{n}\left[P^*/P - 1\right]^2 + 2\sqrt{n}\left(P^*/P - 1\right)o_p(1) + O_p(n^{-1/2}) = O_p(\sqrt{n}),$$

where $P^* := \mathbf{tr}\left[-\mathbf{H}\left(\boldsymbol{\theta}_n^p\right)^{-1}\mathbf{J}\left(\boldsymbol{\theta}_n^p\right)\right]$. Then the order of the power of BMT is no less than $O_p(\sqrt{n})$.

BMT has several nice properties. First, compared with IM, IOS, and IOS_A, BMT is based on the MCMC output. When the optimization of the likelihood function is difficult but the MCMC draws are available, BMT is easier to compute than IM, IOS, and IOS_A. Second, when $\sqrt{n}(\mathrm{BIMT}/q - 1)^2$ does not have the size distortion problem, it is likely that BMT will not suffer from size distortion. As a result, we do not need to use the bootstrap method, then avoid intensive computational effort. In addition, by incorporating BIMT into J_0, there is no need to get the asymptotic variance of BIMT which is complicated and difficult to calculate.

11.3 Posterior-Based Model Selection Criteria

The practice of model selection stands as a pivotal aspect of statistical inference. Many penalty-based information criteria have been proposed to select from candidate models in the literature. A famous example is AIC which requires that MLE is available. In the Bayesian context, the Deviance Information Criterion (DIC), introduced by Spiegelhalter et al. (2002), is a prominent model selection tool, formulated on the posterior deviance distribution. It has several desirable features. Firstly, DIC can be readily computed from the posterior output, such as MCMC output, when the likelihood function is explicitly defined. Secondly, DIC is applicable to a wide range of statistical models. Third, in contrast to Bayes Factors (BFs), DIC is not affected by Jeffreys–Lindley–Bartlett's paradox and remains valid even with improper priors.

In this section, we will review the DIC for Bayesian model selection, especially the frequentist justification of DIC.

11.3.1 DIC for Bayesian Model Selection

A useful measure of how well the model fits the data, based on both the frequentist and Bayesian approach, is the deviance

$$D(\boldsymbol{\theta}) = -2\ln p(\mathbf{y}|\boldsymbol{\theta}).$$

A small value of $D(\boldsymbol{\theta})$ corresponds to a large value of the log-likelihood, indicating the model fits the data well. Deviance measures the in-sample predictive performance of the model and a more complex model will always yield smaller values than a simple model. Deviance itself is not a good choice for model selection because it does not penalize overfitting, meaning that the most complex model will always be selected. But complex models are not always better since their estimates can be highly variable, for instance, the standard errors of the model parameter can be very large from the frequentist viewpoint and the posterior distributions of parameters may be highly diffuse from the Bayesian viewpoint. For the out-of-sample predictive performance, meaning how well the model predicts future data, simple models often perform better.

The most well-known frequentist approximation to the out-of-sample prediction is the Akaike Information Criterion (AIC):

$$\text{AIC} = -2\ln p\left(\mathbf{y}|\hat{\boldsymbol{\theta}}(\mathbf{y})\right) + 2P,$$

where $\hat{\boldsymbol{\theta}}(\mathbf{y})$ is the MLE estimator of the parameters, P the number of parameters. The smaller AIC is, the better the model. The first term is deviance evaluated at $\hat{\boldsymbol{\theta}}(\mathbf{y})$, which decreases as the fit of the model improves. The term $2P$ is called the "penalty" term or the degrees of freedom, which increases as the complexity of the model grows. Thus, in AIC, there is a trade-off between model fit and model complexity.

Spiegelhalter et al. (2002) proposed the DIC for Bayesian model comparison. The criterion takes the form of

$$\text{DIC} = D(\bar{\boldsymbol{\theta}}) + 2P_D, \tag{11.9}$$

where P_D, used to measure the model complexity and also known as "effective number of parameters", is defined as the difference between the posterior mean of the deviance and the deviance evaluated at the posterior mean of the parameters:

$$P_D = \overline{D(\boldsymbol{\theta})} - D(\bar{\boldsymbol{\theta}}) = -2\int [\ln p(\mathbf{y}|\boldsymbol{\theta}) - \ln p(\mathbf{y}|\bar{\boldsymbol{\theta}})]\, p(\boldsymbol{\theta}|\mathbf{y})d\boldsymbol{\theta}, \quad (11.10)$$

with $\bar{\boldsymbol{\theta}}$ being the posterior mean of $\boldsymbol{\theta}$. Note that $D(\boldsymbol{\theta})$ is a function of $\boldsymbol{\theta}$ and thus has a posterior distribution.

Decision-Theoretic Justification for DIC

Let $g(\mathbf{y})$ be the data generating process of $\mathbf{y}$, $\mathbf{y}_{rep} = (y_{1,rep}, \cdots, y_{n,rep})'$ denote the future replicate data with $\mathbf{y}$, and $\boldsymbol{\theta}_n^p$ be the pseudo-true value that minimizes the KL loss between the DGP and the candidate model

$$\boldsymbol{\theta}_n^p = \arg\min_{\boldsymbol{\theta}\in\boldsymbol{\Theta}} \frac{1}{n}\int \ln \frac{g(\mathbf{y})}{p(\mathbf{y}|\boldsymbol{\theta})} g(\mathbf{y})dy,$$

where $\{\boldsymbol{\theta}_n^p\}$ is the sequence of minimizers that are interior to $\boldsymbol{\Theta}$ uniformly in n. The quantity that measures how well a candidate model predicts the replicate data is the KL divergence between $g(\mathbf{y})$ and $p(\mathbf{y}_{rep}|\mathbf{y})$:

$$\begin{aligned} KL\left[g\left(\mathbf{y}_{rep}\right), p\left(\mathbf{y}_{rep}|\mathbf{y}\right)\right] &= E_{\mathbf{y}_{rep}}\left[\ln \frac{g\left(\mathbf{y}_{rep}\right)}{p\left(\mathbf{y}_{rep}|\mathbf{y}\right)}\right] \\ &= \int \left[\ln \frac{g\left(\mathbf{y}_{rep}\right)}{p\left(\mathbf{y}_{rep}|\mathbf{y}\right)}\right] g\left(\mathbf{y}_{rep}\right) d\mathbf{y}_{rep} \\ &= \int \ln g\left(\mathbf{y}_{rep}\right) g\left(\mathbf{y}_{rep}\right) d\mathbf{y}_{rep} \\ &\quad - \int \ln p\left(\mathbf{y}_{rep}|\mathbf{y}\right) g\left(\mathbf{y}_{rep}\right) d\mathbf{y}_{rep}, \end{aligned} \quad (11.11)$$

where $p\left(\mathbf{y}_{rep}|\mathbf{y}\right)$ denote a generic predictive distribution. The smaller this KL divergence, the better the candidate model in predicting $g(\mathbf{y}_{rep})$.

If we choose $p\left(\mathbf{y}_{rep}|\mathbf{y}\right)$ to be the plug-in distribution $p\left(\mathbf{y}_{rep}|\hat{\boldsymbol{\theta}}(\mathbf{y})\right)$ where $\hat{\boldsymbol{\theta}}(\mathbf{y})$ is the MLE estimator of $\boldsymbol{\theta}_n^p$ under the data $\mathbf{y}$, then (11.11) can be rewritten as

$$KL\left[g\left(\mathbf{y}_{rep}\right), p\left(\mathbf{y}_{rep}|\hat{\boldsymbol{\theta}}_n(\mathbf{y})\right)\right] = E_{\mathbf{y}_{rep}}\left[\ln \frac{g\left(\mathbf{y}_{rep}\right)}{p\left(\mathbf{y}_{rep}|\bar{\boldsymbol{\theta}}(\mathbf{y})\right)}\right]$$

$$= E_{\mathbf{y}_{rep}}\left[\ln g\left(\mathbf{y}_{rep}\right)\right] + E_{\mathbf{y}_{rep}}\left[-\ln p\left(\mathbf{y}_{rep}|\hat{\boldsymbol{\theta}}(\mathbf{y})\right)\right],$$

where the expectation $E_{\mathbf{y}}$ and $E_{\mathbf{y}_{rep}}$ are related to $g(\mathbf{y})$ and $g(\mathbf{y}_{rep})$, respectively. Since $g(\mathbf{y}_{rep})$ is the true DGP and $E_{\mathbf{y}_{rep}}(\ln g(\mathbf{y}_{rep}))$ is the same across all candidate models, it can be dropped from the preceding equation.

Assumption 10: $\mathbf{H}_n(\boldsymbol{\theta}_n^p) + \mathbf{B}_n(\boldsymbol{\theta}_n^p) = o(1)$.

Assumption 10 is a generalization of the definition of "information matrix equality"; see White (1996). It was used as an indicator of no model misspecification. Under Assumptions 1–8 and 10, it is well known that

$$E_{\mathbf{y}}E_{\mathbf{y}_{rep}}\left[-2\ln p\left(\mathbf{y}_{rep}|\hat{\boldsymbol{\theta}}_n(\mathbf{y})\right)\right] = E_{\mathbf{y}}\left[\text{AIC} + o_p(1)\right] = E_{\mathbf{y}}\left[\text{AIC}\right] + o(1),$$

which means that AIC is an unbiased estimator of $E_{\mathbf{y}}E_{\mathbf{y}_{rep}}\left[-2\ln p\left(\mathbf{y}_{rep}|\hat{\boldsymbol{\theta}}(\mathbf{y})\right)\right]$ asymptotically; for details, see Burnham and Anderson (2002).

Recently, under Assumptions 1–10, Li et al. (2024) provided a frequentist justification of DIC similar to that of AIC. If the plug-in predictive distribution based on replicate data is $p\left(\mathbf{y}_{rep}|\bar{\boldsymbol{\theta}}(\mathbf{y})\right)$ where $\bar{\boldsymbol{\theta}}(\mathbf{y})$ is the posterior mean of $\boldsymbol{\theta}_n^p$ conditional on the data $\mathbf{y}$, consider the following KL divergence:

$$KL\left[g(\mathbf{y}_{rep}), p\left(\mathbf{y}_{rep}|\bar{\boldsymbol{\theta}}(\mathbf{y})\right)\right] = E_{\mathbf{y}_{rep}}\left[\ln\frac{g(\mathbf{y}_{rep})}{p\left(\mathbf{y}_{rep}|\bar{\boldsymbol{\theta}}(\mathbf{y})\right)}\right]$$

$$= E_{\mathbf{y}_{rep}}\left[\ln g(\mathbf{y}_{rep})\right] + E_{\mathbf{y}_{rep}}\left[-\ln p\left(\mathbf{y}_{rep}|\bar{\boldsymbol{\theta}}(\mathbf{y})\right)\right].$$

Under Assumptions 1–8 and 10, Li et al. (2024) showed that

$$E_{\mathbf{y}}E_{\mathbf{y}_{rep}}\left[-2\ln p\left(\mathbf{y}_{rep}|\bar{\boldsymbol{\theta}}(\mathbf{y})\right)\right] = E_{\mathbf{y}}\left[\text{DIC} + o_p(1)\right] = E_{\mathbf{y}}\left[\text{DIC}\right] + o(1),$$

which implies that, asymptotically, DIC serves as an unbiased estimator for $E_{\mathbf{y}}E_{\mathbf{y}rep}\left[-2\ln p\left(\mathbf{y}rep|\bar{\boldsymbol{\theta}}(\mathbf{y})\right)\right]$. The decision-theoretic underpinning of DIC indicates its capacity to select a model which asymptotically minimizes the expected KL divergence between the DGP and the plug-in predictive distribution $p\left(\mathbf{y}_{rep}|\bar{\boldsymbol{\theta}}(\mathbf{y})\right)$ where the expectation is taken with respect to the DGP.

The asymptotic unbiasedness of AIC hinges on several conditions: firstly, the candidate models must closely approximate the true data generating process (DGP), as outlined in Assumption 10. Secondly, the consistency and asymptotic normality of MLE are crucial, detailed in Assumptions 1–8. Lastly, Assumption 9 pertains to the expression for the asymptotic variance of the MLE. For an in-depth exploration, refer to Li et al. (2024). A notable distinction between AIC and DIC lies in their respective predictive distributions, which are based on different estimators of $\boldsymbol{\theta}_n^p$. AIC employs the ML estimate, represented as $\hat{\boldsymbol{\theta}}(\mathbf{y})$, whereas DIC utilizes the Bayesian posterior mean, denoted as $\bar{\boldsymbol{\theta}}(\mathbf{y})$. This distinction is the basis for referring to DIC as the Bayesian analogue of AIC. Under Assumptions 1–9, Li et al. (2024) demonstrated that

$$\bar{\theta} = \hat{\theta} + O_p(n^{-1}), \tag{11.12}$$

$$\bar{\mathbf{H}}_n\left(\bar{\theta}\right) = \bar{\mathbf{H}}_n\left(\hat{\theta}\right) + o_p\left(1\right). \tag{11.13}$$

From (11.12), the Bayesian posterior mean has the same asymptotic distribution as the MLE and (11.13) ensures the validity of the expression for its asymptotic variance. That is why we can obtain the asymptotic unbiasedness of DIC under Assumptions 1–10.

The Effect of Prior Information on P_D

The deviance information criterion method offers a valuable approach for assessing model complexity within the context of Bayesian analysis, particularly when prior information is integrated into the model, as discussed by Brooks (2002). In contrast, AIC quantifies model complexity using the number of degrees of freedom, denoted as P which is also the number of parameters. However, in Bayesian settings, the incorporation of prior information typically introduces further constraints on the parameter space. Consequently, the effective degrees of freedom, P_D, potentially adjusted by the prior, may not align closely with P, especially for a finite sample size n.

Li et al. (2024) proposed high-order approximation for P_D and DIC to see the effect of prior information. For convenience, we let $\bar{\mathbf{H}}_n^{(j)}\left(\boldsymbol{\theta}\right) = \frac{1}{n}\sum_{t=1}^{n} l_t^{(j)}\left(\boldsymbol{\theta}\right)$ for $j = 3, 4, 5$. Let $\pi\left(\boldsymbol{\theta}\right) = \ln p\left(\boldsymbol{\theta}\right), p^{(j)}\left(\boldsymbol{\theta}\right), \pi^{(j)}\left(\boldsymbol{\theta}\right)$ be the jth-order derivatives of $p\left(\boldsymbol{\theta}\right)$, $\pi\left(\boldsymbol{\theta}\right)$ for $j = 1, 2$. When there is no ambiguity, we write $\hat{\boldsymbol{\theta}}(\mathbf{y})$ as $\hat{\boldsymbol{\theta}}$. Under some regularity conditions, Li et al. (2024) proved that

$$P_D = P + \frac{1}{n}C_1 + \frac{1}{n}C_2 + O_p\left(n^{-2}\right), \tag{11.14}$$

$$\text{DIC} = \text{AIC} + \frac{1}{n}D_1 + \frac{1}{n}D_2 + O_p\left(n^{-2}\right), \tag{11.15}$$

where

$$C_1 = \frac{1}{4}\mathbf{tr}\left[A_2\right] - \frac{1}{6}\mathbf{tr}\left[A_3\right], \quad C_2 = -C_{22},$$

$$D_1 = -\frac{1}{4}A_1 + \frac{1}{2}\mathbf{tr}\left[A_2\right] - \frac{1}{3}\mathbf{tr}\left[A_3\right],$$
$$D_2 = C_{21} - 2C_{22} - C_{23},$$

$$A_1 = vec\left(\bar{\mathbf{H}}_n\left(\hat{\theta}\right)^{-1}\right)' \bar{\mathbf{H}}_n^{(3)}\left(\hat{\theta}\right)\bar{\mathbf{H}}_n\left(\hat{\theta}\right)^{-1}\bar{\mathbf{H}}_n^{(3)}\left(\hat{\theta}\right)' vec\left(\bar{\mathbf{H}}_n\left(\hat{\theta}\right)^{-1}\right),$$

$$A_2 = \left[\bar{\mathbf{H}}_n\left(\hat{\theta}\right)^{-1} \otimes vec\left(\bar{\mathbf{H}}_n\left(\hat{\theta}\right)^{-1}\right)\right]' \bar{\mathbf{H}}_n^{(4)}\left(\hat{\theta}\right),$$

$$A_3 = \bar{\mathbf{H}}_n^{(3)}\left(\hat{\theta}\right)'\left(\bar{\mathbf{H}}_n\left(\hat{\theta}\right)^{-1} \otimes \bar{\mathbf{H}}_n\left(\hat{\theta}\right)^{-1}\right)\bar{\mathbf{H}}_n^{(3)}\left(\hat{\theta}\right)\bar{\mathbf{H}}_n\left(\hat{\theta}\right)^{-1},$$

$$C_{21} = \pi^{(1)}\left(\hat{\theta}\right)'\bar{\mathbf{H}}_n\left(\hat{\theta}\right)^{-1}\bar{\mathbf{H}}_n^{(3)}\left(\hat{\theta}_n\right)' vec\left(\bar{\mathbf{H}}_n\left(\hat{\theta}\right)^{-1}\right),$$

$$C_{22} = \mathbf{tr}\left[\bar{\mathbf{H}}_n\left(\hat{\theta}\right)^{-1}\pi^{(2)}\left(\hat{\theta}\right)\right], C_{23} = \pi^{(1)}\left(\hat{\theta}\right)'\bar{\mathbf{H}}_n\left(\hat{\theta}\right)^{-1}\pi^{(1)}\left(\hat{\theta}\right),$$

where vec is the columnwise vectorization. From (11.15), the difference between DIC and AIC is $O_p(n^{-1})$, then DIC can be regarded as a Bayesian version of AIC. The effect of the prior information on P_D can be approximated by $C_2 = -\mathbf{tr}\left[\bar{\mathbf{H}}_n\left(\hat{\theta}\right)^{-1}\pi^{(2)}\left(\hat{\theta}\right)\right]$ where $\bar{\mathbf{H}}_n\left(\hat{\theta}\right)$ and $\pi^{(2)}\left(\hat{\theta}\right)$ represent the information from the model and prior, respectively.

The preceding analysis can be illustrated by the following simple example:

$$y_i = \theta + u_i, \tag{11.16}$$

where $u_i \sim_{i.i.d.} N(\theta, \lambda^{-1} + \tau_i^{-1})$ for $i = 1, \ldots, n$. The likelihood function is

$$p(\mathbf{y}|\theta) = \prod_{i=1}^{n}\sqrt{\frac{1}{2\pi}\frac{\tau_i\lambda}{\tau_i + \lambda}}\exp\left(-\frac{1}{2}\frac{\tau_i\lambda}{\tau_i+\lambda}(y_i - \theta)^2\right). \tag{11.17}$$

Let the prior of θ be $N(\mu_0, \tau_0^{-1})$. Then the posterior, based on the likelihood function (11.17) and the prior of θ, is given by

$$p(\theta|\mathbf{y}) = \frac{p(\mathbf{y}|\theta)p(\theta)}{\int p(\mathbf{y}|\theta)p(\theta)d\theta} = \sqrt{\frac{\tau^o}{2\pi}}\exp\left(-\frac{\tau^o}{2}(\theta - \mu^o)^2\right).$$

Hence, the posterior mean is

$$\bar{\theta} = E(\theta|\mathbf{y}) = \mu^o = (\tau^o)^{-1}\left(\sum_{i=1}^{n}\frac{\tau_i\lambda}{\tau_i+\lambda}y_i + \tau_0\mu_0\right), \tau^o = \sum_{i=1}^{n}\frac{\tau_i\lambda}{\tau_i+\lambda}+\tau_0,$$

and the posterior variance is $(\tau^o)^{-1}$. Then we have

$$\begin{aligned}\overline{D(\theta)} &= -2\int \ln p(\mathbf{y}|\theta)p(\theta|\mathbf{y})d\theta \\ &= n\ln 2\pi - \sum_{i=1}^{n}\ln\frac{\tau_i\lambda}{\tau_i+\lambda} - \sum_{i=1}^{n}\frac{\tau_i\lambda}{\tau_i+\lambda}\left((y_i - \mu^o)^2 + \frac{1}{\tau^o}\right),\end{aligned}$$

$$D(\bar{\theta}) = -2\ln p(\mathbf{y}|\bar{\theta}) = n\ln 2\pi - \sum_{i=1}^{n}\ln\frac{\tau_i\lambda}{\tau_i+\lambda} - \sum_{i=1}^{n}\frac{\tau_i\lambda}{\tau_i+\lambda}(y_i - \mu^o)^2,$$

$$P_D = \overline{D(\theta)} - D(\bar{\theta}) = \frac{1}{\tau^o}\sum_{i=1}^{n}\frac{\tau_i\lambda}{\tau_i+\lambda}$$
$$= \left(\sum_{i=1}^{n}\frac{\tau_i}{\tau_i+\lambda}+\frac{\tau_0}{\lambda}\right)^{-1}\sum_{i=1}^{n}\frac{\tau_i}{\tau_i+\lambda},$$

and

$$\begin{aligned}\text{DIC} &= D(\bar{\theta}) + 2P_D \\ &= n\ln 2\pi - \sum_{i=1}^{n}\ln\frac{\tau_i\lambda}{\tau_i+\lambda} - \sum_{i=1}^{n}\frac{\tau_i\lambda}{\tau_i+\lambda}(y_i-\mu^o)^2 \\ &+2\left(\sum_{i=1}^{n}\frac{\tau_i}{\tau_i+\lambda}+\frac{\tau_0}{\lambda}\right)^{-1}\sum_{i=1}^{n}\frac{\tau_i}{\tau_i+\lambda}.\end{aligned} \tag{11.18}$$

The log-likelihood function is

$$\ln p(\mathbf{y}|\theta) = -\frac{n}{2}\ln 2\pi + \frac{1}{2}\sum_{i=1}^{n}\ln\frac{\tau_i\lambda}{\tau_i+\lambda} - \frac{1}{2}\sum_{i=1}^{n}\frac{\tau_i\lambda}{\tau_i+\lambda}(y_i-\theta)^2, \tag{11.19}$$

the MLE estimator of θ is

$$\hat{\theta} = \left(\sum_{i=1}^{n}\frac{\tau_i\lambda}{\tau_i+\lambda}\right)^{-1}\sum_{i=1}^{n}\frac{\tau_i\lambda}{\tau_i+\lambda}y_i. \tag{11.20}$$

From (11.19) and (11.20), we have

$$\bar{\mathbf{H}}^{(-2)}\left(\hat{\theta}\right) = -n\left(\sum_{i=1}^{n}\frac{\tau_i\lambda}{\tau_i+\lambda}\right)^{-1}. \tag{11.21}$$

It can be shown that $C_1 = 0$ since the third and fourth derivatives are both zero. Note that the logarithm of the prior density function is

$$\ln p(\mathbf{y}|\theta) = -\frac{n}{2}\ln 2\pi + \frac{1}{2}\ln\tau_0 - \frac{1}{2}\sum_{i=1}^{n}\tau_0(\theta-\mu_0)^2.$$

Then we have

$$\pi^{(2)}\left(\hat{\theta}\right) = -\tau_0. \tag{11.22}$$

From (11.21) and (11.22),

$$C_2 = -\mathbf{tr}\left[\bar{\mathbf{H}}_n\left(\hat{\boldsymbol{\theta}}\right)^{-1}\pi^{(2)}\left(\hat{\boldsymbol{\theta}}\right)\right] = -\left(\frac{1}{n}\sum_{i=1}^{n}\frac{\tau_i\lambda}{\tau_i+\lambda}\right)^{-1}\tau_0.$$

Hence we can show that

$$
\begin{aligned}
P_D &= \frac{1}{\tau^o}\sum_{i=1}^{n}\frac{\tau_i\lambda}{\tau_i+\lambda} = \left(\sum_{i=1}^{n}\frac{\tau_i\lambda}{\tau_i+\lambda}+\tau_0\right)^{-1}\sum_{i=1}^{n}\frac{\tau_i\lambda}{\tau_i+\lambda} \\
&= \left(\frac{1}{n}\sum_{i=1}^{n}\frac{\tau_i\lambda}{\tau_i+\lambda}+\frac{\tau_0}{n}\right)^{-1}\frac{1}{n}\sum_{i=1}^{n}\frac{\tau_i\lambda}{\tau_i+\lambda} \\
&= \left(1+\left(\frac{1}{n}\sum_{i=1}^{n}\frac{\tau_i\lambda}{\tau_i+\lambda}\right)^{-1}\frac{\tau_0}{n}\right)^{-1} \\
&= 1-\left(\frac{1}{n}\sum_{i=1}^{n}\frac{\tau_i\lambda}{\tau_i+\lambda}\right)^{-1}\frac{\tau_0}{n}+O_p\left(\left[\left(\frac{1}{n}\sum_{i=1}^{n}\frac{\tau_i\lambda}{\tau_i+\lambda}\right)^{-1}\frac{\tau_0}{n}\right]^2\right) \\
&= P+\frac{1}{n}C_1+\frac{1}{n}C_2+O_p\left(n^{-2}\right)
\end{aligned}
$$

with $C_1 = 0$ and the number of parameters $P = 1$.

For the models that $\overline{D(\theta)}$ and P_D do not have a closed-form expression, such as the normal model with unknown sampling precision, Equation (11.14) provides a generalized method for measuring the effect of the prior on P_D. Spiegelhalter et al. (2002) used some specific tricks to derive the relationship between P_D and P for this kind of model, but these tricks are difficult to use for other models. For more details, see Li et al. (2024).

11.3.2 DIC for Latent Variable Models and Misspecified Models

In this section, we first discuss how to obtain DIC when the model includes latent variables. Second, we introduce a new version of DIC for misspecified models.

DIC with Data Augmentation

Consider $\mathbf{y} = (y_1, \ldots, y_n)$ as the observed data originating from a probability measure P_0 within the probability space (Ω, F, P_0). Let $\mathbf{z} = (\mathbf{z}_1, \mathbf{z}_2, \cdots, \mathbf{z}_n)'$ represent the latent variables. In this context, the latent variable model is characterized by a parameter vector of dimension P, denoted as $\boldsymbol{\theta}$. The likelihood function based on the observed data is expressed as $p(\mathbf{y}|\boldsymbol{\theta})$, while the complete-data likelihood function, incorporating both observed and latent variables, is denoted by $p(\mathbf{y}, \mathbf{z}|\boldsymbol{\theta})$. The relationship between these two likelihood functions is given by

$$
p(\mathbf{y}|\boldsymbol{\theta}) = \int p(\mathbf{y}, \mathbf{z}|\boldsymbol{\theta})d\mathbf{z}. \tag{11.23}
$$

The integral in (11.23) usually does not have an analytical form. For many latent variable models, the dimension of $\mathbf{z}$ is as high as the sample size of the observed data, making it very difficult to accurately approximate the integral numerically. Consequently, the ML method and hence, AIC are difficult to use because doing so requires the calculation of $p(\mathbf{y}|\boldsymbol{\theta})$ for each value of $\boldsymbol{\theta}$ during numerical optimizations.

For the Bayesian analysis based on the observed-data likelihood function $p(\mathbf{y}|\boldsymbol{\theta})$, one would end up with the same problems as in ML, and DIC is also difficult to calculate since $\ln p(\mathbf{y}|\boldsymbol{\theta})$ does not have a closed form either. For the purpose of enhancing posterior analysis, the data-augmentation approach, as proposed by Tanner and Wong (1987), is frequently employed. This technique expands the parameter space to include both $(\boldsymbol{\theta}, \mathbf{z})$, thereby modifying the likelihood function to $p(\mathbf{y}|\boldsymbol{\theta},\mathbf{z})$. Typically, this adjusted likelihood function is characterized by a closed-form expression, facilitating easier analytical or computational handling. Denote the posterior mean of $\mathbf{z}, \boldsymbol{\theta}$ by $\bar{\mathbf{z}}, \bar{\boldsymbol{\theta}}$, obtained from the joint posterior distribution $p(\boldsymbol{\theta}, \mathbf{z}|\mathbf{y})$. Applying DIC developed earlier to the data-augmented MCMC output leads to

$$\text{DIC}^{DA} = D(\bar{\mathbf{z}}, \bar{\boldsymbol{\theta}}) + 2P_D^{DA}, \tag{11.24}$$

$$\begin{aligned} P_D^{DA} &= \overline{D(\mathbf{z}, \boldsymbol{\theta})} - D(\bar{\mathbf{z}}, \bar{\boldsymbol{\theta}}) \\ &= -2\int [\ln p(\mathbf{y}|\mathbf{z}, \boldsymbol{\theta}) - \ln p(\mathbf{y}|\bar{\mathbf{z}}, \bar{\boldsymbol{\theta}})]\, p(\mathbf{z}, \boldsymbol{\theta}|\mathbf{y}) \mathrm{d}\mathbf{z}\mathrm{d}\boldsymbol{\theta}, \end{aligned} \tag{11.25}$$

where $D(\mathbf{z}, \boldsymbol{\theta}) = -2\ln p(\mathbf{y}|\mathbf{z}, \boldsymbol{\theta})$ is a formulation typically accessible in a closed form. This method of calculating DIC is the preferred approach in WinBUGS, as recommended by Spiegelhalter et al. (2002). The adoption of data augmentation not only simplifies the process of MCMC sampling but also streamlines the computation of DIC from MCMC outputs. As acknowledged in Spiegelhalter et al. (2014), this standard approach for calculating DIC from $p(\mathbf{y}|\boldsymbol{\theta}, \mathbf{z})$ in the contex of latent variable models is employed primarily "only to make the technique computationally feasible."

From a theoretical perspective, DIC^{DA} encounters several issues. A primary concern is the substantial increase in the dimensionality of the parameter space for certain models, such as stochastic volatility models, where it expands from P to $n+P$. This expansion leads to the well-documented incidental parameter problem in econometrics where the information about the incidental parameters stops accumulating after a finite number of observations when the dimension of the parameter space grows proportionally to the number of observations; see Neyman and Scott (1948) and Lancaster (2000). In scenarios where the parameter space expands with the number of observations, both the MLE estimator and the posterior mean may become inconsistent, and the Bernstein–von Mises theorem becomes invalid. Consequently, in such cases, DIC^{DA} might fail to provide an asymptotically unbiased estimation of the Kullback–Leibler (KL) divergence up to a constant.

To understand this problem, let us consider the following random effect model from Celeux et al. (2006),

$$y_i = z_i + \varepsilon_i, \tag{11.26}$$

where $z_i \sim N(\theta, \lambda^{-1})$ and $\varepsilon_i \sim_{i.i.d.} N(0, \tau_i^{-1})$ for $i = 1, \ldots, n$, z_i and ε_i are mutually independent for all i. For simplicity, let λ and τ_i be known. Different from Celeux et al. (2003) where an improper prior is used for θ, we assume the prior for θ is $N(\mu_0, \tau_0^{-1})$. If we treat z_i as parameters, then the complete-likelihood function is

$$p(\mathbf{y}|\theta, \mathbf{z}) = \prod_{i=1}^{n} p(\mathbf{y}|\theta, z_i) = \prod_{i=1}^{n} \sqrt{\frac{\tau_i}{2\pi}} \exp\left(-\frac{1}{2}\tau_i \left(y_i - z_i\right)^2\right), \tag{11.27}$$

and the prior of $\theta, \mathbf{z}$ is

$$p(\theta, \mathbf{z}) = p(\mathbf{z}|\theta) p\left(\theta\right) = \prod_{i=1}^{n} p(z_i|\theta) p\left(\theta\right).$$

The posterior density is

$$p(\theta, \mathbf{z}|\mathbf{y}) = \frac{p(\mathbf{y}|\theta, \mathbf{z}) p(\theta, \mathbf{z})}{p(\mathbf{y})},$$

where

$$p(\mathbf{y}) = \int p(\mathbf{y}|\theta, \mathbf{z}) p(\theta, \mathbf{z}) d\theta\, d\mathbf{z}.$$

Then, the joint posterior density of $\theta, \mathbf{z}$ is

$$\begin{aligned} &p(\theta, \mathbf{z}|\mathbf{y}) \\ &\propto \left[\prod_{i=1}^{n} \sqrt{\frac{\tau_i}{2\pi}} \exp\left(-\frac{\tau_i}{2}\left(y_i - z_i\right)^2\right) \sqrt{\frac{\lambda}{2\pi}} \exp\left(-\frac{\lambda}{2}\left(z_i - \theta\right)^2\right)\right] \\ &\sqrt{\frac{\mu_0}{2\pi}} \exp\left(-\frac{\tau_0}{2}\left(\theta - \mu_0\right)^2\right), \end{aligned}$$

and the posterior densities are

$$\begin{aligned} \theta|\mathbf{y} &\sim \mathbf{N}\left(\mu^o, (\tau^o)^{-1}\right), \\ z_i|\theta, \mathbf{y} &\sim \mathbf{N}\left(\frac{y_i\tau_i + \lambda\theta}{\tau_i + \lambda}, \frac{1}{\tau_i + \lambda}\right), \end{aligned}$$

where

$$\mu^o = (\tau^o)^{-1}\left(\sum_{i=1}^{n} \frac{\tau_i \lambda}{\tau_i + \lambda} y_i + \tau_0 \mu_0\right), \tau^o = \sum_{i=1}^{n} \frac{\tau_i \lambda}{\tau_i + \lambda} + \tau_0.$$

Hence, the posterior means of $\theta, \mathbf{z}$ are

$$\bar{\theta} = \mu^o,$$
$$\bar{z}_i = E\left[E\left(z_i|\theta, \mathbf{y}\right)\right] = \frac{y_i \tau_i + \lambda \mu^o}{\tau_i + \lambda} \text{ for } i = 1, 2, \ldots, n.$$

Since $\{z_i\}_{i=1}^n$ are treated as parameters, they are incidental in the sense of Neyman and Scott (1948). From (11.27), the MLE of z_i is $\hat{z}_i = y_i = z_i + \varepsilon_i$. While it is correctly centered at z_i, it is inconsistent because $\hat{z}_i - z_i$ does not go to zero in probability as n goes to infinity. For the posterior mean $\bar{z}_i$, we have

$$\bar{z}_i = \frac{\tau_i}{\tau_i + \lambda} y_i + \frac{\lambda}{\tau_i + \lambda} \mu^o = y_i - \frac{\lambda}{\tau_i + \lambda}\left(y_i - \mu^o\right),$$

and

$$\begin{aligned}\bar{z}_i - z_i &= -\frac{\lambda}{\tau_i + \lambda} z_i + \frac{\tau_i}{\tau_i + \lambda} \varepsilon_i + \frac{\lambda}{\tau_i + \lambda} \mu^o \\ &= -\frac{\lambda}{\tau_i + \lambda}\left(z_i - \mu^o\right) + \frac{\tau_i}{\tau_i + \lambda} \varepsilon_i.\end{aligned}$$

Therefore, the posterior mean $\bar{z}_i$ is neither centered at the MLE nor consistent. Clearly, both the standard ML large sample theory and the Bernstein–von Mises theorem fail to hold. These results are not surprising since only one observation (i.e., y_i) contains information about z_i.

To compute P_D^{DA}, we use

$$\begin{aligned}\overline{D(\mathbf{z}, \theta)} &= n \ln 2\pi - \sum_{i=1}^{n} \ln \tau_i \\ &\quad + \int \left[\sum_{i=1}^{n} \tau_i \int \left(y_i - z_i\right)^2 p\left(z_i|\theta, \mathbf{y}\right) dz_i\right] p\left(\theta|\mathbf{y}\right) d\theta \qquad (11.28) \\ &= n \ln 2\pi - \sum_{i=1}^{n} \ln \tau_i + \sum_{i=1}^{n} \frac{\tau_i}{\tau_i + \lambda} \\ &\quad + \sum_{i=1}^{n} \frac{\tau_i \lambda^2}{(\tau_i + \lambda)^2}\left(\sum_{i=1}^{n} \frac{\tau_i \lambda}{\tau_i + \lambda} + \tau_0\right)^{-1} + \sum_{i=1}^{n} \frac{\tau_i \lambda^2}{(\tau_i + \lambda)^2}\left(y_i - \mu^o\right)^2,\end{aligned}$$

$$D(\bar{\mathbf{z}}, \bar{\theta}) = n \ln 2\pi - \sum_{i=1}^{n} \ln \tau_i + \sum_{i=1}^{n} \tau_i \left(y_i - \frac{y_i \tau_i + \lambda \mu^o}{\tau_i + \lambda}\right)^2 \qquad (11.29)$$

$$= n\ln 2\pi - \sum_{i=1}^{n} \ln \tau_i + \sum_{i=1}^{n} \frac{\tau_i \lambda^2}{(\tau_i+\lambda)^2} (y_i - \mu^o)^2 .$$

Then

$$\begin{aligned} P_D^{DA} &= \overline{D(\mathbf{z},\theta)} - D(\bar{\mathbf{z}},\bar{\theta}) \\ &= \sum_{i=1}^{n} \frac{\tau_i}{\tau_i+\lambda} + \left(\sum_{i=1}^{n} \frac{\tau_i}{\tau_i+\lambda} + \frac{\tau_0}{\lambda}\right)^{-1} \sum_{i=1}^{n} \frac{\tau_i}{\tau_i+\lambda}\frac{\lambda}{\tau_i+\lambda}. \end{aligned}$$

Hence, DIC^{DA} takes the form

$$\begin{aligned} \mathrm{DIC}^{DA} &= D(\bar{\mathbf{z}},\bar{\theta}) + 2P_D^{DA} \\ &= n\ln 2\pi - \sum_{i=1}^{n} \ln \tau_i + \sum_{i=1}^{n} \frac{\tau_i \lambda^2}{(\tau_i+\lambda)^2} (y_i - \mu^o)^2 \\ &\quad +2\left(\sum_{i=1}^{n} \frac{\tau_i}{\tau_i+\lambda} + (\tau^o)^{-1} \sum_{i=1}^{n} \frac{\tau_i\lambda}{(\tau_i+\lambda)^2}\right). \end{aligned} \tag{11.30}$$

The KL divergence is

$$2KL\left[g\left(\mathbf{y}_{rep}\right), p\left(\mathbf{y}_{rep}|\bar{\mathbf{z}}(\mathbf{y}),\bar{\theta}(\mathbf{y})\right)\right] = C + E_{\mathbf{y}}E_{\mathbf{y}_{rep}}\left[-2\ln p\left(\mathbf{y}_{rep}|\bar{\mathbf{z}}(\mathbf{y}),\bar{\theta}(\mathbf{y})\right)\right],$$

where

$$\begin{aligned} & E_{\mathbf{y}}E_{\mathbf{y}_{rep}}\left[-2\ln p\left(\mathbf{y}_{rep}|\bar{\mathbf{z}}(\mathbf{y}),\bar{\theta}(\mathbf{y})\right)\right] \\ &= n\ln 2\pi - \sum_{i=1}^{n} \ln \tau_i + \sum_{i=1}^{n}\left[\tau_i E_{\mathbf{y}}E_{\mathbf{y}_{rep}}\left[\left(y_{i,rep} - \frac{\tau_i}{\tau_i+\lambda}y_i - \frac{\lambda}{\tau_i+\lambda}\mu^o\right)^2\right]\right] \\ &= n\ln 2\pi - \sum_{i=1}^{n} \ln \tau_i + 2\sum_{i=1}^{n}\frac{\tau_i+\lambda}{\lambda} + \sum_{i=1}^{n} \frac{\tau_i \lambda^2}{(\tau_i+\lambda)^2}\left(E_{\mathbf{y}}\left[(y_i-\mu^o)^2\right]\right). \end{aligned} \tag{11.31}$$

It can be shown that DIC^{DA} takes the form

$$\begin{aligned} E_{\mathbf{y}}\left(\mathrm{DIC}^{DA}\right) &= n\ln 2\pi - \sum_{i=1}^{n} \ln \tau_i + \sum_{i=1}^{n} \frac{\tau_i \lambda^2}{(\tau_i+\lambda)^2}\left(E_{\mathbf{y}}\left[(y_i-\mu^o)^2\right]\right) \\ &\quad +2\left(\sum_{i=1}^{n} \frac{\tau_i}{\tau_i+\lambda} + \tau^{o-1} \sum_{i=1}^{n} \frac{\tau_i\lambda}{(\tau_i+\lambda)^2}\right). \end{aligned} \tag{11.32}$$

From (11.31) and (11.32),

$$\begin{aligned} E_{\mathbf{y}}\left(\mathrm{DIC}^{DA}\right) &= E_{\mathbf{y}}E_{\mathbf{y}_{rep}}\left[-2\ln p\left(\mathbf{y}_{rep}|\bar{\mathbf{z}}(\mathbf{y}),\bar{\theta}(\mathbf{y})\right)\right] \\ &\quad +2\left(\sum_{i=1}^{n}\left(\frac{\tau_i}{\tau_i+\lambda} - \frac{\tau_i+\lambda}{\lambda}\right) + (\tau^o)^{-1}\sum_{i=1}^{n} \frac{\tau_i\lambda}{(\tau_i+\lambda)^2}\right). \end{aligned}$$

Thus, DIC^{DA} is not an asymptotically unbiased estimator of $E_{\mathbf{y}}E_{\mathbf{y}_{rep}}\left[-2\ln p\left(\mathbf{y}_{rep}|\bar{\mathbf{z}}(\mathbf{y}),\bar{\theta}(\mathbf{y})\right)\right]$ in this case. For illustration, let $\tau_i=\lambda=1$ and $\tau_0=0$. Then

$$\sum_{i=1}^{n}\left(\frac{\tau_i}{\tau_i+\lambda}-\frac{\tau_i+\lambda}{\lambda}\right)=-1.5n,$$

$$(\tau^o)^{-1}\sum_{i=1}^{n}\frac{\tau_i\lambda}{(\tau_i+\lambda)^2}=\frac{1}{2}.$$

As a result, the difference between $E_{\mathbf{y}}\left(\mathrm{DIC}^{DA}\right)$ and $E_{\mathbf{y}}E_{\mathbf{y}_{rep}}\left[-2\ln p\left(\mathbf{y}_{rep}|\bar{\mathbf{z}}(\mathbf{y}),\bar{\theta}(\mathbf{y})\right)\right]$ has order $O\left(n\right)$. See the appendix for a detailed proof.

Second, sometimes a statistical model without latent variables can be represented by another model with latent variables. For example, the model (11.16) can be rewritten as (11.26) with latent variables since the observed-likelihood function of (11.26) can be obtained by integrating $\mathbf{z}$ from the joint density of $\mathbf{y},\mathbf{z}$ conditional on θ, $p(\mathbf{y},\mathbf{z}|\theta)$

$$p(\mathbf{y}|\theta)=\int p(\mathbf{y},\mathbf{z}|\theta)d\mathbf{z}=\prod_{i=1}^{n}\int p(y_i,z_i|\theta)dz_i \tag{11.33}$$
$$=\prod_{i=1}^{n}\sqrt{\frac{1}{2\pi}\frac{\tau_i\lambda}{\tau_i+\lambda}}\exp\left(-\frac{1}{2}\frac{\tau_i\lambda}{\tau_i+\lambda}\left(y_i-\theta\right)^2\right)$$

which is just the likelihood function given by (11.16). Obviously, (11.30) is different from (11.18) even if the marginal densities, $p(\mathbf{y})$ from these two models are the same. In practice, it is well-known that the Student's t distribution can be reformulated as a normal-inverse-gamma distribution where the variance is treated as a latent variable that follows an inverse-gamma distribution. For example, the asset pricing model

$$R_t=\boldsymbol{\beta}'F_t+\varepsilon_t,\varepsilon_t\sim t[0,\boldsymbol{\Sigma},\nu] \tag{11.34}$$

where R_t is the excess return of portfolio at period t with $N\times 1$ dimension, F_t a $K\times 1$ vector of factor portfolio excess returns, $\boldsymbol{\beta}$ a $N\times K$ vector of scaled covariances, ε_t the random error, $t=1,2,\cdots,n$, $\boldsymbol{\Sigma}$ a diagonal matrix and $\nu=3$, the degree of freedom of t distribution. It can be shown that (11.34) can be rewritten as the normal-inverse-gamma distribution form

$$R_t=\boldsymbol{\beta}'F_t+\boldsymbol{\varepsilon}_t,\boldsymbol{\varepsilon}_t\sim N(0,\boldsymbol{\Sigma}/\omega_t),\omega_t\sim\Gamma\left(\frac{\nu}{2},\frac{\nu}{2}\right) \tag{11.35}$$

where ω_t is a latent variable. Models given by (11.34) and (11.35) are identical. If we apply DIC to the t distribution model and DIC^{DA} to the normal-inverse-gamma distribution model, it often leads to different values even under the same priors; one can refer to Li et al. (2020) for a detailed illustration.

Third, DIC^{DA} is usually sensitive to transformations of latent variables since the dimension of the parameter space is much larger due to data augmentation. Consider the following alternative model to model (11.26):

$$y_i = \ln \eta_i + \varepsilon_i, \tag{11.36}$$

where $\eta_i \sim LN(\theta, \lambda^{-1})$, $\varepsilon_i \sim_{i.i.d.} N(0, \tau_i^{-1})$ for $i = 1, \ldots, n$, η_i, and ε_i are mutually independent for all i, with LN denoting the log-normal distribution. It is clear that the two models given by (11.26) and (11.36) are identical, as the logarithm of the log-normal distribution is the normal distribution. The complete-likelihood function of (11.36) is

$$p(\mathbf{y}|\theta, \eta) = \prod_{i=1}^{n} p(\mathbf{y}|\theta, \eta_i) = \prod_{i=1}^{n} \sqrt{\frac{\tau_i}{2\pi}} \exp\left(-\frac{1}{2}\tau_i (y_i - \ln \eta_i)^2\right).$$

If the prior of θ is also $N(\mu_0, \tau_0^{-1})$, then the posterior density of θ, η is

$$\begin{aligned} & p(\theta, \eta|\mathbf{y}) \\ & \propto \left[\prod_{i=1}^{n} \sqrt{\frac{\tau_i}{2\pi}} \exp\left(-\frac{\tau_i}{2}(y_i - \ln \eta_i)^2\right) \sqrt{\frac{\lambda}{\eta_i^2 2\pi}} \exp\left(-\frac{\lambda}{2}(\ln \eta_i - \theta)^2\right)\right] \\ & \sqrt{\frac{\mu_0}{2\pi}} \exp\left(-\frac{\tau_0}{2}(\theta - \mu_0)^2\right). \end{aligned}$$

Hence, we have

$$\begin{aligned} \theta|\mathbf{y} &\sim N\left(\mu^o, (\tau^o)^{-1}\right), \\ \eta_i|\theta, \mathbf{y} &\sim LN\left(\frac{y_i\tau_i + \lambda\theta}{\tau_i + \lambda}, \frac{1}{\tau_i + \lambda}\right), \end{aligned}$$

where

$$\mu^o = (\tau^o)^{-1}\left(\sum_{i=1}^{n} \frac{\tau_i\lambda}{\tau_i + \lambda} y_i + \tau_0\mu_0\right), \tau^o = \sum_{i=1}^{n} \frac{\tau_i\lambda}{\tau_i + \lambda} + \tau_0.$$

For $i = 1, 2, \ldots, n$, the posterior means of θ and η_i are

$$\begin{aligned} \bar{\theta} &= E(\theta|\mathbf{y}) = \mu^o \\ \bar{\eta}_i &= E(\eta_i|\mathbf{y}) = \exp\left(\frac{1}{2(\tau_i + \lambda)}\right)\left[\exp\left(\mu^{*o} + \frac{1}{2}\tau^{*o-1}\right)\right], \end{aligned}$$

where

$$\mu^{*o} = \frac{y_i\tau_i}{\tau_i + \lambda} + \frac{\lambda}{\tau_i + \lambda}\mu^o, \ \tau^{*o-1} = \left(\frac{\lambda}{\tau_i + \lambda}\right)^2 (\tau^o)^{-1}.$$

To compute P_D^{DA}, we have

$$\begin{aligned}
&\overline{D(\eta,\theta)} \qquad (11.37)\\
&= n\ln 2\pi - \sum_{i=1}^{n}\tau_i + \sum_{i=1}^{n}\frac{\tau_i}{\tau_i+\lambda}\\
&\quad + \sum_{i=1}^{n}\frac{\tau_i\lambda^2}{(\tau_i+\lambda)^2}\left(\sum_{i=1}^{n}\frac{\tau_i\lambda}{\tau_i+\lambda}+\tau_0\right)^{-1} + \sum_{i=1}^{n}\frac{\tau_i\lambda^2}{(\tau_i+\lambda)^2}(y_i-\mu^o)^2\\
&= \overline{D(\mathbf{z},\theta)}.
\end{aligned}$$

$D(\bar{\eta},\bar{\theta})$ can be expressed as

$$D(\bar{\eta},\bar{\theta}) = D(\bar{\mathbf{z}},\bar{\theta}) + C_d, \qquad (11.38)$$

where

$$\begin{aligned}
C_d = &-\sum_{i=1}^{n}\tau_i\frac{\lambda}{(\tau_i+\lambda)^2}(y_i-\mu^o) - (\tau^o)^{-1}\sum_{i=1}^{n}\tau_i\left(\frac{\lambda}{\tau_i+\lambda}\right)^3(y_i-\mu^o)\\
&+\sum_{i=1}^{n}\frac{\tau_i}{4(\tau_i+\lambda)} + \sum_{i=1}^{n}\frac{\tau_i}{2(\tau_i+\lambda)}\left(\frac{\lambda}{\tau_i+\lambda}\right)^2(\tau^o)^{-1}\\
&+\frac{1}{4}\sum_{i=1}^{n}\tau_i\left(\frac{\lambda}{\tau_i+\lambda}\right)^4(\tau^o)^{-2}.
\end{aligned}$$

Let $P_{D,z}^{DA}$ and DIC_z^{DA} be P_D^{DA} and DIC^{DA} for model (11.26). Let $P_{D,z}^{DA}$ and DIC_z^{DA} be $P_{D,\eta}^{DA}$, DIC_η^{DA} for model (11.53). From (11.37) and (11.38), we have

$$\begin{aligned}
P_{D,\eta}^{DA} &= \overline{D(\eta,\theta)} - D(\bar{\eta},\bar{\theta}) = \overline{D(\mathbf{z},\theta)} - D(\bar{\mathbf{z}},\bar{\theta}) - C_d\\
&= P_{D,z}^{DA} - C_d,
\end{aligned}$$

$$\begin{aligned}
\mathrm{DIC}_\eta^{DA} &= D(\bar{\eta},\bar{\theta}) + 2P_{D,\eta}^{DA} = D(\bar{\mathbf{z}},\bar{\theta}) + C_d + 2P_{D,z}^{DA} - 2C_d\\
&= \mathrm{DIC}_z^{DA} - C_d.
\end{aligned}$$

For illustration, let $\tau_i=\tau$, $\rho=\frac{\tau}{\tau+\lambda}$, $\tau_0=0$. Then $\mu^o=\bar{y}$, $\tau^o=n\lambda\rho$. It can be shown that

$$C_d = \frac{1}{4}n\rho + \frac{\lambda}{2(1-\rho)^2} + \frac{\tau(1-\rho)^4}{4n\lambda^2\rho^2}.$$

Clearly, the difference in both P_D^{DA} and DIC^{DA} is very large (with the order $O(n)$) between models (11.26) and (11.53) although they represent identical models. See the appendix for a detailed proof.

DIC_L for Latent Variable Models

For latent variable models, while DIC^{DA} is easier to calculate, it suffers from several theoretical and practical problems. DIC has rigorous theoretical justification, but it is difficult to compute for latent variable models since the observed likelihood function cannot be expressed in closed form. Li et al. (2020) introduced a new version of DIC (DIC_L) for latent variable models which has a valid justification and is feasible to compute. DIC_L is given by

$$\text{DIC}_L = D(\bar{\boldsymbol{\theta}}) + 2P_L, \tag{11.39}$$

where

$$P_L = \mathbf{tr}\left\{\mathbf{I}(\bar{\boldsymbol{\theta}})V(\bar{\boldsymbol{\theta}})\right\}, \tag{11.40}$$

and

$$\mathbf{I}(\boldsymbol{\theta}) = -\frac{\partial^2 \ln p(\mathbf{y}|\boldsymbol{\theta})}{\partial\boldsymbol{\theta}\partial\boldsymbol{\theta}'}, V(\bar{\boldsymbol{\theta}}) = E\left[\left(\boldsymbol{\theta} - \bar{\boldsymbol{\theta}}\right)\left(\boldsymbol{\theta} - \bar{\boldsymbol{\theta}}\right)' |\mathbf{y}\right].$$

Li et al. (2024) showed that under some regularity conditions, DIC_L is an asymptotically unbiased estimator of $E_{\mathbf{y}}E_{\mathbf{y}_{rep}}\left[-2\ln p\left(\mathbf{y}_{rep}|\bar{\boldsymbol{\theta}}(\mathbf{y})\right)\right]$.

Li et al. (2020) proved that, under some regularity conditions,

$$P_L = P + \frac{1}{n}C_{1,L} + \frac{1}{n}C_{2,L} + O_p\left(\frac{1}{n^2}\right), \tag{11.41}$$

$$\text{DIC}_L = \text{AIC} + \frac{1}{n}D_{1,L} + \frac{1}{n}D_{2,L} + O_p\left(\frac{1}{n^2}\right), \tag{11.42}$$

where

$$C_{1,L} = \frac{1}{2}C_{11,L} - \frac{1}{2}C_{12,L}, \quad C_{2,L} = -C_{22,L},$$

$$D_{1,L} = C_{11,L} + \frac{5}{4}C_{12,L}, \quad D_{2,L} = C_{21,L} - 2C_{22,L} - C_{23,L},$$

$$C_{11,L} = \mathbf{tr}\left[\left(\bar{\mathbf{H}}_n^{-1}\left(\hat{\boldsymbol{\theta}}\right) \otimes vec\left(\bar{\mathbf{H}}_n^{-1}\left(\hat{\boldsymbol{\theta}}\right)\right)'\right)\bar{\mathbf{H}}_n^{(4)}\left(\hat{\boldsymbol{\theta}}\right)\right],$$

$$C_{12,L} = vec\left(\bar{\mathbf{H}}_n^{-1}\left(\hat{\boldsymbol{\theta}}\right)\right)'\bar{\mathbf{H}}_n^{(3)}\left(\hat{\boldsymbol{\theta}}\right)\bar{\mathbf{H}}_n^{-1}\left(\hat{\boldsymbol{\theta}}\right)\bar{\mathbf{H}}_n^{(3)}\left(\hat{\boldsymbol{\theta}}\right)' vec\left(\bar{\mathbf{H}}_n^{-1}\left(\hat{\boldsymbol{\theta}}\right)\right),$$

$$C_{21,L} = \pi^{(1)}\left(\hat{\boldsymbol{\theta}}\right)'\bar{\mathbf{H}}_n^{-1}\left(\hat{\boldsymbol{\theta}}\right)\bar{\mathbf{H}}_n^{(3)}\left(\hat{\boldsymbol{\theta}}\right)' vec\left(\bar{\mathbf{H}}_n^{-1}\left(\hat{\boldsymbol{\theta}}\right)\right),$$

$$C_{22,L} = \mathbf{tr}\left[\bar{\mathbf{H}}_n^{-1}\left(\hat{\boldsymbol{\theta}}\right)\pi^{(2)}\left(\hat{\boldsymbol{\theta}}\right)\right], \quad C_{23,L} = \pi^{(1)}\left(\hat{\boldsymbol{\theta}}\right)'\bar{\mathbf{H}}_n^{-1}\left(\hat{\boldsymbol{\theta}}\right)\pi^{(1)}\left(\hat{\boldsymbol{\theta}}\right).$$

From (11.41) and (11.42), DIC_L can also be regarded as a Bayesian version of AIC and the effect of the prior on P_L is $C_{2,L} = -\mathbf{tr}\left[\bar{\mathbf{H}}_n^{-1}\left(\hat{\boldsymbol{\theta}}\right)\pi^{(2)}\left(\hat{\boldsymbol{\theta}}\right)\right]$.

In the context of latent variable models, while DIC^{DA} is trivial to calculate but cannot be justified, DIC is justified but difficult to compute. DIC_L solves this dilemma because it is justified and straightforward to compute. The corresponding deviance is based on the observed-data likelihood function and the latent variables are not treated as parameters.

To illustrate this idea, let us first consider models given by (11.26) and (11.36). It can be shown that

$$\mathbf{I}(\bar{\theta}) = -\sum_{i=1}^{n}\frac{\tau_i\lambda}{\tau_i+\lambda}, V(\bar{\theta}) = \left(\sum_{i=1}^{n}\frac{\tau_i\lambda}{\tau_i+\lambda}+\tau_0\right)^{-1},$$

for both models since they share the same observed-data likelihood. Then we have

$$\begin{aligned} P_{L,z} = P_{L,\eta} &= \sum_{i=1}^{n}\frac{\tau_i\lambda}{\tau_i+\lambda}\left(\sum_{i=1}^{n}\frac{\tau_i\lambda}{\tau_i+\lambda}+\tau_0\right)^{-1} \\ &= 1-\frac{1}{n}\left(\frac{1}{n}\sum_{i=1}^{n}\frac{\tau_i\lambda}{\tau_i+\lambda}\right)^{-1}\tau_0 + O_p\left(n^{-2}\right). \end{aligned}$$

These two values are close to one (the number of parameters in the model) if τ_0 goes to zero, which means that the prior is vague.

It should be noted that DIC_L is calculable from the output of MCMC output. Although DIC_L does not treat latent variables as parameters, the data augmentation technique can be employed in MCMC simulations without compromising the asymptotic validity of DIC_L.

DIC for Misspecified Models

Both DIC and DIC_L require that all candidate models be good approximations to DGP (Assumption 10). In many applications, this requirement is too strong. Li et al. (2020) relaxed this requirement and proposed a new version of DIC (namely DIC_M) to compare misspecified models.

If a candidate model is misspecified, the expected KL divergence between the DGP and $p\left(\mathbf{y}_{rep}|\hat{\boldsymbol{\theta}}(\mathbf{y})\right)$ can be expressed as

$$\begin{aligned} &E_{\mathbf{y}}\left\{2\times KL\left[g\left(\mathbf{y}_{rep}\right),p\left(\mathbf{y}_{rep}|\hat{\boldsymbol{\theta}}(\mathbf{y})\right)\right]\right\} = 2C + E_{\mathbf{y}}E_{\mathbf{y}_{rep}}\left[-2\ln p\left(\mathbf{y}_{rep}|\hat{\boldsymbol{\theta}}(\mathbf{y})\right)\right] \\ &= 2C + E_{\mathbf{y}}\left\{-2\ln p\left(\mathbf{y}|\hat{\boldsymbol{\theta}}(\mathbf{y})\right) - 2\mathbf{tr}\left\{\mathbf{B}_n\left(\boldsymbol{\theta}_n^p\right)\mathbf{H}_n^{-1}\left(\boldsymbol{\theta}_n^p\right)\right\}\right\} + o(1), \qquad (11.43) \end{aligned}$$

where $\hat{\boldsymbol{\theta}}(\mathbf{y})$ denotes the MLE of $\boldsymbol{\theta}_n^p$ in the misspecified model and C is a constant across all candidate models. As before, we write $\hat{\boldsymbol{\theta}}(\mathbf{y})$ as $\hat{\boldsymbol{\theta}}$. Based on (11.43), the Takeuchi information criterion (TIC) is defined as

$$\text{TIC} = -2\ln p\left(\mathbf{y}|\hat{\boldsymbol{\theta}}\right) + 2P_T, \tag{11.44}$$

where P_T is a consistent estimator of $-\mathbf{tr}\left\{\mathbf{B}_n\left(\boldsymbol{\theta}_n^p\right)\mathbf{H}_n^{-1}\left(\boldsymbol{\theta}_n^p\right)\right\}$; see Takeuchi (1976). Takeuchi information criterion is an asymptotically unbiased estimator of the expected KL divergence minus $2C$ when a candidate model is misspecified. The penalty term P_T which is a consistent estimator of $-\mathbf{tr}\left\{\mathbf{B}_n\left(\boldsymbol{\theta}_n^p\right)\mathbf{H}_n^{-1}\left(\boldsymbol{\theta}_n^p\right)\right\}$ takes the form

$$P_T = -\mathbf{tr}\left\{\bar{\Omega}_n\left(\hat{\boldsymbol{\theta}}\right)\bar{\mathbf{H}}_n^{-1}\left(\hat{\boldsymbol{\theta}}\right)\right\}, \tag{11.45}$$

where $\bar{\mathbf{H}}_n^{-1}\left(\hat{\boldsymbol{\theta}}\right)$ is a consistent estimator for $\mathbf{H}_n^{-1}\left(\boldsymbol{\theta}_n^p\right)$, and a heteroskedasticity and autocorrelation consistent (HAC) estimator of $\mathbf{B}_n\left(\boldsymbol{\theta}_n^p\right)$ is defined by

$$\bar{\Omega}_n\left(\hat{\boldsymbol{\theta}}\right) = \frac{1}{n}\sum_{t=1}^{n}\sum_{\tau=1}^{n}\mathbf{s}_t\left(\hat{\boldsymbol{\theta}}\right)\mathbf{s}_\tau\left(\hat{\boldsymbol{\theta}}\right)' k\left(\frac{t-\tau}{\gamma_n}\right),$$

where $k(\cdot)$ is a kernel function and γ_n is the bandwidth (Newey and West (1987)). We require three more assumptions to ensure the consistency and positive semidefiniteness of $\bar{\Omega}_n\left(\hat{\boldsymbol{\theta}}\right)$ and the consistency of P_T; for more details, see De Jong and Davidson (2000).

Assumption 11: Assume the kernel function $k(\cdot) \in \mathcal{H}$, where

$$\mathcal{H} = \left\{\begin{array}{c} k(\cdot): R \to [-1,1], k(x) = k(-x), \text{for any } x \in R, \\ \int_{-\infty}^{+\infty}|k(x)|\,dx < \infty,\ \int_{-\infty}^{+\infty}\psi(\xi)\,d\xi < \infty, \\ k(\cdot) \text{ is continuous at 0 and at all but a finite number of points in } R \end{array}\right\},$$

where

$$\psi(\xi) = (2\pi)^{-1}\int_{-\infty}^{+\infty} k(x)\,e^{i\xi x}dx.$$

Assumption 12: The bandwidth parameter γ_n is an increasing function of sample size n and $\gamma_n = o\left(n^{1/2}\right)$.

Assumption 13: The expectation of the score function $E\left(\mathbf{s}_t\left(\boldsymbol{\theta}_n^p\right)\right) = 0$ for any t.

Assumptions 11 and 12 ensure that $\bar{\Omega}_n\left(\hat{\boldsymbol{\theta}}\right)$ is positive semidefinite with probability 1 (Andrews, 1991), and together with Assumption 10, $P_T = P + o_p(1)$. The Assumptions 1–8 and 11–13 imply that

$$\bar{\Omega}_n\left(\hat{\boldsymbol{\theta}}\right) - \mathbf{B}_n\left(\boldsymbol{\theta}_n^p\right) \xrightarrow{p} 0,$$

which in turn implies that

$$P_T + \mathbf{tr}\left\{\mathbf{B}_n\left(\boldsymbol{\theta}_n^p\right)\mathbf{H}_n^{-1}\left(\boldsymbol{\theta}_n^p\right)\right\} \xrightarrow{p} 0.$$

If the model is estimated by a Bayesian method, Li et al. (2020) proved that $nV\left(\bar{\boldsymbol{\theta}}\right)$ and $\bar{\Omega}_n\left(\bar{\boldsymbol{\theta}}\right)$ are consistent estimators of $\mathbf{H}_n^{-1}\left(\boldsymbol{\theta}_n^p\right)$ and $\mathbf{B}_n\left(\boldsymbol{\theta}_n^p\right)$, respectively. Hence, DIC is defined as

$$\mathrm{DIC}_M = D\left(\bar{\boldsymbol{\theta}}\right) + 2P_M \text{ with } P_M = \mathbf{tr}\left\{n\bar{\Omega}_n\left(\bar{\boldsymbol{\theta}}\right)V\left(\bar{\boldsymbol{\theta}}\right)\right\}, \quad (11.46)$$

where $\bar{\boldsymbol{\theta}}$ is the posterior mean of $\boldsymbol{\theta}$. Li et al. (2020) proved that DIC_M is an asymptotically unbiased estimator of $E_{\mathbf{y}}E_{\mathbf{y}_{rep}}\left[-2\ln p\left(\mathbf{y}_{rep}|\bar{\boldsymbol{\theta}}(\mathbf{y})\right)\right]$ when a candidate model is misspecified. Under Assumptions 1–9 and 11–12, DIC_M and TIC are asymptotically equivalent, that is,

$$P_M = P_T + o_p\left(\frac{1}{n}\right), \mathrm{DIC}_M = \mathrm{TIC} + o_p\left(\frac{1}{n}\right), \quad (11.47)$$

and

$$\bar{\Omega}_n\left(\bar{\boldsymbol{\theta}}\right) - \bar{\Omega}_n\left(\hat{\boldsymbol{\theta}}\right) \xrightarrow{p} 0.$$

Thus, DIC_M can be regarded as a Bayesian version of TIC.

The conditions to obtain the asymptotic unbiasedness of TIC include the consistency and asymptotic normality of MLE (Assumptions 1–8), and the consistent estimator of $-\mathbf{tr}\left\{\mathbf{B}_n\left(\boldsymbol{\theta}_n^p\right)\mathbf{H}_n^{-1}\left(\boldsymbol{\theta}_n^p\right)\right\}$ based on MLE (Assumptions 11–13). From (11.12), the Bayesian posterior mean the estimator is consistent and asymptotic normal under Assumptions 1–9. And (11.47) shows that P_M is a consistent estimator of $-\mathbf{tr}\left\{\mathbf{B}_n\left(\boldsymbol{\theta}_n^p\right)\mathbf{H}_n^{-1}\left(\boldsymbol{\theta}_n^p\right)\right\}$ under Assumptions 11–13. That is the intuition why DIC_M is an asymptotically unbiased estimator of $E_{\mathbf{y}}E_{\mathbf{y}_{rep}}\left[-2\ln p\left(\mathbf{y}_{rep}|\bar{\boldsymbol{\theta}}(\mathbf{y})\right)\right]$.

Given that DIC_M is applicable to both correctly specified and misspecified models, in contrast to DIC_L, which is suitable only for correctly specified models, there might be a preference for employing DIC*M* over DIC_L in model selection scenarios. Nonetheless, it's important to consider that DIC_M necessitates the Fisher information matrix, which is usually easier to compute than the Hessian information matrix required by DIC_L.

11.4 Concluding Remarks

In this chapter, we provided an overview of some approaches developed in recent years for specification testing and model selection. For specification testing, we summarized two posterior-based tests proposed by Li et al. (2018) and their asymptotic properties; the first method is the posterior-based version of IOS_A test and the second method was motivated by the power enhancement technique. For model selection, we provided an overview of the well-known DIC and its extensions, such as DIC_L for latent variable models and DIC_M for misspecified models. We showed that these approaches not only have good theoretical properties, but also are reasonably simple to compute from posterior output. Hence, with the advance of MCMC and SMC techniques and expanding computing capabilities, these approaches can be applied for a variety of complex models, especially latent variable models. We also illustrated the problem with the commonly used calculation of DIC in practice based on the random effect model.

11.5 Appendix

11.5.1 DIC^{DA} for the Random Effect Model (11.26)

The joint posterior density of $\theta, \mathbf{z}$ is

$$
\begin{aligned}
& p(\theta, \mathbf{z}|\mathbf{y}) \qquad (11.48)\\
& \propto \left[\prod_{i=1}^{n} \sqrt{\frac{\tau_i}{2\pi}} \exp\left(-\frac{\tau_i}{2}(y_i - z_i)^2\right) \sqrt{\frac{\lambda}{2\pi}} \exp\left(-\frac{\lambda}{2}(z_i - \theta)^2\right)\right] \\
& \quad \sqrt{\frac{\mu_0}{2\pi}} \exp\left(-\frac{\tau_0}{2}(\theta - \mu_0)^2\right) \\
& \propto \exp\left\{-\frac{1}{2}\sum_{i=1}^{n}\left[(\tau_i + \lambda) z_i^2 - 2(\tau_i y_i + \lambda\theta) z_i + \tau_i y_i^2 + \lambda\theta^2\right]\right\} \\
& \quad \exp\left(-\frac{\tau_0}{2}(\theta - \mu_0)^2\right) \\
& = \exp\left\{-\frac{1}{2}\sum_{i=1}^{n}(\tau_i + \lambda)\left[\left(z_i - \frac{\tau_i y_i + \lambda\theta}{\tau_i + \lambda}\right)^2 - \left(\frac{\tau_i y_i + \lambda\theta}{\tau_i + \lambda}\right)^2 \right.\right. \\
& \quad \left.\left. + \frac{\tau_i y_i^2 + \lambda\theta^2}{\tau_i + \lambda}\right]\right\} \\
& \quad \times \exp\left(-\frac{\tau_0}{2}(\theta - \mu_0)^2\right) \\
& = \exp\left\{-\sum_{i=1}^{n}\frac{\tau_i + \lambda}{2}\left(z_i - \frac{\tau_i y_i + \lambda\theta}{\tau_i + \lambda}\right)^2\right\} \\
& \quad \exp\left\{-\frac{1}{2}\sum_{i=1}^{n}\left[-\frac{(\tau_i y_i + \lambda\theta)^2}{\tau_i + \lambda} + \tau_i y_i^2 + \lambda\theta^2\right]\right\} \\
& \quad \times \exp\left(-\frac{\tau_0}{2}(\theta - \mu_0)^2\right) \\
& = \exp\left\{\sum_{i=1}^{n} -\frac{\tau_i + \lambda}{2}\left(z_i - \frac{\tau_i y_i + \lambda\theta}{\tau_i + \lambda}\right)^2\right\}
\end{aligned}
$$

$$\exp\left\{-\frac{1}{2}\sum_{i=1}^{n}\frac{\tau_i\lambda}{\tau_i+\lambda}(y_i-\theta)^2\right\}\times\exp\left(-\frac{\tau_0}{2}(\theta-\mu_0)^2\right).$$

Then the density of z_i conditional on $\theta, \mathbf{y}$ is

$$z_i|\theta,\mathbf{y}\sim\mathbf{N}\left(\frac{\tau_i y_i+\lambda\theta}{\tau_i+\lambda},\frac{1}{\tau_i+\lambda}\right). \tag{11.49}$$

The posterior density of θ conditional on $\mathbf{y}$ can be obtained by integrating out $\mathbf{z}$ from (11.48):

$$\begin{aligned}
p(\theta|\mathbf{y}) &\propto \exp\left\{-\frac{1}{2}\sum_{i=1}^{n}\frac{\tau_i\lambda}{\tau_i+\lambda}(y_i-\theta)^2\right\}\exp\left(-\frac{\tau_0}{2}(\theta-\mu_0)^2\right)\\
&= \exp\left\{-\frac{1}{2}\sum_{i=1}^{n}\frac{\tau_i\lambda}{\tau_i+\lambda}(y_i-\theta)^2-\frac{\tau_0}{2}(\theta-\mu_0)^2\right\}\\
&\propto \exp\left\{-\frac{1}{2}\left[\left(\sum_{i=1}^{n}\frac{\tau_i\lambda}{\tau_i+\lambda}+\tau_0\right)\theta^2-2\left(\sum_{i=1}^{n}\frac{\tau_i\lambda}{\tau_i+\lambda}y_i+\tau_0\mu_0\right)\theta\right]\right\},
\end{aligned}$$

that is,

$$\theta|\mathbf{y}\sim\mathbf{N}\left(\mu^o,(\tau^o)^{-1}\right), \tag{11.50}$$

where

$$\mu^o=(\tau^o)^{-1}\left(\sum_{i=1}^{n}\frac{\tau_i\lambda}{\tau_i+\lambda}y_i+\tau_0\mu_0\right), \tau^o=\sum_{i=1}^{n}\frac{\tau_i\lambda}{\tau_i+\lambda}+\tau_0.$$

From (11.49) and (11.50), we have

$$\begin{aligned}
\bar{\theta} &= \mu^o,\\
\bar{z}_i &= E\left(\frac{\tau_i y_i+\lambda\theta}{\tau_i+\lambda}|\mathbf{y}\right)=\frac{\tau_i y_i+\lambda\mu^o}{\tau_i+\lambda}.
\end{aligned}$$

To compute DIC^{DA}, we have

$$\begin{aligned}
\overline{D(\mathbf{z},\theta)} &= n\ln 2\pi-\sum_{i=1}^{n}\ln\tau_i+\int\left[\sum_{i=1}^{n}\tau_i\int(y_i-z_i)^2 p(z_i|\theta,\mathbf{y})\,dz_i\right]p(\theta|\mathbf{y})\,d\theta\\
&= n\ln 2\pi-\sum_{i=1}^{n}\ln\tau_i\\
&\quad+\int\left[\sum_{i=1}^{n}\tau_i\int\left(y_i-\frac{y_i\tau_i+\lambda\theta}{\tau_i+\lambda}+\frac{y_i\tau_i+\lambda\theta}{\tau_i+\lambda}-z_i\right)^2 p(z_i|\theta,\mathbf{y})\,dz_i\right]p(\theta|\mathbf{y})\,d\theta
\end{aligned}$$

$$
\begin{aligned}
&= n\ln 2\pi - \sum_{i=1}^{n} \ln \tau_i \\
&\quad + \int \left[\sum_{i=1}^{n} \tau_i \left(y_i - \frac{y_i\tau_i + \lambda\theta}{\tau_i + \lambda} \right)^2 + \sum_{i=1}^{n} \frac{\tau_i}{\tau_i + \lambda} \right] p(\theta|\mathbf{y})\, d\theta \\
&= n\ln 2\pi - \sum_{i=1}^{n} \ln \tau_i + \sum_{i=1}^{n} \frac{\tau_i}{\tau_i + \lambda} + \sum_{i=1}^{n} \tau_i \int \left(y_i - \frac{y_i\tau_i + \lambda\theta}{\tau_i + \lambda} \right)^2 p(\theta|\mathbf{y})\, d\theta \\
&= n\ln 2\pi - \sum_{i=1}^{n} \ln \tau_i + \sum_{i=1}^{n} \frac{\tau_i}{\tau_i + \lambda} + \sum_{i=1}^{n} \tau_i \int \left(y_i - \frac{y_i\tau_i}{\tau_i + \lambda} - \frac{\lambda}{\tau_i + \lambda}\theta \right)^2 p(\theta|\mathbf{y})\, d\theta \\
&= n\ln 2\pi - \sum_{i=1}^{n} \ln \tau_i + \sum_{i=1}^{n} \frac{\tau_i}{\tau_i + \lambda} + \sum_{i=1}^{n} \tau_i \int \left(\frac{\lambda}{\tau_i + \lambda} y_i - \frac{\lambda}{\tau_i + \lambda}\theta \right)^2 p(\theta|\mathbf{y})\, d\theta \\
&= n\ln 2\pi - \sum_{i=1}^{n} \ln \tau_i + \sum_{i=1}^{n} \frac{\tau_i}{\tau_i + \lambda} + \sum_{i=1}^{n} \frac{\tau_i\lambda^2}{(\tau_i + \lambda)^2} \int (y_i - \theta)^2 p(\theta|\mathbf{y})\, d\theta \\
&= n\ln 2\pi - \sum_{i=1}^{n} \ln \tau_i + \sum_{i=1}^{n} \frac{\tau_i}{\tau_i + \lambda} + \sum_{i=1}^{n} \frac{\tau_i\lambda^2}{(\tau_i + \lambda)^2} \int (y_i - \mu^o + \mu^o - \theta)^2 p(\theta|\mathbf{y})\, d\theta \\
&= n\ln 2\pi - \sum_{i=1}^{n} \ln \tau_i + \sum_{i=1}^{n} \frac{\tau_i}{\tau_i + \lambda} \\
&\quad + \sum_{i=1}^{n} \frac{\tau_i\lambda^2}{(\tau_i + \lambda)^2} (\tau^o)^{-1} + \sum_{i=1}^{n} \frac{\tau_i\lambda^2}{(\tau_i + \lambda)^2} (y_i - \mu^o)^2,
\end{aligned}
$$

$$
\begin{aligned}
D(\bar{\mathbf{z}}, \bar{\theta}) &= n\ln 2\pi - \sum_{i=1}^{n} \ln \tau_i + \sum_{i=1}^{n} \tau_i \left(y_i - \frac{y_i\tau_i + \lambda\mu^o}{\tau_i + \lambda} \right)^2 \\
&= n\ln 2\pi - \sum_{i=1}^{n} \ln \tau_i + \sum_{i=1}^{n} \frac{\tau_i\lambda^2}{(\tau_i + \lambda)^2} (y_i - \mu^o)^2, \\
P_D^{DA} &= \overline{D(\mathbf{z}, \theta)} - D(\bar{\mathbf{z}}, \bar{\theta}) \\
&= \sum_{i=1}^{n} \frac{\tau_i}{\tau_i + \lambda} + \sum_{i=1}^{n} \frac{\tau_i\lambda^2}{(\tau_i + \lambda)^2} (\tau^o)^{-1} \\
&= \sum_{i=1}^{n} \frac{\tau_i}{\tau_i + \lambda} + \left(\sum_{i=1}^{n} \frac{\tau_i}{\tau_i + \lambda} + \frac{\tau_0}{\lambda} \right)^{-1} \sum_{i=1}^{n} \frac{\tau_i}{\tau_i + \lambda} \frac{\lambda}{\tau_i + \lambda}, \\
\mathrm{DIC}^{DA} &= D(\bar{\mathbf{z}}, \bar{\theta}) + 2P_D^{DA} \qquad (11.51) \\
&= n\ln 2\pi - \sum_{i=1}^{n} \ln \tau_i + \sum_{i=1}^{n} \frac{\tau_i\lambda^2}{(\tau_i + \lambda)^2} (y_i - \mu^o)^2 \\
&\quad + 2\left(\sum_{i=1}^{n} \frac{\tau_i}{\tau_i + \lambda} + \sum_{i=1}^{n} \frac{\tau_i\lambda^2}{(\tau_i + \lambda)^2} \tau^{o-1} \right).
\end{aligned}
$$

Note that

$$
\begin{aligned}
& E_{\mathbf{y}} E_{\mathbf{y}_{rep}} \left[-2 \ln p \left(\mathbf{y}_{rep} | \bar{\mathbf{z}}(\mathbf{y}), \bar{\theta}(\mathbf{y})\right)\right] \\
&= n \ln 2\pi - \sum_{i=1}^{n} \ln \tau_i + \sum_{i=1}^{n} \left[\tau_i E_{\mathbf{y}} E_{\mathbf{y}_{rep}} \left(y_{i,rep} - \frac{\tau_i}{\tau_i + \lambda} y_i - \frac{\lambda}{\tau_i + \lambda} \mu^o \right)^2 \right] \\
&= n \ln 2\pi - \sum_{i=1}^{n} \ln \tau_i + \sum_{i=1}^{n} \tau_i \left[E_{\mathbf{y}} \left[E_{\mathbf{y}_{rep}} \left(y_{i,rep} - \frac{\tau_i}{\tau_i + \lambda} y_i - \frac{\lambda}{\tau_i + \lambda} \mu^o \right)^2 \right] \right] \\
&= n \ln 2\pi - \sum_{i=1}^{n} \ln \tau_i + \sum_{i=1}^{n} \tau_i \left[E_{\mathbf{y}} \left[E_{\mathbf{y}_{rep}} \left(\begin{array}{c} y_{i,rep} - \theta \\ + \theta - \frac{\tau_i}{\tau_i + \lambda} y_i - \frac{\lambda}{\tau_i + \lambda} \mu^o \end{array} \right)^2 \right] \right] \\
&= n \ln 2\pi - \sum_{i=1}^{n} \ln \tau_i + \sum_{i=1}^{n} \tau_i E_{\mathbf{y}} \left[E_{\mathbf{y}_{rep}} \left[(y_{i,rep} - \theta)^2 \right] \right] \\
&\quad + \sum_{i=1}^{n} \tau_i E_{\mathbf{y}} \left[\left(\theta - \frac{\tau_i}{\tau_i + \lambda} y_i - \frac{\lambda}{\tau_i + \lambda} \mu^o \right)^2 \right] \\
&= n \ln 2\pi - \sum_{i=1}^{n} \ln \tau_i + \sum_{i=1}^{n} \frac{\tau_i + \lambda}{\lambda} \\
&\quad + \sum_{i=1}^{n} \tau_i E_{\mathbf{y}} \left[\left(\theta - \frac{\tau_i}{\tau_i + \lambda} y_i - \frac{\lambda}{\tau_i + \lambda} \mu^o \right)^2 \right] \\
&= n \ln 2\pi - \sum_{i=1}^{n} \ln \tau_i + \sum_{i=1}^{n} \frac{\tau_i + \lambda}{\lambda} + \sum_{i=1}^{n} \tau_i E_{\mathbf{y}} \left[\left(\theta - y_i + \frac{\lambda}{\tau_i + \lambda} (y_i - \mu^o) \right)^2 \right] \\
&= n \ln 2\pi - \sum_{i=1}^{n} \ln \tau_i + \sum_{i=1}^{n} \frac{\tau_i + \lambda}{\lambda} \\
&\quad + \sum_{i=1}^{n} \tau_i E_{\mathbf{y}} \left[(\theta - y_i)^2 \right] + \sum_{i=1}^{n} \frac{\tau_i \lambda^2}{(\tau_i + \lambda)^2} E_{\mathbf{y}} \left[(y_i - \mu^o)^2 \right] \\
&= n \ln 2\pi - \sum_{i=1}^{n} \ln \tau_i + \sum_{i=1}^{n} \frac{\tau_i + \lambda}{\lambda} \\
&\quad + \sum_{i=1}^{n} \frac{\tau_i + \lambda}{\lambda} + \sum_{i=1}^{n} \frac{\tau_i \lambda^2}{(\tau_i + \lambda)^2} E_{\mathbf{y}} \left[(y_i - \mu^o)^2 \right],
\end{aligned} \tag{11.52}
$$

where we have used the fact that $y_i \sim N\left(\theta, \tau_i^{-1} + \lambda^{-1}\right)$ and $y_{i,rep} \sim N\left(\theta, \tau_i^{-1} + \lambda^{-1}\right)$.

From (11.51) and (11.52), we have

$$
\begin{aligned}
E_{\mathbf{y}} \left(\mathrm{DIC}^{DA} \right) &= E_{\mathbf{y}} E_{\mathbf{y}_{rep}} \left[-2 \ln p \left(\mathbf{y}_{rep} | \bar{\mathbf{z}}(\mathbf{y}), \bar{\theta}(\mathbf{y})\right)\right] + 2 \sum_{i=1}^{n} \left(\frac{\tau_i}{\tau_i + \lambda} - \frac{\tau_i + \lambda}{\lambda} \right) \\
&\quad + 2 \sum_{i=1}^{n} \frac{\tau_i \lambda^2}{(\tau_i + \lambda)^2} (\tau^o)^{-1}.
\end{aligned}
$$

11.5.2 DIC^{DA} for the Random Effect Model with the Log-Normal Distribution

The complete-likelihood function is

$$p(\mathbf{y}|\theta,\eta) = \prod_{i=1}^{n} p(\mathbf{y}|\theta,\eta_i) = \prod_{i=1}^{n} \sqrt{\frac{\tau_i}{2\pi}} \exp\left(-\frac{1}{2}\tau_i (y_i - \ln\eta_i)^2\right).$$

Since the prior of θ is $N(\mu_0, \tau_0^{-1})$, the posterior density of θ, η is

$$\begin{aligned}
&p(\theta,\eta|\mathbf{y}) \qquad\qquad (11.53)\\
&\propto \left[\prod_{i=1}^{n} \sqrt{\frac{\tau_i}{2\pi}} \exp\left(-\frac{\tau_i}{2}(y_i - \ln\eta_i)^2\right) \sqrt{\frac{\lambda}{\eta_i^2 2\pi}} \exp\left(-\frac{\lambda}{2}(\ln\eta_i - \theta)^2\right)\right] \sqrt{\frac{\mu_0}{2\pi}} \exp\left(-\frac{\tau_0}{2}(\theta-\mu_0)^2\right)\\
&= \left[\prod_{i=1}^{n} \sqrt{\frac{\lambda}{\eta_i^2 2\pi}} \sqrt{\frac{\tau_i}{2\pi}} \exp\left(-\frac{\tau_i}{2}(y_i - \ln\eta_i)^2 - \frac{\lambda}{2}(\ln\eta_i - \theta)^2\right)\right] \sqrt{\frac{\mu_0}{2\pi}} \exp\left(-\frac{\tau_0}{2}(\theta-\mu_0)^2\right)\\
&= \left[\prod_{i=1}^{n} \sqrt{\frac{\lambda}{\eta_i^2 2\pi}} \sqrt{\frac{\tau_i}{2\pi}} \exp\left(-\frac{1}{2}\left[(\tau_i+\lambda)(\ln\eta_i)^2 - 2(\tau_i y_i + \lambda\theta)\ln\eta_i + \tau_i y_i^2 + \lambda\theta^2\right]\right)\right]\\
&\quad\times \sqrt{\frac{\mu_0}{2\pi}} \exp\left(-\frac{\tau_0}{2}(\theta-\mu_0)^2\right)\\
&= \left[\prod_{i=1}^{n} \sqrt{\frac{\lambda}{\eta_i^2 2\pi}} \sqrt{\frac{\tau_i}{2\pi}} \exp\left(-\frac{\tau_i+\lambda}{2}\left[(\ln\eta_i)^2 - 2\frac{\tau_i y_i + \lambda\theta}{\tau_i+\lambda}\ln\eta_i + \frac{\tau_i y_i^2 + \lambda\theta^2}{\tau_i+\lambda}\right]\right)\right]\\
&\quad\times \sqrt{\frac{\mu_0}{2\pi}} \exp\left(-\frac{\tau_0}{2}(\theta-\mu_0)^2\right)\\
&= \left[\prod_{i=1}^{n} \sqrt{\frac{\lambda}{\eta_i^2 2\pi}} \sqrt{\frac{\tau_i}{2\pi}} \exp\left(-\frac{\tau_i+\lambda}{2}\left[\left(\ln\eta_i - \frac{\tau_i y_i + \lambda\theta}{\tau_i+\lambda}\right)^2 - \left(\frac{\tau_i y_i + \lambda\theta}{\tau_i+\lambda}\right)^2 + \frac{\tau_i y_i^2 + \lambda\theta^2}{\tau_i+\lambda}\right]\right)\right]\\
&\quad\times \sqrt{\frac{\mu_0}{2\pi}} \exp\left(-\frac{\tau_0}{2}(\theta-\mu_0)^2\right)\\
&= \left[\prod_{i=1}^{n} \sqrt{\frac{\lambda}{\eta_i^2 2\pi}} \sqrt{\frac{\tau_i}{2\pi}} \exp\left(-\frac{\tau_i+\lambda}{2}\left[\left(\ln\eta_i - \frac{\tau_i y_i + \lambda\theta}{\tau_i+\lambda}\right)^2 + \frac{\tau_i\lambda}{(\tau_i+\lambda)^2}(y_i-\theta)^2\right]\right)\right]\\
&\quad\times \sqrt{\frac{\mu_0}{2\pi}} \exp\left(-\frac{\tau_0}{2}(\theta-\mu_0)^2\right)\\
&= \left[\prod_{i=1}^{n} \sqrt{\frac{\lambda}{2\pi}} \sqrt{\frac{\tau_i}{2\pi}} \sqrt{\frac{1}{\eta_i^2 2\pi}} \exp\left(-\frac{\tau_i+\lambda}{2}\left(\ln\eta_i - \frac{\tau_i y_i + \lambda\theta}{\tau_i+\lambda}\right)^2\right)\right]\\
&\quad\times \prod_{i=1}^{n} \exp\left(-\frac{1}{2}\frac{\tau_i\lambda}{\tau_i+\lambda}(y_i-\theta)^2\right) \sqrt{\frac{\mu_0}{2\pi}} \exp\left(-\frac{\tau_0}{2}(\theta-\mu_0)^2\right).
\end{aligned}$$

Then we have

$$\begin{aligned}
p(\theta|\mathbf{y}) &= \int p(\theta,\eta|\mathbf{y})d\theta \qquad\qquad (11.54)\\
&\propto \prod_{i=1}^{n} \exp\left(-\frac{1}{2}\frac{\tau_i\lambda}{\tau_i+\lambda}(y_i-\theta)^2\right) \sqrt{\frac{\mu_0}{2\pi}} \exp\left(-\frac{\tau_0}{2}(\theta-\mu_0)^2\right).
\end{aligned}$$

From (11.53) and (11.54), the posterior densities of θ and η_i can be written as

$$\theta|\mathbf{y} \sim \mathbf{N}\left(\mu^o, (\tau^o)^{-1}\right),$$
$$\eta_i|\theta, \mathbf{y} \sim \mathbf{LN}\left(\frac{y_i\tau_i + \lambda\theta}{\tau_i + \lambda}, \frac{1}{\tau_i + \lambda}\right),$$

where

$$\mu^o = (\tau^o)^{-1}\left(\sum_{i=1}^{n} \frac{\tau_i\lambda}{\tau_i + \lambda} y_i + \tau_0\mu_0\right), \tau^o = \sum_{i=1}^{n} \frac{\tau_i\lambda}{\tau_i + \lambda} + \tau_0,$$

and

$$E(\eta_i|\theta, \mathbf{y}) = \exp\left(\frac{y_i\tau_i + \lambda\theta}{\tau_i + \lambda} + \frac{1}{2(\tau_i + \lambda)}\right),$$

$$\begin{aligned} Var(\eta_i|\theta, \mathbf{y}) &= \left[\exp\left(\frac{1}{\tau_i + \lambda}\right) - 1\right] \exp\left(2\frac{y_i\tau_i + \lambda\theta}{\tau_i + \lambda} + \frac{1}{(\tau_i + \lambda)}\right) \\ &= \left[\exp\left(\frac{1}{\tau_i + \lambda}\right) - 1\right] \exp\left(\frac{1}{(\tau_i + \lambda)}\right) \exp\left(2\frac{y_i\tau_i + \lambda\theta}{\tau_i + \lambda}\right). \end{aligned}$$

The posterior mean of θ is $\bar{\theta} = E(\theta|\mathbf{y}) = \mu^o$. The mean of η_i conditional on $\theta, \mathbf{y}$ is

$$E(\eta_i|\theta, \mathbf{y}) = \exp\left(\frac{y_i\tau_i + \lambda\theta}{\tau_i + \lambda} + \frac{1}{2(\tau_i + \lambda)}\right).$$

Then the posterior mean of η_i can be expressed as

$$\bar{\eta}_i = E[E(\eta_i|\theta, \mathbf{y})] = \exp\left(\frac{1}{2(\tau_i + \lambda)}\right) E\left[\exp\left(\frac{y_i\tau_i + \lambda\theta}{\tau_i + \lambda}\right)|\mathbf{y}\right], \tag{11.55}$$

for $i = 1, 2, \ldots, n$. Note that

$$\frac{y_i\tau_i + \lambda\theta}{\tau_i + \lambda} = \frac{y_i\tau_i}{\tau_i + \lambda} + \frac{\lambda}{\tau_i + \lambda}\theta.$$

Then

$$\frac{y_i\tau_i + \lambda\theta}{\tau_i + \lambda}|\mathbf{y} \sim \mathbf{N}\left(\mu^{*o}, \tau^{*o-1}\right),$$

where

$$\mu^{*o} = \frac{y_i\tau_i}{\tau_i + \lambda} + \frac{\lambda}{\tau_i + \lambda}\mu^o, \ \tau^{*o-1} = \left(\frac{\lambda}{\tau_i + \lambda}\right)^2 (\tau^o)^{-1}.$$

since $\theta|\mathbf{y} \sim \mathbf{N}\left(\mu^o, (\tau^o)^{-1}\right)$. Hence we have

$$\exp\left(\frac{y_i\tau_i + \lambda\theta}{\tau_i + \lambda}\right)|\mathbf{y} \sim \mathbf{LN}\left(\mu^{*o}, \tau^{*o-1}\right).$$

Then, from (11.55), we have

$$\bar{\eta}_i = \exp\left(\frac{1}{2(\tau_i + \lambda)}\right)\left[\exp\left(\mu^{*o} + \frac{1}{2}\tau^{*o-1}\right)\right]. \tag{11.56}$$

To compute P_D^{DA}, we have

$$\begin{aligned}
&\overline{D(\boldsymbol{\eta}, \theta)} \qquad (11.57)\\
&= n\ln 2\pi - \sum_{i=1}^{n}\ln\tau_i + \int\left[\sum_{i=1}^{n}\tau_i\int(y_i - \ln\eta_i)^2 p(\eta_i|\theta, \mathbf{y})\,d\eta_i\right]\\
&\quad p(\theta|\mathbf{y})\,d\theta\\
&= n\ln 2\pi - \sum_{i=1}^{n}\ln\tau_i\\
&\quad + \int\left[\sum_{i=1}^{n}\tau_i\int(y_i - E(\ln\eta_i|\theta, \mathbf{y}) + E(\ln\eta_i|\theta, \mathbf{y})\right.\\
&\quad \left.- \ln\eta_i)^2 p(\eta_i|\theta, \mathbf{y})\,d\eta_i\right]p(\theta|\mathbf{y})\,d\theta\\
&= n\ln 2\pi - \sum_{i=1}^{n}\ln\tau_i + \sum_{i=1}^{n}\tau_i\int(y_i - E(\ln\eta_i|\theta, \mathbf{y}))^2 p(\theta|\mathbf{y})\,d\theta\\
&\quad + \sum_{i=1}^{n}\tau_i\int Var(\ln\eta_i|\theta, \mathbf{y})\,p(\theta|\mathbf{y})\,d\theta\\
&= n\ln 2\pi - \sum_{i=1}^{n}\ln\tau_i + \sum_{i=1}^{n}\tau_i\int\left(y_i - \frac{y_i\tau_i + \lambda\mu^o}{\tau_i + \lambda}\right)^2 p(\theta|\mathbf{y})\,d\theta\\
&\quad + \sum_{i=1}^{n}\tau_i\int Var(\ln\eta_i|\theta, \mathbf{y})\,p(\theta|\mathbf{y})\,d\theta\\
&= n\ln 2\pi - \sum_{i=1}^{n}\ln\tau_i + \sum_{i=1}^{n}\frac{\tau_i\lambda^2}{(\tau_i + \lambda)^2}\tau^{o-1}\\
&\quad + \sum_{i=1}^{n}\frac{\tau_i\lambda^2}{(\tau_i + \lambda)^2}(y_i - \mu^o)^2 + \sum_{i=1}^{n}\frac{\tau_i}{\tau_i + \lambda},
\end{aligned}$$

which is the same as $\overline{D(\mathbf{z},\theta)}$. And $D(\bar{\boldsymbol{\eta}},\bar{\theta})$ is

$$\begin{aligned}
D(\bar{\boldsymbol{\eta}},\bar{\theta}) &= n\ln 2\pi - \sum_{i=1}^{n}\ln\tau_i + \sum_{i=1}^{n}\tau_i\left(y_i - \ln\bar{\eta}_i\right)^2 \\
&= n\ln 2\pi - \sum_{i=1}^{n}\ln\tau_i + \sum_{i=1}^{n}\tau_i\left(y_i - \ln\left(\exp\left(\frac{1}{2\left(\tau_i+\lambda\right)}\right)\left[\exp\left(\mu^{*o} + \frac{1}{2}\tau^{*o-1}\right)\right]\right)\right)^2 \\
&= n\ln 2\pi - \sum_{i=1}^{n}\ln\tau_i + \sum_{i=1}^{n}\tau_i\left(y_i - \ln\left(\exp\left(\frac{1}{2\left(\tau_i+\lambda\right)}\right)\left[\exp\left(\mu^{*o} + \frac{1}{2}\tau^{*o-1}\right)\right]\right)\right)^2 \\
&= n\ln 2\pi - \sum_{i=1}^{n}\ln\tau_i + \sum_{i=1}^{n}\tau_i\left(y_i - \frac{1}{2\left(\tau_i+\lambda\right)} - \mu^{*o} - \frac{1}{2}\tau^{*o-1}\right)^2 \\
&= n\ln 2\pi - \sum_{i=1}^{n}\ln\tau_i + \sum_{i=1}^{n}\tau_i\left(y_i - \frac{1}{2\left(\tau_i+\lambda\right)} - \mu^{*o} - \frac{1}{2}\tau^{*o-1}\right)^2 \\
&= n\ln 2\pi - \sum_{i=1}^{n}\ln\tau_i + \sum_{i=1}^{n}\tau_i\left(y_i - \frac{1}{2\left(\tau_i+\lambda\right)} - \frac{y_i\tau_i}{\tau_i+\lambda} - \frac{\lambda}{\tau_i+\lambda}\mu^o - \frac{1}{2}\left(\frac{\lambda}{\tau_i+\lambda}\right)^2\left(\tau^o\right)^{-1}\right)^2 \\
&= n\ln 2\pi - \sum_{i=1}^{n}\ln\tau_i + \sum_{i=1}^{n}\tau_i\left(y_i - \frac{y_i\tau_i}{\tau_i+\lambda} - \frac{\lambda}{\tau_i+\lambda}\mu^o - \frac{1}{2\left(\tau_i+\lambda\right)} - \frac{1}{2}\left(\frac{\lambda}{\tau_i+\lambda}\right)^2\left(\tau^o\right)^{-1}\right)^2 \\
&= n\ln 2\pi - \sum_{i=1}^{n}\ln\tau_i + \sum_{i=1}^{n}\tau_i\left(\frac{\lambda}{\tau_i+\lambda}\left(y_i-\mu^o\right) - \frac{1}{2\left(\tau_i+\lambda\right)} - \frac{1}{2}\left(\frac{\lambda}{\tau_i+\lambda}\right)^2\left(\tau^o\right)^{-1}\right)^2 \\
&= n\ln 2\pi - \sum_{i=1}^{n}\ln\tau_i + \sum_{i=1}^{n}\frac{\tau_i\lambda^2}{\left(\tau_i+\lambda\right)^2}\left(y_i-\mu^o\right)^2 + C_d,
\end{aligned} \tag{11.58}$$

where

$$\begin{aligned}
C_d = &-\sum_{i=1}^{n}\tau_i\frac{\lambda}{\left(\tau_i+\lambda\right)^2}\left(y_i-\mu^o\right) - \left(\tau^o\right)^{-1}\sum_{i=1}^{n}\tau_i\left(\frac{\lambda}{\tau_i+\lambda}\right)^3\left(y_i-\mu^o\right) \\
&+\sum_{i=1}^{n}\frac{\tau_i}{4\left(\tau_i+\lambda\right)} + \sum_{i=1}^{n}\frac{\tau_i}{2\left(\tau_i+\lambda\right)}\left(\frac{\lambda}{\tau_i+\lambda}\right)^2\left(\tau^o\right)^{-1} \\
&+\frac{1}{4}\sum_{i=1}^{n}\tau_i\left(\frac{\lambda}{\tau_i+\lambda}\right)^4\left(\tau^o\right)^{-2}.
\end{aligned}$$

Note that

$$D(\bar{\mathbf{z}},\bar{\theta}) = n\ln 2\pi - \sum_{i=1}^{n}\tau_i + \sum_{i=1}^{n}\frac{\tau_i\lambda^2}{\left(\tau_i+\lambda\right)^2}\left(y_i-\mu^o\right)^2.$$

Then, by (11.58), we have

$$D(\bar{\boldsymbol{\eta}},\bar{\theta}) = D(\bar{\mathbf{z}},\bar{\theta}) + C_d. \tag{11.59}$$

From (11.57) and (11.58), we can get

$$
\begin{aligned}
P_D^{DA} &= \overline{D(\boldsymbol{\eta}, \theta)} - D(\bar{\boldsymbol{\eta}}, \bar{\theta}) \\
&= \sum_{i=1}^{n} \frac{\tau_i}{\tau_i + \lambda} + \sum_{i=1}^{n} \frac{\tau_i \lambda^2}{(\tau_i + \lambda)^2} \left(\sum_{i=1}^{n} \frac{\tau_i \lambda}{\tau_i + \lambda} + \tau_0 \right)^{-1} \\
&\quad + \sum_{i=1}^{n} \tau_i \frac{\lambda}{(\tau_i + \lambda)^2} (y_i - \mu^o) + (\tau^o)^{-1} \sum_{i=1}^{n} \tau_i \left(\frac{\lambda}{\tau_i + \lambda} \right)^3 \\
&\quad (y_i - \mu^o) - \sum_{i=1}^{n} \frac{\tau_i}{4\,(\tau_i + \lambda)} \\
&\quad - \sum_{i=1}^{n} \frac{\tau_i}{2\,(\tau_i + \lambda)} \left(\frac{\lambda}{\tau_i + \lambda} \right)^2 (\tau^o)^{-1} \\
&\quad - \frac{1}{4} \sum_{i=1}^{n} \tau_i \left(\frac{\lambda}{\tau_i + \lambda} \right)^4 (\tau^o)^{-2}, \\
\text{DIC}^{DA} &= D(\bar{\boldsymbol{\eta}}, \bar{\theta}) + 2P_D^{DA}.
\end{aligned}
$$

Let $\tau_i = \tau$, $\rho = \frac{\tau}{\tau + \lambda}$, $\tau_0 = 0$. Then $\mu^o = \bar{y}$, $\tau^o = n\lambda\rho$, and

$$
\begin{aligned}
\overline{D(\boldsymbol{\eta}, \theta)} &= n \ln 2\pi - n\tau + n\rho \\
&\quad + \lambda n\rho\,(1 - \rho)\,(n\lambda\rho)^{-1} + \lambda\rho\,(1 - \rho) \sum_{i=1}^{n} (y_i - \bar{y})^2 \\
&= n \ln 2\pi - n\tau + n\rho + (1 - \rho) + \lambda\rho\,(1 - \rho) \sum_{i=1}^{n} (y_i - \bar{y})^2,
\end{aligned}
$$

$$
\begin{aligned}
D(\bar{\boldsymbol{\eta}}, \bar{\theta}) &= n \ln 2\pi - n\tau + \frac{\tau\lambda^2}{(\tau + \lambda)^2} \sum_{i=1}^{n} (y_i - \bar{y})^2 + C_d \\
&= n \ln 2\pi - n\tau + \lambda\rho\,(1 - \rho) \sum_{i=1}^{n} (y_i - \bar{y})^2 + C_d,
\end{aligned}
$$

where

$$
\begin{aligned}
C_d &= -\rho\,(1 - \rho) \sum_{i=1}^{n} (y_i - \bar{y}) - (\tau^o)^{-1} \tau\,(1 - \rho)^3 \sum_{i=1}^{n} (y_i - \bar{y}) \\
&\quad + 4n\rho + \frac{1}{2}\,(n\lambda\rho)^{-1}\, n\rho\,(1 - \rho)^2\, \frac{1}{4}\,(n\lambda\rho)^{-2}\, n\tau\,(1 - \rho)^4 \\
&= \frac{1}{4} n\rho + \frac{\lambda}{2\,(1 - \rho)^2} + \frac{\tau\,(1 - \rho)^4}{4n\lambda^2\rho^2},
\end{aligned}
$$

since $\sum_{i=1}^{n}(y_i - \bar{y}) = 0$. Hence, we have

$$P_{D,\eta}^{DA} = \overline{D(\boldsymbol{\eta},\theta)} - D(\bar{\boldsymbol{\eta}},\bar{\theta}) = \overline{D(\mathbf{z},\theta)} - D(\bar{\mathbf{z}},\bar{\theta}) - C_d$$
$$= P_{D,z}^{DA} - C_d,$$

$$\begin{aligned}\mathrm{DIC}_{\eta}^{DA} &= D(\bar{\boldsymbol{\eta}},\bar{\theta}) + 2P_D^{DA} = 2\overline{D(\boldsymbol{\eta},\theta)} - D(\bar{\boldsymbol{\eta}},\bar{\theta}) \\ &= 2\overline{D(\mathbf{z},\theta)} - D(\bar{\mathbf{z}},\bar{\theta}) - C_d \\ &= \mathrm{DIC}_z^{DA} - C_d.\end{aligned}$$

Bibliography

Akaike, H. (1973). Information theory and an extension of the maximum likelihood principle. In *Second international symposium on information theory*, Volume 1, pp. 267–281. Springer.

Andrews, D. W. (1987). Consistency in nonlinear econometric models: A generic uniform law of large numbers. *Econometrica: Journal of the Econometric Society 55*(6), 1465–1471.

Berg, A., R. Meyer, and J. Yu (2004). Deviance information criterion for comparing stochastic volatility models. *Journal of Business and Economic Statistics 22*(1), 107–120.

Breusch, T. S. and A. R. Pagan (1980). The Lagrange multiplier test and its applications to model specification in econometrics. *The Review of Economic Studies 47*(1), 239–253.

Burnham, K. and D. Anderson (2002). *Model selection and multi-model inference: A practical information-theoretic approach*. Springer.

Celeux, G., F. Forbes, C. Robert, and D. Titterington (2006). Deviance information criteria for missing data models. *Bayesian Analysis 1*(4), 651–674.

Chan, J. C. and E. Eisenstat (2018). Bayesian model comparison for time-varying parameter VARs with stochastic volatility. *Journal of Applied Econometrics 33*(4), 509–532.

Chan, J. C. and A. L. Grant (2016). Modeling energy price dynamics: Garch versus stochastic volatility. *Energy Economics 54*, 182–189.

De Jong, R. M. and J. Davidson (2000). Consistency of kernel estimators of heteroscedastic and autocorrelated covariance matrices. *Econometrica 68*(2), 407–423.

Fan, J., Y. Liao, and J. Yao (2015). Power enhancement in high-dimensional cross-sectional tests. *Econometrica 83*(4), 1497–1541.

Gallant, A. R. and H. White (1988). *A unified theory of estimation and inference for nonlinear dynamic models*. Blackwell.

Lancaster, T. (2000). The incidental parameter problem since 1948. *Journal of Econometrics 95*(2), 391–413.

Li, Y., X. B. Liu, and J. Yu (2015). A Bayesian chi-squared test for hypothesis testing. *Journal of Econometrics 189*(1), 54–69.

Li, Y., J. Yu, and T. Zeng (2018). Specification tests based on MCMC output. *Journal of Econometrics 207*(1), 237–260.

Li, Y., J. Yu, and T. Zeng (2020). Deviance information criterion for latent variable models and misspecified models. *Journal of Econometrics 216*(2), 450–493.

Li, Y., S. K. Mallick, N. Wang, J. Yu and T. Zeng (2024). Deviance Information Criterion for Bayesian Model Selection: Theoretical Justification and Applications. Working Paper.

Newey, W. K. and K. D. West (1987). Hypothesis testing with efficient method of moments estimation. *International Economic Review 28*(3), 777–787.

Neyman, J. and E. L. Scott (1948). Consistent estimates based on partially consistent observations. *Econometrica: Journal of the Econometric Society 16*(1), 1–32.

Presnell, B. and D. D. Boos (2004). The IOS test for model misspecification. *Journal of the American Statistical Association 99*(465), 216–227.

Spiegelhalter, D., N. Best, B. Carlin, and A. Van Der Linde (2002). Bayesian measures of model complexity and fit. *Journal of the Royal Statistical Society Series B 64*(4), 583–639.

Spiegelhalter, D. J., N. G. Best, B. P. Carlin, and A. Linde (2014). The deviance information criterion: 12 years on. *Journal of the Royal Statistical Society: Series B (Statistical Methodology) 76*(3), 485–493.

Takeuchi, K. (1976). Distribution of informational statistics and a criterion of model fitting. *Suri-Kagaku (Mathematic Sciences) 153*(2), 12–18. (In Japanese).

White, H. (1982). Maximum likelihood estimation of misspecified models. *Econometrica 50*(1), 1–25.

White, H. (1987). *Specification testing in dynamic models*, Volume 1. Cambridge University Press.

White, H. (1996). *Estimation, inference and specification analysis*. Cambridge University Press.

Wooldridge, J. M. (1994). Estimation and inference for dependent processes. *Handbook of Econometrics 4*, 2639–2738.

Index

For EU product safety concerns, contact us at Calle de José Abascal, 56–1°, 28003 Madrid, Spain or eugpsr@cambridge.org.

www.ingramcontent.com/pod-product-compliance
Lightning Source LLC
LaVergne TN
LVHW101456200926
848483LV00001B/141
* 9 7 8 1 1 0 8 8 4 3 2 9 4 *